Resources for Teaching

Tenth Edition

THE COMPACT BEDFORD INTRODUCTION TO LITERATURE

Reading • Thinking • Writing

Resources for Teaching

Tenth Edition

THE COMPACT BEDFORD INTRODUCTION TO LITERATURE

Reading • Thinking • Writing

Michael Meyer
University of Connecticut

Stefanie Wortman
Rhode Island College

Ellen Darion

Kathleen Morgan Drowne
University of North Carolina, Chapel Hill

Jill McDonough
Boston University

Ellen Kuhl Repetto
University of Massachusetts, Boston

Quentin Miller
Suffolk University

Julie Nash
University of Connecticut

Anne Phillips
Kansas State University

John Repp
Edinboro University of Pennsylvania

Robert Spirko
University of North Carolina, Chapel Hill

BEDFORD/ST. MARTIN'S   BOSTON ◆ NEW YORK

Manufactured in the United States of America.

8 7 6 5 4 3
f e d c b a

For information, write: Bedford/St. Martin's, 75 Arlington Street, Boston, MA 02116 (617-399-4000)

ISBN 978-1-4576-6453-3

Preface

This instructor's manual is designed to be a resource of commentaries, interpretations, and suggestions for teaching the works included in *The Compact Bedford Introduction to Literature*, Tenth Edition. The entries offer advice about how to approach individual selections and suggest possible answers to many of the questions raised in the text. No attempt has been made to generate definitive readings of the works; the text selections are rich enough to accommodate multiple approaches and interpretations. Our hope is that instructors will take what they find useful and leave the rest behind. Inevitably, instructors will disagree with some of the commentaries, but perhaps such disagreements will provide starting points for class discussion.

In addition to offering approaches to selections, many of the entries suggest topics for discussion and writing. The format of the entries varies from itemized responses to specific questions to essays that present overviews of individual works. This flexibility allows each entry to be more responsive to the nature of a particular work and the questions asked about it in the text. The "Connections to Other Selections" questions posed in the text are answered in the manual, and every entry includes suggestions for further connections. The manual includes selected bibliographies for authors treated in depth, and critical readings are mentioned throughout the manual when they are felt to be particularly useful resources for teaching a work. For more general bibliographic guides, see the annotated list of electronic sources on pages 370–95.

The manual also provides additional resources for teaching selections in the Albums of Contemporary Humor and Satire. There is a preface to each of the albums that includes suggestions for teaching this potentially unfamiliar material, and most of the connections questions posed in the text for these selections, with the exception of questions that explicitly ask students to write an essay, are answered in the manual. In addition, the manual provides plenty of similar suggestions for each of the Case Studies in the book — detailed introductory essays as well as itemized responses to questions.

Introductions in this manual offer suggestions for approaching *The Compact Bedford Introduction to Literature*'s editorial discussions in class and a number of "Tips from the Field" — class-tested teaching suggestions from instructors who have taught from previous editions. If you have a teaching tip that you would like to submit for the next edition of this instructor's manual, please send it to the attention of Amanda Legee, Editorial Assistant, at Bedford/St. Martin's, 75 Arlington Street, Boston, MA 02116. Your teaching suggestion should be approximately fifty words long and suggest ways of teaching a particular author or selection that have been especially effective in your classroom experience. If we use your teaching suggestion, we will be happy to acknowledge you in the manual and pay you an honorarium.

The appendices for this manual provide a List of Perspectives that organizes many of the book's Perspectives into critical strategies: formalist, biographical, psychological, historical, gender, mythological, reader-response, and deconstructionist strategies. To provide additional options for teaching *The Compact Bedford Introduction to Literature*, Tenth Edition, Appendix A features a thematic table of contents (pp. 352–63). With over thirty thematic groupings such as Home and Family, Nature, and Science and Technology, this useful tool offers instructors extra flexibility in their teaching and the option to change their course's focus at any time based on personal taste or students' response. A list of Bedford/St. Martin's literary reprint titles available to adopters of the anthology is located in the back of this manual.

Throughout this edition of the manual are icons that highlight selections available on

Web *The Book Companion Site for The Compact Bedford Introduction to Literature*. Tenth Edition, at **bedfordstmartins.com/meyerlit**

The manual is conveniently arranged by genre and follows the organization of the text. Page references corresponding to the text are included at the top of each right page of the manual and after the title of each entry.

Contents

Resources for Teaching

Tenth Edition

THE COMPACT BEDFORD INTRODUCTION TO LITERATURE

Reading · Thinking · Writing

FICTION

The Elements of Fiction

1

Reading Fiction

In connection with the introductory material in Chapter 1, it may be useful to engage students in a comparison of the ways in which they read. For instance, how does the text on the back of a cereal box differ from a story in a news magazine? We read differently depending on our interest in the subject, our acceptance of a writer's style and voice, and our environment. Some students may read primarily while they are on the treadmill at the recreation center; others need quiet in which to concentrate. Even students who wouldn't identify themselves as readers might discover that they actually rely on reading skills more than they realize.

After focusing on the reader, students might consider the reading material. Encourage them to consider how reading fiction may be different from reading a newspaper. What different demands are being made on the reader in these contexts? Fiction invites the reader to enter a world that may or may not be familiar to them; it also asks them to think not only about the words on the page but also about their implications. Fiction is, in a sense, not only about what the writer tells the reader but also what the writer doesn't tell the reader. It's up to the reader to invest the spaces between the words with creative (yet reasonable) meanings. The sample close reading in the chapter will go a long way in helping students visualize the demands of active reading. The annotations to "The Story of an Hour" demonstrate the process of a reader questioning and thinking carefully about a work of literature while reading it. But be sure to remind your students that the annotations are those of an experienced reader, not a student, or they might conclude that the task is beyond their abilities.

Finally, students will profit from learning that sharing their interpretations with each other can be intensely rewarding. Because they bring different experiences and values to their readings, they may discover different significant aspects of a given text. To practice building their interpretive skills, students might bring in a letter to the editor in a local newspaper, or a comic strip, or some other reading material, and explain what they think is of interest about their "text." (This may be particularly successful for students in small groups.) Students may be surprised to discover the differences among their readings — or even their similarities. An ironic editorial or a purposely ambiguous (or especially political) cartoon may provide diverse yet reasonable readings. In discussing those readings, students begin to develop the skills that will make their experience with fiction successful and rewarding.

Web Ask students to research the authors in this chapter or take quizzes on their works at **bedfordstmartins.com/ meyerlit**.

KATE CHOPIN, *The Story of an Hour* (p. 15)

Katherine (Kate) Chopin was born in 1851 and was educated in St. Louis. The mother of six children, she produced her first novel, *At Fault*, in 1890. *Bayou Folk*

1

(1894) and *A Night in Acadie* (1897), both collections of short stories, were followed in 1899 by Chopin's most well-known work, *The Awakening*, a work denounced by critics and judged to be "immoral." At the time of her death in 1904, Chopin left unpublished a novel, *Young Dr. Gosse*, and a short story collection, *A Vocation and a Voice*, from which "The Story of an Hour" is taken. Her fiction commonly depicts heroines who attempt to balance personal independence with the demands of marriage, motherhood, and society.

Web Ask students to explore contexts for Kate Chopin and this story — and a sample close reading — at **bedfordstmartins.com/ meyerlit**.

As you begin to consider this story, lead the class into a discussion of Mrs. Mallard's character. What do they think of her? Even for the twenty-first century, this is in certain ways a bold story, and there are likely to be students who will describe the protagonist as callous, selfish, unnatural — even, in Mrs. Mallard's own words, "monstrous" — because of her joyous feeling of freedom after her initial grief and shock. Go through the text with the class, looking for evidence that this radical shift in feeling is genuine. To demonstrate her grief and subsequent numbness, you might point to Mrs. Mallard's weeping with "sudden, wild abandonment" (para. 3), the "physical exhaustion that haunted her body . . . and soul" (4), the way she sat "motionless, except when a sob came up into her throat and shook her, as a child who has cried itself to sleep continues to sob in its dreams" (7), and her look, which "indicated a suspension of intelligent thought" (8). Especially important to the defense of Mrs. Mallard's character is her effort to fight off "this thing that was approaching to possess her": "she was striving to beat it back with her will" (10).

Ask students to discuss (or write about) what they imagine Mrs. Mallard's marriage to have been like. If her husband "had never looked save with love upon her" (13), what was wrong with the marriage? The answer can be found in the lines "She had loved him — sometimes. Often she had not. . . . What could love, the unsolved mystery, count for in the face of this possession of self-assertion which she suddenly recognized as the strongest impulse of her being!" (15). The surprise ending aside (some readers may find it manipulative), this story is basically about a woman awakening to the idea that all the love and stability in the world can't compensate for her lack of control over her own life.

Ask the class if they can locate any symbols in the story. "The tops of trees that were all aquiver with the new spring life," sparrows "twittering" (5), "patches of blue sky showing . . . through the clouds" (6), and "the sounds, the scents, the color that filled the air" (9) all suggest the renewal and rebirth that follow.

Students could also write about the ending of the story, specifically the last three paragraphs. What is the tone here? (Ironic. First, Mrs. Mallard suffers a heart attack when she sees her husband, rather than when she learns of his death, which is when everyone originally feared she would have an attack. Second, she does not die of joy, as the doctors claim, but of shock — the shock of having to go back to her old way of life once she has realized there is another way to live.)

Chopin's story offers an opportunity to demonstrate how a reader's own values and assumptions are relevant to literary interpretation. Responses to Mrs. Mallard are — for better or worse — often informed by readers' attitudes toward marriage. Similar issues can also be engaged in the van der Zee and Godwin stories that follow Chopin's. Chapter 48, "Critical Strategies for Reading," includes a variety of approaches to "The Story of an Hour." Students who are exposed to this chapter early in the course will be likely to generate more pointed and sophisticated kinds of questions about the subsequent texts they read.

For additional background material, see Per Seyersted's *Kate Chopin: A Critical Biography* (Baton Rouge: Louisiana State UP, 1969; print.); Marlene Springer's *Edith Wharton and Kate Chopin: A Reference Guide* (Boston: G. K. Hall, 1976; print.); and Carol P. Christ's *Diving Deep and Surfacing: Women Writers on Spiritual Quest* (Boston: Beacon, 1980; print.).

POSSIBLE CONNECTIONS TO OTHER SELECTIONS

Dagoberto Gilb, "Love in L.A." (text p. 430)

Susan Glaspell, *Trifles* (text p. 1038)

A Composite of a Romance Tip Sheet (p. 26)

This tip sheet offers an opportunity to begin discussion of the elements of fiction. Reading a romance novel is not a prerequisite for discussion, because most of us have experienced similar formulas in magazines, popular television programs, or films; also, an excerpt from a romance novel begins on text page 31. Students are usually delighted to recognize the patterns prescribed in the tip sheet and have no trouble recalling stories that fit this description. This gets class discussion off to a good start, provided the emphasis is on why readers derive pleasure from romance formulas rather than on a denigration of such reading.

Contemporary criticism has focused considerable attention on the audience and appeal of romance novels. (See, for example, . . . the excerpt from Kay Mussell's *All About Romance: The Back Fence for Lovers of Romance Novels,* accessed at likesbooks.com/ mussell.html.) Romance readers are typically women ranging in age from their twenties to midforties. Not surprisingly, the age of the heroine usually determines the approximate age of the reader, because the protagonists of Harlequin and Silhouette romances — to name only the two most popular series — are created so that consumers will readily identify with the heroines' romantic adventures in exciting settings as a means of escaping the loneliness and tedium of domesticity. (It's worth emphasizing, of course, that male readers engage in similar fantasies; Philip Larkin's "A Study of Reading Habits" on p. 557 suggests some possibilities.) The heroine is "attractive" rather than "glamorous" because she is likely to appeal to more readers who might describe themselves that way.

Romance readers are often treated to a veritable fashion show, with detailed descriptions of the heroine's clothes. This kind of window-shopping is especially apparent in television soap operas, in which the costumes and sets resemble Bloomingdale's displays more than they do real life. In a very real sense, their audience is shopping for images of success, courtship, and marriage. The hero is a man who may initially seem to be cold and cruel but ultimately provides warmth, love, and security. He is as virtuous as the heroine (if he's divorced, his ex-wife is to blame) but stronger. His being "about ten years" older emphasizes male dominance over female submissiveness, a theme that implicitly looms large in many romances.

The use of sex varies in romances, especially recent ones, in which explicitness seems to be more popular. Nevertheless, suspense and tension are produced in all romances by the teasing complications that keep lovers apart until the end. The major requirement of love scenes between the hero and heroine is that they be culminations of romantic feelings — love — rather than merely graphic sexual descriptions.

The simplified writing style of romances is geared for relatively inexperienced, unsophisticated readers. Probably not very many romance readers cross over to *Pride and Prejudice* or *Jane Eyre*, although some of Austen's and Brontë's readers have certainly been known to enjoy romances. Instructors who share their own reading habits with a class might reassure students that popular and high culture aren't necessarily mutually exclusive while simultaneously whetting students' appetites for the stories to come.

KAREN VAN DER ZEE, *From* A Secret Sorrow (p. 31)

Karen van der Zee was born and grew up in Holland. She published a number of short stories there early in her career. Although the United States is her permanent home, she and her husband, a consultant in agriculture to developing countries, often live abroad. The couple was married in Kenya, their first child was born in Ghana, and their second child arrived in the United States. Van der Zee has contributed more than thirty books so far to the Harlequin line; many of them have been translated into other languages.

The excerpt from *A Secret Sorrow* subscribes to much of the plotting and characterization methods described in the composite tip sheet. Kai and Faye are not definitively brought together until the final chapter, after Faye's secret is revealed and Kai expresses his unconditional love for her. Students should have no difficulty understanding how the heroine's and hero's love for each other inevitably earns them domestic bliss in the "low white ranch house under the blue skies of Texas," where the family "flourished like the crops in the fields" (para. 137). Kai is the traditional dominant, protective male who takes charge of their relationship (albeit tenderly). A good many prepackaged phrases describe him: he has a "hard body" (28), and he kisses her with a "hard, desperate passion" (48), when he isn't speaking "huskily" (49) or lifting her face with his "bronzed hand" (131). In contrast, Faye is "like a terrified animal" and no match for his "hot, fuming fury" when he accuses her of jeopardizing their love.

Despite the predictable action, stereotyped characterizations, clichéd language, and flaccid descriptions of lovemaking (108), some students (perhaps many) will prefer *A Secret Sorrow* to Godwin's "A Sorrowful Woman." But that's natural enough. Van der Zee's story is accessible and familiar material, while Godwin's is puzzling and vaguely threatening because "A Sorrowful Woman" raises questions instead of resolving them. Rather than directly challenging students' preferences and forcing them to be defensive, demonstrate how Godwin's story can be reread several times and still be interesting. *A Secret Sorrow* certainly does not stand up to that test because it was written to be consumed on a first reading so that readers will buy the next book in the series.

POSSIBLE CONNECTIONS TO OTHER SELECTIONS

Edgar Rice Burroughs, From *Tarzan of the Apes* (text p. 70)

Gail Godwin, "A Sorrowful Woman" (text p. 39)

GAIL GODWIN, *A Sorrowful Woman* (p. 39)

Gail Godwin traces her beginnings as a writer to her mother, a teacher and writer, who read stories out of a blank address book, "the special book," as Godwin has called it, "a tiny book with no writing at all in it." Although she frequently contributes essays and stories to publications such as *Harper's, Esquire, Cosmopolitan,* and *Ms.* and has written four librettos, Godwin is primarily known as a novelist; her books include *The Perfectionists* (1970), *The Odd Woman* (1974), *Violet Clay* (1978), *A Mother and Two Daughters* (1982), *The Finishing School* (1985), *A Southern Family* (1987), *Father Melancholy's Daughter* (1991), *The Good Husband* (1994), and *Evenings at Five* (2003). Born in 1937 in Birmingham, Alabama, Godwin was educated at the University of North Carolina and the University of Iowa. She worked as a reporter for the *Miami Herald* and as a travel consultant with the U.S. Embassy in London before pursuing a career as a full-time writer and teacher of writing. She has received a National Endowment for the Arts grant, a Guggenheim fellowship, and an Award in Literature from the American Institute and Academy of Arts and Letters. She was coeditor of *Best American Short Stories* in 1985 and has had her short stories collected in *Dream Children* (1976), *Real Life* (1981), and *Mr. Bedford and the Muses* (1983).

"A Sorrowful Woman" challenges the assumptions that inform romance novels. The central point of *A Secret Sorrow* is that love conquers all and that marriage and motherhood make women "beautiful, complete, [and] whole." In contrast, Godwin's story begins with an epigraph that suggests a dark fairy tale: "Once upon a time there was a wife and mother one too many times." The story opens with a pleasant description of the woman's husband ("durable, receptive, gentle") and child ("a tender golden three"), but she is saddened and sickened by the sight of them. These unnamed characters (they are offered as types) seem to have the kind of life that allows Kai and Faye to live happily ever after, but in Godwin's world, this domestic arrangement turns out to be a deadly trap for "the woman." The opening paragraph shocks us into wanting to read the rest of the story to find out why the woman is repulsed by her seemingly perfect life.

It may be tempting to accept the husband's assessment that "Mommy is sick." Students might be eager to see her as mad or suffering from a nervous breakdown, but if we settle for one of those explanations, the meaning of the story is flattened. We simply don't know enough about the woman to diagnose her behavior in psychological terms. She is, after all, presented as a type, not as an individual. She does appear mentally ill, and she becomes progressively more unstable until she withdraws from life completely, but Godwin portrays her as desperate, not simply insane, and focuses our attention on the larger question of why the sole role of wife and mother may not be fulfilling.

The woman rejects life on the terms it is offered to her, and no one — including her — knows what to make of her refusal. (For a discussion of the nature of the conflict in the story, see pp. 62–63 of the text.) What is clear, however, is that she cannot live in the traditional role that her husband and son (and we) expect of her. She finds that motherhood doesn't fit her and makes her feel absurd (consider the "vertical bra" in paragraph 4). When she retreats from the family, her husband accommodates her with sympathy and an "understanding" that Godwin reveals to be a means of control rather than genuine care. He tells her he wants "to be big enough to contain whatever you must do" (21). And that's the problem. What he cannot comprehend is that she needs an identity that goes beyond being his wife and his child's mother. Instead, he gives her a nightly sleeping draught; his remedy is to anesthetize his Sleeping Beauty rather than to awaken her to some other possibilities.

Neither the husband nor the wife is capable of taking any effective action. The husband can replace his wife with the "perfect girl" to help around the house, and he can even manage quite well on his own, but he has no more sense of what to do about her refusal to go on with her life than she does. Her own understanding of her situation goes no further than her realization that her life did not have to take a defined shape any more than a poem does (22). Her story is a twentieth-century female version of Herman Melville's "Bartleby, the Scrivener" (p. 133); both characters prefer not to live their lives, but neither attempts to change anything or offer alternatives. Instead, they are messengers whose behavior makes us vaguely troubled. The two stories warrant close comparison.

In the end, when spring arrives, the woman uses herself up in a final burst of domestic energy that provides the husband and son with laundry, hand-knitted sweaters, drawings, stories, love sonnets, and a feast that resembles a Thanksgiving dinner. But neither renewal nor thanks is forthcoming. Instead, the boy, unaware of his mother's death, asks, "Can we eat the turkey for supper?" (38). The irony reveals that the woman has been totally consumed by her role.

Ask students why this story appeared in *Esquire*, a magazine for men, rather than, say, *Good Housekeeping*. The discussion can sensitize them to the idea of literary markets and create an awareness of audiences as well as texts. Surely a romance writer for *Good Housekeeping* would have ended this story differently. Students will know what to suggest for such an ending.

For a discussion of Godwin's treatment of traditional role models in the story, see Judith K. Gardiner's " 'A Sorrowful Woman': Gail Godwin's Feminist Parable," *Studies in Short Fiction* 12 (1975): 286–90.

TIP FROM THE FIELD

Because many of my community college students don't understand the distinctions of formulaic writing they are supposed to make between the excerpt from van der Zee's *A Secret Sorrow* and Godwin's "A Sorrowful Woman," I have them focus instead on the similarities and differences between the fairy-tale nature of these two stories. I ask students to consider how each story is a fairy tale or representative of one. Students have little difficulty identifying the fairy-tale elements of Prince Charming rescuing a damsel in distress and living happily ever after in *A Secret Sorrow*. Students have more difficulty recognizing the fairy-tale aspects ("Once upon a time there was a wife and mother one too many times") of "A Sorrowful Woman," but once this heuristic device is in place, good discussion and writing will result. I find this works particularly well with older, traditional students who more readily see the invalidity of the first fairy tale and may be all too familiar with the reality of the second.

— JOSEPH ZEPPETELLO, *Ulster Community College*

POSSIBLE CONNECTIONS TO OTHER SELECTIONS

Emily Dickinson, "Much Madness is divinest Sense — " (text p. 812)

Henrik Ibsen, *A Doll House* (text p. 1250)

Herman Melville, "Bartleby, the Scrivener" (text p. 133)

PERSPECTIVES

KAY MUSSELL, *Are Feminism and Romance Novels Mutually Exclusive?* (p. 44)

This Perspective is good for drawing a historical parallel between feminism and romance novels. It might be useful to ask the class to compare the role of feminism in *A Secret Sorrow* and "A Sorrowful Woman": How is feminism manifested, and how is the traditional role of the female treated? It is important to contrast the goals and attitudes of each of these stories and how feminism is or isn't reflected in them.

You may also want to ask each student to write a short paragraph describing feminism. The number of different answers will reflect the way that "feminist scholars have come to recognize a broader range of female experience," (para. 4) in that feminism no longer has a central agenda, but is the product of many differing viewpoints. These viewpoints will be more or less accepting of the current version of the romance novel, and some good discussion could arise out of these quick-writing sessions.

THOMAS JEFFERSON, *On the Dangers of Reading Fiction* (p. 45)

Draw on any story that was popular in class to argue that reading fiction is time spent "instructively employed" and that reason and good judgment can be improved by reading fiction — in short, to refute Jefferson's argument. Have students tell you what they learned from any of the stories in the anthology and state why they were worth reading. Jefferson's views could also be discussed in light of the book banning and censorship going on in this country today.

ENCOUNTERING FICTION: COMICS AND GRAPHIC STORIES

Most students probably do at least some reading for pleasure, yet they tend to approach "serious" fiction as something mysterious and overly demanding. The comic strips and graphic novels that follow below and throughout *The Compact Bedford Introduction to Literature* should help demystify the short story for your students and remind them that storytelling is, first and foremost, a source of enjoyment for both the teller and the reader.

The selections are accompanied by the same kinds of critical reading and connections questions that follow the other short stories in *The Compact Bedford Introduction to Literature*. Assigning those questions may help students gear up for close readings of more traditional works. At the same time, however, you might want to resist the urge to approach the graphic stories as entry-level literature and allow them instead to simply reinforce the notion that reading is pleasurable. Whichever approach you decide to take, your students will surely enjoy these selections.

2

Writing about Fiction

Beginning to write about literature, students should establish particular goals. First, it is important to start to understand and use the language of literary interpretation — to incorporate references to plot, characterization, setting, and other elements into an argument based on the writer's understanding of one or more literary works. Chapter introductions throughout *The Compact Bedford Introduction to Literature* provide and define key terms (foreshadowing, irony, static vs. dynamic characterization, and other terms); encourage your students not only to learn the terms' meanings but to begin to incorporate them into their active vocabularies. Using the correct terminology, the student establishes a sense of authority, and readers of the student's work are more likely to respect the student's perspective. Second, encourage students to develop a particular analytic focus for each writing task. It isn't enough to simply describe an immediate reaction to a literary work, although first responses are useful in beginning to determine a thesis. (To facilitate analytic approaches to the literature, this anthology invites students to generate "First Responses" after they finish reading each literary work; students then proceed to more specific questions about the texts.) After determining their initial reactions, writers should return to the literature and determine how it provoked their responses. Students' discoveries at this stage in the writing process may well lead to significant observations about the literature. Third, students should decide if a particular writing mode will facilitate explanation of their theses. If comparing two stories, for instance, or a character's perspective at the beginning of a story with his/her perspective at the end, the student should compare *to make a specific point*. The order in which the stories or topics are discussed within a paper should be purposeful; it should also be consistent throughout. Good literary interpretation manifests a sense of purpose; the writer should write to convince readers that certain aspects of a given literary work are significant and/or more complex than those readers might have imagined.

The "Questions for Responsive Reading and Writing" in this chapter, although broad, can provide students with ideas that will allow them to begin critically analyzing works of fiction. This list of questions is extensive and may at first seem overwhelming to your students. It is important, therefore, for students to realize that they shouldn't expect every question to apply to every text in a meaningful way, and that certain questions will apply to certain stories better than others. To make these questions seem more manageable, you might consider asking your students to apply the questions about plot to one story that your class has studied, the questions about character to another story, and so on. Or you might choose one piece of fiction and ask your students to answer (in discussion or in a brief writing assignment) one or two questions from each set. As your students learn to apply these questions to different selections, they will become more comfortable discussing fiction and, as a result, become better able to analyze fiction in their writing. You might also remind students that they must understand the literary terms used in the questions in order to answer the questions intelligently; the Glossary of Literary Terms, included at the back of the text on page 1559, provides concise definitions and examples of these terms.

A NOTE ABOUT USING STUDENT MODELS

Student writing samples are included throughout *The Compact Bedford Introduction to Literature*. Instructors may find it constructive to discuss these samples with their own students; in tracing the authors' writing processes and the development of their ideas, literature students may develop their own strategies for writing about literature. These sample student papers include initial responses, detailed lists, and multiple drafts; they enforce instructors' advice that writing is a labor-intensive process. The final drafts demonstrate the value inherent in struggling to develop and enhance original ideas about literature.

Particularly for students who are unfamiliar with writing about literature, these sample papers demonstrate useful techniques for developing accurate thesis statements and incorporating textual evidence. Instructors might call particular attention to the way evidence supports the thesis in these sample papers. Whether paraphrased or quoted directly, textual evidence distinguishes an unconvincing paper from an effective, thought-provoking one. Competent writers don't rely on textual evidence to make their arguments for them; instead, they subordinate the evidence to their own ideas.

Because the sample papers address materials contained within *The Compact Bedford Introduction to Literature*, students may find themselves inspired to reread the literature discussed. Instructors might find it useful to have students write responses to the student sample papers as a way of generating discussion, both about the literature and about the writing process. Working with the sample papers, readers may understand more about how different elements within the literature combine to create meanings and achieve effects; they should also recognize and appreciate in more substantial ways the subtlety of the authors' techniques.

A SAMPLE PAPER IN PROGRESS

In the sample student paper contained in Chapter 2, Maya Leigh writes about the depiction of marriage in Karen van der Zee's novel *A Secret Sorrow* and in Gail Godwin's short story "A Sorrowful Woman." Students should have read the excerpt from van der Zee's novel and the complete Godwin short story (both contained in Chapter 1). In addition, before introducing students to Leigh's sample paper, you may want to assign or encourage your students to respond to the questions following each text. Having generated some initial ideas about these texts, students might appreciate or understand more of Leigh's writing process.

Also, encourage students to answer the "Questions for Responsive Reading and Writing" at the beginning of Chapter 2 in reference to van der Zee's and Godwin's work. (This might be a productive in-class discussion or small-group assignment.) Gaining confidence in assessing plot, character, setting, point of view, and other literary elements, students will be better prepared to follow Leigh's ideas. They may find the numerous questions in each section overwhelming, but they will most likely develop some ideas about each element whether they answer all or only a few of the questions.

Turning to the "First Response," students should recognize the personal quality of the work. Notice the extensive use of "I" throughout: we learn a great deal about Maya as we read her response. (She has read Harlequin romances before, and she knows what she values about them: the happy endings.) In addition, it might be useful to point out that stories that don't initially meet readers' expectations or satisfy them are often better writing topics than stories that contain no surprises and no mysteries. As Leigh notes, the Godwin story "is a much more powerful story, and it is one that I could read several times, unlike the Harlequin. The Godwin woman bothers me too, because I can't really see what she has to complain about" (para. 2). This response leads directly to Leigh's focus on the roles of the female protagonists and their relationship to marriage. At this point, students might look back at their own — or at each other's — first responses to the van der Zee and Godwin stories. Are there problems or striking reactions that invite the writer to study them in more detail?

After completing her "First Response," Leigh then lists her ideas about the female characters' lives: their observations about marriage, men, children, housework, and other relevant issues. She organizes her list in such a way that comparable topics appear opposite one another. For instance, she compares the female characters' status at the end of each story: in Godwin's story, the woman is "dead in the end"; in van der Zee's, the woman, Faye, is "beautiful, whole, complete in the end." Each woman experiences a crisis, but for Godwin's character, the crisis is "due to fear of always having husband and kid" while for van der Zee's protagonist, the crisis is "due to fear of never having husband and kids." Lists such as Leigh's are a useful way of generating and organizing basic observations about literature. This technique is also useful in estimating how characters develop over the course of a story, or how two characters' dialogue with one another evolves. It can even be useful simply in comparing the first few paragraphs of a story with the final ones. It enables readers to begin to identify key aspects for further study.

Two working drafts follow Leigh's lists. After students have read all of each draft, they may find themselves overwhelmed by the material or unable to explain exactly how Leigh's ideas are evolving. Invite them to break down the drafts — to study the thesis statements separately, to focus on particular paragraphs in order to understand how Leigh's topic is evolving, to see how she begins to incorporate different and more convincing textual evidence. In particular, you may want to call students' attention to the way Leigh refines her approach, corrects details of her observations, and incorporates the terminology of literary analysis as she develops these drafts. Strong papers are accurate, thought provoking, and convincing. Ask students to identify two or three different examples in which Leigh's second draft is an improvement on the first. Dealing with these drafts, you might also call attention to basic elements of technique, among them introducing the authors' full names and story titles in the first paragraph, developing a strong thesis within that paragraph, and properly quoting and citing textual evidence throughout the essay.

Finally, having immersed themselves in Leigh's ideas and writing process, students should turn to the final product of her labor. The introduction to the final draft summarizes Leigh's improvements, particularly involving accuracy, argumentation, and mechanics (transitions, sentence clarity, conclusions). In discussion or in small groups, students could study these aspects of the essay and, additionally, identify what they find convincing or provocative about Leigh's ideas. It might be useful to assign different sections of the essay to different groups in order for students to focus more effectively on the material. In connection with studying this final version, students might return to the Godwin and van der Zee texts; having read Leigh's commentary, what do they notice about the literature that they hadn't been aware of while reading these stories? If students still have objections to her ideas or arguments, you may want to encourage them to formulate these objections in writing. Students might also explain how Leigh could overcome their objections or account for their questions.

Students may even find this sample student paper useful beyond their study of Chapter 2: it can serve as a model for writing about literature throughout the fiction section.

3

Plot

The introductory section of Chapter 3 provides students with specific examples of exposition, rising action, conflict, suspense, climax, and resolution. Students should practice applying these terms not only to the fiction provided in the chapter but also to other "stories" that they encounter in popular culture, including jokes, television shows, comic strips, and other sources. Students might keep a log of their reading or television watching for a week and practice identifying plot

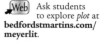 Ask students to explore *plot* at **bedfordstmartins.com/ meyerlit**.

elements. They also might experiment with considering how they might rearrange these elements in a given story to create alternate effects. Students might even work in small groups to compare their readings of the same source and to practice rearranging the elements.

This chapter also explains plot techniques such as flashbacks and foreshadowing. Again, you may wish to invite students to apply these to the "stories" they follow outside of class. It might also be useful to practice in class with texts that most students might already know. Fairy tales, fables, and nursery rhymes are especially fruitful sources for further study of plot. Having "Goldilocks and the Three Bears" begin at the end or in the middle, or investing "Little Red Riding Hood" with foreshadowing in the first paragraph might enable students to discover more meaning both in the original tale and in the retelling.

Web Ask students to research the authors in this chapter or take quizzes on their works at **bedfordstmartins.com/ meyerlit**.

EDGAR RICE BURROUGHS, *From* Tarzan of the Apes (p. 70)

Most of the sixty books Edgar Rice Burroughs wrote recorded bedtime stories he had told his children. In addition to the enormously popular Tarzan series, Burroughs wrote a good deal of science fiction, most notably a series of books that chronicle the adventures of John Carter of Mars. Before making his fortune as a writer, Burroughs was a cowboy, gold miner, policeman, and store manager. His books include *The Princess of Mars* (1917), *Tanar of Pellucidar* (1930), and *Tarzan and the Foreign Legion* (1947). *Tarzan of the Apes* (1914), the first of the Tarzan series, has been translated into more than fifty languages.

Burroughs writes that from Tarzan's "early infancy his survival had depended upon acuteness of eyesight, hearing, smell, touch, and taste far more than upon the more slowly developed organ of reason. The least developed of all in Tarzan was the sense of taste" (paras. 29–30). The description in the excerpt relies heavily on physical detail, almost corresponding to this discussion of Tarzan's acute sensory development. Ask students to isolate one paragraph of the Burroughs excerpt and assess the kind of description included in it. What techniques does Burroughs rely on in successfully presenting such heavy — but not excessive — detail?

Much of the plot in this excerpt functions as a device for revealing the characterizations of Tarzan and Terkoz by providing them with occurrences to which they must react. How would the excerpt change if it were altered to reflect primarily Jane's characterization? What details would be emphasized in such a narrative? Would the plot seem in any way diminished in such a representation?

POSSIBLE CONNECTION TO AN OTHER SELECTION

Karen van der Zee, From *A Secret Sorrow* (text p. 31)

ANNIE PROULX, *Job History* (p. 77)

Proulx's story is centered on the character of Leeland Lee, yet his specific job history takes on an archetypal feeling. This tension between the individual and the general is embodied in the name of Leeland's city, Unique, and the sense he gets while working as a truck driver that "every place is the same" (para. 13). It also informs Proulx's use of the news, which is a constant element in the story that often feels distant from the characters' lives. She often includes references to the news at the ends of paragraphs, as a kind of background or even an afterthought to the more intimate, if smaller-scale, movements of Leeland's life. One exception to this technique occurs in paragraph 10, when news about economic problems dominates the writing, as it dominates Leeland's experience.

Stylistically, Proulx uses the present tense together with a third-person limited perspective to deliver everything as news—though some of these news items are much more subjective than the U.S. and world history unfolding at the same time as Leeland's life. Spanning from the late 1940s to sometime late in the twentieth century, this life happens alongside huge changes in the American landscape. Proulx refers to the expansion of the interstate highway system, which directly affects Leeland's life in Unique, and to the civil rights movement, which affects him less directly. Given the thread of news items that runs through the story, students might want to discuss the final line. Why does Proulx abandon the news at the very end?

While Proulx develops some of Leeland's personal relationships, particularly with his wife, Lori, these connections are largely seen through the filter of his always-changing employment. Leeland's job history is characterized by patterns, which develop as the story continues and prove resistant to change. He has trouble getting along with several different bosses; he longs to own a business, but continually fails when he tries to go to work for himself; and though he tries to leave Unique, he is always drawn back to the town. The final paragraph of the story indicates some changes in Leeland's life, but also some continuity with his old existence. You might ask students whether this ending feels like a break from Leeland's patterns, or an extension of the same.

POSSIBLE CONNECTIONS TO OTHER SELECTIONS

Edgar Rice Burroughs, From *Tarzan of the Apes* (text p. 70; question #1, following)

Annie Proulx, "55 Miles to the Gas Pump" (text p. 470; question #2, following)

CONNECTIONS QUESTIONS IN TEXT (p. 81) WITH ANSWERS

1. Describe the differences you see between the plot of "Job History" and the plot in the excerpt from *Tarzan of the Apes* (text p. 70).

   Both "Job History" and the excerpt from *Tarzan* (text p. 70) are concerned more with external events than with the revelation of internal states. Though readers gain some insight into the characters' minds, they largely learn through inference from the characters' actions. However, Proulx's story moves in unexpected ways, following the characters' lives as they take turns that are sometimes predictable but just as often feel random. By contrast, Burroughs carefully builds tension in the chase scene before giving readers the satisfying triumph in battle.

2. Consider the similarities and differences in plot in this story and Proulx's "55 Miles to the Gas Pump" (text p. 470).

   As in "Job History," the plot of "55 Miles to the Gas Pump" (text p. 470) hinges on the development of a character, and in both Proulx uses external details to suggest the characters' thoughts, desires, suspicions, and even pathologies. At the end of "55 Miles," she includes commentary that establishes an ironic perspective on the characters, casting Croom's crimes as the only way he can find to keep himself entertained. In "Job History," any narrative perspective develops more implicitly. The narrator does not step in to give us a view of Leeland but does seem more sympathetic to his difficulties with finding contentment.

WILLIAM FAULKNER, *A Rose for Emily* (p. 82)

The ending of this mystery story is as chillingly gruesome as it is surprising. Just when we think that the discovery of Homer Barron's body ("what was left of him") is the awful revelation that the narrator has been leading up to, we realize in the final climactic paragraph (and particularly in the last three words) that the strand of "iron-gray hair" on the indented pillow belongs to Emily. The details indicate that she has slept with Homer since she murdered him, because we are told in paragraph 48 that her hair turned gray after Homer disappeared. The closing paragraph produces a gasp of horror in most readers, but by withholding this information until the very end, Faulkner allows us to develop a sympathetic understanding of Emily before we are revolted by her necrophilia.

The conclusion is skillfully foreshadowed: Emily denies her father's death; she buys arsenic; Homer disappears; and there is a terrible smell around the house. These clues are muted, however, by the narrator's rearrangement of the order of events. We learn about the smell before we know that Emily bought arsenic and that Homer disappeared. Hence, these details seem less related to one another than they would if they had been presented chronologically. Faulkner's plotting allows him to preserve suspense in a first reading. On subsequent readings we take delight in realizing how all the pieces fit together and point to the conclusion.

The gothic elements provide an appropriate atmosphere of mystery and are directly related to the conflicts in the story. Emily's decrepit house evokes an older, defunct South that resists the change imposed by garages, gasoline pumps, new construction, paved sidewalks, and a Yankee carpetbagger such as Homer. This exposition is essential to the story's theme because it explains Emily's antagonists. Emily rejects newness and change; her house smells of "dust and disuse." Her refusal to let go of the past is indicated by her insistence that her father did not die and by her necrophilia with Homer. She attempts to stop time, and although the narrator's collective "we" suggests the town's tolerance for and sympathy with such an attitude (as a representative of the North, Homer is powerful but vulgar), the story finally makes clear that living in a dead past means living with death. As much as the narrator realizes that Emily's illusions caused her to reject the changing realities of her life, he — like his fellow citizens — admires Emily with "a sort of respectful affection" (para. 1). She is like a "fallen monument," a reminder of an Old South that could not survive the new order of Reconstruction. Even though she murders Homer, Emily cannot stop the changes brought by the urbanization associated with him.

This story, minus its concerns about change in the South and its tribute — a rose — to Emily's strong sensibilities (in spite of her illusions and eccentricities), fits into the gothic horror tradition, but it would be a far less intriguing work if the formula were to supersede Faulkner's complex imaginative treatment.

POSSIBLE CONNECTIONS TO OTHER SELECTIONS

Stephen Crane, "The Bride Comes to Yellow Sky" (text p. 246)

Emily Dickinson, "The Soul selects her own Society —" (text p. 810)

Ralph Ellison, "Battle Royal" (text p. 226)

PERSPECTIVE ON FAULKNER

WILLIAM FAULKNER, *On "A Rose for Emily"* (p. 89)

Ask students to consider Faulkner's statement "I was simply trying to write about people," which was made in response to a question about symbolism in this story. Have the class look at other stories in which symbols are prevalent, or at least obvious. Are the characters always realistic and convincing? Have you come across any characters who serve a symbolic function but are not entirely credible as far as motivation or behavior goes?

ANDRE DUBUS, *Killings* (p. 93)

At the heart of "Killings" is the issue of the justice of the legal system — a system of arrest, bail, trial, and sentencing — versus the ancient concept of justice known as "an eye for an eye." When Willis and Matt are discussing the matter, Willis argues that the established American legal system will prove unsatisfactory: "Know what he'll do? Five at the most" (para. 16). In the flashback, when Frank returns home after Strout has assaulted him, Matt wants him to press charges, but Frank refuses (38–39). The laws are simply inadequate in many respects for the circumstances surrounding the events of the story; as Matt tells his wife when she objects to Frank's seeing Mary Ann before her divorce is final, "Massachusetts has crazy laws" (58). Later in the story, as Matt forces Strout to pack his belongings, Strout attempts to defend his actions: "I wanted to try to get together with her again. . . . I couldn't even talk to her. He was always with her. I'm going to jail for it; if I ever get out I'll be an old man. Isn't that enough?" (120). In this mock trial, Matt becomes both judge and jury: "You're not going to jail" (121). Matt knows that no system of justice will deny Strout what Strout's action has denied Frank, and the thought of Strout living in freedom at any time in the future is intolerable for Matt: "just thinking of Strout in Montana or whatever place lay at the end of the lie he had told, thinking of him walking the streets there, loving a girl there . . . would be enough to slowly rot the rest of his days" (135). In the end, Matt ensures that Strout's punishment is appropriate to his crime: as Strout shot Frank, so Matt shoots Strout. In the last paragraph, Matt seems to find justice in the knowledge that both Frank and Strout will be covered by the "red and yellow leaves falling on the earth" (169).

Neither Matt nor Strout is really a "killer" (hence the title — "Killings," not "Killers"). By means of the flashbacks and the sequence in which we see Strout's house and hear his "defense," we realize that each of the murders is committed out of love. Matt cannot live with Ruth's daily pain on encountering Strout in town. He is also motivated by the love he continues to feel for his dead son. Remembering how he would stand beneath the tree behind his house as one of his children climbed it, "poised to catch the small body before it hit the earth" (77), Matt carries an undeniable burden of guilt that he could not save his son. After Frank's death, Matt feels "that all the fears he had borne while they [the children] were growing up, and all the grief he had been afraid of, had backed up like a huge wave and struck him on the beach and swept him out to sea" (77). His response to this metaphorical assault is to punish Strout. Matt is constantly reminded of that "huge wave"; as he forces Strout into the car, he recognizes "the smacking curling white at the breakwater" (87). Later, we are told that "over the engine Matt could hear through his open window the water rushing inland under the bridge" (91). Matt uses his awareness of the wave's presence to bolster his courage during his interaction with Strout. Significantly, after he has buried Strout, he throws the gun into a nearby pond (152) and the keys to Strout's car into the Merrimack River (153). In a sense, the water — the force that can drown him in grief and fear unless he opposes it in some way — represents the senseless violence that has destroyed his peaceful existence; his actions serve as defiant gestures against what he feels has "struck him on the beach and swept him out to sea."

As we learn from the interaction between Strout and Matt, Strout has also acted out of love. He attempts to explain to Matt that he wanted Mary Ann and his children back; as the earlier flashback reveals, although his life has been violent and unsuccessful in some aspects, he has not previously demonstrated that he is a "killer." Although Dubus offers these occasional insights into Strout's character, the distance between readers and Strout remains. We have a much greater understanding of Matt's thoughts and feelings than Strout's, and while other characters are referred to throughout the story by their first names, Strout is almost always referred to by his last name only.

How important is the setting? You might ask students what time and place they associate with Frank. When Matt thinks of Frank, he thinks of Frank's job as a lifeguard, of the way he smells of the beach when he comes home, of his tan. Toward the end of the story, Matt and Strout drive past "the Dairy Queen closed until spring, and the two lobster restaurants that faced each other and were crowded all summer and were now also closed" (91). Ask students why this is a significant passage. Certainly the busy summer season, replete with tourists, is associated in Matt's mind with Frank. It is appropriate that the emptiness of the fall season follows Frank's death.

Even though Matt commits a murder in this story, readers may feel tremendous sympathy for him. He is a victim who takes action against the man who caused his grief; he is also portrayed as a man of humanity who takes pains to understand other people's perspectives and the complexities of a situation. Watching his son with Mary Ann, Matt tries to imagine what Frank feels and wants Frank to find the kind of intimacy with Mary Ann that he has established with Ruth. Later, as Matt and Strout go through Strout's house, Matt attempts to understand the situation from Strout's perspective. When he is in bed with Ruth at the end of the story, Matt sees both "Frank and Mary Ann making love in her bed" (169) and Strout's lover: "The other girl was faceless, bodiless, but he felt her sleeping now" (169). Because he is such a finely drawn character, readers may find it difficult to condemn Matt for his actions in "Killings."

POSSIBLE CONNECTIONS TO OTHER SELECTIONS

William Faulkner, "A Rose for Emily" (text p. 82; question #1, following)

Susan Glaspell, *Trifles* (text p. 1038)

Ernest Hemingway, "Soldier's Home" (text p. 166; question #2, following)

CONNECTIONS QUESTIONS IN TEXT (P. 106) WITH ANSWERS

1. Compare and contrast Matt's motivation for murder with Emily's in Faulkner's "A Rose for Emily" (p. 82). Which character made you feel more empathy and sympathy for his or her actions? Why?

    In Faulkner's story, Emily's motivation for murder is to keep things from changing. Her resistance to Homer's leaving her is a more extreme version of her resistance to her father's burial. That earlier abandonment by a man seems to prepare Emily to take extreme measures to prevent Homer from getting away from her. In "Killings," on the other hand, Matt's motivation for murder is to try to return to life as it was before his son was killed. He wants some degree of normalcy not just for himself but also for his wife. Their lives have been shaken by the loss, and seeing their son's killer around town makes it impossible to live with his loss. Though he can't bring Frank back, on some level killing Strout makes it possible to go on with the life they lived before the murder.

2. Explore the father-son relationships in "Killings" and Ernest Hemingway's "Soldier's Home" (p. 166). Read the section on psychological criticism in Chapter 48, "Critical Strategies for Reading." How do you think a psychological critic would interpret these relationships in each story?

Among other things, the perspectives of the two stories make the father-son relationships in them very different. In "Killings," we see the young and promising life of the son from the perspective of his father. In addition to being proud of his son, Matt seems slightly envious or at least nostalgic for youth and the kind of love that comes with it. Frank's murder seems even more devastating from this perspective. By contrast, in "Soldier's Home," the reader sees the father from the perspective of his son. Throughout the course of the story, Krebs and his father never actually interact. The first mention of his father is nearly a page in, and he is introduced when Krebs thinks, "His father was noncommittal" (para. 8). Edicts from the father descend through Krebs's mother, who tells him, "Your father is worried, too . . . He thinks you have lost your ambition" (68). Krebs's father has no active part in his son's life, and this distance between them seems irreparable. Krebs's final thought regarding his father is one of disregard and avoidance: "He would not go down to his father's office. He would miss that one" (95).

PERSPECTIVE

A. L. BADER, *Nothing Happens in Modern Short Stories* (p. 106)

Ask students to read through relatively recent issues of *The New Yorker*, the *Atlantic Monthly*, or *Esquire* until they find a short story they really like. Does anything "happen" in the story? Is there a character change? If not, what do they like about the story?

ENCOUNTERING FICTION: COMICS AND GRAPHIC STORIES

EDWARD GOREY, *From* The Hapless Child (p. 109)

Meyer notes that Gorey "preferred to leave his . . . readers with unanswered questions." This observation is a good starting point for class discussion: What "unanswered questions" trouble your students after reading *The Hapless Child*? What possibilities arise in their minds?

Attempts to analyze Gorey's works tend to dilute their impact. Some students will find themselves drawn toward Gorey's macabre sensibility; others will be quite put off by it. You might want to engage your class in a discussion of how they respond to his work. Do they find it amusing? Depressing? Baffling? Offensive? Why?

POSSIBLE CONNECTIONS TO OTHER SELECTIONS

Kate Chopin, "The Story of an Hour" (text p. 15)

Mark Twain, "The Story of the Good Little Boy" (text p. 484; question #2, following)

Lynda Barry, "Spelling" (text p. 162; question #1, following)

CONNECTIONS QUESTIONS IN TEXT (p. 111) WITH ANSWERS

1. Compare the style of the printed letters in Gorey's drawings and in Lynda Barry's "Spelling" (text p. 162). How is the lettering related to the style and tone of each story?

   The printed letters in Gorey's "Hapless Child" appear as neat, minute script beneath each panel. Because the letters are so organized and mature-looking, they act as a visual cue to readers, telling the audience that this particular narrator is outside of the action of the story, not another child or character from the graphic. The lettering and tone of the text is that of an impartial observer to this story. In Lynda Barry's "Spelling," however, the lettering is blocky and childlike, each word crammed close together and located in a speech bubble, directly occupying space in each frame. Barry uses the lettering to show the reader that the narrator is young and not far removed from the action of each scene.

2. Compare the themes in "The Hapless Child" and in "The Story of the Good Little Boy" by Mark Twain (text p. 484).

Gorey's story is concerned with childhood helplessness and the possibility for his heroine, Charlotte Sophia, gaining some form of control. He ends with a new beginning, as Charlotte Sophia's breaking of the boarding house rules liberates her from a dismal life. When she escapes, she gets away from the adults who loom over her in other panels of the comic. She also changes out of her dark mourning clothes into a white nightgown that recalls the white dress she wears in the beginning, when she was still part of a happy family.

Twain's story is also concerned with rule-breaking, and he presents it as natural behavior for children. By contrast with his irreverent peers, Twain's "good little boy" appears perverse. Even he knows his desire to be good is problematic: "He knew it was not healthy to be too good" (para. 3). Yet he persists because he is in thrall of the didactic literature that Twain satirizes. The tongue-in-cheek ending to the story reinforces the naivety of Jacob's faith in Sunday school books, which never seem to present any useful model for real life. While Charlotte Sophia is similar to Jacob — a good child to whom bad things occur — she learns from her plight that sometimes it is best to break the rules, and by doing so seems to avoid a fate such as Jacob's.

4

Character

In the introductory section for Chapter 4, the sample passage from *Hard Times* demonstrates the intricacies of characterization. Because many students might not be familiar with Dickens's work, it might be fruitful to study the characterization in an example or two drawn from popular culture. For instance, students might decide whether the characters in their favorite television shows are static or dynamic, flat or round. They might compare comedies (typically containing stock, static characters) with dramas (often featuring characters who are allowed to change and grow). Ask students whether the characters on *How I Met Your Mother* are static or dynamic, or whether the characters on *Mad Men* are predictable or surprising in their choices and actions. Commonly, comedy arises from a manipulation of plot in order to force a predictable reaction from a well-established but static character; in contrast, drama's success usually depends on the complexities of characterization. It may be fruitful to discuss why these different "genres" require different manipulations of characterization.

Web Ask students to explore *character* at **bedfordstmartins.com/ meyerlit**.

Encourage students to get into the habit of asking themselves a series of questions about characterization after reading a story. First, is the narrator reliable? Is there any reason provided in the text that the narrator may have a particular agenda that causes her or him to alter or slant the telling of the story? (For instance, in "Bartleby, the Scrivener" [p. 133], what is the lawyer's motivation in telling the story? Is it merely that he found Bartleby an interesting character? Or, does he have something to gain from the telling?) Also, to whom is the narrator telling the story? Occasionally, we have a clear sense of audience. (In a poem such as Robert Browning's "My Last Duchess" [p. 684], for example, we know not only the identity of the listener but also his reaction to the tale.) In addition to the narrator, what other characters are significant to the story? Do the characters change in the course of the narration? Are they static or dynamic? (Sometimes, the most effective way to determine this is through a comparison of the characters.) A character's impression on the reader may be based on what the character says, what the character does, and what other characters say about the character or how they react to her or him. Students might envision themselves as private detectives building case files on each character they encounter in a story; they might share their findings in response to a given story as they develop their skills.

Web Ask students to research the authors in this chapter or take quizzes on their works at **bedfordstmartins.com/ meyerlit**.

CHARLES DICKENS, *From* Hard Times (p. 113)

Charles Dickens (1812–1870) was the author of numerous novels, travel books, and sketches. Many of his most memorable characters are inspired by his memories of childhood, during which time his father was imprisoned for debt. Dickens later acted in amateur theatricals and performed public readings of his work. His novels and other later writings were serialized in both English and American periodicals. Among his works are *Oliver Twist, Bleak House, Great Expectations, A Christmas Carol,* and *A Tale of Two Cities.* He is buried in Poet's Corner, Westminster Abbey.

In this excerpt from *Hard Times*, Dickens's description of "the speaker," Mr. Gradgrind, works to reveal aspects of his character. In addition, other characters' responses to Gradgrind emphasize certain aspects or traits of his character. How does the final paragraph of the excerpt reveal additional information about Gradgrind? How does the information about the other grown-ups in the room convey a specific impression about the children who are assembled there?

As a means of starting discussion of Dickens's characterization of Mr. Gradgrind, ask students to write a short sketch in which they experience a class taught by him. They might enjoy writing about how he would interact with their actual class.

POSSIBLE CONNECTIONS TO OTHER SELECTIONS

Nathaniel Hawthorne, "Young Goodman Brown" (text p. 315)

Mark Twain, "The Story of the Good Little Boy" (text p. 484)

JUNOT DÍAZ, *How to Date a Browngirl, Blackgirl, Whitegirl, or Halfie* (p. 119)

You might begin discussion of this story by asking students why Díaz writes his story in the form of advice. Who might this advice be directed to? A brother or a friend? Someone in whom Yunior sees himself at a younger age?

"How to Date…" is filled with moments in which the reader feels the tension between what Yunior feels and what he says. For example, when he wants to criticize the interracial relationship of one girl's parents, he says instead, "It must have been hard" (para. 14). He also takes care to obscure some of the characteristics of his immigrant family, such as his mother's ability to recognize the smell of tear gas "from the year the United States invaded your island" (10). There are signs, too, that the girls are putting on a persona.

Students should also consider the extent to which they trust Yunior's self-assured analysis of racial differences among young women. Whether or not he is correct about the young women he tries to date, he is also critical of his own relationship to race, especially his tendency to love a white girl's features "more than [he] loves [his] own" (17).

POSSIBLE CONNECTIONS TO OTHER SELECTIONS

John Updike, "A & P" (text p. 201; question #1, following)

David Updike, "Summer" (text p. 295; question #2, following)

CONNECTIONS QUESTIONS IN TEXT (p. 122) WITH ANSWERS

1. Discuss the teenage narrator's relationship to authority in Díaz's story and in John Updike's "A & P" (text p. 201).

   Both of these young men are motivated by sexuality, but they respond in very different ways to authority. Díaz's narrator largely hopes to avoid its power, which is personified in his mother. The story is framed by the lie he tells his mother to get out of a family visit and his measures to cover up what he has been doing while she has been gone. While Yunior is calculating in his escape, Updike's narrator is spontaneous. Sammy makes what he thinks of as a heroic gesture in defiance of the authority of his boss, but his gesture is barely noticed by the girls he intended to impress. He quickly registers that his defiance has much larger implications. It suggests an attitude that will only make his life more difficult.

2. Compare and contrast attitudes toward love and romance in Díaz's story and in David Updike's "Summer" (text p. 295).

   Adolescent love is romanticized in Updike's story, in part perhaps because this story takes place on vacation, in a time and place away from home and normal life. This sense that the central character, Homer, will have to return to that life eventually makes his short connection with Sandra more poignant. By contrast, Díaz's narrator, Yunior, is more realistic; he has to arrange the elements in his everyday life in order to make a romance possible. Neither Homer nor Yunior manage to consummate their relationships, but in "Summer" this emphasizes the tone of longing for a very specific object of affection, while in "How to Date..." the range of possible dates suggests that romantic connections are more provisional and determined by chance as much as by inclination. Ultimately, for both young men, potential romance is related in complicated ways to family connections and friends.

XU XI, *Famine* (p. 123)

The narrator of "Famine" travels from Hong Kong to New York on a mission "to vanquish, once and for all, [her] parents' fear of death and opulence" (para. 35). Their obsession with poverty and hunger becomes her obsession, but after their deaths she wants to move beyond it. Veronica and Kwai-sin both function as foils for the narrator because they experienced wealth and privilege earlier and more easily. Having lived through many more hard years with her parents than she could have imagined, the narrator goes to the opposite extreme, eating her way through New York's most opulent restaurants as if she can cure hunger forever.

Xu Xi wrote about "Famine," "I wanted to merge the faces we wear in public with private longings, and push this idea to its outer limits." The ending of the story achieves a surreal synthesis of public and private with the imaginary feast. The imaginary party in the hotel room takes the actual restaurant tour to strange, dreamlike heights, yet it allows the narrator to have a kind of reconciliation with her parents.

POSSIBLE CONNECTIONS TO OTHER SELECTIONS

Julia Alvarez, "Dusting" (text p. 94)

Nathan Englander, "Free Fruit for Young Widows" (text p. 281; question #2, following)

Mark Halliday, "Young Man on Sixth Avenue" (text p. 492; question #1, following)

CONNECTIONS QUESTIONS IN TEXT (p. 132) WITH ANSWERS

1. Compare the cultural ambitions of the narrator in "Famine" with those of the man in Mark Halliday's "Young Man on Sixth Avenue" (p. 492).

    Though the woman in "Famine" recognizes her parents' anxiety about famine and knows its roots in Chinese society, she wants to free herself from their fears. Her desire for a more comfortable life is intricately connected with her knowledge of English, her experiences of foreign food while in China, and even her conflicted feelings about traditional Chinese dress as readopted by her double, Kwai-sin. While Xu Xi's narrator is occupied with trying to step out of her past, Halliday's "Young Man" seems to arrive out of nowhere. He appears on the avenue tall, handsome, and confident that he will be a success in both business and life. His primary ambition is to make a mark on the huge city that, by the end, passes him without notice.

2. Compare the narrator's symbolic relationship to food in "Famine" with that of the Gezers in Nathan Englander's "Free Fruit for Young Widows" (text p. 281).

    In Xu's story, overindulging in food is a way of rejecting her parents' fears (of opulence and death). It allows her to assert her own personality and to distance herself from their austere ways. Though she carefully chooses her restaurants and her menus, the details of the food don't really matter: "It's not *what* but *how much*" (para. 92). She knows her trip, and the indulgences it affords her, can't go on forever, but she is convinced it can "save [her]" from the life she knew and also, though she doesn't explicitly say this, from her grief over her parents' death (100). In Englander's story, the food that Shimmy Gezer, followed by his son Etgar, gives away is a kind consolation for loss. For the widows of soldiers, the offering of fruit is a kind of reparation; in Tendler's case, it is also a gesture of understanding, or at least of a willingness to accept the violence in his past.

HERMAN MELVILLE, *Bartleby, the Scrivener* (p. 133)

Although students are usually intrigued by Bartleby's bizarre behavior, they are likely to respond to the "inscrutable scrivener" in much the same way that Ginger Nut assesses him: "I think, sir, he's a little *luny*" (para. 49). But to dismiss Bartleby as, say, a catatonic schizophrenic reduces the story to merely a prescient case study and tends to ignore the narrator-lawyer, the other major character. Besides, we don't learn enough about Bartleby to make anything approaching a clinical judgment because, as the lawyer tells us in the first paragraph, "No materials exist, for a full and satisfactory biography of this man." He is as disturbingly mysterious as Godwin's protagonist in "A Sorrowful Woman" (p. 39).

What makes the story so weird — a term that nearly always comes up in discussions of Bartleby — is that the lawyer and the scrivener occupy two radically different fictional worlds. We recognize the lawyer as a character from the kind of fictions that convey at least some of the realistic textures of life, but Bartleby seems to be an allegorical or symbolic intruder in that world. Melville uses Bartleby to disrupt the lawyer's assumptions about life. It's as if a Kafka character suddenly turned up in a novel by Dickens or James. Melville makes us, as much as the lawyer, feel that Bartleby is somehow out of place.

The protagonist is the lawyer; he is a dynamic character who changes while Bartleby, the antagonist, remains static throughout. (Some critics, however, see Bartleby as the story's central character. For alternative readings, see the article by Stern cited at the end of this discussion.) Melville has the lawyer characterize himself in the first few paragraphs so that we understand the point of view from which we will see Bartleby. No champion of truth and justice, the lawyer makes his living doing a "snug business among rich men's bonds, and mortgages, and title-deeds" (2). He is convinced that "the easiest way of life is best"; he is an "eminently safe man" who takes pride in his "prudence," "method," and status (signified by his reference three times in the second paragraph to John Jacob Astor). His other employees, Turkey, Nippers, and Ginger Nut, are introduced to the reader before Bartleby in order to make credible the lawyer's tolerance for eccentric behavior. So long as the lawyer gets some work out of these human copying machines, he'll put up with just about everything — provided they don't publicly embarrass him or jeopardize his reputation. It is significant that he is a lawyer rather than simply a businessman, because the law is founded on precedents and assumptions; Bartleby, however, is "more a man of preferences than assumptions" (149). Because Bartleby is beyond the lawyer's experience, the lawyer does not know how to respond to the scrivener's passive refusal to "come forth" and do "his duty."

Despite the title, the story is the lawyer's, because his sense of humanity enlarges as a result of his experience with Bartleby. "The bond of a common humanity" creates "presentiments of strange discoveries [that] hover[ed] round me" (91). In a sense, the lawyer discovers what Emily Dickinson's speaker describes in "There's a certain Slant of light" (p. 1521), a poem that can help students understand the significance of the lawyer's final comment, "Ah, Bartleby! Ah, humanity!" The lawyer moves beyond his initial incredulity, confusion, anger, and frustration and begins to understand that Bartleby represents a challenge to all his assumptions about life. Finally, he invests meaning in Bartleby instead of dismissing him as eccentric or mad. Melville expects the reader to puzzle out his meaning too.

Bartleby's physical characteristics foreshadow his death. When we first meet him (17), he already seems to have withdrawn from life. He is "motionless" and "pallidly neat, pitiably respectable, incurably forlorn!" He seems scarcely alive and is described as "cadaverous." With nearly all the life gone out of him, he is capable of nothing more than "silently, palely, mechanically" (20) copying until he prefers not to — a refusal that marks the beginning of his increasing insistence on not living.

Bartleby's "I would prefer not to" confuses and enrages the lawyer and his employees. This simple declaration takes on more power and significance as the story progresses (not unlike Edgar Allan Poe's use of "nevermore" in "The Raven"). Bartleby's seemingly mild statement carries with it considerable heft, because "some paramount consideration prevailed with him to reply as he did" (39). His declaration is both humorous and deadly serious.

The Dead Letter Office is essential to understanding what motivates Bartleby's behavior. Although Melville is not specific, he suggests enough about the nature of the thwarted hopes and desires that the scrivener daily encountered in the Dead Letter Office to account for Bartleby's rejection of life. Somehow it was all too painful for him and rendered life barren and meaningless — hence his "dead-wall reveries." The lawyer makes the connection between this experience and Bartleby. But Melville has him withhold that information so that we focus on the effect Bartleby has on the narrator rather than on the causes of Bartleby's rejection of life. By the end of the story, the lawyer has a chastened view of life that challenges his assumption that "the easiest way of life is best."

You may want to ask students to identify the different walls that compose the various settings of this story. (In addition to those in the office, the walls of the prison at the end of the story are significant.) Melville's story is subtitled "A Story of Wall Street" because Bartleby's "dead-wall reveries" represent a rejection of the materialistic values that inform the center of American financial interests. Business and money mean nothing to Bartleby, but they essentially constitute the sum total of the lawyer's life until his encounter with him. Melville sympathizes with the characters while rejecting their responses to life. He clearly does not endorse the lawyer's smug materialism, but neither does he offer Bartleby's unrelenting vision of death as an answer to the dehumanizing, mechanical meaninglessness that walls the characters in. In this story Melville presents issues, not solutions; it is exploratory rather than definitive.

This story can be usefully regarded as a kind of sit-in protest — at least on a metaphysical level — with nonnegotiable demands. Bartleby is a stubborn reminder that the lawyer's world is driven by expediency rather than principle — that the lawyer's satisfaction with life has been based on his previous avoidance of the big issues. Surprisingly, there is some delightful humor in the story as the characters' exasperation with Bartleby's behavior develops. We know that the scrivener is going to get a rise out of them. There is also humor in Bartleby's reply to the lawyer that he is "sitting upon the banister" (195) when the lawyer asks him what he's doing in his office building on a Sunday. And consider the lawyer's suggestions that Bartleby be a bartender, a bill collector, or a traveling companion "to entertain some young gentleman with your conversation" (199–210). A student once suggested that a dramatization of the story should feature Richard Nixon as the lawyer and Woody Allen as Bartleby. Ask students for their own suggestions on who might play these roles; the question encourages them to think of what goes into a characterization.

Students might be asked to trace their reactions to Bartleby while they read, then to compare them with how they respond to him after class discussion of his character.

For an excellent survey of the many varied critical approaches to the story, see Milton R. Stern's "Towards 'Bartleby the Scrivener,' " in *The Stoic Strain in American Literature*, ed. Duane J. MacMillan (Toronto: U of Toronto P, 1979), 19–41.

POSSIBLE CONNECTIONS TO OTHER SELECTIONS

Emily Dickinson, "There's a certain Slant of light" (text p. 1521)

Robert Frost, "Mending Wall" (text p. 843)

Gail Godwin, "A Sorrowful Woman" (text p. 39; question #1, following)

Nathaniel Hawthorne, "Young Goodman Brown" (text p. 315; question #2, following)

CONNECTIONS QUESTIONS IN TEXT (p. 157) WITH ANSWERS

1. Compare Bartleby's withdrawal from life with that of the protagonist in Gail Godwin's "A Sorrowful Woman" (p. 39). Why does each character choose death?

The title characters in both of these stories seem to withdraw as a reaction against demands placed on them, demands that would seem normal to most people. As a clerk, Bartleby is expected to complete the copying work his employer assigns to him, regardless of his preference. The surprise of his refusal, coupled with the gentle manner in which he states it, makes it hard for the narrator of the story to compel him to fulfill his normal role as a worker. Godwin's "Sorrowful Woman" refuses by stages to complete the tasks typical for a wife and mother: cooking, cleaning, getting her child ready for school, etc. She too is mild in her revolt, simply retreating to her bedroom and finally refusing even to see her husband and son. For both characters, death seems to be the final renunciation of the world's expectations.

2. How is Melville's use of Bartleby's experience in the Dead Letter Office similar to Nathaniel Hawthorne's use of Brown's forest encounter with the devil in "Young Goodman Brown" (p. 315)? Why is each experience crucial to an understanding of what informs the behavior of these characters?

Melville uses the Dead Letter Office to suggest a reason for Bartleby's behavior, both to the reader and to the lawyer who narrates the story. We want an explanation for responses to the world that seem abnormal, as Bartleby's certainly does. The idiosyncrasies of the other clerks, though strange perhaps, fit into our understanding of how people cope with oppressive jobs and living situations, but Bartleby's refusal is different. Melville doesn't introduce the Dead Letter Office until the end, which makes it a less certain explanation, one that might be plausible only because some kind of explanation is needed. However, the idea of Bartleby surrounded by letters that cannot find their addressees does give some context to his sense of quiet despair. The forest encounter in "Young Goodman Brown" also helps to explain the main character's later behavior, but Hawthorne spends much more time describing it than Melville does the Dead Letter Office. In this story, the motivating incident is the subject, and it's only at the end, when Brown returns to his family and neighbors, that we see the effect it will have on him. His superior attitude to those around him is perhaps not as mysterious as Bartleby's withdrawal, but Hawthorne makes a vivid story out of his initiation into the dark side of life.

PERSPECTIVES ON MELVILLE

NATHANIEL HAWTHORNE, *On Herman Melville's Philosophic Stance* (p. 158)

After reading Hawthorne's description of Melville, ask students to identify aspects of the description that recall any of the characters or instances from "Bartleby, the Scrivener." In particular, how might Melville's habit of "reason[ing] of Providence and futurity, and of everything that lies beyond human ken" (para. 1) have influenced his portrait of the lawyer? Is there any detail from Hawthorne's description of Melville that recalls Bartleby's characterization?

DAN McCALL, *On the Lawyer's Character in "Bartleby, the Scrivener"* (p. 158)

McCall's topic lies at the heart of any interpretation of Melville's story: How do we perceive both Bartleby and the lawyer? While McCall presents numerous critical opinions on the subject, he fails (in this excerpt) to apply his own argument to the text itself. Ask students to rely on specific examples from the story in explaining whether they find the lawyer sympathetic or unsympathetic.

McCall's article can also provide students with an out-of-class project. Where he focuses on the lawyer's character, encourage students to identify and explain the range of responses to Bartleby himself. How has the perception of either Bartleby or the lawyer changed over the years?

ENCOUNTERING FICTION: COMICS AND GRAPHIC STORIES

LYNDA BARRY, *Spelling* (p. 162)

The attitudes and behaviors of this strip's central character, Marlys, bear out Barry's assertion that a person's mastery of one small aspect of life does not "mean their life is perfect because of it." In just four panels, Barry manages to evoke a familiar annoyance with people who base a sense of personal superiority on trivial accomplishments. At the same time, *Spelling* threatens lifelong consequences for trivial social transgressions and offers empathy for a socially inept young girl. You might want to ask your students what universal fears and desires Marlys personifies. Why is her obsession with spelling so funny?

POSSIBLE CONNECTION TO ANOTHER SELECTION

Herman Melville, "Bartleby, the Scrivener" (text p. 133)

5

Setting

Several aspects of setting are described in the introduction to Chapter 5. Setting may include the time, the location, and the social environment in which a story takes place; moreover, it may contribute additional significance to the meaning of the story. In addition, setting may involve traditional associations. Students might practice identifying their associations with a given place, time of day, and time of year. For instance, what do they associate with Seattle, or Birmingham, Alabama? With midnight? With autumn? Commonly, the general connotations that readers associate with a given setting are those the author has in mind as well. When a setting is specified, students should get in the habit of considering why that setting might be significant. When a setting is not specified, students should also consider the writer's rationale. It might be useful to briefly discuss in class why a writer might or might not specify a setting for a particular story.

Web Ask students to explore *setting* at **bedfordstmartins.com/ meyerlit**.

The stories in this chapter all contain settings that operate on a metaphorical level to contribute to their meaning. Throughout recent history, Yugoslavia has been known for violence and social upheaval; appropriately enough, in Fay Weldon's "IND AFF," it serves as the backdrop for a young woman's life-changing personal decisions. The title of Ernest Hemingway's story, "Soldier's Home," might refer in general to Harold Krebs's small Oklahoma town. It might also call readers' attention to the conditions Krebs encounters in his own family's house — their inability to understand his war experiences. Moreover, the title suggests a particular time — Krebs's return after the war ("Soldier is Home"). The sample stories in this chapter all enable students to reach beyond a literal setting and think more figuratively about the meanings of these works.

Web Ask students to research the authors in this chapter or take quizzes on their works at **bedfordstmartins.com/ meyerlit**.

ERNEST HEMINGWAY, *Soldier's Home* (p. 166)

This is a war story that includes no physical violence because Hemingway focuses on the war's psychological effects on the protagonist. A truce ended the wholesale butchery of youth fighting during World War I, but the painful memory of it has made Krebs a prisoner of war. Although the story's setting is a peaceful small town in Oklahoma, Hemingway evokes the horrors that Krebs endured and brought back home with him. In a sense the real setting of this story is Belleau Wood as well as the sites of the other bloody battles Krebs experienced. (A brief student report summarizing the nature of these battles and the casualties they produced can provide a vivid context for class discussion of the story.)

Krebs cannot talk about his experiences at home because people in town have "heard too many atrocity stories to be thrilled by actualities" (para. 4). He has been affected as a result of his experiences in a way they'll never be, and therein lies the story's conflict. The fraternity brother who went off to war in 1917 with romantic expectations returns knowing what the real picture is (consider the ironic deflation produced by the two photographs in paragraphs 1 and 2). Krebs knows that popular visions of the glory of war are illusions and that the reality consists more typically of sickening fear. An inadvertent hint of that comes from his sister, who calls him "Hare," a nickname that suggests fright and flight. (For a poem with a similar theme see Wilfred Owen's "Dulce et Decorum Est," p. 633.) Krebs prefers silence to lying.

Krebs refuses to engage in the familiar domestic patterns of life expected of him. He also rejects the "complicated" world of the young girls in town. (Krebs's rejection of whatever is "complicated" is related to Hemingway's style on p. 265 in the text.) Nothing really matters very much to him; he appears numb and unwilling to commit himself to what he regards as meaningless, trivial games. He feels more at home remembering Germany and France than living in his parents' house. Reading a history of the battles he's been in gives him a feeling of something more real than his life at home, which strikes him as petty, repressive, and blind. His father's permission to use the family car, for example, is neither wanted nor needed. (For a discussion of the symbolic significance of home in the story, see p. 220 in the text.)

Krebs's mother brings the conflict to a climax. She speaks for the family and the community, urging Krebs to get back to a normal life of work, marriage, and "being really a credit to the community." Krebs finds his mother's values little more than sentimental presuppositions that in no way relate to the person he has become. The only solution to the suffocating unreality imposed on him by his family and town is to leave home. He can neither love nor pray; he's no longer in "his Kingdom" (63). There's no going back to that prewar identity as an innocent fraternity brother from a Methodist college. The story's title, then, is ironic, for Krebs cannot go home again, because home seems to be either a lie or a place stunningly ignorant of what he discovered in the war.

Possible Connections to Other Selections

James Joyce, "Eveline" (text p. 407)

Wilfred Owen, "Dulce et Decorum Est" (text p. 633; question #1, following)

Flannery O'Connor, "Good Country People" (text p. 367)

John Updike, "A & P" (text p. 201)

Muriel Spark, "The First Year of My Life" (text p. 475, question #2, following)

Connections Questions in Text (p. 171) with Answers

1. Contrast the attitudes toward patriotism implicit in this story with those in Wilfred Owen's "Dulce et Decorum Est" (p. 633). How do the stories' settings help to account for the differences between them?

   The ideas of home and country are important in both Hemingway's "Soldier's Home" (p. 166) and Wilfred Owen's "Dulce et Decorum Est" (p. 633). In "Soldier's Home," patriotism is aligned with the dramatic or the pictorial. The citizens at home want the newsreel version of World War I, complete with both the atrocities of the Axis powers and the heroism of the Allied soldiers to help define what is American. It's significant that Krebs identifies with the losing side; when thinking about the countries he saw during the war, he confesses, "On the whole he had liked Germany better. He did not want to leave Germany. He did not want to come home" (para. 14). After his war experience, he is outside of the American mainstream, just as he is outside God's "Kingdom" (63).

   Owen's poem "Dulce et Decorum Est" also shatters the romanticized view of war that civilians cling to. The young men in the poem are separated from America while they fight on the front lines of World War I. These soldiers are struggling under immense suffering, "Bent double, like old beggars under sacks, / Knock-kneed, coughing like hags" (1–2). Their physical pain and exhaustion drive all thoughts of higher purpose out of their minds: "All went lame, all blind; / Drunk with fatigue" (6–7). The speaker describes a gas attack and the resulting death of his companion who did not get his mask on quickly enough. He is haunted by this image, and admits "In all my dreams before my helpless sight / He plunges at me, guttering, choking, drowning" (15–16). The speaker ultimately rejects stereotypical, blind patriotism; the realities of war have made the reasons for it inconsequential, and ultimately insufficient.

2. How might Krebs's rejection of his community's values be related to Sammy's relationship to his supermarket job in John Updike's "A & P" (p. 201)? What details does Updike use to make the setting in "A & P" a comic, though nonetheless serious, version of Krebs's hometown?

Krebs refuses the usual activities expected of a man his age: he won't get a job, and he shows no interest in girls. Hemingway describes Krebs's hometown as a pageant, which Krebs watches but does not participate in. For example, he likes to see "the girls that were walking along the other side of the street" (para. 15), but he doesn't want to get too close to them. At the end he gives in to the expectations of his family and society, resigning himself to getting a job and rejoining community life, but his decision does not promise a real integration back into the values of the society.

Sammy's break from his community is caused not by a deeply traumatic event like war, but by an incident that could appear insignificant to many people. The force of his reaction compared to the relatively minor humiliation of the girls suggests that he was already questioning the community norms. As he quits his job, he knows that his family and friends will not understand his actions properly as a rejection of the power dynamic between the store owners and the young customers, but he feels that he has to make the gesture anyway.

3. Explain how the violent details that Muriel Spark uses to establish the setting in "The First Year of My Life" (p. 475) can be considered representative of the kinds of horrors that haunt Krebs after he returns home.

Though Hemingway never overtly presents any of Krebs's frightening experiences, they are a constantly present undercurrent of the story. The reader can tell that those experiences haunt Krebs by his fascination with books about the war. Not only does he find them to be the "most interesting reading he had ever done," but he thinks that through them he is "really learning about the war" (para. 16). Krebs has to put his terrifying memories into the context of the clearly and calmly presented narrative of the history books. This is one way to try to control his "nausea," which we infer comes from the horrors he has seen (6).

In Muriel Spark's "The First Year of My Life," the narrator is an omniscient infant born in the final year of World War I. From the distant safety of her bed, she can see all the horrors of the front lines, while Krebs toils amongst them. Though she is not actually there, she can see what Hemingway's protagonist experiences, and describes it vividly: "The Western Front on my frequency was sheer blood, mud, dismembered bodies, blistered crashes, hectic flashes of light in the night skies, explosions, total terror" (10). When the German Spring Offensive begins, she says only, "Infinite slaughter" (11). This infinite slaughter was Krebs's life for months on end. Spark's speaker also describes how ". . . soldiers leapfrogged over the dead on the advance and littered the fields with limbs and hands, or drowned in the mud" (16). The reader is given the final tallies of war's accomplishments: "On all the world's fighting fronts the men killed in action or dead of wounds numbered 8,538,315 and the warriors wounded and maimed were 21,219,452" (19). Learning the sheer number of human lives destroyed forces one to contemplate how many men a soldier like Krebs must have seen murdered on a daily basis. Knowing the sheer brutality of the war enhances one's understanding of Krebs's attitude toward life and the seemingly cruel things he says to his mother.

PERSPECTIVE

ERNEST HEMINGWAY, *On What Every Writer Needs* (p. 172)

Ask students to discuss a character (from any story) who does not have a "shit detector." How might this character think and behave differently if he or she did have such "radar"?

FAY WELDON, *IND AFF, or Out of Love in Sarajevo* (p. 173)

In this brief cautionary tale, Weldon manages to question the nature of fate and individual will, desire, and imagination, as well as question the relationship between the apparently political and the apparently personal. It is not so much the "sad story" promised by the first line as it is a fable about taking responsibility for one's actions and understanding the essentially interconnected nature of all events.

When the twenty-five-year-old unnamed narrator fell in love with her forty-six-year-old thesis director (who was already married and the father of three children), she fell in love with her idea of him rather than with him as a man. The narrator, who tells her story from the perspective of one who has learned her lesson and is now simply imparting it, has come to understand that she had confused "mere passing academic ambition with love" (para. 48), believing this man's assessment of the world and of herself ("He said I had a good mind but not a first-class mind and somehow I didn't take it as an insult" [4]) when she should have been coming up with her own conclusions. Weldon comments in another story concerned with a young woman's infatuation with a much older man that "it was not her desire that was stirred, it was her imagination. But how is she to know this?" What the narrator wishes to believe about her lover — that this is "not just any old professor-student romance" — and what she actually feels about him are two different things.

Peter Piper (the name itself should indicate a certain lack of respect on the part of the author for such characters), the Cambridge professor who has been married to a swimming coach for twenty-four years, likes to "luxuriate in guilt and indecision" and has taken his student/mistress with him on a holiday to see whether they are "really, truly suited," to make sure that it is "the Real Thing" before they "shack up, as he put it." The narrator is desperately drawn to her teacher because he represents much more than he actually offers. To maintain her affection for Peter, she overlooks his stinginess ("Peter felt it was less confusing if we each paid our own way" [44]), his whining ("I noticed I had become used to his complaining. I supposed that when you had been married a little you simply wouldn't hear it" [12]), the fact that often when she spoke "he wasn't listening," the fact that he might not want her to go topless at the beach ("this might be the area where the age difference showed"), and his "thinning hair" because he seems authoritative (speaking in "quasi-Serbo-Croatian") and powerful. He "liked to be asked questions" and obviously adores the adoration of his student. She loves him with "inordinate affection," she claims. "Your Ind Aff is my wife's sorrow" (27), Peter moans, blaming a girl who was born the first year of his marriage for his wife's unhappiness, absolving himself from any blame.

The question of whether particular events happen because of the inevitable build-up of insurmountable forces or, instead, because of a series of particular moments that might have been avoided with care, caution, or consideration is brought to bear not only on the narrator's relationship with Peter but on the question of World War I. With the background material effortlessly supplied by Weldon, even readers unfamiliar with the story of Princip's assassination of the archduke will be able to see the way Princip's tale parallels that of the narrator. Was the war inevitable? Was it, as Peter Piper claims, bound to "start sooner or later" because of the "social and economic tensions" that had to find "some release"? Along the same lines of reasoning, is the twenty-four-year marriage between Peter and the woman who is known only as Mrs. Piper doomed to failure, or is it instead pressured into failure by the husband's infidelity? Is it, as the narrator's sister Clare (herself married to a much older professor) claims, a fact that "if you can unhinge a marriage, it's ripe for unhinging, it would happen sooner or later, it might as well be you" (36)? Is it, in other words, the narrator who is assassinating the Piper marriage?

The climax of the story occurs when the narrator and Peter are waiting to be served wild boar in a private restaurant. She notices a waiter whom she describes as being "about my age" (showing her keenly felt awareness of the difference in age between herself and Peter). She has felt desire for Peter in her mind, and has learned to feel "a pain in her heart" as an "erotic sensation," but in looking at the virile, handsome man her own age, she feels "quite violently, an associated yet different pang which got my lower stomach." She describes this desire as the "true, the real pain of Ind Aff!" Her desire for the waiter has nothing to do with his position, his authority, or his power. It has to do with his "flashing eyes, hooked nose, luxuriant black hair, sensuous mouth" (38). She asks herself in a moment of clear vision, "What was I doing with this man with thinning hair?" (41). She thinks to herself, when she automatically tells Peter that she loves him, "How much I lied." She has freed herself from the confines of his authority and declares in opposition to him that "if Princip hadn't shot the archduke, something else, some undisclosed, unsuspected variable, might have come along and defused the whole political/military situation, and neither World War I nor II ever happened" (43). She then gets up to go "home."

"This is how I fell out of love with my professor," declares the narrator, describing their affair as "a silly, sad episode, which I regret." She sees herself as silly for having confused her career ambitions with desire and silly for trying to "outdo my sister Clare," who has married her professor (but has to live in Brussels as a sort of cosmic penance). Piper eventually proves spiteful and tries to refuse the narrator's thesis, but she wins her appeal and, delightfully, can confirm for herself that she does indeed have a "first-class mind." She feels, finally, a connection to poor Princip, who should have "hung on a bit, there in Sarajevo" because he might have "come to his senses. People do, sometimes quite quickly" (48).

POSSIBLE CONNECTIONS TO OTHER SELECTIONS

Mark Halliday, "Graded Paper" (text p. 680)

Nathaniel Hawthorne, "The Birthmark" (text p. 333; question #2, following)

D. H. Lawrence, "The Horse Dealer's Daughter" (text p. 506; question #3, following)

Katherine Mansfield, "Miss Brill" (text p. 254)

Susan Minot, "Lust" (text p. 274; question #1, following)

CONNECTIONS QUESTIONS IN TEXT (p. 179) WITH ANSWERS

1. Compare and contrast "IND AFF" and Susan Minot's, "Lust" (p. 274) as love stories. Do you think that the stories end happily, or the way you would want them to end? Are the endings problematic?

    As love stories, both "IND AFF" and "Lust" may feel foreign to students. First, encourage students to define for themselves what a "love story" actually is. Is it solely about romantic love? Or can it be about learning self-love? In Weldon's "IND AFF" there is a relationship, but it ends; in Minot's "Lust," the relationships are fleeting and leave the narrator feeling downtrodden. Because of these conclusions, some students will see these both as depressing stories or will wish they had ended differently. However, one could argue that stories perhaps do not end happily, but instead productively. In "IND AFF," the main character realizes that she only initiated an affair with Peter, her professor, because she had confused "academic ambition with love" (para. 48) and was trying to one-up her younger sister. She decides to leave as soon as she has this realization, and still earns her PhD. despite jilting her thesis advisor.

    Minot's narrator catalogs her early relationships in a disaffected manner, saying, "You wonder how long you can keep it up" (64). She's clearly unhappy in these relationships, and sex is especially devastating to her sense of self: "After sex, you curl up like a shrimp, something deep inside you ruined, slammed in a place that sickens at slamming, and slowly you fill up with an overwhelming sadness, an elusive gaping worry" (79). Despite her despair, she continues to enter into new relationships with different men, restarting her love story over and over again, but never finding the happy ending. The ultimate love story for this narrator would be to learn to do what makes her happy and helps her fulfill her own wants and needs.

2. Explain how Weldon's concept of "Ind Aff" — "inordinate affection" — can be used to make sense of the relationship between Georgiana and Aylmer in Nathaniel Hawthorne's "The Birthmark" (p. 333).

Aylmer, the "mad scientist" of Hawthorne's "The Birthmark," might aver that his feeling for Georgiana is what Weldon describes as the opposite of "Ind Aff": "A pure and spiritual, if passionate, concern for her soul" (para. 26). Yet given his obsession with Georgiana's physical characteristic — the birthmark tellingly shaped as a human handprint — he might more accurately be described as displaying "Ind Aff." The long-suffering Georgiana, on the other hand, displays a love that is more pure and spiritual. It is possible that like Weldon's professor, who refuses to acknowledge his own responsibility when he tells the protagonist that "your Ind Aff is my wife's sorrow" (27), Aylmer may never perceive or accept his own responsibility for the events leading to Georgiana's death.

3. How does passion figure in "IND AFF" and in D. H. Lawrence's "The Horse Dealer's Daughter" (p. 506)? Explain how Weldon's and Lawrence's perspectives on passion suggest differing views of love and human relationships.

Weldon's story is primarily passionless — certainly there is little sexual energy or warmth between the narrator and the professor, for whom she feels at most a sentimental and intellectual attachment. The only real passion in this story comes when the narrator looks at the young waiter: "Instead of the pain in the heart I'd become accustomed to as an erotic sensation, [I] now felt, quite violently, an associated yet different pang which got my lower stomach" (para. 38). In contrast, Mabel and Fergusson, the protagonists of Lawrence's story, seem to be affecting each other even before their symbolically loaded journey into the muddy pond. However, readers may have the sense that while Mabel and Fergusson's future will continue to be sparked by their almost raw emotional response to each other, they'll never quite banish the odor of the brackish water. Ask students to compare the tone of the final paragraphs of each story: How much does each paragraph convey about the protagonists' choices, perspectives, and futures?

PERSPECTIVE

FAY WELDON, *On the Importance of Place in "IND AFF"* (p. 179)

Weldon's Perspective on her story, taken from an interview almost ten years after it was published, invites readers to apply biographical strategies to "IND AFF." Students might first describe the aspects of the story that seem relevant to Weldon's commentary. Second, they might consider her assessment of setting in this story. Given the political and cultural instability of this region in the 1990s, culminating in the arrival of the UN peacekeeping force, what additional meaning might be drawn from "IND AFF"?

MAY-LEE CHAI, *Saving Sourdi* (p. 181)

"Saving Sourdi" is a coming-of-age tale about the story's narrator, Nea, as she grows from a spirited but naive girl into a young woman who has gained some understanding of herself, her family, and her life in America. You might want to begin class discussion by asking your students who the story is about. Although Chai's focus might seem, at first, to be on Sourdi's arranged marriage and what happens to her as a result of it, a careful reading makes it clear that the protagonist is, indeed, the younger sister.

Point your students to the text's discussion of characterization to help them understand why Nea is the more central figure in the story. Although her name figures in the title, Sourdi is a flat character: the story begins and ends with her meekly accepting the role assigned to her by her mother (and, by extension, her culture). She does not question her fate, let alone struggle against it, despite Nea's desperate attempts to get her to fight for herself. Nor does Chai give her readers much insight into Sourdi's emotional

landscape. We can tell that she is afraid of some things, particularly men and the authorities she believes will put her and her sisters into foster homes if they do not behave as
they are expected to. And we can tell that she has chosen not to fight, although we don't
know how she feels about that decision. But everything we know about Sourdi is filtered
through Nea's perceptions. Indeed, Sourdi's character is most significant in how she
serves as a foil for Nea's: Sourdi is everything that her little sister is not.

Readers are fully aware, however, of how Nea feels about her situation. She is a
fully rounded character whose perceptions of herself and of the world change drasti-
cally by the story's end. At the same time, her narration makes it clear that she is
confused and frightened by life in South Dakota. She doesn't know what to make of
it at all, but she is determined to imagine herself as brave and in control of her surroundings. Notice, for example, how she introduces herself: she reports that she
"stabbed" (para. 1) a man when she was eleven, although we learn later that she
managed only to nick him through the fabric of his jacket. Nea thinks of herself as
a brave protector capable of violence. She refuses to acknowledge her fear, but her
actions betray her terror of life in America. (This raises the question of how reliable
she is as a narrator.)

You can probably generate a very interesting class discussion by asking your students what Nea is afraid of: Is it America, men, authority, the possibility of losing her
sister, adulthood, marriage, motherhood, something else? If Nea is the story's protagonist, then who — or what — is her antagonist? What, exactly, does she think she is saving Sourdi *from*? In attempting to protect her sister, is she revealing a desire to protect
herself as well? You might want to ask your students, also, why Nea is so determined to
protect her older sister yet shows no concern for her younger sisters. How does that
observation influence their interpretation of her fears?

Another interesting avenue for discussion is the narrator's name. Meyer discusses
at some length how the names of characters can suggest important information about
them. Like *Sourdi*, *Nea* sounds like a traditional Cambodian name, but it is also a feminine form of *neo*, the Latin word for *new*. A common theme in immigrant literature is
the conflict between the old world and the new. With this in mind, how can the story
of Nea's fears and struggles — and her defiant efforts to form her own ideas and to
define life on her own terms — be read as a story about adapting to life in a new country with an unfamiliar culture?

Possible Connections to Other Selections

Julia Alvarez, "Queens, 1963" (text p. 897; question #1, following)

John Updike, "A & P" (text p. 201; question #2, following)

Connections Questions in Text (p. 194) with Answers

1. Discuss the process of immigrants becoming Americanized in this story and in
   Julia Alvarez's poem "Queens, 1963" (text p. 897).

   Alvarez's poem dramatizes the process by which different groups of immigrants
   become "melted into" (63) the United States of America. The fate of the German,
   Jewish, and Dominican families on the block offers hope for the newly arrived
   African American family, but Alvarez does not diminish the difficulty of their position. The speaker of the poem notices, and recognizes from her own experience,
   their air of "hardness mixed with hurt" (65).

   In "Saving Sourdi," Chai shows her characters negotiating their status as outsiders,
   largely through their relation to Sourdi's boyfriend, Duke. Even at his most sympathetic, Duke can't become a full confidant for Sourdi and Nea. Their shared, and
   separate, experience is focused in the story of survival that Sourdi tells to her sister,
   about carrying Nea across a minefield, being willing to "walk on bones" to save her
   (para. 178).

2. Compare the characterization of Nea in "Saving Sourdi" and of Sammy in John Updike's "A & P" (p. 201). In what sense do both characters see themselves as rescuers?

Both Nea and Sammy do what they think of as heroic deeds for people who either don't appreciate or are unaware of what they've done. Both of their "rescues" fail, and both of them suffer negative consequences (Nea is rejected by her sister and will almost certainly be punished by her mother; Sammy loses a secure job). At the same time, neither character is acting purely out of disinterested concern for the people they are trying to help. Nea, at some level, perceives that her sister's situation could be her own fate if she doesn't fight it; Sammy objects to the store manager's humiliating treatment of the three girls not only for their own sake but because he had derived a certain amount of pleasure from observing their bodies and their rebellious behavior. Both Nea and Sammy, indeed, are as much rebelling against custom as they are helping somebody else.

6

Point of View

After reading the introduction to Chapter 6, students should be able to distinguish a first-person point of view from a third-person point of view. Is the narrator a major or minor character in the story or a witness to it? Does the narrator have access to the inner thoughts of all the characters? One of the characters? None of the characters? Students should practice identifying the point of view in the stories they study. Then, they should analyze the author's choice of point of view. In addition, point of view is related to characterization in significant ways. Students should be aware that a narrator may have a particular agenda — that the telling of the story is slanted in some respect. Is the narrator trying to make himself look more important? Generally, point of view is designed to showcase a dynamic (rather than a static) character. Students should know why an author chooses a particular point of view; they should also imagine the effect of changing the point of view within a given story. What would be lost or gained in changing a particular story's point of view?

Web Ask students to explore *point of view* at **bedfordstmartins.com/ meyerlit**.

Web Ask students to research the authors in this chapter or take quizzes on their works at **bedfordstmartins.com/ meyerlit**.

JOHN UPDIKE, *A & P* (p. 201)

John Updike is one of those rare writers who command both popular acclaim and critical respect. The prolific novelist, short story writer, and poet was born in Shillington, Pennsylvania, in 1932, completed a bachelor's degree at Harvard University (where he worked for a time as a cartoonist for the Harvard *Lampoon*), and spent a year at Oxford University studying at the Ruskin School of Drawing and Fine Arts. After returning from England in 1955, he worked at *The New Yorker*, where he began publishing his short fiction. He left the magazine in 1957 to write full-time, and wrote prolifically until his death in 2009.

Updike's great subject was the relationship between men and women, especially in marriage. The Rabbit novels (*Rabbit, Run*, 1960; *Rabbit Redux*, 1971; *Rabbit Is Rich*, 1981; and *Rabbit at Rest*, 1990; named for their protagonist, Harry "Rabbit" Angstrom) constitute perhaps the best-known examples of this preoccupation. Updike received numerous awards, including the National Book Award, the Pulitzer Prize, and the Creative Arts Medal for Lifetime Achievement from Brandeis University. His collections of stories include *Pigeon Feathers* (1962) and *Trust Me* (1987); his novels include *The Centaur* (1963), *The Coup* (1978), and most recently, *The Widows of Eastwick* (2008). His poetry collections include *The Carpentered Hen and Other Tame Creatures* (1958) and *Tossing and Turning* (1977); his nonfiction works include a collection of essays and criticism, *Hugging the Shore* (1983), and the memoir *Self-Consciousness* (1989).

Sammy's voice is what pulls us into "A & P," thanks to his engaging first-person narration. Ask the class to describe his voice — the tone he uses, the things he thinks and says, the way he says them. What kind of a person is Sammy?

While Sammy is not exactly an all-American boy — he's too much of a smart aleck and disrespectful to his elders and to women (when he's not telling us about "sheep" or "houseslaves," he's focused on someone's belly or shoulders or "sweet broad soft-looking can") — he is funny, and we excuse most of his prejudices on the ground of youth. (He *is* young. It is difficult to imagine the more mature, responsible Stokesie, for example, quitting his job over this incident.) Updike's mastery of the vernacular makes Sammy all the more appealing: we enjoy hearing him talk and think, and his observations about protocol in the A & P and his small town are mercilessly accurate. At the same time Sammy is critical of this context, however, he is also a part of it: "We're [the A & P is] right in the middle of town, and the women generally put on a shirt or shorts or something before they get out of the car into the street.... Poor kids, I began to feel sorry for them, they couldn't help it" (para. 10–11). He understands how the little world he lives in works, and he knows it is inappropriate for the girls to be wearing bathing suits in the A & P.

Ask the class to identify the climax of the story (Sammy quitting his job) and to discuss why Sammy quits. Sammy hasn't given us any evidence that he hates his job. He has a friend there, and his wonderful description of using the cash register suggests he gets a certain amount of pleasure from his mastery of the machine. He is bored, however. (His descriptions of the store's regular clientele and the view from the front of the store demonstrate this.) And, without realizing it, he's probably looking for a cause, or at least something to react to. He does, after a while, feel bad for the girls, and quitting becomes a heroic gesture. In his mind, he isn't defending the honor and dignity of just these three embarrassed girls but of everyone, including himself, who feels humiliated or restricted by the narrow parameters of the silly, limited, limiting town or society in which they live.

Ask the class what Sammy gains from quitting. In acting on what has suddenly become principle, does he gain anything? On the surface, he certainly loses more than he gains. The gesture is lost on the girls, who hightail it out of the store too fast even to hear him. And, of course, he loses his job. But for the moment, anyway, he retains his dignity — and the last line of the story suggests he has already gained some perspective.

Ask the class whether they think Sammy should have quit and whether they agree that "once you begin a gesture it's fatal not to go through with it" (31). How do they imagine Updike feels about this statement? The relatively somber tone of the story's last three paragraphs, along with the narrator's dramatic last line, suggest that Updike does not agree with Sammy on this point. Sammy's going to learn from this experience, but he's learning the hard way. (This can lead to an interesting paper: exploring the roles and attitudes of the two minor characters, Stokesie and Lengel, by comparing them with Sammy.)

POSSIBLE CONNECTIONS TO OTHER SELECTIONS

May-Lee Chai, "Saving Sourdi" (text p. 181)

Ernest Hemingway, "Soldier's Home" (text p. 166)

Flannery O'Connor, "Revelation" (text p. 381)

MAGGIE MITCHELL, *It Would Be Different If* (p. 206)

Mitchell's story begins with two conditional statements, one in the title (It would be different *if*...) and another in the first lines (*If* I could hate you...). The story never really leaves that speculative feeling, though the narrator returns most forcefully to it at the end. Though the narrator provides some description of herself, Mitchell largely leaves it to readers to infer Nikki's personality from her way of processing love and loss. She's perceptive enough to realize that others in town, who she once felt were on her side, have long since stopped caring about the love triangle that Nikki continues to obsess over. Not only does she regret losing her ex, to whom she speaks throughout this story, but she seems to feel that her life is still inextricably connected with his. For example, when she fantasizes about her ex, Jeff, entering the salon where she works and leaving behind "traces of [his] reflection in the mirror" (para. 13), readers understand just what she means when she says that Jeff seems to be "everywhere." Nikki's pride in giving Jeff "the best haircut he will ever, ever get" (11) reflects her sense that everything has been wrong in his life since he wronged her. Perhaps her wildest fantasy is that his cheating on his new wife is just a sad condition of a life gone "all wrong" (5) and that he would have been faithful if he'd stayed with her. Compare this with her sense that her name yoked with his: "Nikki Gilbert. It sounded right" (6).

POSSIBLE CONNECTION TO ANOTHER SELECTION

Muriel Spark, "The First Year of My Life" (text p. 475; question #1, following)

CONNECTION QUESTION IN TEXT (p. 475) **WITH ANSWER**

1. In a short essay, compare this narrator's representation of her past to that of the narrator in Muriel Spark's "The First Year of My Life" (text p. 475). What is the relationship between the narrative present and the remembered past in each story? How does it shape the ending in each case?

   Both of these stories are told in first person, and in both the past is filtered through the attitudes and opinions of the narrator. Nikki, in "It Would Be Different If," remembers the past in ways that serve her sense of injustice. Though many years have passed, and though she seems at least partially aware that her side of the story no longer holds the attention of her friends and neighbors, she is largely trapped in her teenage view of events. In Spark's story, we also see a narrator who looks back from the perspective of an older person but still remains captivated by the impressions of her youth. The limitations on the first-person perspective are largely the subject of "The First Year of My Life," and Spark seems to have fun exploring the extremely narrow experience of the baby, who at first can barely even move around, even while she insists that the baby has a radically expanded consciousness of world events.

JUNE SPENCE, *Missing Women* (p. 209)

Though "Missing Women" centers on a mysterious disappearance, the story is less about the fate of the women than about the impact of their disappearance on the community, as the narrator's use of the collective "we" suggests. Spence paints an ugly picture of the town's response, which begins with self-congratulation and moves through suspicion to end with indifference. Each of these successive attitudes seems to spring primarily from the townspeople's desire to look like they're doing the right thing: "All of us admirable, the way we rally together" (para. 8).

Spence contrasts the mystery-story details in the first paragraph with the assertion that "details are not clues" (2). Theory and observations never turn into any revelation. The same holds true for the many motives the townspeople imagine for each of the women to disappear. These never go beyond speculation. In spite of all the stories that circulate and the scrutiny of the principal characters, the observers of this crime drama unfolding in their town find that they "cannot rule out anything" (6).

The narrator identifies most of the characters in the story not by name but by their positions in the community or in the story — for example, the hostess of the party where the teenage girls were last seen, the hostess's parents, and her boyfriend. However, she identifies by name Kay, the vanished mother; Vicki, her daughter; and Adele, Vicki's friend. These decisions on Spence's part contribute to the feeling that while the missing women are characters in some bizarre story, the real action is not what individuals do, but how a group of people function — or fail to function — together as "Our community" (8).

POSSIBLE CONNECTION TO ANOTHER SELECTION

William Faulkner, "A Rose for Emily" (text p. 214; question #1, following)

CONNECTION QUESTION IN TEXT (p. 82) **WITH ANSWER**

1. Discuss how point of view is used to characterize the respective communities in "Missing Women" and in William Faulkner's "A Rose for Emily" (text p. 82).

Both Faulkner's and Spence's stories capture the collective fascinations and judgments of a town. In both cases, an anomaly in the social landscape obsesses the citizens and functions as a stark contrast by which they define what is "normal" in their lives. However, the positions of the characters at the center of these scandals are very different. In Faulkner's story, the townspeople are pleased to see the privileged Emily Grierson "humanized," first by spinsterhood and then by grief (para. 26). Their chorus of "Poor Emily" conveys satisfaction with her problems more than sympathy. By contrast, the three women in Spence's story are quite ordinary members of the community. Only their disappearance gives them a mysterious quality that sets them apart and makes them the subject of so much speculation.

ENCOUNTERING FICTION: COMICS AND GRAPHIC STORIES

MARJANE SATRAPI, *"The Trip," from* Persepolis (p. 216)

Given prevailing twenty-first-century images of Iranian culture, students will likely be surprised by the attitudes portrayed by Satrapi in her graphic novel. Although Americans are encouraged to view Iran's culture as backward and violent, Satrapi's characters are remarkable for the "Americanness" of their middle-class values and for their complete lack of interest in fundamentalist messages; the mother "couldn't care less" about political developments — at least not until they have a direct impact on the way she lives her life. It's worth noting that the family's conflict stems not from a disagreement about cultural values but from the ways those values threaten to disrupt their daily lives.

You might want to ask your students who Satrapi is writing for. If necessary, point out that her graphic novel is written in English, that the characters' appearance is ethnically neutral, and that the novel was published in 2003. What might she have hoped to accomplish with *Persepolis* and its sequel?

7

Symbolism

The three stories in Chapter 7 invite the reader to consider the complexity of symbolism. After reading the introduction, students should be aware of the difference between symbolism and allegory; they should also begin to appreciate the nuances of symbolism. In addition to the common cultural symbols described in the introduction, students might generate a list of other familiar symbols from their daily experience. For instance, what traditional, conventional, or public meanings do students associate with water? (Possible associations range from baptism rites to the territory of the unconscious.) What possible meanings are associated with dragons? In Western cultures, dragons have commonly symbolized danger or obstacles to success. In Eastern cultures, in contrast, they are often perceived to be symbols of good luck. In order to demonstrate the sophistication and breadth of common symbols, instructors might introduce students to reference works such as J. E. Cirlot's *A Dictionary of Symbols* (Philosophical Library, 1971). However, as explained in the introduction, common sense should be a reader's guide in determining the meaning of literary symbols.

 Ask students to explore *symbolism* at **bedfordstmartins.com/ meyerlit**.

 Ask students to research the authors in this chapter or take quizzes on their works at **bedfordstmartins.com/ meyerlit**.

TOBIAS WOLFF, *That Room* (p. 222)

The narrator of Wolff's story becomes a field hand because he is looking for a more authentic life. His search leads him to a revelatory experience in a motel room. As Wolff's title suggests, that room plays an important role in the story; it expands to represent any turning point in life, especially those brought on by an encounter with death. The narrator seems to cast forward to later experiences — being drafted into military service, learning his daughter has been in a car accident — all of which metaphorically bring him back to "that room" where he first confronted his mortality.

Students might begin discussion of the story by talking about the narrator's relationships to the farmer and his nephew, Clemson, and the two Mexican workers, Eduardo and Miguel. He occupies a middle position between them, not allied with the owner of the farm, but still in a more privileged position than the brothers. The ending suggests that he ultimately identifies with Eduardo and Miguel in spite of his terrifying experience in the motel, and in spite of the fact that Miguel seems to associate him with the farmer's mistreatment.

POSSIBLE CONNECTIONS TO OTHER SELECTIONS

Ralph Ellison, "Battle Royal" (text p. 226; question #1, following)

John Updike, "A & P" (text p. 201; question #1, following)

CONNECTION QUESTION IN TEXT (p. 225) WITH ANSWER

1. Discuss the similarities and differences related to the nature of what the protagonist learns about life in "That Room" and in either John Updike's "A & P" (text p. 201) or Ralph Ellison's "Battle Royal" (text p. 226).

36

All three of these are, in different ways, coming-of-age stories. In "That Room" and "Battle Royal," violence plays a central role. Wolff's narrator encounters it when he realizes the anger of the disenfranchised worker. This surprising moment produced a revelation about mortality that is more or less universal. Ellison's narrator, on the other hand, faces a more complicated set of social and political institutions. In fact, he says he will have to go to college before he'll really start to appreciate the implications of his experience. As the story unfolds, he is still in the process of understanding his position, especially how the favors the white men offer him (like the scholarship) depend on his enduring their sadistic punishments. While the young man in Updike's story has his moment of awaking during a more mundane scene, working at his grocery store job, he defies authority, as Wolff's narrator does at the end of "That Room."

RALPH ELLISON, *Battle Royal* (p. 226)

The opening paragraph of this story is fairly abstract and may be difficult for some students to grasp on first reading. But by the story's end the narrator's comments in this paragraph should have become very clear. Throughout this story Ellison is concerned with the masks, roles, and labels people impose on one another in this society. The narrator is invisible because the town's white citizens don't see him (or anyone else black) for what he is — which is, simply, a human being. What they see is a black man, or, in their vocabulary, a "nigger," "coon," or "shine." And "niggers," to their minds, are to be treated a certain way; mainly, they are to be publicly humiliated and abused. It is bitterly ironic that these men can bestow a great honor on this boy (the college scholarship) and simultaneously treat him worse than they would treat their dogs. It is equally ironic that, despite the brutal treatment the narrator receives at the hands of these men, he still wants to give his speech and is still proud to receive their gift.

The horrifying battle royal can be seen as a metaphor for the society the narrator lives in, in which nothing makes sense. Ten black boys are viciously used by some of the most important men of the town; they are forced to provide a freak show — first in the boxing ring, later on the electrified rug. In both cases they are jerked around like puppets on a string. They are, in fact, puppets; the white men are the puppeteers. If the boys refuse to fight one another, or to grab for the money with sufficient enthusiasm, it is clear the drunken white mob will hurt them much worse than they will hurt one another. White men have the power and make the decisions in this society, so the boys do as they are told. And not once do any white men — the very source of all this angry violence and confusion — get hurt.

The boys are brought in front of the naked blonde in an attempt to make them feel as uncomfortable as possible; they are not supposed to look at white women, and, left to their own devices, they wouldn't, especially in a room full of drunken white men. The blonde, with her ironic American flag tattoo, suggests all the things the boys (who are supposed to be Americans too) can't have simply because they are black: dignity, self-respect, freedom of choice, the freedom not to beat each other up or be beaten up by the white citizens present.

The blonde also serves another, very different function: at the same time that she is supposedly superior to the boys by virtue of the color of her skin, she is being used by the men; she too is a puppet. In paragraph 9, when she is being tossed into the air, the narrator sees the same "terror and disgust in her eyes" that he and the other boys are feeling.

As a high-school graduate, the narrator is extremely naive and believes that these men really respect him as he gives his speech after the battle, barely able to talk because he is choking on his own blood. In retrospect, as an educated adult, he realizes that he could not possibly have gotten an ounce of respect from any of them, and that, if he had known better at the time, he would not have respected himself. He realizes now that he was a laughing stock and that the white men were sending him the very message he read in his dream: "Keep This Nigger-Boy Running." In retrospect, too, he is able to understand his grandfather's dying words. His grandfather meant that a black man in this society didn't stand a chance by fighting racism openly. Instead, he believed blacks should pretend to play the game; white people had so much power that it was only by working within their system (by receiving scholarships to black colleges, for example, and then leading black people "in the proper paths") that blacks could hope to accomplish anything in the fight for equality. Dignity and self-respect, meanwhile, could come from within, since you would know you were agreeing them "to death and destruction" (2).

POSSIBLE CONNECTIONS TO OTHER SELECTIONS

William Faulkner, "A Rose for Emily" (text p. 82; question #1, following)

Flannery O'Connor, "Revelation" (text p. 381)

CONNECTION QUESTION IN TEXT (p. 236) WITH ANSWER

1. Compare and contrast Ellison's view of the South with William Faulkner's in "A Rose for Emily" (p. 82).

    Ellison's view of the South is that it punishes any difference from the norms of the group in power. The young black men in the story are forced to put on a humiliating show for the white audience. Also, though she is part of their torture, the blonde woman who stands before them naked is also fearful of the men in power. Even positive differences, such as the narrator's facility in making speeches, are punished, as the audience singles him out for special ridicule. Faulkner's South, on the other hand, is one that seems to protect difference, even when it leads to horrible results. Though the townspeople gossip among themselves about the eccentric Emily, they also want to shield her from the intrusions of her northern suitor and her out-of-town cousins. They may not respect her, but they do think she has a right to live as she wants. Of course, her family's former position and wealth guarantee a protection to her that would probably not be granted to a woman of the lower class.

P E R S P E C T I V E

MORDECAI MARCUS, *What Is an Initiation Story?* (p. 236)

Ask students to apply one of Marcus's three categories of initiation to a story they are familiar with. Their response should explain how the initiation in the story they have chosen fits one of Marcus's categories but not the other two.

For a more creative response, ask students to write short sketches that depict one of Marcus's types of initiation. They might follow up their fictional sketches with short explanations of how their sketches fit Marcus's definitions.

MICHAEL OPPENHEIMER, *The Paring Knife* (p. 240)

For the couple in Oppenheimer's story, the paring knife becomes the symbol of an uncharacteristically violent fight, which the male narrator recounts in a flashback. The full import of the paring knife remains ambiguous, contributing to what is mysterious about the end of the story. Students may come up with many possible ways to interpret the woman's final action, returning the knife to its place beneath the refrigerator. Does it suggest that she would prefer not to remember? Or that she doesn't want to undo the fight? The many open-ended questions Oppenheimer leaves at the end of the story show how a symbol like the knife can be both easily determined and essentially indeterminate.

POSSIBLE CONNECTIONS TO OTHER SELECTIONS

Raymond Carver, "Popular Mechanics" (text p. 269; question #2, following)

Susan Glaspell, *Trifles* (text p. 1038)

Maggie Mitchell, "It Would Be Different If" (text p. 206; question #1, following)

CONNECTIONS QUESTIONS IN TEXT (p. 241) WITH ANSWERS

1. Compare the narrator's emotions at the end of this story and in Maggie Mitchell's "It Would Be Different If" (p. 206).

    The emotion Oppenheimer's narrator feels at the end of the story is understated, but the way he recounts the fight and how it was resolved suggests a feeling of relief that, after the fight, the mess of dishes on the floor allowed the couple to laugh and go back to bed together. The woman's response, which he mentions abruptly and without comment, seems to suggest that she is less confident in the resolution of the fight than he is — and that this comes as a surprise to the narrator.

    At the end of Maggie Mitchell's "It Would Be Different If," we've moved away from the narrator's bitter recollections of the past. Instead of dwelling on the night when her boyfriend left her for another girl, she creates a fantasy scenario of their reunion. Though it's difficult to tell at times how much of this fantasy is based on actual fact, it causes the reader to sympathize with the narrator. Her enduring hope and determination to wait for her love is both potentially foolish and admirable. Like Oppenheimer's conclusion, the reader is left unsure of whether or not to share the narrator's confidence in this reunion.

2. Explain how symbolism is central to understanding the resolution of the conflicts in "The Paring Knife" and in Raymond Carver's "Popular Mechanics" (p. 269).

    In Oppenheimer's story, the knife is certainly a symbol of the violent argument between the two characters, but it is worth noting that it is a modest knife. A paring knife is smaller but does finer work than, for example, a butcher's knife. As a symbol, it may suggest that the couple's argument was small and yet potentially dangerous. Oppenheimer takes a mundane physical object and invests it with a complex set of meanings.

    By contrast, the symbolism of Carver's story is not attached to a single object. Rather, it draws on the well-known Bible story about King Solomon's solving a dispute over a baby by suggesting that the child be cut in half with a sword. Solomon's ruse revealed the true mother, who would rather give up her baby than see it killed. In "Popular Mechanics," the two parents' self-serving claims won't allow either to back down, and Carver's ending reverses the happy resolution in the Bible story.

8

Theme

The introduction to Chapter 8 offers seven specific suggestions to help students identify and formulate themes for the stories they read. It might be useful to assign students to apply those hints to stories the class has already discussed. Also, students might practice identifying the theme of a given story before they come to class. Working in small groups or exchanging written statements about the theme, they may realize through studying their own concrete examples that theme is a significant literary element. They also might formulate statements of theme and "morals" for the same story in order to differentiate between them and to learn more about a story's perspective on a given topic.

 Ask students to explore *theme* at **bedfordstmartins.com/ meyerlit**.

 Ask students to research the authors in this chapter or take quizzes on their works at **bedfordstmartins.com/ meyerlit**.

STEPHEN CRANE, *The Bride Comes to Yellow Sky* (p. 246)

In this story Jack Potter is conflicted between the love and duty he feels toward his new wife and the love and duty he feels toward Yellow Sky. As town marshal, protector and defender of, and friend to, Yellow Sky, he feels he has betrayed the town not only by marrying a stranger but by marrying without the town's knowledge as well. Crane is playing with some traditional western myths here — most notably the idea of the lawman's loyalty to his territory above anything else, even personal happiness.

In fact, the title and first paragraph of this story set up our expectations for a typical western. The bride's coming to Yellow Sky supplies the element of adventure and a little bit of tension (how will she react to her new home, and how will the town react to her?). The train and the plains, with their mesquite, cactus, "little groups of frame houses," and the "sweeping" vista all provide the setting we associate with western adventures. But Crane is quick to let us know that he is playing off these traditions rather than adopting them conventionally. Notice that the bride is neither pretty nor young, and that while the newlywed couple is ostensibly very happy, they are practically tortured by embarrassment.

As far as traditional westerns go, something is definitely askew here. Marshals don't usually have brides because women only get in the way in the wild world of gunslingers and Indians. And if there is a wife, she is decidedly young and pretty. She is also in the house, where she belongs, rather than in San Antonio, dragging the marshal miles away from where he belongs, taking care of the local drunk bully. Finally, while we expect this story to end in a shoot-out (though because of the comic tone we don't really expect anyone to get killed), words are exchanged instead of bullets and Scratchy Wilson is "disarmed" by the incredible fact (and sight) of Jack Potter's bride. For all we know, if Mrs. Potter hadn't been standing there, Wilson might not have believed Potter's claim that he had just gotten married (which is also his explanation for why he doesn't have a gun). So Mrs. Potter actually serves as a weapon more powerful than a gun; Wilson takes one look at her and loses interest in shooting.

What kind of shoot-out is this, where no shots are fired? What kind of West is this, with a bride in a cashmere dress (attire we can't imagine women wearing, or even having access to, in that setting)? And we're explicitly told that Scratchy Wilson's gaudy outfit is inauthentic western garb; the shirt came from New York City and the inappropriate boots are, we learn in paragraph 63, "the kind beloved in winter by little sledding boys on the hillsides of New England." The suggestion is that the romantic West of the storybooks is dead, or at least dying fast. Edwin H. Cady, in *Stephen Crane* (New York: Twayne, 1962), notes that " 'The Bride Comes to Yellow Sky' is a hilariously funny parody of neo-romantic lamentations over 'The Passing of the West.' The last marshal is tamed by a prosaic marriage and exempted from playing The Game so absurdly romanticized. . . . His occupation gone, the last Bad Man, a part-time worker anyhow, shuffles off into the sunset dragging boot tracks through the dust like the tracks of the last dinosaur" (102). When Scratchy Wilson says, "I s'pose it's all off now" (88), the specific reference is to his rampage on the town, but the larger implication is that the whole myth of the West is over as well.

Scratchy's comic and ineffective qualities are meant to suggest those same qualities in Yellow Sky, and in any part or member of the West that still adheres to this myth. The drummer in the saloon reinforces this concept; as an outsider to Yellow Sky, he helps dramatize this episode. The fact that he has been many places but hasn't encountered such a situation before suggests how ridiculous this little scene really is; people just don't go around shooting up a town this way anymore (if they ever really did), and Yellow Sky seems to be one of the last places to find this out.

Crane creates suspense by delaying the inevitable meeting between Potter and Wilson; he alternates scenes of the bride and groom en route to Yellow Sky with scenes of what is going on in Yellow Sky at the same moment. But it is a teasing rather than a gripping suspense; Crane's tone is sufficiently mocking and ironic that we don't really believe Wilson, or anybody else, is actually going to kill anyone.

Possible Connections to Other Selections

William Faulkner, "A Rose for Emily" (text p. 82; question #2, following)

Katherine Mansfield, "Miss Brill" (text p. 254; question #1, following)

Jane Martin, *Rodeo* (text p. 1336)

Connections Questions in Text (p. 253) with Answers

1. Although Scratchy Wilson and the title character in Katherine Mansfield's "Miss Brill" (p. 254) are radically different kinds of people, they share a painful recognition at the end of their stories. What does each of them learn? Discuss whether you think what each of them learns is of equal importance in changing his or her life.

    At the end of Crane's story, Scratchy Wilson realizes that his archetypal rivalry with the town sheriff has come to an end. He walks away forlornly, like a boy whose accustomed playmate has announced he's too grown up now to join the game. The sight of Mrs. Potter seems to make Wilson confront the absurdity of his actions. Though we don't know for sure, the end of the story seems to suggest that Wilson will lose his relish for going on shooting sprees. Miss Brill, too, seems to lose a primary source of enjoyment at the end of Mansfield's story. Her people-watching identifies others as actors, "all on the stage" (para. 9). By observing their actions, she can infer their characters, cast them in roles such as "hero and heroine" (11). However, the overheard conversation of the young couple makes her realize that she too is just an actor in the scene, and not its director.

2. Write an essay comparing Crane's use of suspense with William Faulkner's in "A Rose for Emily" (p. 82).

    Both Crane and Faulkner use plot structure to create suspense for the reader, but they do it in very different ways. Crane uses simultaneous narratives to point the readers toward the inevitable climax. The first section follows Potter and his new wife on their journey, while the second and third describe a typical afternoon in the life of Yellow Sky. Both narratives are moving toward the Potter home, where

Scratchy Wilson confronts the sheriff. Faulkner, on the other hand, breaks up traditional narrative structure. By relating the story out of sequence, he delays the funeral and the surprise that follows. Faulkner's is a different kind of suspense because the reader doesn't have as clear a sense of the climax to come as he or she does in "The Bride Comes to Yellow Sky." However, Faulkner's careful use of details suggests to readers that something is not right, and makes us anticipate some revelation.

KATHERINE MANSFIELD, *Miss Brill* (p. 254)

Mansfield's characterization of Miss Brill is a portrait of an elderly woman alone. We never learn her first name because there is no one to address her familiarly. She carefully observes the crowds in the park because they are the only people in her life, aside from the students she tutors or the old gentleman for whom she reads the newspaper. She notices that the band conductor wears a new coat, and she looks forward to her special seat in the park, which is for "sitting in other people's lives just for a minute while they talked around her" (para. 3). By silent participation in other people's lives — even if they are only a husband and wife quarreling over whether one of them should wear spectacles — her life is enriched.

Miss Brill is content with her solitary life of observations. She is not merely a stock characterization of a frail old lady. She prides herself on her ability to hear and watch others. She sorts out the children, parents, lovers, and old people and vicariously participates in their lives, but she does not see herself in the same light as the other people who sit on the benches: "they were odd, silent, nearly all old, and from the way they stared they looked as though they'd just come from dark little rooms or even — even cupboards!" (5). Miss Brill believes she is more vital and alive than that.

Life in the park offers all the exciting variety of a theater production to Miss Brill. She regards herself as part of a large cast, every member of which plays an important role. She feels a sense of community with them that makes her want to sing with the band. The music seems to be a confirmation of her connection with people and a fitting expression of her abiding concern that kindnesses be observed: she wants to rebuke a complaining wife; she disapproves of the haughty woman who rejects the violets picked up for her by a little boy; and she regards the man who blows smoke in the face of the woman with the ermine toque as a brute. Her reactions to these minor characters reveal her decency and sensitivity.

At the climactic moment, when she feels elated by the band's music, she is suddenly and unexpectedly made to realize that the young "hero and heroine" (actually the story's antagonists) who sit nearby regard her as an unwelcome intrusion in their lives. She hears herself described as a "stupid old thing" and the fur that she so fondly wears is dismissed as merely "funny" (11–14). This insensitive slight produces the conflict in the story and changes Miss Brill because she is suddenly made aware of how she is like the other old people in the park. She returns home defeated, no longer able to delight in the simple pleasure of a honeycake. "Her room [is] like a cupboard," where she places her fur in a box. When "she put the lid on she thought she heard something crying" (18). Her fur — Miss Brill's sense of herself — expresses for her the painful, puzzled sense that she is less vitally a part of the world than she had assumed. Her life appears to be closed down — boxed up — at the end. Having denied herself the honeycake, it seems unlikely that she'll return to the park the following Sunday. If she does, her role in the "play" she imagined will have been significantly diminished because she no longer perceives herself as an astute observer of other characters but as one of them, "odd, silent," and "old."

As a writing assignment, you might ask students to discuss the function of the minor characters mentioned in the story. They can analyze the way Mansfield uses these characters to reveal Miss Brill's character.

There is almost no physical description of Miss Brill in the story. Another writing assignment might be to develop a detailed description that is consistent with Miss Brill's behavior.

Possible Connections to Other Selections

Stephen Crane, "The Bride Comes to Yellow Sky" (text p. 246)

James Joyce, "Eveline" (text p. 407; question #2, following)

Fay Weldon, "IND AFF, or Out of Love in Sarajevo" (text p. 173; question #1, following)

Connections Questions in Text (p. 258) **with Answers**

1. Compare Miss Brill's recognition with that of the narrator in Fay Weldon's "IND AFF, or Out of Love in Sarajevo" (p. 173).

    Both moments of recognition happen suddenly, through a chance encounter with a stranger. Miss Brill overhears a young couple referring to her as "that stupid old thing" and making fun of her clothes (para. 13). Their conversation makes her realize that people see and judge her only from the outside, just as she has seen them as they move through the park. Weldon's narrator experiences a moment of recognition, not by having herself revealed, but by suddenly seeing her lover clearly. Her attraction to the young waiter makes her realize the falseness of "the pain in the heart [she'd] become accustomed to as an erotic sensation" (38). The young man stands in contrast to "this man with thinning hair" (41), whose limitations she has seen but not really acknowledged until in Sarajevo.

2. Write an essay comparing the themes in "Miss Brill" and James Joyce's "Eveline" (p. 407).

    One theme of "Miss Brill" is that while each person feels like the center of her own universe, she is actually just a minor figure in the theater of other people's lives. As Miss Brill sits and watches the people pass through the park, she is struck by how much they are like characters. The music of the band, accompanying their movements, further serves to make the strollers look like part of a tableau. However, because of the young couple's careless remarks, she suddenly realizes not only that she is a part of the scene, but that she is not its center. Her self-image, as an acute observer and a lively presence in the drama, contrasts starkly with the young man's view that "no one wants her."

    Joyce's story deals not just with the places we occupy in others' lives, but the duties we owe them. His protagonist, Eveline, is unhappy living with her father, but she feels responsible for taking care of him after her mother's death. She wants to escape with her fiancé, Frank, but her wish to let him "save her" (para. 18) also turns into a sense of obligation. She's not sure she can change her mind about leaving with him "after all he [has] done for her" (19). Ultimately, Eveline chooses her primary obligation to her father, but the reader is left with the sense that, either way, her sense of duty to the men in her life will "drown her" (22).

DAGOBERTO GILB, *Romero's Shirt* (p. 258)

Gilb's story begins as a sparse catalog of the life of one hardworking man as he attempts to provide for his family. On closer inspection, students will find that this seemingly simple story is replete with symbols. Romero's titular shirt is the most obvious one; it represents his remaining pride in himself and his appearance, his ability to be practical and still "in style." However, Romero's house is also a symbol; it might represent Romero's determination to work hard and provide for his family, and to be satisfied with the bare essentials. The juniper bush, on the other hand, might stand for Romero's repressed longing for something better. The way Romero nurtures and cares for the juniper, even while ignoring other parts of his yard and lawn, conveys this last hope for true material wealth. One could argue the symbolic status of the old man or Romero's car as well. Students might analyze these items and others to help them understand what kind of man Romero is and what kind of life he's lived.

POSSIBLE CONNECTIONS TO OTHER SELECTIONS

Dagoberto Gilb, "Shout" (text p. 433; question #1, following)

Annie Proulx, "Job History" (text p. 77; question #2, following)

Jan Beatty, "My Father Teaches Me to Dream" (text p. 988; question #3, following)

Michael Chitwood, "Men Throwing Bricks" (text p. 989; question #3, following)

CONNECTIONS QUESTIONS IN TEXT (p. 263) WITH ANSWERS

1. Discuss the treatment of domestic life, and in particular the image of the fathers, in "Romero's Shirt" and in Gilb's "Shout" (p. 433).

    The fathers in Gilb's two stories are superficially similar and incorporate autobiographical elements from the author. They are both men who endure physical labor to provide for their families, both are Mexican Americans, both are struggling to find a better life. However, in "Romero's Shirt," there is virtually no relationship shown between Romero and his family. Romero is a quiet, distant man who does not have any close emotional relationships. He makes money to support his family and take care of the house, but Gilb never portrays him as talking with his wife or playing with his children. Throughout the story, it's almost as if Romero is completely alone, except for the old man who comes by. Gilb describes this to the reader toward the end of the story, saying Romero had "...lost many words, avoided many people, kept to himself, alone, almost always, even when his wife gave him his meals" (para. 13).

    The unnamed husband and father in "Shout" has the opposite personality as Romero. He enters the house loudly, banging and yelling, talking and demanding attention even as he tells everyone, "Shut up and be quiet!" The irony in his repeated attempts to silence his family is that he's the loudest one in the group. This father talks almost constantly, even when no one is answering him. Rather than the silence and stillness of domestic life in Romero's family, here Gilb shows his audience a hectic, brash, loud family life. Despite the yelling and aggression, Gilb uses the final scene to show his readers how protective this father is of his family, how tender he is toward his wife, and how much he loves her.

2. Compare the working lives of the protagonists in "Romero's Shirt" and Annie Proulx's "Job History" (p. 77). What significant similarities and differences do you find in the protagonists' responses to work?

    Early in the story, Gilb describes Romero's professional life as a handyman: "He hangs wallpaper and doors, he paints, lays carpet, does just about anything someone will call and ask him to do" (para. 2). Romero is satisfied with this type of unstable work because "he's his own boss, and he's had so many bad jobs over those other years, ones no more dependable, he's learned that this suits him" (2). Leeland Lee is similar, though Proulx never spells it out quite as clearly. Leeland tries multiple times through his life to start his own business and be his own boss like Romero, but financial instability always forces him back into the work force. Frequently, Leeland "can't seem to get along" (5) with his bosses. He tries, like Romero, to provide for his family, but they are constantly struggling.

    However, it seems as though unlike Romero, Leeland is constantly getting in his own way. The business ventures he attempts are often not well planned, and Leeland never keeps a safety net in savings for himself and his family. They'll spend all the money on a failed business and then have to start from the bottom once again. Romero, on the other hand, favors whatever level of stability he can gain through working odd jobs. While Romero might look more responsible by not spending his family's savings on starting a business, one can also argue that Romero has given up on finding anything better, whereas Leeland, even after losing his parents and his wife, is still trying.

3. Consider the ending and tone of "Romero's Shirt," keeping in mind the two following poems about work: Jan Beatty's "My Father Teaches Me to Dream" (p. 988) and Michael Chitwood's "Men Throwing Bricks" (p. 989). Which of the two poems do you think seems to describe Romero's sensibilities more completely?

Answers will vary, and students can make a convincing argument for either of these poems. Students may point out lines from Beatty's poem, like "You don't look from side to side. / You keep your eyes straight ahead. / That way nobody bothers you — see?" (lines 5–7) as embodying Romero's silent, distant work ethic. However, one could also use Beatty's line "There's no handouts in this life" (13) as proof that her poem does not embody Romero's sensibilities, because Romero does offer a handout to the old man when he makes him lunch and pays him an extra two dollars to trim the juniper. Some students may believe that Chitwood's description of two men performing physical labor is more similar to Romero's life. Others might think that Chitwood imbues this simple action with too much beauty by using vocabulary like "chime" (9) and phrasing such as "to accept them like a gift" (7).

9

Style, Tone, and Irony

The introduction to Chapter 9 describes the intricacies of style, tone, and irony. Students might experiment individually with style, tone, and irony first by rereading some of their own work and establishing some assessment of their own natural style and tone. Second, they might learn more about these tools by rewriting common fairy tales in different voices. For instance, how might "Goldilocks and the Three Bears" sound as told by a Sam Spade character (from Dashiell Hammett's *The Maltese Falcon*)? A Walter Mitty? A politician? Students might also practice writing excuses why a paper might be late in different modes — both sincere and ironic. You may even want to introduce students to such landmark examples of irony as Jonathan Swift's "A Modest Proposal." Though the irony in literature is rarely as exaggerated as Swift's, it provides the reader with information about the story that might dramatically affect their interpretations. Inventing and practicing their own examples of different styles, tones, and ironic works, and reading other examples embodying them, students will become more confident at recognizing and responding to these literary tools in the work of professional authors.

Web Ask students to explore the literary elements in the chapter at **bedfordstmartins.com/ meyerlit**.

Web Ask students to research the authors in this chapter or take quizzes on their works at **bedfordstmartins.com/ meyerlit**.

RAYMOND CARVER, *Popular Mechanics* (p. 269)

"Popular Mechanics" describes a stark domestic situation with a startling conclusion. For an interesting reading of "Popular Mechanics," see "Physical and Social Laws in Ray Carver's *Popular Mechanics*," by Norman German and Jack Bedell, *Critique* 29.4 (Summer 1988): 257–60. This entry incorporates several of their ideas.

What connections do students make when they think of the term *popular mechanics*? One possibility is the contemporary "how-to" magazine *Popular Mechanics*, which contains suggestions and instructions for "home improvement" projects. In its form, Carver's story reminds us of such a "how-to." Consisting of a series of very brief paragraphs, or "steps," it contains no complicated instructions or convoluted sentences. It's only when we look beneath the surface and consider the story's implications that we discover its complexities. There is a certain "mechanical" nature to the story as well, as Carver describes the couple's physical grappling over the baby: "in the near-dark he worked on her fisted fingers with one hand and with the other hand he gripped the screaming baby up under an arm near the shoulder" (para. 31); "She caught the baby around the wrist and leaned back" (34). As German and Bedell point out, the baby functions as some sort of wishbone during this scuffle (258). Holding him over the stove, and pulling at him from each side, the husband and wife focus solely on their own wishes rather than the baby's safety. Ask students how they interpret the last line: "In this manner, the issue was decided" (36). German and Bedell suggest that "issue" refers both to the argument and to the baby as the parents' offspring (258). As the last line implies, in this struggle there can only be losers.

Minor details of the story contribute to its effect. In the first paragraph it is "getting dark" both inside and out; the light has faded away by the end of the story. In paragraph 10, the husband looks "around the bedroom before turning off the light"; in paragraph 31, we are told that "the kitchen window gave no light." The scuffle intensifies in proportion to the increasing darkness in the house — and, as German and Bedell note, the sound level rises proportionally to the decreasing light (259). The argument over the baby's picture foreshadows the struggle in the kitchen and reveals the parents' tendency to objectify everything in their attempts to hurt each other. The flowerpot serves as yet another example of this: the symbol of a domestic harmony that has ceased to exist for these people, the pot is knocked off the wall by the parents' mutual efforts. In this story, the baby (often referred to as "it") becomes just one more object.

In class, explain the story of Solomon (1 Kings 3) and ask students to compare its outcome with Carver's conclusion. (Neither of Carver's adult characters is willing to take any responsibility: notice that the wife says, "You're hurting the baby" [29] instead of "We're hurting the baby.") Whereas 1 Kings 3 is ultimately a story about a mother's love and selflessness, "Popular Mechanics" reveals the animosity and selfishness of both parents.

POSSIBLE CONNECTIONS TO OTHER SELECTIONS

Dagoberto Gilb, "Love in L.A." (text p. 430)

Nathaniel Hawthorne, "The Birthmark" (text p. 333; question #2, following)

Ernest Hemingway, "Soldier's Home" (text p. 166; question #1, following)

CONNECTIONS QUESTIONS IN TEXT (p. 270) WITH ANSWERS

1. Compare Carver's style with Ernest Hemingway's in "Soldier's Home" (p. 166).

    Both Carver and Hemingway use a spare, unadorned style, avoiding complicated explanations of the characters' thoughts or motivations. Far from ignoring psychology, this style allows the writers to examine the characters with a sharp vision. Since Carver and Hemingway attend almost solely to external events, they leave the readers to puzzle out the implications of the scenes they present. However, because Carver's story is so brief, he is necessarily even more limited in his choice of details than Hemingway. For example, we never learn the names of the couple, but only know them as "he" and "she." The anonymity of the characters, as well as the appropriately gloomy setting, reinforce the allegorical feeling of "Popular Mechanics."

2. How is the ending of "Popular Mechanics" similar to the ending of Nathaniel Hawthorne's "The Birthmark" (p. 333)?

    Carver's story ends on an ironic note that echoes the Solomon story which informs the plot, revealing the biblical story behind this modern tale. Carver's use of cold, businesslike language at the end also throws the scary reality of the climax into relief. The actual injury of the child seems to be lost in the negotiations of the fighting couple. In Hawthorne's story, Aylmer's insistence on ethereal perfection similarly denies Georgiana's physical existence. He is so thrilled by the disappearance of her birthmark that he doesn't notice her condition deteriorating. Hawthorne's final note is ironic too: "Thus ever does the gross fatality of the earth exult in its invariable triumph over the immortal essence" (para. 90). In both stories, the main characters treat other people as tools to be used, and in both there are tragic consequences.

PERSPECTIVE

JOHN BARTH, *On Minimalist Fiction* (p. 271)

Is minimalism defined more by a "terse, oblique, realistic or hyperrealistic" quality (para. 1) or by the inclusion of numerous references to contemporary popular culture? Students should identify a selection from the fiction section that in their opinion fits Barth's definition and explain why it does so. In their responses, they should explain whether the story they have chosen to write about is minimalistic in form, style, or material.

SUSAN MINOT, *Lust* (p. 274)

Beginning their study of this story, students might look up the meaning of *lust* in the dictionary. Definitions of the term range from "pleasure, delight" to "intense sexual desire: lasciviousness." Ask the students whether these denotations really apply to Minot's story. (They might wonder *whose* lust is referred to here.) Though they might initially be overwhelmed by the numerous sexual encounters described by the narrator, they should examine in particular the narrator's selection of metaphors and similes in order to reach some conclusions about the meaning of the story. Studying the narrator's analogies, readers become aware of the irony inherent in the title.

Trace the narrator's references to her encounters throughout the story. Describing her initial sexual experience, she claims that she "flipped" (para. 1), implying a certain exhilaration about discovering her sexuality. Being sexually active is for her a way of asserting her independence and maturity, particularly when she compares herself to her mother: the narrator states, "[I] kept the dial [of birth control pills] in my top drawer like my mother and thought of her each time I tipped out the yellow tablets in the morning before chapel" (31). However, her sexual experiences don't enhance her self-confidence; rather, they steadily diminish her. She later tells us that during and after sex, she felt like "a body waiting on the rug" (6), that she was "filled absolutely with air, or with a sadness that wouldn't stop" (28). Elsewhere, she tells us, "you wonder how long you can keep it up. You begin to feel as if you're showing through, like a bathroom window that only lets in grey light, the kind you can't see out of" (64). In many of her analogies, she compares herself to a piece of meat (recalling derogatory terms for the body): "Then you start to get tired. You begin to feel diluted, like watered-down stew" (44); "you wonder about things feeling a little off-kilter. You begin to feel like a piece of pounded veal" (72); "after sex, you curl up like a shrimp, something deep inside you ruined, slammed in a place that sickens at slamming, and slowly you fill up with an overwhelming sadness, an elusive gaping worry" (79). It's evident that the narrator's encounters with these young men increasingly make her feel more like an object than a person. It is significant that she is an unnamed narrator, that none of her partners (not lovers) ever calls her by her name. The structure of the story, fragmented by her experiences with different men, also illustrates her fragmentation of self.

In addition to revealing her personal feelings through her analogies, the narrator provides some sense of the larger, cultural assumptions about gender. She asserts that there are different "rules" of behavior for young men and young women: "The more girls a boy has, the better. He has a bright look, having reaped fruits, blooming. He stalks around, sure-shouldered, and you have the feeling he's got more in him, a fatter heart, more stories to tell. For a girl, with each boy it's as though a petal gets plucked each time" (43). You may want to ask students to compare the language of these descriptions and to examine the description in paragraph 48. Here, the narrator explains the typical roles for boys and girls:

> On weekends they play touch football while we sit on the sidelines, picking blades of grass to chew on, and watch. We're always watching them run around. We shiver in the stands, knocking our boots together to keep our toes warm, and they whizz across the ice, chopping their sticks around the puck. When they're in the rink, they refuse to look at you, only eyeing each other beneath low helmets. You cheer for them, but they don't look up, even if it's a face-off when nothing's happening, even if they're doing drills before any game has started at all.

In other words, men are those who act; women are those who observe. Men have the authority in their interaction with women. The narrator describes the way her partners take the initiative: " 'Come here,' he says on the porch. . . . He kisses my palm then directs my hand to his fly" (12–15); they focus on their own needs and interests rather than on hers: ". . . trying to be reasonable, in a regular voice, 'Listen, I just want to have a good time.' So I'd go because I couldn't think of something to say back that wouldn't be obvious, and if you go out with them, you sort of have to do something" (25–26). The narrator uses words such as "surrender" (28) to describe the way she feels about these encounters. She doesn't demonstrate any sense of personal authority in dealing with men: "I thought the worst thing anyone could call you was a cock-teaser. So, if you flirted, you had to be prepared to go through with it" (38). The one time she tries to achieve more of a relationship with the boy she's sleeping with, his response is "What the hell are you talking about?" (60). Ask students to explain the irony in the narrator's comment "I hate those girls who push away a boy's face as if she were made out of Ivory soap, as if she's that much greater than he is" (68).

Students might discuss the way the girls in this story interact with each other. What are their value systems? We get two glimpses of the narrator with her friends Giddy and Jill. In the first, the other girls cannot imagine that the narrator is unhappy, because she "always [has] a boyfriend" (36). (Students might explain the narrator's reaction to her friends' comments here.) In the second, all three are talking with the housemother, Mrs. Gunther, whose own life history doesn't promise anything more for these young women. Having married her first boyfriend (because she was pregnant, we wonder?), she affirms for Jill, Giddy, and the narrator the passiveness of women and the centrality of male attention. Students might discuss the circumstances of the narrator's school and family life — there are certainly very few adults who seem aware of her experiences or their ramifications. In this predominantly upper-class setting, in which the narrator and her companions attend prep schools, go on ski trips, and stay at family apartments and summer houses, there is surprisingly little positive, constructive interaction with adults. The few adults who take notice of her sexual activity — the school doctor, Mrs. Gunther, the headmaster — never offer her any constructive alternative choices.

In connection with "Lust," students might consider whether the narrator's assertions about the gender roles described in Minot's story reflect their own experience. In this context, it might be useful to discuss the roles of male and female characters in popular fairy tales. Compare, for instance, the roles of Prince Charming and Sleeping Beauty, or even those of the characters in "Little Red Riding Hood." Can students think of a fairy tale in which the female character takes an authoritative stance? Two excellent essays on the subject might be relevant to such a discussion: Marcia K. Lieberman's " 'Some Day My Prince Will Come': Female Acculturation through the Fairy Tale," and Karen E. Rowe's "Feminism and Fairy Tales," both reprinted in Jack Zipes's *Don't Bet on the Prince: Contemporary Feminist Fairy Tales in North America and England* (New York: Methuen, 1986).

Minot's story also seems relevant to recent studies such as Mary Pipher's *Reviving Ophelia* (New York: Ballantine, 2002) and other studies about girls' loss of confidence during their teenage years. Significantly, the narrator tells us, "I could do some things well. Some things I was good at, like math or painting or even sports, but the second a boy put his arm around me, I forgot about wanting to do anything else, which felt like a relief at first until it became like sinking into a muck" (19).

POSSIBLE CONNECTIONS TO OTHER SELECTIONS

David Updike, "Summer" (text p. 295; question #1, following)

Fay Weldon, "IND AFF, or Out of Love in Sarajevo" (text p. 173; question #2, following)

CONNECTIONS QUESTIONS IN TEXT (p. 281) WITH ANSWERS

1. Compare the treatments of youthful sexuality in "Lust" and David Updike's "Summer" (p. 295). Do you prefer one story to the other? Why?

The teenage characters in David Updike's "Summer" are still innocent at the end of the story; their lust has gone unconsummated. Their attraction to one another appears to be more romantic or sentimental than physical — neither character feels the need to commit to a physical gesture. Indeed, we are told in "Summer" that for Homer, the protagonist, "to touch [Sandra], or kiss her, seemed suddenly incongruous, absurd, contrary to something he could not put his finger on" (para. 14). In contrast, the narrator of "Lust" has had only physical experience, not psychological or emotional involvement. Her partners demonstrate no desire for any relationship other than a physical one; hence, the tone of the end of "Lust" is one of disillusionment and regret. In contrast, the tone of "Summer" is upbeat, emphasizing Homer's new awareness and his joy that Sandra has returned his interest. Theirs is a much more reciprocal relationship, albeit unconsummated, than any of the encounters the narrator describes in "Lust."

2. Write an essay explaining the sort of advice the narrator of Fay Weldon's "IND AFF, or Out of Love in Sarajevo" (p. 173) might give to the narrator of "Lust." You might try writing this in the form of a letter.

    The narrator of Weldon's story comes to her revelation by taking a clearer look at her true feelings about love and about the man with whom she thought she was in love. Though she has been aware of his faults all the time, she finally realizes how they affect her in the relationship. She might tell Minot's narrator to think of the impact all the men she gets involved with have on her. The woman in "Lust" seems to have the beginning of this knowledge. She notices the way she feels the next day: "you'd be in a total fog, delirious, absent-minded, crossing the street and nearly getting run over" (para. 42), or "You begin to feel diluted, like watered-down stew" (44), or finally, "You seem to have disappeared" (83). However, she continues to be persuaded by the beginning of flirtation, when "You stare into their eyes. They flash like all the stars are out" (81).

NATHAN ENGLANDER, *Free Fruit for Young Widows* (p. 281)

Englander begins this story by placing it in a series of increasingly specific contexts. He begins with the international scale of the conflict between Egypt and Israel and then zooms in to reveal the central characters, Shimmy Gezer and Professor Tendler, Israeli soldiers coping with Egyptian troops as temporary allies. As a whole, "Free Fruit for Young Widows" deals with personal tragedy — Tendler's loss of his biological family in concentration camps and betrayal by his surrogate family after he returned home — set against the historical backdrop of the Holocaust and the Second World War.

As Shimmy relates Tendler's story to his son, Etgar, the contrast between the personalities of Tendler and Etgar becomes clear. Shimmy acts as a kind of mediator between Tendler's learned, academic philosophy and Etgar's more practical outlook. Philosophers have to see gray shades, not just black and white, and Shimmy performs a kind of instruction for his son, teaching him to make subtle distinctions. At the end of his story, he undermines simple conclusions, even as Etgar grasps for them. The difference between the two philosophical systems leads to two very different kinds of lives for Shimmy's friend and his son, though eventually Etgar finds a way to sympathize with Tendler's choice to murder his betrayers.

As a storyteller, Shimmy dramatizes Tendler's emotional attachment to the home through the details of the comfortable feast scene in the family kitchen. Ask students to think about why Englander chooses to tell the story from Shimmy's perspective, so that Tendler's feelings and reactions are all related secondhand. This might lead to questions about how Shimmy takes possession of the story. Under what circumstances might Professor Tendler tell his friend about these events? How does it change the story to have it narrated by someone who wasn't directly involved?

POSSIBLE CONNECTIONS TO OTHER SELECTIONS

Andre Dubus, "Killings" (text p. 93; question #1, following)

Muriel Spark, "The First Year of My Life" (text p. 475; question #2, following)

CONNECTIONS QUESTIONS IN TEXT (p. 290) WITH ANSWERS

1.   Discuss and evaluate the rationales for murder in this story and in Andre Dubus's "Killings" (text p. 93).

In both stories, the justification for murder hinges on survival, though the characters have broader definitions of survival than students might expect. In "Killings," Matt is under no threat from his son's killer, but he insists that in order to preserve his life and, more importantly, his wife's life as she has known it, he has to eliminate Stout. His idea of survival is largely psychological, and he focuses on the impact on Ruth of seeing the murderer around town and having to relive her son's death over and over.

2.   Compare the way horrific facts and events are presented in Englander's story and in Muriel Spark's "The First Year of My Life" (text p. 475).

In Englander's story, Etgar serves to test Tendler's rationale while his father tries to make him understand. Like Dubus's character, Tendler feels that in order to start a life again after surviving the horrors of the concentration camp, he needs to achieve a kind of psychological safety. The betrayal of the last people he thought loved him is, in Tendler's mind and in Shimmy's too, justification for killing them. These murders are Tendler's way of removing a final threat to his being.

Both stories are matter-of-fact about the violence that occurs during war. Englander narrates all of Tendler's murders in a straightforward style. At the beginning, for example, Tendler "[takes] up his gun and [shoots] each of the commandos in the head" (para. 3). Later, he leaves his "last bullet" in the farm family's "fat baby girl" (95). While the audience, like Etgar, might recoil from such violence, the narrator presents it plainly. Spark also looks unflinchingly at the horrors of war, but unlike Englander she often details them in list fashion. For example, in the separate cities of "Berlin and Vienna the people were starving, freezing, striking, rioting, and yelling in the streets" (11). Her style suggests the way that, even for a sensitive viewer, such awful sights begin to blur together.

ENCOUNTERING FICTION: COMICS AND GRAPHIC STORIES

MATT GROENING, *Life in Hell* (p. 518)

Groening's *Life in Hell* earned him a loyal following long before he created *The Simpsons* and *Futurama*, but many of his biggest television fans are unaware of the existence of his "bulgy-eyed rabbits with tragic overbites." Although his earlier characters look very similar to Homer, Marge, Bart, Lisa, and Maggie, the *Life in Hell* series tends to make the dark side of Groening's humor more apparent, as this example illustrates.

POSSIBLE CONNECTIONS TO OTHER SELECTIONS

Jack London, "To Build a Fire" (text p. 518; question #4, following)

Annie Proulx, "55 Miles to the Gas Pump" (text p. 470)

CONNECTION QUESTION IN TEXT (p. 292) WITH ANSWER

3.   Discuss the perspective on death in Groening's strip and in Jack London's "To Build a Fire" (p. 518).

For Groening and London, death is an inevitability outside of human determination; we cannot stave off what nature has in store for us. In Groening's comic, death becomes something absurd and meaningless, a truth best dismissed if one is to live. The *Life in Hell* strip asserts that the true power of death lies in its ability to sharpen the pleasures of life. Groening's mother rabbit tries to convince her son that death is what "makes life so precious! Because it's so short! That's why you mustn't brood about your death! There's too much to experience before your time runs out! So cheer up, gloomy! There's love, laughs, and picnics!" London's protagonist struggles against the cold and focuses on each small movement and minute task to keep himself alive. However, no matter what he does, he is defeated by nature, or perhaps fate. Though he avoids most ice-traps, he finally falls into one and soaks his feet. And though he starts a fire to thaw himself, snow from a tree falls and extinguishes it, signing his death warrant. Even Groening's optimistic mother rabbit does not escape the reality of death unscathed; she finds herself unable to sleep.

10

Combining the Elements of Fiction: A Writing Process

Even if you have taught this anthology in the exact order in which it is printed, paying strict attention to each element as it appears in the book (and let's be honest — most instructors skip around a bit, according to their own course needs), you have probably already combined the elements of fiction in your discussion of the stories. For example, it is hard to imagine discussing William Faulkner's "A Rose For Emily" strictly in terms of plot, ignoring such important elements of the story as setting, character, and symbolism. In fact, any story worth inclusion in a literature anthology can best be understood in light of the way the elements of literature work together to create a total effect. This chapter invites students to analyze David Updike's "Summer" for this total effect and to see the way one student writer brainstorms a thesis about the story.

Web Ask students to explore the literary elements in this chapter at **bedfordstmartins.com/meyerlit**.

In order to emphasize the importance of combining the elements of fiction, you might first study the story in light of each individual element. Either as a class or in groups, examine the way each element functions in Updike's story. Following are some questions to ask to generate discussion. (A general discussion of the story follows these questions.)

Plot: Does "Summer" have a clear beginning, middle, and end? Is the plot straightforward? Fragmentary? What is the conflict in the story?

Character: How realistic are the story's characters? Are they dynamic or static? Which character(s) do you identify with most? Why? What information does Updike provide about the characters and what does he leave out? What effect do these choices have on the reader?

Setting: Describe the setting. What details does Updike use to convey the tone of the setting? How important is the setting to the narrative as a whole?

Point of View: How would we read this story if it were told from Sandra's point of view? What information would an omniscient third-person narrator reveal that we do not receive here? Would the story differ significantly if Homer were the actual narrator?

Symbolism: Consider the following symbols: summer, heat, the characters' names, Sherlock Holmes. What other symbols can your students identify? How important are they to their reading of the story?

Theme: What is the story's theme? Is it stated explicitly or implicitly?

Style, Tone, and Irony: Identify the tone. Is it nostalgic, ironic, objective? A combination? Cite textual examples.

When you have finished examining each individual element, ask your students what is gained by studying a story in light of more than one element. How do the elements work together to create the total effect of the story? Are all the elements equally important in analyzing this story? If they were to include this story in a different chapter of the book, which one would it be? Why?

The rest of the Fiction unit of this anthology contains stories that may emphasize one element or another, but that should be read in the context of all the elements together.

DAVID UPDIKE, *Summer* (p. 295)

"Summer" is a celebration of both a time of year and a time of life. This story of teen protagonist Homer's subtle pursuit of Sandra, his friend Fred's sister, is vitalized by the descriptions of the lake and the characters' youthful energy. From the opening description of the way Homer and Fred pass their time (in athletics, predominantly) to the closing description of the final night at the lake, Updike lavishes description on the images of summer. His story is replete with references to images that evoke all the senses. Students might trace them throughout the story.

Web Ask students to research David Updike or take a quiz on this work at **bedfordstmartins.com/meyerlit**.

Even the characters' names allude to aspects of the summer. "Homer" — as if from home run — reminds us of one of the boys' favorite activities. (Baseball players are known as "the boys of summer.") Updike's characters play some form of baseball indoors as well as outside, as detailed by the first paragraph: "a variant of baseball adapted to the local geography: two pine trees as foul poles, a broomstick as the bat, the apex of the small, secluded house the dividing line between home runs and outs. On rainy days they swatted bottle tops across the living room floor." Is "Homer" also an indication that the summer — and the adventure — will end in a satisfying way? The name for the female love interest is equally apt: "Sandra" evokes the sandy beaches of summer. The other prominent name contained in Updike's story also emphasizes the theme: here, Thyme equals "time." Not only is summer ending and autumn arriving, but there is the sense that Homer and his friend Fred are at the peak of their vitality. Their sense of indestructibility (drinking for the first time, "wrestl[ing] the car" [para. 11]) and their energy (manifested through their many athletic activities) are relevant indeed. It is during this summer that they become "unofficial [tennis] champions of the lake by trouncing the elder Dewitt boys, unbeaten in several years" (13). It is no coincidence that "glum Billy Dewitt" attributes his loss to the boys' youth. Homer thinks that although Dewitt jests, he also is "hiding some greater sense of loss" (13); indeed, Dewitt's metaphorical "summer," his career as champion, is over.

Although Homer doesn't acknowledge his longing for Sandra until the end of paragraph 9, readers are given many clues that he has a crush on her prior to that point in the story. For instance, Homer lavishes description on Sandra. Instead of saying, "Sandra never tanned," he savors her image: "When she first came in her face was faintly flushed, and there was a pinkish line around the snowy band where her bathing suit strap had been, but the back of her legs remained an endearing, pale white, the color of eggshells, and her back acquired only the softest, brownish blur" (5). The words "endearing" and "softest" indicate his affection for her. He also notes with frustration that she is "strangely indifferent to his heroics" (6).

Of course, there are several hints in the story that Sandra is less oblivious to Homer's crush than he imagines. Although he hopes to impress her by winning the tennis match, she utterly distracts him by leaving at the crucial moment: "Homer watched her as she went down the path, and, impetus suddenly lost, he double faulted, stroked a routine backhand over the back fence, and the match was over" (6). Worst of all, she doesn't even focus on him as he tells her about it afterward. All she says is, "I wish I could go sailing" (7). Coming home from the hike up the mountain, she keeps "his elbow hopelessly held in the warm crook of her arm" (10). Readers must wonder how much of Sandra's summer has been a subtle, friendly campaign to drive Homer to distraction — after all, she's described more than once as appearing in front of him from nowhere, stretching or calling attention to her body in some way, teasing him with her laughter as they cruise home after her shift at the bowling alley. His favorite words for approximating her attraction are "indifference" and "oblivious": "as silently as she arrived, she would leave, walking back through the stones with the same casual sway of indifference" (5); "her life went on its oblivious, happy course without him" (10); "Homer sat at the counter and watched her serve up sloshing cups of coffee, secretly loathing the leering gazes of whiskered truck drivers, and loving her oblivious, vacant stare in answer, hip cocked, hand on counter, gazing up into the neon air above their heads" (12). As the final paragraph of the story reveals, however, Sandra has been anything but indifferent or oblivious throughout Homer's visit to the lake. Looking back on the story after having read it all, students will appreciate the humor and irony of the passages that stress her disregard for Homer.

Homer admits that "to touch her, or kiss her, seemed suddenly incongruous, absurd, contrary to something he could not put his finger on"; "he realized he had never been able to imagine the moment he distantly longed for" (14). Ask students to discuss Homer's motivation here. Why doesn't he kiss Sandra? Why doesn't he need to demonstrate his affection for her in some tangible way? What is there in the story that indicates that longing itself is enough? Is there any connection between his distanced affection for Sandra and his interest in the girl in the canoe who waves to them at the end of the summer? He tells us, "there was something in the way that she raised her arm which, when added to the distant impression of her fullness, beauty, youth, filled him with longing as their boat moved inexorably past, slapping the waves, and she disappeared behind a crop of trees" (15). Is this in some sense a metaphor for the ending of his pursuit of Sandra as the summer comes to a close?

Midway through this story, Homer, the teenage protagonist, reads one of Sir Arthur Conan Doyle's Sherlock Holmes stories (4). In many ways, "Summer" is also a detective story in which Homer discovers that his interpretation of the events at the lake has not been accurate. For an entertaining comparison, students might look up "A Scandal in Bohemia," the one Sherlock Holmes story in which Holmes meets his match, in a woman, Irene Adler. Sandra's outmaneuvering of Homer is in many ways reminiscent of both the mystery and the romance of "A Scandal in Bohemia." One of Holmes's favorite expressions for the thrill of the mystery is "the game's afoot!" Here, the game of teen romance enacted by Sandra and Homer is most satisfyingly, indeed, by the end of the story literally "afoot."

POSSIBLE CONNECTIONS TO OTHER SELECTIONS

Dagoberto Gilb, "Love in L.A." (text p. 430; question #2, following)

John Updike, "A & P" (text p. 201; question #1, following)

CONNECTIONS QUESTIONS IN TEXT (p. 299) WITH ANSWERS

1. Compare David Updike's treatment of summer as the setting of his story with John Updike's use of summer as the setting in "A & P" (p. 201).

    Both stories detail the characteristics of summer, both as a time of year and as a time of life. Their endings particularly, however, differ. "Summer" is romantic while "A & P" is realistic. Although both stories focus on young male protagonists who are infatuated with the idea of the young women they encounter, Homer's experience is playful; in contrast, Sammy's encounter with Queenie and her friends leads him initially to make the gesture of quitting his job and then to realize that the consequences of his actions may be more significant than he realized. For both protagonists, the end of summer is the end of innocence, but the tone with which each author invests that realization is significantly different.

2. Discuss "Summer" and Dagoberto Gilb's "Love in L.A." (p. 430) as love stories. Explain why you might prefer one over the other.

Both Gilb and Updike's protagonists may pursue what the women they encounter represent more than the women themselves. Gilb's protagonist, Jake, is in love with his own sense of himself as a manipulator of other people; his pursuit of Mariana is based on his desire to avoid paying for the damage he's inflicted on her Toyota. Updike's protagonist, however, is less egotistical than young: he's infatuated with the idea of infatuation. However, Homer doesn't hurt Sandra in any way. Indeed, there's a playful reciprocity to their relationship that's missing from Mariana's encounter with Jake.

Approaches to Fiction

11

A Study of Nathaniel Hawthorne

In the following chapters, students have the opportunity to develop some expertise in the works of Nathaniel Hawthorne and Flannery O'Connor. In addition to studying more than one work by the same author, here they have the opportunity to engage with the critics. In the chapters for each author, there appear not only numerous Perspectives (some general, some specific to the stories contained in each chapter) but also excerpts from two critiques of the same story ("Complementary Critical Readings").

Instructors may want to encourage their students to study the multiple approaches to interpretation of literature in Chapter 48 before beginning to discuss the critical commentary. After some introduction to psychological, feminist, formalist, and other strategies for interpretation, students might more readily identify individual critics' ideologies or better understand their intellectual approaches to the literature as well as their ideas about the content (their close readings) of these stories. Comparing the critical stances exemplified by the examples in these chapters, particularly in connection with multiple stories by the same authors, students will enhance both their reading and their critical thinking skills. They may also appreciate more deeply the diverse possibilities for interpretation of these compelling stories.

 Ask students to research Nathaniel Hawthorne or take quizzes on his works at **bedfordstmartins.com/ meyerlit**.

NATHANIEL HAWTHORNE

Young Goodman Brown (p. 315)

Brown's name conveys several meanings that can be determined after reading this story. This is a point worth stressing with students so they do not mistakenly assume that they should perceive the following meanings on a first reading. "Young" suggests the protagonist's innocent, simple nature at the beginning of the story, when he has an as-yet-untested, abstract faith in life. "Goodman," in addition to being a seventeenth-century honorific somewhat like "mister," takes on an ironic meaning when Brown meets the devil. "Brown" is a common name that perhaps serves to universalize this character's experience. If Hawthorne had chosen the name "White" or "Black," he would have cast the protagonist in too absolute a moral role. "Gray" would do, but "Brown" has the additional advantage of associating the protagonist with the forest, particularly in the fall, an appropriate season for the story's movement from innocence to experience.

Web Ask students to explore contexts for Nathaniel Hawthorne and "Young Goodman Brown" at **bedfordstmartins.com/ meyerlit**.

The opening paragraphs provide important contrasts between the village and the forest. The village represents the safe, predictable landscape of home, associated with light, faith, goodness, and community. In paragraph 8 the forest is dreary, dark, gloomy, narrow, and threatening; it represents a moral wilderness in which skepticism and evil flourish. Brown journeys into the forest to meet the devil. No specific reason is given for the journey, but most of us can understand Eve's curiosity about biting into the apple. Brown assumes that he will be able to cling to "Faith" after his encounter with the devil (although students may never have heard of this story, most will grasp its allegorical nature very quickly). But of course Brown turns out to be wrong because when he sees that the rest of the community — from all the respectable deacons, select-men, and religious leaders to his family and beloved Faith — share the impulses he has acted on, his faith is shattered.

We know that Brown's meeting is with a supernatural figure because the old man explains that he had been in Boston only fifteen minutes before his meeting in the forest outside Salem village. His devilish nature is conveyed by his serpentine staff; indeed, he even sits under "an old tree" (para. 10) that suggests the tree of knowledge in Genesis. We don't have to believe, however, that Brown has a literal encounter with the devil. Hawthorne tells us that the staff's wriggling like a snake probably was only an "ocular deception" (13). This kind of calculated ambiguity is used a number of times in the story to accommodate readers who are wary of supernatural events and prefer "reality" in their fiction.

Students should be asked to locate other instances of ambiguity — such as Faith's ribbons and the question at the end concerning whether Brown simply dreamed the entire sequence of events. It seems that the answer to this question doesn't really matter because in the final paragraph Hawthorne dismisses such questions and instead emphasizes the terrible results of Brown's belief that he has been betrayed by everyone in the community. Brown's life is ruined; he becomes as stern and dark as the moral wilderness he abhors. Because he turned away from life and lost faith, "his dying hour was gloom." There is no absolute evidence either to relieve the community of responsibility for its involvement with evil or to pronounce it innocent. (A reader can, however, draw on Hawthorne's other works to demonstrate that he viewed humankind as neither wholly corrupt nor perfect; see, for example, "The Birthmark," text p. 333.)

Even if Faith has some knowledge of evil or is tempted by it, that does not mean that "evil is the nature of mankind" (65) as the devil (not Hawthorne) falsely claims. When she joyfully meets her husband on the village street, Hawthorne paints on Faith's face no ironic smile, which would indicate hypocrisy or deception. And she has her pink ribbons. There is no actual reason for Brown to shrink "from the bosom of Faith" (72). He does so because he refuses to tolerate any kind of ambiguity. He is a moral absolut-ist who mistakenly accepts the devil's view of humanity. In a psychological sense his rejection of the world may be seen as a projection of his own feelings of guilt, and so he repudiates all trust, love, and especially faith, because he now sees faith as a satanic joke.

The built-in ambiguities in "Young Goodman Brown" have encouraged many read-ings of the story. For a convenient sample of twelve different readings see *Nathaniel Hawthorne: Young Goodman Brown*, edited by Thomas E. Connolly (Columbus: Merrill, 1968). If a dozen students are asked to read and summarize varying interpretations, the class will have an opportunity to debate the story in detail and develop an idea of what makes one interpretation more valid than another. It's also useful for them to realize that critics can disagree.

Possible Connections to Other Selections

Nathaniel Hawthorne, "The Birthmark" (text p. 333; questions #2 and #3, following)

——, "The Minister's Black Veil" (text p. 324)

Herman Melville, "Bartleby, the Scrivener" (text p. 133; question #1, following)

CONNECTIONS QUESTIONS IN TEXT (p. 324) **WITH ANSWERS**

1. Compare and contrast Goodman Brown's reasons for withdrawal with those of Melville's Bartleby (p. 133). Do you find yourself more sympathetic with one character than the other? Explain.

Goodman Brown withdraws from society because he has received an insight into the sinfulness of mankind, but he does not share in that fallibility. He becomes a "stern, a sad, a darkly meditative, a distrustful, if not a desperate man" (para. 72) because he feels morally superior to the other townspeople. Bartleby's withdrawal does not appear to be moral in nature, but he too is "a desperate man." If we take the Dead Letter Office as one reason for his behavior, it seems that his withdrawal is prompted by the futility of life. Just as the letters cannot find their proper destinations, Bartleby has an intuition of the aimlessness of people's lives, which he feels himself.

2. To what extent is Hawthorne's use of dreams crucial in this story and in "The Birthmark" (p. 333)? Explain how Hawthorne uses dreams as a means to complicate our view of his characters.

Because the satanic mass that Hawthorne describes might be only Goodman Brown's dream, it leaves open the possibility that he has only imagined the grave sins of all his fellow citizens. He lets those perceived sins affect the way he thinks of and behaves toward them, so that at his death, those around him are somewhat relieved to have a break in the "gloom" (para. 72). Instead, he should take his dreams as a warning, as Faith seems to do at the beginning of the story. When her husband is about to leave, she asks him to stay because "A lone woman is troubled with such dreams and such thoughts that she's afeared of herself sometimes" (3). If he had put stake in her dreams, he would have been spared the life-altering experience in the woods.

In "The Birthmark," Aylmer's dream marks a change in both characters' lives, which have subsequently been agitated by the surfacing of Aylmer's subconscious. It disrupts the calm of their marriage by voicing his obsession with the removal of his wife's birthmark, "affrighting this actual life with secrets that perchance belong to a deeper one" (14). Through Aylmer's dream, his wife, Georgiana, is made aware of his hateful feelings toward her birthmark and is determined to rid herself of it to salvage her marriage and her life. His dream also serves as a warning to Aylmer of the significance of this birthmark to his wife's life; "its tiny grasp appeared to have caught hold of Georgiana's heart" (14).

3. What does Goodman Brown's pursuit of sin have in common with Aylmer's quest for perfection in "The Birthmark" (p. 333)? How do these pursuits reveal the characters' personalities and shed light on the theme of each story?

Goodman Brown falters in his pursuit of sin, but as he makes his journey through the forest, he is largely influenced by the thought, and later by the appearance, of members of his community, who he had previously thought were pure and holy. It is significant that Hawthorne sets this story not in his own time, but in an earlier time, closer to America's Puritan roots. Hawthorne uses Brown's personality to critique the piety of Puritanism. In "The Birthmark," Hawthorne turns his critique on a narrow-minded vision of science. Aylmer is a classic overreacher in the tradition of Faust, and thus his pursuit is bound to end in tragedy. His obsession with his wife's birthmark blinds him to her other charms, and his hubris in thinking he can remove something so deeply ingrained in her leads eventually to her death.

The Minister's Black Veil (p. 324)

Nathaniel Hawthorne's "The Minister's Black Veil" presents readers with unanswerable questions: Why does the minister wear the black veil? What does the veil represent? A first-person point of view would destroy the ambiguity, and therefore the intellectual challenge, of the tale. If Mr. Hooper told his congregation and Hawthorne's readers why he made the choice to wear the veil, it is likely that neither group would be affected by his action. Because Mr. Hooper does not reveal his motivation, students are forced to propose their own theories for it.

If, as Edgar Allan Poe and other critics have suggested, Mr. Hooper wears the veil as a penance for a specific sin, possibly in connection with the young woman whose funeral he conducts, he exacts a heavy toll from his parishioners. From the first moment he appears wearing the veil, "two folds of crape, which entirely concealed his features, except the mouth and chin, but probably did not intercept his sight, farther than to give a darkened aspect to all living and inanimate things" (para. 6), he casts a cloud upon his parishioners' faces and spirits. They cannot return his greeting. The traditional atmosphere of the church is disrupted by the congregation's horror, and after church many of Mr. Hooper's listeners reverse their normally decorous behavior to gawk or gossip: "Some talked loudly, and profaned the Sabbath-day with ostentatious laughter" (13). Later the same day, even the corpse in the coffin shudders as Mr. Hooper bends over it, though a black veil is appropriate for the occasion. The minister then officiates at a wedding, but "the same horrible black veil, which had added deeper gloom to the funeral . . . could portend nothing but evil to the wedding" (22). The groom shivers, and the bride is so pale that she is associated with the dead maiden of the earlier funeral. These are short-term effects of the minister's decision to wear the black veil; a long-term effect of it on his parishioners is the breakdown of his communication with them. The good people of his church are accustomed to guiding him in church matters as well as to being led by him: "Hitherto, whenever there appeared the slightest call for such interference, he had never lacked advisers, nor shown himself averse to be guided by their judgment" (24). Yet when they approach him to discuss his reason for wearing the veil and call his attention to its adverse effect on the church, they are unable to influence him. Not even his wife-to-be, Elizabeth, can convince him to remove his mask, even for a moment. Though she is noted for her "calm energy" (25) and has a "firmer character than his own" (36), she too is affected by the veil: "But, in an instant, as it were, a new feeling took the place of sorrow: her eyes were fixed insensibly on the black veil, when, like a sudden twilight in the air, its terrors fell around her" (36). If the minister dons the black veil as a penance for his unknown sin, the fear, distrust, and isolation it inspires are greater evils that seem to defeat his purpose.

If Mr. Hooper dons the black veil to symbolize the sins of his secretive flock, he exacts a heavier toll upon himself. On the first Sunday of its appearance, the veil isolates him not only from his parishioners but from God: "It threw its obscurity between him and the holy page, as he read the Scriptures; and while he prayed, the veil lay heavily on his uplifted countenance" (10). God cannot reach him, and his congregation chooses to avoid him: "None, as on former occasions, aspired to the honor of walking by their pastor's side. Old Squire Saunders, doubtless by an accidental lapse of memory, neglected to invite Mr. Hooper to his table, where the good clergyman had been wont to bless the food, almost every Sunday since his settlement" (13). As he continues to wear the veil, the people not only avoid him but express their opinions of him in bewilderment and scorn: "Our parson has gone mad!" (9); "it was reckoned merely an eccentric whim" (44); "but with the multitude, good Mr. Hooper was irreparably a bugbear" (44). Even though he becomes a renowned speaker, and people come from great distances to hear his church services, they come for dubious, clearly not religious, reasons: "With the mere idle purpose of gazing at his figure, because it was forbidden them to behold his face" (45). The people in his village go out of their way to avoid him in the streets, while children flee at his approach. Far from being a holy man, he has become a monster. His personal life is in no better condition after Elizabeth decides not to marry him. He himself is frightened at his reflection in the mirror. In the end, the black veil has cost him his link with humanity: "It had separated him from cheerful brotherhood and woman's love, and kept him in that saddest of all prisons, his own heart" (47). Mr. Hooper addresses this awful personal cost on his deathbed when he cries, "Why do you tremble at me alone? . . . Tremble also at each other" (58). This is his final intimation that the wearing of the veil is connected with his parishioners' spiritual welfare.

One other possible motive is a self-righteous and total obsession with wearing the black veil — he is unable to give it up for his lover, his congregation, or his God. On his deathbed he speaks of the supposed meaning of the veil and of man's fundamental tendency to hide sins. If he is purely self-motivated, this deathbed speech is hypocritical. He has worn the black veil at an inestimable cost.

Hawthorne suggests that at the funeral over which Mr. Hooper presides, the veil is "an appropriate emblem" (18). Does Mr. Hooper's lifelong appearance in the veil suggest an ongoing funeral for the town's spirituality? What is the meaning of the minister's constant smile? Is it genuine, ironic, or the sign of a crazed intellect? In what real-life situations do people wear veils? How does Mr. Hooper's application of the black crape conform to or contrast with these traditional uses? As students attempt to answer these questions, ask them to explain how "The Minister's Black Veil" is, as Hawthorne claims, a parable. Students' definitions of the term may lead them to their own answers to these questions and their own interpretations of the story.

POSSIBLE CONNECTIONS TO OTHER SELECTIONS

Nathaniel Hawthorne, "The Birthmark" (text p. 333; questions #2 and #3, following)

——, "Young Goodman Brown" (text p. 315; questions #1 and #2, following)

CONNECTIONS QUESTIONS IN TEXT (p. 333) WITH ANSWERS

1. How might this story be regarded as a sequel to "Young Goodman Brown" (p. 315)? How are the themes similar?

    Both stories deal with the way an individual's relationship to his community is affected by his experience of sin. In "Young Goodman Brown," we see the pious man's first real encounter with evil. Though he resists the devil, he returns home changed; he can no longer relate to his fellow townspeople or even his wife because he perceives them as sinners. In "The Minister's Black Veil," Hooper separates himself from the congregation by putting on his veil. As he admits to Elizabeth, the veil is "a type and a symbol" (para. 30). That is, it represents some boundary between himself and others. However, it also works on the literal level to alienate his congregation; not being able to see his eyes, they begin to fear him. Hooper seems more sorrowful than Brown and there is a note of self-recrimination in his isolation. However, both characters make the mistake of disassociating themselves from the community, which serves to amplify their faults.

2. Explain how Faith in "Young Goodman Brown," Georgiana in "The Birthmark" (p. 333), and Elizabeth in "The Minister's Black Veil" are used to reveal some truth about the central male characters in each story. Describe the similarities that you see among these female characters.

    Faith in "Young Goodman Brown," as her name suggests, is the most allegorical of these three female characters. With her cheerful pink ribbons, she stands for goodness in a world of sin. It is Goodman Brown's fear that she has given in to the devil that makes him continue on his "errand" into the forest. His despair that Faith has been lost continues even after he wakes alone and returns home. Once he has connected her in his mind with evil, he shies away from her. Elizabeth, in "The Minister's Black Veil," is a more realistic character; rather than functioning mostly as a symbol, she reveals the main character by her reaction to his symbolic veil. While the other townspeople are afraid to ask Hooper why he has put it on, Elizabeth simply and kindly asks him about it. However, her lighthearted questions give way to serious fears when he refuses to remove it even for a moment when he is alone with her. She finally reacts with horror, leaving Hooper alone behind his veil. Unlike Elizabeth, Georgiana in "The Birthmark" lacks the strength to challenge her husband. Her utter devotion to Aylmer allows him to pursue his narcissistic goals, and the self-loathing she develops because of the birthmark puts her in the position of his experimental subject. Georgiana puts herself entirely in Aylmer's hands, and her death is a consequence of his folly.

3. Compare Hawthorne's use of symbol in "The Minister's Black Veil" and "The Birthmark" (p. 333). Write an essay explaining which symbol you think works more effectively to evoke the theme of its story.

The type of veil worn by Minister Hooper is usually a symbol for grief, but interestingly, it is traditionally worn by women. As one of the members of Hooper's congregation notes, "a simple black veil, such as any woman might wear on her bonnet, [becomes] such a terrible thing on Mr. Hooper's face!" (para. 14). Though we never learn exactly what he is mourning, Hooper is haunted by something. The symbol of the hand-shaped mark on Georgiana's cheek in "The Birthmark" represents an imperfection in her otherwise flawless looks and character. It also raises questions about what is made by God and what is made by men's hands. Aylmer is infuriated by the birthmark because it seems to be the mark of humanity on his bride. He wants to imagine her as a pure spirit, but ironically, he attempts to change her appearance through his own scientific work.

The Birthmark (p. 333)

Aylmer (a variant of Elmer, meaning "noble") in this story is neither evil nor mad. An eighteenth-century scientist, he embodies the period's devotion to science and reason. However, his studies supersede all else in his life; they are his first love — even before his wife. His choice of science over love identifies him as the kind of Hawthorne character who displays an imbalance of head and heart. His intellect usurps his common sense and feelings. He loses sight of Georgiana's humanity in his monomaniacal quest to achieve an ideal perfection in her person.

Aylmer is shocked by Georgiana's birthmark because he sees it as a "visible mark of earthly imperfection" (para. 5). To him the "crimson hand" (a sign perhaps that humankind's fallen nature is imprinted by the devil [original sin] on all human beings) symbolizes the "fatal flaw of humanity" and is a sign of mortality, "toil and pain" (8). This extreme perspective differs from the more normal views of the birthmark in paragraph 7.

Georgiana (whose name is appropriately associated with the earthy rather than the ideal) loves her husband so completely that she is willing to risk her life to win his approval. Her feelings serve as a foil to his obsessive efforts to perfect her; she loves him despite his willingness to dehumanize her. She is unaware of his blasphemous pride, which the reader sees clearly: "What will be my triumph when I shall have corrected what Nature left imperfect in her fairest work!" (19). Though the story is set in the 1700s, Georgiana can be seen as a prototype of many nineteenth-century female characters — passive and incapable of changing the course of events that will inevitably destroy her. She becomes a martyr to her love for Aylmer. Students are likely to see her as hopelessly weak rather than nearly perfect. When Georgiana reads Aylmer's journal and observes that "his most splendid successes were almost invariably failures, if compared with the ideal at which he aimed" (51), many readers wonder why this and other grim foreshadowings about the nature of his work (see 32–37) do not alarm her. Hawthorne, however, stresses her loyal devotion to her husband more as a virtue than as a weakness.

Aminadab is also an obvious foil to Aylmer. His name spelled backward is, interestingly enough, *bad anima* (bad soul or life principle). He represents the opposite of Aylmer's aspirations for the ideal: "He seemed to represent man's physical nature." His physical features — his grimy, shaggy, low stature and "indescribable earthiness" — are in stark contrast to Aylmer's "slender figure, and pale, intellectual face," which make him "a type of the spiritual element" (25). Aminadab's "smoky aspect" is the result of his tending Aylmer's "hot and feverish" furnace, which seems demonic and evokes the destructive nature of Aylmer's efforts to spiritualize matter (57).

Although Aylmer's motives are noble, his egotism blinds him to a central fact that his science ignores, for according to Hawthorne, there can be no such thing as mortal perfection. The story's theme argues that the nature of mortal existence necessarily means humanity's "liability to sin, sorrow, decay, and death" (8). For Hawthorne, no science can change that fact of life. As soon as the birthmark fades from Georgiana's face, her life fades because mortality and perfection do not coexist. Aylmer lacks the profound wisdom to embrace the human condition. Like Young Goodman Brown, he fails to accept the terms on which life offers itself.

Students may find provocative a discussion (or writing assignment) about this story as a modern version of our obsession with attaining physical perfection, through exercise, cosmetic surgery, or some other means. Hawthorne's theme of human imperfection is largely a philosophical issue, but it can also be addressed through psychological and sociological perspectives.

POSSIBLE CONNECTIONS TO OTHER SELECTIONS

Emily Dickinson, "Success is counted sweetest" (text p. 803)

Nathaniel Hawthorne, "The Minister's Black Veil" (text p. 324)

——, "Young Goodman Brown" (text p. 315; question #1, following)

Flannery O'Connor, "A Good Man Is Hard to Find" (text p. 356)

Fay Weldon, "IND AFF, or Out of Love in Sarajevo" (text p. 173)

CONNECTION QUESTION IN TEXT (p. 344) WITH ANSWER

1. Compare Aylmer's unwillingness to accept things as they are with Goodman Brown's refusal to be a part of a community he regards as fallen.

   Both of these characters are doomed by their striving after perfection. Aylmer cannot see his wife's beauty because he is obsessed with her one flaw. Though other men see the birthmark as adding to her charm, he becomes increasingly disgusted by it. Georgiana begins to adopt his attitude, and she too develops a hatred for it so strong that eventually she would rather die than continue living with it. Thus, Aylmer's need for perfection destroys his wife's life. In a similar way, Goodman Brown's intimation of the sins of his fellow townspeople poisons his opinion of their good acts. Once he has connected them with sin, he can no longer see what he first admired in them. In his case, though, the entire community stands against his scorn of their imperfection. Rather than conforming to his view, they are relieved when he dies and they no longer have to deal with his sense of superiority.

PERSPECTIVES ON HAWTHORNE

NATHANIEL HAWTHORNE, *On Solitude* (p. 344)

Students can use this letter to get a sense of how Hawthorne worried about his self-imposed solitude and how he used "nothing but thin air to concoct my stories." Ask students if tensions in the letter are manifested in any of the Hawthorne stories included in this chapter.

NATHANIEL HAWTHORNE, *On the Power of the Writer's Imagination* (p. 346)

The light of a writer's imagination cast on familiar objects and events changes our perceptions of things. Good writing causes us to encounter not merely observable facts but also meanings supplied by the author. Hawthorne's purposes as a writer go beyond a realistic presentation of the world; he sought to invest his work with his own reading of "the truth of the human heart."

NATHANIEL HAWTHORNE, *On His Short Stories* (p. 347)

Hawthorne seems a bit nervous and uncertain about characterizing his stories because he anticipates his public's objection to their ambiguities and sometimes puzzling themes. He is aware that a weird tale such as "The Minister's Black Veil" is radically different from the popular sunny magazine sketches of robust American life contemporary with it.

HERMAN MELVILLE, *On Nathaniel Hawthorne's Tragic Vision* (p. 348)

Melville admired Hawthorne's exploration of the darker side of human potential. He dedicated *Moby-Dick* to Hawthorne because he recognized in him a kindred spirit willing to risk an outward-bound voyage, even if it meant the possibility of being lost.

GAYLORD BREWER, *The Joys of Secret Sin* (p. 348)

Students might find that, after reading Hawthorne's stories, this poem is in line with their sympathies. Through his choice of words, Brewer suggests that the solitary sorrows of Goodman Brown and Mr. Hooper are actually somewhat aggressive. These two are "soldiers of melancholy" (line 3), acting "smugly" (6) toward their friends and neighbors. Their overbearing sadness "soils" (4) the earth, leaving "her name / sullied" (7–8). Though the two characters seem to experience real grief, Brewer thinks that their secret pleasure in isolation is essentially morbid.

12

A Study of Flannery O'Connor

With their grotesque characters, bizarre situations, religious imagery, and astute (if dark) worldview, Flannery O'Connor's stories are both interesting to read and satisfying to teach. This anthology enables students to study this complicated writer in depth because it contains three of her stories and a number of Perspectives on her unique writing style. O'Connor's own comments on her faith and the choices she made as a writer, combined with a number of critical views, will be helpful to students who want to make sense of the strange southern world of damnation and redemption that O'Connor presents to her readers.

> **Web** Ask students to research Flannery O'Connor or take quizzes on her works at **bedfordstmartins.com/meyerlit**.

FLANNERY O'CONNOR

A Good Man Is Hard to Find (p. 356)

This story may initially puzzle students. It certainly defies easy interpretation. As they analyze the grandmother's and the Misfit's characters, they may understand more of the story, but even after discussion, students might have more questions than answers.

At the beginning of the story, the grandmother dwells on the past. Her manners and attire are ladylike: "The grandmother had on a navy blue straw sailor hat with a bunch of white violets on the brim and a navy blue dress with a small white dot in the print. Her collars and cuffs were white organdy trimmed with lace and at her neckline she had pinned a purple spray of cloth violets containing a sachet" (para. 12). She is a hard contrast to the mother, a young woman in slacks who represents the contemporary woman, and the rude granddaughter, June Star, the woman of the future. The grandmother's stories, about former beaus, lost opportunities, and secret panels in houses long gone, emphasize her preoccupation with the past. Even her humor involves the past: " 'Where's the plantation?' John Wesley asked. 'Gone With the Wind,' said the grandmother. 'Ha. Ha' " (23–24). She seems incapable of accepting the present or preparing for the future. She can only focus on her personal affairs and desires.

The Misfit is striking because he forces the grandmother beyond her obsession with herself and her past. As soon as she sees him, she focuses on identifying him. Then, trying to save herself and her family, she attempts to convince him that he is (note present tense) a good man. The Misfit and the grandmother are similar in one sense: he, too, dwells on his past. His grievances about his criminal record highlight his human past, and his observations about Jesus reflect a more universal human past. After hearing his "confession," the grandmother attempts to preserve both of their futures by "saving" the Misfit: "If you would pray . . . Jesus would help you" (118). Even though the Misfit refuses her help, they are both shaken out of their selfish memories. The grandmother becomes a more Christian woman because of her encounter with the Misfit. In truth, as the Misfit explains, "She would of been a good woman, . . . if it had been somebody there to shoot her every minute of her life" (140). Jesus taught the people by his good example and his raising of the dead; the Misfit enlightens the woman by his evil example and his execution of her.

This story obviously foreshadows its violent ending by its constant references to death in the plot, the dialogue, and the setting. The grandmother dresses up for the journey so that if she is in an accident, "anyone seeing her dead on the highway would know at once that she was a lady" (12). The last city that the family drives through is Toombsboro. The Misfit and his henchmen drive a car associated with funerals: "A big black battered hearse-like automobile" (70). Is the Misfit the death the story foreshadows, or is O'Connor simply leading up to the deaths of the family?

Does "A Good Man Is Hard to Find" seem like a genuine story, or is the plot too coincidental? Are the characters and events believable? The power of surface appearances is constantly emphasized: the old woman is a lady because of the way she dresses; she recognizes the Misfit as one of her children only after he dons the shirt worn previously by Bailey Boy. Why does O'Connor call attention to these surface appearances and their effects? If this story is an allegory, what do the Misfit and the grandmother (for whom other, more specific names are never indicated) represent? What is the effect of the epigram at the beginning of the story? It may merely warn the reader about the journey this family is making; there may, however, be added significance to the source and the religious nature of its message. What might the dragon represent?

TIPS FROM THE FIELD

I always do a "talk show" after teaching the section on O'Connor. I have five or six students assume characters from each of the O'Connor stories and have the rest of the class prepare questions for the "guests" on the talk show. This exercise is always popular and is especially fun if you choose "hams" to play the characters.

— ROBERT CROFT, *Gainesville College*

From my experiences trying to teach Flannery O'Connor to a class including several Japanese and Swedish students, I came to realize that a number of American students — even southern ones — also have trouble with O'Connor's use of dialect. I found that having these students read aloud some scenes from "Good Country People" and "A Good Man Is Hard to Find" effectively broke through the dialect barrier. Their ears seem to be able to make sense of O'Connor's dialogue even when their eyes can't.

— JAMES H. CLEMMER, *Austin Peay State University*

POSSIBLE CONNECTIONS TO OTHER SELECTIONS

Nathaniel Hawthorne, "The Birthmark" (text p. 333; question #1, following)

Flannery O'Connor, "Revelation" (text p. 367)

CONNECTION QUESTION IN TEXT (p. 367) WITH ANSWER

1. What makes "A Good Man Is Hard to Find" so difficult to interpret in contrast, say, to Nathaniel Hawthorne's "The Birthmark" (p. 333)?

   O'Connor leaves much more unresolved at the end of her story than Hawthorne does, making the readers' interpretations less determinate. At the crucial moment of the story, we know that the grandmother has some kind of revelation, but the nature of this sudden enlightenment is a mystery. She sees the Misfit as "one of [her] own children" (para. 136), but does she mean this figuratively, in the sense that all people are related to one another by Christ? Or is she so distraught over her own son's death that she's delusional? Where Hawthorne's narrative voice fills in many of the thematic connections of his story, with O'Connor, we have only the characters' statements to go on. Whether the grandmother really would have been a better person "if it had been somebody there to shoot her every minute of her life" (140) is up to the reader to decide.

Good Country People (p. 367)

The central conflict in this story is between Hulga, who believes herself to be vastly superior to everyone around her, and the Bible salesman, Manley Pointer, whom Hulga and her mother at first take to be simple, naive, "good country people." Hulga wants to seduce Pointer to shatter his alleged innocence, both physical and spiritual. She wants him to believe in nothing, as she does. Her initial impulse is mean-spirited, but even her first thoughts of seducing him include a fantasy of being with him once she has enlightened him about her version of the truth: "She imagined that she took his remorse in hand and changed it into a deeper understanding of life. She took all his shame away and turned it into something useful" (para. 91). Despite her facade of nastiness, which she uses as a sort of defense mechanism, Hulga really does want warmth, respect, admiration, and even love. She begins to recognize these feelings in herself, ironically, as Pointer is convincing her to show him her artificial leg. She is moved by what she perceives to be his innocence, which has enabled him (she thinks) to see the truth about her: that she "ain't like anybody else" (128).

But the joke is on Hulga. No sooner does Pointer get his hands on her leg than all his apparent innocence and tenderness disappear. It was the leg he wanted all along, for his collection; the sexual activity would have been a nice fringe benefit, but he is perfectly willing to leave without it. When Hulga asks him, in paragraph 136, "aren't you just good country people?" she is, ironically, clinging to the very values that she previously denounced and satirized. She is forced to acknowledge that civility and common decency (which Pointer has flouted by taking her leg) do matter. She has been deceiving herself by pretending that these things are dispensable, that she does not need affection, and that she does not believe in, or need to believe in, anything. It has taken someone more cynical and evil than herself to make her aware of the truth.

Hulga now realizes that, compared with Pointer, she is the innocent one. O'Connor's suggestion is that Hulga will soon get the same message we do from Pointer's last words: the result of "believing in nothing" is the kind of depravity of spirit Pointer exhibits, and if she wants to save herself from that, she'd better start believing.

Hulga's two names represent her inner conflict between everything she is and everything she is repressing. The name "Joy," of course, is just another of her mother's empty clichés, so she changes it to Hulga (which suggests some combination of the words *ugly, huge,* and *hulk*). By denying the "nice" name her mother gave her, she can deny the "niceness" in herself. She can, in fact, create a new self: hostile, angry, and abusive — all to hide the pain she feels because of what she is repressing. Mrs. Hopewell's name emphasizes the shallowness of her beliefs that "nothing is perfect" (11) and that "people who looked on the bright side of things would be beautiful even if they were not" (17). And Mrs. Freeman's name suggests that she is free in a way that both Joy and her mother are not.

Mrs. Freeman sees through Hulga as her mother can't; direct the class to paragraph 16, where we learn that Mrs. Freeman calls the girl "Hulga" rather than "Joy": "Mrs. Freeman's relish for using the name only irritated [Hulga]. It was as if Mrs. Freeman's beady steel-pointed eyes had penetrated far enough behind her face to reach some secret fact." This secret fact is that, as O'Connor says in "On Theme and Symbol" (text p. 396), "there is a wooden part of [Hulga's] soul that corresponds to her wooden leg." Mrs. Freeman's statement at the story's end, "Some can't be that simple," suggests that she has seen through the Bible salesman as well. That Mrs. Hopewell repeatedly refers to Mrs. Freeman with condescension as "good country people" becomes increasingly ironic in light of the fact that Mrs. Freeman is much smarter and a much better judge of human nature than either her employer or her employer's daughter.

The older women are introduced before Hulga so that her character can be developed in relation to theirs. By the time Hulga appears, we are as alienated by her mother's insipid thoughts and conversation as Hulga is, so we can empathize with the girl somewhat. The last two paragraphs of the story depict an unchanged, vapidly optimistic Mrs. Hopewell, who knows nothing of what has gone on between Hulga and Pointer in the barn. Her cheerful ignorance contrasts sharply with Hulga's "churning face" and emotions in the preceding paragraph; it is Mrs. Hopewell who has the most to learn.

The limited omniscient point of view lets O'Connor alternate between Mrs. Hopewell's and Hulga's perspectives, giving us access to the actions and thoughts of both characters and allowing us to make informed judgments that we would not be able to make if we were limited to Hulga's point of view.

POSSIBLE CONNECTIONS TO OTHER SELECTIONS

Nathaniel Hawthorne, "Young Goodman Brown" (text p. 315; question #2, following)

Ernest Hemingway, "Soldier's Home" (text p. 166; question #1, following)

Flannery O'Connor, "Revelation" (text p. 381)

CONNECTIONS QUESTIONS IN TEXT (p. 381) WITH ANSWERS

1. How do Mrs. Hopewell's assumptions about life compare with those of Krebs's mother in Hemingway's "Soldier's Home" (p. 166)? Explain how the conflict in each story is related to what the mothers come to represent in the eyes of the central characters.

    Mrs. Hopewell's name sums up her outlook on life; she is unswervingly optimistic. Yet she is also realistic in her views. The narrator ironically comments that "Mrs. Hopewell had no bad qualities of her own, but she was able to use other people's in such a constructive way that she never felt the lack" (para. 4). Just as she manages Mrs. Freeman by allowing her to have her hand in everything, she also wants to manage her daughter's life and convince her to be less cynical. Yet for Hulga, her mother's optimism is naive. The changing of her name illustrates how she has rejected her mother's "Joy" for a name that sounds like "the broad blank hull of a battleship" (14). In "Soldier's Home," the mother represents all the norms of the community from which Krebs has been alienated by his experience of war. Her emotional pleas for him to rejoin normal life just serve to make him more disgusted by it. At the end he gives in and agrees to return to the world of work and family, but his decision is prompted not by his desire but by her demands.

2. Discuss the treatment of faith in this story and in Hawthorne's "Young Goodman Brown" (p. 315).

    Hulga's rejection of faith is part of what makes her different and, in her mind, superior to the other people in her community. Still, we see that she is not immune to spiritual feeling. When Manley Pointer says she "ain't like anybody else" (para. 128), she has a feeling that is "like losing her own life and finding it again, miraculously, in his" (129). O'Connor's language in this paragraph mirrors the language some Christians use to talk about being born again. Thinking that Manley has understood some deep truth about her, Hulga has her own kind of religious experience. However, her conception of herself is shattered when Manley suddenly turns hateful and takes her prosthetic leg. His parting remark to her destroys her newfound faith: "[Y]ou ain't so smart. I been believing in nothing ever since I was born" (145).

    In Hawthorne's story, Goodman Brown begins as a man of faith, and though his belief in God remains intact, his faith in the moral uprightness of his neighbors is destroyed by his night in the woods. Though he goes out at night with the purpose of meeting the devil, he is surprised to see that other members of the community are there as well. He can accept a view of himself as a sinner, but he refuses to accept the same fallibility in the elders of his church or in his deceased father.

Revelation (p. 381)

As a member of "the home-and-land owner" class, Mrs. Turpin believes herself to be superior to "niggers," "white-trash," and mere "home-owners" (para. 24). She takes pride in her position in the community, and far worse in O'Connor's credo, she takes pride in what she perceives to be her privileged position in relation to God. In paragraph 74 she thinks, "He had not made her a nigger or white-trash or ugly! He had made her herself and given her a little of everything. Jesus, thank you! she said. Thank you thank you thank you!" She believes that she was singled out to have this high station, along with her other virtues. In other words, she believes that she is saved and has nothing to worry about on Judgment Day. The gospel music on the radio in the doctor's office adds an extra ironic twist. Note, in paragraph 21, that Mrs. Turpin can supply the song's "last line mentally"; this is a gesture of routine rather than one that comes from the heart. Mrs. Turpin takes God and his mercy for granted; she might as well be singing along with a toothpaste commercial.

Among the signals Mrs. Turpin misses but we comprehend is the parallel between the doctor's waiting room and Mrs. Turpin's pig parlor. A close reading of paragraphs 173–181 will reveal that Mrs. Turpin sees the hogs as interchangeable rather than individuals. She is unable, however, to make the connection to the group of people in the doctor's office, or to humanity in general — which she still, this late in the story, insists on dividing into classes. It is in this context, too, that we understand Mrs. Turpin's hired woman's comment, "You just had you a little fall" (147). It suggests that she has fallen from God's grace, at least in part because she thought she could earn and control it.

In paragraphs 178–186 Mrs. Turpin is addressing God; her anger and confusion stem from the fact that she really does believe herself to be a good person; it is not until the end of the story that she realizes her prideful hypocrisy. So at this point she feels that the message that she is a warthog from hell is unwarranted, that God has tricked her somehow and is being cruel and unfair. The truth is revealed to her in the story's last two paragraphs, when "a visionary light settled in her eyes" (191). According to Frederick Asals, the "abysmal" knowledge Mrs. Turpin receives is that "those like herself, who had possessed 'good order and common sense and respectable behavior,' who had been blessed with a 'God-given wit,' discover that although these gifts are apparently their worldly responsibility, they have no final value in themselves." But the message is also "life-giving," or at least has the potential to be so:

> The visionary procession of "Revelation" clearly carried into eternity...the purifying action of the fire itself. Indeed...the imaginary fire in O'Connor's fiction...is most often purgatorial...and what it signals is the infliction of a searing grace, the onset of a saving pain. (Frederick Asals, *Flannery O'Connor: The Imagination of Extremity* [Athens: U of Georgia P, 1982], 225–26)

We see that Mrs. Turpin has at least a chance for redemption, although there will be a high price to pay.

Mary Grace attacks Mrs. Turpin partly because she is a messenger from God, partly because she is disturbed, and partly, we suspect, because she recognizes (perhaps through her God-given vision as a lunatic) Mrs. Turpin for the hypocrite she is. Mary Grace's name, of course, suggests redemption. Because she is ugly and nasty, Mrs. Turpin feels superior to her, so it is fitting that Mary Grace deliver the divine message: that Mrs. Turpin might as well be a warthog from hell for all the good her "virtues" will do her on Judgment Day. Further irony comes from the title of Mary Grace's textbook; in O'Connor's Catholic vision, human development can't be studied, or controlled, by humans; it is all in the hands of God. (If it could be controlled, why would the little boy have an ulcer? Why would Mary Grace be a lunatic?)

The humor in this story (as well as in the rest of O'Connor's work) is bitter, but it helps to cut the pain of the characters by introducing a measure of buoyancy, a light at the end of the tunnel. O'Connor's is a tragicomic vision; she recognized that while humanity's folly is great, it is also funny. But humor, in literature and in life, has always operated as a defense mechanism, to help people bear their trials and tragedies. This is one of the reasons O'Connor's work resonates even for readers with no religious faith. Humor is universal, as are O'Connor's concerns with hypocrisy and truth.

POSSIBLE CONNECTIONS TO OTHER SELECTIONS

Emily Dickinson, "What Soft — Cherubic Creatures — " (text p. 809)

Ralph Ellison, "Battle Royal" (text p. 226; question #3, following)

Flannery O'Connor, "Good Country People" (text p. 367; question #1, following)

——, "A Good Man Is Hard to Find" (text p. 356)

John Updike, "A & P" (text p. 201; question #4, following)

CONNECTIONS QUESTIONS IN TEXT (p. 395) WITH ANSWERS

1. Compare and contrast Mary Grace with Hulga of "Good Country People" (p. 367).

   Like Hulga, Mary Grace is bookish and has experienced life outside of the South. This perspective makes her dismissive of provincial points of view and even, as we see at the end of the story, enraged by them. The two young women have mothers who are similar as well. Both Mary Grace's and Hulga's mothers believe that women should be well-mannered and concerned more with having a good time than with learning. Both daughters act out against these potentially limiting ideas of how women should act.

2. Explain how "Revelation" could be used as a title for any of the O'Connor stories you have read.

   In each of the O'Connor stories in this chapter, the main character is forced to reconsider her beliefs and think beyond the narrow scope of her experiences. In "A Good Man Is Hard to Find," the grandmother's mysterious declaration that the Misfit is one of her children shows that in her fear she has moved beyond her strictly delineated ideas about good and bad people. Similarly, Mrs. Turpin's revelation forces her to reconsider her place in the system of "classes" that she so likes to think about. Hulga in "Good Country People" has equally fixed beliefs, though they are based less on social conventions than on the rejection of such strictures. Even so, her revelation occurs when she realizes she has too quickly assumed she knows the type of person she is dealing with in Manley Pointer.

3. Discuss Mrs. Turpin's prideful hypocrisy in connection with the racial attitudes expressed by the white men at the "smoker" in Ralph Ellison's "Battle Royal" (p. 226). How do pride and personal illusions inform these characters' racial attitudes?

   Mrs. Turpin's ideas about race are frequently revealed by her game of imagining what she would do if Jesus had asked her to choose what kind of person she could be. Though she amuses herself with these mental games, they serve only to make her more proud; she doesn't seem able to really imagine living under different circumstances. Her brand of prejudice is less overtly destructive than that of the white men in Ellison's story, but she does adopt a superior attitude toward the people around her. That kind of attitude, taken to an extreme, can lead to the dehumanization of others. When the men at the smoker set the narrator and the other young black men fighting, the white men act almost as if it were a cock fight. They see the fighters not as people but just as things that are there for their entertainment and that can be discarded when they have had enough.

4. Explore the nature of the "revelation" in O'Connor's story and in John Updike's "A & P" (p. 201).

   Mrs. Turpin's revelation challenges her self-satisfied notions about race and class. As she is sitting in the waiting room, we see that she does not hesitate to speak for other people. She claims to know, for example, that African Americans wouldn't want to go back to Africa and that what they all want is to "improve their color" (para. 68). However, Mary Grace's violent reaction to her complacent attitudes makes her rethink how much she knows about other people. The revelation of the narrator in Updike's story is as much about the atmosphere he lives in as about his own values. However, he too is struck by how little he knows of other people's ideas and motives. He hopes that the girls will thank him for the grand gesture of quitting his job, but by the time he goes outside, they have disappeared, and he is left alone in his rejection of the community that scorned them.

PERSPECTIVES ON O'CONNOR

FLANNERY O'CONNOR, *On Faith* (p. 396)

At the end of "Good Country People," Hulga appears to be a likely candidate to "cherish the world at the same time that [she struggles] to endure it." Ask the students to explain how and why this change comes about.

FLANNERY O'CONNOR, *On Theme and Symbol* (p. 396)

O'Connor argues that "the peculiar problem of the short-story writer is how to make the action he describes reveal as much of the mystery of existence as possible" (para. 2), and she cautions against our overlooking the literal resonance of her work in pursuit of symbolic meaning. Encourage students to identify both the literal and symbolic significance of some aspect of O'Connor's fiction. For instance, Mary Grace's response to Mrs. Turpin in "Revelation," "Go back to hell where you came from, you old warthog" (112), has literal as well as symbolic impact. What is especially apt about O'Connor's choice of language here?

JOSEPHINE HENDIN, *On O'Connor's Refusal to "Do Pretty"* (p. 398)

What are the differences between the example referred to by Hendin and the instances in O'Connor's fiction in which a character refuses to "do pretty"? What exactly is O'Connor refusing in this anecdote? What are characters such as Mary Grace in "Revelation" objecting to? Are there other significant differences between the fictional and biographical examples?

CLAIRE KATZ, *The Function of Violence in O'Connor's Fiction* (p. 398)

Ask students to assess the types of violent acts that occur in O'Connor's fiction. Is there a pattern to this violence? Do certain characters experience more violent acts than others? How would students define "violence" within the context of O'Connor's stories?

EDWARD KESSLER, *On O'Connor's Use of History* (p. 399)

Kessler asserts that "in O'Connor's fiction, the past neither justifies nor even explains what is happening" (para. 1). Ask students to identify O'Connor's characters' perspectives on their histories — for instance, what does the Misfit's description of his past in "A Good Man Is Hard to Find" explain about his behavior? How often are the characters' pasts in some way a source for the prideful behavior that leads to their downfalls? Based on such examples, do students agree or disagree with Kessler's argument?

Time Magazine, *On "A Good Man Is Hard to Find"* (p. 400)

The idea that O'Connor's fiction is "unladylike" should provoke lively discussion. You might begin by having your class talk about how the other adjectives in the blurb— "brutal," "slam-bang," "balefully direct"—reveal what the reviewer would consider ladylike in writing. You might also have them discuss why O'Connor's publishers would have chosen this blurb to publicize the work. Though it wasn't exactly meant as praise, they must have had the idea that it would interest readers in her writing.

13

A Cultural Case Study:
James Joyce's "Eveline"

As the introduction to Chapter 13 explains, students should learn to study literary texts not only from a formalist perspective (practicing close readings) but also from other extratextual perspectives. In Chapter 13, students are provided with several resources that might help them learn more about the context in which Joyce wrote "Eveline." Though this story might seem simple and straightforward, particularly until the final paragraph, students are bound to wonder why the protagonist changes her mind at the last minute. The accompanying sources — a photograph, a temperance tract, a letter from an Irish immigrant to a family member, and a synopsis of *The Bohemian Girl* — all help students understand more about the character, time, place, and situation depicted in this story. In combination with the materials about Joyce that lead into the story, these "cultural contexts" help students interpret "Eveline."

Web Ask students to research James Joyce or take a quiz on this story at **bedfordstmartins.com/ meyerlit**.

JAMES JOYCE, *Eveline* (p. 407)

After reading the story, and before studying the materials that follow it, invite students to discuss the ways in which the introduction to Joyce's life and work (including the chronology) is particularly helpful in understanding "Eveline." For instance, Joyce's experiences as an expatriate may inform his characterization of the protagonist. In addition, how do the references to Ireland's political and religious situation at the time Joyce was writing the stories that compose *Dubliners* add depth to the story? Finally, ask students to discuss their ideas about why the material in Joyce's story might have been controversial or subject to censorship. Are there any details in the story that seem particularly libelous?

After reading this story, students may be eager to debate the reasons Eveline refuses to accompany Frank to Buenos Aires. Most of the story leads the reader to expect that she will leave, as it focuses on the many reasons she is unhappy. It would seem that she has nothing to look forward to in Dublin: her father continually harangues her, and the members of her family whom she has truly loved are dead. Her job is not rewarding, and her manager enjoys humiliating her. Why, then, does Eveline decide to stay with her father in Dublin? Readers must examine the text closely to discover the reason for her decision.

Eveline has witnessed the gradual displacement of much of her familiar surroundings. Physically, the place where she has grown up has become more urbanized and modern, resulting in a loss of connections between the people who live there: "One time there used to be a field there in which they used to play every evening with other people's children. Then a man from Belfast bought the field and built houses in it — not like their little brown houses but bright brick houses with shining roofs. The children of the avenue used to play together in that field" (para. 2). In addition, her spiritual community of family and friends has been equally fragmented. The people she has loved most — Ernest and her mother — are dead. The children she once played with are either dead or have left the country. As Eveline comes to realize, "Everything changes. Now she was going to go away like the others, to leave her home" (2). Her choice is perhaps less between Frank and her family than between leaving behind the last vestiges of her community — a particular place in Dublin and a particular state of mind — or maintaining it in some fashion.

She has seen what happens when people leave Dublin — they are forgotten by those who remain behind. A good example of this is her father's friend, the priest, whose picture hangs in Eveline's house. She knows that, according to her father, "He is in Melbourne now" (4), but "during all those years she had never found out the name of the priest" (3). What can Eveline expect to be said about her if she leaves for Buenos Aires with Frank, particularly since her father dislikes Frank and has forbidden her to see him? Such a separation from her family would augment the dissolution of the only community she has known.

Students should consider what Frank represents and what he offers to Eveline. Frank has taken her to places she wouldn't ordinarily go, like the theater, and he wants to take her out of the country. He himself is foreign to her experience: he actively enjoys life, calls her by a nickname, and sings. How does he contrast with Eveline's family? What about him attracts her to begin with? How can we reconcile her quiet appreciation of his "foreign" qualities with her ultimate decision to remain in familiar surroundings?

Eveline is reminded of certain familial obligations and attachments as she waits for the evening departure time. The music of the street organ outside reminds her of the night her mother died and of Eveline's "promise to keep the home together as long as she could" (14). At that time, Eveline agreed to uphold her mother's commitment to keeping the family together in some fashion; if she leaves, she will have failed to honor her mother and her mother's values. Since her mother's death she has "had hard work to keep the house together and to see that the two young children who had been left to her charge went to school regularly and got their meals regularly" (9). However, as she thinks about the demands that have been placed upon her, she does not find her life "wholly undesirable" (9). Despite her father's violent propensities, she has observed his tender side: "Her father was becoming old lately, she noticed; he would miss her" (13). In particular she remembers two instances in which he demonstrated a commitment to his family: "Not long before, when she had been laid up for a day, he had read her out a ghost story and made toast for her at the fire. Another day, when their mother was alive, they had all gone for a picnic to the Hill of Howth. She remembered her father putting on her mother's bonnet to make the children laugh" (13). With these familial bonds before her, she prepares to leave with Frank.

The key to Eveline's decision to stay might be found in paragraph 19. Waiting for the boat's departure, "out of a maze of distress, she prayed to God to direct her, to show her what was her duty." In the end, Eveline is motivated by duty to her father and mother, and to her familiar surroundings; she cannot deny her responsibilities. While students may not agree with her decision, a well-rounded discussion of her complex motivations can be thought-provoking and rewarding.

Possible Connections to Other Selections

Ernest Hemingway, "Soldier's Home" (text p. 166; question #2, following)

D. H. Lawrence, "The Horse Dealer's Daughter" (text p. 506; question #1, following)

Connections Questions in Text (p. 410) with Answers

1. How does Eveline's response to her life at home compare with that of Mabel in D. H. Lawrence's "The Horse Dealer's Daughter" (p. 506)? Write an essay that explores the similarities and differences in their efforts to escape to something better.

   Eveline's life at home is one of hard and mostly unappreciated labor. After her mother's death, she assumes the duties of the wife of the household, not just cooking and cleaning for her father, but also taking care of her younger siblings. Because of the limited opportunities open to women at the time in which the story is set, her only hope for escaping this life is to attach herself to another man. Yet at the moment she is about to leave, she decides to stay in her father's home. The woman in Lawrence's story, Mabel, is also largely unappreciated. Living in a house full of men, she seems to have retreated into herself. Her refusal to state her preferences is mysterious, but it may indicate that she thinks her preferences matter very little to her brothers. Her attempted suicide reveals how few her options in life are after she loses the protection of her father. The dramatic way she reacts to being saved by the doctor shows that she has transferred to him the responsibility of caring for her.

2. Write an essay about the meaning of "home" to the protagonists in "Eveline" and Hemingway's "Soldier's Home" (p. 166).

    For both of these main characters, home entails a number of demands and expectations that are hard to fulfill. Though the difficulties of her home life make Eveline want to run away, she also feels a strong sense of duty to her family. Her decision to stay at the end of the story reveals how family ties win out even over her personal happiness. The returned soldier in Hemingway's story, however, no longer feels a similar sense of duty. Krebs knows what his family expects of him, but his experiences in the war make the tasks of everyday small-town life seem trivial. When he decides at the end to go along with convention, it is less out of a sense that he is doing the right thing than out of simple exhaustion. He doesn't know how to resist the role society expects him to play, so he acquiesces to his mother's wishes, even while he no longer values his choice.

DOCUMENTS

THE ALLIANCE TEMPERANCE ALMANACK, *On the Resources of Ireland* (p. 412)

Students should focus on the way the authors of this temperance tract shape their argument about the condition of Ireland. (Study the use of pronouns: *we* and *our* refer to the English.) For the English, this tract is designed to arouse indignation about the waste of resources and the lack of productivity by the Irish people. Since the English, as landlords and overseers for the Irish, resent the loss of their profits and the depreciation of their property as a result of the Irish people's excessive consumption of alcohol (note that the opening line of the tract emphasizes its writers' chief concern with "the great decay of her trade and manufacturers"), you may want to ask students to explore the possible motivations for this tract. In essence, the argument is not founded in humanitarianism. If the Irish were to stop drinking and start producing linens and other commodities mentioned in the tract, they still would reap very little of the profits of their labors. Instead, the English landlords would accumulate the wealth. Why, then, would the Irish find it worthwhile to change their habits?

In connection with this text, students should explore how an awareness of the Irish propensity for alcoholism adds meaning to "Eveline." This tract is of particular relevance to Eveline's characterization of her father and her economic circumstances. Mr. Hill is commonly drunk and abusive: "Even now, though she was over nineteen, she sometimes felt herself in danger of her father's violence. She knew it was that that had given her the palpitations. When they were growing up he had never gone for her, like he used to go for Harry and Ernest, because she was a girl; but latterly he had begun to threaten her and say what he would do to her only for her dead mother's sake" (para. 9). Her father's alcoholism is longstanding, although Eveline convinces herself that during her childhood, he was "not so bad" (2). It is also an economic reality for her that the majority of the family's financial resources (including all of her own salary and some of her brother's, as well as whatever her father earns) are to be pocketed by her father and used for alcohol. Though he gives her some funds for family groceries, he consumes a substantial amount of the family's resources. It is ironic that he refuses to give Eveline money because "he wasn't going to give her his hard-earned money to throw about the streets" (9); he himself is going to waste the same money in the local pubs.

In addition, in the closing paragraph of the excerpt, the authors reveal an inherent rivalry with the Americans (previously in the position of the Irish, tenants of the British): "Have we nothing to learn from America, where, by the associated efforts of the sober and intelligent for the purpose of discouraging the use of ardent spirits, their consumption is already diminished one-third throughout the whole Union?" (6). Students might compare the reaction of the American colonists to English rule (revolution) with the response of the Irish (despair, submission, inebriation). Students also should decide whether the tract writers are motivated more by concern for their fellow man or by greed.

In connection with this tract, written from the English perspective, it might be useful to introduce the students to all or part of Jonathan Swift's famous and satiric essay "A Modest Proposal." Swift, an Irishman, writes with intensity about the English people's disregard for Irish citizens. His proposal that the English begin to consider Irish children as a food source highlights his indignation at the way English landlords are running Ireland and consuming its natural resources. Students might find helpful connections among this satire, the temperance tract, and Joyce's short story.

BRIDGET BURKE, *A Letter Home from an Irish Emigrant* (p. 415)

In "Eveline," the protagonist prepares two letters before she leaves to meet Frank. One is addressed to her father; the other is to her brother, Harry. This alerts the reader to Eveline's close ties to her family, even when she is thinking of eloping with Frank. Students should explore the ways in which Bridget Burke's letter to her brother John also demonstrates a deep devotion to family and home. First, Bridget repeatedly asks for news of home: "I often Have a Walk with Patt & Has a long yarn of Home" (para. 1); she adds, "we often Have some fun talking of the Old times at Home" (1). In the final paragraph of her letter, she begs for information about home, family, and friends: "Now John I must ask you for all my Aunts & Uncles Cousins friends & Neighbours sweet Harts & all also did Cannopy die yet." She concludes, "Lett me know all about Home." Although one paragraph of her letter does focus on Bridget's observations about Australia, the majority of her letter concerns family and home in Ireland. Reading this real immigrant's reaction to life in a foreign country, we understand more about why Eveline cannot leave her home at the end of Joyce's story.

Though Bridget is living in Australia, it is clearly not a "home" to her. She goes walking with her brother, and occasionally visits her uncle and his family. She confesses, however, that she "cannot make free with any body" (1). Though the country offers success to "a Young person that can take care of himselfe" (2), Bridget nonetheless finds it "verry strange" (1). She seems to have traveled out of Ireland for economic reasons; nonetheless, she finds Australia emotionally and psychologically unsatisfying.

A Plot Synopsis of The Bohemian Girl (p. 416)

In "Eveline," Frank takes Eveline to the opera, an uncommon experience for her: "she felt elated as she sat in an unaccustomed part of the theatre with him" (para. 10). In this respect, the opera itself is irrelevant: the opportunity to get away from her father's abuse, the humiliation of her position at The Stores, and the unending work of raising her younger siblings is most significant. However, the choice of the particular opera is also relevant. (Joyce's decision to identify the opera specifically by name indicates its relevance to the characterization and themes of his story.) "Bohemian" has several definitions: it may refer to a specific geographic area, a group of people (wanderers, Gypsies), or a lifestyle (usually an unconventional one). For instance, if Eveline were to run off with Frank to Buenos Aires, she might be seen as participating in a bohemian rejection of family connections and church strictures about marriage. (Eloping in itself might be seen as a "bohemian" act.)

Like Joyce's short story, Balfe's opera involves a heroine's choice of husband and connection to family. The Bohemian girl, Arline, falls in love with her rescuer, Thaddeus. Eveline, in similar fashion, regards Frank as her rescuer. Arline is taken from her home; Eveline is considering eloping with Frank to South America. Eventually, Arline is able to return home with the man she loves and receive the blessings of her father. Perhaps Eveline fantasizes about such an outcome. In any case, the opera offers her the possibility of a sentimental, satisfying resolution.

Incidentally, students might not understand why Thaddeus dashes his drink to the ground in the first act. He is "a Polish exile," a "fugitive from the Austrian troops" (1). When the Count proposes a toast to "the Emperor," he is demonstrating an alliance with the forces that are pursuing Thaddeus. Thus, not only is *The Bohemian Girl* a romance; it also depicts a political division. Thaddeus and the Count are on opposing sides of the conflict; metaphorically, Frank and Mr. Hill also represent different factions between which Eveline must choose.

14

A Study of Dagoberto Gilb:
The Author Reflects on Three Stories

The collection of stories, essays, and interviews in this chapter gives students a chance to examine the work of a contemporary author, giving it the kind of in-depth study often devoted to authors long since declared classics. Students can study Gilb's fiction and also get insights into his writing process, the way he thinks about art in his own life, and the role he sees MexAm art playing within the larger culture. (See his discussion of this term on p. 445.)

Web For more information on Dagoberto Gilb or for quizzes on his stories, visit **bedfordstmartins.com/meyerlit**.

His essays, as well as his work at the Centro Victoria, suggest Gilb wants to bring more exposure to Mexican Americans as a unique culture and artistic tradition. He hopes to help address the problem he identifies in "On Distortions of Mexican American Culture": "we have no images in our nation's history other than as foreigners" (para. 1). Challenging the strict identification of Mexican Americans as immigrants, he shows a blended tradition indigenous to the southwestern United States. His own work shows how varied this culture is (encompassing different economic classes, life experiences, etc.) and also reveals how it interacts with other cultures—for example, the Armenian neighbors who live upstairs in "Shout," or the Asian shop owners from Erick's neighborhood in "Uncle Rock."

While Gilb writes compelling female characters, these stories are notably perceptive about the lives of men and the expectations for masculine behavior. His characters reflect the pressures of work and supporting a family, the pleasures of dreaming about beautiful cars and beautiful women, and the complications of growing up male with a mother who draws a lot of male attention. For some further discussion of masculinity, students might consult Gilb's essay on being "macho" and what that accusation really means: **http://www.barcelonareview.com/44/e_dg.htm**.

DAGOBERTO GILB, *How Books Bounce* (p. 428)

Though Gilb admits even he finds himself "a curious representative of literature," he is tongue-in-cheek when he describes the pedigrees and the breeding of "real writers." There is also humor in the list of questions he asks in paragraph 4 about his vocation: "Am I the product of some secret government experiment that maybe went wrong?" Ultimately, Gilb's essays undermine such questions. This one in particular shows how anyone can fall in love with reading and writing—even if he or she never expected it. Gilb believes that when it comes to stories, "we *each* have one, no matter to what breeding or privilege we were born" (para. 6).

The author himself was not bred for literary stardom, as he suggests with his comparison of books with balls. As a young man, books were foreign while balls were familiar and presented a range of possibilities: "I bounced them, hit them, caught them, guarded them, blocked them, kicked them, jump shot them" (1). When he discovers literature, what he falls in love with is, in part, a similar feeling of possibility. Often reading seems to offer him secrets that had been forgotten or unknown. Gilb professes a love for books "forgotten in quirky, cramped bottom corners, and ones that took tall ladders to touch, and ones that saw so little light their covers seem to have recast inward" (3). After students have read Gilb's other essays, particularly "On Distortions of Mexican

American Culture," you might ask them to elaborate on what it means to Gilb to love a "forgotten" book.

DAGOBERTO GILB, *Love in L.A.* (p. 430)

"Love in L.A." might be interpreted as "California Dreamin.'" Set in the shadow of the Hollywood Freeway, it is all about pretending to be someone different and attempting to attract an audience. Although Jake drives a '58 Buick (without insurance), he dreams of "something better": a "crushed velvet interior with electric controls for the L.A. summer, a nice warm heater and defroster for the winter drives at the beach, a cruise control for those longer trips, mellow speakers front and rear of course, windows that hum closed, snuffing out that nasty exterior noise of freeways" (para. 1). Given the centrality of cars and freeways in Southern California, this is an apt metaphor for the kind of life of wealth and status that Jake would like to lead, the person he'd be if only the reality of his situation lived up to his imagination. Instead of sitting in "a clot of near motionless traffic" (1), he'd be cruising through life. Tellingly, the "green light" (2) of his imagination is more real than the actual traffic in front of him. Lost in his fantasy, he rear-ends the car ahead of him.

Jake is conscious of "performance" throughout his encounter with Mariana. He stalls for time while he prepares lines based on both his inability (and unwillingness) to make financial reparation and his attraction to her. He also considers at least two options for escaping the situation. Students can deduce from this significant information about his character that Jake is not the upstanding individual he appears to be at the start of his conversation with Mariana. Jake's performance is further undermined by the information that emphasizes his scam in action. For instance, Jake tells Mariana, "I really am sorry about hitting you like that" (12), but the text following this ("he sounded genuine" [12]) implies that he is trying to pull some sort of scam. His deception becomes more obvious throughout the exchange. After acting sincere, Jake "exaggerated greatly" (20) about his lack of identification and his vocation as a musician; later, "he lied" about whether he had insurance (28). He might think he's been convincing ("back in his car he took a moment or two to feel both proud and sad about his performance" [38]). Ask students to consider whether or not Jake feels guilty for his deceitful actions. Exactly what might he feel sad about?

Ask students to characterize the cars featured in "Love in L.A." Jake's aging Buick is big and sturdy and mechanically reliable, and he regards its lack of nicks or dents as "one of his few clearcut accomplishments over the years" (3). Mariana's car is a newer Toyota with Florida plates. As Jake puts it, these cars are "so soft they might replace waterbeds soon" (12). There are unmistakable parallels between the cars and their owners' personalities. Jake dresses in "less than new but not unhip clothes" (6), and while he appears to be having a conversation about the damage to Mariana's car, he's really more interested in whether he can get her into bed. It's no accident that while Jake talks, he "fondle[s] the wide dimple" (12) in Mariana's (car's) rear end.

Although he seems to think he won over Mariana because she gives him her phone number, the final paragraph reveals that she hasn't been influenced by his act. It won't do her any good to trace the license number that she copies off the plate on his car, but then, he's not going to drive off thinking that his deception worked. In fact, one could argue that each character has attempted to scam the other. Jake plays his "genuine" act to escape from responsibility, while Mariana may have relied on her beauty in order to coerce him into giving her the information she needs. Neither character will be satisfied. Love, in this story, is less about genuine affection and attraction than it is about running (and deflecting) a scam. Ultimately, Jack is yet another kind of used-car salesman, and his encounter with Mariana will be only another hit-and-run statistic.

POSSIBLE CONNECTION TO ANOTHER SELECTION

Fay Weldon, "IND AFF, or Out of Love in Sarajevo" (text p. 173)

DAGOBERTO GILB, *Shout* (p. 433)

Gilb conveys a great deal about the couple in this story through their dialogue. The husband comes home shouting and cursing, but there are introspective moments as well, such as the conversation in which the wife reveals the results of her trip to the clinic. Readers also get a lot of insight into the main character in the first paragraph, as he stands waiting for his wife to unlock the door. While he waits, his mind casts back over interactions with his coworkers and looks forward to the pleasant routine of his evening at home.

In his commentary, Gilb writes that "there are not a lot of stories about men like the main character in 'Shout.'" He is perhaps foremost a big talker. From the moment he comes home, he pours out questions, criticisms, and commentary on his family. His quick tongue is turned in their defense, however, when a neighbor complains about the baby's crying. Though this character is something of a hothead, he also has contemplative moments. In the quiet after the children have gone to bed, he apologizes for his yelling and acknowledges he is "getting too old" to get into fights (para. 31).

Gilb also notes in "On *Shout*" that the short story form may have more in common with poetry than with the novel. In discussing the story, you might have students pick out passages that seem to them to embody what Gilb identifies as poetic: compressed language or the single image that evokes a wealth of feeling. Where in the story does Gilb do the most with just a few words?

DAGOBERTO GILB, *Uncle Rock* (p. 438)

Gilb describes the main character of this story, Erick, as having "gone mute" in response to his situation, particularly the way men look at his beautiful mother ("On *Uncle Rock*," para. 7). The young boy is very perceptive of her attitudes toward the men who approach her, noting that she is much more likely to show interest in a man wearing a suit than in one wearing a uniform (2). He resents the way these men pretend friendship with him to get on his mother's good side and her willingness to play along with their chumminess. He understands, too, the difference between the respectful affection of Roque and the presumptuous advances of men like the baseball player, who offers Erick's mother the number of his hotel room.

Yet Erick, like his mother, sometimes gets swept up in these men's attention. While he is skeptical about her series of boyfriends, Erick also seems to understand her inability to commit to Roque, who even the young boy understands is "too willing and nice, too considerate and generous" (7). On some level, he knows why his mother would try to use her primary source of power, her beauty, to reach a status she might be barred from otherwise. In the end, though, he has sympathy for Roque: "It wasn't his fault he wasn't an engineer" (14).

In his commentary on this story, Gilb describes the fiction writer's craft as similar to creating a mosaic. This image helps him to answer complex questions about autobiography and imagination in fiction. For this author, fiction is always grounded in memory and experience, which make up the fractured tiles he will cobble together into a story. Yet the final product is, as the mosaic analogy suggests, carefully composed. It may have autobiographical pieces but it is far from a simple reflection of the author's life.

PERSPECTIVES

DAGOBERTO GILB, *On Physical Labor* (p. 444)

Our current economic system is often called an information economy because so many people work with only their brains while their bodies stay inert in a chair. In this excerpt, Gilb reminds us that physical work is not only necessary, but often satisfying and rewarding. He is careful to separate justified complaints about working conditions or wages from dissatisfaction with work itself, which he doesn't think is a necessary response to hard labor.

The Detroit poet he refers to is Philip Levine, who was named poet laureate in 2011. Students might be interested to compare the attitudes toward work in his poems with Gilb's assertions in this essay. As a starting place, Levine's poem "Making It Work," about the factory Gilb mentions, is available at **http://www.poemhunter.com/best-poems/philip-levine/making-it-work/**.

DAGOBERTO GILB, *On Distortions of Mexican American Culture* (p. 445)

While Americans are used to thinking about "binary" relationships in other parts of the country — particularly the interaction of white and black cultures in the deep South — Gilb suggests that we are somehow blind to a similar relationship at work in the Southwest, where "brown and white" converge. He hopes to open our eyes not just to the presence of people of Mexican descent but also to the extent to which Mexican American is a distinct culture — not an import from Mexico, but a longstanding presence in the American landscape. He insists that Americans extend our appreciation of cultural inheritance beyond "oversized enchilada plates and the bountiful bowls of tortilla chips" that, along with inaccurate movie westerns and kitschy "folklorico" dress, form our stereotypes of Mexican American culture.

POSSIBLE CONNECTIONS TO OTHER SELECTIONS

John Updike, "A & P" (text p. 201; question #1, following)

David Updike, "Summer" (text p. 295; question #1, following)

CONNECTIONS QUESTIONS IN TEXT (p. 452) WITH ANSWERS

1. How might "Love in L.A." or "Shout" be considered love stories but very different from John Updike's "A & P" (text p. 201) or David Updike's "Summer" (text p. 295)? Choose one of Gilb's stories and one of the Updikes' stories to compare the social setting, conflicts, protagonists, and tone.

   Both "A & P" and "Summer" are stories of adolescent love. Their protagonists are young men, for whom desire becomes a kind of turning point, forcing them to reevaluate themselves or their lives. Like both of the Updike stories, "Love in L.A." describes a love that is potential but never realized. However, while "A & P" and "Summer" both hold on to the possibility that desire is transformational, Gilb makes readers question whether genuine love is even possible, or at least whether real love can spring up among the strivers and showmen in L.A. "Shout" portrays both the deepest and most adult love out of all these stories, and for this reason it offers a much less romanticized picture of a relationship than, for example, "Summer." The couple's genuine attachment to one another has to survive in the midst of economic struggles, worries about where to work and live, and the pressures of raising children.

2. Explain how Gilb's perspective "On Physical Labor" (p. 444) can be used as a means of tracing some shared themes about work among the poems in Chapter 38, "A Thematic Case Study: The World of Work" (text p. 985).

   The poems in the "World of Work" case study display varied attitudes toward work, several of which may be usefully compared with Gilb's comments on physical labor. A few of these poems, including Wormser's "Labor" and Chitwood's "Men Throwing Bricks," celebrate hard work as graceful and clear in its intentions. Students could write well about the similarity between these poems and Gilb's description of cultures that revere work as an essential part of life. By contrast, a poem like Ignatow's "The Jobholder" portrays a very different kind of work — the kind that only occurs in the mind. Compared to the full life of labor and family Gilb describes, the routine of Ignatow's worker looks hollow and soulless.

15

A Thematic Case Study: The Literature of the South

This chapter, which reprints essays by such writers as W. J. Cash, Flannery O'Connor, Margaret Walker, and Irving Howe, as well as photographs, paintings, and movie stills, provides contexts for the southern literature in the anthology. Before embarking on an examination of the chapter's southern theme, you might want to engage your students in an attempt to define what southern literature is. What makes a work of fiction "southern"? Is it a matter of geography, of identity, of sensibility? Is a story set in the South automatically a work of southern literature? What about a story written by a southerner but set in another part of the country? What if the author hails from the North or the West but some of or all the characters identify themselves as southern (as is the case with Andrea Lee's "Anthropology")? What about the work of southern-born writers who migrated north, or northern-born writers who settled in the South? Is race a factor? Students' answers to these questions will almost certainly vary as much as the definitions of the "South" attempted by John Shelton Reed and Dale Volberg Reed. After they've spent some time grappling to define southern literature, students will be much better able to appreciate the attempts represented by the critics in this chapter.

Almost every essay in this case study is accompanied by at least one image from fine art or popular culture. If you are having any trouble getting your students to read and relate to literature, this visual portfolio should help them start making connections between fiction, criticism, and the world around them. The visual aspect of this chapter will be more rewarding for your students if they go beyond notions of art as decoration. Encourage them to approach these images as texts and to think about them critically. The questions that accompany each selection should help your students actively engage with the images and the ways in which they enrich and complicate the critics' arguments.

In addition to the selections listed on page 454, you might also want to look at the following stories, poems, and plays that might be considered examples of southern literature:

Kate Chopin, "The Story of an Hour" (text p. 15)

Ernest Hemingway, "Soldier's Home" (text p. 166)

Lisa Parker, "Snapping Beans" (text p. 546)

Cathy Song, "The White Porch" (text p. 639)

Walt Whitman, "Cavalry Crossing a Ford" (text p. 624)

JOHN SHELTON REED AND DALE VOLBERG REED, *Definitions of the South* (p. 455)

Map: **U.S. BUREAU OF THE CENSUS, *The South*** (p. 454)

The Reeds' brief overview of "three of the most common definitions" of the South "and what's wrong with them" is from the introduction to *1001 Things Everyone Should Know About the South* (1996), an irreverent encyclopedia of southern history and culture. The authors, both academics, hint at but don't address an important question: Why is it important to define the South in the first place? The origins of the definitions they dismiss offer some suggestions: the South, difficult as it is to pinpoint on a map, has a distinct history and culture that in many ways distinguishes it from the rest of the United States. But their proposed alternative, that the South is "where people think they're in the South" isn't particularly satisfying. Ask your students what they think the authors mean by this and work with them to try to articulate what, besides geography, marks the South as a separate region with its own identity.

The U.S. Census map is a useful tool for getting your students thinking about what states make up the South. They may be surprised, for example, to see Delaware included but not Missouri. Texas and Oklahoma are often classified as western states instead of (or in addition to) southern ones. Ask your students what states they would add to or remove from the map, and why. Is it possible to draw a map of the South that the entire class agrees on?

W. J. CASH, *The Old and the New South* (p. 455)

Movie still: **METRO-GOLDWYN-MAYER,** *Gone with the Wind* (p. 457)

Lithograph: **Currier and Ives,** *The Old Plantation Home* (p. 458)

For W. J. Cash, the southern mindset embodies an impossible paradox. Although it may have become somewhat modernized as a result of urbanization and industrial growth, he says, the region imagines itself as the product of a rarefied past (exemplified by *Gone with the Wind* and the Currier and Ives print) that never truly existed. Cash argues that the South looks backward in order to move forward, that "it has actually always marched away, as to this day it continues to do, from the present toward the past" (para. 6). In other words, the South resists the inevitability of modernization by striving to revert to an imagined past.

Your students are likely to have a difficult time with this selection. Cash presumes that his readers possess a good deal of historical knowledge, and his vocabulary and sentence structure are complex. You may need to work through a few of the passages with your students to help them grasp the meaning of his comparisons. At the same time, his argument itself might be a little puzzling to students. It will help to outline the stages of his argument in class: he defines the myth of the Old South (paragraphs 1–3), then the myth of the New South (4), before debunking both of those legends (5–6). He attempts to resolve the paradox of the Old and the New South by asserting that they have always coexisted.

The two images that accompany Cash's essay offer an excellent illustration of his point. Both picture Civil War–era plantations but were produced many years after "the Old South is supposed to have been destroyed" (4). The backgrounds for Scarlett O'Hara and the happy slaves portray the "large and stately mansions, preferably white and with columns and Grecian entablature" (2) that Cash evokes in his description of "the Old South of the Legend" (1). These backward glances at "Old World splendor and delicacy" (2) embrace a past more peaceful and harmonious than it really was.

POSSIBLE CONNECTIONS TO OTHER SELECTIONS

William Faulkner, "A Rose for Emily" (text p. 82)

Flannery O'Connor, "Revelation" (text p. 381)

IRVING HOWE, *The Southern Myth* (p. 458)

Painting: **John Richards,** *The Battle of Gettysburg, 1863* (p. 460)

In this selection Howe proffers a popular explanation for the South's cultural distinctiveness. Southern identity, he argues, is indelibly shaped by the region's defeat in the Civil War (or, as it is known to many in the South, the War Between the States). As Howe sees it, the cultural memory of loss colors the modern southern experience and shapes the region's perceptions. As the loser, the South was marginalized and forced to develop on its own path; "living on the margin of history" (para. 2), the region was able to offer the rest of the country a fresh perspective on American life. At the same time, Howe believes that the destruction of the war provides southern writers "a compact and inescapable subject" (3). Writers of the South, he argues, cannot avoid writing about "the defeat of the homeland"; what's more, this ubiquitous subject gives the southern writer an edge by offering a sense of history and community unavailable to writers in other parts of the country.

Much of Howe's argument plays out in John Richards's painting of the Battle of Gettysburg (on July 3, 1863). The Union army dominates the picture, and the battery of northern soldiers forms an impenetrable wall. The Confederate soldiers, on the other hand, are relegated to the left margin and the deep background of the image. Whereas the Union men stand erect and in organized files, carry coffins with their heads up, or sit relaxed, the defeated soldiers are ushered away, heads down and backs hunched over. Half of the southern men are only partially shown, and they are markedly smaller than their foes. The confident organization and progress of the North contrasts with the dejection and exit of the South.

"The Southern Myth" was written more than fifty years ago. You might want to ask your students whether Howe's argument is still valid (or whether it was when he wrote it in 1951). Can a watershed event a hundred and fifty years in the past still claim a strong hold on a region's consciousness?

POSSIBLE CONNECTIONS TO OTHER SELECTIONS

William Faulkner, "A Rose for Emily" (text p. 82; question #2, following)

Walt Whitman, "Cavalry Crossing a Ford" (text p. 624)

CONNECTION QUESTION IN TEXT (p. 461) WITH ANSWER

2. Explain how the South's memory of the Civil War is woven into the plot of Faulkner's "A Rose for Emily" (p. 82). How is this memory related to the story's theme?

   Miss Emily lives her life among the "stubborn and coquettish decay" of the antebellum South (2), and when she dies she lies in the graveyard among the soldiers. Though Faulkner mentions the war overtly at only a few points, memories of the Civil War are a constant undercurrent in the story. The community's reaction to the intrusion of the Yankee, Homer Barron, shows that they still have a deep suspicion of the North. In his essay, Howe argues that the South retained a regional identity longer than other areas of the country, and that it "worked desperately to keep itself intact" and separate as an entity (para. 1). He also suggests that one possibility for southern subject matter is the South's "partial recapture of power through humiliating alliances with Northern capital" (4). The relationship between Miss Emily and Homer Barron enacts those negotiations on a personal level, and her willingness to form a partnership with a Yankee makes her neighbors pity her. Because they expect her to be hurt or wronged by him, they never seem to suspect his murder.

FLANNERY O'CONNOR, *The Regional Writer* (p. 461)

Painting: CLYDE BROADWAY, *Trinity—Elvis, Jesus, and Robert E. Lee* (p. 462)

As Flannery O'Connor describes it here, great literature explores distinct regional realities to tell universal truths. She pinpoints identity as a crucial element in forming a writer's consciousness and responds to concerns—such as those articulated by Donald R. Noble (text pp. 466–67)—that southern identity is losing its meaning. Her solution is to define regional identity more precisely by small, identifiable allegiances (such as "being a Georgia writer" [para. 2]) than by larger, more amorphous connections such as being from the South.

At the same time, O'Connor is careful to remind her readers that romanticized notions of the South as a land of aristocratic gentility overlook the "hookworm and bare feet and muddy clay roads" (3) that defined the South for far more of its residents. She looks to "the hidden and often the most extreme" (3) for the nexus of any region's identity, asserting that deep within the soul is the place where truth resides and that artists are best equipped to draw that truth out.

O'Connor died shortly after *Mystery and Manners* (from which this piece is taken) was published. She would likely have been relieved to see that southernness has retained its meaning even as that meaning has shifted; she would probably have enjoyed the humor that masks more serious concerns in Clyde Broadway's painting *Trinity—Elvis, Jesus, and Robert E. Lee.* Broadway's satiric art acknowledges the South's iconic past (as epitomized by the Civil War general Robert E. Lee) but puts history and faith on the same level as the region's extraordinarily influential popular culture. Before your students dismiss *Trinity* as merely a humorous commentary on southern culture, press them to view it in O'Connor's terms: How does it explore "the hidden and the most extreme" (3) components of southern identity? What "qualities that endure, regardless of what passes" (3) are shared by the painting's three figures?

POSSIBLE CONNECTIONS TO OTHER SELECTIONS

William Faulkner, "A Rose for Emily" (text p. 82)

Flannery O'Connor, "A Good Man Is Hard to Find" (text p. 356; question #2, following)

———, "Good Country People" (text p. 367; question #2, following)

———, "Revelation" (text p. 381; question #2, following)

CONNECTION QUESTION IN TEXT (p. 462) WITH ANSWER

2. O'Connor asserts that southern identity is "not made from the mean average or the typical, but from the hidden and often the most extreme." How is this idea manifested in O'Connor's "A Good Man Is Hard to Find" (p. 356), "Good Country People" (p. 367), or "Revelation" (p. 381)?

   Students' answers will vary according to which of O'Connor's stories they choose to focus on, of course, but all three illustrate her predilection for using extremes in fiction. O'Connor's fiction often eschews the "typical" for the surreal; by portraying wildly unlikely episodes, she forces her readers to contemplate the deeper meanings they embody.

MARGARET WALKER, *The Southern Writer and Race* (p. 463)

Photo: ERNEST C. WITHERS, *"Bus Station, Colored Waiting Room, Memphis, Tennessee,"* c. 1960s (p. 463)

Photo: LIBRARY OF CONGRESS, *Elizabeth Eckford at Little Rock Central High School,* September 4, 1957 (p. 464)

Photo: ERNEST C. WITHERS, *"Sanitation Workers' Strike, Memphis, Tennessee,"* 1968 (p. 464)

With justifiable anger, Walker argues that although southern writers consistently grapple with issues of race, southern literature is inherently racist. Slavery, she notes, dehumanized African Americans; Jim Crow compounded the problem by establishing separate social and cultural worlds for whites and blacks and instilling hatred of blackness in both races. The psychological conflicts that result from dehumanization and segregation, she notes, "can be seen in the literature" (para. 2) of white and black writers.

Walker's argument emerges directly from the civil rights movement. The photographs that accompany her argument should help your students appreciate its cultural context. The hatred and resentment Walker describes are clearly visible in the image provided by Ernest C. Withers. All the same, your students might find some of Walker's assertions — for example, that "the white writers [of the nineteenth century] were writing apologies for slavery and the Black writers were protesting against the inhumanity of the slave system" (2) — debatable. Rather than question the truth of her argument, consider asking your students what Walker is responding to and what she might be trying to accomplish.

POSSIBLE CONNECTIONS TO OTHER SELECTIONS

Ralph Ellison, "Battle Royal" (text p. 226; question #3, following)

William Faulkner, "A Rose for Emily" (text p. 82; question #2, following)

Flannery O'Connor, "Revelation" (text p. 381)

Margaret Walker, "The Southern Writer and Race" (text p. 463)

August Wilson, "Fences" (text p. 1420)

Collage: **ROMARE BEARDEN,** *Watching the Good Trains Go By* (p. 465)

An astounding number of African Americans responded to Jim Crowism by removing themselves from the environment altogether. Between 1910 and 1920, about 500,000 black men and women left the South in what historians refer to as the Great Migration. But as Romare Bearden's collage suggests, black southern men felt ambivalent about moving north. Although the home portrayed in the collage is in poor shape and the land apparently barren, the figure on the left gazes at the viewer with a look of defiant determination to stay, while the figure on the right looks in the direction the train is traveling (northward) with an expression that combines anticipation and doubt. The figure in the background, the only one looking directly at the train, is quietly going about his business, seemingly unimpressed by the promise of migration. It is important that the men in this image are "watching the good trains go by" but not riding on them: the implication is that they have chosen to stay.

CONNECTIONS QUESTIONS IN TEXT (pp. 465–466) WITH ANSWERS

2. Consider Faulkner's characterization of Tobe in "A Rose for Emily" (p. 82). Using Walker's terms, explain why you think Tobe is a wooden stereotype or a realistic portrayal of a black man.

   Although he is not explicitly portrayed as "flat, mindless, and caricatured as [a] buffoon" (para. 1), there is no question that Tobe's character is a "wooden stereotype." His name is mentioned only once; where he does appear he is usually referred to as "the Negro." A loyal servant who never questions Miss Emily's directives but simply performs his duties, Tobe is given no individual personality traits; instead, he is described (twice) as "going in and out with a market basket," unable "to keep a kitchen properly," and "doddering." Indeed, Faulkner implies that as the only person besides Miss Emily to enter the house in decades, Tobe was aware of her crime and her perversity but chose—like a good, loyal servant—to do nothing about it.

3. Walker observes that under segregation "the Black child was educated to imitate a white world as superior to his and thus taught to hate himself." How is this dramatized in Ellison's "Battle Royal" (p. 226)?

Despite his notable academic accomplishments, Ellison's protagonist has internalized the racist assumptions of the town's white leaders to the point that he willingly participates in their ritual humiliation of black boys. Although the experience is excruciating and confusing for him, he doesn't think to protest his treatment and continues to believe that he can earn the respect of the very men who take such pleasure in demeaning him.

DONALD R. NOBLE, *The Future of Southern Writing* (p. 466)

Using anecdotal observations as starting points, Noble attempts to predict how southern literature will change in the near future. As he sees it, southern writers will shift their focus from the communal to the personal, creating a ripple effect in the treatment of race and gender. At the same time, he imagines that the traditionally quirky elements of southern identity will slowly lose their significance and therefore their centrality in the literature.

Because this essay was first published in 1985, it will be interesting to discuss how much of Noble's vision has proved accurate and where he might have missed the mark. You might also want to ask your students whether they consider Noble's predictions optimistic or pessimistic. How does he seem to feel about the changes he anticipates? How do your students feel about them?

POSSIBLE CONNECTION TO ANOTHER SELECTION

W. J. Cash, "The Old and the New South" (text p. 455; question #1, following)

CONNECTION QUESTION IN TEXT (p. 467) WITH ANSWER

1. How does Noble's characterization of the South differ from W. J. Cash's assessment (p. 455)? According to Noble, what has caused the greatest changes in the South?

   Whereas Noble sees the South as a continually evolving region that is slowly losing some of its distinctiveness and inevitably becoming more like the rest of the country, Cash asserts that the South will always resist the very changes Noble anticipates by clinging to an imagined past. For Cash, the South is the product of a unique blend of nostalgia and progress; but from Noble's perspective the influence of nostalgia is eroding as economic developments permanently alter the demographic landscape. It is significant, of course, that the two descriptions were written forty-four years apart: possibly the intervening years have worked to loosen the psychological grip of the region's nineteenth-century history.

LEE SMITH, *On Southern Change and Permanence* (p. 467)

The novelist Lee Smith uses contemporary statistics about southern demographics and economy to describe a New South that would be unrecognizable to past generations of southerners. The region has been transformed from a poor, rural farming environment to an urban landscape of immigrants, shopping malls, and new kinds of jobs. As a result, she argues, the themes and characterizations of traditional southern literature are no longer relevant; indeed, she dismisses them as "trite" (para. 7). Despite these seismic changes to the southern experience, however, Lee believes that "some things never change" (4). Even with a shifting population and a new economic structure, Lee claims, southern identity still carries with it a tendency toward religiosity, violence, and hard work.

More significant, Lee asserts that storytelling is an enduring southern trait that will survive any changes in the region. "Narrative is as necessary to us as air," she writes; the story "gives a recognizable shape to the muddle and chaos of our lives" (8). Lee anticipates, then, that southern literature will retain a distinct regional flavor even if the flavor itself changes. You might want to ask your students whom Lee includes in the "us" and "our" of her final paragraph. Does her assessment apply to the rising numbers of immigrants and migrants, or is she, perhaps, clinging to a southern identity threatened by the changes she outlines?

POSSIBLE CONNECTION TO ANOTHER SELECTION

Donald R. Noble, "The Future of Southern Writing" (text p. 466; question #3, following)

CONNECTION QUESTION IN TEXT (p. 468) **WITH ANSWER**

3. Compare Smith's ideas about the changing nature of the South with Donald R. Noble's view (p. 466). Do you think they essentially agree or disagree in their assessment of the South? Explain.

    Essentially, Smith and Noble seem to agree that the New South is defined by changes in the region's demographics and industry and that those changes are characterized by much greater diversity and a significantly improved economy. But Noble's emphasis is on predicting how those changes will alter the focus of southern literature, whereas Smith's focus is on how the enduring qualities of the literature will help the southern reader cope with the changes.

16

A Thematic Case Study: Humor and Satire

Students will probably have no trouble appreciating the humor in this chapter, but they may need help figuring out how to analyze the humorous aspects of literature. They might be able to pick out the characteristics of comedy more easily if they start by thinking about stand-up. What kinds of jokes are typical of stand-up comedy? What makes them funny? Most stand-up depends heavily on stereotypes: women who max out their credit cards on shoes; country folk who marry their cousins. Does this feature of comedy extend to literature as well? To what extent does humor in writing rely on stock characters? Some of the funny characters in this chapter, like Twain's Jacob, are static "types," while others, like the narrator of "My Kid's Dog," are more fully developed. Do these stories constitute different kinds of humor?

You might also find it useful to have a discussion about the differences between humor and satire. Satire tends to be more pointed, as the writer uses humor in order to critique some aspect of society. Several of the stories in this chapter attempt that kind of critique: Spark's story takes political issues as one of its subjects, for example. Do the others make more subtle comments on society?

ANNIE PROULX, *55 Miles to the Gas Pump* (p. 470)

This "story" is composed of two related fragments — Rancher Croom's suicide and his wife's discovery of "the corpses of Mr. Croom's paramours" (para. 2). In two short paragraphs and a sentence, Proulx manages to evoke an entire marriage with its years of secrets, resentments, and violent betrayals. The phrase "just as she thought" reveals that Mrs. Croom is not even surprised to find several moldy bodies in her attic, "all of them used hard, covered with tarry handprints, [and] the marks of boot heels" (2).

Although the West is traditionally associated with lawlessness and violence, the sick, sexual serial killings in this story come as a shock. Whose voice is that of the final line, "When you live a long way out you make your own fun"? Is it Rancher Croom justifying his acts? Is it Mrs. Croom? Obviously the voice is an ironic one, but what does the final line say about people who "live a long way out"?

POSSIBLE CONNECTIONS TO OTHER SELECTIONS

Raymond Carver, "Popular Mechanics" (text p. 269; question #1, following)
Stephen Crane, "The Bride Comes to Yellow Sky" (text p. 246; question #2, following)
Mark Twain, "The Story of the Good Little Boy" (text p. 484; question #3, following)

CONNECTIONS QUESTIONS IN TEXT (p. 471) WITH ANSWERS

1. Despite their brevity, how do "55 Miles to the Gas Pump" and Carver's "Popular Mechanics" (p. 269) manage to create compelling fictional worlds?

   Proulx and Carver write in very different styles. While Carver's prose is spare and straightforward, Proulx uses complicated sentence structure and a profusion of adjectives. However, what allows both writers to convey so much in so few words is their ability to make single actions stand in for a lifetime of choices. The image of

Mrs. Croom sawing a hole in her roof to confirm what she has long suspected about her husband is both sad and horrifying. The relationship in "Popular Mechanics" is allegorical but no less revealing. The way the two characters talk about "the baby" and "this baby" without using his name shows just how little concern they actually have for him.

2. Compare Proulx's treatment of the West with Crane's in "The Bride Comes to Yellow Sky" (p. 246).

Crane uses his story to deflate some mythical ideas about the West. The archetypal situation in which the sheriff enters a showdown with the notorious local ruffian is diffused by the presence of the sheriff's new wife. She does not have a traditional place in the story, and so she makes it impossible for the two men to carry out the script. By contrast, Proulx's story gives us a more gruesome interpretation of received ideas. Her last line about people who "live a long way out" (para. 3) suggests the isolation and independence we often associate with the West, but the way that this lonely life makes Mr. Croom behave is more horrible than the behavior in any typical western.

3. Consider the use of irony in Proulx's story and in Mark Twain's "The Story of the Good Little Boy" (p. 484). Explain why you find the endings of the stories similar or different in tone.

Proulx's story ends with a line that almost sounds, with its aphoristic quality, like the moral of the story. However, it gives the reader no real insight into either Mr. Croom's sexually driven murders or his wife's apparent willingness to pretend she didn't know there was something wrong. The irony of this ending is in the very idea that these behaviors could be explained. Twain's story also reveals the falsity of such morals. His protagonist, Jacob, tries to be as good as the children in Sunday school books, but his attempts to do right are constantly misinterpreted or go awry. Yet Twain argues at the end of the story, "Every boy who ever did as he did prospered except him. His case is truly remarkable" (para. 11). Underneath this irony, Twain seems to suggest that the attempt to do good in a fallen world is naive.

RON HANSEN, *My Kid's Dog* (p. 472)

You might begin discussion of this story by asking students about the tone the narrator takes toward himself. He casts the dog as the villain of the story, and the range of generic names he uses to refer to the pet shows his disdain: "Sparky" (para. 2), "little Foo-Foo" (7), "Fido" (10), "Rover" (11). However, the narrator also depicts himself behaving in less-than-heroic ways. The "standard patriarchal shout" (10) he directs at the dog shows his tendency to be commanding, and his self-characterization as "a man of depth, perspicacity, and nearly Olympian strength" (22) is humorous precisely because he seems shallow and easily defeated. Hansen also uses the narrator to lampoon suburban life, pointing out his brand-name clothes (Brooks Brothers) and calling his wife's shopping by the elevated term "provisioning" (11). Like a prototypical suburban father, this man spends his free time "futzing with the hinges on the front-yard gate" (10). In fact, as the story progresses, the reader gets the sense that his frustration with the dog is deeply connected to his frustrations with middle-class family life.

POSSIBLE CONNECTION TO AN OTHER SELECTION

Edgar Allan Poe, "The Cask of Amontillado" (text p. 536; question #2, following)

CONNECTIONS QUESTIONS IN TEXT (p. 475) WITH ANSWERS

1. Compare the opening lines of this story with the openings of several others in this anthology. Discuss how their respective writers immediately engage their readers' interest.

The first lines of this story are terse and colloquial. They don't sound particularly literary but instead convey the speech of this middle-class, American narrator. They also begin the story at a place where many others would end. For example, compared with Andre Dubus's first sentence of "Killings," (p. 93) which immediately introduces the conflict with Steve's statement, "I should kill him" (para. 1), Hansen's opening suggests completed action. Also, by characterizing the narrator through speech, it takes a more indirect route than a story like "Young Goodman Brown." (p. 315) Hawthorne's first few sentences introduce the title character and his wife by name in addition to establishing the setting. His exposition is more direct, while Hansen leaves more to the reader's inference.

2.   Compare the tone of this revenge story with that of Edgar Allan Poe's "The Cask of Amontillado" (p. 536).

"The Cask of Amontillado" is not just a revenge story; it is a story that reflects, in its first paragraph, on the nature of revenge and how it can be exacted. As such, it serves as a foil for Hansen's humorous take on the revenge story. The narrator even refers to Poe sarcastically within "My Kid's Dog," which is a good indication of the difference in tone between the two stories. That is, Hansen's tale is a kind of mock revenge story. While Poe's narrator indignantly recounts "the thousand injuries of Fortunato" (para. 1) to gothic effect, Hansen uses a similar tone to poke fun at his narrator's sense of injury.

MURIEL SPARK, *The First Year of My Life* (p. 475)

At the beginning of her story, Spark surprises readers with an unexpected central character: a baby who is not, as we might expect, innocent and unaware of her surroundings. Instead, this baby asserts that all babies are omniscient, and that what she is about to describe is a common human experience, though one that is blotted out in all but those cultures or situations most open to mystical experience. This baby is very deliberate about her development, taking in food so that she can gain strength, working her limbs for better control, cutting her teeth, etc. She describes babyhood as a kind of illness that she has to struggle to conquer, and she prepares herself carefully for this struggle, seeming to take as her own the wartime motto "*Tout le monde à la bataille!*" (para. 15).

Just as the baby looks unflinchingly on her own helplessness, she turns without fear to observe the harsh realities of war. In fact, she prefers the "sheer blood, mud, dismembered bodies, blistered crashes, hectic flashes of light in the night skies, explosions, total terror" of the Western Front (10) to the well-articulated but perhaps false speeches she hears when she turns to the Parliament. She speaks of world events as if they were a series of radio channels she can selectively tune in to, and of all the channels, which also give her insight into important writers of the time, the channel on the Western Front feels the most real.

The British Prime Minister H. H. Asquith plays an important role in the story's resolution. Asquith was known as a skilled politician during peacetime, but he was charged with being hesitant and even weak when it came to conducting a war. This particular speech, however, not only emphasizes a purification of Europe through violence but also strikes a nationalistic note in celebrating Britain's involvement. Something about this combination seems to lead to the baby's first smile, though her reaction may be almost as hard for readers to understand as it is for her family, who mistakenly attribute the smile to the candles on her birthday cake. After discussing Asquith in particular, you might ask students what they think of the baby's general attitude toward adults. What does she respect in adults and what causes her disdain?

POSSIBLE CONNECTIONS TO OTHER SELECTIONS

Ernest Hemingway, "Soldier's Home" (text p. 166; question #1, following)

E. E. Cummings, "next to of course god america, i" (text p. 673; question #2, following)

Wilfred Owen, "Dulce et Decorum Est" (text p. 633; question #2, following)

1. Use the historical context as a means of explaining Krebs's behavior in Ernest Hemingway's "Soldier's Home" (text p. 166).

   Spark vividly portrays the horrors of WWI, including the brutality of the fighting and the sense that humanity had created for itself the darkest time in history. In Hemingway's story, Krebs's difficulty functioning back in his hometown seems to be largely due to his inability to deal with the contrast between those horrific memories of war and the apparent normalcy to which he has returned. Hemingway expresses this dissonance in Krebs's feeling of being out of place. For example, he enjoys watching girls from a distance but feels that "the world they were in was not the world he was in" (para. 15). Similarly, when his mother tries to get him to rejoin society as a productive member, he insists, "I'm not in [God's] Kingdom" (63). His realization at the end of the story, about the truth of the war versus the lies that everyday life requires, echoes with the sense in Spark's story that the awful sights of the Western Front are in some ways easier to deal with than the dissembling discussions of war at home.

2. Write an essay comparing the themes of Spark's story with those in E. E. Cummings's "next to of course god America, i" (text p. 673) and Wilfred Owen's "Dulce et Decorum Est" (text p. 633).

   Like "Soldier's Home," Owen's poem "Dulce et Decorum Est" concerns the "lie" that war breeds. In this case, lies justify as glorious and right a war that Owen portrays as brutal and disgusting. Cummings's poem also focuses on how war and conflict get cast as part of a heroic narrative. "next to of course god America, i" partakes of the rhetoric of America's founding and its defense of liberty, but it turns these glorifying sentiments into a jumbled and incoherent mass. The final line suggests that the speaker is anxious or overwrought in his repetition of these confused slogans. Spark's story, too, hinges on a statement meant to justify the importance of war. Asquith talks about war in terms of a "cleansing and purging" of the evils of the world, but he also valorizes the part Britain played in the war as a "privilege" (para. 26).

JOYCE CAROL OATES, *Hi Howya Doin* (p. 481)

Oates's mention of the police report in the first sentence of "Hi Howya Doin" does not reveal how the story will resolve, but it does hint that the overzealous jogger will confront some kind of trouble on the jogging path. It creates suspense by making the reader wait for something dramatic to happen. Though the setting of the story stays the same, Oates signals the passage of time by changes in the central character's outfits. These changes, in addition to his accumulating encounters with other joggers, move the reader steadily toward that dramatic climax.

Oates's decision not to use sentence breaks mimics the act of jogging by creating a kind of continuous forward movement. The setting of the story on the jogging path is also well-suited to the way Oates introduces characters and then lets them go by. For example, Madeline Hersey is first described physically, and then her reaction to the jogger's greeting reveals more about her thoughts. Though readers might start to feel that she is a central character because of this extended discussion, she does not become the subject of the story because Oates turns her attention elsewhere. This technique of linking character sketches also contributes to the surprise of the ending, in which one of the incidental characters along the trail becomes crucial to the plot.

POSSIBLE CONNECTIONS TO OTHER SELECTIONS

Ron Hansen, "My Kid's Dog" (text p. 472; question #1, following)

Rick Moody, "Boys" (text p. 532; question #2, following)

1. Compare the tone of the humor in this story with that in Ron Hansen's "My Kid's Dog" (p. 472).

   Students might begin by commenting on the different styles these two stories were written in—Hansen's clear, traditional first-person narrative and Oates's unusual, stream-of-consciousness flood of words. These two approaches directly affect how humor is conveyed through each story. The humor in "My Kid's Dog" originates largely from the narrator's descriptions of the situations he finds himself in. A perfect example of this is when, after burying the deceased dog, he receives a phone call from his wife's friend, asserting the dog had bitten her son and demanding he take it to the vet to check it for rabies. Rather than hope the animal did not pass on an illness to the child, instead he finds himself "wondering what toxicity lurked in the child's leg and to what extent the poison was culpably responsible for our adored pet's actionable extinction, a loss we would feel for our lifetimes" (19). Due to his earlier profession of hatred for this animal, the narrator's sarcasm is apparent. Through his narrator, Hansen is able to make jokes that are slightly off-color, but clear and straightforward, easy for even the most casual reader to pick up on.

   Oates's story has only black humor that's more insidious than Hansen's open playfulness. Much of it derives from the multiple descriptions of the male jogger who issues the eponymous greeting to other runners. Though unnamed, he's described in great detail, from his "size-twelve Nikes" to his "big horsey teeth" (p. 612). Oates frequently mentions his athleticism, the clothes he's wearing, his weight, even his body odor. These details start to seem redundant, but every so often Oates will throw in a phrase like "as the initial police report will note" (p. 612), which keeps readers intrigued. Finally the punch line comes as Oates transitions her narrative voice from third- to second-person, drawing the reader in for the final climactic moment, and finishing the story with the sarcastic response, "That's how I'm doin."

2. Comment on the ways in which style is related to content in "Hi Howya Doin" and in Rick Moody's "Boys" (p. 532).

   Both of these stories push the limits of prose writing. Both are written as one long, unbroken paragraph, so they resist division into a series of separate episodes or discrete moments. However, while Moody works variations on one sentence, Oates writes her whole story as a single sentence with a final period coming only at the end. In "Boys" that one sentence makes the individual characters seem largely representative of broader movements in human life. "Hi Howya Doin" is much more dependent on describing unique characters, each of whom helps to reveal the interesting central figure.

MARK TWAIN, *The Story of the Good Little Boy* (p. 484)

Upon reading this title, students may expect a simple morality tale for children, and that's what Mark Twain's story is — in a way. Readers who are familiar with Twain's more famous youthful characters, Tom Sawyer and Huckleberry Finn, will already sense that Twain is not one to celebrate perfect obedience to the adult value system. Jacob Blivens is everything Huck and Tom are not: "He always obeyed his parents, no matter how absurd and unreasonable their demands were" (para. 1), Twain writes ironically. He is honest, hardworking, and churchgoing. In short, he is so morally upright that other children believe he is "afflicted" (1).

Twain is not satirizing obedient children in his story so much as the Sunday-school books that depict overly perfect children who die sentimentally in the last chapter and are mourned in a grand funeral. "Jacob," we are told, "had a noble ambition to be put in a Sunday-school book" (3). Twain's descriptions of these books are hilarious, and you might ask one of your students to read paragraphs 2 and 3 out loud so your class will have a good sense of what was considered to be appropriate children's litera-ture in the nineteenth century. What are Twain's objections to these stories? How likely is it that nineteenth-century children took them as seriously as Jacob Blivens does? How do these stories compare to ways our culture uses literature and the media to teach children its values?

Students may be startled to learn of Jacob's very *un*sentimental fate. Like his role models, he succeeds in dying for his goodness, but he is blown up before he is able to make an inspirational dying speech. Nor is Jacob sentimentally mourned; as Twain wryly notes, "You never saw a boy scattered so" (10). What is your students' response to Twain's humorous treatment of the death of a child (and a "good" one at that!)?

POSSIBLE CONNECTIONS TO OTHER SELECTIONS

Raymond Carver, "Popular Mechanics" (text p. 269)

Stephen Crane, "The Bride Comes to Yellow Sky" (text p. 246; question #2, following)

Ralph Ellison, "Battle Royal" (text p. 226; question #1, following)

CONNECTIONS QUESTIONS IN TEXT (p. 487) WITH ANSWERS

1. Compare Jacob's fate with that of the central character in Ellison's "Battle Royal" (p. 226).

    Both of these characters do everything they think is expected of them, but rather than being rewarded for their actions, they are punished or humiliated. However, the difference in the perspective of the narrators makes readers react differently to the stories' outcomes. Twain is an omniscient narrator, relating Jacob's actions from a distance. The good little boy's failures are more humorous due to this dis-tance. Ellison's first-person narrator, on the other hand, requires that the audience identify with his aspirations and with his pain when he is disappointed. Though in the end he is awarded a scholarship by the white men in the audience, the nar-rator's dream reveals his knowledge of their real motives.

2. Write an essay explaining the extent to which this story and Crane's "The Bride Comes to Yellow Sky" (p. 246) are dependent on a reader's familiarity with the formulaic qualities of Sunday-school stories or traditional western stories.

    Twain's story depends on the conventions of Sunday-school books, but a reader who has never read any gets plenty of hints from Twain about what kind of char-acters and situations they contain. By describing Jacob's thoughts about the Sunday-school stories, Twain both supplies the reader with this information for comparison and characterizes Jacob as a naive but strangely ambitious child. By the time the reader gets to the wild ending of "The Good Little Boy," he or she knows that this is an incident far removed from the prototypical scenes of kind-ness toward dogs and poor women that fill Jacob's favorite books. Crane also gives the reader some hints about the type of story that he is parodying in "The Bride Comes to Yellow Sky." By placing an outsider in the saloon, he gives the characters in the story the chance to explain the pattern of their lives, which conforms neatly to the standard western tale. Their overblown stories of Scratchy's meanness make his defeat at the end even more humorous.

17

A Thematic Case Study:
Remarkably Short-Short Stories

In their introduction to an anthology called *Short Shorts,* Irving Howe and Ilana W. Howe claim that the form is "like most ordinary short stories, *only more so.*" Their definition refers to the limits on character development and plot action that differentiate short stories from novels and that are even more constrained in very short stories, such as the ones contained in this chapter. Howe and Howe argue that in short shorts "circumstance eclipses character, fate crowds out individuality, an extreme condition serves as emblem of the universal." One question you might pose to your students is how well this definition explains, for example, Kim Addonizio's meditation on death in "Survivors" or Mark Budman's mockery of modern-day priorities in "The Diary of a Salaryman." To what extent are the characters in these stories revealed by their unique thoughts and voices, and to what extent do they become representative? Since short-short fiction, under many different names, has become increasingly popular in recent years, another question to begin with is what might account for this trend: What might authors like about the limitations the form puts on them? How do short shorts appeal to readers differently than longer fiction?

Web Ask students to research the authors in this chapter or take quizzes on their works at **bedfordstmartins.com/meyerlit**.

KIM ADDONIZIO, *Survivors* (p. 489)

Addonizio's title seems to shift meanings as this story progresses. At first it sounds like an affirmation, but it comes to express the character's worries about being left behind. It suggests that he is concerned not with surviving the disease but rather with outliving his partner. In the course of the story, the reader's sense of the character shifts as well. At first he might seem quibbling or even petty in his concerns, but by the end we understand his fear and sorrow at the thought of losing his partner.

Addonizio has to be very economical in such a short space; through her description of the apartment, with its loving portrait of the couple, kitschy decorations, and pet parrot, she conveys details of the couple's life together. The lover's background is also sketched quickly through the main character's impressions of his parents, both of them disapproving of the fact that he is gay, though they express their disapprobation in different ways.

Students are likely to see the parrot, and the act of freeing it, as symbolic — of death as offering freedom from the illness, for example. They might need to be prompted to think first about what the pet literally means for this character. How might it provide company to him? To what extent would a parrot make a satisfying companion? What might motivate the character to release the parrot into the wild? Not only is the parrot simply a mimic of human speech, able to reproduce it without really being able to respond, but the departed lover's voice might be among those it can imitate.

POSSIBLE CONNECTION TO AN OTHER SELECTION

Peter Meinke, "The Cranes" (text p. 496; question #1, following)

1. Compare the themes in "Survivors" and in Peter Meinke's "The Cranes" (text p. 496).

   "Survivors" and "Cranes" concern the lives couples build together — and in both cases the partners seem so bound together that neither person can think of living without the other. As in Addonizio's story, Meinke suggests the texture of this shared life through small details, like the story about the husband drunkenly confronting a priest. However, the perspectives are very different. In Addonizio's story, the reader is granted access to the character's mind, and we observe all of his thoughts — loving, selfish, fearful, etc. By contrast, Meinke paints a picture of his characters primarily through their dialogue. We learn about their personalities, and their affection for one another, through the way they talk to each other.

RON CARLSON, *Max* (p. 490)

This story begins by describing Max the dog, but it quickly becomes clear that the real subject is Maxwell, the pretentious art curator, whom the narrator unmasks to show readers a "simple crook" (para. 5). Even though Maxwell is making money by damaging art works and then collecting the insurance, he speaks in ways that both romanticize museum work — "hectic and lovely" (4) — and disparage all of his fellow workers. Max the dog is the perfect foil for Maxwell because he has an instinctual drive that breaks down civilized exteriors. As the narrator says, "He can ruin a cocktail party faster than running out of ice" (1).

You might ask students about the nature of the relationship the narrator and his wife have with Maxwell. In the beginning of the story, the narrator introduces him as "our friend" (2), yet it's clear that he doesn't like Maxwell. The scotch-drinking, jewelry-wearing curator has nothing in common with the beer-drinking narrator, who seems more knowledgeable about baseball than art. Yet the couple seems to be amused by Maxwell's pretenses. They react to his frequent topics of conversation as if they were a kind of Greatest Hits, gleefully anticipating what he will say next. Maxwell's faults seem to both repel the couple and bind them to him.

POSSIBLE CONNECTIONS TO OTHER SELECTIONS

Howard Nemerov, "Walking the Dog" (text p. 968; question #2, following)

Joyce Carol Oates, "Hi Howya Doin" (text p. 481; question #1, following)

CONNECTIONS QUESTIONS IN TEXT (p. 491) WITH ANSWERS

1. Discuss the point of view and tone of the narration in "Max" and Joyce Carol Oates's, "Hi Howya Doin" (p. 481).

   The narrator of "Max" takes a matter-of-fact tone from the first sentence, in which he bluntly labels Max a "crotch dog" (para. 1). His satirical moments are reserved for Maxwell and, to a lesser extent, for his new girlfriend. Unlike the traditional first-person narration of "Max," Joyce Carol Oates's "Hi Howya Doin" utilizes a stream-of-consciousness point of view. Oates does use an omniscient point of view, revealing choice facts about each new runner, such as the many problems of Dr. Rausch: "departmental budget cuts! his youngest daughter's wrecked marriage! his wife's biopsy next morning at eleven A.M." Oates uses this intimate point of view and her attention to minute details to draw the reader into the narration.

2. Compare the narrator's relationship to his dog in "Max" and in Howard Nemerov's "Walking the Dog" (text p. 968).

   Carlson's narrator sees the problems with his dog's behavior, but he mostly seems to admire Max's unerring ability to take someone down a notch. In fact Max, with his "powerful instinct and insistent snout" (para. 1), serves as the perfect foil to Maxwell, who is overly refined and ultimately untrustworthy. At the beginning of the story, the reader might not guess that the narrator would enjoy seeing Maxwell "ruin a cocktail party faster than running out of ice" (1). By the end, however, it is clear that he gleefully uses Max to ruin the unpleasant evening with Maxwell. The speaker of "Walking the Dog" seems similarly pleased to be a witness to his pet's very unhuman way of experiencing the world, even pleased to go along with him on his poop-sniffing explorations. Though he recognizes that dog and man inhabit "Two universes" (line 1), the speaker also appreciates that they can coexist, bound together by the leash.

MARK HALLIDAY, *Young Man on Sixth Avenue* (p. 492)

The prose in Halliday's story, with its repetition and its simple declarative sentences, takes on the self-assured tone of the young man in the title. He is at the beginning of his life and feels confident that in both work and personal life he will be a force to be reckoned with. The repetition of the year "1938" also suggests that the young man's hopeful attitude is part of a larger cultural feeling. At the end of a decade of economic crisis, he believes that things will have to take a turn for the better in "the big brazen decade ahead" (para. 2). Though Halliday abruptly turns the story toward the end of his main character's life, it is still essentially about that young man in the city, or about the gap between what that young man thought his life would bring and how it has changed in the intervening years.

The author of "Young Man on Sixth Avenue" is best known as a poet, so this story might provide an opportunity to discuss the intersection of short-short fiction and prose poems, two genres that are often linked in journals or anthologies.

POSSIBLE CONNECTIONS TO OTHER SELECTIONS

Raymond Carver, "Popular Mechanics" (text p. 269; question #2, following)

Dagoberto Gilb, "Love in L.A." (text p. 430)

Rick Moody, "Boys" (text p. 532)

Xu Xi, "Famine" (text p. 123; question #1, following)

CONNECTIONS QUESTIONS IN TEXT (p. 494) WITH ANSWERS

1. Discuss the significance of the Manhattan setting in "Young Man on Sixth Avenue" and in Xu Xi's "Famine" (p. 123).

   For the narrator of "Famine," the culinary promise of Manhattan stands in for larger possibilities but also represents an escape from her parents' austere lifestyle. Compared with the poverty of other countries and with her modest upbringing, Manhattan represents wealth, plenty, and even the excess of "Western diets" (para. 7). In Halliday's story, Manhattan is also a symbol of possibility and progress. Its bustling atmosphere makes the young man feel more important as he strides across the streets. However, at the end, it makes the man feel smaller and slower, as he concedes to wait while the city's younger inhabitants pass by.

2. Write an essay comparing the ending of Halliday's story with that of Raymond Carver's "Popular Mechanics" (p. 269). What is the effect of the ending on your reading of each story?

   The ending of Halliday's story recalls the beginning, but, as he imagines his younger self still striding across the avenue, the older man has a new perspective on his role in Manhattan. This turn serves to change the reader's understanding of the title of the story, which refers not just to the young man's confidence and pride but also to how the same man later reflects on himself and what the city meant in his life. Carver's story ends at its climax, when he suggests that the mounting argument between the parents will result in the child being torn apart. Readers probably realize only at this last moment that Carver is writing a new "Popular" fiction version of the Solomon story from the Bible.

MARK BUDMAN, *The Diary of a Salaryman* (p. 494)

One way to begin discussion of this story is to ask students what they would expect from the diary form. Some of the qualities of a diary are present in Budman's work: the story is written in the first person, presumably from personal experience, and the writing is casual, structured as a series of fragments rather than formal sentences. However, students might notice that some features of a diary are missing, notably the intimacy or sense of emotional revelation that the diary writer usually employs.

Instead of the character's feelings about work, Budman gives readers absurd details of office life. One significant detail falls right in the middle of the story: the narrator meets another employee who has been in a very similar position for years, yet they have never met or known of the other's existence. Even the titles the salaryman gets promoted to seem repetitive and meaningless. Similarly, the information we get about his personal life (or lack of one) is structured in repetitive yet vague sentences. The salaryman seems to have a hard time following his wife's and children's actions and interpreting what they mean.

Given the story's emphasis on work, it is telling that the narrator experiences a sexual awakening that changes his attitudes, making it impossible for him to go back to work when he receives an offer. The sources of pleasure at the end of the story (not only sex, but the bath and the strawberries) are opposed to the sterility of office life. The narrator describes his new activities as keeping him pleasantly "busy," though it is a very different type of business that occupies him.

POSSIBLE CONNECTIONS TO OTHER SELECTIONS

Mark Halliday, "Young Man on Sixth Avenue" (text p. 492; question #1, following)

Annie Proulx, "Job History" (text p. 77; question #2, following)

CONNECTIONS QUESTIONS IN TEXT (p. 495) WITH ANSWERS

1. Write an essay that discusses the plot and style of Budman's story and Mark Halliday's "Young Man on Sixth Avenue" (text p. 492).

   Both Budman's and Halliday's stories concern the passage of time, and both use extreme compression to show how quickly time goes by for their protagonists. Budman conveys the rushing of time by repeating sentences with slight variations, so that the changes of life seem to pass in a blur. Halliday draws out the moment of youth and confidence, the man's invincible feeling, in five paragraphs, as a means of contrasting it with the speed of the sixth paragraph, which encompasses many years in the man's life: war and peacetime, several jobs, the growth of a family, and the death of the man's wife. An important difference between the two stories is what makes the time pass quickly: in spite of a vague feeling of regret about not achieving his literary ambitions, Halliday's character seems to have lived a full life, while Budman's character only discovers the richness of life outside of the office near the end of his time.

2. Consider the similarities and differences in tone and theme concerning the versions of life in "The Diary of a Salaryman" and in Annie Proulx's "Job History" (p. 77).

   Budman's salaryman and Proulx's protagonist Leeland Lee both sacrifice their personal lives for the sake of work. However, Budman's character seems to have the luxury of a steady income, which allows the family he has created to go on without him. Even though he misses important milestones in his children's lives, he still has five grandchildren to play with in the end and a wife who is pleased to see him reject his old work habits. Leeland, on the other hand, becomes too wrapped up in just trying to keep his family afloat financially to ever truly enjoy his family. Soon his wife Lori has died of cancer, his oldest son is suffering from addiction and "no one knows how to reach [him]," and his two daughters "both married now, curse Leeland" (24). Though his family survives Lori's death and is reunited, they're still more focused on business ventures than being together. Proulx drives this preoccupation with work home with her last line: "Nobody has time to listen to the news" (25).

PETER MEINKE, *The Cranes* (p. 496)

Meinke tells his story almost completely through the conversation of the elderly couple. The reader, left on the outside, has to try to figure out what the "wrong thing" is that they're considering (para. 8). Their talk seems so central that on a first reading it is easy to skip over the telling details: "the shower curtain spread over the front seat" (3), the "object wrapped in a plaid towel" (26), the "somehow sinister" (43) look of the lone car. These hints all lead up to their suicides. There are clues within the dialogue as well. The husband's quoting of the famous line from *Casablanca*, for example, signals that they are about to end their love affair.

The cranes that they watch as they talk become symbolic of the couple's relationship. They can't remember how the birds court one another (as courting is in their distant past), but they do remember "that they mate for life and live a long time" (25). The husband further extends the connection, imagining that the cranes have problems similar to their own: "Their feathers are falling out and their kids never write" (25). Rather than describing the moment of their suicides, Meinke allows the cranes to illustrate it through the image of the two birds "[plunging] upward, their great wings beating the air and their long slender necks pointed like arrows toward the sun" (44). The direction of the birds' flight subtly suggests the ascension of the two humans' souls after their deaths.

POSSIBLE CONNECTIONS TO OTHER SELECTIONS

Kate Chopin, "The Story of an Hour" (text p. 15; question #1, following)

Gail Godwin, "A Sorrowful Woman" (text p. 39; question #1, following)

Dylan Thomas, "Do Not Go Gentle into That Good Night" (text p. 747)

CONNECTION QUESTION IN TEXT (p. 498) WITH ANSWER

1. Consider how symbols convey the central meanings of "The Cranes" and of Kate Chopin's "The Story of an Hour" (p. 15) or Gail Godwin's "A Sorrowful Woman" (p. 39).

   The cranes in Meinke's story represent the couple in the car. Though we can glean some information from their conversation, much of what we know about them comes from the parallel between their commitment to each other and that of the cranes, which "mate for life and live a long time" (para. 25). At the end, the birds' flight upward, with "their long slender necks pointed like arrows toward the sun" (44), represents the couple's transcendence of their earthly problems.

   In Godwin's story, the symbolism comes largely from its fairy-tale underpinnings. The "sleeping draught," for example, provides relief to the woman, but also reminds the reader of the spells and potions used to sedate Snow White and Sleeping Beauty. The son's game of "[pretending] he was a vicious tiger" (6) is just make-believe, but it scares her nonetheless because he represents a kind of threat. Finally, when she separates herself from her family by moving into the nanny's room, the woman becomes "a young queen, a virgin in a tower" (22). Though her isolation seems self-imposed, the connection with fairy tales suggests that she has actually been imprisoned by a villain, and in this story the only villain we can identify is her husband or something he represents.

TERRY L. TILTON, *That Settles That* (p. 498)

Tilton's story may provoke debate in your class. It hinges on a metafictional move; here, the character's action deliberately creates a story. Because of the story's very short length, students may resist the self-reflexive element more, or they may find it clever. Either way, this story may be a particularly good testing ground for Howe and Howe's definition of a short short. (See introduction to this chapter on p. 94.) Since Tom is only vaguely sketched as a character and Sam is not described at all, how much do their characters matter to readers? If Sam and his motivation aren't the point of the story, then what is? Do these two characters take on allegorical significance? What is most arresting, interesting, or, perhaps, infuriating about the climax of the story? And to what extent does it offer resolution, as the title suggests?

POSSIBLE CONNECTIONS TO OTHER SELECTIONS

Rich Orloff, *Playwriting 101: The Rooftop Lesson* (text p. 1346)
Mark Twain, "The Story of the Good Little Boy" (text p. 484)

18

A Collection of Stories: Stories for Further Reading

In Chapter 18, "Stories for Further Reading," students have the opportunity to apply what they have learned about plot, characterization, setting, irony, and other literary elements in the earlier chapters of *The Compact Bedford Introduction to Literature*. The stories in this chapter are not accompanied by specific questions, "Connections" topics for discussion, or writing exercises. Instructors might want students to prepare their own questions in connection with the readings in this chapter (after all, after responding to the questions provided in all the earlier chapters, students should have developed some knowledge about how to pose questions, as well as how to respond to them). This might make a good group project; separate groups might be responsible for presenting questions for individual stories. In addition, students might follow their readings in this chapter by generating their own "First Response" questions (either for themselves or for their classmates). As they may have learned by following the exercises provided in earlier chapters, identifying an immediate response to a story and then building an understanding of how the work provokes such a response may enable them to find additional meaning in the work or learn more about an author's technique. In effect, this collection enables the students to become the instructors — to develop a more immediate relationship with the literature — without finding themselves limited to the ancillary materials provided in earlier chapters.

Web Ask students to research the authors in this chapter or take quizzes on their works at **bedfordstmartins.com/ meyerlit**.

ZORA NEALE HURSTON, *Spunk* (p. 502)

Like much of Hurston's work, this story is rooted in her knowledge of oral storytelling practices. The men who gather at the store are not only characters in "Spunk" — they narrate the story of Spunk, Lena, and Joe as it progresses. "Spunk" begins with the sense that the story they are telling is ongoing; the onlookers at the store seem not to be surprised at all when they see Spunk and Lena walking down the street together. The story ends, too, with the community beginning to discuss the next chapter in Lena's life. The narration of this tale extends beyond the boundaries of the written story.

The two men at the center of the story have larger-than-life personae. Especially after Joe's death, their feud takes on a supernatural scale. It seems to extend beyond the grave, with Joe taking on strange new forms — or so the townspeople come to believe. They imagine the fight going on after Spunk's death as well: "If spirits kin fight, there's a powerful tussle goin' on somewhere ovah Jordan" (para. 58). Their fight is not simply about a woman, but about two different ways of relating to the world, and which is ultimately better. Compared to the two men, Lena is a marginal character. She is also much more realistic. By contrast with the onlookers in the store and with the two leading men, she speaks very little. It is significant that the only time Hurston includes her voice is to show Lena's claim over her house, the one thing that neither Joe nor Spunk seem to be able to take over as their own.

The characters spend a great deal of time comparing the personalities of Joe and Spunk, so you might start discussion by having students do the same. Do they have the same sense of what behavior on the part of these men is admirable and what is blameworthy? Why do the onlookers seem to revise their opinion of Joe after his death? Finally, to what degree are big talkers like Walter and Elijah responsible for the deaths of both Joe and Spunk?

D. H. LAWRENCE, *The Horse Dealer's Daughter* (p. 506)

D. H. Lawrence was born in 1885 in the Nottinghamshire village of Eastwood, in England's industrial Midlands. Although he grew up feeling closer to his book-loving mother, Lawrence would finally regard his miner father's rough vitality with deep respect, and he imbued a number of his male characters with his father's qualities of mind and behavior, qualities he came to see as essentially masculine. Further, the depictions of marriage in his mature works echo the "union of opposites" embodied in his parents' relationship. No "true marriage" — no true relationship, really — could exist, Lawrence thought, without fundamental conflict.

After finishing high school, Lawrence became a clerk, then an elementary-school teacher; he spent two years at Nottingham University College, earning a teacher's certificate in 1908. During this time he worked on his first novel (*The White Peacock*, published in 1911), wrote poetry and short fiction, and read constantly. He got a job as a schoolteacher in a suburb of London and stayed for four years, until he fell in love with Frieda von Richthofen, the German wife of a professor at Nottingham. They married in Germany in 1914, by which time Lawrence's autobiographical second novel, *Sons and Lovers*, had been published to both good reviews and good sales.

The couple returned to England early in World War I. Lawrence's vehement opposition to the war (it didn't help that Frieda was German) led to trouble with the English authorities. This was, in fact, only the first in what was to become a lifelong series of conflicts with the established order. *The Rainbow* was banned soon after its publication in 1915 because of its depictions (frank for the time) of sexuality. When the war ended, Lawrence left England with his wife, only to spend the rest of his life looking for a community where he felt welcome. Often very ill with the tuberculosis that eventually killed him, Lawrence lived and wrote in Italy, Australia, Mexico, France, and New Mexico. After his death his ashes were scattered near the ranch house where he had lived outside Taos, New Mexico.

Lawrence's works include *Women in Love* (1920), *Aaron's Rod* (1922), *Kangaroo* (1923), *The Plumed Serpent* (1926), *Lady Chatterley's Lover* (1928), and *Studies in Classical American Literature* (1923).

Some students will be confused or even disturbed by Lawrence's vision of love, life, and death as presented in this story. For this reason an attempt to answer the concrete question "Why does Mabel attempt suicide?" might be a good way to move toward a discussion of the themes. What about Mabel's life is so oppressive, unbearable, and meaningless? What, prior to the opening of the story, had made her life worthwhile?

Mabel's life has been grim since her widowed father remarried, an action that set Mabel "hard against him" (para. 97). (Presumably Mabel felt the marriage violated her father's original love for her mother, who had died thirteen years before this story takes place.) Before he remarried, Mabel had been contented enough, attending her father and living "in the memory of her mother, . . . whom she had loved" (97). But with her father's death went the family fortune — the one thing that had made Mabel feel "established," "proud," and "confident" (96). Her brothers had always been "brutal and coarse" (96) and had never shown any interest in her. She had no friends or acquaintances, both her parents were dead, and her poverty made her feel completely degraded. The only place she felt secure was in the churchyard where her mother was buried; her only source of happiness was tending her mother's grave and anticipating "her own glorification, approaching her dead mother, who was glorified" (98). The fact is, Mabel has been leading a sort of living death.

This analysis of Mabel's situation should give students better insight into her character and can lead to a more sophisticated discussion of, or writing assignment on, the use of symbols in the story. Students should now be able to identify many of the symbolic aspects of the setting: the large house, servantless and desolate; the empty stables; the "gray, wintry day, with saddened . . . fields and an atmosphere blackened by the smoke of foundries not far off"; and "a slow, moist, heavy coldness sinking in and deadening all the faculties" (99, 106). Yet while all of these suggest death, the story contains just as many symbols of life: the horses, with their "swinging . . . great rounded haunches" and their "massive, slumbrous strength" (6); "the working people," who provide Fergusson with excitement, stimulation, and gratification (106); and Mabel herself, who is literally brought back to life by Fergusson, but who also, figuratively, brings him to life: "He could never let her go away. . . . He wanted to remain like that forever, with his heart hurting him in a pain that was also life to him" (154).

This introduction to the interrelated themes of life and death and love should enable students to discuss the story more fully. You could also ask students to write about the main characters: Do they change during the course of the story, and if so, how? What brings about these changes? Why does Mabel ask Fergusson if he loves her when she does? Why does he react to her question "amazed, bewildered, and afraid" (147)? What does the last paragraph of the story suggest about Mabel and Fergusson's future, and about Lawrence's vision of relationships between men and women?

Another fruitful topic might be a discussion of point of view. Ask students to identify and discuss the type of narration used. Could the story have been told exclusively from Mabel's point of view, or Fergusson's? Why or why not?

POSSIBLE CONNECTIONS TO OTHER SELECTIONS

Fay Weldon, "IND AFF, or Out of Love in Sarajevo" (text p. 173)

James Joyce, "Eveline" (text p. 407)

JACK LONDON, *To Build a Fire* (p. 518)

London conveys the feeling of intense cold through careful recording of details like the way "spittle crackled" (para. 4) in the air or the fact that the character has to carry biscuits next to his skin to keep them from freezing. The narration is very thoughtful, attentive, and even, at moments, philosophical. Yet the thoughts of the character are quite simple. They consist largely of repeated acknowledgements of the cold and a changing assessment of advice he got from an "old-timer" (20) who had more experience in the Alaskan wilderness. The contrast between the narrator's voice and the character's thoughts is especially clear when the man starts to realize that he will not survive. As the narrator puts it, "He sat up and entertained in his mind the conception of meeting death with dignity" (35). London then gives the character's version of the thought: "His idea of it was that he had been making a fool of himself, running around like a chicken with its head cut off" (35). The narrator also has some access to the dog's thoughts or, it may be more accurate to say, the dog's instinctive reactions. The narrative deliberately switches to the dog's perspective in the end. Have students discuss the effect of this ending. What does the turn away from the human perspective mean?

POSSIBLE CONNECTION TO ANOTHER SELECTION

Annie Proulx, "55 Miles to the Gas Pump" (text p. 470)

KATHERINE MANSFIELD, *The Fly* (p. 528)

In "The Fly," six years have passed since the main character's son died in war. After being reminded of his son's grave by a former employee, the man, who is only identified as "the boss," wants to feel grief. He has in the past experienced some relief from weeping, but in spite of his insistence that time would not alleviate his suffering, it seems to have done so because now he cannot cry.

One aspect of the story you'll want to take time to discuss is the structure. Is the father's loss of his son at the emotional center of the story as well as at its literal center? If so, why does Mansfield begin with a different character, Mr. Woodifield, and his ill health? The boss's character, in contrast, is stronger and more powerful, though he is five years older than Woodifield. Does this knowledge of him change our view of later events?

Ask your students why the fly distracts the boss's attention at the end. What does his attitude toward it illustrate about the man's character? Though he can feel the loss of his own son, he looks on the fly's struggles with detached curiosity. His decision to extend a kind of patriarchal mercy on the fly comes too late.

POSSIBLE CONNECTION TO ANOTHER SELECTION

Emily Dickinson, "I heard a Fly buzz — when I died —" (text p. 814)

RICK MOODY, *Boys* (p. 532)

In "Boys," Moody creates a whole story from variations on a single sentence collected in a single paragraph. This technique makes even more apparent the differing sentence lengths that are one of the greatest pleasures of prose. For example, the short sentence "Boys enter the house calling for mother" (p. 532) is followed by a much longer sentence about how the boys bury their sister's dolls. The repetition also highlights the point at which the two main characters change most dramatically, when the death of their father finally makes them "no longer boys" (p. 535).

Through his variations, Moody traces the lives of the two boys as they grow from babies into children, teenagers, and finally adults. Their story is as archetypal as it is rich and detailed. Though we learn the specifics of the boys' antics, including the disgusting mixture they concoct out of kitchen odds-and-ends and try to convince their sister to eat, we never know their names. Nor do we learn much about their individual personalities, though Moody suggests that one is more athletic and the other more artistic. We see the boys' sexual awakening, see them become more independent from one another, and see them make decisions about how their adult lives will be. As they grow up, the always-present conflict between the boys stops being physical and becomes ideological. This conflict seems to come in large part from the inevitable distance between them. Each at times "misses his brother horribly, misses the past, misses a time worth being nostalgic over, a time that never existed" (p. 535), just as "each is devoted and each callous" (p. 535) to the other. In "Boys" the sadness of the losses to death (of the father and sister) is mirrored by the loss of what bound the two brothers together.

POSSIBLE CONNECTION TO ANOTHER SELECTION

Mark Halliday, "Young Man on Sixth Avenue" (text p. 492)

EDGAR ALLAN POE, *The Cask of Amontillado* (p. 536)

This classic revenge story is also classic Poe — narrated calmly in the first person by a man who kills his enemy by sealing him alive in his vaults. This story will fascinate and sicken any reader with even the most mild claustrophobia or fear of being buried alive. (Isn't this a universal fear?) Although the outcome of the story is in little doubt — we sense that the narrator will succeed in exacting revenge for Fortunato's insult — Poe maintains suspense by withholding the murderer's exact plan until the end.

This story is ripe with irony. Fortunato is led to his death by his own insistence. The narrator plays upon his enemy's greatest weakness — his pride in connoisseurship of wine. When Fortunato hears that his "friend" has acquired a cask of the rare Amontillado, he insists upon seeing it for himself to determine if it is the true vintage. Your students may enjoy locating lines in which the narrator is gracious and overly solicitous of Fortunato. He several times refers to Fortunato as "my friend," and feigns concern about the effects of the damp vaults on his health. "Come . . . we will go back; your health is precious" (para. 35). The reader will not miss the double meaning in Fortunato's reply, "I shall not die of a cough," or the narrator's all-too-accurate answer, "True — true . . . and indeed, I had no intention of alarming you unnecessarily" (36–37). Careful readers will also pick up on the narrator's claim that he is a mason. While Fortunato refers to the brotherhood of Freemasons, the narrator is referring to the masonry he is about to perform, in which he will build the wall that imprisons his enemy in the crypt.

Note how Poe builds suspense in the terrifying final paragraphs. The narrator chains Fortunato to the granite and "begins vigorously to wall up the entrance of the niche" (75). Poe then leads the reader through Fortunato's responses — first shock, then crying, then silence, then resistance. The narrator pauses during his work in order to experience "more satisfaction" (76) in his enemy's struggle. After more agonized screaming and vigorous resistance, Fortunato is eventually silent. Is the narrator finally "satisfied"? How do your students account for his sick feeling at the story's end? How do they feel about the story's main characters? Who is the protagonist and who is the antagonist? Poe never reveals Fortunato's original "insult" to the narrator. Why not? Would your students have reacted differently if they had known what "crime" Fortunato committed?

Your students might want to discuss this story as a "horror story," comparing it to contemporary books and films of the same genre. Poe's work is horrifying in the same way that Alfred Hitchcock movies are (as opposed to "slasher" films). There is very little physical violence in the story itself, and the murder of Fortunato is far less disturbing than the psychological torment which he undergoes as he realizes what is happening to him.

POSSIBLE CONNECTIONS TO OTHER SELECTIONS

William Faulkner, "A Rose for Emily" (text p. 82)

Nathaniel Hawthorne, "The Birthmark" (text p. 333)

——, "Young Goodman Brown" (text p. 315)

Flannery O'Connor, "A Good Man Is Hard to Find" (text p. 356)

POETRY

The Elements of Poetry

19

Reading Poetry

Perhaps the most difficult part of any introductory literature course is convincing the students that they can, in fact, read poetry. Students are often intimidated by previous experiences, either in high school or in other college courses; they have often accepted that they "just don't get it." Thus it is important to develop students' confidence in themselves as readers. One way to do this is to get students to articulate what they see actually happening in the poem, to read what is "on the page."

This chapter contains several poems that lend themselves to such an application. Robert Hayden's "Those Winter Sundays" and John Updike's "Dog's Death," among others, are poems that have a clear scene or situation that grounds them: they mean what they say in a concrete way. Other meanings and issues can be raised, of course, but Updike's poem, for instance, is first and foremost about the death of a pet. Students will often "get" this level of the poem but distrust their reading, figuring that it isn't what the poem is "really about." A good reading, however, is grounded in such particulars. You might want to have students offer a one- or two-sentence summary of the action of such poems: "The speaker in Updike's poem describes, the sudden death of the family dog." Students can then be encouraged to build on these readings once their "fear of poetry" has been deflated somewhat.

Web Ask students to research the poets in this chapter at **bedfordstmartins.com/ meyerlit**.

Even such poems as Robert Morgan's "Mountain Graveyard" can become more accessible; what may seem to some as mere wordplay will be more powerful if students slow down and picture the scene evoked by the title.

In some cases, you may be confronted by students who already have all the answers. Such students can easily intimidate a class. A useful exercise can be done with Robert Frost's "The Road Not Taken" (Chapter 31, text p. 840). Many students have encountered this poem in high school; most have "learned" that it is a poem about making a brave choice that leads the speaker to a life of independence or a poem of regret at lost possibilities. As the text points out, however, close attention to the verb tenses in the final stanza reveals a more ambiguous reading. You may want to distribute a copy of this poem (without commentary) to the class, and ask, "How old is the speaker in the poem?" Focusing attention on the last two stanzas can prove instructive even to experienced readers and can emphasize the importance of careful attention and multiple readings.

There are two strategies you may find effective in working with students' resistance to poetry and helping them understand the poems they are faced with: reading aloud and short writings. On the surface, this sounds obvious, but having to understand a poem well enough to read it or hearing it spoken can make a difference in students' appreciation of poetry. Tips on encouraging reading aloud can be found in this manual in the introduction to Chapter 25.

Similarly, you might want to assign students short, informal writing to help them think through some of the issues you want to cover in class. These writings can be based on questions in the text, questions of your own, or even student-generated questions based on issues that seem to interest them in discussion. Writing before class discussion can help students frame ideas to share. You may want to grade these assignments only on a pass/fail basis to give students the chance to do experimental thinking in a low-stakes environment. Chapter 48 of the text has a number of questions and strategies you might find useful in these assignments.

LISA PARKER, *Snapping Beans* (p. 546)

This poem, in the voice of a college student returning home to Grandma's, contrasts the familiarity of family with new knowledge of the outside world. "Snapping Beans" is a kind of shorthand for the tenuous middle ground the speaker and grandmother share, with Grandma's home still comforting and beautiful to the speaker. Students will probably be able to relax with Parker's straightforward narrative, simple vocabulary, accessible imagery, and earnest tone. The sudden violent dispatch of the leaf from the tree and Grandma's observation of it provide a parallel to the speaker's separation from the grandmother's world.

Students are likely to be familiar with the distance between loved ones and the shifts that occur when we grow up and move away from our families. Consider asking them to spend ten or fifteen minutes engaged in a journal-writing exercise that examines how their own relationships with family members have changed since they left for college. Asking them to read aloud selections from their writing could establish a sense of community in the classroom.

POSSIBLE CONNECTION TO AN OTHER SELECTION

Robert Frost, "Birches" (text p. 848)

ROBERT HAYDEN, *Those Winter Sundays* (p. 547)

Useful comparisons can be made between any of the poems in this text that speak of love's transcendence or amplitude and any others, like this one and Scott Hightower's "My Father" (text p. 662), that speak of its difficulty — the time it sometimes takes to recognize love. Hayden's speaker looks back at his father's unappreciated Sunday labor, at last knowing it for what it was and knowing, too, that the chance for gratitude has long since passed. The poem gives a strong sense, especially in its final two lines, that the speaker has tended to "love's austere and lonely offices" (line 14). The repetition of "What did I know?" seems to be a cry into the silence not only of the past but of the poet's present situation as well. The poem plays the music of the father's furnace work, the hard consonant sounds "splintering, breaking" (6) as the poem unfolds and disappearing entirely by the poem's end.

You might begin discussion by asking students to describe the speaker's father in as much detail as possible based on the speaker's spare description. From the poem's second word, *too*, the poem reaches beyond itself to suggest something about the man without naming it. What other details contribute to our impression of him? Following that discussion, you could also ask for a description of the speaker. What does his language reveal about his character? And how does this character contrast with his father's character?

POSSIBLE CONNECTION TO ANOTHER SELECTION

Scott Hightower, "My Father" (text p. 662)

JOHN UPDIKE, *Dog's Death* (p. 548)

This narrative poem subtly traces a family's emotional response to the illness and death of their pet dog. Ask students to find the events that lead to the dog's death. How does the speaker relate these events? He tells us the dog's age when he talks about her toilet training and immediately establishes the family's relationship to her by repeating their words: "Good dog! Good dog!" (line 4). Alliteration and assonance soften the story; after they have identified these sound patterns, ask students why the repeated sounds are appropriate to the subject matter. Direct their attention to the enjambment in lines 12–13. Why does the sentence span two stanzas? Might the speaker be reluctant to tell us the dog died?

When he relates his wife's reaction to the death, the speaker describes her voice as "imperious with tears" (14). After they have established a definition of the word *imperious,* ask students to determine why it might be used here. The ambiguous "her" and "she" in the final two lines of the stanza make us puzzle out for a moment the pronouns' referent. Is the speaker talking about his wife or the dog? Are both implied? How does this distortion of identity work in a discussion of death?

The final stanza reads as a eulogy; the consonants become harder — "drawing" (18), "dissolution" (18), "diarrhoea" (19), "dragged" (19) — perhaps because the speaker is working at closing off the experience. In a writing assignment, you might ask students to discuss the three uses of "Good dog." How does the last one differ from the first two? How does the poem prepare us for the change?

POSSIBLE CONNECTION TO ANOTHER SELECTION

Jane Kenyon, "The Blue Bowl" (text p. 636)

WILLIAM HATHAWAY, *Oh, Oh* (p. 550)

The reader's delight in the surprise ending of this poem hinges on the mood set up by the language of the first fifteen lines. Which words create this idyllic mood? What happens to the poem if you replace these words with others? For example, what words could replace "amble" (line 1)? How might one wave besides "gaily" (10)? How could the caboose pass other than with a "chuckle" (15)? How does the poem read with your revisions?

Does the poet give any clues as to what lies ahead? What about the "black window" in line 9, the exact center of the poem? A writing activity dealing with denotation and connotation could develop from a study of this poem. Have students consider a picture (one of an old house works well) and describe it first as though it might be used as a setting for *Nightmare on Elm Street,* then for an episode of *The Brady Bunch.* Discuss the word choices that set the different moods.

ROBERT FRANCIS, *Catch* (p. 552)

This poem casts metaphor-making as a game of catch between two boys. If you are using the poem to examine metaphor, you might ask students what is missing from the central metaphor that Francis creates: that is, when two boys are playing catch, they are tossing a ball to each other. If we interpret the two players of this game as the poet and the reader, does the game of catch seem one-sided, as though one player is firing a number of balls at the other? Once you catch the ball in a game of catch, you throw it back. Does the relationship between reader and poet work the same way?

Encourage students to enjoy listening to this poem. Like a good pitcher, Francis finds various ways of throwing strikes. Consider, for example, line 3, with its "attitudes, latitudes, interludes, altitudes," or "prosy" and "posy" later in the poem.

POSSIBLE CONNECTIONS TO OTHER SELECTIONS

Emily Dickinson, "Portraits are to daily faces" (text p. 805)
Robert Francis, "The Pitcher" (text p. 711)

PHILIP LARKIN, *A Study of Reading Habits* (p. 557)

This poem about a speaker's developing disillusionment with reading is a clever satire of the speaker's attitude. Note the poem's intricate rhyme pattern. The poet's use of a complex poetic form while having the poem's speaker use slang and trite phrases provides an excellent opportunity to make students aware of the difference between the poet and the speaker of a poem. Does the slang used in Larkin's poem help to identify the speaker with a particular time period? With what current words would your students replace such words as *cool* (line 4), *lark* (8), *dude* (13), *chap* (15)? Is any of the slang used in this poem still current?

After your students have read Larkin's poem, you might ask them to discuss their previous (and present) reading habits or have them write a short essay on this subject. What do they expect to gain from reading? Escape? Pleasure? Knowledge?

POSSIBLE CONNECTIONS TO OTHER SELECTIONS

Anne Bradstreet, "The Author to Her Book" (text p. 647)

Billy Collins, "Introduction to Poetry" (text p. 564)

ROBERT MORGAN, *Mountain Graveyard* (p. 558)

Ask students if they agree with the assertion that "Mountain Graveyard" is "unmistakably poetry." If they think it is poetry, is it a good poem? Meyer's strong argument in the text may be intimidating, but students should be encouraged to develop their own sense of what poetry is as they work through these chapters. Further, this poem and the next afford opportunities (because of their highly unorthodox forms) to lead students into a discussion of the authority of the printed word: Is a piece of literature good because "the book says so"? Is a story "art" because it is anthologized? It might be useful to return to these questions when your class finishes its consideration of poetry.

As a writing activity, have students choose another setting (college campus, supermarket, playground) and develop a set of anagrams for the new locale. Do different arrangements of the anagrams change the overall meaning of the set? Are any of the arrangements poetry?

POSSIBLE CONNECTIONS TO OTHER SELECTIONS

Helen Chasin, "The Word *Plum*" (text p. 712)

E. E. Cummings "l(a" (text p. 559; following)

E. E. CUMMINGS, *l(a* (p. 559)

E. E. Cummings was born in Cambridge, Massachusetts, the son of a Congregationalist minister. He earned a degree from Harvard University and began writing his iconoclastic poems after coming upon the work of Ezra Pound. His experimentation with syntax and punctuation reflects a seriously playful attitude toward language and meaning and a skepticism about institutional authority.

At first glance, "l(a" seems to be a poem spewed out by a closemouthed computer held in solitary confinement. As with Morgan's "Mountain Graveyard," however, the poem comes into its own as the reader not only deciphers but brings meaning to the text. Implied here is a simile between a falling leaf and loneliness. The use of a natural image to suggest an emotion recalls Japanese haiku (see Chapter 27 of this manual).

The vertical quality of the poem illustrates the motion of a single leaf falling. Students might also point out the repetition of the digit *one* (indistinguishable in some texts from the letter *l*), along with other "aloneness" words, such as *a* and *one*. If ever a poem's medium enhanced its message, this one surely does.

POSSIBLE CONNECTION TO ANOTHER SELECTION

Robert Morgan, "Mountain Graveyard" (text p. 558; preceding)

ANONYMOUS, *Western Wind* (p. 560)

Students should be aware that, in England, the coming of the west wind signifies the arrival of spring. How is the longing for spring in this lyric connected to the overall sense of longing or to sexual longing? These brief four lines contain examples of several poetic devices worth noting. Ask students to consider the effects of the apostrophe and the alliteration in the first line. Many modern poets would think these techniques artificial and overdone, but this poet seems to be interested in making a strong statement in just a few words. Does it work? Also, consider the use of the expletive "Christ" (line 3). This word makes the reader feel the intensity of emotion being conveyed and turns the poem into a kind of prayer—it is both sacred and profane.

For purposes of comparison, discuss this poem in conjunction with another lyric that uses the same apostrophe, Percy Bysshe Shelley's "Ode to the West Wind" (text p. 756). Students should note that "Western Wind" is much more personal and less formal in diction than Shelley's poem.

POSSIBLE CONNECTIONS TO OTHER SELECTIONS

Robert Herrick, "Delight in Disorder" (text p. 728)

Percy Bysshe Shelley, "Ode to the West Wind" (text p. 756)

REGINA BARRECA, *Nighttime Fires* (p. 561)

This narrative poem has a recurrent theme, indicated by the repetition of the word *smoke*. Smoke is the end of the father's quest, but what, exactly, is he looking for? His daughter, the speaker, provides a clue when she tells us that her father lost his job, so he had time to pursue fires. Smoke is the father's assurance that there is justice in the world because fires destroy rich and poor people alike. Ask students to look at the images the speaker uses to describe her father: What kind of man is he? How would they characterize the daughter's relationship to him? Does the mother also think of these drives as "festival, carnival" (line 15)? In some respect, the carnival is the father's performance before his family, in which the "wolf whine of the siren" (9) is matched by his "mad" (8) expression.

In a writing assignment, you might ask students to examine the metaphors describing the father. What do these figures tell us about his life? For example, in the final image of the father, his eyes are compared to "hallways filled with smoke" (31). Why is he likened to a house? What might this image tell us about his life?

POSSIBLE CONNECTION TO ANOTHER SELECTION

Robert Hayden, "Those Winter Sundays" (text p. 547)

BILLY COLLINS, *Introduction to Poetry* (p. 564)

Using a series of colorful metaphors, the speaker of this poem—a poetry instructor—describes his (or her) frustration with student expectations in an introductory poetry class. Depending on the reader's point of view, the speaker's attitude might be amusing or insulting. As a teacher you probably find yourself nodding with recognition of the instructor's foiled attempts to get students to appreciate poetry for what it is, but your students might see things differently.

"Introduction to Poetry" offers you an excellent opportunity to gauge your own students' expectations of your role in the course. Ask them if they think the speaker is being fair. Do they believe the speaker uses the poem's metaphors literally in classroom assignments, or are they simply meant to describe the instructor's wishes? Do the metaphors make sense to your students?

Ask your students, also, whether they see a little bit of themselves or their peers in the poem's students. As new readers of poetry, it's likely that they do, indeed, want to know what a poem "means." Do they see humor in the speaker's confession metaphor, or do they cling to the notion that they must discover what Meyer calls the "definitive reading" of a poem?

For a writing exercise, have your students respond to the speaker. How would they characterize the instructor's expectations?

POSSIBLE CONNECTIONS TO OTHER SELECTIONS

Mark Halliday, "Graded Paper" (text p. 680)
Richard Wakefield, "In a Poetry Workshop" (text p. 1025)

ENCOUNTERING POETRY: IMAGES OF POETRY IN POPULAR CULTURE

Students often come into an introductory poetry course intimidated and frightened. Despite their familiarity with song lyrics, they're often convinced that lyric poetry is "beyond" them. Others bring with them the assumption that writing and reading poetry is an elite undertaking that has no application to their daily lives.

The "Encountering Poetry" section (text pp. A–H) should help to dispel some of your students' preconceptions. Poetry is all around us. We run across it on public transportation, in advertisements, on product packaging, online, even on our friends' refrigerators. You might be tempted to use the poems in this portfolio as a way to get students comfortable with interpreting poetry, but it's best to resist the urge. Spend your first class, or your first couple of classes, simply getting your students to appreciate poetry as a source of pleasure that they'll find in unexpected places. You might even want to assign your students to bring in their own examples of poetry from their personal environments. By getting them to think of poetry as something fun and accessible, you'll have gone a long way toward teaching them how to dig deeper into its pleasures.

HELEN FARRIES, *Magic of Love* (p. 566)

Note the ways in which this poem fulfills the greeting-card formula, especially with its "lilting" anapests, internal rhymes, and tried-and-true (and terribly trite) metaphors, all designed to lift the reader's spirits.

You might begin discussion by asking why this poem has withstood the test of time (as greeting-card verse). The pleasure of this specific poem comes not as much from its theme, which is nothing particularly new, as from its elements of sound, especially its internal, and full, end-stopped rhyme. Because poetry evolved, at least partly, from an oral tradition — using rhymes as mnemonic devices — you may even use this poem as a vehicle for discussing the very basic history of poetry. You may ask, for example, *why* strict rhyme and meter serve as such an effective mnemonic device. Does this poem use its devices pleasurably?

POSSIBLE CONNECTION TO ANOTHER SELECTION

Emily Dickinson, "If I can stop one Heart from breaking" (text p. 800)

JOHN FREDERICK NIMS, *Love Poem* (p. 566)

Greeting cards must speak to the anonymous masses. Nims's poem, while maintaining a simplicity of diction and a directness of sentiment, is far stronger than the greeting-card verse, in part because it is addressing a specific person.

The poem is obviously not a piece to be carved on the pedestal of some faceless ideal; students will probably have at least some curiosity about a poem that begins "My clumsiest dear." After they have become accustomed to this violating of poetic convention, ask them to review the poem for other refreshing and surprising uses of language. They might mention, for example, the use of "shipwreck" as a verb in line 1, the play on "bull in a china shop" (line 3), or the projective quality of "undulant" in line 8 to describe the floor as it appears to the drunk. Again, unlike conventional verse, this poem concludes with an almost paradoxical twist to the most salient feature of this woman who breaks things: her absence would cause "all the toys of the world [to] break."

In a writing assignment, you might ask students to compare this poem with Shakespeare's sonnet "My mistress' eyes . . ." (text p. 743).

POSSIBLE CONNECTIONS TO OTHER SELECTIONS

Margaret Atwood, "you fit into me" (text p. 645)

William Shakespeare, "My mistress' eyes are nothing like the sun" (text p. 743)

BRUCE SPRINGSTEEN, *Devils & Dust* (p. 568)

In this song, Springsteen employs symbols that carry deep cultural significance. In the third stanza, the appearance of "blood and stone" (line 18) and "mud and bone" (22) suggests a barren landscape that has been ravaged by violence or war. The two words in Springsteen's title, especially, have biblical connections. "Dust" is associated with death but also with a return to origins, as in the phrase from a funeral prayer: "ashes to ashes, dust to dust." However, paired with "devils," the cycle associated with "dust" becomes more malign and more frightening. "Devils & Dust" is itself a cycle. It begins with the speaker's "finger on the trigger" (1), a phrase that returns near the end to emphasize the speaker's ongoing struggle.

Springsteen also uses rhetorical reversals in the song to give new meaning to familiar phrases. For example, "We're a long, long way from home" (line 5) is a common phrase, but in the next line, Springsteen writes, "Home's a long, long way from us" (6). This change in phrasing seems to emphasize not only the physical distance but the strangeness of the place in which the speaker finds himself.

POSSIBLE CONNECTION TO ANOTHER SELECTION

Jim Stevens, "Schizophrenia" (p. 657)

S. PEARL SHARP, *It's the Law: A Rap Poem* (p. 569)

In a meter and vernacular that will likely be familiar to your students, this poem provides an analysis of what our nation's laws reveal about our collective behavior. This analysis is followed by disgust for the behavior that made the laws necessary. The poem ends with an optimistic response, rendering the laws impotent by presenting "rules" that focus on producing positive, creative behavior rather than forbidding negative, destructive behavior.

Sharp states more than once her analysis of what our laws reveal about our cultural behavior: "The rules we break are the laws we make / The things that we fear, we legislate" (lines 3–4); "The laws we make are what we do to each other / There is no law to make brother love brother" (18–19). This absence of a law enforcing love is the impetus for Sharp's creation of the more positive "rules": the distinction between "rules" and "laws" provides an alternative to the despair of legislation. This is an insistent poem, attacking its point from several angles. Sharp emphasizes the importance of her rules as a counterbalance to the distressing lessons our laws teach us, urging her readers to "Listen up!" (25). The rules emphasizing education, kindness, and sobriety underscore the need for personal responsibility and self-respect.

You might want to compare other features of rap with more traditional poetic conventions: end rhyme, allusion, alliteration, meter, and clever turns of phrase. Ask students to describe these conventions and to give examples of them from this poem. If you have worked with other twentieth-century poetry, contrast the types of conventions apparent in rap and in other modern poems.

POSSIBLE CONNECTION TO ANOTHER SELECTION

Gwendolyn Brooks, "We Real Cool" (text p. 614)

PERSPECTIVE

ROBERT FRANCIS, *On "Hard" Poetry* (p. 571)

Discussing hard poetry through its opposite, soft poetry, may be the best way into a discussion of this piece. Hard poetry does not use excess words, does not lapse into sentimentality, does not have an undefined or loose form. The hard poem sustains tension between poet and speaker, reader and text. You may want to put Francis's ideas to the test by asking students to find specific lines from "Devils & Dust" that support an argument about whether the lyrics can be characterized as "hard" poetry. Are the speaker's tone and the images used in the song sentimental — or "soft"? Students should be able to point to a number of lines that allow for multiple interpretations — that challenge the reader and create some "resistance." You might ask students whether they feel the lyrics are tightly organized. How effective is Springsteen's use of rhyme and repetition?

POSSIBLE CONNECTIONS TO OTHER SELECTIONS

Helen Farries, "Magic of Love" (text p. 566)

Bruce Springsteen, "Devils & Dust" (text p. 568)

MARY OLIVER, *The Poet with His Face in His Hands* (p. 572)

One aspect of Oliver's poem you might point out to students is her use of enjambment to suspend the reader's expectations or to reinforce the tone of the poem. In the first stanza, the line break after "your" (line 1) delays the cause of the cry, and the break after "world" (2) holds out for a moment the grammatical possibility that the world is the subject that does the truth-telling. In stanza two, the line breaks draw our attention to "can't" (4), a word that is key to Oliver's portrait of the petulant poet.

In drawing this portrait, Oliver occasionally uses a sarcastic tone, as in "if your pretty mouth can't / hold it in" (5-6). By giving in to self-pity, the poet misses out on the exuberant "water fun" (11) of the falls as well as the thrush's apprehension of "the perfect, stone-hard beauty of everything" (18). That is, he loses both life and art by turning inward. In contrast to the mocking tone, Oliver also takes on the voice of a high lyric at points in the poem when she describes the sublime landscape of the waterfall. However, her vision of the sublime sends readers back to her title. The poet in despair, who puts his face in his hands, can't see the world this poem describes.

POSSIBLE CONNECTIONS TO OTHER SELECTIONS

Emily Dickinson, "A Bird came down the Walk —" (text p. 693)

Robert Frost, "Design" (text p. 856; question #1, following)

John Keats, "Ode to a Nightingale" (text p. 713)

CONNECTION QUESTION IN TEXT (p. 572) WITH ANSWER

1. Compare the thematic use of nature in Oliver's poem and in Robert Frost's "Design" (p. 856).

   Mary Oliver's "The Poet with His Face in His Hands" uses nature to drive home the insignificance of human strife. Oliver's subject is in emotional turmoil, and the speaker says, "You want to cry aloud for your / mistakes. But to tell the truth the world / doesn't need any more of that sound" (1–3). The speaker then encourages her subject to lose him or herself in nature, which is completely indifferent to the subject's suffering. Beneath the waterfall, one can "roar all you // want and nothing will be disturbed" (12–13). The "stone-hard beauty of everything" (18) does not cease or soften in the face of human suffering. Oliver's speaker sees the beauty and indifference of nature as a positive thing, because it puts our suffering into perspective; no matter what tragedy happens in life, the splendor of the natural world endures.

The thematic use of nature in Robert Frost's "Design" is much more ominous. The speaker describes a scene of beautiful death, a spider "On a white heal-all, holding up a moth/Like a white piece of rigid satin cloth—" (2–3). Unlike Oliver's poem, where nature is an unstoppable force of life, Frost uses this scene to describe nature as "Assorted characters of death and blight" (4) or "Like the ingredients of a witches' broth—" (6). The speaker wonders why he has been greeted with this display of nature's drive towards death, saying "What but design of darkness to appall?— / If design govern in a thing so small" (13–14). He is questioning what kind of higher power, if there is one, would create things only to watch them destroy one another. Rather than Oliver's life affirming, eternal nature, Frost's speaker sees the death and destruction that plays out between all living things.

JIM TILLEY, *The Big Questions* (p. 572)

In "The Big Questions," Tilley uses humor to illustrate his topic, following an extended simile that shows that there are big questions and then there are *big* questions—a question can be big "only in the moment" (4), like when one hikes a trail and comes face to face with a hungry grizzly bear. Here the poet takes a seemingly lighter look at a serious topic, and he reaches a truth or "answer" through the associations made in the poem.

Tilley plays with the idea of what a "big question" is. He does this largely by repetition and by looking at the idea of a "big question" through different lenses. Ask students what they think of Tilley ending with an "answer" that is, in fact, a question: When the answer to a big question is finally found, who will find it and how? "Might it not be a person like you / staring down a bear looking for lunch?" (25).

POSSIBLE CONNECTIONS TO OTHER SELECTIONS

Billy Collins, "Introduction to Poetry" (text p. 564)

Mary Oliver, "The Poet with His Face in His Hands" (text p. 572; question #1, following)

CONNECTION QUESTION IN TEXT (p. 573) WITH ANSWER

1. To what extent does Mary Oliver's poem "The Poet with His Face in His Hands" also raise the existential question of "why you are here"?

   Tilley boils down the definition of a big question to whether or not it can be answered; an answerable question is in fact "a defining moment, / but not a big question, / because no one ever figures those out" (20–22). In some cases, Tilley says you may find your "answer" instinctively or out of self-preservation. Oliver, as well, says there are bigger questions out there than the poet's personal preoccupations. Her advice is for the poet to go where the world surrounds him or her, where the thrush seems to understand its own insignificance, singing out about "the stone-hard beauty of everything" (18).

ALBERTO RÍOS, *Seniors* (p. 573)

You might begin your discussion of this poem by asking students to talk about its use of slang, particularly in the first stanza. The slang establishes the speaker's environment as well as his conversational tone. As the poem progresses, it focuses on the speaker, and the tone becomes more meditative. Although they modify his relationship to other people, the images of cavities, flat walls, and water (particularly in stanza 3) distance the speaker from the social realm, until he is left "on the desert" (32) in the last stanza.

Students might write an essay on these images. How does their evocation of sexual experience prepare us for the poem's last line? What is the speaker trying to say about sex? About life? How does the language of the final stanza compare with that of the first stanza? What might this changed diction indicate in the speaker's attitude toward himself and the world?

POSSIBLE CONNECTION TO ANOTHER SELECTION

T. S. Eliot, "The Love Song of J. Alfred Prufrock" (text p. 1006; question #1, following)

CONNECTION QUESTION IN TEXT (p. 574) WITH ANSWER

1. Think about "Seniors" as a kind of love poem, and compare the speaker's voice here with the one in T. S. Eliot's "The Love Song of J. Alfred Prufrock" (p. 1006). How are these two voices used to evoke different cultures? Of what value is love in these cultures?

   J. Alfred Prufrock's voice bespeaks an empty culture, characterized by "sawdust restaurants" and "yellow smoke" as well as by empty conversations and rituals. "Prufrock" is a poem about love that never comes to be because the speaker is too fearful to act: "Do I dare / Disturb the universe?" Ríos's speaker also describes a lost culture, particularly in his use of slang and his references to materialism in the first two stanzas. In fact, many of the images in "Seniors" are complemented by similar, though starker, images in "Prufrock." In each poem, love symbolizes the speaker's individual feelings of loss and the collective emptiness of the culture.

ALFRED, LORD TENNYSON, *Crossing the Bar* (p. 575)

Tennyson wrote "Crossing the Bar" near the end of his life, and though he went on to write other poems, he requested that this be the last poem published in any collection of his work. The speaker expresses a calm acceptance of death but is aware of its contradictions. Tennyson's use of nautical imagery conveys some of this ambiguity, the voyage standing both for entering a frightening unknown and embarking on an exciting journey. The speaker's trip takes him both away from and toward home. Ask students what it means to identify God as a "Pilot" (line 15) if the speaker has been separated from him up to this point.

The figure of the sandbar in this poem functions as a boundary line. Separating the safe waters near land and the rougher sea beyond, the bar also separates life from death or from the afterlife. It interrupts the continuous flow of the tide as the "clear call" (2) and the "evening bell" (9) interrupt the passage of time. The horizontal is bisected by a vertical axis. You might discuss with students the religious significance of these images. The Christian idea of resurrection depends on a vertical movement out of "Time and Place" (13). Call students' attention to the fact that these two words, in addition to *Pilot,* are capitalized in the last stanza.

POSSIBLE CONNECTIONS TO OTHER SELECTIONS

John Donne, "A Valediction: Forbidding Mourning" (text p. 658)

Randall Jarrell, "The Death of the Ball Turret Gunner" (text p. 591)

Dylan Thomas, "Do Not Go Gentle into That Good Night" (text p. 747; question #1, following)

CONNECTION QUESTION IN TEXT (p. 575) WITH ANSWER

1. Compare the speaker's mood in "Crossing the Bar" with that in Dylan Thomas's "Do Not Go Gentle into That Good Night" (p. 747).

Both speakers confront death bravely, but their views of what death will bring are very different. Tennyson's speaker approaches death as if it were a wise and trustworthy captain. Not only does he not fear his fate, but he looks forward to a peaceful journey. The speaker in Thomas's poem, on the other hand, wants to defy death. Rather than accepting fate gracefully as Tennyson's speaker does, Thomas's speaker urges his dying father to fight as long and as hard as he can. Thomas's tone is angry and rebellious. While Tennyson's speaker takes a filial stance toward death, acting dutifully and respectfully, the loyalty of Thomas's speaker is to his human father. He challenges the traditional view of the supernatural father figure by subverting the natural order of birth and death.

EDGAR ALLAN POE, *The Raven* (p. 575)

Edgar Allan Poe was an American poet and storyteller who aligned himself with the American Romantics. The natural world (particularly the darker aspects) and the supernatural world often figure prominently in the work of the American Romantics, as does the value of one's emotions over reason. Poe's work inspired other renowned poets and writers, particularly French poet Charles Baudelaire and many of the French Symbolists. Consider his triangular construct of the speaker, his dead love, and the bird, and ask students how Poe's poem fits into the general tenets of the American Romantics.

"The Raven" is a long narrative poem written in regular six-line stanzas. The sixth line acts as a refrain, repeating the "nothing more" and then, more famously, the "nevermore" of each stanza. To start discussion, ask students to recount the parts of the poem that they find most memorable. How do the rhythms (largely trochaic octameter) and rhymes influence their recollections? What do students find most compelling—is it the tone of the unfolding story, the effect and variations of repetitions, the central image of the raven, or something else?

POSSIBLE CONNECTIONS TO OTHER SELECTIONS

John Keats, "La Belle Dame sans Merci" (text p. 1015)

Mary Oliver, "The Poet with His Face in His Hands" (text p. 572; question #1, following)

CONNECTION QUESTION IN TEXT (p. 578) WITH ANSWER

1. Compare Poe's treatment of pain and suffering with Mary Oliver's in "The Poet with His Face in His Hands" (p. 572).

   Poe does exactly what Oliver says not to do in "The Poet with His Face in His Hands," since he does "drip with despair all afternoon" (14). Poe's raven reminds him of his personal loss, while Oliver exhorts the poet to hear the thrush singing by the falls, to take his face out of his hands for a minute.

CORNELIUS EADY, *The Supremes* (p. 578)

This savagely cynical poem describes the fatalism of schoolchildren, who are "born to be gray" (line 1)—to conform. The poem, which continues to rely on dull-toned colors to paint its picture, is all about a soul-killing conformity that causes children to point out and ridicule any differences that exist between themselves and others. A good place to begin discussion is with the "long scream" (5, 18) that exists in the back of the schoolchildren's minds. Is this a scream of protest? Of angst? Of outrage? Students are likely to have experienced or witnessed the type of divisiveness that exists between the students in this poem. Where does it come from? Where does Eady think it comes from? There are a few possible answers to this question: the parents who "shook their heads and waited" (13) for their children to conform, the sometimes mind-numbing institution of primary education, the children themselves, the undefined "they" of line 25, or something like fate. In what sense can the wigs, lipstick, and sequins of the final lines be considered "self-defense"? How do the last three lines change our understanding of the speaker, or his classmates?

Possible Connections to Other Selections

Emily Dickinson, "From all the Jails the Boys and Girls" (text p. 818)

Judy Page Heitzman, "The Schoolroom on the Second Floor of the Knitting Mill" (text p. 656; question #1, following)

Louis Simpson, "In the Suburbs" (text p. 616)

Connection Question in Text (p. 579) **with Answer**

1. Discuss the speakers' memories of school in "The Supremes" and in Judy Page Heitzman's "The Schoolroom on the Second Floor of the Knitting Mill" (p. 656).

    In Heitzman's poem, the schoolteacher, Mrs. Lawrence, is singled out for her cruelty to children. Her desire to keep children "in line" is institutionally sanctioned, but her criticism of the speaker's leadership skills is unthoughtful. There is no "Mrs. Lawrence" to blame in "The Supremes." The children are victimized as much by their own human nature as they are by any one teacher, or by elementary school more generally.

20

Writing about Poetry

Comments often overheard in introductory literature classes suggest that many students believe that they are simply incapable of understanding poetry. Thus their attempts to find meaning in poems are often hindered by their feelings of intimidation and ineptness. The Questions for Responsive Reading and Writing in Chapter 20 may prove to be particularly useful to these insecure students because they break down general poetry analysis into smaller components, which students may feel better able to manage. These questions can also aid more confident and capable students in their analysis and interpretation of poetry by offering specific places for them to begin their literary investigations.

You might also use these questions in class to teach your students how to approach writing about poetry. Have your students work individually or in small groups, exploring possible answers to these questions using assigned poems. Brief written responses to these questions might lead to longer, more detailed interpretations at a later time. Of course, not every question will relate meaningfully to every poem. To help students learn to apply a certain type of question in their analysis, you might devise an exercise in which your students decide which questions are best suited to which particular poems in a set. You might also remind them that these questions about poetry are open-ended and often require more than a one-word or one-sentence response. Ask them to provide evidence for their answers by quoting directly from the poems they have chosen to analyze. Also, it is important for students to feel comfortable using the terminology that describes particular elements of poetry; be sure to refer them to the Glossary of Literary Terms included in the anthology (text p. 1559) if they are having trouble understanding any of these terms.

Chapter 20 includes a brief sample student paper analyzing Elizabeth Bishop's poem "Manners" (text p. 585). Ask your students to read the poem and then discuss how they might approach the assignment that was given to this student writer. What specific aspects of the poem might they choose to explore? What would they do differently from the writer of the sample? You may consider assigning your class a writing task similar to the one described in this chapter, using any poem your students have studied. The sample paper, while not necessarily a blueprint for effective poetry analysis, may offer your students a useful model of strong student writing that they may try to emulate. At the same time, you might ask your students to treat the sample student paper as an unfinished draft of an essay and have them suggest revisions that would make the paper even more effective.

Web Ask students to explore contexts for Elizabeth Bishop at **bedfordstmartins.com/ meyerlit**.

21

Word Choice, Word Order, and Tone

Because poetry depends for its effects on the concentrated use of language, word choice can play a pivotal role in determining the meaning of a poem. For instance, in Martín Espada's "Latin Night at the Pawnshop" (text p. 598), the choice of the word *apparition* as the first noun in the poem echoes Ezra Pound's "In a Station of the Metro." One word sets up an allusion to a key imagist poem and thus puts Espada's poem in the context of that tradition. Still, students may remain unconvinced that word choice is all that important to a poem.

Web Ask students to explore the poetic elements in this chapter at **bedfordstmartins.com/ meyerlit**.

As an exercise to emphasize the importance of word choice, you might have students type a short poem or section of a poem on a word processor. Most word processors come with a thesaurus function that allows the user to replace a word with a synonym provided from a list. Have students replace either a couple of key words in the poem or a word in each line with the synonyms offered, and then read their new poems to the class. After a few examples, it should become clear how important word choice is to the overall effect of the poem.

You might try a similar exercise for word order with some of the selections. Having students think hypothetically about other options for a poem can help them develop an appreciation for the reasons a poem is the way it is. In general, counterfactuals help sharpen critical thinking skills.

The reasons a poem conveys a certain tone are sometimes hard to pin down and can initially prove frustrating for students. You might find it helpful to encourage students to look at not only word choice but also other features of the poem in their discussions of tone.

The pairing of Thomas Hardy's and David R. Slavitt's poems about the *Titanic* can very effectively show students the workings of diction. The popularity of the James Cameron movie *Titanic* will ensure that students know something about the event itself. A similar grouping that can prove interesting is Joanne Diaz's "On My Father's Loss of Hearing" (p. 609), Mary Oliver's "Oxygen" (p. 610), and Cathy Song's "The Youngest Daughter" (p. 611). Each of these poems is told from the perspective of someone with an ailing or aging family member. Students may have difficulty articulating how and why each speaker has a different relationship with and perspective on his or her loved one, but this exercise will help them understand how theme and tone are related.

RANDALL JARRELL, *The Death of the Ball Turret Gunner* (p. 591)

Randall Jarrell attended Vanderbilt University and so became influenced by the Agrarian literary movement, an anti-industrial movement that sought to reinstate the values of an agricultural society. Jarrell's poem probably reflects on personal experience, as he was an air force pilot from 1942 until the end of World War II. Like most of his poems, however, this one evokes universal human pain and anguish, regardless of its specific circumstances.

The textual discussion of this poem calls attention to Jarrell's intentional use of ambiguity in some of his word choices, but is the overall tone of the poem ambiguous?

How would you describe the speaker's attitude toward his subject? Have students look at Alfred, Lord Tennyson's "The Charge of the Light Brigade" (text p. 733) for another depiction of death in war. What are the word choices Tennyson makes in order to create the tone he wants? How does the tone of Tennyson's poem compare with that of Jarrell's?

The scene depicted in Jarrell's poem might almost be a synopsis of one of the major story lines in Joseph Heller's novel *Catch-22*. Compare Jarrell's word choices and the mood created by them with Heller's depiction of the gunner in Chapter 5 of *Catch-22*:

> That was where he wanted to be [atop the escape hatch, ready to parachute to safety] if he had to be there at all, instead of hung out there in front like some goddam cantilevered goldfish in some goddam cantilevered goldfish bowl while the goddam foul black tiers of flak were bursting and billowing and booming all around and above and below him in a climbing, cracking, staggered, banging, phantasmagorical, cosmological wickedness that jarred and tossed and shivered, clattered and pierced, and threatened to annihilate them all in one splinter of a second in one vast flash of fire. (New York: Dell, 1974; print; 50)

POSSIBLE CONNECTIONS TO OTHER SELECTIONS

Wilfred Owen, "Dulce et Decorum Est" (text p. 633)

Alfred, Lord Tennyson, "The Charge of the Light Brigade" (text p. 733)

COLETTE INEZ, *Back When All Was Continuous Chuckles* (p. 594)

Much of the surprise in this poem comes from the juxtaposition of humor and death. Some words fall obviously on one side or the other: "cemetery" (line 6), "hilarious" (7), "ghost" (8), "Silly billies" (12). What are the connotations of more ambiguous words, such as "helpless" (1) or "grinding" (5)? Do they foreshadow the pretending in the last stanza?

You might ask students about the forms jokes take. What kind of expectations do they set up, and do the jokes in this poem meet those expectations? The disconnect between joke and punch line, which produces an "'I don't get it'" (10), is a figure for the way the child's expectations of life are overturned. The author of the poem was an orphan herself, living first in an orphanage in Belgium and then with several foster families in the United States. The jokes she writes into this narrative work as a line of defense against painful realities, both personal (Doris's mother's cancer) and public (the war).

POSSIBLE CONNECTION TO ANOTHER SELECTION

Gwendolyn Brooks, "We Real Cool" (text p. 614; question #1, following)

CONNECTION QUESTION IN TEXT (p. 595) WITH ANSWER

1. Discuss the tone of this poem and that of Gwendolyn Brooks's "We Real Cool" (p. 614).

   Both Inez and Brooks use light tones that conflict with their grave subject matter. Inez's tone is playful as it attempts to re-create the joking of the two young girls. Brooks's tone is as cool as her characters. Her reticence mimics their fatalistic pose. For both poets, the tone is a barrier between the self and the trauma at the center of the poem. At the same time, their use of the colloquial brings death down from grand abstraction and places it squarely among the elements of everyday life.

MARILYN NELSON, *How I Discovered Poetry* (p. 595)

In "How I Discovered Poetry," the speaker discovers the power of words, which can be both beautiful and destructive. She experiences poetry's sensual and spiritual beauties, two sides of the pleasure of poetry that come together in the phrase "soul-kissing" (line 1). She and her teacher are engaged with high literary culture, as is suggested by the paraphrase of Wordsworth in "Mrs. Purdy and I wandered lonely as clouds" (4). However, Mrs. Purdy also introduces the dialect poem filled with degrading stereotypes for the speaker to read. Her smile, which becomes "harder and harder" (10), starts to feel threatening to the young speaker as the teacher insists that she read. Through this humiliating moment of reading, Nelson links poetic sensitivity, which separates the speaker from her classmates, with the greater separation of race between her and the all-white class.

POSSIBLE CONNECTIONS TO OTHER SELECTIONS

Judy Page Heitzman, "The Schoolroom on the Second Floor of the Knitting Mill" (text p. 656)

Patricia Smith, "What It's Like to Be a Black Girl (for Those of You Who Aren't)" (text p. 634)

Ronald Wallace, "Miss Goff" (text p. 826; question #1, following)

CONNECTION QUESTION IN TEXT (p. 595) WITH ANSWER

1. How does Nelson's description of discovering poetry compare with Ronald Wallace's in "Miss Goff" (p. 826)?

   Both Nelson and Wallace choose the sonnet form in these poems. Its compression helps to make the discovery of poetry into a dramatic moment of self-discovery. Both also suggest that poetry is a lonely occupation — either enjoyed in solitude or in incongruous pairs. Both are allusive, as Nelson mentions a Wordsworth poem and Wallace refers to Dickinson's definition of poetry as whatever makes you feel as if "the top of [your] head were taken off." However, Nelson's poem has a political dimension that is not present in Wallace's.

KATHARYN HOWD MACHAN, *Hazel Tells LaVerne* (p. 596)

You might begin discussing this poem by talking about names and how they, too, have connotative value. Would our expectations be the same if the poem were titled "Sybil Speaks with Jacqueline"? By and large this poem does a good job at getting across its meaning through denotative language. But the fact that Hazel does use language almost exclusively in denotative terms is in itself a sign of her personality. As in a dramatic monologue by Robert Browning, Hazel tells more about herself, her social class, and her impenetrably matter-of-fact outlook on life than she does about her encounter with the frog. We as readers then fill in the gaps of the speaker's perceptions as well as piece together her outlook and attitude.

You might ask students to respond to Hazel's personality. She is likable; her matter-of-factness cuts through any of the fairy tales the world might try to sell her, and she's funny. Students can probably provide examples of characters from TV shows who are like Hazel and whose humor derives from their plainspoken concreteness. We all admire the survivor who cannot be duped.

POSSIBLE CONNECTION TO ANOTHER SELECTION

Robert Browning, "My Last Duchess" (text p. 684; question #1, following)

1. Although Robert Browning's "My Last Duchess" (p. 684) is a more complex poem than Machan's, both use dramatic monologues to reveal character. How are the strategies in each poem similar?

   The speakers of each poem reveal something about themselves as they try to narrate a story. The speaker of this poem repeats the line "me a princess," indicating that her bravado is just a front for her dreams. The speaker of Browning's poem uses more sophisticated language, and he believes that he is in control of the narrative situation, but the more he talks the more he reveals about his true desires and motives. His asides are what give him away; as he pauses to consider how he should express something, he gives us the opportunity to analyze not only the content of his speech but his expression of it as well.

MARTÍN ESPADA, *Latin Night at the Pawnshop* (p. 598)

This imagist poem describes what the speaker sees in the window of a pawnshop. In the instruments suspended there, he sees the apparition of a salsa band. He compares the price tags on the instruments to a toe tag on a dead man.

There is nothing apparently "difficult" about this poem, so students may be quick to dismiss it, feeling that they "get the point" instantly. The challenge for discussion then becomes to fill in the considerable space around the poem. The liveliness of a salsa band coupled with the fact that the poem takes place on Christmas, a day of celebration, contribute to the poem's blunt emotional overtones. What does the speaker's presence at a pawnshop on Christmas suggest? The speaker is implicitly mourning the passage of something vital. Unlike the Christmas ghosts of a character students are familiar with, Dickens's Scrooge, this apparition does not seem to provide any comfort or hope for the future. The apparition is the *absence* of the band, with its instruments apparently sold cheaply. As a way of pointing out what exactly has been lost, emphasize all the economic allusions in the poem (pawnshop, Liberty Loan, golden, silver, price tags). Does the poem seek to make a broad point about class and culture in contemporary America? Consider the title as a follow-up to this question. Students may think of other examples of the various ways in which immigrants in America must "sell out" their culture for more fundamental survival needs (i.e., money).

POSSIBLE CONNECTION TO ANOTHER SELECTION

Louis Simpson, "In the Suburbs" (text p. 616)

PAUL LAURENCE DUNBAR, *To a Captious Critic* (p. 599)

The vocabulary of this poem may pose a challenge for your students, so remind them to look up words they don't know, like "captious," "deplores" (line 1), and "abdicate" (4). Otherwise, they will miss Dunbar's witty insult to his critic. Depending on their preconceived ideas about poetry, students may be surprised to find it serving such a function. If they are surprised, ask them if "To a Captious Critic" reminds them of something else they've seen or heard, maybe on TV or the Internet. How would a twenty-first-century critic be likely to respond?

In opening up this small poem, it might help your students to know that Dunbar, one of the first African American poets to achieve wider recognition, wrote both in standard English poetic language and in black folk dialect. Why does he choose the former in writing this response? What does that choice say about the critic? Some of the formality in the poem, such as the "dear" in the first line, is ironic, but does it also give Dunbar greater authority in answering his detractor?

POSSIBLE CONNECTIONS TO OTHER SELECTIONS

Anne Bradstreet, "The Author to Her Book" (text p. 647)

David McCord, "Epitaph on a Waiter" (text p. 751)

ROBERT HERRICK, *To the Virgins, to Make Much of Time* (p. 599)

Robert Herrick, son of a well-to-do London goldsmith, rather halfheartedly became an Anglican clergyman assigned to Dean Prior in Devonshire, in the west of England. He wrote poems secretly, inventing for many of them alluring, exotic, phantom mistresses. After losing his position when the Puritans rose to power, Herrick published his only book, containing some 1,200 poems, in 1648.

This is one of the better-known poems of the *carpe diem* (seize the day) tradition. Here Herrick is advising young women in a tone of straightforward urging to make the most of their opportunities for pleasure while they are in the prime of youth and beauty. These "virgins," Herrick implies, are like the sun at its zenith or a flower in full bloom; they will soon begin to decline and may never have the same opportunities for marriage again. The word *virgins,* rather than *women,* accommodates the advice in the last stanza to "go marry" and carries with it as well the connotation of sought-for sexual fulfillment. Some of your students might point out how a young woman's situation is much more complex today than it apparently was in Herrick's time, as "seizing the day" can and often does mean pursuing opportunities for career over those for marriage.

One possible way to enter a discussion of the poem is to consider the arrangement of the argument. The speaker has a definite intent: to communicate bits of wisdom to the "virgins" of the title. What effect does the order of his points of argument have on the way the poem reads? What would happen if we were to rearrange the first three stanzas: Would the message of the poem remain exactly the same?

ANDREW MARVELL, *To His Coy Mistress* (p. 601)

After graduating from Cambridge University in 1639, Andrew Marvell left England to travel in Europe. Almost nothing is known of his life from this time until he became the tutor of the daughter of a powerful Yorkshire nobleman in 1650. Most of his poems seem to have been written during the next seven years. He served for a short time as John Milton's assistant when Milton was Latin secretary for the Commonwealth, and he represented Hull, his hometown, in Parliament from 1659 until he died.

This seduction poem is structured with a flawless logic. Marvell's speaker begins with a hypothetical conjecture, "Had we but world enough, and time," which he then disproves with hyperbole, promising his "mistress" that he would devote "an age at least" (line 17) to praising her every part. Time is, of course, far more limited, and the poem's second section makes clear time's ravages on beauty. The third section expounds the *carpe diem* theme: if time is limited, then seize the day and triumph over life's difficulties with love.

Web Ask students to explore contexts for Andrew Marvell and this poem — as well as a sample close reading — at **bedfordstmartins.com/ meyerlit**.

From his initial tone of teasing hyperbole, the poet modulates to a much more somber tone, employing the metaphysically startling imagery of the grave to underscore human mortality. Lines 31–32 are an example of understatement, calculated to make the listener react and acknowledge this world as the time and place for embracing.

Some classes may need help in recognizing that the verbs in the first part of the poem are in the subjunctive mood, while those in the last are often in the imperative. At any rate, students should easily recognize that the last section contains verbs that all imply a physical vigor that would seize time, mold it to the lovers' uses, and thus "make [time] run" (46) according to the clock of their own desires.

The poem seems far more than a simple celebration of the flesh. It confronts human mortality and suggests a psychological stance that would seize life (and face death) so that fulfilling one's time would be a strategy in confronting time's passing.

As a writing topic you might ask students to explain the radical and somewhat abrupt change in tone between the opening twenty lines and the rest of the poem. Marvell offers more than one reason for his speaker to temper his initial levity.

TIP FROM THE FIELD

I use point-of-view writing assignments that ask students to assume a persona in a poem or story and respond to the other characters or situations in the selection accordingly. For example, I have students read Andrew Marvell's "To His Coy Mistress" and then write an essay from the point of view of the wooer or the wooee.

— SANDRA ADICKES, *Winona State University*

POSSIBLE CONNECTION TO ANOTHER SELECTION

John Keats, "Ode on a Grecian Urn" (text p. 612)

ANN LAUINGER, *Marvell Noir* (p. 603)

In this poem, Lauinger transports Marvell's *carpe diem* into the crime-filled world of film noir. Instead of feeling rushed by impending death, the speaker in "Marvell Noir" feels the pressure of the police who will come to take away his "Sweetheart" (line 1). By recounting the woman's story in broad outline, Lauinger calls on some of the typical aspects of the crime movie, especially the character of the femme fatale. As the female poet takes on a male voice, she can more effectively satirize Marvell's original plea to his lover. At the same time, she critiques how women are portrayed in noir movies as both tragic "angel face[s]" (19) and dangerous sexual predators. You might have your class discuss where their sympathies lie after they've read the poem. The woman is clearly a perpetrator, but is the speaker innocent? What does the language he uses suggest about him?

POSSIBLE CONNECTION TO ANOTHER SELECTION

Andrew Marvell, "To His Coy Mistress" (text p. 601; question #1, following)

CONNECTION QUESTION IN TEXT (p. 604) WITH ANSWER

1. Compare the speaker's voice in this poem with that of the speaker in "To His Coy Mistress" (p. 601). What significant similarities and differences do you find?

    Though some of Marvell's language is unfamiliar to modern readers, the voice in his poem is not rarefied. While his mistress remains standoffish, the speaker's plea has to be direct and immediate. Even when he talks about abstract concepts like eternity, he invents metaphors to give them a physical presence, as he does in the last lines: "Thus, though we cannot make our sun / Stand still, yet we will make him run" (lines 45–46). Lauinger's parody of the poem attempts to retain this down-to-earth voice, but translate it into the modern idiom of film noir. The voice in her poem is worldly, slangy, and straightforward. The sentences are short and declarative, largely avoiding figurative language. As in "To His Coy Mistress" they suggest a speaker who sees beyond romanticized ideas about love.

SHARON OLDS, *Last Night* (p. 604)

Olds's aubade is more internal than any of the other poems in this group. She doesn't directly address the "you" of the poem until almost halfway through (line 12), and even then she focuses mainly on the experience of the speaker. Rather than trying to seduce, as Marvell does, Olds explores the meaning of sex. The image of the chrysalis (7) and the phrase "without language" (8) provide keys to understanding the tone of this poem. Feelings during sex are indescribable, enclosing the speaker inside of her own senses; they exist outside of regular human interaction.

While Herrick urges young people to marry while they are vital and full of life, Olds describes sex in terms of death; it is not tender, but "like killing, death-grip / holding to life, genitals / like violent hands clasped tight" (13–15). The brutality of this section helps readers to understand "I am almost afraid" in the first line. You may wish to mention to your students the tradition that equates orgasm with a kind of death. The French, in particular, use the euphemism *le petit mort*, suggesting that a lover is emptied or negated in some way at climax. This view of sex sets the stage for the end of Olds's poem, in which the couple reemerges "clasped, fragrant, buoyant" (28). The awakening the next morning becomes a resurrection. Though the middle section of the poem uses the language of death, Olds ends up affirming the resilience of life.

Since Olds presents a female perspective on the love poem, you might have students look at "Last Night" in conjunction with Marvell's "To His Coy Mistress" (text p. 601). Does the speaker's relation to her partner, who "secured" (26) and kept her "sealed" (24), bear any resemblance to the relationship Marvell implies?

POSSIBLE CONNECTIONS TO OTHER SELECTIONS

Robert Herrick, "To the Virgins, to Make Much of Time" (text p. 599; question #1, following)

Andrew Marvell, "To His Coy Mistress" (text p. 601; questions #1 and #2, following)

CONNECTIONS QUESTIONS IN TEXT (p. 605) WITH ANSWERS

1. How does the speaker's description of intimacy compare with Herrick's and Marvell's?

    In their *carpe diem* poems, both Herrick and Marvell glorify youth as the natural time for intimate relationships. Herrick characterizes youth as warm and sunny while the prospects for old age are dreary. Marvell, too, understands love in terms of the passing day and argues the urgency of loving while the day is, or while the lovers are, young. Marvell suggests that death is naturally solitary, that a couple cannot exist beyond the grave. Therefore, the young should rush to embrace life rather than wait patiently while death approaches. Olds, on the other hand, does not see sex and death as mutually exclusive. While Herrick and Marvell use the sun to symbolize youthful intimacy, the action of Olds's poem takes place at night and is only reflected upon in the light of morning. Intimacy is warm for Herrick, but unpleasantly hot for Olds, who imagines herself and her partner as "dragonflies / in the sun" (lines 2–3). In "Last Night," *eros* is mixed up with *thanatos*, the death drive. Rather than holding death at bay, intimacy allows Olds's speaker to die and be reborn.

2. Compare the speaker's voice in Olds's poem with the voice you imagine for the coy mistress in Marvell's poem (p. 601).

    Given Marvell's counterarguments in "To His Coy Mistress," we expect that the mistress has appealed to patience and reason in rebuffing the speaker. Her function in this relationship is to maintain propriety. The speaker tries to convince her to give up caution and allow herself to be ruled by passion. The speaker in Olds's poem is also concerned with control over the situation, but in this case she has already released it. She loses herself in the sexual act, and the next day she has to consider its meaning. Both the coy mistress and the speaker of Olds's poem have anxieties about intimacy that contrast with the purely positive views put forward by Marvell's speaker.

THOMAS HARDY, *The Convergence of the Twain* (p. 606)

Between the ages of fifteen and twenty-one, Thomas Hardy was apprenticed to an architect in his native Dorchester, an area in southwest England that he was to transform into the "Wessex" of his novels. He went to London in 1862 to practice as an architect and pursue a growing interest in writing. Though he enjoyed a successful career as a novelist, Hardy stopped writing fiction after publishing *Jude the Obscure* in 1895, concentrating instead on the poetry that ranks him among the major English poets.

This poem ushers in an event that some consider to be the beginning of the modern era: the sinking of the *Titanic*. The final two stanzas support this idea. What is the true significance of the event, according to the speaker? What are the implications of a God who is described as both "The Immanent Will that stirs and urges everything" (line 18) and "the Spinner of the Years" (31)? On a superficial level, the "twain" of the title signifies the ship and the iceberg; what are some of the word's connotative meanings?

The *Titanic* as described in this poem is "gaily great" (20) in its luxurious opulence, but Hardy also stresses the ship's "vaingloriousness" (15), planned by the "Pride of Life" (3). It is as though in this dramatic gesture of invention and design, humanity became the tragic overreacher. In a writing assignment, you might ask the class to compare the tones of the speakers in this poem and in Percy Bysshe Shelley's "Ozymandias" (text p. 1022).

The "marriage" between ship and iceberg is suggested through the use of several words and phrases, such as "sinister mate" (19), "intimate welding" (27) — as in "wedding" — and "consummation" in the final line.

Hardy assigns the disaster to Fate, or as he allegorizes it, the "Immanent Will" (18) that directs all things and the "Spinner of the Years" (31), who decides when time has run out.

POSSIBLE CONNECTIONS TO OTHER SELECTIONS

Stephen Crane, "A Man Said to the Universe" (text p. 673)

David R. Slavitt, "Titanic" (text p. 608)

DAVID R. SLAVITT, *Titanic* (p. 608)

Although Slavitt's poem acknowledges the power of fate, it focuses on human attitudes rather than cosmic forces. The first stanza, for example, calls attention to our gullibility; its weary yet affectionate tone originates in the "this is how we are" shrug of the two *who* clauses. The speaker ponders death, deciding that because "we all go down" (line 4), it would be better to do so with some company and some notice from the rest of the world. But the speaker's gentle urging that it wouldn't be "so bad, after all" (11) to go "first-class" (14) includes some simple, unambiguous descriptions of what such a mass loss of life would actually be like: "The cold water" (11–12), which would be "anesthetic and very quick" (12); the "cries on all sides" (13). Death always wins, "we all go down, mostly / alone" (4–5), so wouldn't it be fine to die "with crowds of people, friends, servants, / well fed, with music" (5–6)?

You might ask students to compare in a short paper the attitudes toward fate in "Titanic" and Hardy's "The Convergence of the Twain" (text p. 820) and how each poem's diction and tone contribute to the communication of these attitudes.

POSSIBLE CONNECTION TO ANOTHER SELECTION

Thomas Hardy, "The Convergence of the Twain" (text p. 606; questions #1 and #3, following)

1. How does "Titanic" differ in its attitude toward opulence from "The Convergence of the Twain" (p. 606)?

   In Hardy's poem the opulence of the passengers aboard the *Titanic* is emblematic of their lack of humility, and it seems partially responsible for the crash. Slavitt's poem, at least on the surface, celebrates the style with which the same passengers exited the world, arguing that, as long as we have to die, we might as well be having fun while we do it.

3. Compare the speakers' tones in "Titanic" and "The Convergence of the Twain."

   Hardy's poem is serious, formal in its use of language, form, and rhyme. "Titanic" is much more colloquial, less brooding in its tone and its language. Both poems could be described as philosophical, but Slavitt's brand of philosophy is more homespun and optimistic.

JOANNE DIAZ, *On My Father's Loss of Hearing* (p. 609)

The epigram Diaz chooses for this poem underscores the benefit she sees to her father's hearing loss. Rather than focusing on the heightening of other senses that we sometimes associate with deafness or blindness, she believes his blessing is in the reduction of sensory information. Her question, "What else / is there but loss?" (lines 7–8), sounds despairing, but by the end of the poem, she suggests that this loss is merciful. Her father is "Abled differently" (1) in an emotional sense; he becomes less susceptible to the exhausting demands of his children and the surface patter of "sarcastic jokes, the snarky dialogue / of British films" (9–10). Hearing loss also disconnects him from the natural world, as he can't hear the "crack of thawing ice" (16) or "the scrape of his / dull rake in spring" (17–18). It creates a distance between him and the world that allows him to free his desires, "released like saffron pistils in the wind" (20), and to free his love, which "hurts much less" (28) when its demands are less immediate.

Though the poem praises the loss of senses, Diaz's careful description of the impressions her father no longer receives seems to celebrate them as well. You might have your students discuss in what ways this poem contradicts itself. Would the poet be content to lose her hearing? How does she use imagery as a way of imagining her father's experience?

POSSIBLE CONNECTIONS TO OTHER SELECTIONS

John Milton "When I Consider How My Light Is Spent" (text p. 1019; question #1, following)
William Carlos Williams, "To Waken an Old Lady" (text p. 655)

CONNECTION QUESTION IN TEXT (p. 610) WITH ANSWER

1. Compare Diaz's treatment of the father's deafness with John Milton's treatment of his own blindness in "When I consider how my light is spent" (p.1019).

   These poems approach the loss of a major sense in very different ways, beginning with perspective. In Diaz's poem, a father's deafness is described by his child in the context of how his family life is impacted. The speaker describes the many sounds her father cannot hear: "He's lost the humor of / sarcastic jokes, the snarky dialogue / of British films eludes him" (8–10), as well as sounds he himself causes, like "the scrape of his / dull rake in spring" (17–18). The father's deafness is not entirely negative, however; because of it, "No noisome cruelty, no baffled rage, / no aging children sullen in their lack" can affect him (26–27). Though bereft of hearing, the father has gained a layer of protection from the verbal violence perpetrated by others.

   In "When I consider how my light is spent," John Milton describes the experience of blindness as being given a resource from God that is now "Lodged with me useless" (4). Milton is writing from his own experience and in a first person point of view, unlike Diaz. Additionally, his religious themes are very different from Diaz's focus on the physical world and modern life. Milton's speaker is concerned not with his own inability to see, but with how his blindness may hamper his ability to properly do God's work on earth. He questions, "Doth God exact day-labor, light denied?" (7). As in Diaz's poem, the speaker does not think of his loss only as a disability, but instead as an altered state of living. He concludes that while others must take action to serve God, "They also serve who only stand and wait" (14).

MARY OLIVER, *Oxygen* (p. 610)

Oliver's poem points out that air, the most basic necessity for life, is also entirely invisible to us. Because we can't see air, other senses—particularly the sense of hearing—take precedence in this poem. Oliver plays on the contradiction between the sound of breath and the silence as air settles into "quietude" (line 22). This contrast also arises in connection with the labored but "beautiful sound" (13) of the partner's breathing and the thought of its eventual end. Oliver's description of the fire's "singing, deep-red / roses" (20–21) completes her speaker's meditation on the sound of air infusing energy and life into matter, as she imagines that the crackling noise of the fire becomes an artful song.

"Oxygen" is, in one sense, a prayer to breath. The speaker's posture as she "[kneels] / before the fire" (5–6) recalls a physical gesture of supplication. The prayer is also directed to her partner in the upstairs room. At the end of the poem, the combination of flame and roses, both potent religious symbols, gives the fire an almost iconic status.

POSSIBLE CONNECTION TO ANOTHER SELECTION

Alice Jones, "The Larynx" (text p. 615)

CATHY SONG, *The Youngest Daughter* (p. 611)

This poem describes the experience of a grown woman who has stayed at home to take care of her aging mother. The speaker is bound by duty to stay in the family home until her mother dies. The long-standing nature of her situation is presented early on in images: "The sky has been dark / for many years" (lines 1–2). The escape planned at the end of the poem is symbolized by the thousand paper cranes in the window, flying up in a sudden breeze. The speaker suggests ambivalence about her mother through the "sour taste" in her mouth in line 26 and the "almost tender" (30) way the speaker soaps the blue bruises of her mother's body. The toast to the mother's health following an acknowledgment that the speaker is not to be trusted demonstrates the ambivalence further: once the mother dies, the youngest daughter can leave home; the sour taste and tenderness for her circumstances, the familiar silence and the migraines, will all change for both better and worse.

Asking students to analyze their own ambivalence about their parents in journal entries could help them establish a connection with Song's narrative. Spend a little time before the writing period suggesting circumstances that could provide context for their writing. Their departures for college may provide illustration of their changing relationships with their parents.

POSSIBLE CONNECTION TO ANOTHER SELECTION

Lisa Parker, "Snapping Beans" (text p. 546)

JOHN KEATS, *Ode on a Grecian Urn* (p. 612)

The speaker's attitude toward this object of beauty is a rapt expression of awe at its evocative and truth-bearing power and presence. Life portrayed on the urn is forever in suspended animation: no one gets old; the "wild ecstasy" goes undiminished; the love, never consummated, is yet never consumed and wearied of. Keats seems to admire this portrait of the sensuous ideal, which exists unmarred by mortality or the vagrancy of human passion.

The significant question about this ode beyond the meaning of the closing two lines and whether the speaker or the urn pronounces all or a part of them appears to rest with "Cold Pastoral!" (line 45) and the ambivalence these words imply. Earlier, in stanza 3, Keats had admired the love "for ever warm and still to be enjoyed" (26) that was portrayed on the urn. Has the temperature of the urn changed by stanza 5? Has the speaker discovered, in essence, that even though the urn portrays a sensuous ideal of courtship and pursuit, it is still merely a cold form that, because it is deathless, can never feel the warmth of human life?

Still one of the best studies on this ode is the essay bearing the same title as the ode by Earl R. Wasserman in *The Finer Tone: Keats's Major Poems* (Baltimore: Johns Hopkins UP, 1953, 1967; print; 11–63.). For the record, Wasserman argues that the closing lines are spoken by the poet to the reader; as Wasserman explains, the ode is *on* a Grecian urn, not *to* the urn. Hence "it is Keats who must make the commentary on the drama" (59).

POSSIBLE CONNECTIONS TO OTHER SELECTIONS

Emily Dickinson, "Success is counted sweetest" (text p. 803)

John Keats, "To Autumn" (text p. 637; question #2, following)

Andrew Marvell, "To His Coy Mistress" (text p. 601; question #1, following)

CONNECTIONS QUESTIONS IN TEXT (p. 614) WITH ANSWERS

1. Write an essay comparing the view of time in this ode with that in Marvell's "To His Coy Mistress" (p. 601). Pay particular attention to the connotative language in each poem.

    In Keats's ode, time wastes human beings but does not affect art. Art provides hope, friendliness, and beauty to human beings, making their misery more understandable in its "truth." In Marvell's poem, which dwells much more on the physicality of human experience, the speaker urges his listener to "make [the sun] run" (line 46), because time will destroy her anyway. The difference in the poems' treatments of time results from their different subjects. Whereas Keats's ode discusses art versus human existence, Marvell's work claims that human existence is all we have.

2. Compare the tone and attitude toward life in this ode with those in John Keats's "To Autumn" (p. 637).

    In "To Autumn" Keats celebrates a moment at the end of fall, asking us to appreciate the passage of time in his timeless work of art. In a sense the Grecian urn, a celebration of timeless beauty in art, competes with the ephemeral season of autumn. The poems are perfectly juxtaposed; one celebrates finitude, the other immortality. "To Autumn" appeals directly to the senses, whereas in "Ode on a Grecian Urn" the urn stands between the speaker and his audience, and between the audience and the ephemeral experience frozen forever on the urn. "Ode on a Grecian Urn" creates a sense of esthetic distance and self-consciously questions the meaning and value of art in a way that "To Autumn" does not.

GWENDOLYN BROOKS, *We Real Cool* (p. 614)

Gwendolyn Brooks, who grew up in Chicago and who won the Pulitzer Prize in 1950, was a deeply respected and influential African American poet.

In this poem, Brooks sets forth a tableau in a montage of street language. The poetic conventions she uses include alliteration, assonance, and internal rhyme. Students may be so taken with the sounds of the poem that they will be surprised that it has a decidedly somber focal point. How does the rest of the poem prepare us for the final line? Is there a "message" implicit in the poem? If so, how is the message affected by the poem's spare yet stunning language?

The repeated "we" sounds the menacing note of the communal pack, its members secure perhaps only when they are together. The truncated syntax reflects both a lack of and a disdain for education, yet the poem celebrates the music of its vernacular, a quality that would be mostly lost were the pronouns to appear at the beginnings of lines.

Brooks's attitude toward this chorus that finds strength in numbers is a measured anger against its self-destructiveness. The absence of "we" in the final line is a silent prophecy of their future, moving us toward an understanding of the poem's theme: death (burial/shovel) at an early age and the corruption of a golden opportunity to spend youth more wisely. The "Golden Shovel" also bespeaks an ironic promise that the events of the last line sadly belie.

POSSIBLE CONNECTION TO ANOTHER SELECTION

Langston Hughes, "Jazzonia" (text p. 939)

JOAN MURRAY, *We Old Dudes* (p. 615)

Murray's parody uses the techniques of Brooks's poem, but to comical effect. Her characters are funny because they are based on conventional notions of old men. They have the proper accessories (white shoes and dentures), hang out in the right places (the mall and Palm Beach), and enjoy the standard hobbies (playing golf and voting Republican). One thing you might have your class discuss is whether Murray maintains her humorous tone throughout, or whether the poem takes a turn toward the end. Does she make the men so ridiculous that we don't care about their death, or does their death remind us that there are individuals behind the stereotype?

POSSIBLE CONNECTION TO ANOTHER SELECTION

Gwendolyn Brooks, "We Real Cool" (text p. 614; question #1, following)

CONNECTION QUESTION IN TEXT (p. 615) **WITH ANSWER**

1. Compare the themes of "We Old Dudes" and Brooks's "We Real Cool" (p. 614). How do the two poems speak to each other?

   Brooks's poem comments on both the hopelessness of the young men and the society that puts them in that position. Though she doesn't mention it outright, readers know that part of the reason these men live such freewheeling yet dangerous lives is the institutionalized racism that closes many possibilities for them. Murray's portrait of old men who "vote red," then, enters a conversation with Brooks's poem about politics and privilege. Both groups of men are close to death, but Murray's "old dudes" have lived long lives and have achieved a certain degree of stereotypical middle-class success. Their superficial activities are the occupations of people who have lived full lives and retired. The men in Brooks's poem, on the other hand, participate in similarly superficial activities, but because they are so young, their idleness takes on a sense of foreboding, and their deaths are tragically premature.

ALICE JONES, *The Larynx* (p. 615)

The long breathy sentence of this poem focuses attention on the reader's own larynx when the poem is read aloud. Having a student read the poem to the class could help students see the function the long sentence structure serves. The complex mechanisms involved in creating a single tone are described in both scientific terms and poetic phrases. The scientific language, like "transparent sacs knit / with small vessels into a mesh" (lines 7–8), progresses into the more poetic phrases of the final third of the poem: "they flutter, / bend like birds' wings finding / just the right angle to stay / airborne" (23–26).

Ask students how their understanding of the poem would be different if Jones had left out the explicit mention of song. The explication of how the voice works comes to a clear culmination; without it, students might have got lost in reading the poem. Asking which lines provide hints that the poem is leading toward song could help direct discussion.

POSSIBLE CONNECTIONS TO OTHER SELECTIONS

Helen Chasin, "The Word *Plum*" (text p. 712)

Alice Jones, "The Foot" (text p. 727; question #1, following)

CONNECTION QUESTION IN TEXT (p. 616) WITH ANSWER

1. Compare the diction and the ending in "The Larynx" with those of "The Foot" (p. 727), another poem by Jones.

    Jones takes advantage of rich anatomical vocabulary in both poems. "The Larynx" uses phrases such as "epiglottic flap" (line 1) and "bronchial / fork" (3–4) to introduce an instructive tone before departing for more figurative language. "The Foot" makes a litany of "calcaneus, talus, cuboid, / navicular, cuneiforms, metatarsals, / phalanges" (3–5) to introduce the oblique evolution that produced this miraculous support. While "The Larynx" examines the process by which the larynx produces sounds, "The Foot" takes a journey of discovery through the anatomy of the foot to arrive at "the distal nail" (22), the reminder of our cave-dwelling ancestors and their claws.

LOUIS SIMPSON, *In the Suburbs* (p. 616)

Students may resist this spare poem's desolate presentation of the fate of the American suburbanite. The suburban phenomenon began a dozen years before Simpson published his poem, but the poem is as relevant as ever because Americans continue to move to the suburbs. At least some of your students are likely to be from suburban households. A discussion of the American Dream may be a productive place to begin, perhaps even before students have read the poem. It might also be useful to have them define "middle class," in terms of both yearly income and lifestyle choices. Once you have established (and perhaps complicated) their sense of the middle class in America, you can work your way into the poem: Where does the speaker of this poem get off equating a middle-class existence with a "waste" (line 2) of life? Does "middle-class" (3) necessarily mean suburban or vice versa? Is the situation as fatalistic as the poet suggests it is? (Half of the poem's six lines contain the phrase "were born to" [lines 2, 3, 5], and the first line is "There's no way out.")

This apparently simple poem is complicated considerably by the final two lines. The poet connects a suburban lifestyle with one of religious devotion. Because of the negative diction ("no way out" in line 1, "waste" in line 2, for example), the comparison invites a discussion not only of the worst aspects of middle-class existence but of religion, too. But what alternatives are there? Consider, too, the positive aspects of suburbia and religion. What connotations does the poem's last word, "singing," carry? At the end of the discussion you might point out how powerful word choice can be for generating ideas in a simple, spare poem like this one.

Comparisons of this poem to John Ciardi's "Suburban" (text p. 965) are likely to yield observations of a stark difference in tone. Ciardi's poem is funny; Simpson's is quite serious. Yet do the poems share a similar attitude about what is important in life? Does the speaker of "Suburban" lead a typical middle-class life? Does the speaker in "In the Suburbs"? How do the differences in speaker and point of view affect the reader's reception of each poem?

John Ciardi, "Suburban" (text p. 965; question #1, following)

Florence Cassen Mayers, "All-American Sestina" (text p. 750)

CONNECTION QUESTION IN TEXT (p. 617) WITH ANSWER

1. Write an essay on suburban life based on this poem and John Ciardi's "Suburban" (p. 965).

   Based on the speakers' attitudes in these two poems, the suburbs are, ostensibly, devoid of life, or repressed. Mrs. Friar, the neighbor in Ciardi's poem, fails, out of an overdeveloped sense of propriety, to value the "organic gold" (line 11) of the dog's "repulsive object" (5). The speaker in Simpson's poem regards suburban, middle-class life as a "waste [of] life" (2). Yet each poem concludes on a hopeful note, stressing the life that is beneath an otherwise sterile-seeming appearance: Simpson's poem concludes with the hopeful last word, "singing" (6), and Ciardi's hints at the "resurrection" (20) into plant life of even the foul "repulsive object."

GARRISON KEILLOR, *The Anthem* (p. 617)

Garrison Keillor, writer and host of the popular radio show "A Prairie Home Companion," wrote a series of amusing poems for the *Atlantic*, in which he imagined the voices of different American poets penning "The Star Spangled Banner." This version of the U.S. national anthem, written in the voice of Robert Frost, is full of gentle humor, riffing on lines from Frost's well-known poem "Stopping by Woods on a Snowy Evening" (text p. 853). In it, the speaker replaces the woods with the flag and substitutes battleground imagery for the idyllic setting in "Stopping by Woods...." This verse is colloquial, emphasized by the words he chooses for his end rhymes and in the vocabulary of his last stanza. For example, a funny, conversational interjection like "hip hooray" (line 17) or the insertion of the odder diction of "derrière" (9) helps cultivate the humor and rhymes of the poem.

When discussing "The Anthem," ask students what lines or images they remember of "The Star Spangled Banner," and consider how Keillor's verses allude to the original. Ask students to look at "Stopping by Woods on a Snowy Evening" and note how Keillor mimics Frost's end rhymes.

POSSIBLE CONNECTIONS TO OTHER SELECTIONS

E. E. Cummings, "next to of course god america i" (text p. 673)

Robert Frost, "Stopping by Woods on a Snowy Evening" (text p. 853)

A NOTE ON READING TRANSLATIONS

SAPPHO, *Hymn to Aphrodite* with three translations by HENRY T. WHARTON, THOMAS WENTWORTH HIGGINSON, and MARY BARNARD (pp. 619–621)

In this appeal to Aphrodite, Sappho asks that the lover who has spurned her be afflicted with yearning and filled with desire for Sappho. All but one of these versions of this poem, Sappho's most famous, try to conform to the original's stanzaic form — a form that has come to be known as the sapphic. A sapphic is three eleven-syllable lines followed by one five-syllable line, or two eleven-syllable lines followed by one sixteen-syllable line. The Greeks used a metrical system based on syllable length rather than stress: thus a Greek metric foot would consist of a combination of short and long syllables rather than unstressed and stressed syllables. This metric system, called quantitative, is difficult in English, where it is usually replaced—as in these versions—with a more familiar accentual-syllabic approximation.

Despite their common formal aims and their dedication to accurately rendering the original, each of these poems is unique. Both Wharton's and Higginson's versions sound high-flown and a bit archaic—almost biblical—to our ears, and they wouldn't have sounded like ordinary speech to nineteenth-century readers, either. Compare, for instance, Higginson's elaborate cry, "Weigh me not down with weariness and anguish / O Thou most holy!" (lines 3–4) with Barnard's "Don't, I beg you, / cow my heart with grief!" (3–4). Where Higginson's version is grandiose, full of ornate phrasing, Barnard's is colloquial and sisterly. Barnard stresses the ties between the speaker and the goddess in her closing, where Aphrodite acts as a confidante, whereas in other versions she is cast in a less consoling role: as military ally (in Wharton); as venerated deity, "Sacred protector" (28) in Higginson.

Studying this poem makes clear how much of translation is interpretation, how much a translator is limited or informed by the context in which he or she is writing. You might want to discuss Higginson's editorial decision to change the pronoun for Sappho's lover from "she" to "he" in the sixth stanza, though the lover was certainly a woman in the original. The practice of editing poems in such a way was not uncommon in previous centuries—even Shakespeare was not immune. Although students may find this sort of obvious editing troubling, it is interesting to note the extent to which these translators' choice of a style or a level of diction changes the poem in equally—or more—profound ways.

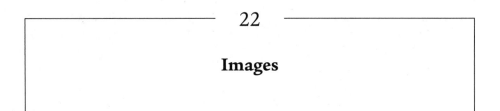

22

Images

Students are already very familiar with imagery through advertising. You may find it an interesting exercise to have students compare ads and poems dealing with similar subject matter: a recruitment commercial and Owen's "Dulce et Decorum Est," for instance. This may prove to be a controversial exercise — be prepared for students' resistance. You may instead (or additionally) want to have students focus on several advertisements or television shows and write a short response to the imagery they find there. This exercise can be beneficial because it will show students they already know how to read imagery, and it will also help sharpen their critical thinking skills by applying analysis in an area they are unused to.

 Ask students to explore *imagery* at **bedfordstmartins .com/meyerlit**.

Still, students can sometimes have trouble with very imagistic poems: such poems may require more effort on the part of readers than they suspect. It often may help to ask students to consider why it is that a poet focuses so closely on a given scene or object. Walt Whitman's "Cavalry Crossing a Ford" can seem like just a pretty scene unless one puts it in the context of the Civil War and realizes the possible fate in store for these men — a fate of which Whitman was all too aware from his work in a hospital. If students can be helped to see that poets often use images to emphasize significance or preserve a fleeting moment, they may appreciate the poems more.

Ask students to research the poets in this chapter at **bedfordstmartins .com/meyerlit**.

Another important point in this chapter is that images need not be exclusively visual. Sally Croft's "Home-Baked Bread" and Cathy Song's "The White Porch" both use a variety of imagery to enhance the sensual themes of the poems. William Blake's "London" and Matthew Arnold's "Dover Beach" are full of auditory images.

You may find that it helps to have students experiment with their own writing in this chapter: they could be asked to write a descriptive paragraph or poem concretely rendering an object, a scene, or an activity. This can serve to emphasize ideas raised in class about the significance of detail.

The paragraph from T. E. Hulme at the end of the chapter can also be useful in this regard, as it highlights some of these ideas. It can also provide a good starting place for discussions either now or later in the class about the distinction between poetry and prose.

WILLIAM CARLOS WILLIAMS, *Poem* (p. 623)

William Carlos Williams was born and lived most of his life in Rutherford, New Jersey, a town near Paterson, the city that provided the title and much of the subject matter of his "modern epic" poem *Paterson*. He had a thriving medical practice for fifty years, delivering more than two thousand babies and writing his poems, novels, short stories, and essays at night and in the moments he could snatch between patient visits during the day.

This poem is an imaged motion, but the verse has a certain slant music, too. Notice the *t*-sounds that align themselves in the second tercet, the consonance in "hind" (line 8) and "down" (9), the repetitions in "pit of" (10), "empty" (11), and "flowerpot" (12). Sound also helps convey the poem's sense of agility and smoothness.

Students may initially resist this poem because, being apparently simple, it may not conform to their expectations. If this situation arises, or perhaps even if it doesn't, you can use this opportunity to ask the question "What should poetry do or be?" In all likelihood, you can convince skeptics that Williams's poem does what they don't think it does. In any case, it is an opportunity to refine a definition of poetry while exploring its power to appeal to our imagination.

POSSIBLE CONNECTION TO AN OTHER SELECTION

Matsuo Bashō, "Under cherry trees" (text p. 753)

WALT WHITMAN, *Cavalry Crossing a Ford* (p. 624)

Walt Whitman is, with Emily Dickinson, one of the two poetic giants of the American nineteenth century. Born in Huntington, Long Island, he grew up in Brooklyn, leaving school at age eleven for a job as an office boy in a law firm. His poetry grew out of his experiences as a reporter, teacher, laborer, and Civil War nurse. He self-published the first edition of his book — his life's work, really — *Leaves of Grass* in 1855.

Whitman's descriptive words lend a colorful, paradelike quality to this scene. The flashing arms with their musical clank along with the guidon flags fluttering gaily create an image that suggests liveliness and energy. Yet "Behold" in lines 3 and 4, with its biblical overtones and its arresting sense of absorbing the sight ("be-hold"), is more stately than *look* or *see* and, with its long vowels, is almost ministerial. How does Whitman manage these two apparently contrasting tones?

The speaker in this poem (we can assume Whitman himself) seems to be fairly distant from the scene and possibly slightly elevated to see the entire picture. He scans the troops with a panning gaze that is, nonetheless, able to come in for some close-ups as he looks at the brown-faced men, "each group, each person, a picture" (4).

A productive discussion of this poem might take into account Whitman's lines and how their rhythm contributes to the description in the poem. Does the momentum of the lines have anything to do with the movement of the troops? To what degree is the description "arranged," and to what degree does it mirror the speaker's perception of the scene as it impresses itself on him?

POSSIBLE CONNECTION TO ANOTHER SELECTION

William Carlos Williams, "Poem" (text p. 623)

DAVID SOLWAY, *Windsurfing* (p. 624)

"Windsurfing" is a poem full of action and motion. The poem begins with "It"; the poet does not pause long enough to even explain exactly what "it" is, but instead allows the motion of the poem to mirror the motion of the windsurfer. The man who is windsurfing is referred to directly only twice; the man and the windsurfer move so forcefully together that the two share a single identity. The intensity of the motion of the windsurfer as it careens across the water is suggested through the carefully chosen verbs ("plunge" [line 20], "lunging" [27], "snapping" [37], "lashing" [38], "shearing" [39], etc.), which reveal the violence, grace, and beauty of the scene.

Because "Windsurfing" conveys one particular scene vividly, you may wish to ask students to compare the water imagery, the fluidity of motion between the man and his windsurfer, and the sensual imagery to those of other poems with similar settings (such as Matthew Arnold's "Dover Beach" [text p. 626]).

POSSIBLE CONNECTIONS TO OTHER SELECTIONS

Robert Frost, "Birches" (text p. 848; question #1, following)
Cathy Song, "Girl Powdering Her Neck" (text p. F; question #2, following)

CONNECTION QUESTIONS IN TEXT (p. 626) WITH ANSWERS

1. Consider the effects of the images in "Windsurfing" and Robert Frost's "Birches" (text p. 848). In an essay, explain how these images elicit the emotional responses they do.

   Solway's imagery moves fluidly, one metaphor leading into another with active verbs. Frost's imagery is slower, with a distinctly melancholy feel. The speaker in "Birches" seems to be an adult man who is reminiscing about his youth as he stares at the birch trees in the forest. He describes how the birches are bent under the weight of ice each winter, but says, "I should prefer to have some boy bend them" (23). He reveals that this is an activity he did in his youth: "So was I once myself a swinger of birches" (41). The speaker infuses his imagery with longing and loneliness, saying, "And life is too much like a pathless wood / Where your face burns and tickles with the cobwebs / Broken across it, and one eye is weeping / From a twig's having lashed across it open" (44–47). These images convey the solitary pain the speaker has experienced throughout his life. He wishes for a chance to start life over, imagining dying and returning to life as the same as climbing a birch.

2. Compare the descriptions in "Windsurfing" and Cathy Song's "Girl Powdering Her Neck" (text p. F). How does each poet appeal to your senses to describe windsurfing and the image of the girl?

   Solway provides the reader with metaphors that change at rapid-fire pace, mimicking the movement of the windsurfer. For example, the speaker describes the windsurfer as "Part of the sleek apparatus" (18), and then says, "And now the mechanism's wholly / dolphin, springing toward its prey" (28–29) a few lines later. Song's poem does not spring so quickly from one metaphor to the next, but instead lingers on the minutest details of the girl, embellishing with simple similes and metaphors.

MATTHEW ARNOLD, *Dover Beach* (p. 626)

Matthew Arnold was born in the English village of Laleham, in the Thames valley. His father was a clergyman and a reformist educator, a powerful personality against whom the young Arnold rebelled in a number of ways, including nearly flunking out of Oxford. After several years as private secretary to a nobleman, in 1851 Arnold became an inspector of schools, a post he held for thirty-five years. For the characteristic jauntiness of his prose style, Walt Whitman once referred to him as "one of the dudes of literature."

Many of us have had the experience of looking out on a landscape and registering its beauty (and possibly its tranquility) and its undercurrent of something lost or awry. Such is the case for the speaker of "Dover Beach" as he looks out at the shore awash in moonlight. The private moment has its wholeness, for he stands in the "sweet" night air with his beloved (line 6). But all the security and peace he could expect to feel are shaken by his concerns beyond the moment and his awareness of the ravages that history brings to bear on the present. We are not fragments of our time alone, the poem seems to say; we are caught in the "turbid ebb and flow / Of human misery" (17–18) that Sophocles heard so long ago.

In the third stanza Arnold goes beyond commenting on the sadness that seems an inevitable part of the human condition, as his thoughts turn to the malaise of his own time. Faith, which once encircled humanity, is now only the overheard roar of its waters withdrawing to the rock-strewn edges of the world. In short, for whatever happens there is no solace, no consolation, nor reason to hope for any restoration, justice, or change. Humankind is beyond the tragic condition of Sophocles, and in this poem Arnold seems to be tipping the balance toward a modernist existential worldview. The tone of the poem barely improves by the final stanza, for the image Arnold leaves us with is that of "ignorant armies" clashing in the night (37) — the sound and fury once again signifying nothing.

The images of Dover Beach or some other imagined seascape work well to evoke the tone that Arnold is trying to convey. In discussion, or perhaps as a writing topic, you might ask the class to review the poem for natural details and images (in lines 9–14 or most of the third stanza, for example) that suggest the dreary, stark, and ominous portrait Arnold is painting here.

General essays on this poem appear in A. Dwight Culler's *Imaginative Reason: The Poetry of Matthew Arnold* (New Haven: Yale UP, 1966; print.) and James Dickey's *Babel to Byzantium* (New York: Farrar, 1968; print.).

POSSIBLE CONNECTION TO ANOTHER SELECTION

Wilfred Owen, "Dulce et Decorum Est" (text p. 633; question #1, following)

CONNECTION QUESTION IN TEXT (p. 627) WITH ANSWER

1. Explain how the images in Wilfred Owen's "Dulce et Decorum Est" (p. 633) develop further the ideas and sentiments suggested by Arnold's final line concerning "ignorant armies clash[ing] by night."

   The crippled soldiers in Owen's poem illustrate the final line of Arnold's, their decrepitude confirming what Arnold only hinted at. Owen's gruesome images — "coughing like hags" (line 2), "blood-shod" (6), "choking, drowning" (16) — graphically demonstrate the consequences of those "ignorant armies clash[ing] by night."

RUTH FORMAN, *Poetry Should Ride the Bus* (p. 627)

The strength of Forman's "Poetry Should Ride the Bus" lies in the clarity of her message, revealed in concrete images. The speaker champions a poetry of everyday, known things. Through personification, she shows exactly who and what this poetry should be. Decked out beautifully in a "polka dot dress" (line 1), "bright red lipstick" (5), or "fine plum linen suits" (9), her poetry is entangled with the stark or coarse images of "the yellow crackhouse" (4), the men "shootin craps" (8), or the conversation on the front porch. Pretty in a realistic way, it never transcends its gritty daily experience.

And it not only rides the bus but travels in the most undignified manner — "in a fat woman's Safeway bag" (14). The details are precise, right down to the other items in the bag and the day of the week the Safeway food will be served. It's clear that this is a poetry that cares in a familial way, for who else would "drop by a sweet potato pie" (17) and "sit through a whole photo album" (19)?

Only at the end does the poem move beyond concrete imagery. There is music in the rhythms and rhymes throughout, but ask students how the speaker whispers her own "electric blue magic" (26) in the last stanza, repeating certain sounds: for example, the *l* in "blue," "life," and "soul." Students should consider the slant and true rhymes of "soul," "while," and "smile" in the last lines. Rhythm and rhyme can also appeal to the senses, becoming the "red revolution love songs" (21) she mentions.

POSSIBLE CONNECTIONS TO OTHER SELECTIONS

Billy Collins, "Introduction to Poetry" (text p. 564; question #1, following)

Gary Snyder, "How Poetry Comes to Me" (text p. 653)

Richard Wakefield, "In a Poetry Workshop" (text p. 1025)

CONNECTION QUESTION IN TEXT (p. 628) WITH ANSWER

1. How does Forman's speaker's view of poetry compare with that of the speaker in Billy Collins's "Introduction to Poetry" (text p. 564)?

Both Collins and Forman believe that "poetry should ride the bus." Collins makes this clear when he introduces poetry by asking the reader to experience the poem physically: "press an ear against its hive" or "feel the walls for a light switch." The introduction should involve the senses for both, and both portray a vibrant and knowable poetry.

The reader of poetry is approached differently in each, however. Collins refers to poetry's reader in the third person, while Forman addresses the reader intimately, in second person.

The endings of the poems also differ greatly. For Collins, the introduction inevitably fails, with the poem being "tortured" by the reader who begins "beating it with a hose" to force out its meaning. Forman ends with a "yeah," a positive note. In the penultimate stanza, she says poetry should sing to the reader, and then in the final stanza, she lets it sing again.

AMY LOWELL, *The Pond* (p. 628)

The first three lines of Lowell's poem consist of direct description of the natural world: the leaves, the water, and the sound of the frogs. Following the dash at the end of the third line, she moves into metaphor, comparing the frogs' croaking to "Cracked bell-notes" (line 4). At the end of the poem the man-made object intrudes on the natural scene. However, the human creation is broken, and this brokenness is the reason it is able to mimic the animal sound. You might ask your students why Lowell introduces the metaphor in the last line. Do they read it as a comment on the act of writing poems?

Possible Connection to An Other Selection

Mary Oliver, "The Poet With His Face in His Hands" (text p. 572)

RUTH FAINLIGHT, *Crocuses* (p. 629)

As one of the first flowers to come up at the beginning of spring, the crocus symbolizes the promise of winter's end and a coming season of rebirth. In her poem, Fainlight plays on these associations with adjectives like "tender" (line 1), "shivering" (3), and "naked" (4). These descriptors take on a new meaning once the poem's central figure has been revealed. By comparing the crocuses to bodies bearing traces of violence, Fainlight juxtaposes the idea of spring with the reality of death. Like the crocus blooms, the bodies are fragile and vulnerable, but, in addition to the harsh elements, they also face the "shouted order" that leads to a "crack of gunfire" (7). The burst of sounds at the end of the poem further highlights the difference between the mute natural world and the human world, which is loud, violent, and self-destructive.

Possible Connections to Other Selections

William Blake, "Infant Sorrow" (text p. 100)

John Milton, "On the Late Massacre in Piedmont" (text p. 1018)

MARY ROBINSON, *London's Summer Morning* (p. 629)

This poem, set in eighteenth-century London, refers to the act of listening to "the busy sounds / Of summer's morning" (lines 1–2). Aural details convey the sounds of the street: shouting "chimney-boy" (4), rattling "milk-pail," "tinkling bell" (7), and "the din of hackney-coaches" (10). Robinson moves on to visual details, listing the "neat girl" (19) walking with a hat box, the sunlight "on the glitt'ring pane" (21), and "pastry dainties" (27). The sounds have roused the speaker, who now watches the street. The opening line invites the reader to acknowledge the familiarity of these sights and sounds, then pulls the focus from the street to the bedroom, where "the poor poet wakes from busy dreams" (41) to write the poem, and concludes with an image of the poet in the act of writing.

When your students try to work on their own listings of the morning's events, draw their attention to the use of aural and visual detail; Robinson's poem does not get tangled in narrative but focuses on sight and sound. What are some of the ways in which other senses could enter this litany? As a preparatory writing exercise, you might want to ask your students to move through the poem, expanding it to include other details such as the taste of the vegetables the vendors offer, the smells of the horses pulling the hackney coaches, and the weight of the "busy mop" (18) in the hands of the housemaid.

POSSIBLE CONNECTIONS TO OTHER SELECTIONS

William Blake, "London" (text p. 631; question #1, following)

William Wordsworth, "London, 1802" (text p. 656)

CONNECTION QUESTION IN TEXT (p. 630) WITH ANSWER

1. How does Robinson's description of London differ from William Blake's "London," (p. 631) the next poem? What would you say is the essential difference in purpose between the two poems?

   Blake opens his vision of London with "I wander" (line 1); Robinson constructs her poem around the sounds and visions available through a bedroom window. Robinson's poem is a cheerful list of images accompanied by the music of a busy street on a summer morning, while Blake sets his poem in "midnight streets" (13). Blake's vision of London is essentially a negative view of a corrupt city; Robinson's vision is positive and innocent of Blake's bleak account.

WILLIAM BLAKE, *London* (p. 631)

William Blake's only formal schooling was in art, and he learned engraving as an apprentice to a prominent London engraver. After his seven years' service, Blake made his living as a printer and engraver, writing poetry on the side. The private mythology that came to dominate his poems was worked out in almost total obscurity: at the time of his death Blake had acquired some notice for his art but almost none for his writing.

This poem may seem pessimistic, but is it entirely so? If students would go so far as to call it "apocalyptic," does their knowledge of history help them to discern where the speaker's attitude comes from? The use of "chartered" (line 1) to describe streets and the River Thames makes all the boundaries in the poem seem unnatural and rigid; the cries heard are cries of pain and sadness. Like the rigidities of the chartered streets, the legislation of the "mind-forged manacles" (8) does nothing to promote civil liberty and happiness. Blake implies here that the "manacles" of religion and government that should protect individuals fail miserably to ensure good lives. Children are sold into near slavery as chimney sweeps, their own dark and stunted faces casting a pall (appall) on the benevolent state and the Christian tradition. Soldiers sent off to war die or kill other soldiers. Sexual restrictions invite prostitution and thus promote disease, which may, in turn, afflict marriages and resulting births. Social regulations ("manacles") thus induce societal ills.

The image of the soldier dying for the state, for example (11–12), is described in a condensed and effective manner that suggests not only his lucklessness (or helplessness) but also the indifference of a government removed from the individual by class ("Palace" [12]), its insularity ("walls" [12]), and the imperturbable security of law.

Comparison of the two versions of the final stanza provides an excellent writing topic. Notice, though, how much more endemic the societal failings and wrongdoings appear in the second (revised) version. Instead of "midnight harlot's curse," the phrase becomes the "midnight streets" (13) (evil as pervasive) and "the youthful Harlot's curse" (14) (a blighting of innocence at an early age). By reversing "marriage hearse" and "infant's tear," Blake suggests not a mere (and societally sanctioned) cause-effect relation between marriage and the birth of afflicted infants but the presence of syphilis in even the youngest members of society and the conditions that would sustain its presence.

How do the urban ills of contemporary society compare with those of Blake's time? It might be an interesting exercise to ask students to write a poem about contemporary social ills, either urban or rural, in Blake's style. What has changed?

POSSIBLE CONNECTION TO AN OTHER SELECTION

George Eliot, "In a London Drawingroom" (text p. 1006)

WILFRED OWEN, *Dulce et Decorum Est* (p. 633)

This poem is an argument against war, not against a country. So often war is an act surrounded by image-making words of glory and honor and flanked by the "nobility" of slogan sentiments. Here Owen has presented the actuality of battle and death by a particularly dehumanizing and agonizing weapon: poison gas. He wants his audience to know a little more exactly what war entails.

This famous indictment of war centers on the experiences and emotions of a disillusioned World War I soldier. It might be necessary to provide a little background about the nature of warfare during "the war to end all wars." The ground war was fought mostly in trenches, where not only did close and relentless combat last much longer than anyone initially expected, but the threat of illness from decomposing bodies and diseases that bred in the mud of the trenches was very real. You are likely to push some buttons by doing so, but you may want to try to discuss the final lines first.

Owen seems to want to collar and talk to each reader directly. After the vividness of his description, some of which is in the present tense, Owen's attitude toward the "lie" (line 28) that his "friend" (26) might tell is disdainful, and understandably so.

You may want to ask students where the notion that it is noble to fight for one's country comes from. Under what circumstances does such a notion break down? Is war still glamorized by way of songs, films, and poetry?

POSSIBLE CONNECTION TO ANOTHER SELECTION

Matthew Arnold, "Dover Beach" (text p. 626)

PATRICIA SMITH, *What It's Like to Be a Black Girl (for Those of You Who Aren't)* (p. 634)

Using vernacular with a matter-of-fact tone, Smith defines race and gender in very personal terms, examining, simultaneously, how the speaker's race shapes her sexuality and how her gender and sexuality affect her understanding of her race. The poem uses a second-person perspective to establish an immediate connection with the reader; it conveys a sense that "you're not finished" (line 2). There are forces that make "something, / everything, wrong" (3–4), your own physical appearance is insufficient, and blue food coloring and "a bleached / white mophead" (6–7) would be preferable to your own eyes and hair. This is also a coming-of-age poem, moving from "being 9 years old" (1) to "finally having a man reach out for you" (18). Sexuality, physicality, athleticism, and profanity are all present and fiercely accounted for. The final image, caving in around a man's fingers, presents a good opportunity for discussion: Is the speaker responding to the man's touch in relief or in defeat? Ask students to defend their opinion with reference to other lines in the poem.

You might want to ask students to attempt a freewriting exercise that defines them in terms of their gender and ethnicity. What's it like being a White Boy? An Asian Girl? How do gender and ethnicity work to define us all?

Margaret Atwood, "you fit into me" (text p. 645)

Gwendolyn Brooks, "We Real Cool" (text p. 614)

RAINER MARIA RILKE, *The Panther* (p. 635)

Born in Austria-Hungary (now the Czech Republic), Rainer Maria Rilke was educated in Catholic schools but later rebelled against his faith. He migrated to Munich after studying philosophy at Prague. In 1909 he went to Paris, a gathering place for many artists at the time. Rilke's images have been described as having classical plasticity: precise, chiseled, and visual. His mixture of squalor and art may have come from the time he spent in Paris.

The form and content of "The Panther" unite to indicate increasing confinement. In each of the stanzas, Rilke moves from exterior to interior and from action to inaction, leaving the reader with something more finite to consider each time — paralleling the confinement experienced by the panther. The first line of the first stanza refers to the world beyond the bars: by the end of the stanza, there are only "a thousand bars; and behind the bars, no world" (line 4). In the first line of the second stanza, the panther is moving "in cramped circles, over and over" (5); at the end of the stanza, we find "a mighty will [which] stands paralyzed" (8). The third stanza traces the path of an image as it penetrates "the curtain of the pupils" (9) until it "plunges into the heart and is gone" (12). This final image is so far within the panther that it remains unidentifiable. As a result, like the panther, we are forced by the form of the poem into a stillness and a recognition of our inability to control the situation. In a sense, Rilke is dropping the curtain over our own pupils.

POSSIBLE CONNECTION TO ANOTHER SELECTION

Emily Dickinson, "A Bird came down the Walk —" (text p. 693; question #1, following)

CONNECTION QUESTION IN TEXT (p. 635) WITH ANSWER

1. Write an essay explaining how a sense of movement is achieved by the images and rhythms in this poem and in Dickinson's "A Bird came down the Walk —" (p. 693).

   Dickinson's bird moves with jerky movements, reflected in her brief, restless lines, until the end of the poem when the bird's movements are compared to rowing. Rilke's panther is at once more graceful and more cramped. His "ritual dance around a center / in which a mighty will stands paralyzed" (lines 7–8) is almost hypnotic so that we are especially surprised by the unexplained rushing image in the final stanza.

JANE KENYON, *The Blue Bowl* (p. 636)

The speaker of this poem recounts how she and someone else (presumably a husband or lover) buried their dead cat the day before the poem was written. The burial is ritualistic; the speaker compares herself and her fellow undertaker to "primitives" (line 1). Though they go about the burial rather methodically, the event has affected them deeply. They are "silent" (12) the rest of the day and seemingly empty: "we worked, / ate, stared, and slept" (12–13).

The title of this poem provides its most challenging point of interpretation. In addition to asking about the blueness of the bowl, ask students why the title focuses on the seemingly inconsequential bowl at all; why not entitle the poem "The Burial"? The bowl's blueness calls attention to other colors in the poem that may have otherwise been overlooked: the cat's "long red fur" (7) and the incongruous "white feathers / between his toes" (7–8). There is something *off*, something unsettling about the entire poem. Note how the first sentence, read alone, raises fundamental questions about meaning: Do primitives bury cats with bowls? The speaker has difficulty communicating; she interrupts her description ("long, not to say aquiline, nose" [9]) in the same way that the robin or the neighbor of the final simile says "the wrong thing" (17).

Burial is meant to be a neat, finalizing procedure, but death is a messy business, both physically and emotionally. Nothing about it can be satisfying. In discussing the psychological implications of burial and comparing this poem to John Updike's "Dog's Death" (text p. 548), students may be reluctant to leap over the next level of taboo into a comparison of human burial to pet burial. How might the nature of "The Blue Bowl" have changed if the speaker were burying a person rather than a pet? How might it have remained the same?

POSSIBLE CONNECTION TO AN OTHER SELECTION

John Updike, "Dog's Death" (text p. 548; question #1, following)

CONNECTION QUESTION IN TEXT (p. 636) WITH ANSWER

1. Write an essay comparing the death of this cat with the death of the dog in Updike's "Dog's Death" (p. 548). Which poem draws a more powerful response from you? Explain why.

    One difference is that the cat of Kenyon's poem is never described as it was when it was alive. We do not see it die, whereas we witness the death of the dog in Updike's poem firsthand. Kenyon's speaker states that "there are sorrows keener than these" (line 11) as she buries the cat, but Updike's speaker shows us the grief of the family. It is likely that students will find Kenyon's poem unsettling and will find Updike's poem viscerally upsetting or pathetic.

SALLY CROFT, *Home-Baked Bread* (p. 636)

This poem describes a seduction by way of cooking, cleverly departing from the title of the source of the epigraph, *The Joy of Cooking*, into another popular text from the 1970s, *The Joy of Sex*. The great-aunt of the second stanza is an interesting inroad. Great-aunts are generally associated more with cooking than with seduction: Is this one figured into the poem as a contrast to the amorous speaker, or does she reinforce the idea that all women have their "cunning triumphs" (line 2), which are sometimes hidden or only suggested?

"Cunning triumphs," appearing amid the measured dryness of a cookbook text, certainly has the potential to arrest someone's poetic sensibilities. *Cunning* seems more appropriately applied to the feats of Odysseus than to the food in *The Joy of Cooking*. At any rate, "cunning triumphs" rises, as it were, beyond the limits of technical discourse. It shines, it sparkles, it almost titillates the kitchen soul.

"Insinuation" (3), too, is a pivotal word in the poem. It looks back on the questioning attitude of the opening lines and points toward the wily, winding seductiveness of what will follow.

At first we hear the speaker reading and questioning the cookbook. Then we hear the speaker transformed into a new identity — of Lady Who Works Cunning Triumphs. She is addressing someone she would charm and seduce.

The poem achieves a unity through the repetition of certain images, such as the room that recalls the great-aunt's bedroom as well as the other reiterated images, of honey, sweet seductiveness, warmth, and open air.

POSSIBLE CONNECTIONS TO OTHER SELECTIONS

Elaine Magarrell, "The Joy of Cooking" (text p. 661)
Cathy Song, "The White Porch" (text p. 639)

JOHN KEATS, *To Autumn* (p. 637)

"To Autumn" was the last major lyric Keats wrote. But despite its tone and imagery, particularly in the last stanza, there is no indication that Keats had an exact foreknowledge of his impending death.

Personification is a major device in this poem. In stanza 1, which suggests the early part of the day, autumn is the "bosom-friend" (line 2) of the sun and a ripener of growing things. In stanza 2, which has a midday cast, autumn is a storekeeper and a harvester or gleaner. In the final stanza, which reflects "the soft-dying day" (25), the image of autumn is less directly named, but the idea of the contemplative is suggested. One sees things ripening in the opening stanza; in stanza 2, autumn feels the wind and drowses in the "fume" (17) of poppies; in the final stanza, autumn and the reader both are invited to listen to the special music of the close of the day and of the year.

In his brief poetic career, Keats seems to have grown into a more serene acceptance of death, preferring the organic ebb and flow of life over the cool, unchanging fixity of the artifact.

POSSIBLE CONNECTIONS TO OTHER SELECTIONS

Robert Frost, "After Apple-Picking" (text p. 847; question #1, following)

John Keats, "Ode on a Grecian Urn" (text p. 612)

Dave Lucas, "November" (text p. 978; question #2, following)

CONNECTIONS QUESTIONS IN TEXT (p. 638) WITH ANSWERS

1. Compare this poem's tone and perspective on death with those of Robert Frost's "After Apple-Picking" (p. 847).

    More metaphoric, perhaps, than literal, the apple picker's description of the recent harvest in "After Apple-Picking" could be a summary of his life. Already drowsy, he allows the time of day and the season to ease him into a reverie. The harvest he contemplates is a personal one—the apples he picked or let fall. This musing might occasion more brooding than is found in "To Autumn," in which the poet surveys more impersonally the season's reign and the year's end. "To Autumn" captures the last moments before winter, preserving them in all their ripeness and sensuality. Although both poems imply that death is near, Keats's speaker is far less willing to yield to it before appreciating the last moments of life as fully as he can.

2. Write an essay comparing the significance of this poem's images of "mellow fruitfulness" (line 1) with that of the images in Dave Lucas's "November" (text p. 978). Explain how the images in each poem lead to very different feelings about the same phenomenon.

    The images in "To Autumn" provide a sharp contrast to those in "November." Lucas's version of fall is mired in gloom and decay; the first image is of dead leaves "raked to the curb in copper- and shale- / stained piles, or the struck-match-sweet / of sulfur // becoming smoke" (3–6). On the surface, sulfur and smoke simply connote homeowners burning leaves, but it can also call to mind images of hell. Rather than Keats's cheerful images of "mellow fruitfulness" (1), Lucas's speaker focuses on death, decay, and emptiness. He drives these themes home in the last image of the sky, and "Hung across it, aghast surprise / of so many clotted, orphaned nests" (8–9).

CATHY SONG, *The White Porch* (p. 639)

The speaker in this poem establishes a conversation with her listener in the first stanza: "your" (line 10), "think" (12). She projects her listener into the future even as she captures the present moment through the description of her newly washed hair. The second stanza moves the conversation toward sexual innuendo, comparing the speaker's arousal to a flower, a flock of birds, and a sponge cake with peaches. Ask students to determine how these images give us a sense of what the speaker is like. What is her relationship to the listener? The final stanza returns us to the initial image of hair, but whereas the first stanza moves toward the future, the third plunges us back into the past. Students will enjoy comparing the images describing the mother to those describing the lover in the final lines. Like the rope ladder (an allusion to Rapunzel?), the poem is column-shaped, inviting its listener into the experience of reading it as it talks about a sexual relationship.

In a writing assignment, ask students to examine the concrete nouns and participial verbs in the poem. How do they evoke the speaker's message? How do images of domestic life summon the speaker's more "philosophical" side?

POSSIBLE CONNECTION TO AN OTHER SELECTION

Sally Croft, "Home-Baked Bread" (text p. 636; question #1, following)

Sharon Olds, "Last Night" (text p. 604; question #2, following)

CONNECTION QUESTION IN TEXT (p. 640) WITH ANSWER

1. Compare the images used to describe the speaker's "slow arousal" (line 22) in this poem with Sally Croft's images in "Home-Baked Bread" (p. 636). What similarities do you see? What makes each description so effective?

    Croft also uses domestic images to talk about sexual intimacy and poetry writing. Both "Home-Baked Bread" and "The White Porch" invite the listener into the experience, promising food and warmth; each poem, for example, uses peaches to seduce its listener. The imagery is full of anticipation and ripeness. There is an element of danger, too, in each poem, enticing the audiences into delicious but forbidden experiences.

2. Write an essay comparing the images of sensuality in this poem with those in Sharon Old's "Last Night" (text p. 604). Which poem seems more erotic to you? Why?

    Both of these poems are undeniably sensual, but students may have differing opinions on which they find more so. Song's "The White Porch" builds tension through the detailed images of the speaker's mundane tasks, coupled with images such as, "I feel the strain of threads, / the swollen magnolias / heavy as a flock of birds / in the tree" (26–29) and "I'll watch you / drench your slice of it / in canned peaches / and lick the plate clean" (34–37). The imagery of Olds's poem is more overt in its discussion of intimacy, especially in lines such as, "No kiss, / no tenderness — more like killing, death-grip / holding to life, genitals / like violent hands clasped tight" (12–15). Some students may find Song's subtlety more appealing, while others may prefer Olds's overt, even violent, imagery.

MELANIE McCABE, *Paperboy* (p. 640)

"Paperboy" is a recollection of what it was like to be a twelve-year-old girl in love with a seventeen-year-old boy. Ask students what details in the poem give it emotional power. McCabe offers fragments — "his bicep in the twilight" (line 3), "the huge shadow of the hickory" (9), "a shutter, unhinged" (28). How do these fragmented images convey the perceptions of a twelve-year-old, or of an older woman looking back on the emotional experience of a not-quite-child, not-quite-adult?

One way to begin a discussion of imagery in "Paperboy" is to ask about the speaker's perspective. What tone do her images convey and what's their cumulative effect? The imagery reflects McCabe's overall intent: ask students to think about the effect of words like "violated" (5) and "loitering" (7), or images of "red embers" (26) and "a warped door" (28). Ask how the language of the poem points to the speaker's perceptions and her emotional state. What's revealed when she chooses to call herself "a straw" (18) or when she says she is "lodged like a splinter in his day" (24)? Students might also consider how sound marries sense here, in the effect of repeated images and words like *hickory*, *longing*, and *beat*.

POSSIBLE CONNECTIONS TO OTHER SELECTIONS

Emily Dickinson, "Wild Nights — Wild Nights!" (text p. 809)

Christopher Marlowe, "The Passionate Shepherd to His Love" (text p. 954)

Andrew Marvell, "To His Coy Mistress" (text p. 601)

Edna St. Vincent Millay, "Recuerdo" (text p. 958)

CONNECTION QUESTION IN TEXT (p. 641) WITH ANSWER

1. Write an essay on the nature of desire in "Paperboy" (text p. 640) and in Joan Murray's "Play-by-Play" (text p. 959).

   Students will approach this comparison / contrast from a variety of angles, but they will explore the difference between how the young speaker in "Paperboy" and the older women in "Play-by-Play" experience desire. They might focus on the contemplative tone in "Play-by-Play" versus the direct, impassioned voice of "Paperboy." The speaker in "Paperboy" is consumed and baffled by her desire: "He smelled of something // I knew. Like nothing I knew. He came to me" (20–21). Murray's speaker has the wisdom of age to shape her feelings and understanding: "Who better than these women, with their sweaters / draped across their shoulders, their perspectives / honed from years of lovers, to recognize / the beauty that would otherwise / go unnoticed on this hill?" (23–27). The speaker in "Paperboy" is fractured by her overwhelming feelings ("something broken beat and beat the air — / a shutter, unhinged — a warped door that wouldn't close" [27–28]), while the narrator of "Play-by-Play" can sit back and consider the reaction of the object of her desire.

PERSPECTIVE

T. E. HULME, *On the Differences between Poetry and Prose* (p. 641)

As a class exercise, you might ask students to bring in examples of prose that contradict Hulme's claims. Students might want to bring in examples of prose they read elsewhere. In another writing assignment, you might ask students to flesh out Hulme's theory with especially vivid examples of poems that "hand over sensations bodily."

23

Figures of Speech

The material in this chapter can build on issues raised in the previous two: considerations of word choice, tone, and images both influence and reflect choices in figurative speech. You might have your students draw these connections explicitly by having them select a poem from this chapter and analyze it in terms of its figurative language and also in terms of concepts discussed earlier. Doing so will help them understand how various elements make up the poem's total effect.

> **Web** Ask students to explore the poetic elements in this chapter at **bedfordstmartins.com/meyerlit**.

Another possible exercise for this chapter would be to have students, working either alone or in small groups, think about and list instances of figurative language used in their everyday speech. You might have them do this at the beginning of the chapter (after a brief discussion of figurative language) and again at the end. The difference in the number of instances they derive should be encouraging.

It is likely that students are already aware of the difference between simile and metaphor; the distinction will become important to them only if they can understand that it has some significance. Similes tend to call attention to the comparison itself, as in Margaret Atwood's "you fit into me" or William Wordsworth's "London, 1802": the comparison becomes an important feature of the poems, foregrounding the "you and me" in Atwood's case, or John Milton in Wordsworth's. Conversely, metaphors tend to focus on the *content* of the comparison, shifting the focus from the separate entities being compared to the nature of those entities, as in Dickinson's "Presentiment—is that long Shadow—on the lawn—."

> **Web** Ask students to research the poets in this chapter at **bedfordstmartins.com/meyerlit**.

Metonymy and synecdoche can be difficult for students to grasp; for some reason, they find it more difficult to remember "metonymy" than "metaphor." You might find it useful to point out (or to have students point out) uses of metonymy in everyday language: "The White House confirms" or "University A beat University B" or "The Chancellor's office responded." This can help students get a grasp of the concepts involved and defuse their anticipation of being unable to understand these terms.

Paradox and oxymoron can be useful tools to encourage students' critical thinking skills. Puzzling out paradoxes and explaining oxymorons often require students to think in unusual ways. Poems that lend themselves to this are Donne's "Batter My Heart" and "Death Be Not Proud," as well as nearly any poem by Emily Dickinson.

WILLIAM SHAKESPEARE, *From* Macbeth *(Act V, Scene v)* (p. 644)

After asking students to identify each of the things to which Shakespeare's Macbeth compares life, and to consider how life is like each of them, have them decide which of these figures of speech is the most effective. Does one overpower the others, or does the overall effect depend on the conjunction of all of them?

Have students recall other things to which they have heard life compared. Are these common images examples of strong figurative language or merely clichés? For example, "Life is a bed of roses" conveys the idea that life is easy and beautiful, but it is such a well-worn phrase that it now lacks the impact it might once have had. As a writing assignment, have students come up with their own similes and metaphors and explain how life is like the image they have created.

See Robert Frost's " 'Out, Out—' " (text p. 850) for one example of how a modern poet has made use of Shakespeare's famous passage. Students familiar with William Faulkner's *The Sound and the Fury* might be able to comment on how another twentieth-century writer has used the reprinted passage from *Macbeth*.

POSSIBLE CONNECTION TO ANOTHER SELECTION

Robert Frost, " 'Out, Out—' " (text p. 850)

MARGARET ATWOOD, *you fit into me* (p. 645)

Students may need help with the allusions called up by the first two lines of this poem: the hook and eye that fasten a door shut; the buttonhook used to fasten women's shoes in the early twentieth century. You might ask students to compose a poem in which a figure of speech produces first pleasant associations and later unpleasant or, as in Atwood's poem, lurid ones. You might also ask the class to determine in a brief writing assignment how the simile and its expansion work. Would the poem be as successful, for example, if "eye" were not a part of the human anatomy?

POSSIBLE CONNECTION TO ANOTHER SELECTION

Emily Dickinson, "Wild Nights—Wild Nights!" (text p. 809)

EMILY DICKINSON, *Presentiment—is that long Shadow—on the lawn —* (p. 646)

As noted in the text, Dickinson uses richly connotative words such as *shadow* and *darkness* to express in a few words the sense of fear and danger inherent in her "Presentiment." You might explore with your students other connotations of the word *presentiment.* Are all premonitions warnings about negative occurrences? Have any of your students had premonitions about good things? What kinds of words might one want to use in order to express—economically—the possibility of pleasant surprise? You could have students, individually or in groups, try to identify specific words and then a controlling metaphor that would be appropriate to express this alternative kind of surprise.

POSSIBLE CONNECTION TO ANOTHER SELECTION

Emily Dickinson, "Success is counted sweetest" (text p. 803)

ANNE BRADSTREET, *The Author to Her Book* (p. 647)

This speaker regards her collection of poetry as though it were her child, considering both its penchant for brattiness and the mother's affection for it. Ask students to trace the extended metaphor in this poem, pointing out the way that diction influences tone. What, for example, do the words *ill-formed* and *feeble* (line 1) tell us about the speaker's attitude toward her work? Does this attitude change at all as the poem progresses? Although her initial attitude toward the book is disdain, the speaker's reluctance to part with her creation in the final lines could be the result of both modesty and affection.

Sound patterns and meter are also good topics for discussion of this poem. The meter is iambic pentameter, but there are variations in rhythm that are linked to meaning. Line 15 presents the problem of metrical arrangement, providing an example in line 16: "Yet still thou run'st more hobbling than is meet."

In a writing assignment, you might ask students to discuss the way this poem talks about the writing process. How does Bradstreet suggest a book is written?

POSSIBLE CONNECTIONS TO OTHER SELECTIONS

William Shakespeare, "Not marble, nor the gilded monuments" (text p. 955)

Ronald Wallace, "Building an Outhouse" (text p. 660)

RICHARD WILBUR, *The Writer* (p. 647)

In discussion, ask students what Wilbur is equating with the act of writing at the beginning of the poem (and which writer the title refers to). In the first three stanzas, phrases such as "the prow of the house" (line 1), "a chain hauled over a gunwale" (6), and "a great cargo" (8) all convey the image of a buoyant, well-stocked ship beginning its voyage. As the narrator/father considers this image, he emphasizes its positive aspects by wishing his daughter a "lucky passage" (9).

Yet the ship is not the controlling metaphor of "The Writer" (as students may notice when they compare the third and the last stanzas of the poem). It may be useful to point out the pronoun shift that occurs in the first half of the poem from the "I" of the first three stanzas — the "I" of the narrator — to the "she" who asserts herself in the fourth and fifth stanzas. The shift is reinforced in the fourth stanza by the words *but, as if to reject,* and *a stillness,* which reveal the daughter's refusal to accept the speaker's "easy figure" (11) of speech, despite its positive connotations. The pace of his daughter's typing, which moves from "a stillness" to "a bunched clamor," inspires the narrator to revise his metaphor. The ship is transformed into the dazed starling that was once "trapped" in the room where his daughter now writes. This memory of the starling supplies the remainder of the poem with its direction, and with a harsher tone. Note the contrast in stanzas seven through nine between light and dark, hope and despair, as the "sleek, wild, dark" starling would "batter against the brilliance" of the room, "drop like a glove / To the hard floor," "wait . . . humped and bloody / For the wits to try it again" (21–26).

In the end, though, this is not a pessimistic poem, but a realistic one. With its "smooth course for the right window," the starling sails into the world, not unscathed but headed toward the freedom, light, and life. Reminded of the "battering" humans also experience as they journey through life (and emphasizing the connection by rhyming "starling" with "darling" in the final stanza), the narrator reiterates his wish for his daughter with a greater awareness of the hazards as well as the rewards that lie ahead of her.

POSSIBLE CONNECTIONS TO OTHER SELECTIONS

Jan Beatty, "My Father Teaches Me to Dream" (text p. 988; question #1, following)

Emily Dickinson, "A Bird came down the Walk" (text p. 693)

CONNECTION QUESTION IN TEXT (p. 648) WITH ANSWER

1. Compare the speaker's use of metaphor in "The Writer" with the father's method of offering advice in Jan Beatty's "My Father Teaches Me to Dream" (text p. 988). What's the essential difference between how the two fathers express themselves?

    While Beatty's father proffers statements to his child about "what work is," Wilbur's narrator listens quietly to his daughter's struggle with her "work." In "My Father. . ." the statement is made that life is repetitive, while in "The Writer," the speaker fears the unknown journey his daughter is embarking on; both poems, however, acknowledge a difficult process, as seen in Beatty's line "There's no hand-outs in this life" (line 13), and in Wilbur's metaphor of the "humped and bloody" bird trying to clear the "sill of the world."

EDMUND CONTI, *Pragmatist* (p. 649)

As a writing assignment, you might ask the class to discuss whether the mixed tone of this poem is successful. Is, for example, "coming our way" (line 2) too liltingly conversational for the idea of apocalypse?

Samuel Taylor Coleridge, "What Is an Epigram?" (text p. 751)

William Hathaway, "Oh, Oh" (text p. 550)

DYLAN THOMAS, *The Hand That Signed the Paper* (p. 650)

Dylan Thomas's *Eighteen Poems,* published in 1934, when he was twenty, began his career as a poet with a flourish: here, it seemed, was an answer to T. S. Eliot, a return to rhapsody and unembarrassed music. Thomas's poems became more craftsmanlike as he matured, but they never lost their ambition for the grand gesture, the all-embracing, bittersweet melancholy for which the Romantics strove. Thomas lived the role of the poet to the hilt: he was an alcoholic, a philanderer, a wonderful storyteller, a boor, and a justly celebrated reader of his own poems and those of others. Although he never learned to speak Welsh (he was born and grew up in Swansea, Wales), it is said that his poems carry the sounds of that language over into English. He died of alcohol poisoning during his third reading tour of the United States.

Although Thomas seems to be referring to no specific incident in this poem, the date (1936) indicates a possible concern with the political machinations leading up to the outbreak of World War II. The "five kings [who] did a king to death" (line 4) may even recall the five major powers who signed the Treaty of Versailles to end World War I but in their severe dismantling of Germany set the stage for another war. Some critics suggest that the poem, especially in the last two stanzas, refers to a wrathful God. Which words or phrases would lend credence to this reading? Students may suggest other situations in which a person in power can, by performing a seemingly simple act, adversely affect people at long range.

Discuss the title's allusion to the saying "The hand that rocks the cradle rules the world." Both phrases make observations about the power inherent in the acts of a single person. How are the acts to which they refer alike and different? How does the allusion to motherhood create irony in the poem? (Students familiar with the 1992 horror film *The Hand That Rocks the Cradle,* which deals with a deranged babysitter, may have their own associations with this poem.)

Alice Jones, "The Foot" (text p. 727)

Carl Sandburg, "Buttons" (text p. 677)

JANICE TOWNLEY MOORE, *To a Wasp* (p. 651)

Discuss with students how an awareness of the intensity and seriousness of purpose that usually accompany the use of apostrophe affects their reading of this poem, which is, after all, about a common insect. In what way is the fist in the last line being waved at both the speaker and the wasp? Whose fist is it? How does the word *chortled* in the first line help us understand the speaker's view of the wasp? Discuss the paradox inherent in the notion of "delicious death" (line 11).

John Donne, "The Flea" (text p. 1005)

David McCord, "Epitaph on a Waiter" (text p. 751)

J. PATRICK LEWIS, *The Unkindest Cut* (p. 653)

Students will enjoy this humorous quatrain that is a play on the saying "The pen is mightier than the sword." To open discussion, ask students to point out the paradox inherent in this simple poem. Discuss also the title of the poem, pointing out that the title is an allusion to Shakespeare's *Julius Caesar* (III.ii.188).

Paul Laurence Dunbar, "To a Captious Critic" (text p. 599)

GARY SNYDER, *How Poetry Comes to Me* (p. 653)

Snyder's characterization of poetry departs from the traditional view of inspiration. Rather than coming in a flash of insight, poetry is "blundering" (line 1) and "Frightened" (3). Instead of being overtaken by poetry, the author retains control of the situation and has to "go to meet it" (5). The poem also calls upon the scene of a camper being encroached on by dangerous animals, but the meekness of poetry in Snyder's view makes this a very different story. Poetry is not an animal from which we need protection, but rather a cowering thing likely to be scared away.

You might have your students discuss the images of light and dark in this poem. Poetry belongs to the realm of the dark. If the speaker wants to find it, he has to venture out to the "Edge of the light" (6). The meeting must take place in the border area between light and darkness. What does the campfire, the light that holds poetry at a distance, symbolize? What does it provide for the speaker and what does it prevent?

POSSIBLE CONNECTION TO ANOTHER SELECTION

Richard Wakefield, "In a Poetry Workshop" (text p. 1025)

WILLIAM CARLOS WILLIAMS, *To Waken an Old Lady* (p. 655)

The image of the birds in winter at first suggests a bleak meaning for old age. The "bare trees" (line 5) and "snow glaze" (6) don't seem to offer much refuge. However, Williams observes that winter provides the birds with rest and with seeds to eat. The barren elements of the landscape, including the "harsh weedstalks" (11) and "dark wind" (9), are made bearable, "tempered / by a shrill / piping of plenty" (16–18). Williams seems to suggest that old age, though it may seem harsh, has its share of comforts.

POSSIBLE CONNECTION TO ANOTHER SELECTION

Colette Inez, "Back When All Was Continuous Chuckles" (text p. 594; question #1, following)

CONNECTION QUESTION IN TEXT (p. 655) WITH ANSWER

1. Discuss the shift in tone in "To Waken an Old Lady" and in Colette Inez's "Back When All Was Continuous Chuckles" (p. 594).

   In Williams's poem, the shift in tone occurs partly through the change in the use of verbs. The first half is marked by anxious verbals—"cheeping" (line 3), "skimming" (4), "Gaining and failing" (7). After the turn, Williams uses present perfect and present tense verbs to create a calmer mood—"has rested" (12), "is covered" (14), and "is tempered" (16). This switch to the present perfect and present tenses suggests an acceptance of old age as largely backward looking. However, Williams returns to the *-ing* ending in the last line, this time in the form of a noun rather than a verb. The actions of the first half have now become a static element, one that contributes to the comforts of the winter scene.

   "Back When All Was Continuous Chuckles" begins in the voice of the young narrator. Her reflections are interspersed with examples of the jokes she told with her friend, and the diction draws from her vocabulary, with words like "moron" (line 2), "Freaky" (7), and "crabby" (14). As the poem progresses, the quoted jokes stop, and the language becomes less tied to the words of the young girl. Here the adult poet takes over to express feelings that her younger self did not know how to deal with. Though the friends go back to "flipping through joke books" (23), it is no longer important that we hear the jokes. Instead, we are left with the mature knowledge that the names on the cemetery headstones would soon become familiar.

ERNEST SLYMAN, *Lightning Bugs* (p. 655)

This three-line poem casts lightning bugs (also called "fireflies") as spies who invade the speaker's backyard. It might be difficult to sustain a discussion about such a short poem, but you could begin by asking students to describe the speaker, the conditions under which he might make this observation, and the sights and sounds that surround him. Does his paranoia come from his sense that he is alone or from his sense that he is all too crowded?

Without the title, we would think this poem is about people. The title frames the experience by identifying the image to be captured in the lines that follow. Then, the image of the "peepholes" (line 2), coming as it does before the "snapshots" (3), makes us first imagine the bugs as human beings who require peepholes to see who is outside. When mention of snapshots is added to this image, the bugs become like tourists, waiting for someone to come out of the house so they can take a picture. This is ironic, for it is really the bugs who are the celebrities, fascinating the speaker, who watches them.

JUDY PAGE HEITZMAN, *The Schoolroom on the Second Floor of the Knitting Mill* (p. 656)

This small, quiet poem demonstrates the impact the words of adults can have on the young; the speaker, an adult, is still haunted by a teacher's judgment. In the first stanza the reader is led to believe that the speaker holds Mrs. Lawrence tenderly in her memory; seeing the cardinals makes the speaker miss her. However, the details given in the first stanza include only Mrs. Lawrence's classroom manicure and a blueprint of the building that housed her classroom. The image of the teacher as she "carved and cleaned her nails" (line 2) can be read most immediately as an indictment of her teaching technique, but it can also be seen as an implied metaphor that foreshadows the harm Mrs. Lawrence can do. The nails can be read as claws, the cleaning and carving the daily maintenance of her weapons.

Another image that conveys a sense of the teacher's physical and pedagogical characteristics is the simile at the conclusion of the poem: "Her arms hang down like sausages" (22). Here Mrs. Lawrence is a figure to be pitied, a tired, defeated person who is totally oblivious to the effects of her words. The carving and cleaning of nails, the hanging arms, the quiet statement about Judy's poor leadership — all are mundane images. Harm is present all the time, ready to inflict lasting damage at any moment. You might want to ask your students to consider other insidious sources of quiet but serious harm. They are likely to have their own stories of how quickly words can hurt, regardless of the speaker's awareness or intent.

POSSIBLE CONNECTION TO ANOTHER SELECTION

Mark Halliday, "Graded Paper" (text p. 680)

WILLIAM WORDSWORTH, *London, 1802* (p. 656)

William Wordsworth was born in the English Lake District, in Cockermouth, West Cumberland, and grew up roaming the countryside. He completed his undergraduate degree at Cambridge University in 1791 and spent a year in revolutionary France. By the age of twenty-seven, he had settled in Somersetshire to be near Samuel Taylor Coleridge, with whom, in 1798, he published one of the most influential volumes in the history of English poetry, *Lyrical Ballads*. Wordsworth enjoyed increasing public reward as a poet (becoming poet laureate in 1843) even as his private life suffered from frequent tragedy and disappointment.

The metonymic nouns following the colon in line 3 of "London, 1802" all point to areas within British culture and civilization that Wordsworth thinks have declined since

John Milton's day. All things have suffered loss—from the strength of the church, the army, or the accomplishment of writers to the more immediate and individual quality of home life—in particular an "inward happiness" (line 6), along with a sense of strength and security.

Milton seems to have represented for Wordsworth an epitome of the heroic, a kind of guiding star apart from other human beings, with a voice that was expansive, at one with the sublime in nature, and morally incorruptible.

POSSIBLE CONNECTIONS TO OTHER SELECTIONS

William Blake, "London" (text p. 631)

George Eliot, "In a London Drawingroom" (text p. 1006)

JIM STEVENS, *Schizophrenia* (p. 657)

The ways in which personification, stanzaic form, and title combine to create meaning in this poem can be a fruitful approach to discussion. Stevens personifies the house as a victim suffering from the turmoil of its inhabitants. You might ask students to find examples of ways in which the house is physically "hurt" by their activities (see especially lines 2–5 and 17–20). The sequencing and relative lengths of the stanzas draw the reader to important statements of meaning in the poem. The poem is framed by two identical statements that "it was the house that suffered most." Moving toward the center from these identical lines, lines 2–5 and 17–20 deal specifically with physical things happening to the house. The next two stanzas toward the center, lines 6–9 and 13–16, depict the people doing things to the house, using it as a means of carrying out their aggressions toward one another. The very center of the poem, set off by a three-line stanza when the ones surrounding it have contained four lines, specifies what has been going on between the people themselves.

It is the title, however, that brings the poem together as a whole and allows us to relate the suffering *of* the house to the suffering *in* the house. *Schizophrenia* literally means a split mind; it is a psychosis characterized by radical changes in behavior. Have the students notice the change in behavior and its effects on the house between the beginning and end of the poem. In the first nine lines, the house is being violently abused: doors and dishes are slammed around, the carpets are intentionally scuffed, and grease, much harder to deal with than plain dirt, is ground into the tablecloth. In lines 5–9, the pattern moderates slightly: the slammed doors get locked, the dishes remain dirty instead of being slammed around, the feet stand still instead of scuffing. The third long stanza provides a transition into a mode of behavior radically opposite to what has come before. It casts the turmoil in terms of the inhabitants' violence toward one another but also indicates that this violence is no longer occurring. Instead, what we see in lines 12–15 is the people dividing the house between them, splitting it between them to stay out of one another's way and put an end to the fighting. Note the ominous tone of line 15, an allusion to the biblical warning that "a house divided against itself cannot stand." Indeed, the effects on the house of this new kind of warfare are all seen in terms of things splitting apart—the paint coming away from the wood, the windows breaking into pieces, the front door coming loose from its hinges, and the roof tiles coming off the roof. The last word (*madhouse*) of the poem proper, before the refrain of the last line, brings the reader back to the title. You might discuss with your students whether the word refers to the house itself, which the speaker contends is suffering, or whether it means a house that contains mad people, or both. Is the idea of "home," the combination of house and people, the real victim of the madness? Would "Madhouse" have been a better title than "Schizophrenia"?

POSSIBLE CONNECTION TO ANOTHER SELECTION

Edgar Allan Poe, "The Haunted Palace" (text p. 667)

WALT WHITMAN, *A Noiseless Patient Spider* (p. 658)

In this poem, Whitman participates in a fairly long and distinguished tradition, starting with the homely tropes of Edward Taylor or Anne Bradstreet, that explores analogies between lower forms of natural life and the human condition. In this instance the analogy is effective because both soul and spider are isolated — and are trying to reach across vast space to forge connections between themselves and the rest of the world. The emphasis within the soul seems to be a reflective activity (*musing, venturing, throwing, seeking*), while the activity of the spider seems more a physical compulsion, especially with the repetition of "filament."

POSSIBLE CONNECTION TO ANOTHER SELECTION

Emily Dickinson, "I heard a Fly buzz — when I died —" (text p. 814)

JOHN DONNE, *A Valediction: Forbidding Mourning* (p. 658)

The questions in the text show how richly metaphorical this metaphysical poem in fact is. Virtually every statement here is made through a comparison. The lovers should tolerate their separation with the same grace with which "virtuous men" leave this earth (line 1). They are not like the "Dull sublunary" lovers (13) who need physical presence to sustain each other; they represent something finer. This sense of refinement is picked up and developed further in the simile in line 24, when the strength of the love between Donne and his wife is compared to gold, which does not shatter when beaten but expands to delicate, fine plate. Donne concludes his poem with the well-known compass metaphor. You might have to explain at this point what sort of compass Donne is describing, since we live in an age of computer graphics, not drafting skills. Because the compass here is used to draw circles, it is a most appropriate simile to describe unity and perfection.

POSSIBLE CONNECTIONS TO OTHER SELECTIONS

Anne Bradstreet, "To My Dear and Loving Husband" (text p. 956)

John Donne, "The Flea" (text p. 1005)

William Shakespeare, "Shall I compare thee to a summer's day?" (p. 743)

KAY RYAN, *Hailstorm* (p. 660)

In Ryan's compressed poem, the figurative language conveys a complex theme. By comparing the hailstorm to hornets, Ryan describes the frenetic movement of the ice pellets, reminiscent of the insects' flight. The movement inherent in this image sets up the contrast with the stillness of the storm's end. The sting of the hornets also becomes blunter and harder in the "fists and punches" (line 12) that the hail releases on the ground. By calling the hail "little white planets" (3), Ryan opens her meteorological poem to larger scientific language, including the earth's "crust" (10) on which the hailstones land. The images of the planets also reveal the otherworldliness of a hailstorm's aftermath, with its perfectly shaped white spheres that quickly melt away.

POSSIBLE CONNECTIONS TO OTHER SELECTIONS

Matsuo Bashō, "Under cherry trees" (text p. 753)

Robert Frost, "Design" (text p. 856)

Timothy Steele, "Waiting for the Storm" (text p. 723)

RONALD WALLACE, *Building an Outhouse* (p. 660)

Students will likely enjoy the scatological humor of this poem, which compares poetry to a toilet and, to a degree, to excrement. The last line, with its repetition of "sit on it" and its unmistakable reference to shit, is almost guaranteed to provoke laughter in class. You should have no trouble, either, in getting students to find the poem's many sophomoric puns and comparisons, such as "sweet smell" (line 4), "fly" (8), "load" (8), and the "nub" of a "pencil" (11).

If you'd rather avoid an extended classroom discussion of bodily functions, try to focus your students on the date of the poem (1991). At the writing of this sonnet (itself a form considered by many to be outdated), outhouses were obsolete in all but the poorest of American communities. Knowing that, what is Wallace implying about "building a poem" (1)?

POSSIBLE CONNECTIONS TO OTHER SELECTIONS

Anne Bradstreet, "The Author to Her Book" (text p. 647)

Katharyn Howd Machan, "Hazel Tells LaVerne" (text p. 596)

ELAINE MAGARRELL, *The Joy of Cooking* (p. 661)

This grisly poem is from the point of view of a disgruntled sibling who has, on a literal level, cooked parts of her sister and brother. On a metaphorical level, she is attacking their attributes which have injured her. Ask students whether they think the poem is humorous or horrifying. They are bound to recall some news story or horror movie featuring cannibalism, even of one's family members. Is the speaker's fantasy tempered by these incidents, or does her tone and her reliance on the discourse of cookbooks make it impossible to accept the poem as anything but a metaphor with humorous intent?

The tongue and heart are extended metaphors for the siblings. The sister is described as needing spices to make her more interesting. We can imagine that hers is not an effervescent personality. The brother, characterized as a heart, seems heartless. Whereas most hearts feed six, his "barely feeds two" (line 16). He is "rather dry" (10), requiring stuffing to make him palatable. Neither sibling is complete enough when left alone to warrant the speaker's unadorning description; she must "doctor them up" to make them palatable to her audience and herself.

POSSIBLE CONNECTION TO ANOTHER SELECTION

Sally Croft, "Home-Baked Bread" (text p. 636; question #1, following)

CONNECTION QUESTION IN TEXT (p. 661) WITH ANSWER

1. Write an essay that explains how cooking becomes a way of talking about something else in this poem and in Sally Croft's "Home-Baked Bread" (p. 636).

   Croft at first questions *The Joy of Cooking*, wondering why it should treat its subject as one would a human mystery. Carried away by the language, she moves into the role of seductress, luring her listener into the erotic sensuality of her poem. Magarrell's adaptation from the same book takes an entirely different form. Her tone is bitter. Rather than seducing her listeners, she startles and perhaps alienates them through her arresting images.

SCOTT HIGHTOWER, *My Father* (p. 662)

Hightower offers a rich list of metaphors that give the reader a way to "know" the titular father. In class discussion, ask students to attempt a literal description of the father, based on the figurative descriptions of him. Students may refer to the innate complexities in the pairing of "sugar man" and "teamster," or in the series "Siberian / tiger" (4–5), "lamb" (5), and "horse's ass" (6). Discuss the thread of association that Hightower seems to follow from word to word, line to line, stanza to stanza. An entire life can be boxed into a stanza, covering a range of behavior and emotion: "He stomps and hurls lightning bolts. / Has slipped away. Passed away. / My father was passé. My father" (22–24). Ask students which metaphors feel expected or unexpected.

While it's important to note the ways in which figurative language speaks about the subject at hand, these metaphors ultimately reveal things about the *I* of the poem. Perhaps because his father encompasses so many specific things, the speaker finds himself bound by the demands of metaphor, having "no use for / similes" (31–32). Because of his father, the speaker "hungers" after his own metaphors in order to address such complicated, intimate subjects.

POSSIBLE CONNECTIONS TO OTHER SELECTIONS

Billy Collins, "Introduction to Poetry" (text p. 564)

Ruth Forman, "Poetry Should Ride the Bus" (text p. 627)

PERSPECTIVE

JOHN R. SEARLE, *Figuring Out Metaphors* (p. 663)

In a writing assignment, ask students to find two poems in which the metaphors work and two in which they don't. Students should explain their choices in these essays — that is, define the metaphors in the poems and explain why they work (or why they don't). If possible, students should speculate about the characteristics of a successful metaphor based on the evidence of the poems they have chosen.

A class exercise or another writing assignment might involve students finding metaphors in sources other than poems — in the newspaper, for example, or in popular songs or television programs. Once found, these examples could also be analyzed as successful or unsuccessful metaphors.

24

Symbol, Allegory, and Irony

The discussion of symbol and allegory can follow naturally from the discussion of figurative language. In a sense, symbols are metaphors with one term left open, and it is up to the reader to complete them. Many of the poems in the previous chapter lend themselves well to symbolic readings—a good transition between the chapters might have students select a previously covered poem and examine its symbols.

 Ask students to explore the poetic elements in this chapter at **bedfordstmartins.com/meyerlit**.

Another exercise that can be useful is to have students brainstorm a list of symbols found in popular culture and articulate the connotations that surround them: what the American flag means, for instance. (This exercise can also illustrate how symbols can have different meanings for different groups.) This can help give students a sense of how symbols work, and how they can be simultaneously specific and general.

Students often seem to believe that every poem is immediately symbolic, which can be simultaneously encouraging and frustrating in their zeal to leap to the "real" meaning of the poem. Alternately, they may be committed to a kind of relativism, in which they believe that some poems can be symbolic of anything. While it is true that some symbols are more loosely focused than others, one of the challenges of discussion in this chapter is to encourage students to offer well-thought-out readings. It is a difficult line to walk between putting pressure on students to read critically and shutting down all discussion because the students come to believe that the teacher has "the right answer," and unless they can provide this they are better off keeping quiet. In fact, students may use silence as a tactic to bring out "the right answer" from the teacher. In this chapter it is perhaps better to err on the side of caution and try to draw out students' own interpretations, even if these interpretations are initially somewhat off track. You may find it useful to avoid giving your own interpretations at all, relying instead on student input shaped by questions from you and from other students. Students may find this frustrating at first, particularly when they are used to being given answers by authorities, but ultimately it will sharpen their abilities as readers.

Irony can be difficult to explain directly—in this case, examples are a great help. Irony often depends on an understanding of the context, as Kenneth Fearing's "AD" illustrates. Without some understanding of want ads, the irony in this poem will not be evident. It may be useful to compare some kinds of irony to an inside joke in that they depend on a shared bit of information before the audience can "get it." Students may in fact be quite familiar with situational irony, as in Jane Kenyon's

Web Ask students to research the poets in this chapter at **bedfordstmartins.com/meyerlit**.

"Surprise." They may be able to readily call incidents to mind in which all was not as it initially seemed. For an interesting take on irony, you might look at Linda Hutcheon's book *Irony's Edge: The Theory and Politics of Irony* (New York: Routledge, 1994; print.), which is an occasionally dense but well-supported argument about the place of irony in contemporary society.

ROBERT FROST, *Acquainted with the Night* (p. 665)

This poem investigates the mind of a speaker who has seen a part of humanity and of nature that he cannot overlook. His experience has led him to see things that other people have not necessarily seen. The poem invites us to read it on more than one level, as is the case with many of Frost's poems. You might ask students to discuss in a two-page essay how the clock functions in this poem. How does its presence modify the poem's tone? Do we read it literally, symbolically, or as a mixture of both?

POSSIBLE CONNECTIONS TO OTHER SELECTIONS

T. S. Eliot, "The Love Song of J. Alfred Prufrock" (text p. 1006)

Robert Frost, "Stopping by Woods on a Snowy Evening" (text p. 853)

EDGAR ALLAN POE, *The Haunted Palace* (p. 667)

Edgar Allan Poe was born in Boston, the son of itinerant actors. He lived an often harrowing life marked by alcoholism, disease, and misfortune, managing to eke out a rather precarious existence primarily as an editor for a number of newspapers and periodicals in Philadelphia, New York, and Baltimore. Although he was renowned in his lifetime as the author of "The Raven," his most abiding ambition was to be a respected critic. He died after collapsing in a Baltimore street.

Students may have had little exposure to allegory, since it is not frequently used by modern writers. Thus it might be useful to explicate at least one stanza of the poem, discussing how a particular part of the palace corresponds to a particular part of the human body or mind. Notice the two "characters" actually personified by Poe in the poem: Thought (line 5) and Echoes (29). Does there seem to be a particular reason for singling out these two?

What is the purpose of using such archaic expressions as "Porphyrogene" (22) and "red-litten" (42)? What other words in the poem seem especially well chosen for their connotative meanings?

As a short writing assignment or subject for further class discussion, ask your students to contrast the depictions of the "windows" and the "door" of the palace when they first appear in the poem (stanzas 3 and 4) with their portrayal in the last stanza, after the coming of the "evil things" (33). How do the windows and door seem to change?

POSSIBLE CONNECTION TO ANOTHER SELECTION

Jim Stevens, "Schizophrenia" (text p. 657)

EDWIN ARLINGTON ROBINSON, *Richard Cory* (p. 669)

Edwin Arlington Robinson became a professional poet in the grimmest of circumstances: his father's businesses went bankrupt in 1893, one brother became a drug addict and another an alcoholic, and Robinson could afford to attend Harvard University for just two years. He eked out a livelihood from the contributions of friends and patrons, finally moving to New York City, where his work received more critical attention and public acceptance. He won three Pulitzer Prizes for his gloomy, musical verse narratives.

As a writing assignment, you might ask students to analyze how Robinson achieves the power of the final line of "Richard Cory," paying special attention to the regal language that describes Cory as well as the strong contrasts in the couplets of the final stanza.

POSSIBLE CONNECTION TO ANOTHER SELECTION

Percy Bysshe Shelley, "Ozymandias" (text p. 1022)

KENNETH FEARING, *AD* (p. 672)

How does the double meaning inherent in the title of the poem — "AD" is an abbreviation for "advertisement" as well as for "in the year of the Lord" — prepare the reader for the satire that follows? Notice how even the type used for this poem contributes to its meaning. The italicized words and phrases might occur in any high-powered advertising campaign. How is the effect of the advertising words undercut by the words in standard type? What is the effect of the reversal of type patterns in the last line?

Students should be aware that the poem alludes, in part, to the Uncle Sam "I want you" army recruiting posters. Discuss whether the purpose of the satire in "AD" is to expose a situation that exists, to correct it, or both. Is the situation to which the poem refers — the attempt to draw people into a horrifying occupation by making the work sound exciting and rewarding — confined to the pre–World War II era?

Possible Connection to Another Selection

Wilfred Owen, "Dulce et Decorum Est" (text p. 633)

E. E. CUMMINGS, *next to of course god america i* (p. 673)

The speaker of this poem is trapped by jingoistic clichés that render his speech almost meaningless. His intent is to manipulate his audience, convincing them that the men who have sacrificed their lives in war are "heroic" and "happy" (line 10). As a writing assignment, you might ask students to analyze how Cummings portrays character without using direct description.

Possible Connection to Another Selection

Florence Cassen Mayers, "All-American Sestina" (text p. 750)

STEPHEN CRANE, *A Man Said to the Universe* (p. 673)

What sort of answer does the man in the poem expect to get from the universe? What does that say about the man? What other emotions, besides amusement, does this poem evoke? How does a reader's own perception of how the universe operates affect his or her response to the poem? Students are likely to concur that the more distance they feel between themselves and the man, the more amusing they find the poem.

Possible Connections to Other Selections

Robert Frost, "'Out, Out —'" (text p. 850)
Langston Hughes, "Lenox Avenue: Midnight" (text p. 939)

BOB HICOK, *Making it in poetry* (p. 674)

You might begin by asking your students why Hicok chooses such short lines in this poem. How do the frequent stops contribute to the humor of the poem and the attitude toward its subject? Because of these short lines, the repeated answer "Because I write poems" is broken differently each time the speaker gives it. The first time, "I write" carries the primary meaning of the sentence: it is the reason the poet has those checks. The second time, it is necessary to have "I write poems" together as a unit. The addition of the final word explains the speaker's obscurity.

You might also discuss what effect the poem's inclusion in this anthology has on its meaning. What would Hicok say about having his work reprinted here?

Possible Connections to Other Selections

Alexander Pope, From *An Essay on Criticism* (text p. 707)
Richard Wakefield, "In a Poetry Workshop" (text p. 1025, question #1, following)

1. Compare the life of the poet in Hicok's poem and in Richard Wakefield's "In a Poetry Workshop" (p. 1025).

   Poetry is a small part of the public life of the speaker in Hicok's poem, as evidenced by the small sums of money he receives from the journals that publish his work. He knows that writing poems is not the kind of public act that would make the bank teller recognize him. Wakefield's narrator has a very different experience because poetry is part of his public persona — he has to teach it. While Hicok worries that poetry is unknown to most people, Wakefield thinks it is overrun with useless rules. Both poems take an ironic stance toward poetry. The fact that we, as the audience, are reading Hicok's poem undercuts the idea that no one cares about his work, and Wakefield contradicts his own advice by creating a pattern of rhyme and rhythm.

JANE KENYON, *Surprise* (p. 675)

From the perspective of the woman "surprised," this poem encompasses many of the conflicting emotions of a surprise party in spare, deliberate imagery. Distracted by the unnamed male, and oblivious to the gathering elsewhere, the speaker notes all the changes around her as a result of the onset of spring. The last three lines of the poem reverse the mood, suggesting that the speaker's surprise comes at the ease with which her husband/lover has deceived her, opening up the possibility that there is something wrong with their relationship.

It might be useful to begin by asking students if they have ever been involved in a surprise party — either as the "victim" or as the scheming organizer. A discussion of what a surprise party intends to do leads naturally into a discussion of what it often actually does. Similarly, the poem leads us from the mundane — "pancakes at the local diner" (line 1), "casseroles" (4) — to the surprising renewal of nature in springtime, to the woman's astounding realization that the man has had such an easy time lying to her. The word "astound" (10), with its connotations of bewilderment, directs our attention away from the surprise party and into speculation about the relationship between them. The irony centers on the renewal of the spring birthday juxtaposed against some almost funereal undertones (consider "spectral" in line 8 and "ash" in line 9, for example). The tension among images enables us to interpret their relationship in a novel, surprising way.

Possible Connection to Another Selection

William Hathaway, "Oh, Oh" (text p. 550; question #1, following)

Connection Question in Text (p. 675) with Answer

1. Write an essay on the nature of the surprises in Kenyon's poem and in Hathaway's "Oh, Oh" (p. 550). Include in your discussion a comparison of the tone and irony in each poem.

   "Oh, Oh" is much more humorous than this poem, but the effects are similar. In both cases the final line tells us something that we didn't know, something that causes us to rethink the rest of the poem, especially the title. In Hathaway's poem we know that something is coming, though, because the title clues us in. In this poem we may at first take the "surprise" to be simply the surprise party, so we are especially surprised to learn that there is something amiss between this couple who seem to have enjoyed their breakfast and spring walk.

MARTÍN ESPADA, *Bully* (p. 675)

Espada's bitter poem builds on the irony that an elementary school named for Theodore Roosevelt — who before becoming the twenty-sixth president of the United States led his "Rough Riders" to victory in Cuba during the Spanish-American War

(1896–98) — is now dominated by Latino children. Although your students will be able to formulate a basic understanding of the irony from the details provided by the poet, a more thorough understanding of the Spanish-American War and the Boston school system in 1987 will help them gain a much more nuanced appreciation of the poem. It would be well worthwhile to assign them the Critical Strategies question (#3) in the text as a brief writing or oral report assignment before tackling the poem in class; you may want to divide responsibilities so that some students look up the Spanish-American War, some research Roosevelt's role in it, and some try to find information on the Boston public school system of the late 1980s, rather than overwhelming them with a major research project.

Students should be able to find a serviceable overview of the Spanish-American War and Roosevelt's role in it in a good encyclopedia (even online) or an American history survey textbook. The context of the Boston public schools in the late 1980s is likely to prove more elusive, especially because Espada has taken some liberties with fact for the purpose of his poem (the Roosevelt Elementary School in Hyde Park, a predominantly white working-class neighborhood on the edge of Boston, is actually named after Franklin Delano Roosevelt). The Boston public school system was found guilty of running racially segregated schools and forced by court order to desegregate in the 1970s: the busing program that ensued sparked riots and severe racial tensions that continue to linger. By the late 1980s schools in disadvantaged communities were still suffering from lack of funds (especially compared with schools in wealthier areas), and the city struggled to find a solution to the public school system's reputation for poor levels of education. Yet in September 1987, thirteen years after the controversial busing order was put into effect, a federal appeals court concluded that the city had shown a good effort to desegregate and decided that Boston no longer needed to follow racial guidelines in school assignments — essentially ending the era of court-ordered busing.

POSSIBLE CONNECTION TO ANOTHER SELECTION

Judy Page Heitzman, "The Schoolroom on the Second Floor of the Knitting Mill" (text p. 656)

KEVIN PIERCE, *Proof of Origin* (p. 676)

Pierce's title plays on several words central to the debates between creationists and those who believe in human evolution. "Origin" recalls Darwin's pivotal work *The Origin of Species*. "Proof" evokes the scientific method but also serves as a reminder that it is impossible to find irrefutable proof of either case. Science offers evidence, not proof, and the subject of the creation story is beyond the realm of proof. Pierce's take on the controversy highlights one piece of scientific evidence for evolution: the opposable thumbs that seem to separate more evolved mammals from others. However, even while using these appendages, the creationists adhere to the idea that humans were created in the form we see today rather than developing from some earlier species.

POSSIBLE CONNECTIONS TO OTHER SELECTIONS

Paul Laurence Dunbar, "Theology" (text p. 752)

Paul Humphrey, "Blow" (text p. 710)

Alice Jones, "The Foot" (text p. 727)

CARL SANDBURG, *Buttons* (p. 677)

This poem examines a topic that continues to be present whenever the media examine the costs of war; televised coverage of the wars in Vietnam and the Persian Gulf instigated similar commentary since this poem was written in 1915. Sandburg's poem hinges on the "laughing young man, sunny with freckles" (line 3), seemingly unaware of the meaning of his actions as he marks the day's casualties on the map "slammed up for advertising" (1) in a newspaper office. The map itself is a symbol for the war losses; the absence of gravity in the actions of the man who works to update that symbol is the inconsistency that drives the poem. The parenthetical examination of the "buttons" of the poem's title demonstrates the distance between the thoughtlessness of the young man and the tragic events played out on the actual battlefield.

Students are likely to be familiar with other media and their relationship to tragedy: How do television and radio announcers convey the gravity of the deaths they report? How do doctors and police officers on television series vary their emotional responses to crime and death depending on context?

POSSIBLE CONNECTIONS TO OTHER SELECTIONS

Kenneth Fearing, "AD" (text p. 672; question #1, following)

Henry Reed, "Naming of Parts" (text p. 682; question #1, following)

CONNECTION QUESTION IN TEXT (p. 677) WITH ANSWER

1. Discuss the symbolic treatment of war in this poem, Kenneth Fearing's "AD" (p. 672), and Henry Reed's "Naming of Parts" (p. 682).

   Sandburg's poem establishes the symbol of buttons for the losses of wartime, with a parenthetical examination that imagines the actual deaths and wounds beyond the map and its markers of victory and loss. Fearing's poem symbolizes the burgeoning Nazi movement by imagining the absurdity of a help-wanted ad detailing the attributes required of would-be Nazis. Reed's poem focuses on a small task, part of a soldier's training; this task is explicitly nonviolent, an exercise in vocabulary and mechanics, not related to death and wounds. All three authors focus on some small detail of wartime, real or imagined, that allows the reader to grasp the actual horror of war.

DENISE DUHAMEL, *How It Will End* (p. 677)

When watching movies, viewers tend to project their own personal baggage onto the characters being portrayed. They come to expect many clichés in films involving the breakdown or renewal of a love relationship, and Duhamel's readers are invited to join the speaker and husband in "How It Will End" as they watch a public drama unfold. It is "as good as a movie" (line 4), readers are told. The poem's dialogue begins with typical assumptions about what's in front of them: "Boy, he's sure in for it" (9) and "He deserves whatever's coming to him" (10). The speaker and her husband begin to fight, too, as they watch the lifeguard and girl fight and become more involved in their own observations. Duhamel reveals a good deal about the relationship of the speaker and husband through dialogue, since they end up expressing their own thinly veiled disappointments and frustrations with each other.

The bookend symbol of the red flag is important, adding a bit of sexual innuendo and comedy, since it "slaps against his station" (17) at the beginning of the fight and at the end "hangs limp" (47).

The situation in the poem is ironic because the speaker and husband begin as if they are watching a movie and end up finding themselves in one of their own making—however, there is uncertainty about where their fighting will lead, since "no one is watching us" (49). Add to that the irony that Duhamel is well aware her readers are watching her husband and wife very carefully.

POSSIBLE CONNECTIONS TO OTHER SELECTIONS

Robert Frost, " 'Out, Out—' " (text p. 850)

Jane Kenyon, "Surprise" (text p. 675; question #1, following)

1. Compare the tensions that are exposed in this poem and in Jane Kenyon's "Surprise" (text p. 675).

   Hidden tensions are revealed between the couples in both "How It Will End" and "Surprise." In Duhamel's poem, the speaker and her husband watch a couple's public fight, and it is "as good as a movie." Kenyon's poem begins with the "he" suggesting a walk, to look at the flowers. Quickly, both poems begin to reveal a discord in the couples' relationships. The husband and wife in "How It Will End" begin to bicker about the reason for the younger couple's fight. The imagery in "Surprise" goes slightly askew for a lovely spring walk, with ferns in the "ditches," and "spectral leaves" being pushed aside. In the end, the young couple in "How It Will End" makes up, while the speaker and husband are still fuming at each other. The speaker in "Surprise" is "astounded" at the ease with which her partner has "lied."

JULIO MARZÁN, *Ethnic Poetry* (p. 679)

The phrase "The ethnic poet said" begins each of the poem's five stanzas, followed by a quotation and the response of the "ethnic audience." In each case the poet speaks in language or imagery that isn't "conventional"—it seems to disrupt conventions of typical Western poetry or thought. In each case the audience responds by eating ethnic food or playing on ethnic instruments. In the final stanza, though, the poet quotes from Robert Frost's "Mending Wall," and the audience's response is to "deeply [understand] humanity" (line 20).

The poem invites us to consider the "proper" response to poetry as it satirizes the notion that poetry is a philosophical venture, that it is supposed to evoke in its listeners a deep understanding of human nature. The irony (and subtle humor) is made thicker by the fact that Frost's poem is about divisions between neighbors and that this poem begins with the assumption that there are differences between ethnic and other poetry. It might be interesting to apply the notion that poetry is meant to evoke a deep understanding about human nature to the poems excerpted within each stanza of "Ethnic Poetry." Is it possible to do so? Why does the "ethnic audience" choose to respond differently? What assumptions are made about the ethnicity of the poet and the audience in each stanza?

This poem may tend to touch off discussions of the "proper" response to poetry and the proper way to construct a poem. Ruth Forman's poem "Poetry Should Ride the Bus" (text p. 627) can deepen this discussion because it suggests that poetry is out of touch with everyday life. Is it implicitly so? Has our perception of poetry made it an elitist form? This is a good opportunity to get students to consider the nature of the barriers between "high" and "low" culture: Where do they experience poetry in their lives besides in college courses? And what is their response to it? Do they ever *read* poetry "for fun," or do they know anyone who does? Have they ever been to a poetry reading? Is the emphasis in contemporary music on lyrics or on melody, instrumentation, and so forth? Would students' responses to the lyrics of their favorite band be altered if those lyrics were presented in a classroom? (The general question: Does our understanding of poetry depend more on the context in which we read it or on the nature of the poetry itself?)

POSSIBLE CONNECTION TO ANOTHER SELECTION

Robert Frost, "Mending Wall" (text p. 843)

MARK HALLIDAY, *Graded Paper* (p. 680)

This poem takes the theme of a professor's written comments on a paper and examines them for poetic content. Using humor and taking advantage of the diction used in academic contexts, the poem establishes a connection between professor and student, examining the ways in which the graded paper serves as a communiqué between generations, a kind of love note shuffled back and forth. In its conclusion, the speaker acknowledges that, despite the student's difficulty with semicolons, the real problem is that "You are not / me, finally" (lines 34–35). The "delightful provocation" (38) this presents is the crux of the poem.

The grader of the paper is characterized as intelligent and familiar with academic culture but ultimately willing to allow room for honesty in the teacher-student relationship, opening the way for examination of a larger possibility. The final lines, beginning with "And yet" (29), offer an excuse for the fine grade awarded: anyone who is having trouble with semicolons, opaque thinking, and confused syntax shouldn't be getting an A-, but the "impressive . . . cheeky" (33) confidence of the student overrides the professor's initial "cranky" reaction.

POSSIBLE CONNECTION TO ANOTHER SELECTION

Robert Browning, "My Last Duchess" (text p. 684; question #1, following)

CONNECTION QUESTION IN TEXT (p. 681) WITH ANSWER

1. Compare the ways in which Halliday reveals the speaker's character in this poem with the strategies used by Robert Browning in "My Last Duchess" (p. 684).

   Halliday and Browning both use formal speech in the first lines of their poems and then settle into a more honest, revealing informality. Halliday moves from "your thinking becomes, for me, / alarmingly opaque" (lines 7–8) to "you are so young, so young" (37) over the course of his poem; Browning moves from the formal niceties of a host—"Will't please you sit and look at her?" (5)—to a vivid description of jealousy and the implication, in "I gave commands" (45), of murder.

CHARLES SIMIC, *The Storm* (p. 681)

In "The Storm," Simic personifies beings in nature to show how they sense and respond to the coming storm. Only the static blue sky and the collective "we" who "know nothing" (line 13) fail to respond quickly to the changes in the air. Simic's choice of "spellbound" (14) to describe the people suggests that they not only are oblivious to nature but are held under some power they do not control. In his use of personification, however, Simic makes the animals and especially the plants in the landscape seem human in their concerns and behaviors. The weeds worry over what is coming, and the trees bend slightly in a show of social nicety. In the world of "The Storm," these entities are far more sensitive and thoughtful than people are.

POSSIBLE CONNECTIONS TO OTHER SELECTIONS

Emily Dickinson, "Presentiment—is that long Shadow—on the lawn—" (text p. 646)

Timothy Steele, "Waiting for the Storm" (text p. 723)

CONNECTION QUESTION IN TEXT (p. 681) WITH ANSWER

1. Write a comparative analysis of the themes of "The Storm" and Emily Dickinson's "Presentiment—is that long Shadow—on the lawn—" (p. 646).

   Simic attributes human behaviors to the elements of the natural world in order to compare their reactions with humans' sensitivity to changes in the environment before a storm. Dickinson makes a similar move in describing the grass as "startled" (line 3). However, her very compact poem also depends on the complex ideas behind the abstract noun "Presentiment." One concept this word suggests is the foreknowledge that Simic's details hint at in "The Storm," but Dickinson's use of abstraction gives her poem a more cerebral feeling than Simic's with its conversational tone. Also, though both authors write about sensing a coming change, Dickinson's poem looks forward more directly to death as the source of change.

JAMES MERRILL, *Casual Wear* (p. 682)

Merrill has been called a conversational poet. His familiarity with the lives of American aristocrats may result from his wealthy background, which especially influenced his earlier poetry.

Jeans, of course, are "casual wear," and by implication, this act of random terrorism appears to be a casual flourish of some unseen hand. That relation in sum seems to be the import of this poem. Because of the enjambment of lines between stanzas, students may not at first observe that the stanzas rhyme with an *abba* pattern — except the middle two lines of the first stanza. But then, what would rhyme with "Ferdi Plinthbower"? Rhyme, however — along with odd, lengthy names; precise statistics; and descriptions of human beings as proper demographic models — detracts from our ability to feel the weight of this crime against humankind and our intuitive understanding of the moral workings of the universe. The inverse parallels between "tourist" and "terrorist" seem just too chillingly neat.

So what might Merrill actually be saying in this poem? Perhaps he is not so much speaking out against terrorist activity as talking about the media, with its formulaic scenarios, and the number-plotting social scientists, who surround such an event with their own dehumanizing mist of facts and figures. In the final irony of the poem, we know the name of the clothing designer but not that of the terrorist's victim.

Comments on Merrill's poetry include *James Merrill: Essays in Criticism,* edited by David Lehman and Charles Berger (Ithaca: Cornell UP, 1983; print.), and Judith Moffet's *James Merrill: An Introduction to the Poetry* (New York: Columbia UP, 1984; print.).

POSSIBLE CONNECTION TO ANOTHER SELECTION

Peter Meinke, "The ABC of Aerobics" (text p. 774; question #1, following)

CONNECTION QUESTION IN TEXT (p. 682) WITH ANSWER

1. Compare the satire in this poem with that in Peter Meinke's "The ABC of Aerobics" (p. 774). What is satirized in each poem? Which satire do you think is more pointed?

   Meinke's satire directs itself at the frantic health-conscious exercising that has become a part of our culture. Merrill's addresses a different aspect of the same culture, the materialism and media hype that eradicate the individual, leaving us with facts, figures, and wardrobe reports. Merrill's poem has a sobering life-and-death message, whereas Meinke's seems to have more hope for immediate change. Merrill's speaker is bitter; Meinke's satire is comical.

HENRY REED, *Naming of Parts* (p. 682)

The irony of this poem is situational. The instructor (no doubt an army sergeant addressing a group of raw recruits) is filled with self-importance as he drones on about naming the rifle parts, wholly oblivious to the silent beauty of the spring day. The season, though, arouses in the young recruit's thoughts reminders of a world far more vibrant than that of weaponry. Students should be able to distinguish between sergeant and recruit in the exchange of voices. The recruit's musings begin in the second half of the fourth line of each stanza, and the final line works to deflect the authoritative tone of the earlier part of the stanza. Discussion of rifle parts summons up with ironic aptness physical allusions, which the young recruit inevitably thinks of as he looks at the beautiful gardens in spring, assaulted by the vigorous bees.

ALLEN BRADEN, *The Hemlock Tree* (p. 683)

A naturalistic picture of the world builds to, and then recedes from, Braden's italicized line: *"for the living shall consume / the flesh of the living"* (lines 9–10). His philosophical statement applies to all living things — people, animals, plants. His first example is of an owl that leaves the hemlock to "devour a wild dove" (3). The dove was under the illusion of protection: "tamed by Safeway birdseed" (3). All that is left as evidence of the dove's death is "a wreath of down and drops of blood" (12), both an accurate description of what's left of the bird and a biblical allusion, as is the reference to a "covenant with nature" (8), which echoes the Old Testament idea of a covenant with God. In this way, Braden implies that "you" (4) must have faith that this is the truth of the matter. He suggests that you "might be wondering" (13) about the wisteria blooming around the tree. It is lovely and transient, yet it strangles the tree "with its gradual, constrictive, necessary beauty" (18). There is an implied beauty in the life and death of all that the poem speaks of, and it is interesting to note that the most beautiful (and necessary) is the strangling wisteria.

Braden uses the image of the hemlock tree throughout: it is the place from which the owl stalks its prey and the tree the wisteria climbs and destroys. Ask students what they know of hemlock and its properties. Why would a hemlock tree be a fitting symbol for a world in which one meets death at the hands of a fellow creature? Students may mention Socrates being forced to drink hemlock, and that discussion may then touch upon the martyrdom of Christ. Students may wish to look at the poem from a naturalist's viewpoint, examining only the perfect and "inevitable / circuit of hunger" (6–7), but consider also the Christian symbolism throughout—references to the dove, the covenant, the wreath and blood, and the italicized line which has some intimation of the Eucharist: "this is my body and blood."

POSSIBLE CONNECTIONS TO OTHER SELECTIONS

Gerard Manley Hopkins, "Pied Beauty" (text p. 1012)

A. E. Housman, "Loveliest of trees, the cherry now" (text p. 738)

Andrew Hudgins, "The Cow" (text p. 709)

Mary Oliver, "Wild Geese" (text p. 983)

Paul Zimmer, "What I Know about Owls" (text p. 982)

CONNECTION QUESTION IN TEXT (p. 684) WITH ANSWER

1. Compare the view of nature expressed in this poem and in any poem of your choice from Chapter 37, "A Thematic Case Study: The Natural World" (text pp. 975–984).

    Students might choose "What I Know about Owls" or "November" to compare its subject or tonal similarities. They might choose something like "Wild Geese" and discuss the natural order of things and our response to it. Any comparison should focus on images or symbols of the natural world and our place in it.

ROBERT BROWNING, *My Last Duchess* (p. 684)

Robert Browning lived with his parents in a London suburb until he married Elizabeth Barrett at age thirty-four; he had previously left home only to attend boarding school and for short trips abroad. He and his wife lived in Italy for fifteen years, a period in which he produced some of his first memorable poems. *Men and Women,* published in 1855, gained Browning the initial intimations of his later fame. The poet returned to England after his wife died in 1861. His work continued to elicit increasing public (if not always critical) acclaim.

Ironically, the speaker is talking about the portrait of his last duchess (how many went before?) to the marriage broker, who is handling the current arrangement between the duke and the broker's "master," the father of the bride-to-be.

The last wife's principal fault was that she was too democratic in her smiles; she did not reserve them for the duke alone. The duke holds no regard for kindness and thoughtfulness; he thinks only of money, rank, and name. He treats women as objects and possessions.

The visitor seems to want to leave early, perhaps to warn his master of the unfeeling tyrant who would marry the master's daughter at a cut rate (cf. lines 47–54).

Students may have already read this dramatic monologue in high school. The second time around they should appreciate the irony even more as the duke reveals so much of his own character while ostensibly controlling the situation.

POSSIBLE CONNECTIONS TO OTHER SELECTIONS

Mark Halliday, "Graded Paper" (text p. 680)

Katharyn Howd Machan, "Hazel Tells LaVerne" (text p. 596; question #1, following)

CONNECTION QUESTION IN TEXT (p. 686) WITH ANSWER

1. Write an essay describing the ways in which the speakers of "My Last Duchess" and Katharyn Howd Machan's "Hazel Tells LaVerne" (p. 596) inadvertently reveal themselves.

    In both cases the speaker has a story to tell, and both speakers are trying to paint a favorable picture of themselves as they do so. The speaker of Browning's poem gets himself in trouble as he continues to talk, indicating the fate of his last duchess through unsuppressed expressions of his own unfulfilled desire. As he describes the portrait, he eventually gets away from art and into the character of the duchess, wondering all the while how he should express himself. The speaker of "Hazel Tells LaVerne" reveals her unconscious desire to be taken away from her situation as she repeats the line "me a princess," focusing (without meaning to do so) on herself rather than on the frog whose story she is narrating. Students with a background in psychology might be able to flesh out the motivations behind these speakers' tales even more.

RICHARD WILBUR, *A Finished Man* (p. 686)

The opening line "Of the four louts who threw him off the dock" sets the stage in "A Finished Man"—no matter what the old man in Wilbur's poem goes on to do, he continues to be haunted by the embarrassing or troubling things that have happened to him. Ask students what they make of this man who tries to "walk today with heart at ease" (line 13) to receive accolades, yet whose mishaps take up three-fifths of the poem.

Wilbur's ironic title suggests his man is polished or perfected, but also that his life is all but over. (Additionally, Wilbur's iambic pentameter gives his verse a "finish," or a sense of perfection, and solidly "finishes" the thought of each line.) His man is "finished" as the college, to which he's presumably given money, decides to name a building for him. Basking in this life accomplishment, he "feels the warm sun sculpt his cheek" (17). In this way, he turns into a monument himself as he hears the "young president" (18) get up to speak. Ask students to discuss the irony of Wilbur's statement: "If the dead die, if he can but forget, / If money talks, he may be perfect yet" (19–20). What do they make of this man who has waited until the end of his life to overcome his insecurities, but only does so by outliving or outspending his contemporaries?

POSSIBLE CONNECTIONS TO OTHER SELECTIONS

Emily Dickinson, "Success is counted sweetest" (text p. 803)

Edwin Arlington Robinson, "Richard Cory" (text p. 669; question #1, following)

CONNECTION QUESTION IN TEXT (p. 686) WITH ANSWER

1. Compare the themes in "A Finished Man" and in Edwin Arlington Robinson's "Richard Cory" (text p. 669).

    Both poems revolve around men who appear (or want to appear) as what they are not. Each is a "finished man." Robinson's Cory "glittered when he walked" in front of the townspeople; Wilbur's old man "feels the warm sun sculpt his cheek." Despite these images of vibrancy, Cory goes home and "put[s] a bullet in his head," while Wilbur's old man, one senses, has almost no time left.

WILLIAM BLAKE, *The Chimney Sweeper* (p. 687)

There is an ironic distance in this poem between the speaker, who seems to be too young to make judgments, and Blake, who through his ironic perspective underscores the harm that comes from too meekly doing one's duty, not to mention the evil of a society indifferent to the plight of "thousands of sweepers" whose only pleasure is in dreams. Needless to say, sacrificing one's hair for the sake of on-the-job cleanliness is not a principle Blake would endorse.

On the surface the poem could be interpreted as a dream of desire for some beneficent angel to release the boys from their "coffins of black" (line 12) — that is, the chimneys. More likely, the dream expresses a desire for release through death from the tortuous and life-threatening trials of sweeping soot from chimneys. Here again, irony operates, in that a dream of death makes it easier for the boy to face his life the next morning.

PERSPECTIVE

EZRA POUND, *On Symbols* (p. 688)

Consider Pound's use of the word *natural* in the first line of the passage. Does he mean that a symbol should be drawn from an object in nature or that a symbol should have a natural, easy relationship to the idea it is meant to symbolize? Students might suggest other interpretations. Does Pound's example of the hawk at the end of the passage help to clarify his meaning? Ask students what a hawk might symbolize. Choose a poem from this chapter and, identify the symbols the poet uses and discuss whether they are "natural" in either sense of the word. Look at Edgar Allan Poe's "The Haunted Palace" (text p. 667), wherein the human mind and head are compared to a house, or Henry Reed's "Naming of Parts" (text p. 682), in which there is a symbolic contrast between rifle instruction and the beauty of nature, as examples to discuss which method of using symbols they think conveys meaning most effectively.

25

Sounds

Encouraging students to read aloud is vital for this chapter. Although initially you may have to lead by example, you will probably want to shift the focus onto student readers at some point. In some cases you may find yourself confronting a considerable degree of resistance, particularly if there has not been much reading aloud previously. Much of this resistance stems from fear of embarrassment, and dealing with it requires either the creation of a "safe space" in which students can read without fear of others snickering or a slightly raucous classroom environment in which students don't feel as much pressure to be "cool."

Web Ask students to explore *sound* at **bedfordstmartins.com/ meyerlit**.

If you have a group of particularly shy students, you might find it helpful to assign students poems in advance, so that they have a chance to read the poem through a couple of times before being called on to speak out before the class. If you have a mix of extraverts and introverts, you might schedule the class so that the extraverts read "cold" and announce at the end of class the poems the introverts will read in the next session, to give them fair warning.

In most cases the addition of student voices to the classroom will help increase involvement and raise the energy level. If you have not featured much student reading in the class so far, this chapter would be an appropriate time to do so.

In addition to including student voices in the classroom, this chapter affords an opportunity to include the voices of the poets as well: the poems of Hopkins, Carroll, and Pope are available on audio recordings. It is perhaps a judgment call as to whether you should introduce these readings before students have done much reading on their own, in order to provide models of reading for them, or to wait until after students have some experience, to keep from intimidating them into silence. If you have included recordings in previous chapters, this may not be an issue here. In any event, recordings can be very useful in giving students a sense of the reality of the people "behind the page." You may find it appropriate to do readings or bring in recordings of poems that have been popular with students earlier in the class and evaluate the poets' use of sound in relation to the students' own preference of these poems.

Web Ask students to research the poets in this chapter at **bedfordstmartins.com/ meyerlit**.

Thematically, there are some interesting poems in this chapter. If you do not want the focus on reading to overwhelm a discussion of these poems, you could use the reading as a springboard to raise the class's interest and energy, and to give them specific features to discuss when they make connections between the sound of a poem and its "message."

ANONYMOUS, *Scarborough Fair* (p. 690)

Your students may or may not be acquainted with the Simon and Garfunkel version of this ballad that was used in the 1960s as an antiwar song, and the use of this traditional ballad in that context may lead to some interesting discussion about the difference between the oral and written tradition.

As a ballad, "Scarborough Fair" follows a clear pattern: four feet to a line with an *abab* rhyme scheme and repeated second and fourth lines. In addition, in all but the first stanza, the first words of the stanza are "Tell her to" followed by the introduction of an impossible task that, if performed, will reconcile the speaker of the poem to the "bonny lass" (line 3) who was once his true lover. The impossible nature of these tasks is perhaps a clue as to how much hope the speaker in the poem has of reconciliation.

The effect of the refrain is soothing—readers and listeners come to expect the repeated lines, and the rhythm of these lines is peaceful. The herbs that are mentioned in the refrain are associated with female power (parsley was used to decorate tombs, sage represents wisdom, rosemary is for memory, and thyme is thought to enhance courage). In addition, both sage and rosemary had the connotation of growing in gardens where women ruled the households. Why might the poet have chosen these herbs as repeated symbols in this ballad? What message might the poet have been trying to convey?

POSSIBLE CONNECTIONS TO OTHER SELECTIONS

Anonymous, "Bonny Barbara Allan" (text p. 999)

John Donne, "A Valediction: Forbidding Mourning" (text p. 658)

JOHN UPDIKE, *Player Piano* (p. 691)

This poem is a listening exercise in how to translate the sounds poetry can produce to musical analogues we have already heard. From light ditties through more somber 1920s chase-scene music, perhaps, to a medley of chords and light cadences, this poem explores a player piano's repertoire. In doing so, does the poem do anything *besides* impress us with its sounds? Does reading the poem allow us anything beyond the sheer joy of the sounds of words and the way they can be manipulated?

MAY SWENSON, *A Nosty Fright* (p. 692)

Because "A Nosty Fright" is much more about sound than sense, be sure to read it, or have students read it, aloud (this may be more difficult than one might anticipate, for the transposed consonants often have the effect of creating tongue-twisters). Does the fractured diction have any purpose other than humor? Remind students that people who are upset or frightened often find it difficult to speak clearly.

Notice that sometimes the poetic technique used here results in transpositions that are actual words. Do any of these seem appropriate in this poem, for instance, "Bat" in line 24 or "fright" in line 25? Do any of them seem out of place, like "mitten" (20)? Have students suggest definitions for some of the nonsense words and phrases, based on their sounds. Compare the poem with Lewis Carroll's "Jabberwocky" (text p. 704). Are the techniques for creating new words the same in both poems?

POSSIBLE CONNECTION TO ANOTHER SELECTION

Lewis Carroll [Charles Lutwidge Dodgson], "Jabberwocky" (text p. 704)

EMILY DICKINSON, *A Bird came down the Walk—* (p. 693)

Silent reading of this poem, followed by reading it aloud, will reinforce the connection between sound and sense. In particular, students should hear the difference between the irregular movement of the first three stanzas and the smoothness of the last six lines, a difference created visually by punctuation but even more obvious when the poem is heard.

One of the poetic techniques that characterizes Emily Dickinson's poetry is her use of unexpected words and images. Consider her depiction of the bird's eyes and of his flight. How can eyes be "rapid" (line 9)? How can they hurry (10)? How can feathers "unroll" (15)? How is flight like rowing (16)? What is the effect created by the use of unusual language to describe an ordinary creature?

Compare the way the sounds of poetry are used to create a sense of an animal's movement in this poem and in Rilke's "The Panther" (text p. 635). Are the panther's movements in any way like the bird's?

POSSIBLE CONNECTIONS TO OTHER SELECTIONS

Gerard Manley Hopkins, "The Windhover" (text p. 1012)

Rainer Maria Rilke, "The Panther" (text p. 635)

ANYA KRUGOVOY SILVER, *French Toast* (p. 697)

"French Toast" is a poem radiant in alliteration. Consider the musical assonance found in "thick" and "milk" (line 1) or "drenching every yeasted / crevice"(4–5). Not all rhymes are perfect; also discuss with students the musicality of slant rhymes, like "remember" (7) and "butter" (9).

The sound of what's being described enhances the vividness of the images found here. Silver engages the senses with word and sound combinations—"spongiest challah" in "foaming cream" (3). The words are onomatopoeia-like: all is "dipped," "drenched," "sodden," or "soak[ed]." Sound mimics sense as the bread is "fringed with crisp lace of browned egg and scattered sugar" (2). Ask students to identify the consonance and assonance in this line and others.

Also discuss the consequence of starting with a foreign phrase. Silver brings the poem full circle when the last lines about the speaker's life echo the opening note, "*pain perdu.*" Ask students to hear the phrase *pain perdu* in their heads and observe where the echo occurs: "I turn / toward you under goose down after ten years / of marriage, craving, still, that sweet white immersion" (10–12).

POSSIBLE CONNECTIONS TO OTHER SELECTIONS

Helen Chasin, "The Word *Plum*" (text p. 712)

Sally Croft, "Home-Baked Bread" (text p. 636)

Diane Lockward, "Linguini" (text p. 703)

Elaine Magarrell, "The Joy of Cooking" (text p. 661)

RICHARD ARMOUR, *Going to Extremes* (p. 698)

What are the "extremes" to which this poem goes? How does the poet connect the two words that describe the extremes?

Even if students are unfamiliar with scansion, they should be able to detect a difference in the way words are emphasized in lines 1 and 3 as opposed to lines 2 and 4. Ask them to describe how the sound shifts coincide with the action of the poem. In speaking lines 1 and 3 aloud, one can almost feel the sharp movements of the bottle. In lines 2 and 4, it is as though the bottle is at rest, with the person who has been shaking it now waiting to see whether or not the catsup will come. Having students actually "shake" an imaginary catsup bottle as they recite the poem might be an effective way to connect sound to sense.

POSSIBLE CONNECTION TO ANOTHER SELECTION

Margaret Atwood, "you fit into me" (text p. 645)

ROBERT SOUTHEY, *From "The Cataract of Lodore"* (p. 698)

Although Robert Southey is now known chiefly for his association with some of the great poets of the Romantic period, such as Wordsworth and Coleridge, he was very popular in his own time and became the poet laureate of England in 1813. He is also credited with the first published version of the children's story *The Three Bears.*

In a twenty-three-line introductory stanza that is not excerpted here, the poet reveals that his son and daughter had requested him to tell them — in verse — about the water at Lodore. He also introduces himself as the poet laureate. Does having this information in any way change your students' response to the poem that follows?

Are any lines in the poem especially memorable? Why is it appropriate that line 69, with its thirteen syllables, is metrically the longest line of the poem?

TIP FROM THE FIELD

One tip I've found helpful in teaching sound in poetry is to have students stand in a tight circle and recite the excerpt from "The Cataract of Lodore" in round-robin fashion, one after another. Each student reads a line in the order of the poem, repeating the poem several times, faster each time. The results, in terms of student response, are remarkable.

— NANCY VEIGA, *Modesto Junior College*

POSSIBLE CONNECTION TO ANOTHER SELECTION

A. E. Housman, "Loveliest of trees, the cherry now" (text p. 738)

PERSPECTIVE

DAVID LENSON, *On the Contemporary Use of Rhyme* (p. 701)

You might ask students to find contemporary poems that make subtle use of rhyme. Philip Larkin's poems are good examples of the effective use of slant rhyme and enjambment to camouflage the rhymes in a poem. Conversely, you might ask students to look for songs that don't use rhyme.

Students might be interested in speculating on why writers are returning to rhyme. Is more formal poetry appropriate for our time and culture? Or is it simply a question of rebelling against the norm (in our time, unrhymed poetry)?

GERARD MANLEY HOPKINS, *God's Grandeur* (p. 702)

Gerard Manley Hopkins was a deeply religious man, a Jesuit ordained in 1877. He had previously graduated from Oxford University and joined the Roman Catholic Church in 1866. He served a number of parishes before being appointed a professor of classics at University College, Dublin. Although he tried to keep his poetic vocation from interfering with his spiritual one, he wasn't successful, and he suffered greatly because of this conflict, once burning all his finished work and another time forsaking poetry for seven years.

Although this poem follows sonnet form and an exact rhyme scheme, the first eight lines still read very roughly. How does the poet achieve this effect? Note the disruptions in rhythm as well as the use of cacophonic sounds. Have students try reading line 4 aloud to better appreciate its difficulty. Is there any change in the level of disruption or the level of cacophony in the last six lines? What is the effect of the inserted "ah!" in the last line?

Compare the halting beginning and smooth ending of this poem with the similar transition that occurs in Emily Dickinson's "A Bird came down the Walk —" (text p. 693). How does Dickinson's bird compare with the bird image Hopkins evokes in the last two lines?

POSSIBLE CONNECTION TO ANOTHER SELECTION

William Wordsworth, "he World Is Too Much with Us" (text p. 742)

DIANE LOCKWARD, *Linguini* (p. 703)

"Linguini" is a poem that, like a recipe, makes use of lists. Lockward peppers her writing with Italian phrases that add to the atmosphere and the musicality of what she writes about. This is a poem steeped in things Italian: in love, in language, and in the foods that illuminate the relationship being described. Ask students to consider the effect of repetition in this poem. How would the poem be different if, as in "French Toast" (text p. 697), the poem began with the word *linguini* and then it wasn't heard again until the very end? Discuss how the repetition allows for movement within the poem and lets Lockward explore the dimensions of her subject. Also consider how these choices go hand in hand with Lockward's decision to write her poem as one long stanza.

POSSIBLE CONNECTIONS TO OTHER SELECTIONS

Helen Chasin, "The Word *Plum*" (text p. 712)

Sally Croft, "Home-Baked Bread" (text p. 636)

Elaine Magarrell, "The Joy of Cooking" (text p. 661)

Anya Krugovoy Silver, "French Toast" (text p. 697; question #1, following)

CONNECTION QUESTION IN TEXT (p. 704) WITH ANSWER

1. What similarities and differences do you find in the use of sound in "Linguini" and in Silver's "French Toast" (text p. 697)?

    Both writers make use of another language that the reader may or may not be acquainted with for effect, and both are writing about foods that originated in a foreign country. Silver uses a French phrase to begin her poem and returns to it at the end, while Lockward interweaves Italian vocabulary throughout. Both use words that imitate sounds: in "French Toast," those of cooking, in "Linguini," eating. Both are heavily alliterative.

LEWIS CARROLL [CHARLES LUTWIDGE DODGSON], *Jabberwocky* (p. 704)

"'Jabberwocky' is no mere piece of sound experimentation but a serious short narrative poem describing a young man's coming of age as he seeks out and kills the tribal terror." Test that description on your students, and they will, one hopes, turn around and tell you that the fun of this poem and the justification for its being reside in its sound and word creations.

Carroll kept his own glossary for some of the words in this poem, which Alice read through her looking glass. The glossary entries and copious notes about the poem are provided by Martin Gardner in *The Annotated Alice* (New York: Bramhall House, 1960; print; 191-97.). The notes are too extensive to include here, but as a sampling, here is the first stanza "translated":

'Twas time for making dinner (bryllyg — to broil),
    and the "smooth and active" (slimy + lithe) badgers

Did scratch like a dog (gyre — giaour)
    and drill holes (gimble) in the side of the hill:

All unhappy were the Parrots (now extinct; they lived on veal and
    under sundials),

And the grave turtles (who lived on swallows and oysters) squeaked.

Reality bores its head through the hills and holes of "Jabberwocky," and certain words in the poem have their place in the *OED*. These include *rath,* an Irish word for a circular earthen wall; *Manx,* a Celtic name for the Isle of Man; *whiffling,* smoking, drinking, or blowing short puffs; *Caloo,* the sound and name of an arctic duck; *beamish,* old form of *beaming; chortled,* Carroll's own coinage, meaning "laughed"; and *gallumphing,* another of Carroll's creations, which according to him is a cross between *gallop* and *triumphant* and means "to march on exultantly with irregular bounding movements."

POSSIBLE CONNECTION TO ANOTHER SELECTION

May Swenson, "A Nosty Fright" (text p. 692; question #1, following)

CONNECTION QUESTION IN TEXT (p. 705) WITH ANSWER

1.   Compare Carroll's strategies for creating sound and meaning with those used by Swenson in "A Nosty Fright" (p. 692).

     Whereas Swenson transposes letters to create amusing sound patterns and effects, Carroll combines and alters words to invent a new language for his speaker. Carroll's technique is harder to translate word for word; it requires more of his audience's imaginative effort.

WILLIAM HEYEN, *The Trains* (p. 705)

For students who don't know, explain that Treblinka is the name of a Nazi concentration camp located near Warsaw, Poland. To illustrate Heyen's use of sound, you may want to open discussion by reading the poem aloud to your class. By repeating the word *Treblinka,* and by relying on choppy words with sharp, hard consonant sounds, Heyen creates the sound and rhythm of the wheels of a train — a rhythm that is intensified with the repetition of *Treblinka* until it resonates within the reader. In this way the poet uses sound and rhythm to affect the reader. Ask students to provide specific examples from the poem of how sound is used to intensify the horror of Treblinka.

At first, Heyen tells the facts of the story, listing with detachment and distance the statistics of what was removed from Treblinka on freight trains. As the poem continues, however, the statistics gain strength and the reader's horror mounts with each new revelation: Clothing became paper (line 7), watches were saved and kept (8), and women's hair was used for mattresses and dolls (9).

In the fourth stanza, Heyen implies that many people are indirectly linked to the atrocities of Treblinka through the legacy of the material goods culled from the Holocaust. He suggests that the words of his poem might "like to use some of that same paper" (10); "One of those watches may pulse in your own wrist" (11), much like the rhythm of breathing or a pulse; and that someone the reader *knows* may "collect dolls, or sleep on human hair" (12). Ask students to consider the effect of this stanza. Is the poet implying a collective guilt for the Holocaust? Or is he implying that the horror of Treblinka lives on through the material legacy of the dead? In the end, no one escapes Heyen's indictment, and although Commandant Stangl of Treblinka may be dead at last, his legacy lives on in word and sound within anyone who hears the story.

POSSIBLE CONNECTION TO ANOTHER SELECTION

Ruth Fainlight, "Crocuses" (text p. 629)

JOHN DONNE, *Song* (p. 706)

This poem explores a number of supposed impossibilities, ending with "a woman true, and fair" (line 18). The poem is at once bawdy and cynical; women are promiscuous, but the speaker also feels that they cannot be otherwise. Once students have discerned the speaker's attitude and his tone, take some time to investigate the way the speaker builds his argument. What types of mysteries does he use for comparison in the first stanza?

Donne manages to mix cynicism and lightheartedness here as he verbally throws up his hands at the possibility of finding an honest mind or a woman who is both true and fair. You might spend some time in class discussion exploring how he holds at bay the darker tones of his cynicism. Can we identify with Donne's dilemma today, or have attitudes toward women changed too much? What does the humor in the poem tell us about his fundamental attitude toward women? Students will probably appreciate the hyperbole in the poem. It is as though Donne were saying, "You might as well get with child a mandrake root, as find an honest mind."

The last stanza is especially humorous. Donne claims he would not even go next door to see this reputedly loyal woman. Her reputation for loyalty might hold long enough for his friend to write a letter describing her, but by the time the speaker arrived, she would have been false to two or three other lovers.

As a writing assignment, you might ask students to discuss the humor in this song, humor that would definitely include Donne's use of hyperbole. Students should then try to anticipate a listener's reaction to the speaker and decide whether the speaker is perfectly "straight" in his observations.

POSSIBLE CONNECTION TO OTHER SELECTIONS

Anonymous, "Scarborough Fair" (text p. 690)

John Donne, "The Flea" (text p. 1005)

ALEXANDER POPE, *From* An Essay on Criticism (p. 707)

Alexander Pope was born in London and, after age twelve, grew up in Windsor Forest. Because his family was Catholic and because he had been afflicted with tuberculosis of the spine, most of his education was completed at home. Catholics couldn't attend university or hold office — chief routes to patronage in those days — so Pope became by necessity as well as by desire and talent the first writer to show that literature could be one's sole support. His work, beginning with translations of the *Iliad* and the *Odyssey,* was both critically approved and financially profitable.

You might begin discussion of this selection by reminding students that the debate over which should take precedence, sound or sense, has been of greater concern to poets than many of us realize or recall.

Pope enjoys a little self-reflective mockery in these lines, like the bumper sticker that reads "Eschew Obfuscation." What he says, he does: the iambs march with strict, tuneful regularity in line 4. The word *do* in line 10 is an expletive, or meter filler. Line 11 presents a parade of monosyllables. "Chimes" in line 12 sets up the anticipated "rhymes" in line 13, and line 21 exceeds its bounds, albeit slowly, with the long alexandrine. Line 20 ("A needless Alexandrine") is also a clever play on Pope's name and on himself.

Line 23 uses assonance and some alliteration to suggest what it means; line 24 is a fine example of "easy vigor," straightforward and brief enough; lines 32 and 33 imitate the thought through the manipulation of sounds, particularly the sibilance of the *s* sound, the growling of the *r*s, and the forcefulness of the blocks of heavy-stressed words, as in "when loud surges lash."

In line 34 the sounds get stuck in one's throat ("rock's vast weight") and reflect this resisting struggle. Accents in line 35 on "líne tóo lábors" and on "wórds móve slów" create an almost plodding rhythm that imitates the sense of the words. These lines contrast with lines 36 and 37, which contain far more light-stressed words and use a much more direct and smooth syntax.

Careful reading of much contemporary poetry will reveal the continuing validity of Pope's observations. In any case, the power of words fashioned into lines with close attention to sound can be amply demonstrated by observing the structure of popular songs and advertisements.

HAKI R. MADHUBUTI, *The B Network* (p. 708)

Because Madhubuti's poem does not follow conventional capitalization and punctuation rules, the instances where he does use capitals or punctuation are more emphatic. You might discuss why he chooses to capitalize the words he does: *West, Black, Comprehend, While.* What are the important forces at work in this poem, and how do they interrelate?

It might help to give your class a little background on the Black Arts movement, in which Madhubuti was a prominent figure. In the 1960s, the Black Arts movement was closely connected to the political aims of Black Power. Its proponents wanted to forge a new esthetic, separate from any ideas about art brought down from European models. "The B Network" argues for this kind of new cultural identity. Like many other works from the Black Arts period, it also draws on African American speech patterns for its musical qualities. Your students will certainly notice the alliteration in the poem, which Madhubuti hints at with his title, and will probably hear the many internal rhymes and assonance. They may also recognize this style of poetry, with its affinity to performance, as a predecessor to rap music. The last line of the poem, however, departs from the style of the rest of the poem: "write the exam" (line 34) sounds more prosaic than anything that has come before, and Madhubuti emphasizes the shift by setting the single line on its own. However, he continues the play of sounds by slant-rhyming "exam" with "brotherman." How significant a change in tone is this last line? What does the poet accomplish there?

POSSIBLE CONNECTION TO ANOTHER SELECTION

Claude McKay, "America" (text p. 929; question #1, following)

CONNECTION QUESTION IN TEXT (p. 709) WITH ANSWER

1. Compare the style and themes of "The B Network" with those of Claude McKay's "America" (p. 929).

   While both pieces have a musical quality when read, McKay's piece is much more traditional. Madhubuti uses alliteration, slang, and nontraditional punctuation to create his musicality, while McKay uses rhyming couplets and straightforward diction. Both poets are describing the difficulty of living in the United States as black Americans and advocating for acceptance, but in different eras and different ways. McKay's speaker admits, "I love this cultured hell that tests my youth" (4). He can withstand the hatred of American society and even mourns the possibility of its future decline: "Darkly I gaze into the days ahead, / And see her might and granite wonders there, / Beneath the touch of Time's unerring hand, / Like priceless treasures sinking in the sand" (11–14). On the other hand, Madhubuti calls for African Americans to embrace their blackness and difference, rather than resigning themselves to the cruelty of prejudice. His speaker encourages other African Americans, saying, "brothers need to bop to being Black & bright & above board" (27).

ANDREW HUDGINS, *The Cow* (p. 709)

As the question in the text points out, this poem was published in the humor issue of *Poetry.* The humor in "The Cow" comes from its juxtaposition of naive affection with a matter-of-fact attitude toward slaughter. For example, the narrator, who says "I love the red cow / with all of my heart" (lines 1–2), seems to feel no disjunction when he says later, after the disemboweling and skinning of the cow, "We all love beefsteak" (23). The humor is hard to separate from the poem's moments of horror. The last image, of putting the cow's "own creamy butter" (32) on her meat, has a grotesque irony. The short lines and simple rhymes that Hudgins uses heighten both the childlike quality of the poem and the jarring distance between the voice and the quotidian acts of slaughter that it describes.

PAUL HUMPHREY, *Blow* (p. 710)

The class may not be familiar with the term *luffed* (line 4), which is a nautical word meaning "to turn the head of the ship into the wind." The woman here is metaphorically transformed into a sailing ship—appropriately enough as both would be spoken of as "she." The marvelous final line gives a blow to the gesture of the speaker trying to quell the woman's wind-filled skirt. Here the alliteration creates a kind of humor, and the quick end-stopped monosyllables with their *t* sounds emphasize the deftness that marks the woman's movements. Point out to the class how these short, light sounds are used, almost as a verbal photograph, to capture the moment.

Possible Connection to Another Selection

Robert Herrick, "Upon Julia's Clothes" (text p. 739)

ROBERT FRANCIS, *The Pitcher* (p. 711)

This poem ostensibly describes a baseball pitcher's art, but the poet seems also to be describing the art of poetry. When poems discuss poetry, it is always important to consider whether their claims are meant to be universal or whether they are meant to apply only to a specific type of poetry, usually the poetry that the poet favors. You might also discuss how the poem functions on a literal level: Does the metaphor ever break down? In what sense is a reader analogous to a batter?

If a pitcher is too obvious, the batter will easily figure out how to hit the balls he throws. The pitcher and batter play a cat-and-mouse game in which the pitcher must stay within the boundaries but not pitch directly to the hitter. While the other players throw directly to one another, he must seem to throw a fast ball only to throw a curve and vice versa. But he cannot throw wildly, or he has failed to do his job. In a similar way, the poet's play with language must "avoid the obvious" (line 3) and "vary the avoidance" (4). Line 4, almost (but not quite) a repetition of line 3, does what it says by avoiding the repetition.

Like the pitcher's task of avoidance within bounds, the rhymes in the poem are not quite but almost there. We have the sense of a potential never actualized. The final lines illustrate the perfect rhyme that is avoided in the previous lines, indicating the completed pitch and the finished poem.

The poet, like the pitcher, chooses his words and delivers them as he feels he must, making the reader wait patiently. Ironically, the pitcher is on the defensive side, although he appears to be on the offensive as he aims at his target. This fact may lead us to question the real relationship between poet and audience suggested in this analogy.

Possible Connection to Another Selection

Robert Francis, "Catch" (text p. 552; question #1, following)

Connection Question in Text (p. 711) with Answer

1. Write an essay comparing "The Pitcher" with another work by Francis, "Catch" (p. 552). One poem defines poetry implicitly, the other defines it explicitly. Which poem do you prefer? Why?

   "Catch," which explicitly compares baseball to poetry, takes a playful approach and uses sound to emphasize the fun of the boys' game. "The Pitcher" is implicit; as you read the poem it slowly becomes apparent that it's not just about baseball. "The Pitcher" is less overtly playful, but Francis obviously takes delight in using near rhymes and couplets to mirror the interaction between a pitcher and batter. The goal of the poet/pitcher in the two poems is different as well. In "Catch" the game is played between two equals who share the same goals of throwing and catching. The relationship in "The Pitcher," on the other hand, is more adversarial: the protagonist (the poet) tries to prevent the batter (the reader) from hitting the ball.

HELEN CHASIN, *The Word* Plum (p. 712)

The title of this poem suggests that it is about words. The relationship of the word *plum* to the object plum will generate an interesting discussion of the nature of language. Do words correspond to objects? Does poetry do more than point dimly to the sensuous realm?

The alliteration and assonance make our lips move the way they might when we are eating a plum. They also call attention to the sound of the poem, so that it is also about writing poetry.

POSSIBLE CONNECTION TO ANOTHER SELECTION

Anya Krugovoy Silver, "French Toast" (text p. 697)

RICHARD WAKEFIELD, *The Bell Rope* (p. 712)

Wakefield rhymes "The Bell Rope" like a poem in quatrains, and he chooses true rhymes rather than slant rhymes throughout. However, his choice to make the poem one long verse paragraph instead of dividing it visually into stanzas as well as his use of enjambment to place the rhyme words in different positions in his sentences serve to mute the rhymes. Wakefield achieves both a lyrical quality and a feeling of direct storytelling.

Like many poems about childhood, "The Bell Rope" uses a seemingly small incident to indicate larger issues that continue into adulthood. Here, the church bell and the rope that the speaker pulls to ring it are physical manifestations of prayer, and they suggest a way prayer can be answered. The boy in the poem hears in church about the saints and how they are "uplifted" (line 12), but the actual feeling of swinging from the rope gives him a more intimate understanding of what that word means. The sensation is so striking that, even years later, he can still remember it clearly.

POSSIBLE CONNECTIONS TO OTHER SELECTIONS

Robert Frost, "Birches" (text p. 848; question #1, following)

Judy Page Heitzman, "The Schoolroom on the Second Floor of the Knitting Mill" (text p. 656)

CONNECTION QUESTION IN TEXT (p. 713) WITH ANSWER

1. Compare the images and themes of "The Bell Rope" with those in Robert Frost's "Birches" (p. 848).

   Both "The Bell Rope" and "Birches" use concrete imagery to consider the idea of heaven and how humans might ascend to it. The child's perspective in both is a significant choice: it allows the poet to reimagine the received idea of heaven by looking at it from an innocent perspective. Wakefield's poem uses the bell rope as a concrete example of spiritual uplift, and Frost's imagines a boy using birch trees in a similar manner. One interesting difference between the two is that Frost's speaker articulates his desire both to ascend and to come back to earth again, and the birch trees serve this purpose by holding him up only until his weight pulls him down again. Both images — the tree and the rope — contain a force and counterforce. When Wakefield's speaker rings the bell, his pull downward is countered by the rope's swinging up. For both poets, these complex images suggest a spiritual life that involves some give-and-take between humans and the divine.

JOHN KEATS, *Ode to a Nightingale* (p. 713)

Earl R. Wasserman in *The Finer Tone: Keats's Major Poems* (Baltimore: Johns Hopkins UP, 1953, 1967; print.) discusses this ode at length and places it in context with other Keats poems, including "Ode on a Grecian Urn" and "La Belle Dame sans Merci." He finds here a set of impossible contradictions, for it appears that happiness or ecstasy can be achieved only by an annihilation of self. As Wasserman writes, "By attempting to gain 'happiness,' one is brought beyond his proper bound, and yet, being mortal, he is still confined to the earthly; and thus he is left with no standards to which to refer, or rather, with two conflicting sets of standards" (183).

As a result of his complete empathic entrance into the bird's state, the poet finds himself "too happy in thine happiness" (line 6). The poet has exceeded his own mortal bounds. In stanza 2 he longs for escape from this world — through an inebriation from the waters of poetic inspiration. Such a fading or leave-taking would be a means of fleeing from the strain of mortality (stanza 3). The bird, which at first had signified beauty and oneness with nature, is now becoming identified with immortality and the ability to transcend the mortal state. The speaker admits his fascination with "easeful Death" (52), but at the close of stanza 6, he realizes the ultimate dilemma: if he did die, the bird would go on singing but the speaker would be as responsive as "sod" (60).

The introduction of Ruth in line 66 is interesting, because she symbolizes life, family, and generational continuity. Having lost her husband, she stayed with her mother-in-law in an alien land, remarried, and bore a son.

The word *forlorn* recalls the speaker to his senses in stanza 8, for he realizes that in this world of death, spirit, and the imagination — this ethereal world of transcendent essences — he is as nothing, and the word *forlorn*, like a bell, not only recalls him to himself but could also serve as his death summons. Note how many of the poem's attractive sensuous details exalt physical, mortal life. At the close of stanza 5, for example, Keats rescues even the flies for our poetic appreciation.

POSSIBLE CONNECTION TO ANOTHER SELECTION

Percy Bysshe Shelley, "Ode to the West Wind" (text p. 756)

HOWARD NEMEROV, *Because You Asked about the Line between Prose and Poetry* (p. 716)

The title of Nemerov's poem indicates that this is an address to another person. Who does Nemerov mean by "you," and is this the same person he addresses in the second line? What questions would readers have about the difference between the genres? The poem is oblique in its answer to these questions, so you might have your students talk about how individual words or phrases characterize this difference. For one thing, Nemerov revises the question posed to him by introducing the idea of a "gradient" (line 3). The genres are not separated by a line but rather exist on a continuum as does the precipitation as it changes from rain to snow, "From silver aslant to random, white, and slow" (4). That the gradient is "invisible" (3) suggests the difficulty of distinguishing poetry from prose, and Nemerov dramatizes this problem in the fifth line: "There came a moment that you couldn't tell." However, in the next moment one can "clearly" (6) tell. We know that the snowflakes that "flew instead of fell" (6) represent poetry, but why would Nemerov choose this metaphor? In what way is prose earthbound and poetry flighted?

POSSIBLE CONNECTION TO ANOTHER SELECTION

Billy Collins, "Introduction to Poetry" (text p. 564)

26

Patterns of Rhythm

As in Chapter 25, reading aloud can be of great benefit here. Abstract discussions of prosody will almost certainly turn students off. However, if students can understand how rhythm contributes to the overall impression a poem makes, they will be more likely to show interest in questions of meter. One way to emphasize this impression is to have students read these poems aloud.

These readings will also show that even the strictest metrical forms are not absolute — no one really reads iambic meter da-dum da-dum da-dum, and students will find attempts to do so unnatural (and perhaps humorous). There are variations in rhythm built into the language, and often into the meter of the poems themselves. Once students understand this, they can approach prosody as a descriptive rather than prescriptive activity and can see scansion as a way of understanding effects rather than as an end in itself.

You may want to encourage this perception in the kinds of writing you have students do in this chapter. Critics almost never use exclusively prosody-based arguments about poems; students would be well advised to do the same. You might craft the writing assignments to have students talk about prosody among other features of a poem that contribute to its overall effect or meaning. This kind of assignment has the added advantage of keeping skills students have developed in previous chapters alive by continued use.

This chapter also lends itself well to the inclusion of popular culture — rap music, for instance, can be very sophisticated metrically. Students will probably immediately understand the difference in feeling between songs with a heavy beat (for instance, Rihanna's "Please Don't Stop the Music") and ones where the rhythms are lighter and more trippingly phrased (MGMT's "Time to Pretend"). Depending on the tastes of your class, the students themselves may be able to provide better and more current examples.

> **Web** Ask students to research the poets in this chapter at **bedfordstmartins.com/ meyerlit**.

Another exercise you might try would be to have students look for patterns of rhythm in other kinds of language — Martin Luther King Jr.'s "I have a dream" speech lends itself particularly well to this application and can be compared in structure to the selection from Walt Whitman's "Song of the Open Road."

WALT WHITMAN, *From "Song of the Open Road"* (p. 718)

Walt Whitman's poem proclaims the glorious freedom of the open road, but its form is not completely "free." The stanzas are nontraditional, rather than totally anarchic. Ask students to look for links within and between the two stanzas, for patterns that hold them together. The first stanza, after beginning with the foreign word *Allons,* uses several exclamatory phrases, many of which begin with the word *let.* The second stanza also begins with a foreign word — *Camerado* — and after one transitional exclamation proceeds with three phrases that repeat the word *give.* In addition, the second stanza mentions several items that are supposedly left behind in the first and replaces these old values with new ones: "my love" is offered as a replacement for money (lines 4 and 8), "myself" for preaching and law (6 and 9).

Ask students to recall other places where they have seen repetition used as a rhetorical device. They might mention speech making, legal documents, or the Bible. Discuss the implications of Whitman's use of a technique that characterizes the very things he wishes to abandon.

Ask students whether they find the narrator's attitude attractive or repulsive. Does he seem naive or insightful? Are they drawn to the idea of leaving books, laws, and religion behind for the "Open Road"?

POSSIBLE CONNECTIONS TO OTHER SELECTIONS

Alfred, Lord Tennyson, "The Charge of the Light Brigade" (text p. 733)

Walt Whitman, From "I Sing the Body Electric" (text p. 763)

WILLIAM WORDSWORTH, *My Heart Leaps Up* (p. 721)

The text discusses the enjambment in lines 8–9. What is the effect of the enjambment in the first two lines? Note that all the lines between are end-stopped. Is there a thematic connection between the pairs of enjambed lines? Between the end-stopped lines?

Ask students to discuss what they think Wordsworth means by "the child is father of the Man" (line 7). Do any current songs or other elements of popular culture reflect this same sentiment, or is it dismissible as a nineteenth-century Romantic impulse?

POSSIBLE CONNECTION TO ANOTHER SELECTION

William Blake, "The Lamb" (text p. 731)

TIMOTHY STEELE, *Waiting for the Storm* (p. 723)

The text thoroughly discusses the poem's metrics and how they contribute to its meaning. In addition, you may wish to discuss word choices in the poem. How can darkness be "wrinkling," as stated in line 1? Why do you suppose Steele uses such a prosaic title for a poem so full of poetic images? You might have students examine the individual images and discuss the senses to which they appeal. Is the poem mostly auditory, visual, tactile, or does it touch all the senses? Why does Steele start and end with the images he does? Can your students suggest other prestorm sensations the poet might have included? Would their inclusion alter the poem's mood? You might have students decide on a topic for description and brainstorm to produce images that draw on each of the senses. Are some senses harder to utilize than others?

POSSIBLE CONNECTION TO ANOTHER SELECTION

William Butler Yeats, "That the Night Come" (text p. 725)

WILLIAM BUTLER YEATS, *That the Night Come* (p. 725)

William Butler Yeats was born in Dublin and spent his youth in Dublin, London, and Sligo (his mother's family's home) in the west of Ireland. After graduating from high school, Yeats decided to attend art school (his father, J. B. Yeats, was a painter) and made poetry an avocation. He dropped out soon after and at age twenty published his first poems in the *Dublin University Review*. His poetic influences include Spenser, Shelley, Blake, and the pre-Raphaelite poets of 1890s London, but a perhaps equally important shaping force was his religious temperament. Never satisfied with Christian doctrine, he invented, piecemeal, a mythology that informs his poetry in often obscure ways. For range and power, no twentieth-century poet equals Yeats.

Discuss the central metaphor of the poem: that the woman's longing for death is like a king's longing for the consummation of his marriage. Note especially the word *desire* (line 2). How can the desire for death possibly be equated with the desire for sex? Compare this poem to one of the *carpe diem* poems students have read. In the *carpe diem* tradition sexuality is opposed to death; in this poem is sexuality equated with death? Why does the speaker call death "proud" (3)? Does the speaker see death as a proud bridegroom awaiting his bride? Is this an allusion to Donne's "Death Be Not Proud" (text p. 781)?

POSSIBLE CONNECTION TO ANOTHER SELECTION

John Donne, "Death Be Not Proud" (text p. 781)

JOHN MALONEY, *Good!* (p. 726)

Maloney has chosen a sonnet form, which complements the intense sports-commentator-like narration of the poem. The tension of the moment is amplified in his end rhymes. There is something very sonnet-like about the play happening here. To begin a discussion, ask how the back and forth movement, the fakes, the dribbling, and the final "SHOOT" (12) to the net is very like what happens within a sonnet—perhaps look at other traditional sonnets when making the comparison.

Students may be curious about the complexity of a poem like "Good!" since it is so accessible. Ask students if they are moved by this poem or if there are any surprises within it. Do they see this moment in a basketball game differently because of Maloney's compression of it? If poetry can be about any subject, examine what about this arrangement of words would be called poetic.

POSSIBLE CONNECTIONS TO OTHER SELECTIONS

Robert Francis, "Catch" (text p. 552)
David Solway, "Windsurfing" (text p. 624)

CONNECTION QUESTION IN TEXT (p. 726) WITH ANSWER

1. Compare the diction and tone in "Good!" and in Jim Tilley's "The Big Questions" (p. 572).

    In John Maloney's "Good!" the diction and tone reflect the action of the poem. Maloney's speaker employs basketball terminology like "dribbles" (3), "calls the play" (4), "a pick" (7), and "baseline" (10). These terms might be unfamiliar to students who aren't interested in basketball, but they lend an air of authenticity to the poem. By describing the action this way, Maloney's tone follows the fast-paced movement of a basketball game. Additionally, the diction uses onomatopoeia to add to the descriptions of the player's movements, including the "clicking seconds" (3) and the way the rim "rattles" (13). The tone is serious but appreciative of the player's final accomplishment, when the ball falls "into the net, trippingly drop two points" (14).

    Jim Tilley's "The Big Questions" does not feature a specific set of terms in the way "Good!" does. Instead, the speaker relies on simple, straightforward language, creating a wry but thoughtful tone. The speaker's diction often creates some humor, as when he says, "and you encounter a mammoth / grizzly who hasn't had lunch / in a fortnight, and he eyes you / as the answer to his only big question" (6–10). The tone and diction makes the poem speculative and almost whimsical as the speaker muses on what constitutes a "big question" versus a "defining moment" (20). The tone is in direct contrast to the serious subject matter of not only contemplating questions that "have never been answered" (2), but also the idea of "staring down a bear looking for lunch" (25). While Tilley's subject matter is downright dire, Maloney's tone in "Good!" is more urgent.

WILLIAM TROWBRIDGE, *Drumming behind You in the High School Band* (p. 726)

Ask students if they can detect a beat in Trowbridge's lines. Where do they find a regular drum beat? Where does the rhythm deviate or lengthen? There are many lines of regular iambic tetrameter: "we measured off the football field" (line 2) or "How left was left, how right was right!" (8). These ground the poem and reflect the title. When Trowbridge varies the stress within the meter, it's usually for an effect that mirrors meaning and reflects his assertion: "We had a rhythm all our own" (9). Consider the insertion of one small "and" that sets everything askew: "and my heart kept stepping on my heels" (13). Ask students to consider the final lines together without the "and." Discuss how one small word, one slight shift in stress or meter, can have a big effect on the listener. With another line, Trowbridge might have worked within a sonnet structure. For a further point of discussion, consider reasons the poet might have had for sidestepping a regular form.

ALICE JONES, *The Foot* (p. 727)

The anatomical terms make "The Foot" scholarly and intellectually precise. The speaker of the poem clearly knows a great deal about the foot — the scientific terminology communicates much more than most people know about their feet. Given that poems are scanned in metrical feet, you might suggest to your students that this poem can be read as a pun; the metrical feet of a poem, such as iambs, support the poem just as human feet support people. The scholarly and foreign terms used to describe the subject of the poem obscure the function of the foot, just as overly scholarly terminology about scansion can obscure the function (and enjoyment) of a poem.

Certainly, the poem can be read not only as a pun. The first line does reveal the speaker's surprise about the human foot — that it is "our improbable support" — and the ending returns to this sense of mystery when it alludes to our connection to "an ancestor" (line 23) with a "wild / and necessary claw" (24–25). It might be interesting to have students explore one or more of the following questions in writing: What effect does the poet achieve by using language the common reader does not understand? Likewise, why would a poet write about a familiar object and make it seem foreign? Does the poet intend to humble readers by suggesting that despite all our learning we still are rooted in a past that contains ancestors with claws rather than feet?

POSSIBLE CONNECTION TO ANOTHER SELECTION

Alice Jones, "The Larynx" (text p. 615)

A. E. HOUSMAN, *When I was one-and-twenty* (p. 728)

The basic metrical pattern here is iambic trimeter. The first stanza is tightly rhymed, with only two rhyming sounds. The second stanza picks up on the first rhyming word of stanza 1 (*twenty*), but Housman in this stanza uses more rhyming words (four sounds in the eight lines), as though he were opening up to experience. Appropriately, given his unhappy romance, "rue," "two," and "true" echo one another in rhyme. Love in both stanzas is metaphorically treated with marketplace terminology. In the first stanza the wise man advises the speaker to keep his fancy free. In the second stanza the wise man observes that the heart "was never given in vain" (line 12), and moreover the cost of buying or selling this seat of affection is immeasurable. The repetition of " 'tis true" (16) is like a shaking of the head, of one in a state of "endless rue" (14).

You might enter a discussion of this poem by asking students about their reactions to advice from elders. They will probably have stories about how they had to learn through experience, not advice. If that is the case, what is our relationship to the speaker of the poem? Are we meant to reject his advice, too, in favor of learning on our own? Is the speaker somewhat foolish, because he believes he has aged so much in just one year?

POSSIBLE CONNECTION TO ANOTHER SELECTION

Robert Frost, "Birches" (text p. 848)

ROBERT HERRICK, *Delight in Disorder* (p. 728)

The speaker of this poem prefers in women a slightly disheveled appearance to one that presents the wearer as though she is perfect. Not coincidentally, the poem's strength is not only in its artfulness, its reliance on poetic conventions like end rhyme and alliteration, but also in the slight disorderliness of his rhythm. Vague impressions of court life in seventeenth-century England may be sufficient to initiate a discussion of the importance of dress at the time. If you are also discussing Ben Jonson's "Still to Be Neat," the next poem in this section, you might be able to get some mileage out of a discussion of the relationship between the two arts of fashion and poetry and the way they interact.

You might begin discussion of this poem by asking students what connotations the word *neat* holds for them. Then explore Herrick's use of *disorder* (line 1), as contrasted with our word *disorderly*, along with *wantonness* (2). Clearly, disorder and wantonness arouse in the speaker here a "fine distraction" (4) and exercise a certain appeal that would not be present if the person addressed were prim and proper.

The speaker is bewitched but not bothered by his lady's "sweet disorder" (1). Words are chosen to indicate a tantalizing of the passions by "erring" lace (5), "tempestuous" petticoats (10), and shoestrings tied with a "wild civility" (12).

Herrick subtly illustrates his theme by working changes in the basic iambic tetrameter rhythm. Iambs change to trochees (cf. lines 2 and 4, for example), and in line 10 dactyls appear.

Ask students to turn back to the second question in the text and in a writing assignment analyze how patterns of rhyme and consonance work to create a subtle and pleasing artistic order.

POSSIBLE CONNECTIONS TO OTHER SELECTIONS

Ben Jonson, "Still to Be Neat" (text p. 729)
John Frederick Nims, "Love Poem" (text p. 566)

BEN JONSON, *Still to Be Neat* (p. 729)

Stepson of a bricklayer, Jonson was one of the first English writers to make his living by his pen. Admired for his lyrical poetry and literary criticism, Jonson is perhaps best known for his satiric comedies — including *Volpone* (1605), *The Alchemist* (1610), and *Bartholomew Fair* (1614) — and for the elaborate masques he created with designer Inigo Jones for the court of James I.

It may seem odd then that Jonson would choose to reject the elaborate fashions of the time, yet that is what he is doing in this poem. The speaker dislikes the artful manners and dress of the woman. "Sweet" (line 6) refers both to her smell, which is sweet, and their relationship, which presumably has some difficulties, perhaps because of her preoccupation with her appearance. The speaker is suspicious about the reason for this preoccupation.

He asks the woman to be more sincere in her attentions to him, to pay less attention to her appearance. Neglecting herself is "sweet" (10) to him because it is more natural, less deceptive. Words such as *adulteries* (11) and *face* (7) play with the relationship between art and nature, intimating that the woman's efforts to make herself into a beautiful object only mar her natural beauty.

The disruptions in the rhythms reinforce Jonson's point until the final line. In line 6 the rhythm and the caesura in the middle of the line force the reader to slow down, emphasizing the speaker's insistence that the woman stop her artful motion and remove the mask. In the final line the iambic tetrameter brings the speaker's point home in a succinct statement of his case.

POSSIBLE CONNECTION TO ANOTHER SELECTION

Robert Herrick, "Delight in Disorder" (text p. 728; questions #1 and #2, following)

CONNECTIONS QUESTIONS IN TEXT (p. 730) WITH ANSWERS

1. Write an essay comparing the themes of "Still to Be Neat" and Herrick's preceding poem, "Delight in Disorder." How do the speakers make similar points but from different perspectives?

   Herrick's speaker asks for a similar absence of artistry and an emphasis on irregularity. But the poems seem to treat the art–nature dichotomy differently. For Herrick, a "sweet disorder" (line 1) may be part of the art, whereas for Jonson the relationship between art and nature is more troubled. Jonson's speaker does not want his beloved to be artful; Herrick's simply asks that the art not be "too precise in every part" (14).

2. How does the rhythm of "Still to Be Neat" compare with that of "Delight in Disorder"? Which do you find more effective? Explain why.

   With trochees interrupting the iambic rhythm throughout, Jonson's poem is more insistent than Herrick's. The speaker in "Still to Be Neat" is calling for an end to false art. Herrick's smoother rhythm and more easily flowing syllables suggest the speaker's delight in observing the disorder of his lady's dress. The differences in meter are in keeping with the different relationship between art and nature in the two poems.

SONIA SANCHEZ, *Summer Words of a Sistuh Addict* (p. 730)

Sanchez's use of lowercase letters, unconventional spellings, and erratic punctuation give "Summer Words" a sense of unpolished directness. They also contribute to the creation of an individual voice that tells the story. However, after the first voice has been established, there are several changes in speaker near the end of the poem. At line 14 the speaker seems to switch to a narrator chronicling the story of the "sistuh," and, again at line 19, the speaker changes to a character that comes in direct contact with her. These changes in who is telling the story are important to understanding both the woman at the heart of the poem and the way outside observers relate to her. They feel sorry for her, but they also feel distanced from her and her problems.

The singing at the end of the poem seems to circle back to the church in the beginning. Now, the unnamed "we" (26) listen to the addict's story and share a communal feeling of sadness over the "sistuh's young tears" (line 25). Unlike the church at the beginning, which does not seem to have any effect on the woman who will become an addict, the music at the end gives the feeling of a real blessing.

WILLIAM BLAKE, *The Lamb* (p. 731) and *The Tyger* (p. 731)

These two poems when paired make excellent examples of diction, rhythm, and sound and how these elements enhance tone. Ostensibly, each poem uses a four-stress pattern of trochaic feet, but the gliding *l* sounds of the opening of "The Lamb" make the first stress on "Little" seem much lighter than the emphasis "Tyger" receives. The rhyme in the opening two lines of "The Lamb" is feminine, again unlike the stressed rhyme in "The Tyger." Only one question ("Who made Thee?") is asked of the lamb, and that question is repeated several times, giving the poem a sense of childlike simplicity and innocence. In this poem, moreover, there is a figural pattern of exchangeable identities between Lamb and Creator (Lamb of God), and speaker as child and Christ as God's child. Unlike the fearful symmetry of "The Tyger," this poem reflects a wholeness and innocence through the cohesiveness of these identities.

"The Tyger" poses far more questions about the creation of this powerful, regal beast, including the question in line 20: "Did he who made the Lamb make thee?" Ways of reading that question include the debate over the presence of evil in a God-created universe and the possibility of a second creator from whom darkness, evil, and fierce energy emanate. Could not the tiger stand for positive expressions of power? By and large, though, the questions in "The Tyger" go unanswered. Notice, for example, the substitution of *dare* in the final line for *could* in line 4.

As a writing assignment, you might ask students to examine several elements in each poem, including rhythm, patterns of consonance and assonance, pace, tone, and even levels of ambiguity so that they are able on a fairly sophisticated level to articulate the differences between the two lyrics.

POSSIBLE CONNECTIONS TO OTHER SELECTIONS

William Blake, "Infant Sorrow" (text p. 1001)

William Wordsworth, "I Wandered Lonely as a Cloud" (text p. 1027)

CARL SANDBURG, *Chicago* (p. 732)

You might begin by introducing your class to the idea of the invocation. Traditionally, a poet would invoke the muse at the beginning of the work, asking for help with the task at hand. The root of invocation is *vocare*, "to call." Here the higher power being called upon is also the subject of the poem, the city of Chicago. How does the power of the city differ from that of a muse or god? How does Sandburg characterize the city in these first lines? Some of his epithets reappear in the last lines of the poem. Here they take on a new character as the city itself takes possession of the names, "proud" to answer to them (line 23).

Sandburg's poem contains both short, heavily accented lines, as in the invocation, and long lines with a prose cadence. Like Whitman, he structures the prose sections with the rhetorical device of anaphora, beginning sentences with repeated words or phrases. These repetitions enhance the rhythm of the long lines. As an exercise, you might have your students reline the poem, breaking the long sentences into four- or five-beat lines. Then have them discuss how these changes alter the tone of the poem. What is gained or lost from the original?

POSSIBLE CONNECTION TO ANOTHER SELECTION

William Blake, "London" (text p. 631; question #1, following)

CONNECTION QUESTION IN TEXT (p. 733) WITH ANSWER

1. Compare "Chicago" with William Blake's "London" (p. 631) in style and theme.

    Both "Chicago" and "London" are concerned with the darker side of city life. Sandburg sees Chicago as "wicked" (line 6), "crooked" (7), and "brutal" (8), and Blake hears in London a chorus of crying, sighs, and curses. However, the poems take different turns. In spite of the ugliness it contains, Chicago is "proud to be alive and coarse and strong and cunning" (10). Sandburg's looser structure and long lines seem to convey some of the reckless exuberance he admires in the city. Blake, on the other hand, uses a stricter form as a way of maintaining order in the face of chaos. His poem does not find anything to praise in the city. Its images grow increasingly grim until he ends on the sad oxymoron, the "Marriage hearse" (line 16).

ALFRED, LORD TENNYSON, *The Charge of the Light Brigade* (p. 733)

This poem praises and honors the light brigade, those "noble six hundred" men who charge "into the valley of Death" even though they know that they will die. The poem raises questions about the nature of bravery during wartime; the soldiers are praised for their glory, their honor, their nobility, but there is a nagging sense that their deaths could have been avoided. They knew that "Some one had blundered" (line 12), but this logic is tempered by the sentiment behind the famous lines "Their's not to make reply, / Their's not to reason why, / Their's but to do and die" (13–15).

The rhyme and meter make the poem sound like a typical poem celebrating the heroes of war. The phrase "six hundred" is rhymed repeatedly, with "thundered" (21), "wondered" (31), and "sundered" (36); the word "blundered," which sounds a discordant note in the second stanza, is nearly buried by what appears to be the poem's laudatory tone. Students may debate about whether the poem focuses on praising the brigade for its courage or on criticizing the brigade for its blind obedience, which leads many of them to death. The effect would certainly be different if the sentiment of the second stanza were to come at the end of the poem. Because it doesn't, questions about the poem's tone and the speaker's attitude must take into consideration both the poem as a whole and the second stanza in particular. The "honor" that is proposed for the "noble six hundred" in the final stanza is altered not only by the second stanza but by the fact that the six hundred are less than six hundred in stanzas 4 and 5.

POSSIBLE CONNECTIONS TO OTHER SELECTIONS

Wilfred Owen, "Dulce et Decorum Est" (text p. 633; question #1, following)

Walt Whitman, "Cavalry Crossing a Ford" (text p. 624)

CONNECTION QUESTION IN TEXT (p. 735) WITH ANSWER

1. Compare the theme of "The Charge of the Light Brigade" with that of Wilfred Owen's "Dulce et Decorum Est" (p. 633).

    The tone of "Dulce et Decorum Est" makes its theme much more obvious; would students go so far as to say that the speakers of the two poems share the same attitude but that they simply differ in their degrees of subtlety? Is there a certain nobility associated with the warfare Tennyson describes, with its charges on horseback and sabers, as opposed to Owen's description of World War I with its invisible enemy, its lethal gas, and the horrors of trench warfare?

PERSPECTIVE

LOUISE BOGAN, *On Formal Poetry* (p. 735)

You might ask students to compare Bogan's questions about form as repression with Whitman's assertion that "[t]he rhyme and uniformity of perfect poems show the free growth of metrical laws and bud from them as unerringly and loosely as lilacs or roses on a bush, and take shapes as compact as the shapes of chestnuts and oranges and melons and pears, and shed the perfume impalpable to form" (p. 764). Students could write an essay about these perspectives on "form" in poetry, using two or three examples from Chapter 39, "A Collection of Poems."

27

Poetic Forms

There is some degree of controversy over the role of form in poetry. The movement calling itself New Formalism advocates a widespread return to form and criticizes what it calls the status quo of open form. (A possible introduction to this position is in Dana Gioia's "Notes on the New Formalism" in the Autumn 1987 *Hudson Review*, reprinted in *Can Poetry Matter?* Also, see Timothy Steele's *Missing Measures* [Fayetteville, AR: University of Arkansas Press, 1990; print.].) There are also, however, several defenses of open form (perhaps the best of which is Stanley Plumly's "Chapter and Verse" in the 1978 January–February and May–June issues of *American Poetry Review*). You might find it interesting to introduce your students to this controversy and have them find their own positions on the matter. This exercise can help students understand that there are reasons for the choice to write in or out of traditional forms, and that traditional forms are not always or necessarily conservative. In addition, it emphasizes the idea that poetry is a dynamic genre, full of conflict and contradiction.

As in previous chapters, this material will likely be most appealing to students in terms of its relation to the overall impact of a poem — form takes on meaning only when married to content and presented in context. Quizzes that ask students to give the structure of a Petrarchan sonnet tend not to work as well as those that ask students to explain how the form of a particular sonnet contributes to its overall effect. (Some historical notes might be useful in this chapter, as the importance of traditional forms has as much to do with the history of those forms as with each current instance of the form.)

Web Ask students to research the poets in this chapter at **bedfordstmartins.com/ meyerlit**.

The section on sonnets is particularly good at emphasizing the different uses to which the form was put; each use draws on the structure of the sonnet to help create meaning and coherence in the poem. Mark Jarman's "Unholy Sonnet," in conjunction with the sonnets from Donne found in Chapter 39, make good test cases. Students can see how the sonnet form allows Jarman to engage in a cross-century and cross-faith debate with Donne; the sonnet ensures that despite the historical and religious differences, the discussion takes place on the same terrain.

Another example that can help students understand the union of form and content can be found in the section on the villanelle — the kinds of repetition this form requires can be used for emphatic statement, as both Dylan Thomas's and Edwin Arlington Robinson's poems demonstrate.

A. E. HOUSMAN, *Loveliest of trees, the cherry now* (p. 738)

The speaker in this poem greets life with a warmhearted joie de vivre. Although he is young, he already has a sense of life's limits. He means to enjoy the beauty of life every minute he is alive. Even then, he claims, he could not absorb all the beauties of life. The connotations of rebirth and spring are reinforced by the mention of Eastertide in line 4.

Yet behind the gaiety and cheerful resolve is an awareness of the imminence of death. You might explore, either in class discussion or as a writing assignment, the question of whether this could be considered a *carpe diem* poem.

Robert Frost, "The Road Not Taken" (text p. 840)

Robert Herrick, "To the Virgins, to Make Much of Time" (text p. 599)

ROBERT HERRICK, *Upon Julia's Clothes* (p. 739)

Herrick uses so many of the elements of poetry—rhyme, rhythm, the sound and choice of words—so well in this brief lyric that it is worth taking some class time to analyze. The first tercet of iambic tetrameter is absolutely regular and thus suggests the sweet*ly* flow*ing* l*i*quefaction of Julia's clothes. In the second tercet, trochees interrupt the established pattern to capture in rhythmic terms "that brave vibration" (line 5). *Brave* is used here in the sense of "making a fine show or display," as in a banner waving.

POSSIBLE CONNECTION TO ANOTHER SELECTION

Paul Humphrey, "Blow" (text p. 710; question #1, following)

CONNECTION QUESTION IN TEXT (p. 740) WITH ANSWER

1. Compare the tone of this poem with that of Paul Humphrey's "Blow" (p. 710). Are the situations and speakers similar? Is there any difference in tone between these two poems?

   The situations are dissimilar in that Herrick's subject is "my Julia" (line 1) but the speaker of Humphrey's poem has no relationship with his subject. He is more self-deprecating than Herrick's speaker is; when the woman laughs and leaves in the final lines, we sense that she is laughing at him rather than at her situation. His gallantry becomes buffoonery. Herrick's emphasis is on the speaker's reverie; he is ecstatic rather than ridiculous.

S O N N E T

JOHN KEATS, *On First Looking into Chapman's Homer* (p. 741)

The principal theme of Keats's sonnet is discovery; he uses the sudden and unexpected discovery of the Pacific Ocean by early explorers of the Americas as a metaphor for those moments in life when we feel that a previously held view has been radically shaken.

You might ask students whether they have experienced a moment of discovery similar to that which Keats describes. After they have read Keats's poem, give them a few minutes to write about a moment when they felt a sense of revelation similar to that felt by "stout Cortez" (line 11) and his men, and then discuss the results.

A comparison of Keats's sonnets provides ample evidence of the poet's continual experimentation with form during his brief career. In "Chapman's Homer," Keats utilizes the characteristic division of the Italian sonnet into octave and sestet, with the opening eight lines setting up a situation or argument and the remaining six resolving it. You may wish to compare Keats's use of the sonnet form in "Chapman's Homer" with his use of the form in other poems in Chapter 39. In some sonnets Keats favors the Italian or Petrarchan form, but in "When I have fears" (text p. 1014) he uses the English or Shakespearean rhyme scheme (three quatrains and a couplet).

WILLIAM WORDSWORTH, *The World Is Too Much with Us* (p. 742)

Like Hopkins in "God's Grandeur" (text p. 702), Wordsworth is protesting here the preoccupation with worldliness—banking, buying, getting, spending—that makes it increasingly difficult to feel the mystery and power in the natural world. Proteus (a god of the sea) and Triton (another sea god, who stirred up storms) lie dormant, their power to kindle in the human soul a spirit of awe suppressed in the commercialized world, where people have bartered their hearts away. "Great God!" (line 9) is the speaker's spontaneous and ironic response to the decline of spirituality, for it appears that the pagan world possessed a stronger sense of godliness.

POSSIBLE CONNECTIONS TO OTHER SELECTIONS

Matthew Arnold, "Dover Beach" (text p. 626)

Gerard Manley Hopkins, "God's Grandeur" (text p. 702; question #1, following)

CONNECTION QUESTION IN TEXT (p. 742) **WITH ANSWER**

1. Compare the theme of this sonnet with that of Gerard Manley Hopkins's "God's Grandeur" (p. 702).

   Both Wordsworth's sonnet and "God's Grandeur" draw from the social and industrial worlds to discuss the greatness of creation and the human threat to that greatness. The speaker in Hopkins's sonnet places his faith in the creator, who can overcome the destructive actions of human beings. Wordsworth's sonnet returns to pagan myths for comfort, although the speaker has little hope of overcoming the bleakness of the world that is "too much with us." Hopkins dwells on bleak images of all "seared with trade" (line 6), but he is convinced that nature is still available to us and that even humanity can be redeemed.

WILLIAM SHAKESPEARE, *Shall I compare thee to a summer's day?* (p. 743)

The speaker in this sonnet praises his beloved not only for her loveliness but also for her temperateness of manner. Unlike nature, which is forever changing, she shows a steady devotion. Moreover, the speaker tells us that this love will extend well into the future, even beyond the grave. Such love, like the art that celebrates it, confers a measure of immortality on the lovers and, self-reflexively, on the sonnet. Notice, for example, how the stressed words in the couplet reinforce this idea. *Long* is stressed in both lines of the couplet, along with other significant words that link continued "life" with "this," the sonnet that confers immortality, and "thee," the object the sonnet addresses.

POSSIBLE CONNECTIONS TO OTHER SELECTIONS

John Frederick Nims, "Love Poem" (text p. 566)

William Shakespeare, "My mistress' eyes are nothing like the sun" (text p. 743)

WILLIAM SHAKESPEARE, *My mistress' eyes are nothing like the sun* (p. 743)

Students may have read this sonnet in high school, and you might begin by asking them what they think the mistress looks like. Some clarification of Shakespeare's use of the term *mistress* (beloved or chosen one) may be in order. This sonnet plays with the conventions and clichés of the Petrarchan sonnet, which elaborated on the extraordinary qualities of the maiden's eyes as compared to the splendor of the sun. But Shakespeare refuses to do this and thus argues for a poetry that avoids cliché and the excess metaphor that tries to outdo reality. He is, in fact, asserting the beauty of his beloved in the last line. She is as attractive as any other woman who has been "belied" (made to seem more beautiful) by false comparison.

POSSIBLE CONNECTION TO ANOTHER SELECTION

William Shakespeare, "Shall I compare thee to a summer's day?" (text p. 743)

SHERMAN ALEXIE, *The Facebook Sonnet* (p. 744)

To begin discussion, ask students what the speaker means when he compares Facebook to the "altar of loneliness" (line 14). Explore how everything mentioned, stanza by stanza, adds up to the final couplet. In this English (or Shakespearean) sonnet, we are told that Facebook, praised for connecting so many people, wields a power that elicits and exposes our most undignified, immature, and lonely sides—and we have come to worship it.

This is a poem of spare images and strong statements that conveys the idea that Facebook taps into the piece of us that craves company and affection, even from "past friends / and lovers, however kind or cruel" (2–3), and appeals to our vanity. Discuss how broken lines, like "Why can't we pretend" (5) or "Let's exhume, resume, and extend" (7), form complete thoughts that carry weight both before and after their enjambment.

POSSIBLE CONNECTIONS TO OTHER SELECTIONS

John Donne, "Batter My Heart" (text p. 1005)
William Wordsworth, "The World Is Too Much with Us" (text p. 742)

CONNECTION QUESTION IN TEXT (p. 744) WITH ANSWER

1. Write an essay comparing the themes of "The Facebook Sonnet" and Emily Dickinson's "The Soul selects her own Society" (text p. 810).

   Both of these pieces deal with the intersection of the private and personal. Despite the difference in time period, each poet is attempting to convey the same message: that some things should be kept personal and secret. Alexie's speaker is pointing out the flaws in Facebook, observing that it can both "undervalue and unmend // The present" (4–5). He draws the reader's attention to the irony of looking for connection through the Internet, where we "Let one's search / For God become public domain" (10–11). He names Facebook as "the altar of loneliness" (14), because it provides only a superficial semblance of actual companionship. Dickinson rejects these false displays of sociability. For her, "The Soul selects her own Society— / Then—shuts the Door" (1–2). For this speaker, friendships and intimacy are meant to be shared selectively and with great care, while to all outsiders one must "close the Valves of her attention" (11).

MARK JARMAN, *Unholy Sonnet* (p. 745)

This poem is an example of an Italian, or Petrarchan, sonnet. You may wish to begin discussion by having students read the poem aloud, since the lines are so heavily enjambed that the rhythm and rhyme occur subtly. In dealing with this piece as a sonnet, you might point out that Italian sonnets are characterized by the usual fourteen lines of iambic pentameter, but unlike other sonnet forms, this type usually contains a shift in content between the octave and the sestet—a movement from suggestion to resolution.

This shift occurs in terms of both style and content in this poem. In the opening octave, many of the lines begin with a dactylic rather than an iambic foot (lines 1–4 each begin this way), and all the lines in the octave have feminine endings. By contrast, the sestet lines each begin with a standard iambic foot and conclude with a masculine ending. In content, the repeated use of the word *after*—which occurs five times in the octave—sets up a sense of suspense in the first part of the poem that is then resolved through the repeated "there is" in the concluding sestet. In addition, the octave uses the pronouns *us* and *our*, while the answering sestet uses the pronouns *you* and *your*. Ask students to consider whether this shift in pronouns affects the reading of the poem. Does it strengthen or detract from the sense of resolution contained in the poem's concluding sestet?

POSSIBLE CONNECTION TO ANOTHER SELECTION

John Donne, "Death Be Not Proud" (text p. 781; question #1, following)

1. Jarman has said that his "Unholy Sonnets" (there are about twenty of them) are modeled after John Donne's *Holy Sonnets* but that he does not share the same Christian assumptions about faith and mercy that inform Donne's sonnets. Instead, Jarman says, he "work[s] against any assumption or shared expression of faith, to write a devotional poetry against the grain." Keeping this statement in mind, write an essay comparing and contrasting the tone and theme of Jarman's sonnet with Donne's "Death Be Not Proud" (p. 781).

   Jarman's sonnet considers the disparity between what we are trying to do through practicing religion and what we actually do. He believes that the rituals of church-going do nothing to eradicate our basic (and base) human nature. The sonnet by Donne describes a much more personal faith on the part of the speaker. Human activity does not interfere with his relationship with God or with his belief in eternal life through faith. The subject in Jarman's poem is collective first person and second person; in Donne's poem, the subject is first-person singular. In writing "a devotional poetry against the grain," Jarman is responding not only to Donne but also to modern views of religion. Yet in terms of form, Jarman's sonnet does work as a kind of inversion of Donne's logic; both poems end with a bold sentiment in the final couplet.

WILLIAM BAER, *Letter of Resignation* (p. 745)

This "letter" is written to a lover, but it is written entirely in the language of the workplace. In contrast, other sonnets in this chapter have a letter-like quality because of the intimacy created by their diction and formal constraints. To begin discussion, look at other poems in this chapter that invoke a particular person ("Upon Julia's Clothes" text p. 739) or offer a description of the "other" ("My mistress' eyes are nothing like the sun" text p. 743) and consider the ways in which they differ from Baer's poem.

Beginning with "Dear [blank]" (line 1), "Letter of Resignation" is devoid of any emotional connection to the "other" he is addressing. Where else does that impersonal quality work in his favor? Ask students to scan the lines and note where Baer shifts stress or meter and consider how he has used form to enhance the distant tone he wants here. Address the irony inherent in the final line, where the speaker claims to have "deep regret" and be "very truly yours" (14) even as he ends his relationship with the recipient.

Possible Connections to Other Selections

Sherman Alexie, "The Facebook Sonnet" (text p. 744)

Billie Bolton, "Memorandum" (text p. 961; question #1, following)

Christopher Marlowe, "The Passionate Shepherd to His Love" (text p. 954)

William Shakespeare, "Shall I compare thee to a summer's day?" (text p. 743)

Connection Question in Text (p. 746) with Answer

1. Compare the form and content of "Letter of Resignation" and Billie Bolton's "Memorandum" (text p. 961).

   Both poems mimic the form indicated in their title (the structure of a formal letter, of a memo), but they differ in style. The numbered points that are featured in Bolton's poem are very prose-like, although quick with association, while Baer's poem is written as formal verse. Both lodge a personal complaint within a businesslike format and are heavily ironic.

R. S. GWYNN, *Shakespearean Sonnet* (p. 746)

In this "Shakespearean Sonnet," R. S. Gwynn has a bit of fun. His title is a pun, and the impetus for the poem comes from a line that was not written by either Gwynn or Shakespeare — it came from the TV listings! The bard's sonnets are not the subject; neither is it an expression of love or loss in that vein. Instead, Gwynn cleverly abridges the themes of some of Shakespeare's best plays. To begin discussion, ask students if they can identify the plays alluded to here. How do students respond to a playful poem such as this? Where is "Shakespearean Sonnet" in line with Shakespearean writing and where is it not? Consider diction, rhyme, and meter when answering these questions.

POSSIBLE CONNECTIONS TO OTHER SELECTIONS

William Shakespeare, "My mistress' eyes are nothing like the sun" (text p. 743)

———,"Shall I compare thee to a summer's day?" (text p. 743)

VILLANELLE

DYLAN THOMAS, *Do Not Go Gentle into That Good Night* (p. 747)

This poem is a villanelle, a French verse form ordinarily treating light topics, whose five tercets and concluding quatrain use only two end rhymes. The first and third lines of the poem must alternatively conclude the tercets and form a couplet for the quatrain. Despite these formal restrictions, Thomas's poem sounds remarkably unforced and reflects quite adequately the feeling of a man who does not want his father to die.

Just as remarkable is the poem's rich figurative language; this villanelle could be used as a summary example of almost all the points outlined in this chapter. Variety is achieved through the metonymies for death, such as "close of day" (line 2), "dark" (4), "dying of the light" (9). The overall effect is to describe death metaphorically as the end of a day and thus, in some sense, to familiarize death and lessen its threat. Even to describe death as "that good night" (1) reduces it to a gesture of good-bye. Other figures of speech include a pun on "grave" men (13) (both solemn and mortal); an oxymoron in "who see with blinding sight" (13); various similes, such as "blaze like meteors" (14); and the overall form of the apostrophe.

Thomas introduces several examples of people who might be expected to acquiesce to death gently but who, nonetheless, resist it. "Wise men" (4) — philosophers perhaps — want more time because so far their wisdom has not created any radical change ("forked no lightning," line 5). Men who do good works — theologians possibly — look back and realize that the sum total of their efforts was "frail" and if they had devoted more time to a fertile field ("green bay"), their deeds might have been more effective (8). "Wild men" (10) — inspired artists, writers — know their words have caught and held time, but they know, too, how in various ways — with their relations with others or perhaps with alcohol and drugs — they have "grieved" the sun (11). "Grave men" (13) at the end of their lives realize too late that joy is one means of transcending time. All these groups experience some form of knowledge that makes them wish they could prolong life and live it according to their new insights.

As a writing assignment you might ask students to analyze a character or group of people that they have read about in a short story who seem to fit into one of the categories Thomas describes. What advice would he give them? How otherwise could they lead their lives?

POSSIBLE CONNECTION TO ANOTHER SELECTION

John Donne, "A Valediction: Forbidding Mourning" (text p. 658)

EDWIN ARLINGTON ROBINSON, *The House on the Hill* (p. 748)

Robinson's villanelle describes the emptiness of the "House" for three stanzas before he tweaks the momentum by asking the question: "Why is it then we stray / Around the sunken sill? / They are all gone away" (lines 10–12). The speaker reiterates the futility of returning to the House in the repeated lines. The final stanza leads the reader to understand the inhabitants have died—it is not just that they have "gone away," but that the House itself has been vacant for some time and is crumbling: "there is ruin and decay" (16). Ask students to read Dylan Thomas's "Do Not Go Gentle into That Good Night" (text p. 982). Reading that villanelle puts the static quality in "The House on the Hill" into high relief, since Thomas's repeated lines take on new meanings and movement from stanza to stanza. Robinson's monotonous repetition works, though, since it leaves a haunting "shut and still" quality lingering throughout the poem.

POSSIBLE CONNECTIONS TO OTHER SELECTIONS

Edgar Allan Poe, "The Haunted Palace" (text p. 667; question #1, following)
———, "The Raven" (text p. 575)

CONNECTION QUESTION IN TEXT (p. 748) WITH ANSWER

1. Compare the images and themes of "The House on the Hill" with Edgar Allan Poe's "The Haunted Palace" (text p. 667).

   "The House on the Hill" is desolate, while the "Haunted Palace" is peopled now with "vast forms that move fantastically / To a discordant melody" (lines 43–44). The House carries an eerie quality, a sense of being haunted, even if it only manifests itself in the "winds blow[ing] bleak and shrill" (5). Both can be read as allegories of a disordered mind, or in "The House on the Hill," a failing or grief-stricken mind.

SESTINA

ALGERNON CHARLES SWINBURNE, *Sestina* (p. 749)

The speaker of this poem finds his pleasure in sleep and dreams; the harsh realities of waking life disappoint and fail to sustain his soul. Swinburne's "Sestina" is an unusual example of the form, in that the end words rhyme (the pattern is *ababab, bababa*). The rhymes connect the repeated words thematically: *day, way,* and *may* are contrasted to *night, light,* and *delight.*

"Sestina" has strong religious overtones, introduced by the poem's focus on the soul and reinforced by references to "wings" (line 4), "lordship" (9), and "heaven" (24). But religion, in this poem, is not necessarily a positive force. The speaker's soul thrives only in a dream state, and he chooses, as a result, to reject the day, possibly a metaphor for religious teaching and certainly a metaphor for reality. The envoy cements the speaker's dejection and loss of faith, asserting that "man hath no long delight" (39) regardless of what pleasures he may find singing under moonlight.

A little cultural history may help your students understand this poem. Swinburne was a London poet of the Victorian era, which was marked by sexual repression and religious emphasis on purity and restraint. But Swinburne was actively homosexual and given to scandalously masochistic behaviors, particularly self-flagellation. Rather than hide his predilections, he flaunted them—often inventing or exaggerating stories about his exploits—and earned a reputation as a decadent poet. His *Poems and Ballads* (1866) were reviled by critics for their overt celebration of things like sadomasochism, homosexuality, and necrophilia, as well as for their decidedly anti-Christian bent. In this context "Sestina" can be read as a celebration of illicit pleasures forbidden by Victorian religion and possible only out of sight of the respectable (daytime) public.

POSSIBLE CONNECTIONS TO OTHER SELECTIONS

Mark Jarman, "Unholy Sonnet" (text p. 745)
Walt Whitman, From "I Sing the Body Electric" (text p. 763)

FLORENCE CASSEN MAYERS, *All-American Sestina* (p. 750)

This poem is in a sense an inverted sestina because the first words of each line (rather than the end words) conform to the conventions of a sestina. The poem runs through a series of American clichés involving the numbers one through six and fits them into this difficult poetic form. Mayers departs from her own scheme a few times, though: What should be "six" in the third stanza is "sixty-" (line 14), and it wraps around to the next line, "four-dollar question"; and "hole in one" (27) in stanza 5 and "high five" (34) in stanza 6 break the pattern of having the number begin the line.

Students might debate about whether this poem raises important themes or whether it's just a clever exercise. You may want to gear discussion toward a consideration of what is particularly "all-American" about the clichés in the poem. (Is the fact that they are clichés all-American?) It might help to try to classify the images; the categories may vary, but most seem to have something to do with a kind of consumer hucksterism, as in "one-day sale" (8), "five-year warranty" (9), and "sixty-four-dollar question" (14–15); or with nostalgia, as in "five-cent cigar" (5) or "one-room schoolhouse" (36); or with excess, as in "six-pack Bud" (7), "two-pound lobster" (17), or "four-wheel drive" (25). Students may come up with entirely different categories. Encourage them to be flexible when creating these categories. Do they see an emerging pattern that might help to define "all-American"? Do any of the phrases not fit neatly into any category? A comparison with Cummings's "next to of course god america i" (text p. 673) may highlight these themes. But does Mayers critique America in the same way that Cummings does? Is it possible to read the poem as a celebration rather than a critique? Or is it simply a neutral portrait? In any case, why does she choose this form to represent it?

POSSIBLE CONNECTIONS TO OTHER SELECTIONS

E. E. Cummings, "next to of course god america i" (text p. 673; question #1, following)

Tato Laviera, "AmeRícan" (text p. 773)

CONNECTION QUESTION IN TEXT (p. 751) WITH ANSWER

1. Describe and compare the strategy used to create meaning in "All-American Sestina" with that used by Cummings in "next to of course god america i" (p. 673).

   Both poems rely on the distance between relatively meaningless American cultural clichés and real ideas to create meaning, but the speaker of Cummings's poem builds toward a definite point. In Mayers's sestina there is little progress. The poem's meaning wouldn't change much if the stanzas were rearranged; meaning comes primarily from the building panorama of clichés. Cummings's speaker begins with hollow phrases and departs from there to try to convince his audience that the war dead performed their duties cheerfully.

EPIGRAM

SAMUEL TAYLOR COLERIDGE, *What Is an Epigram?* (p. 751)

DAVID McCORD, *Epitaph on a Waiter* (p. 751)

PAUL LAURENCE DUNBAR, *Theology* (p. 752)

Note how crucial the technique of word selection becomes in poems that use as few words as these. Have students write in prose the ideas conveyed in each of the first three epigrams. These summaries will probably be considerably more verbose and less witty than the poems from which they stem. Which specific words in each epigram are used to condense meanings that might normally be expressed by means of longer words or phrases?

Also consider how important titles become in the epigrams by McCord and Dunbar. Have students discuss how each epigram would be different if it were presented without its title. McCord's title informs the reader of his subject's occupation and his decease, whereas the poem might refer to anyone who had gone through life exceedingly preoccupied. What does McCord's poem imply about the waiter without saying it specifically? For how much of Dunbar's poem does the title "Theology" seem appropriate? Which words contribute to the serious tone implied by the title? Where does the meaning seem to shift?

LIMERICK

ARTHUR HENRY REGINALD BUTLER, *There was a young lady named Bright* (p. 752)

LAURENCE PERRINE, *The limerick's never averse* (p. 752)

HAIKU

MATSUO BASHŌ, *Under cherry trees* (p. 753)

Bashō is usually considered the greatest of the haiku poets. He was born near Kyoto, growing up as the companion of a local nobleman's son. He moved to Edo (now called Tokyo) when he was twenty-three and eventually became a recluse, living outside the city in a hut. He made several long journeys, always relying for food and shelter on the generosity of local Buddhist temples and on other poets. *The Narrow Road to the Deep North,* a collection of interlocked prose and haiku chronicling one of these journeys, is perhaps his best-known work in the West.

CAROLYN KIZER, *After Bashō* (p. 753)

This poem demonstrates the importance Bashō still has, in many languages, for poets who write haiku. The reference to the "famous" (3) moon indicates the writer's familiarity with the moon as a constant trope in nature poetry in general and haiku in particular. Some Bashō poems that examine the moon include these:

Felling a tree
and seeing the cut end —
tonight's moon.

Harvest moon —
walking around the pond
all night long.

Bashō himself, writing more than a thousand years before Kizer, indicated his awareness of the familiarity of the moon as trope:

It's not like anything
they compare it to —
the summer moon.

ELEGY

BEN JONSON, *On My First Son* (p. 754)

A father's deep grief for his lost child as expressed in this beautiful epitaph needs little explication. However, the poem contains several ideas worthy of class discussion. Why does the poet think that we should envy those who die at an early age? Do your students agree? Do they think the poet believes it himself? How can a child be considered a "best piece of poetry" (line 10)? Have students suggest paraphrases for the last two lines, which are confusing because of the convoluted grammatical construction. Do these lines mean that the poet has learned a lesson about not caring too much for earthly joys, a reading that the use of the word *lent* in line 3 supports? Is he proposing that his great attachment to the child had something to do with his death?

POSSIBLE CONNECTION TO ANOTHER SELECTION

Anne Bradstreet, "Before the Birth of One of Her Children" (text p. 1002)

BRENDAN GALVIN, *An Evel Knievel Elegy* (p. 755)

Galvin's poem for Evel Knievel, published the year after the motorcycle stuntman died, remarks on the significance of his career and his impact on those who watched him. Galvin makes a figurative connection between Knievel's stunts and the more mundane risks that people take in their everyday lives. In the middle of the poem Galvin invokes Icarus, so you may want to refresh students' memories on the myth of Icarus and Daedalus. This version of the story becomes uniquely American in that the overreacher is not an inventor or an innovator, but a daredevil. His downfall is not pride at what he can achieve so much as a lack of fear. In addition to mourning for the stuntman, this elegy also asks what role he played for Americans in general. In fact, at the end of the poem, Galvin turns away from Knievel, joining those audiences who refuse to "suffer the loss / of [his] departure" (lines 30–31) because, while Knievel underwent a public "annealing" (27), they have undergone their own private trials by fire.

POSSIBLE CONNECTION TO ANOTHER SELECTION

Ben Jonson, "On My First Son" (text p. 754)

ODE

PERCY BYSSHE SHELLEY, *Ode to the West Wind* (p. 756)

Percy Bysshe Shelley was born to wealth in Horsham, Sussex. Educated in conventional privileges, he was taunted by his schoolmates for his unconventionality and lack of physical prowess. His rebellion against this environment helped make him both a nonconformist and a democrat. He was expelled from Oxford in 1811 for coauthoring a pamphlet called *The Necessity of Atheism.* He eventually married Mary Wollstonecraft Godwin and in 1818 settled in Italy, where he wrote his most highly regarded works, including "Prometheus Unbound" and "Ode to the West Wind." Shelley drowned while sailing with a friend, and his ashes were buried in a cemetery in Rome near the graves of his son, William Shelley, and John Keats.

The west wind in England is hailed as the harbinger of spring. As an introduction to this ode, you might have students read the anonymous "Western Wind" (text p. 560).

The tercets and couplets that form each section of this ode should pose no problems; basically, the tercets interweave (*aba, bcb, cdc, ded, ee*). Because Shelley is describing wind, the ethereal element, it is appropriate that the sounds of the couplet (*ee*), which appear at the end of every twelfth line in the first three sections, should have an airy, wind-rushed quality, as in "hear," "atmosphere," "fear."

The first three sections describe the powers the wind has in nature — on land in autumn, in the clouds in "the dying year" (winter, line 24), and on the bay (a mixture of land and sea) in the summer. When Shelley turns to his own problems, including his sense of despair and his need for inspiration (sections 4 and 5), the rhyme of the couplet (*ee*) is changed, and a more mournful, weighted sound ("bowed," "proud") is substituted. The rhyme scheme almost makes the poem generalize in the final section, when "Wind" and the promises of spring are bestowed on "mankind" (67).

For a close reading of this ode, see S. C. Wilcox's "Imagery, Ideas, and Design in Shelley's 'Ode to the West Wind,' " *Studies in Philosophy* 47 (October 1950); print; 634–49.

As a three-page writing assignment, ask students to analyze the symbolic meaning of the west wind.

POSSIBLE CONNECTION TO ANOTHER SELECTION

Henry Wadsworth Longfellow, "Snow-Flakes" (text p. 1016)

PARODY

BLANCHE FARLEY, *The Lover Not Taken* (p. 758)

The fun of parodies derives in part from recognition of their sources—in this instance, Frost's "The Road Not Taken" (text p. 840). In Farley's parody, we see again the distressed speaker who wants to have it both ways. As is usually the case with Frost's deliberators, the woman in this poem seems to have many hours to devote to "mulling" (line 2). Farley mimics Frost's faint archaisms with the line (present in both poems) "Somewhere ages and ages hence" (17). She also plays with and lightly satirizes the rigors of Frost's blank-verse line. Notice, for example, how she carries over the key word that would round out the sense of the line between lines 8 and 9, only to accommodate the pentameter scansion. At the close of her poem, Farley plays down the need for choosing and asserts that there was no difference between the lovers. Appropriately for this parody, she closes with a heroic couplet.

PICTURE POEM

MICHAEL McFEE, *In Medias Res* (p. 759)

Students will probably have fun identifying the puns in this portly poem. A handful for consideration: "His waist / like the plot / thickens" (lines 1–3)—just as in a murder mystery, his increasing girth is out to get him, as the darker tone of the second half of this poem implies. "Wedding / pants" (3–4)—do we read this as the pants from the suit he wore at his wedding, no doubt a smaller size, or as the waist "wedding," or uniting, with the waistband of the pants? "Breathtaking" (4) no longer means spellbinding but rather a kind of choking. The "cinch" (5) can be read either as a girth or belt, or a snap, an easy thing to do.

PERSPECTIVE

ELAINE MITCHELL, *Form* (p. 760)

By comparing form to a corset, Mitchell develops the idea that there is a time and a place to use form in poetry and a time and a place not to use it. Ask students to identify in the poem the various moments when the poet suggests that form can be helpful. Responses might include that it can "shape and deceive" (line 5), "It / 's an ace up your sleeve" (7–8), and "it / might be a resource" (12–13) or "your grateful slave" (14). Then ask students to identify places where the poet warns that form can prove too confining, such as "Don't try to force it" (3), "Ouch, too tight a corset" (6), "No need to force it" (9), and "sometimes divorce it" (16). Ultimately, Mitchell seems to be suggesting that poets need to recognize when form works to their advantage and when it is forced. When form is forced, poets need to be willing to abandon it rather than continue to impose form where it doesn't work.

By adhering to poetic form herself (three-line stanzas—except the final stanza—constructed with an *aba* rhyme scheme throughout), the poet forces her poem to conform to the restrictions of form she's set up. Indeed, she creates a very controlled rhythm (dactylic dimeter) and rhyme scheme to provide the poem with structure. Some students may recognize that, ironically, Mitchell forces words together and pulls them apart in totally outrageous ways in order to maintain the form she's established. Ask students to consider whether this effect is intentional.

28

Open Form

Whereas traditional forms depend on the interplay of the poet's current speech and an established form, open form hinges on the poet's (and the reader's) ability to discover a form that works toward the overall effect the poet wishes to produce. Just as in the previous chapter, each of the poems here can form the basis of a rewarding discussion about how form relates to content. With open form, the poet theoretically has absolute control over the form chosen, although some may choose a fairly constraining pattern to guide the poem — witness Peter Meinke's "The ABC of Aerobics." As a result of this freedom, the poem must actually withstand closer and more critical reading, as each formal choice takes on greater significance.

The absence of regular metrics or stanzas does not mean the absence of structure. Tato Laviera's "AmeRícan" demonstrates a use of repetition that is reminiscent of Whitman's and serves to create a similar sense of flow and plenitude.

Web Ask students to explore the poets in this chapter at **bedfordstmartins.com/ meyerlit**.

As an exercise, you might have your students experiment with line breaks by taking a poem from the book and redoing the breaks. They might then give that poem to another student and have that student evaluate the new poem, asking themselves "Has the meaning of the poem (or parts of the poem) changed?" This exercise may help to emphasize felicitous or infelicitous choices in poetic structure. A related exercise might have students create found poems by taking a piece of prose and inserting line breaks. Students could again evaluate the results, looking for meanings that have been altered or significances that have been added by the change in form.

WALT WHITMAN, *From "I Sing the Body Electric"* (p. 763)

Whitman's outpouring is a homage to the body, the soul, and poetry all at once. Whitman offers here an anatomy of wonder.

The rhythm of this portion of the poem is striking. Notice how many of the lines begin with a trochee or a spondee. The initial heavy stresses lend a kind of relentless thoroughness to Whitman's catalog of the human body. You might have the class scan a portion of the poem, say from line 25 to line 30. The lines change from heavily accented to a lighter, roughly iambic rhythm that suggests "the continual changes of the flex of the mouth" (line 28).

The chief difficulty is, of course, discerning the exact relationship between these things. We tend to think of them as separate from each other. Does Whitman's poem help us to unify them in our minds? The poem lists a number of body parts: Do any of them tend to stand out or to form any sort of unexpected patterns?

POSSIBLE CONNECTION TO ANOTHER SELECTION

Algernon Charles Swinburne, "Sestina" (text p. 749)

PERSPECTIVE

WALT WHITMAN, *On Rhyme and Meter* (p. 764)

In addition to assigning Consideration 3 as a writing topic, you might ask students to write a few paragraphs about Whitman's use of catalogs or lists as an element of the organic form he espouses. The excerpt from "I Sing the Body Electric" (text p. 763) is especially useful for this exercise. Why is Whitman's tactic of listing appropriate to his subject?

DAVID SHUMATE, *Shooting the Horse* (p. 766)

Ask students to consider "a force even more austere" than that of a gunshot, "which we have named mercy." With that one word, "mercy," Shumate reverses direction in the poem, which has hurtled, from the title, to the squeezing of the trigger. His speaker is matter-of-fact throughout, with hints that feel like slips into the deeper relationship here ("like a lover about to leave" and "the routine we taught each other long ago"). The simple subject-verb-object sentence structure and use of fragments adds to the weight of what is unspoken. The poem isn't about the horse's suffering, which the shooting is meant to end — the poem is about the speaker's agony before he kills the horse.

POSSIBLE CONNECTIONS TO OTHER SELECTIONS

Emily Dickinson, "After great pain — a formal feeling comes" (text p. 813)

Andrew Hudgins, "The Cow" (text p. 709; question #1, following)

CONNECTION QUESTION IN TEXT (p. 767) WITH ANSWER

1. Compare the treatment of the death of the horse in this poem with that of the bovine in "The Cow" by Andrew Hudgins (text p. 709).

   While the poems both graphically describe the death of an animal at the hands of its owner, grief or awe is implicit in Shumate's poem, while Hudgins's poem takes a humorous tone (the difference is particularly striking in the endings of the poems). Also, the use of third person in Hudgins's poem creates a certain emotional distance, as does the time lapse from beginning to end; "Shooting the Horse" describes a much briefer period of time, from the opening of the stall door to the shooting.

RICHARD HAGUE, *Directions for Resisting the SAT* (p. 767)

Hague's poem undercuts itself when it insists that the reader "follow no directions" (line 14). Once your students have identified the immediate reasons for Hague's revolt — having to spend a "Saturday morning with pencils" (2), the constrictive "rules of gravity, / commas, history" (3–4) — you might have them discuss how his poem works as a direction against directions. Would he encourage the reader to ignore his rules as well?

You might also ask your class to talk about the alternative Hague proposes, living "whole / like an oyster or snail" (12–13). Does that sound like a rewarding existence? What would its benefits be? And how does the image of the snail inform a reading of the last line? Besides the marks that aren't supposed to go outside the SAT bubbles, Hague may also be thinking of the purposeless trails that animals make.

ELLEN BASS, *Gate C22* (p. 767)

Similes can be tricky — when one says that something is "like" something else, the comparison must ring true or it will seem forced or overblown. Ask how Bass's similes raise this scene from the ordinary, magically transforming this kiss on the airport tarmac into the sort of encounter people dream of. What is the effect of layering them—would they have worked if she had used only one? Consider the balance and interplay of an image like "kisses like the ocean" (line 15) next to the mundane (but vivid) image of the passengers, pilots, and "the aproned woman icing Cinnabons" (21). What is the effect of the final image, when the focus lands on the viewers, "tilting our heads up" (35)? Discuss the strength and effectiveness of as many details as possible from line to line, stanza to stanza.

POSSIBLE CONNECTIONS TO OTHER SELECTIONS

John Donne, "A Valediction: Forbidding Mourning" (text p. 658)

Denise Duhamel, "How It Will End" (text p. 677)

George Eliot, "In a London Drawingroom" (text p. 1006; question #1, following)

CONNECTION QUESTION IN TEXT (p. 768) WITH ANSWER

1. Compare the poets' use of setting to establish theme in "Gate C22" and in George Eliot's "In a London Drawingroom" (text p. 1006).

    A view of life is imparted by the observer in both "Gate C22" and "In a London Drawingroom." Without the lovers who are the focus of "Gate C22," the view in the airport terminal might be very similar to that of "In a London Drawingroom." In Eliot's poem, "All hurry on and look upon the ground" (line 13). In "Gate C22," the gaze of the people milling about—"passengers waiting for the delayed flight / to San Jose, the stewardesses, the pilots, / the aproned woman icing Cinnabons, the man selling / sunglasses" (19–22)—might also be turned down, except for the spectacular embrace happening in front of them. In Eliot's poem, no one "rest[s] a little in the lap of life" (12), but in "Gate C22" the viewers eagerly want to become the ones participating in that life, "tilting [their] heads up" (35). One might say that the routine seen daily from the drawingroom allows only a description of stasis, while a scene in an airport leaves the poet with a greater possibility for the unexpected.

NATASHA TRETHEWEY, *On Captivity* (p. 769)

"On Captivity" starts with a journal entry by Jonathan Dickinson, a Quaker merchant who was shipwrecked on the coast of Florida and held for several days by Native Americans. By imagining how the colonists' language reflects back on them, Trethewey's poem reveals several ironies in this captivity narrative. First, their use of the term "savages" (line 3) for the Native Americans is itself a kind of savagery, and Trethewey imagines that they say the word with hatred. Second, while the colonists came to America assuming that their religious mission would protect them, in this situation, they are literally covered up only by pages of the "Good Book" (33). Furthermore, the captives' own names are inscribed on those pages, so their desire to label the previous inhabitants of America is turned back on them when they have to wear their own labels. The stanza shape Trethewey uses allows each stanza to build toward a small climax, giving the poem a repeating structure of tensions built up and then released.

POSSIBLE CONNECTION TO ANOTHER SELECTION

Julio Marzán, "The Translator at the Reception for Latin American Writers" (text p. 770)

JULIO MARZÁN, *The Translator at the Reception for Latin American Writers* (p. 770)

This poem examines the sudden end of a conversation: once the origins of the speaker are known, the new acquaintance loses interest. The imaginative center of the poem is the comparison of the acquaintance to a film director. The speaker imagines the man is disappointed in the "lurid script" (line 19) he sees as the only possible potential for "Puerto Rico and the Bronx" (5). Marzán assumes that readers will recognize the separation between the mundane nature of domestic issues—"dreary streets" (21), "pathetic human interest" (22)—summoned by mention of "Puerto Rico and the Bronx" (5) and the exotic "Mayan pyramid grandeur" (14) associated with other Latin American locales.

The setting helps establish this tension: the reception is "high culture" (23), while "Puerto Rico and the Bronx" (5) represent areas with few economic advantages. This friction sees its result in the abrupt ending of the conversation as the acquaintance seeks other company. The speaker's tone remains amused and detached, however, demonstrating the real separation: readers would likely choose the company of the speaker over the rude, unimaginative man who prefers cheese.

POSSIBLE CONNECTIONS TO OTHER SELECTIONS

Mark Halliday, "Graded Paper" (text p. 680)

Tato Laviera, "AmeRícan" (text p. 773)

ROBERT MORGAN, *Overalls* (p. 771)

Morgan's description of the overalls obviously sets up the comparison of work with war, which he makes explicit in the final line. The overalls are decorated with "medals, badges" (line 8), a "sheath" (10) as if for a sword, and "holsters" (20) like those for guns. But he also uses geographic metaphors, describing the patches as "mesas" (16) in a "cloth topography" (18). Beyond the military comparison, what about the laborer can we infer from Morgan's figures? The geography of the overalls suggests age, and their levels of patches indicate that the wearer has little money for new clothes. This begins to look like the portrait of a downtrodden worker. Yet the final line also points back to the childlike quality described at the beginning of the poem. Though this is war, it is a "playful" one (23).

POSSIBLE CONNECTION TO ANOTHER SELECTION

Robert Hayden, "Those Winter Sundays" (text p. 547)

KEVIN YOUNG, *Eddie Priest's Barbershop & Notary* (p. 771)

This poem is about a neighborhood barbershop and the culture that has sprung up around it. It is important to note that much of Young's intention unfolds through the perspective of race. How does the poet give the reader a sense of place through the setting of scene and use of diction?

Written in free verse and highly alliterative, Young's poem presents some difficulty to the reader because of his lack of punctuation and use of fragment. Discuss how fragments such as "the pain of running / a fisted comb through stubborn / knots is the dark dirty low / down blues   the tender heads / of sons fresh from cornrows all / wonder at losing half their height" (lines 11–16) add up to more than a description of hair—to a bigger picture of a particular shop and of a people. Once students have created some associations with the metaphors and fragmented images at hand, begin to look at the deliberation of Young's line breaks and what they reveal.

POSSIBLE CONNECTIONS TO OTHER SELECTIONS

George Eliot, "In a London Drawingroom" (text p. 1006)

Ruth Forman, "Poetry Should Ride the Bus" (text p. 627)

ANONYMOUS, *The Frog* (p. 772)

Although a number of violations of grammatical rules appear in this poem—such as lack of agreement between subject and verb in "bird . . . are" (line 1), or "he hop" (3), and double negatives in "He ain't got no" (4)—there is a certain structure to its content.

Following the odd assertion that the frog is "a wonderful bird" (1), the poet catalogs the frog's characteristics and follows them up with a list of what the frog lacks. The final line is a sort of culmination of both approaches: "When he sit, he sit on what he ain't got almost" (6). And although the literal meaning of the poem and its ungrammatical sentences might seem confusing, the poet provides a clear image of the frog, almost in spite of the language. The repetition of words such as *almost* and *hardly* and the reliance on many one-syllable words contribute to the overall rhythmic pattern of the work. You might ask students what the effect of comparing a frog to a bird is in this poem.

Possible Connections to Other Selections

Emily Dickinson, "A Bird came down the Walk —" (text p. 693)

Katharyn Howd Machan, "Hazel Tells LaVerne" (text p. 596)

TATO LAVIERA, *AmeRícan* (p. 773)

"AmeRícan" relies on a complex structure and innovative use of language for its power. Encourage students to examine the components and the physical layout of each section of this ever-changing, ever-moving poem. Each of the first three stanzas begins with the phrase "we gave birth to a new generation." The new generation is composed of those AmeRícans who will gather the elements of their culture and move into the mainstream American culture represented by New York. The seventh stanza (lines 21–24) highlights the poem's narrative development and the poet's creative use of language. Marking the transition between native and American culture, the poet embodies the literal movement, the disorientation, and the character of the new environment through the rearrangement and repetition of *across, forth,* and *back.* Appropriately, residence in New York (an island connected by bridges) is indicated by the line "our trips are walking bridges!" (24). What other meaning is indicated by this line?

The eighth stanza breaks from the form established by the preceding stanzas. Ask students why it is appropriate to omit the beginning word "AmeRícan" here. In what way is this physical detail a response to the "marginality that gobbled us up abruptly!" (31)? In what other ways do the content and tone of this stanza contrast with those of the rest of the poem?

The poem is infused with the poet's sense of both Puerto Rican and American cultures. Encourage students to note the comparisons between the first and second halves of this poem, in which Laviera touches on the music, spirit, and language of each culture. Also, students might notice instances (particularly toward the end of this poem) in which the cultures seem fused—for example, in words such as *spanglish* (41).

What is the tone of the final two stanzas? Literally, there is a celebration of the myth of America—"home of the brave, the land of the free." The penultimate stanza alludes to the understanding fostered by our Puritan forefathers that America is God's chosen country, "a city on a hill" that should be an example to all nations. The lines in which Laviera refers to "our energies / collectively invested to find other civili- / zations" (52–54) also touch on our history of manifest destiny. The final stanza conveys the joy experienced by an assimilated AmeRícan, yet there is also considerable loss of identity in the speaker's "dream to take the accent from / the altercation, and be proud to call / [him]self american" (57–59).

Possible Connection to Another Selection

Julio Marzán, "The Translator at the Reception for Latin American Writers" (text p. 770)

PETER MEINKE, *The ABC of Aerobics* (p. 774)

Born in Brooklyn, Peter Meinke often experiments with form, preferring to let the poem dictate its own form. Works whose titles begin "The ABC of . . ." usually are primers designed to teach the basic elements of a subject. You might start discussion of this poem by asking whether it fulfills the expectations its title sets up. In a kind of playful, semisatiric thumbing of the nose at cholesterol-level and heart-rate calculators, the poem at least acknowledges the obligations of its title. The speaker, apparently, has tried to ward off the effects of aging by jogging, but he expends all this effort with a despairing sense of his past sins and the dark forebodings of his genetic history manifested in the portrait of Uncle George. Small wonder, then, that his thoughts turn to Shirley Clark, and the poem concludes with the speaker "breathing hard" (line 26) and gasping for his lost flame at his own "maximal heart rate" (7).

At least two aspects of this poem merit some consideration. One is the carefully controlled use of consonance and alliteration, often for humorous effect. Notice, for example, the alternating *l* and *b* sounds in line 12 followed by the nasal hiss of "my / medical history a noxious marsh." Later, in a spoofing of health and fitness fads, Meinke shows the direction of his true inclinations by exchanging "zen and zucchini" for "drinking and dreaming" (25-26).

The second aspect of this poem that students should feel comfortable enough to enjoy is the humor, which derives in part from the poem's dip into the vernacular. "Probably I shall keel off the john like / queer Uncle George," Meinke unabashedly tells us in lines 16 to 17, while he describes the lucky lover who married the fabled Shirley as a "turkey" (20) who lacks all aesthetic appreciation for her wondrous earlobes. We are inclined to like the speaker in this poem, and both his personality and the radiated humor act as rhetorical devices, helping us to feel the way he feels about "The ABC of Aerobics," which, by the way, takes us to the end of the alphabet with "zen and zucchini."

Critical studies of Meinke's work include Philip Jason's "Speaking to Us All" in *Poet Lore* (Washington, D.C.: Heldref Publications, 1982; print.) and Eric Nelson's "Trying to Surprise God" in *Mickle Street Review* (Camden: Walt Whitman House Association, 1983; print.).

POSSIBLE CONNECTION TO ANOTHER SELECTION

James Merrill, "Casual Wear" (text p. 682)

CHRISTINA GEROGIANNIS, *Headland* (p. 775)

In "Headland," Gerogiannis finds both grammatical and metaphorical means of expressing what is hard to say about loss. The poem reveals a pattern of revising speech: the speaker rethinks "no sadness" (line 1) and offers, instead, "no / definite sadness" (4-5). Similarly, the day in section two becomes "the living day" in section three (11). These repetitions-with-difference give "Headland" the feeling of thoughts turned over and over in grief.

The loss in the poem is also figured as small spaces and wide gulfs. The domestic setting of "Headland" is sketched out through Gerogiannis's attention to small details like the piece of jasper on the dresser or the comforter splashed with bleach. These small interior details contrast with the vast space outside, the acres that surround the house. The title also suggests isolation, for a headland is surrounded on three sides by water.

In discussion, students might want to think about the appearance of memory aids like the slideshow and the "photos on corkboard" (14). Do these forms of remembrance have anything in common with headland? You might also call students' attention to the form of the poem. What is the effect of having the same arrangement of lines in each section? How does this structure — a tercet followed by a couplet — work within the sections?

POSSIBLE CONNECTION TO ANOTHER SELECTION

Emily Dickinson, "The Bustle in a House" (text p. 816; question #1, following)

1. Why are the speaker's sensory perceptions jumbled in this poem? Discuss "Headland" using terms Emily Dickinson identifies in "The Bustle in a House" (p. 816).

   Dickinson's use of the word "Bustle" suggests a kind of hurried activity that helps to keep the mind off a recent loss. In "Headland," the evidence of hurried cleaning — even the ceilings have been bleached — is one of the ways Gerogiannis indicates the presence of grief in the house. The fragmentation of the poem into short sections also suggests that the activity is a way of avoiding sustained attention to the loss. In her second stanza, Dickinson extends the images of household activity so that the work is not just a preoccupation but a way of dealing with emotion: "The Sweeping up the Heart / and putting Love away" (lines 5-6). At the end of "Headland," the cleaning seems to prepare for the later act of starting again.

FOUND POEM

DONALD JUSTICE, *Order in the Streets* (p. 777)

The poem outlines a process, with each step in a separate stanza. As we read the poem, we observe the process with the speaker. The word *jeep,* without an article, is repeated at the beginnings of three stanzas, lending an air of impersonality to its actions, as if there were no driver. The poem is itself impersonal, reducing "Order in the Streets" to a series of mechanized steps, devoid of human presence.

29

Combining the Elements of Poetry:
A Writing Process

Once students have grasped some of the individual elements of a poem, there remains the task of combining these separate insights into a coherent whole. Class discussion in introductory courses often takes up this challenge. While students make specific observations about a poem, the instructor attempts to connect the observations, in order to give students a bigger picture. But this isn't always easy. Asking Questions about the Elements in Chapter 29 (page 779 of the text) may help students who need to add more component elements to their understanding of the poem or those who have a grasp of the components but still need a way of integrating them in discussion or in written assignments. The questions may also help more advanced students. Even if these students have a good understanding of a poem's structure, the questions could suggest ways of structuring their own papers on the poem.

You might also want to use these questions to facilitate class discussion. After determining which questions are particularly useful for a given poem, have separate groups of students explore separate questions. Then have the groups report to the class as a whole. Ask them to support their responses with citations from the poem. In the discussion following, try to engage the groups in dialogue with one another. How do their insights overlap? How might they combine their observations in a paper? This type of exercise should be valuable because it enacts the very task of the chapter.

Web Ask students to research John Donne at **bedfordstmartins.com/ meyerlit**.

Chapter 29 includes a sample student paper explicating John Donne's "Death Be Not Proud." Have your students read Donne's poem and then discuss how they might approach the assignment given to the student writer. You might want to ask them how they would write a similar paper but with a different combination of elements. How would they write such a paper about a different poem? What can they learn about combining elements from this sample paper? You might even ask them to critique the paper and suggest revisions.

APPROACHES
TO POETRY

30

A Study of Emily Dickinson

There are several difficulties in teaching Dickinson. One lies in having students unlearn previous assumptions about her. Emily Dickinson was, in fact, a real person and did, from time to time, get out of the house. Dickinson can be read as a poet of passion and exuberance as well as irony and playfulness. The popular image of her as an agoraphobic introvert has done a disservice to such readings. Emphasizing that she was an actual human being can help students find a juncture between the erotic Dickinson, the death-obsessed Dickinson, the religious Dickinson, the playful Dickinson, and so on.

In addition, students may find many of her poems to be extremely challenging, though some may seem deceptively simple. When you ask students to "get their hands dirty" with these poems, they may find that they can dig much deeper than they initially thought. The challenging poems are often difficult because of Dickinson's use of occasionally unfamiliar vocabulary, wordplay, understatement, and gaps in her poetry. You may find it useful to encourage students to bring to bear all the skills they have developed in previous chapters, including reading the poems aloud and writing about them.

EMILY DICKINSON

If I can stop one Heart from breaking (p. 800) **and** *If I shouldn't be alive* (p. 801)

You might wish to impress on your class the difference in quality between these two poems by means of a prereading experiment. Before your students have read the introductory text for this section, show them copies of the two poems with key words removed, and have them attempt to fill in the blanks. They will probably have no trouble with phrases like "in vain," "Robin," or "his Nest again" in the first poem, but do any of them anticipate "Granite lip" in the second?

You might begin discussion of "If I can stop one Heart . . ." by asking students to consider the comments on sentimentality and the greeting-card tradition in the text (pp. 565). Dickinson's relation to such popular occasional verse is, after all, not so far-fetched, as she is reputed to have honored birthdays and other social occasions by composing poems. Ask students to speculate on why this poem was so popularly successful and then to explore its limitations. The poem's simplicity and the extent to which it recounts what we *think* it should are among its popular virtues. If students have trouble seeing the poem's limitations, ask them if it is possible to live life with only one rule of conduct. Would they consider their entire lives successful if they saved one robin? You might also speculate with students on why the least common denominator of a poet's work is so often what the popular mind accepts. Recall as a parallel Walt Whitman's poem on Lincoln, "O Captain! My Captain!"—a rhymed lyric that has found its way into many high-school anthologies and may be even more popular since its use in the film *Dead Poets Society.*

"If I shouldn't be alive" is much more in keeping with Dickinson's usual ironic mode. In what ways is this poem similar to the previous one? What emotions are evoked by the use of the robin in each poem? Where does "If I shouldn't be alive" break away from the world of sentimentality evoked by "If I can stop one Heart . . ."? What does the speaker's concern that she might be thought ungrateful, suggested by the second stanza, say about her? How do the speakers of these two poems differ?

As a way of enabling students to appreciate the master stroke of the "Granite lip" in the last line, you might have them rewrite the line so that it steers the poem back toward a more conventional expression.

POSSIBLE CONNECTIONS TO OTHER SELECTIONS ("If I shouldn't be alive")

Emily Dickinson, "Because I could not stop for Death —" (text p. 814)

Helen Farries, "Magic of Love" (text p. 566)

The Thought beneath so slight a film — (p. 802)

Just as laces and mists (both light, partial coverings) reveal the wearer or the mountain range, so a veiled expression reveals the inner thought or opinion. Dickinson is here implying that the delicate covering makes the eye work harder to see the form behind the veil; therefore, misted objects appear in sharper outline.

Ask students to suggest other metaphors Dickinson might have used to describe the distinctness of things that are partially hidden. Depending on your class, you might be able to discuss one of the more obvious examples: whether or not seminudity is more erotic than complete nakedness. Why does Dickinson use such totally different metaphors — women's clothing and a mountain range—to make her point here? Is there any connection between the two? Do your students agree with Dickinson's premise? Are things more distinct, or simply more intriguing, when the imagination must become involved? Does one see another person's thoughts more clearly when a "film" necessitates working harder to understand, or is it just as likely that the "understanding" that results is a hybrid of two persons' thoughts?

POSSIBLE CONNECTIONS TO OTHER SELECTIONS

Emily Dickinson, "Portraits are to daily faces" (text p. 805)

——, "Tell all the Truth but tell it slant—" (text p. 817)

To make a prairie it takes a clover and one bee (p. 803)

"To make a prairie . . ." reads like a recipe—add this to that and you will get the desired result. But it could just as well be a call for props in a theater production: take these items and add a little reflective imagination and the result will be a prairie, itself a symbol of open-endedness and freedom of spirit.

To enable students to understand the poem more clearly, you might ask them to explore the idea of essential ingredients by writing their own "recipe" poem: How do you make a family? A term paper? A painting? What happens to each of these entities as various ingredients are removed? What cannot be removed without destroying the entity or changing its character completely?

POSSIBLE CONNECTIONS TO OTHER SELECTIONS

Emily Dickinson, "I felt a Cleaving in my Mind—" (text p. 816)

Robert Frost, "Mending Wall" (text p. 843)

Success is counted sweetest (p. 803)

The power of this poem, to some degree, is its intangibility. We puzzle over how desire enables those who will never succeed to know success better than those who actually achieve it. Ask students to talk about the comparison of success to "a nectar" (line 3). It is odd that the verb *comprehend* should be paired with nectar; what does it mean to comprehend? When your students begin to talk about the pairing of understanding and physical images, ask them to think about "need" (4) as both a physical and an intellectual desire for success.

You might also have students discuss the word *burst* in the final line. Are the failures the true achievers? If so, what is it they achieve?

POSSIBLE CONNECTIONS TO OTHER SELECTIONS

Emily Dickinson, "I like a look of Agony" (text p. 808)

——, "Water, is taught by thirst" (text p. 804)

John Keats, "Ode on a Grecian Urn" (text p. 612; question #1, following)

CONNECTION QUESTION IN TEXT (p. 804) WITH ANSWER

1. In an essay compare the themes of this poem with those of John Keats's "Ode on a Grecian Urn" (p. 612).

   The themes of both "Success is counted sweetest" and "Ode on a Grecian Urn" have to do with wanting. Dickinson holds that success, or as she later calls it, "Victory" (line 8), is "counted sweetest / by those who ne'er succeed" (1–2). In other words, the want of success makes success itself seem better. To use a cliché, the grass is always greener.... Similarly, Keats's image of the lovers forever chasing each other recalls the agony of the unsuccessful listener in Dickinson's poem. Yet the agony is not entirely negative. Consider how sweetly the success in Keats's poem is counted.

Water, is taught by thirst (p. 804)

Thematically, this poem reiterates the contention in previous Dickinson poems, such as "Success is counted sweetest" (text p. 803) and "The Thought beneath so slight a film —" (text p. 802), that the inability to grasp something physically brings its essential qualities into sharper focus. It might be interesting to have students suggest what Dickinson's pattern is in this poem. The first four lines appear to work by oppositions: water is defined by its lack, land by the oceans surrounding it, transport (ecstasy) by agony, and peace by war. But how is "Memorial Mold" related to love (line 5), and how can a bird be defined in relation to snow? The poem's images seem to move from the concrete to the abstract (although the last line seems to subvert this reading). Perhaps the reader is meant to consider the more abstract connotations of the words in the last line. What are some of the ideas or feelings that birds and snow call to mind? Are any of these ideas opposites?

POSSIBLE CONNECTIONS TO OTHER SELECTIONS

Emily Dickinson, " 'Heaven' — is what I cannot reach!" (text p. 807)

——, "I like a look of Agony" (text p. 808)

——, "Success is counted sweetest" (text p. 803; question #1, following)

CONNECTIONS QUESTIONS IN TEXT (p. 804) WITH ANSWERS

1. What does this poem have in common with "Success is counted sweetest" (p. 803)? Which poem do you think is more effective? Explain why.

   Both poems argue that we learn through deprivation. We gain not just through necessity but through experiencing desperate circumstances. Students are likely to argue that this poem is more effective because it emphasizes its theme through repetition and variation. But "Success is counted sweetest" is at once more specific and broader in scope. It might be interesting to revisit this question after you have covered more of Dickinson's poetry or to have students try to isolate what they believe her most effective (or affecting) poem is.

2. How is the crucial point of this poem related to "I like a look of Agony" (p. 808)?

The central point of "Water, is taught by thirst" is that things only become distinct when they have an opposing force to compare them to. People learn to appreciate and understand things as they really are once they've experienced the opposite. A simple example of this is Dickinson's line "Peace—by its battles told" (4). Humans cannot comprehend or fully appreciate peace without first knowing war. Similarly, "I like a look of Agony" is about learning to tolerate and even appreciate things like pain, and to see the positives that agonizing things can bring into one's life. The narrator respects "a look of Agony / Because I know it's true—" (1–2). She does not like pain for its own sake, but rather the reality and honesty it can lead to.

Safe in their Alabaster Chambers— (1859 version) (p. 804) and Safe in their Alabaster Chambers— (1861 version) (p. 805)

Probably the most physically obvious change Dickinson made in revising this poem was the combining of the last two lines in the first stanza into one line. The latter poem seems more regular because its line and rhyme schemes are the same in both stanzas. The change also has the effect of de-emphasizing the more pleasant image of the original last two lines—the satin rafters—and emphasizing the colder, harder image of the stone. The emphasis becomes even more pronounced with the addition of the strong punctuation at the end of line 5 in the 1861 version.

The physical changes in the first stanza, coupled with a complete change of imagery for the second stanza, result in a different tone for the two versions of the poem. In the 1859 version the dead are lamented but life goes on around their tombs in anticipation of their eventual resurrection at the end of the world (note that in line 4 they only "sleep"). In the 1861 version the dead "lie" in their graves, and the larger universe continues in its course as though human deaths are of little importance. The second poem's mention of "Diadems" and "Doges" (9) serves to emphasize that even the fall of the earth's most powerful people has little impact on the universe. The human relationship to nature here is more like that in Stephen Crane's "A Man Said to the Universe" (text p. 673).

You might have students note at this point Dickinson's emphasis on white, translucent things in her imagery. Have students recall such images from earlier poems. They might mention film, lace, mountain mists, or snow. Note the contrast between Dickinson's conviction that we comprehend life more clearly through the mists, and Emerson's idea, for example, that we should ideally become like a "transparent eyeball" in order to know Nature.

POSSIBLE CONNECTION TO ANOTHER SELECTION (1859 version)

Emily Dickinson, "Apparently with no surprise" (text p. 830)

POSSIBLE CONNECTIONS TO OTHER SELECTIONS (1861 version)

Emily Dickinson, "Apparently with no surprise" (text p. 830)
Robert Frost, "Design" (text p. 856; question #1, following)

CONNECTION QUESTION IN TEXT (p. 805) **WITH ANSWER**

1. Compare the theme in the 1861 version with the theme of Robert Frost's "Design" (p. 856).

Both poems have to do with perspective and proportion, focusing first on something small and then pulling back to examine how those smaller things fit into a larger scheme. Frost's spider and moth retain their significance despite the ironic final line, "If design govern in a thing so small." Dickinson's "meek members of the Resurrection" (line 4), by contrast, are rendered insignificant by the entire second stanza. They are faceless and unimportant; the poet does not bother to pause and observe them, unlike Frost's speaker, who concentrates on the spider, moth, and flower in detail before dismissing them.

Portraits are to daily faces (p. 805)

Before asking students to discuss the analogy presented in "Portraits," you might want to remind them of the analogy sections on their ACTs. They probably were at some point taught the strategy of making a connection between one pair of words and trying to apply it to a second pair. What happens when your students try to apply this strategy to Dickinson's poem? One difficulty lies in determining whether the comparison in the first line is meant to be taken in a positive or a negative manner. Is a portrait a daily face that is perfected and idealized, captured so that it never grows old? Or is it a static, posed rendering of something that was meant to be alive and constantly changing? The word *pedantic* in line 3 suggests a negative connotation for the second term in each analogy. The sunshine is ostentatious in its glory—in its "satin Vest" (line 4). Do your students object to the characterization of bright sun as "pedantic"? After all, there is nothing inherently inferior about sunshine—or about living human faces, for that matter.

POSSIBLE CONNECTIONS TO OTHER SELECTIONS

Emily Dickinson, " 'Faith' is a fine invention" (text p. 829)

——, "Tell all the Truth but tell it slant —" (text p. 817)

——, "The Thought beneath so slight a film —" (text p. 802; question #3, following)

Robert Francis, "Catch" (text p. 552; question #1, following)

Robert Frost, "Birches" (text p. 848)

——, "Mending Wall" (text p. 843)

CONNECTIONS QUESTIONS IN TEXT (p. 806) WITH ANSWERS

1. Compare Dickinson's view of poetry in this poem with Robert Francis's perspective in "Catch" (p. 552). What important similarities and differences do you find?

   In both poems the reader must work hard to understand the meaning. Dickinson's poem embodies this circumstance, whereas Francis's illustrates it. But we have the impression that Francis believes in authorial intention, that there is a single "point" that the reader can "get," even if that point is obscure. Dickinson's poem (and her poetry in general) presents wide gaps between the reader and poet; we are not sure if we are meant to understand exactly what one of her poems means or if that meaning can remain stable over multiple readings.

3. How is the theme of this poem related to the central idea in "The Thought beneath so slight a film —" (p. 802)?

   Portraits are held to be superior to "daily faces" presumably because they allow the viewer to interpret them and to regard them with a sense of wonder. The thought beneath a slight film also allows for interpretation and awe. In both cases, art is preferred to quotidian existence.

4. Compare the use of the word "fine" here with its use in " 'Faith' is a fine invention" (p. 848).

   In "Portraits are to daily faces," Dickinson could be using the word "fine" to denote several different things, depending on how students read the poem. If one is inclined to read "Portraits" as a disparaging poem, then "fine" might mean thin, or even sharp. In "'Faith' is a fine invention," Dickinson is using "fine" to mean acceptable or pleasing. Faith is a pleasing concept when the truth of something seems evident; but when a concept becomes more abstract (for example, the existence of germs in Dickinson's time, or God), mankind typically begins to search for concrete proof, using instruments like microscopes.

Some keep the Sabbath going to Church — (p. 806)

One way to help students grasp more concretely the ideas Dickinson posits here is to have them draw up a chart comparing the practices of the "I" and the "Some" in this poem. How does the level of comparison shift between the first two stanzas and the third? The most important comparisons come in the last stanza; like the Puritans, the speaker claims that his or her religious practices result in a direct relationship to God, with no middleman. While the earlier lines may suggest a "to each his own" approach to religion, stanza 3 leaves little room for doubting which experience the speaker considers to be "real" religion. Discuss the distinction made in the last two lines between focusing on the goal one is journeying toward and focusing on the journey itself. Which attitude do your students feel reflects their own outlook?

Possible Connections to Other Selections

Gerard Manley Hopkins, "Pied Beauty" (text p. 1012)

Walt Whitman, "When I Heard the Learn'd Astronomer" (text p. 1026; question #1, following)

Connection Question in Text (p. 806) with Answer

1. Write an essay that discusses nature in this poem and in Walt Whitman's "When I Heard the Learn'd Astronomer" (p. 1026).

    For both poets, nature is sacred and should be approached through direct experience rather than through the filter of other human perspectives. Although both speakers value their direct experience of nature, they contextualize it differently. For Whitman's speaker it is an alternative to science, and for Dickinson's speaker it is an alternative to religion. These contexts give very different meanings to "nature." Science, especially astronomy, is a way of explaining natural phenomena, but religion is a way of providing moral instruction, a human phenomenon. Both speakers demonstrate the same impulse, but their quests differ in specific ways.

"Heaven" — is what I cannot reach! (p. 807)

You might begin discussion of this poem by having students recall other stories they have encountered that deal with the attraction of "forbidden fruit." The first stanza may allude to the story of Adam and Eve or to the myth of Tantalus, who was punished for trying to deceive and humiliate the gods by being placed in a pool in Hades, where the water at his feet receded every time he tried to take a drink and the luscious fruits growing above his head moved away whenever he tried to pluck them to assuage his hunger. Can your students think of other tales that emphasize the same idea? Does this myth affirm or contradict their own experiences? Why does this speaker consider the unattainable to represent heaven? What does this say about him or her?

Besides the apple that is out of reach, what other images of the unattainable does Dickinson use in this poem? The last stanza is particularly difficult in its syntax as well as its diction. How, for example, can "afternoons" (line 9) be a "decoy" (10)?

As a further topic for discussion, or as a writing assignment, students could be asked to consider other Dickinson poems that posit a thesis similar to or different from this one.

POSSIBLE CONNECTIONS TO OTHER SELECTIONS

Emily Dickinson, "I like a look of Agony" (text p. 808)

——, "Water, is taught by thirst" (text p. 804; question #1, following)

Sharon Olds, "Last Night" (text p. 604; question #2, following)

CONNECTIONS QUESTIONS IN TEXT (p. 807) WITH ANSWERS

1. Write an essay that discusses desire in this poem and in "Water, is taught by thirst" (p. 804).

    In " 'Heaven' — is what I cannot reach!" desire seems to be created by unavailability, not just heightened by it. There is almost a perverseness in wanting only what is beyond reach, and Dickinson signals this awareness in her ironic quotes around "Heaven" (lines 1 and 4). In "Water, is taught by thirst," desire is formed not just by absence but also by passing through the opposite of the desired thing. Dickinson implies that gratitude develops through this deprivation.

2. Discuss the speakers' attitudes toward pleasure in this poem and in Sharon Olds's "Last Night" (p. 604).

    For the speaker of this poem, pleasure is always just out of reach. She can presumably *see* the objects of her pleasure, but the experience is frustrating nonetheless, as the allusion to Tantalus makes clear. Whereas Dickinson's speaker cannot reach the apple on the tree, Olds's speaker is fully able to grab her moment of passion, to experience her sexual tryst, and to relive it through memory. Hers is a much less inhibited attitude toward pleasure; she can and does experience it. Dickinson's speaker can neither experience nor enjoy the things she desires.

I felt a Funeral in my Brain (p. 807)

Most of Dickinson's poems are rife with metaphor, and this one is no exception; it leans heavily on the extended metaphor of a funeral. Ask students to consider the individual metaphors line by line that create a vivid world of activity within the abstract "brain."

Students should consider how the senses are evoked here. Are they surprised by the general noisiness and activity (given that this is a "funeral")? How do her metaphors match their perception of funerals and where do they diverge? How does her meter match the noise and experience she's describing? Discuss the reflection of sound and sense in an iambic line like "With those same Boots of lead, again" (line 11). You might point out some of the more striking images that invoke sound — the "Mourners to and fro . . . treading — treading —" (2–3), the "Service, like a Drum —"(6), the tolling of the "Heavens . . . a Bell" (13). Students can describe what they "see" and hear happening in the brain, using various approaches from previous chapters. Also discuss the curious split between the funeral — and the idea of "Being" as "an Ear" (15) — and the speaker who is separate, stranded in "Silence" (16) in the funeral in her brain.

One can read this poem as a description of a breakdown, similar to "I felt a Cleaving in my Mind —" (text p. 816), or as a portrait of one faced with a truth they cannot process. There are hints at these interpretations in her marriages of abstract ideas to concrete images — that the speaker is somehow a corpse being carried across her own brain, that a "Plank in Reason" (17) breaks, and that she drops through worlds that make up a seemingly bottomless grave. With these interpretations in mind, ask students what they make of the "Sense" that breaks through as Mourners pace in her brain. What are they mourning? Discuss how one understands her claim to have "Finished knowing" in the last line, both in terms of what happens when one dies and what happens in particular mental states.

POSSIBLE CONNECTIONS TO OTHER SELECTIONS

Emily Dickinson, "After great pain, a formal feeling comes—" (text p. 813)

——, "Because I could not stop for Death—" (text p. 814; question #1, following)

——, "I felt a Cleaving in my Mind—" (text p. 816)

——, "I heard a Fly buzz—when I died—" (text p. 824)

John Keats, "When I have fears that I may cease to be" (text p. 1014)

William Butler Yeats, "That the Night Come" (text p. 725)

CONNECTION QUESTION IN TEXT (p. 808) WITH ANSWER

1. Compare the themes in this poem and in "Because I could not stop for Death—" (text p. 814).

    There is a sense in both poems that the speaker is powerless over what is happening to her—Death stops to pick her up in his carriage in "Because . . ." and the Mourners move around the immobile *I* in "I felt a Funeral . . .". Each deal with death, but in "Because . . ." the speaker "lives" on in death, while "I felt a Funeral . . ." ends with a burial and "Finished knowing." "Finished knowing" is used as a verb, but because of the enjambment of the lines can be read as a noun—there is a cessation of brain activity in "I felt a Funeral . . ." while "Because . . ." ends with timeless immortality.

I like a look of Agony (p. 808)

You might want to ask your class whether the speaker in this poem has an outlook similar to or different from those of the speakers in other Dickinson poems they have read. Whereas many of the previous speakers have professed a love of things half-seen, this one seems obsessed with certainty. Ask students to point out words that have to do with truth or falsehood; they will be able to find several in this short verse. Is death the only certainty for human beings? Are there any other times when it is possible to be certain that the image a person projects is an accurate one? Note also the words *I like* in line 1 and the characterization of Anguish as "homely" in the last line. Does this speaker actually find pleasure in people's death throes?

Flannery O'Connor once wrote, in justifying her use of violent encounters in her fiction, that "it is the extreme situation that best reveals what we are essentially." What would the speaker of this poem say to such a statement?

POSSIBLE CONNECTIONS TO OTHER SELECTIONS

Emily Dickinson, "The Bustle in a House" (text p. 816)

——, " 'Heaven'—is what I cannot reach!" (text p. 807; question #1, following)

——, "Success is counted sweetest" (text p. 803)

——, "Water, is taught by thirst" (text p. 804)

CONNECTION QUESTION IN TEXT (p. 808) WITH ANSWER

1. Write an essay on Dickinson's attitudes toward pain and deprivation, using this poem and " 'Heaven'—is what I cannot reach!" (p. 807).

    Based on these poems, it would seem that Dickinson is something of an ascetic, if not a masochist. Each poem describes a blissful state that the speaker cannot achieve. Yet each poem also describes a yearning; that is, in each poem the speaker is not content with her state of deprivation and pain so much as she uses that state to gauge her emotions. In this poem the desired condition is not necessarily death but rather honest purity. The same could be said for the other poem as well: on the surface, the speaker inclines toward death, but unadulterated honesty—so rare in our daily lives—is at the heart of her quest.

Wild Nights — Wild Nights! (p. 809)

A class discussion of this poem could focus on a few well-chosen words. Researching the etymology of *luxury* (line 4) will leave no room for doubt as to the intended eroticism of the poem; it comes from the Latin *luxuria,* which was used to express lust as well as extravagant pleasures of a more general sort, which the term has now come to mean. You might also discuss the use of natural imagery in the second and third stanzas. The heart in stanza 2 has no more need of compass or chart. Ask your students what these images mean to them. They seem to imply attention to order, rules, and laws. These images are set aside in the third stanza in favor of Eden and the sea.

A study of "Wild Nights" provides an excellent opportunity to discuss the possibility of disparity between the author of a work and the created narrator who speaks within the work. Students may wish to dismiss the eroticism of this poem if they have stereotyped Dickinson as a pure spinster in a white dress. However, the speaker of this poem cannot be specifically identified as Dickinson. Indeed, it is debatable whether the speaker is male or female.

POSSIBLE CONNECTIONS TO OTHER SELECTIONS

Margaret Atwood, "you fit into me" (text p. 645; question #1, following)
Edna St. Vincent Millay, "Recuerdo" (text p. 958)

CONNECTION QUESTION IN TEXT (p. 809) WITH ANSWER

1. Write an essay that compares the voice, figures of speech, and theme of this poem with those of Margaret Atwood's "you fit into me" (p. 645).

    Atwood's poem is characterized by sarcasm and irony, as though the speaker is trying to flatter her addressee only to deflate him with a wry insult. The speaker of Dickinson's poem is much more sincere, desiring sexual union without anticipating the pain that Atwood's speaker focuses on. The imagery of this poem suggests security, whereas Atwood's imagery upends such security and replaces it with a disturbing image of pain: a fish hook in a human eye.

What Soft — Cherubic Creatures — (p. 809)

A brief discussion of societal expectations for women in the mid-nineteenth century may help students to appreciate Dickinson's satirical intent in this poem. A woman was expected to be "the Angel in the House" who exerted a spiritual influence on those around her and made family life harmonious. In her book *Dimity Convictions: The American Woman in the Nineteenth Century* (Athens: Ohio UP, 1976; print.), which draws its title from this poem, Barbara Welter notes that "religion or piety was the core of woman's virtue, the source of her strength," and that "religion belonged to woman by divine right, a gift of God and nature." Further, woman was to use her "purifying passionless love [to bring] erring man back to Christ." Among other evidence from mid-nineteenth-century women's magazines, Welter cites a poem that appeared in an 1847 issue of *Ladies' Companion.* The title alone — "The Triumph of the Spiritual over the Sensual" (*Dimity Convictions* 21–22) — is enough to convey the sense of disembodied spirituality Dickinson attacks in the poem.

Ask students to notice the particular adjectives the poet uses to describe the "Gentlewomen." They are "Soft," "Cherubic" (line 1), and "refined" (6), but by the end of the poem they are "Brittle" (11). The crucial lines 7–8, which divide the positive from the negative attributes, are especially important. Not only are the women disconnected from both the human and the divine, but their attitudes would seem, by extension, to dissociate them from the central tenet of Christianity, that God became man. The last two lines make it clear that the first stanza is intended to be read satirically. How might the comparisons to "Plush" (3) and to a "Star" (4) be construed negatively? Notice the two uses of the word *ashamed,* in lines 8 and 12. Who is ashamed in each case? What is the effect of the repetition of this word?

Emily Dickinson, " 'Faith' is a fine invention" (text p. 829; question #1, following)

Christina Georgina Rossetti, "Some Ladies Dress in Muslin Full and White" (text p. 1019)

CONNECTION QUESTION IN TEXT (p. 810) WITH ANSWER

1. How are the "Gentlewomen" in this poem similar to the "Gentlemen" in " 'Faith' is a fine invention" (p. 829)?

    Dickinson attacks the false faith of "gentlemen" and "gentlewomen" in these poems. Both groups pretend to be pious, but Dickinson characterizes them as hypocritical and superficial, with no clear sense of redemption and no knowledge of their souls.

The Soul selects her own Society — (p. 810)

You might begin a discussion of this poem by asking students to consider whether the image projected here matches the image of a female who spends her life in near solitude. They are likely to notice that one stereotypically assumes that a woman remains alone because she has no other choice (more so when this poem was written than today), whereas the "Soul" described here operates from a position of power. The verbs associated with the soul are all active: she "selects" (line 1), "shuts" (2), chooses (10), and closes off her attention (11), "unmoved" by chariots (5) or even emperors (7).

How does the meter in lines 10 and 12 reinforce what is happening in the poem at this point? What seems to be the purpose of the soul's restrictions on her society? You might have students discuss both the limitations and the benefits of such exclusiveness. Do they think the advantages outweigh the disadvantages or vice versa? What does the poem's speaker think? How do you know?

POSSIBLE CONNECTIONS TO OTHER SELECTIONS

Emily Dickinson, "I dwell in Possibility—" (text p. 812)

——, "Much Madness is divinest Sense—" (text p. 812)

Much Madness is divinest Sense — (p. 812)

This poem could be the epigram of the radical or the artist. For all its endorsement of "madness," however, its structure is extremely controlled—from the mirror-imaged paradoxes that open the poem to the balancing of "Assent" (line 6) and "Demur" (7) and the consonance of "Demur" and "dangerous" (7). Try to explore with the class some applications of the paradoxes. One might think, for example, of the "divine sense" shown by the Shakespearean fool.

POSSIBLE CONNECTION TO ANOTHER SELECTION

Emily Dickinson, "The Soul selects her own Society—" (text p. 810; question #1, following)

CONNECTION QUESTION IN TEXT (p. 812) WITH ANSWER

1. Discuss the theme of self-reliance in this poem and in "The Soul selects her own Society—" (p. 810).

    In this poem Dickinson scorns conformity, specifically in terms of the often wrongheaded attempt to separate sense from insanity. The theme is that we must try to see beyond the notion that consensus necessarily equals what is right. (You might highlight the fact that the poem was written in 1862, at the start of the Civil War; before this period, slavery was accepted in America because it reflected a majority opinion.) Dickinson focuses on the individual in "The Soul selects her own Society—," turning the focus away from the majority and to the individual, who decides for oneself what is right, good, or just by aligning oneself only with others who share the same beliefs, even if those others represent a minority.

I dwell in Possibility — (p. 812)

In the first two lines of the poem the speaker sets up the general premise that poetry is superior to prose. The imagery used in the next ten lines specifies the reason that the speaker values poetry. One possible strategy for teaching the poem is to explore the metaphor of the house and then return to the original premise and ask students whether they find it convincing.

The imagery in this poem moves outward from man-made, earthly examples to examples from nature to a final image of the supernatural. In lines 3 and 4 the speaker compares poetry to prose as though they were both houses. Why is it important that the comparison focuses specifically on the windows and doors of the house? The second stanza draws the metaphor outward to compare the rooms and roof of the house of poetry to entities in nature. The chambers in the house are likened to cedar trees (line 5), trees known for the durability of their wood and for their longevity. The cedars of Lebanon are also a familiar biblical allusion. According to the first book of Kings, the house of Solomon was built "of the forest of Lebanon . . . upon four rows of cedar pillars, with cedar beams upon the pillars" (2:2); the lover in the Song of Solomon sings, "The beams of our house are cedar" (1:17). The roof of the house of poetry is compared to the sky (7–8), but again the speaker adds a qualifier — the word *everlasting* (7) — to raise this roof to an even higher level. The final word of the poem — *paradise* — ends the comparison at the farthest possible reaches of expansiveness.

Returning to the comparison made in the opening lines, students will probably see that the speaker considers poetry to be the "fairer House" (2) on the basis of its capacity to expand, to open up to ever wider capacities. A fruitful discussion might result from the question of whether or not students agree with the speaker of this poem. Can they think of examples of prose that are expansive, or poetry that is narrow? How does the example of Dickinson's own prose — her letter to Higginson (text p. 820) — fit into this argument?

POSSIBLE CONNECTIONS TO OTHER SELECTIONS

Emily Dickinson, "The Soul selects her own Society—" (text p. 810)

T. E. Hulme, "On the Differences between Poetry and Prose" (text p. 641; question #1, following)

CONNECTION QUESTION IN TEXT (p. 813) WITH ANSWER

1. Compare what this poem says about poetry and prose with T. E. Hulme's comments in "On the Differences between Poetry and Prose" (p. 641).

    Hulme contrasts the symbolic nature of prose with the metaphorical and imagistic properties of poetry. For him, poetry uses a "visual concrete" language. Dickinson argues that poetry is less confined than prose, which is a different point altogether. For her, poetic language is about the endless possibilities for signification in poetry. Her version of poetry is ethereal, taking us through the "Everlasting Roof" of "The Gambrels of the Sky" (lines 7–8), whereas Hulme sees poetry as "a pedestrian taking you over the ground." Of course, for him prose is no more ethereal but simply more direct, like "a train which delivers you at a destination." Prose for Dickinson is simply more constrained than poetry — a house with fewer windows, inferior doors, and an actual roof.

After great pain, a formal feeling comes— (p. 813)

In an interesting inversion of her often-used technique of employing metaphors from life to explore the territory of death and beyond, Dickinson in this poem uses a metaphor of death—the ceremony of a funeral—to evoke an image of one who has dealt with great pain in life. This poem is about survivors and how they are able eventually to get past their pain. In addition to the controlling image of a funeral, the poet uses two other strategies to convey the idea of a place that is past pain. Dickinson's word choices here abound in objects and adjectives that permeate the poem with a sense of numbed feelings. If you ask your students to point out some of these words, they might mention *formal* (line 1), *Tombs* (2), *stiff* (3), *mechanical* (5), *Wooden* (7), *Quartz* and *stone* (9), *Lead* (10), and *Snow* (12), among others.

The entire poem deals with life after the initial sharp pain of loss has subsided. Lines 12–13 concern the movement from palpable discomfort to apathetic stupor to true release. Ask your students if their own experiences with pain confirm or repudiate this scenario. Does the speaker hedge a bit in line 11? Are there other human rituals besides funerals by which we formally let go of pain?

POSSIBLE CONNECTIONS TO OTHER SELECTIONS

Emily Dickinson, "The Bustle in a House" (text p. 816; question #1, following)

Robert Frost, "Home Burial" (text p. 844)

CONNECTION QUESTION IN TEXT (p. 813) WITH ANSWER

1. How might this poem be read as a kind of sequel to "The Bustle in a House" (p. 816)?

   The poems might be looked at as stages one goes through when coping with loss. "The Bustle in a House" describes an immediate return to daily routine following death, almost a denial of the gravity of the situation even though this bustle is the "solemnest of industries / Enacted upon Earth" (lines 3–4). "After great pain . . ." describes the emotions that might follow the immediate need to return to the relative order of everyday life, the gradual process that allows us to let go of our grief.

I heard a Fly buzz—when I died— (p. 814)

This poem is typical of Dickinson's work as a willed act of imagination fathoming life after death and realizing the dark void and limitation of mortal knowledge. David Porter in *Dickinson: The Modern Idiom* (Cambridge: Harvard UP, 1981; print.) observes,

> At a stroke, Dickinson brilliantly extracted the apt metonymical emblem of the essential modern condition: her intrusive housefly. . . . The fly takes the place of the savior; irreverence and doubt have taken the place of revelation. Her fly, then, "With Blue—uncertain stumbling Buzz" is uncomprehension, derangement itself. It is noise breaking the silence, not the world's true speech but, externalized, the buzz of ceaseless consciousness. (239)

You might introduce this idea and then, either in discussion or in a writing assignment, ask the class to explore the tone of this poem and its accordance with Porter's comment.

POSSIBLE CONNECTION TO ANOTHER SELECTION

Walt Whitman, "A Noiseless Patient Spider" (text p. 658; question #1, following)

CONNECTION QUESTION IN TEXT (p. 814) WITH ANSWER

1. Contrast the symbolic significance of the fly with that of the spider in Walt Whitman's "A Noiseless Patient Spider" (p. 658).

The fly in Dickinson's poem is a kind of otherworldly messenger that fills up the space between death and life. Still, there is no connection between the fly and the speaker; nor does the fly seem to belong to the other world, unlike Whitman's spider, whose job is to connect the soul with the world of the living.

Because I could not stop for Death — (p. 814)

Here is one Dickinson poem in which the speaker manages to go beyond the moment of death. The tone changes in the exact center of the poem, from the carefree attitude of a person on a day's leisurely ride through town and out into the country, to the "chill" (line 14) of the realization that he or she is heading for the grave. The final images, however, are not those of horror but of interest in the passage from time to eternity and the ramifications thereof.

The first line makes the reader aware of the speaker's lack of control over the situation; Death is clearly in charge. Still, as Death is described as kind (line 2) and civil (8), and as Immortality is along for the ride, the situation is not immediately threatening. In the third stanza the carriage takes the speaker metaphorically through three stages of life: youth, represented by the schoolchildren; maturity, represented by the fields of grain; and old age, pictured as the setting sun.

Lines 13 and 14, which describe the chill felt as the sun goes down, constitute the turning point of the poem. Both the figurative language and the rhythm pattern signal a change. Dickinson abruptly reverses the alternating four-foot, three-foot metrical pattern of the first twelve lines so that line 13 contains the same number of feet as the line that immediately precedes it. The caesura after "Or rather" serves to emphasize the speaker's double take. You might wish to discuss the speaker's tone as the poem concludes.

Possible Connections to Other Selections

Emily Dickinson, "Apparently with no surprise" (text p. 830; question #1, following)
——, "If I shouldn't be alive" (text p. 801)

Connection Question in Text (p. 815) with Answer

1. Compare the tone of this poem with that of Dickinson's "Apparently with no surprise" (p. 830).

   Both poems cast the process of death as something methodical and mannerly. Yet this poem sounds more philosophical than "Apparently with no surprise," perhaps because its subject is human death as opposed to the cycles of nature. There are also a multitude of dashes in this poem, whereas the other one ends with a period, making it sound more like a clever observation than a deep meditation.

They say that "Time assuages" (p. 815)

This poem acts as a rebuttal to those who insist "time assuages" or "heals all wounds." It is structured with an assumption (what "they" say), Dickinson's refutation, and her clarification of how time functions as heart, body, and soul heal from deep hurt. She uses an analogy that compares what happens emotionally to what happens physically over time in the lines "An actual suffering strengthens / As Sinews do, with age" (lines 3–4). Ask students to think about how sinews "strengthen" with age. What happens to the body as we get older? Suppleness and flexibility come with youth, so it is not that kind of strengthening. Is there any connection between that and the "stiff Heart" and "letting go" described in "After great pain, a formal feeling comes —" (text p. 813)? Keep her lexicon in mind as you consider this brief poem.

In the second stanza, she offers her own definition of time as a "test of trouble." How does a "test" differ from a "remedy" in this context? The verdict is this: if time is a remedy, then there was no "actual suffering" (3). Discuss the type of suffering of which she speaks. Under what circumstances might someone suggest, rightly or wrongly, that time is a panacea?

POSSIBLE CONNECTIONS TO OTHER SELECTIONS

Emily Dickinson, "After great pain, a formal feeling comes" (text p. 813)

——, "The Bustle in a House" (text p. 816)

——, "I felt a Cleaving in my Mind —" (text p. 816)

——, "I felt a Funeral in my Brain —" (text p. 807)

Robert Frost, "Home Burial" (text p. 844)

William Wordsworth, "Mutability" (text p. 1029)

I felt a Cleaving in my Mind — (p. 816)

This poem describes an experience of mental disintegration or serious psychological strain. The speaker relates the feeling that his or her "Brain had split" (line 2), and that as a result the speaker's thoughts become increasingly disjointed. Eventually they seem to unravel, like balls of yarn rolling across the floor. You might discuss with your students this likening of the unraveling balls of yarn (7–8) to a mental breakdown. Ask them what is so effective about connecting the homely, domestic image of yarn with the anguish of psychological decay.

Structured in perfect iambic pentameter and incorporating full rhymes, this Dickinson poem is unusual in its regularity. Much of the power of "I felt a Cleaving" lies in its sharp contrast between form and content. Discuss with your students the disparity between its smooth patterns of rhythm and rhyme and its disturbing theme. Point out that the first stanza reads almost like a jingle — how do the poem's soothing musical qualities increase the horror of the experience? Poetically, the speaker's thoughts are joined together seamlessly, in perfect sequence. Yet this is precisely what the speaker claims is impossible for him or her to do. Ask your students to speculate why Dickinson would write such a smooth poem to describe such a jarring experience.

You might also ask your students to investigate the dictionary meanings of several words in this poem. Interestingly, *cleave* is defined as both "to separate" and "to adhere," and *ravel*, which is actually a synonym for *unravel*, means both "to entangle" and "to disentangle." Ask your students to consider some of the possible implications of these double meanings.

POSSIBLE CONNECTIONS TO OTHER SELECTIONS

Emily Dickinson, "To make a prairie it takes a clover and one bee" (text p. 803; question #1, following)

John Keats, "Ode to a Nightingale" (text p. 713)

CONNECTION QUESTION IN TEXT (p. 816) WITH ANSWER

1. Compare the power of the speaker's mind described here with the power of imagination described in "To make a prairie it takes a clover and one bee" (p. 806).

   The speaker in this poem is relatively powerless. The cleaving of her mind is beyond her control, and she is not able to mend it, as when one wakes from a dream and tries to fall asleep again to see how it will turn out. In "To make a prairie" the mind has the power to create even without the things of the earth, but it is unclear whether the mind has the power to consciously create in itself a state of reverie.

The Bustle in a House (p. 816)

The images in this poem suggest that getting on with mundane, everyday activities helps us to move beyond the pain of death. In contrast, the use of the funeral metaphor in "After great pain" (text p. 813) promotes the idea that a formal ritual helps us to accomplish this purpose. You might ask students which method strikes them as being more effective. Look closely at the diction in line 7. The phrase "We shall not want" echoes the Twenty-third Psalm, a hymn of comfort and confidence in God's support at the time of death. But does the expression also imply that even though we don't want to deal with any thought other than being reunited with the loved one in eternity, the reality may not be so simple?

In *Literary Women* (Garden City: Doubleday, 1976; print.), Ellen Moers claims that "Emily Dickinson was self-consciously female in poetic voice, and more boldly so than is often recognized" (61). Does the imagery in this poem confirm or repudiate Moers's assertion? Ask your students to reflect on the many speakers they have encountered in Dickinson's poems. Is her poetic voice generally identifiable as female? If so, how? If not, how would you characterize her poetic voice(s)?

POSSIBLE CONNECTIONS TO OTHER SELECTIONS

Emily Dickinson, "After great pain, a formal feeling comes —" (text p. 813; question #1, following)

———, "I like a look of Agony" (text p. 808; question #2, following)

CONNECTIONS QUESTIONS IN TEXT (p. 817) WITH ANSWERS

1. Compare this poem with "After great pain, a formal feeling comes —" (p. 813). Which poem is, for you, a more powerful treatment of mourning?

   The poems advance two opposing ideas about how people mourn. "The Bustle in a House" describes a flurry of little tasks that distract the grieving person. "After great pain" discusses a shutting down of functions as the mourner contemplates loss in total stillness. They seem to contradict one another, and your students might find that one or the other is more true to their experiences. However, they may also both be true, describing different types of mourning or different stages of the complicated process of dealing with death.

2. How does this poem qualify "I like a look of Agony" (p. 808)? Does it contradict the latter poem? Explain why or why not.

   The focus of the two poems is slightly different because there is no *I* in this poem. "I like a look of Agony" raises questions about the speaker, whereas this poem states a more objective truth. Yet both poems treat the subject of death and its effects, and in that respect there is a slight contradiction between them because this one ends with the notion of eternity, whereas "I like a look of Agony" concentrates on the physical death of a person without alluding to the state of the soul afterward.

Tell all the Truth but tell it slant — (p. 817)

You might open consideration of "Tell all the Truth" by having students discuss how the speaker characterizes "Truth." The imagery used here centers on the idea of light; in only eight lines, the poet uses "slant" (line 1), "bright" (3), "Lightning" (5), "dazzle" (7), and "blind" (8), besides the punning reference in the word *delight* (3). The speaker considers direct truth to be a light so powerful that it is capable of blinding. Students may suggest other contexts in which they have seen this idea expressed. Biblical stories often recount appearances of God as a light too blinding to be looked at directly. What is it about Truth, which after all only allows us to see things as they really are, that is potentially so destructive?

Don't let your students miss the exquisite word choices in lines 3 and 4 as Dickinson contrasts human fallibility—"our infirm Delight" (De-light?)—with the perfection of "Truth's superb surprise."

How does poetry in general affirm this poem's thesis? Would you expect a writer who believed this premise to prefer writing poetry to writing prose?

POSSIBLE CONNECTIONS TO OTHER SELECTIONS

Emily Dickinson, "I know that He exists" (text p. 829; question #1, following)

——, "Portraits are to daily faces" (text p. 805)

——, "The Thought beneath so slight a film—" (text p. 802)

CONNECTION QUESTION IN TEXT (p. 817) WITH ANSWER

1. How does the first stanza of "I know that He exists" (p. 829) suggest an idea similar to this poem's? Why do you think the last eight lines of the former aren't similar in theme to this poem?

   Both poems argue that the truth is not necessarily obvious or that the deepest truths are cloaked in mystery. The difference in theme between the two poems has to do with the difference of the subjects: the implications of "Truth" are not as grave as the implications of God's existence.

There is no Frigate like a Book (p. 818)

Dickinson had great faith in the transformative power of reading. This poem encapsulates her belief, imagining books and poetry as forms of transportation. Her comparisons suggest reading acts with tremendous speed. You might remind your students to look up "Frigate" (line 1) and "Coursers" (3) to clarify their understanding of these terms. A frigate is a war vessel, but its archaic meaning is a light, quick ship. A courser is a swift horse, often one used in battle. What do your students make of the military connotations of these words? Notice how the adjective "prancing" (4) goes beyond comparison to directly identify poetry with the powerful horse.

Dickinson also uses economic diction, revealing her concerns about the democratic nature of reading. Reading helps the poor to escape the "oppress of Toll" (6). Ask your students what kind of relationship she sets up by rhyming "Toll" (6) with "soul" (8). In this poem it seems that monetary concerns could hinder the development of higher faculties.

POSSIBLE CONNECTIONS TO OTHER SELECTIONS

Anne Bradstreet, "The Author to Her Book" (text p. 647)

Emily Dickinson, "I dwell in Possibility—" (text p. 812; question #1, following)

CONNECTION QUESTION IN TEXT (p. 818) WITH ANSWER

1. Compare the use of extended metaphor in this poem with that of "I dwell in Possibility —" (p. 812). How consistent is the use of extended metaphor in each poem, and what is its effect?

   Dickinson uses figurative language similarly in these poems to suggest the numerous possibilities of poetry and to compare it favorably with other human activities. In "There is no Frigate like a Book," Dickinson develops the extended metaphor of poetry as a means for transportation. Though it has features in common with earthly conveyances like a "Frigate" (line 1) or a set of "Coursers" (3), poetry surpasses any of these and is unfettered by any "Toll" (6). In "I dwell in Possibility —," her metaphor is a house, and poetry's house is the roomiest of all, with the most amenities. One interesting difference between the two poems is Dickinson's introduction of "Prose" (2) in "I dwell in Possibility—." By bringing in a different form to critique, she makes her praise of poetry even more pointed. Dickinson also stretches the limits of her metaphor further in "Possibility." The house to which she compares poetry becomes so expansive that it starts to sound less like a house than like the entire natural world, whose sky is the poet's roof.

From all the Jails the Boys and Girls (p. 818)

Here is a perfect poem for the last day of the semester! Dickinson captures the joy and energy of children released from school by playing trios of images against one another. The "Jails" of the first line and the "Prison" and "keep"—a pun that evokes both a sense of being held and the medieval image of a castle dungeon—in the fourth express the confinement the children endure during the school day. The released prisoners "leap" (line 2), and "storm" and "stun" (5) the world into which they escape. The sense of attacking life to demand everything it has to give is unmistakable, especially when one considers the use of transcendent words such as "ecstatically" (2), "beloved" (3), and "bliss" (6). The triple alliteration of *F*s in the last two lines attempts to bring things back down to earth. You might ask your students whether or not the last two lines have the tempering effect that the bearers of the frowns hope to convey. With which feeling does the end of the poem leave students?

Possible Connections to Other Selections

William Blake, "The Garden of Love" (text p. 1001; question #1, following)

Emily Dickinson, "Much Madness is divinest Sense" (text p. 812)

——, "Wild Nights—Wild Nights!" (text p. 809)

Robert Frost, "'Out, Out—'" (text p. 850; question #2, following)

Richard Hague, "Directions for Resisting the SAT" (text p. 767)

John Keats, "To one who has been long in city pent" (text p. 1014)

William Wordsworth, "I Wandered Lonely as a Cloud" (text p. 1027)

Connections Questions in Text (p. 818) with Answers

1. Compare the theme of this poem with that of William Blake's "The Garden of Love" (text p. 1001).

    Blake's "Garden of Love" has been replaced by organized religion. He encounters Dickinson's "Frowns" there, or vestiges of them, as they have written "Thou shalt not" over the door. Dickinson's children escape their prison into a garden of love, becoming a "Mob of solid Bliss." There's irony in her choice of the word *Foe* in the last line to describe the boys and girls she so obviously enjoys.

2. In an essay discuss the treatment of childhood in this poem and in Robert Frost's "'Out, Out—'" (text p. 850).

    Essays will vary, but many will mention Frost's wish that the boy had been released from his "jail" earlier (that they could have given him "the half hour" from his work). He mentions "those that lifted eyes" early in the poem, indicating that most keep their eyes on their work, in their prison of work. The child in his poem doesn't escape, and meets a brutal death. Dickinson writes of the release of children from their jails, whether work or school or some other prison. For her, the children are all-powerful; "they storm the earth and stun the air" as they revel in their freedom.

PERSPECTIVES ON EMILY DICKINSON

EMILY DICKINSON, *A Description of Herself* (p. 819)

Probably the most immediately evident characteristic of Dickinson's personal correspondence is that, as in her poetry, the language comes in spurts interspersed with an abundance of dashes. Also, as in her poetry, she uses numerous metaphors. Have your students explore some of these metaphors, such as Dickinson's reference to criticism of her poetry as "surgery" (paragraph 2) and her discussion of "undressed" thought (3). Do such metaphors hide or clarify her meaning?

Dickinson's comment that she had written only "one or two" poems before that winter, when in fact she had written nearly three hundred, could lead to a discussion of the constructed self that appears even in personal correspondence. Have your students consider how they might write about last weekend's party in an e-mail to their parents as opposed to a text message to their best friend from high school. Without necessarily being dishonest, we generally shape any presentation of self depending on how we wish to appear to a particular audience. How do you suppose Dickinson appeared to Higginson when he first read this letter?

THOMAS WENTWORTH HIGGINSON, *On Meeting Dickinson for the First Time* (p. 820)

The first part of Higginson's letter to his wife reports his encounter with Emily Dickinson at her home in Amherst in a fairly straightforward fashion. If your students have read the poet's letter describing herself to Higginson, you might ask them to consider how closely the poet's description of herself matches his observations. Although Higginson refers to the poet's manner and appearance as "childlike" three times in a short space, he is also struck by her wisdom when she begins to speak to him.

Dickinson's definition of poetry would be an interesting topic for class discussion. Students might be encouraged to talk about the aptness or limitations of her definition. Should all poetry produce the violent reaction in a reader that she describes? Would Dickinson's own works qualify as poetry according to her definition? The last comments of Dickinson that Higginson records, concerning her relation to the outside world, also merit consideration. Why would she have such an extreme reaction to the thought of mixing in society? Which of her comments might Mrs. Higginson have considered foolish?

MABEL LOOMIS TODD, *The* Character *of Amherst* (p. 820)

While Todd refers to Emily Dickinson both as a character and as a myth, her examples in this letter tend to cast Dickinson more as a ghost; several times she notes that no one ever sees the poet. None of her characterizations of Dickinson is particularly positive. Referring to someone as a "character" usually denotes unusual, even amusing behavior, and portraying that person as a ghost suggests that that person has no substance. Todd does not even use the term *myth* in its powerful, archetypal sense, but more to connote something unreal or not to be believed. The comments in this letter would seem to negate Dickinson's thesis, often stated in her poetry, that things seen half-veiled are more clearly seen than things in plain view. You might ask students what Todd's observations about Dickinson reveal about Todd herself and about the way Dickinson may have been perceived by her Amherst neighbors. As a topic for writing or for class discussion, you may wish to have your students piece together information from this letter and the previous two in order to produce a composite "portrait" of Emily Dickinson. What may emerge from these pieces, however, is the enigmatic quality of her character.

RICHARD WILBUR, *On Dickinson's Sense of Privation* (p. 821)

According to Wilbur, Dickinson's fascination with the concept of want, both human and personal, emerges in her poetry in two ways. Her apprehension of God as a distant, unresponsive deity compels her to write satirical poetry protesting this situation on behalf of other human beings. However, the poet who rages against an uncaring creator on behalf of her fellow creatures also tolerates such privations and emulates such aloofness on a personal level. For Dickinson, "less is more" is merely another Christian paradox to be savored, such as the paradoxes of dying to live or freeing oneself by becoming a slave. In fact, depriving herself of everything possible, especially human companionship, seems to have been Dickinson's technique for achieving that appreciation for and knowledge of what she and other humans were missing that inspired her poetry. You may wish to have your students discuss this second premise more thoroughly; it may be a difficult concept for those not accustomed to dealing with paradox. Do they see any parallels in their own lives or in the culture at large to the idea that, as Wilbur says, "privation is more plentiful than plenty"? Can they think of times when deprivation has produced positive results, or do they feel that Dickinson uses this highly contradictory premise as a rationalization for her own eccentricities?

SANDRA M. GILBERT AND SUSAN GUBAR, *On Dickinson's White Dress* (p. 822)

You might wish to preface your discussion of this piece with a freewriting exercise in which your students explore their own associations with whiteness. Do their connotations mostly involve positive qualities, negative qualities, or nothingness? Gilbert and Gubar contrast William Sherwood's assertion that Dickinson's white dress was a sign of her commitment to the Christian mystery of death and resurrection with Melville's suggestion that whiteness may be the "all-color of atheism." They go on to suggest that whiteness may have been, for Dickinson, the perfect expression of a fascination with paradox and irony, that she was drawn to the color precisely because it was capable of representing opposite ends of any spectrum. You might ask your students whether they find any of the above theories convincing before having them propose their own theories as to why Dickinson wore only white (see question 3 in the text, p. 823).

You might caution your students that Gilbert and Gubar's characterization of the dress on display at the Dickinson homestead as "larger than most readers would have expected" is not shared by all who have seen it. Given the feminist perspective of Gilbert and Gubar's work, why might they emphasize the size of Dickinson's dress in this manner?

CYNTHIA GRIFFIN WOLFF, *On the Many Voices in Dickinson's Poetry* (p. 823)

Wolff acknowledges the multiplicity of voices represented by the speakers in Dickinson's poems, from child to housewife to passionate woman to New England Puritan. She insists, however, that the presence of these different voices affirms cohesion rather than indicates a fragmentation of the poet's psyche. According to Wolff, what the voices have in common is a concern with specific human problems, particularly those problems that threaten "the coherence of the self." Thus the many voices become not a difficulty to be overcome but a tool by which the poet seeks to overcome difficulties. Wolff is especially adamant in her assertion that the voice selected for any particular poem does not represent the poet's particular mood of the moment but is a "calculated tactic," a part of her artistic technique, an aspect of an individual poem that is as carefully chosen as any of the poem's words might be.

In discussing this passage, you might ask your students to consider whether they have different "voices" for different occasions and what determines how they speak at any given time. Do they get a sense of unity in reading Dickinson's poetry? If it is true that Dickinson again and again returns to the idea of encounters that threaten "the coherence of the self," what are some of these encounters, and in what ways are they threatening?

PAULA BENNETT, On "I heard a Fly buzz—when I died—" (p. 824)

To Bennett, the fly in Dickinson's poem represents humankind's ignorance of what awaits us after death. This ignorance is dramatically emphasized in Dickinson's poem by the dying speaker, who, anticipating a divine experience at her death, is shocked when she is assailed by the buzzing of a fly instead. Ask students if they agree with Bennett's assertion that Dickinson's conclusion about death and the afterlife in this poem is that "we do not know much." Are there other ways to interpret Dickinson's depiction of the dying moment? Is Dickinson's poem necessarily, as Bennett puts it, a "grim joke" about the fate of human corpses—to be devoured by flies?

MARTHA NELL SMITH, On "Because I could not stop for Death—" (p. 825)

Smith's central interpretation of Dickinson's most famous poem about death is that it is ultimately a joke. This will undoubtedly be hard for many of your students to swallow. How can a poem about death be comic? It may be useful to have your students discuss how they define "jokes" and what they think makes something funny. Smith notes that Dickinson struggled with the faith that her neighbors reveled in, often finding herself believing that they would be disappointed with any revelations they may have on their deaths. With this in mind, do your students find Dickinson's sense of humor (if they see humor at all) to be morbid, or is there something more cruel or self-serving to it?

RONALD WALLACE, Miss Goff (p. 826)

As a critic, Wallace is considered an authority on the uses of humor in poetry. His book *God Be with the Clown: Humor in American Poetry* (1984) explores the comic aspects of the poetry of such literary giants as Dickinson, Walt Whitman, Robert Frost, Wallace Stevens, and John Berryman. His interest in humor and Emily Dickinson works to good effect in "Miss Goff." (It may interest your students to know that the *OED* states that in the 1860s a "goff" was a clown or a fool.) In this poem a student's tasteless practical joke seems to defeat a "tired" (line 3) old-maid teacher, who passes out in "horror" (4) at the cruelty, but it also inadvertently introduces another student to the wonders of Dickinson's poetry.

Encourage your students to explore the parallels between the characters of Miss Goff and Emily Dickinson. Like Dickinson, Goff is unmarried and socially unskilled. When faced with difficulty, the teacher, like the poet, turns to poetry for solace. And, like Dickinson, Goff transfixes, even if she is unaware of the effect she has on at least one member of her audience (the poem's speaker). Encourage students, also, to discuss the implications of Miss Goff's faint.

The form of Wallace's paean to Dickinson offers another promising avenue for discussion. "Miss Goff" is a sonnet. What's interesting about Wallace's use of the form is that although he does adhere primarily to the iambic pentameter that is usual in sonnets, he strays from it to emphasize elements of the teacher's and the student's personalities. Note, for example, that an extra unstressed syllable at the end of nearly every line (except 6) of the first stanza gives them feminine endings to poetically evoke the femininity of Miss Goff. Anapests in lines 4 ("hór|rŏr, thĕ héart|lĕss"), 5 ("cŭstó|dĭan slý|lў"), and 8 ("Em|ĭlў Dĭck|ĭnsŏn mím|ĕŏs thére") draw attention to the classroom's heartlessness, the custodian's participation in the students' joke, and Dickinson's poems. The lines of the second stanza, on the other hand, end with masculine stresses. The anapests here draw attention to "ŏn thĕ cóld" (10) and "ŏf oŭr héads" (14); both phrases introduce allusions to Dickinson's definition of poetry—"My business is circumference" and "If I feel physically as if the top of my head were taken off, I know that is poetry."

Thomas Wentworth Higginson, "On Meeting Dickinson for the First Time" (text p. 820)

Mabel Loomis Todd, "The *Character* of Amherst" (text p. 820)

ADDITIONAL DICKINSON POEMS ACCOMPANYING QUESTIONS FOR WRITING ABOUT AN AUTHOR IN DEPTH

"Faith" is a fine invention (p. 829)

This poem highlights a witty, even satirical side of Dickinson. Have students note the words that define each of the alternative ways of seeing. "Faith" is an "invention" (line 1), and microscopes are "prudent" (3). When examining Dickinson's diction, it is helpful to note the variety of possible definitions for ordinary words used in an unusual manner. *Invention* not only means a created or fabricated thing but also carries the more archaic sense of an unusual discovery or a find. Likewise, while *prudence* has a rather stilted, utilitarian ring to it in the twentieth century, it once meant having the capacity to see divine truth. You might ask your class whether they feel the speaker favors religion or science. Because both faith and microscopes are meant to help people perceive directly rather than through a mist, is it possible that the poet favors neither side in this argument?

Ask your students what they think of Charles R. Anderson's comment on this poem in *Emily Dickinson's Poetry* (New York: Holt, 1960; print.): "This is a word game, not a poem" (35).

Emily Dickinson, "Portraits are to daily faces" (text p. 805)

——, "What Soft—Cherubic Creatures —" (text p. 809)

I know that He exists (p. 829)

Dickinson here seems to be at the cutting edge of modern sensibility and its dare-seeking fascination with death. The poem begins as a testimony of faith in the existence of a God who is clearly an Old Testament figure. If you ask students how the poem's speaker characterizes this deity, they may note the attributes of refinement, hidden-ness, and removal from the gross affairs of earthly life. With this in mind, the tone of the next stanza, in which God seems to be the orchestrator of a cosmic game of hide-and-seek between Himself and whichever of His creatures will play, and in which the reward is "Bliss" (line 7), may be puzzling to students. The word *fond* in line 6 begins to sow a seed of doubt about the rules of this game. Does it mean "affectionate," or is it being used in its older sense of "foolish"?

In the third stanza the speaker more fully comprehends the meaning of the game: finding God can mean finding oneself in God at the moment of death. Instead of death being a discovery that begins a condition of everlasting bliss, one may be confronted with an abrupt and everlasting ending. "Death's—stiff—stare" (12) caps three lines of halting verse, further emphasized by the hardness of the alliteration (you may wish to read these lines aloud so that students will appreciate their impact). By the third stanza, the ironic barb pierces through the texture of ordinary language. Instead of saying that the joke has gone too far, the speaker in the final line substitutes the verb *crawled,* which summons up the image of the serpent in the Garden of Eden in addition to bringing the lofty language of the first stanza down to earth.

This poem receives a brief but adequate discussion in Karl Keller's *The Only Kangaroo among the Beauty* (Baltimore: Johns Hopkins UP, 1979; print; 63.). Keller observes that the "tone of voice moves from mouthed platitude to personal complaint." Ask your students if they agree with this assessment.

POSSIBLE CONNECTIONS TO OTHER SELECTIONS

Emily Dickinson, "Tell all the Truth but tell it slant —" (text p. 817)

Robert Frost, "Design" (text p. 856)

I never saw a Moor — (p. 829)

This straightforward profession of faith follows a pattern of expansion of imagery from the natural to the supernatural. Despite its simplicity, the poem reflects sound theology; one of the basic theological proofs of the existence of God is the existence of the universe. Ask your students if the poem would be as effective if the first stanza relied on images of man-made things such as the pyramids. Why or why not? How would it change the impact of the poem if the stanzas were reversed?

POSSIBLE CONNECTION TO ANOTHER SELECTION

Emily Dickinson, " 'Heaven' — is what I cannot reach!" (text p. 807)

Apparently with no surprise (p. 830)

While a first reading of "Apparently with no surprise" seems to present the reader with a picture of death in an uncaring, mechanistic universe overseen by a callous God, a closer look reveals a more ambiguous attitude on the part of the speaker. Most of the poem deals with an ordinary natural process, an early morning frost that kills a flower. Framing this event is the viewpoint of the speaker, who acknowledges by means of the word *apparently* that his or her perspective may not be correct. The speaker claims God is not involved in the event, other than to observe and to approve, as the speaker apparently does not. An examination of the adjectives and adverbs used in the poem reinforces the uncertainty of tone for which we have been prepared by the opening word. "No surprise" (line 1), "accidental power" (4), and the sun proceeding "unmoved" (6) suggest a vision of nature as devoid of feeling. However, how can anything proceed and at the same time be *un*moved? How can power be used forcefully, as "beheads" (3) and "Assassin" (5) imply, and yet be accidental? The description of the frost as a "blond Assassin" in line 5 is particularly worth class discussion. Does the noun *Assassin* suggest that the frost is consciously evil? What about the adjective *blond*? You may wish to have your students recall other images of whiteness in Dickinson's poetry. Can they come to any conclusions as to the connotations this color has for her?

POSSIBLE CONNECTIONS TO OTHER SELECTIONS

Emily Dickinson, "Because I could not stop for Death —" (text p. 814)

——, "Safe in their Alabaster Chambers —" (1859 version) (text p. 804)

ADDITIONAL RESOURCES FOR TEACHING DICKINSON

SELECTED BIBLIOGRAPHY

Anderson, Charles R. *Emily Dickinson's Poetry.* New York: Holt, 1960. Print.

Bennett, Paula. *Emily Dickinson: Woman Poet.* Iowa City: U of Iowa P, 1990. Print.

Bloom, Harold, ed. *Emily Dickinson.* New York: Chelsea, 1985. Print.

Chase, Richard. *Emily Dickinson.* New York: William Sloane Assocs., 1951. Print.

Dickinson, Emily. *The Complete Poems of Emily Dickinson.* Ed. Thomas H. Johnson. Boston: Little, 1955. Print.

——. *The Letters of Emily Dickinson.* Ed. Thomas H. Johnson and Theodora Ward. Cambridge: Belknap Press of Harvard UP, 1958. Print.

———. *The Master Letters of Emily Dickinson.* Ed. Ralph W. Franklin. Amherst: Amherst College P, 1986. Print.

Diehl, Joanne Feit. *Dickinson and the Romantic Imagination.* Princeton: Princeton UP, 1981. Print.

Farr, Judith. *The Passion of Emily Dickinson.* Cambridge: Harvard UP, 1992. Print.

Ferlazzo, Paul J., ed. *Critical Essays on Emily Dickinson.* Boston: Hall, 1984. Print.

Johnson, Thomas H. *Emily Dickinson: An Interpretive Biography.* New York: Atheneum, 1955. Print.

Juhasz, Suzanne, ed. *Feminist Critics Read Emily Dickinson.* Bloomington: Indiana UP, 1983. Print.

Leyda, Jay. *The Years and Hours of Emily Dickinson.* New Haven: Yale UP, 1960. Print.

Martin, Wendy. *The Cambridge Companion to Emily Dickinson.* New York: Cambridge UP, 2002. Print.

Orzeck, Martin, and Robert Weisbuch, eds. *Dickinson and Audience.* Ann Arbor: U of Michigan P, 1996. Print.

Patterson, Rebecca. *Emily Dickinson's Imagery.* Amherst: U of Massachusetts P, 1979. Print.

Porter, David. *Dickinson, the Modern Idiom.* Cambridge: Harvard UP, 1981. Print.

Smith, Martha Nell. *Rowing in Eden: Rereading Emily Dickinson.* Austin: U of Texas P, 1992. Print.

Stocks, Kenneth. *Emily Dickinson and the Modern Consciousness: A Poet of Our Time.* New York: St. Martin's, 1988. Print.

Stonum, Gary Lee. *The Dickinson Sublime.* Madison: U of Wisconsin P, 1990. Print.

Wardrop, Daneen. *Emily Dickinson's Gothic: Goblin with a Gauge.* Iowa City: U of Iowa P, 1996. Print.

TIP FROM THE FIELD

I have my students become "experts" on one of the poets treated in depth in the anthology. The students then work in pairs and "team-teach" their poet to two other students who are experts on another poet.

— KARLA WALTERS, *University of New Mexico*

31

A Study of Robert Frost

Like Dickinson, Frost may have a somewhat sanitized image in the minds of some students. The introduction addresses this point, but if students remain unconvinced, "Home Burial" and " 'Out, Out—' " should provide ample evidence of the dark side of Frost.

Many of Frost's poems change on a second or third close reading—the text offers "The Road Not Taken" as an example of this. "Mending Wall" also exhibits this tendency. Frost can provide a good opportunity for students to pay attention to their own reading habits. You might assign short writings that ask students not only to interpret the poems, but also to notice how their interpretations might change between readings.

ROBERT FROST

The Road Not Taken (p. 840)

This poem has traditionally been read as the poet's embracing of the "less traveled" road of Emersonian self-reliance, but the middle two stanzas complicate such a reading. Ask students to read the first and last stanzas alone and then to notice that in the middle two stanzas the speaker actually seems to equivocate as to whether the roads were actually different. After reading those two stanzas, do students trust the assertion that "I took the one less traveled by" (line 19)? In "On the Figure a Poem Makes" (text p. 858), Frost states that a poem can provide "a momentary stay against confusion." Against what kind of "confusion" is the poet working? How do the uses of rhyme, meter, and stanza form work against confusion? Is there a "clarification of life" (another of Frost's claims for poetry) in this poem?

At least three times in this poem (lines 2, 4, and 15) the word *I* disrupts the iambic rhythm. Why would the poet do this? What is the effect of the dash at the end of line 18?

Richard Poirier, in *Robert Frost: The Work of Knowing* (New York: Oxford UP, 1977; print.), claims that Frost's poems are often about the making of poetry. Is there any sense in which this poem could refer to writing poetry? For instance, do a poet's choices of rhyme, meter, or metaphor at the beginning of a poem dictate how the rest of the poem will proceed? Do poets try to choose roads not taken by their predecessors in order to be original? Are they sometimes unable to return to standard forms later, once they have launched out on a new poetic path?

As a writing assignment, you might ask your students to discuss or write about decisions they have made that closed off other choices for them.

POSSIBLE CONNECTION TO ANOTHER SELECTION

Blanche Farley, "The Lover Not Taken" (text p. 758)

The Pasture (p. 842)

Ask students to suggest reasons that Frost chose to place "The Pasture" at the beginning of several volumes of his poetry. What might readers of this poem infer about the poems that followed? Could the references to raking the leaves away and watching the water clear in lines 2 and 3 suggest something more than the performance of spring chores?

Notice that the speaker twice informs the reader that "I shan't be gone long" (lines 4 and 8). The need to return to stable ground after going out and making discoveries is a recurring theme in Frost's poetry, as is evident in "Birches" and "Stopping by Woods on a Snowy Evening." Poems wherein the return is not assured — "Acquainted with the Night," for example — tend to be much more negative in tone. They often foreground what Lionel Trilling called the "terrifying" side of Frost. How does Frost's practice of using a fixed form, such as blank verse or sonnet, yet altering the form by varying the meter or rhyme schemes (something he frequently does through the use of dialogue) demonstrate a similar desire to return to stable ground? Does this put the poet's often-quoted comment that writing free verse is like "playing tennis with the net down" in a different light? Is writing free verse, for Frost, more like casting loose from all one's moorings without an anchor?

POSSIBLE CONNECTIONS TO OTHER SELECTIONS

Robert Frost, "After Apple-Picking" (text p. 847)

Walt Whitman, "One's-Self I Sing" (text p. 1027)

Mowing (p. 842)

This poem offers an amiable meditation on "the sweetest dream that labour knows" (line 13). The "long scythe" (2), so often a symbol of time or death, here establishes the power and pleasure of work. That symbolic resonance combines with references to fairy tales to establish the edge of a forest as a mysterious place where one might receive "the gift of idle hours, / Or easy gold at the hand of fay or elf" (7–8). But the speaker discounts these ephemeral notions: "Anything more than the truth would have seemed too weak" (9). These allusions are secondary to the productive and happy relationship between the speaker and the right tool for the job.

The narrative is more clearly conveyed when the poem is read aloud. The first six lines examine the "whispering" (2) voice of the scythe; the last eight resist the tradition of fairy tales that prefer "idle hours" (7) or "easy gold" (8) to the satisfactions of work well done. The speaker is alone, in "the heat of the sun" (4), but these circumstances are not presented in a negative light; the laboring speaker does not complain but revels in his work.

POSSIBLE CONNECTION TO ANOTHER SELECTION

Robert Frost, "The Pasture" (text p. 842)

Mending Wall (p. 843)

Students may already be familiar with this work from their high school reading. Although the poem is often considered an indictment of walls and barriers of any sort, Frost probably did not have such a liberal point of view in mind. After all, the speaker initiates the mending, and he repeats the line "Something there is that doesn't love a wall." For him, mending the wall is a spring ritual — a kind of counteraction to spirits or elves or the nameless "Something" that tears down walls over the winter. It is a gesture, ritual, and reestablishment of old lines, this business of mending walls. The speaker teases his neighbor with the idea that the apple trees won't invade the pines, but to some measure he grants his conservative neighbor his due.

POSSIBLE CONNECTIONS TO OTHER SELECTIONS

Emily Dickinson, "Portraits are to daily faces" (text p. 805)

———, "To make a prairie it takes a clover and one bee" (text p. 803; question #1, following)

Robert Frost, "Neither Out Far nor In Deep" (text p. 854; question #2, following)

CONNECTIONS QUESTIONS IN TEXT (p. 844) WITH ANSWERS

1. How do you think the neighbor in this poem would respond to Dickinson's idea of imagination in "To make a prairie it takes a clover and one bee" (p. 803)?

   The neighbor in "Mending Wall" might accuse the speaker in Dickinson's poem of being foolish and impractical. Dickinson's speaker does not seem to think that boundaries make people happier, but the neighbor's experience has proved to him that "Good fences make good neighbors" (line 27). The speaker in Frost's poem, more open to the kind of imagination Dickinson celebrates, wants his neighbor to imagine that elves have brought the wall down — but the neighbor probably won't.

2. What similarities and differences does the neighbor have with the people Frost describes in "Neither Out Far nor In Deep" (p. 854)?

   In both poems Frost presents people who seem to be content with a single point of view, resisting new or even alternative views of the world. The neighbor, "like an old-stone savage armed" (line 40), appears to be part of some primeval mystery that fascinates the speaker in "Mending Wall." In contrast, the people in "Neither Out Far nor In Deep" are the ones transfixed by a mystery — that of the vast ocean.

Home Burial (p. 844)

"Home Burial" is a dialogue in blank verse between a husband and wife who have recently lost their child and who have different ways of coping with loss. One way to begin discussion is to consider the form of the poem: Does it seem more like a poem or a miniature play? How does the rhythm of the poem affect its theme? The haunting repetition of the word *don't* in line 32, for example, is realistic dialogue when we consider the tension behind the situation, but it also serves to mark a turning point in the poem. At what other points in the poem do similar repetitions occur, and do they also mark turning points in the dramatic situation, or do they reveal something about the psychological state of the characters?

Biographical criticism is beginning to come back into fashion, and you might remind the class of some of the introductory notes on Frost in this chapter before discussing the poem. Clearly the speaker is more matter-of-fact than his wife, and there is decidedly a communication problem between them. Note how Frost splits their dialogue in the interrupted iambic lines. But doesn't the husband deserve some special commendation for possessing the courage and integrity to initiate a confrontation with his wife? Discussion of the poem might also consider the value that ancients and moderns alike ascribe to a catharsis of emotions.

You might, if the class seems at all responsive, examine the speaker's claim that "a man must partly give up being a man / With women-folk" (lines 52–53). What does this statement mean? Has feminism done anything to challenge what are uniquely man's and uniquely woman's provinces of concern?

POSSIBLE CONNECTIONS TO OTHER SELECTIONS

Emily Dickinson, "After great pain, a formal feeling comes —" (text p. 813)

Robert Frost, " 'Out, Out —' " (text p. 850)

Jane Kenyon, "The Blue Bowl" (text p. 636)

After Apple-Picking (p. 847)

The sense of things undone and the approach of "winter sleep" seem to betoken a symbolic use of apple picking in this poem. Moreover, the speaker has already had an experience this day—seeing the world through a skim of ice—that predisposes him to view things strangely or aslant. At any rate, he dreams, appropriately enough, of apple harvesting. Apples take on connotations of golden opportunity and inspire fear lest one should fall. As harvest, they represent a rich, fruitful life, but as the speaker admits, "I am overtired / Of the great harvest I myself desired" (lines 28–29).

Apples are symbolically rich, suggesting everything from temptation in the garden of Eden, with overtones of knowledge and desire, to the idea of a prize difficult to attain, as in the golden apples of Hesperides that Hercules had to obtain as his eleventh labor. Here they can be read as representing the fruit of experience.

POSSIBLE CONNECTION TO ANOTHER SELECTION

John Keats, "To Autumn" (text p. 637)

Birches (p. 848)

This poem is a meditative recollection of being a boyhood swinger of birches. In the last third of the poem, the speaker thinks about reliving that experience as a way of escaping from his life, which sometimes seems "weary of considerations" (line 43). Swinging on birches represents a limber freedom, the elation of conquest, and the physical pleasure of the free-fall swish groundward. Note, in contrast, Frost's description of what ice storms do to birches. Images like "shattering and avalanching on the snow-crust" (11) suggest a harsh brittleness. The speaker in the end opts for Earth over Heaven because he (like Keats, to some extent) has learned that "Earth's the right place for love" (52).

Frost's blank verse lends a conversational ease to this piece, with its digressions for observation or for memory. A more rigid form, such as rhymed couplets, would work against this ease.

In a writing assignment, students might analyze the different forms of knowing in "Birches," contrasting truth's matter-of-factness (lines 21–22) and the pull of life's "considerations" (43) with boyhood assurance and the continuing powers of dream and imagination.

POSSIBLE CONNECTION TO ANOTHER SELECTION

Emily Dickinson, "Portraits are to daily faces" (text p. 805)

"Out, Out —" (p. 850)

Often when disaster strikes, we tend to notice the timing of events. Frost implies here that "they" might have given the boy an extra half-hour off and thereby averted the disaster. This perspective, coupled with the final line, in which the family seems to go on with life and ordinary tasks, can appear callous. But compare the wife's chastisement of her husband in "Home Burial" (text p. 844). Is the attitude callousness, or is it, rather, the impulse of an earth-rooted sensibility that refuses pain its custom of breaking the routine of life-sustaining chores and rituals? Very little in this poem seems to be a criticism of the survivors; rather, like *Macbeth* and the famous speech that proclaims life's shadowy nature (text p. 644), it seems to acknowledge the tenuous hold we have on life.

POSSIBLE CONNECTIONS TO OTHER SELECTIONS

Stephen Crane, "A Man Said to the Universe" (text p. 673; question #3, following)

Robert Frost, "Home Burial" (text p. 844; question #2, following)

2. Write an essay comparing how grief is handled by the boy's family in this poem and by the couple in "Home Burial" (p. 844).

   Grief separates the couple in "Home Burial," as the wife accuses the husband of being unfeeling when the husband suggests that they must go on living despite their child's death. Miscommunication lingers in the split lines as well as in the situation of the couple, separated by the length of a staircase. In " 'Out, Out —' " the bereaved "turned to their affairs" (line 34), choosing the response of the man in "Home Burial." Death unites them in that it reaffirms their commitment to the duty of living.

3. Compare the tone and theme of " 'Out, Out —' " with those of Stephen Crane's "A Man Said to the Universe" (p. 673).

   " 'Out, Out —' " and Crane's poem share a moral view that there is little ground on which humanity and the universe might meet. Crane's tone is slightly humorous, whereas Frost's approach is more poignant, but both rely heavily on dialogue to make their opinions known. Frost's borrowing from *Macbeth*, as well as the subject of the dead boy, gives his poem a more tragic quality than is present in Crane's sobering message.

The Oven Bird (p. 851)

This poem describes the height of nature's growth in midsummer and how it already forecasts nature's turning into a "diminished thing" (line 14). Frost's puzzling line, "Mid-summer is to spring as one to ten" (5), uses the image of the clock face to make his point about this cycle. While spring is still ripening toward its high point, midsummer is already past the peak, the way one o'clock is past the peak of the day, at noon.

The oven bird is called a "singer" in the first line of the poem, but it is actually more rhetorical than artistic: it "says" several things about the season and eventually poses a question. Frost claims that the bird "knows in singing not to sing" (12). Though the sonnet is a form modeled after song, "The Oven Bird" expresses some reservations about song, or more generally about art's need to make plain facts seem prettier than they are. For Frost, the fact that this bird talks more than sings gives it a kind of authority.

Fire and Ice (p. 852)

With a kind of diabolic irony, the theories for the way the world might end grow as our knowledge and technology increase. Students can probably supply a number of earth-ending disaster theories: overheating of the earth because we are moving sunward; the greenhouse effect with the chemical destruction of the ozone layer; war, apocalypse, or "nuclear winter"; a change in the earth's orbit away from the sun; the return of the ice age; and so on. Frost here also speaks of the metaphoric powers of hatred (ice) and desire (fire) as destroyers of the earth. To say that ice would "suffice" (line 9) to end the world is a prime example of understatement.

Dust of Snow (p. 852)

There is a lightness in this poem, as though the "dust of snow" were some kind of chance blessing or, at the very least, a light slap that commanded a change of mood. The experience happens quickly, and the one sentence elides act and mood and rein-forces the sense of cause and effect that associates the two stanzas.

As an essay topic, you might ask the students to demonstrate to what ends Frost (especially in this poem) uses nature to explore and make bearable the situation of being human.

Matsuo Bashō, "Under cherry trees" (text p. 753)

Allen Braden, "The Hemlock Tree" (text p. 683)

Robert Frost, "Fire and Ice" (text p. 852)

——, "The Pasture" (text p. 842)

Mary Oliver, "The Poet with His Face in His Hands" (text p. 572; question #1, following)

CONNECTION QUESTION IN TEXT (p. 853) WITH ANSWER

1. Compare the themes in "Dust of Snow" and Mary Oliver's "The Poet with His Face in His Hands" (text p. 572).

   In "Dust of Snow," Frost's speaker is the brooding poet Oliver sends out into nature to hear the thrush singing of the "perfect, stone-hard beauty of everything." While he isn't beside a waterfall, the speaker sits in nature and finds his focus on his personal sorrows lifted by the movement of a crow and the falling of the snow. The speaker in Frost's poem learns the lesson imparted in "The Poet"; that sometimes, one must go out and experience nature to soothe mental and spiritual anguish.

Stopping by Woods on a Snowy Evening (p. 853)

With very few words, Frost here creates a sense of brooding mystery as the speaker stops his horse in a desolate landscape between wood and frozen lake. The attraction of the woods is their darkness, the intimation they offer of losing oneself in them. The speaker gazes into them with a kind of wishfulness, while his horse shakes his bells, a reminder to get on with the business of living. The repetition in the last lines denotes a literal recognition that the speaker must move on and connotes that there is much to be done before life ends.

You might use question 4 in the text as a brief writing assignment to show how rhyme relates and interlocks the stanzas and offers in the final stanza (*dddd*) a strong sense of closure.

POSSIBLE CONNECTION TO ANOTHER SELECTION

Henry Wadsworth Longfellow, "Snow-Flakes" (text p. 1016)

The Need of Being Versed in Country Things (p. 854)

In this poem, one is hard-pressed to place the speaker, but one hears him clearly. There is no apparent *I*; birdsong is mentioned as being "more like the sigh we sigh / From too much dwelling on what has been" (lines 15–16). That *we* gives the reader a window on the speaker. The birds continue on their merry way, but the speaker has projected his feeling onto them. There are hints at tone in earlier stanzas in which beauty is intertwined with destruction: a beautiful sunset glow is caused by a fire; the chimney of a house remains but Frost's simile likens it to a ruined flower ("like a pistil after the petals go" [4]). The abandonment of the house is clear in stanza 3, when it is said the barn doors open "no more" (9) for the horses that used to stop there. The omniscient eye of the speaker examines the renewal of nature taking place and vestiges of mankind left behind. The remark that "there was really nothing sad" (21) here must now be taken with a grain of salt, for while that's true "for them" (the birds, the plants, the ruins of the house), someone is able to project sadness onto the scene. Discuss the difference between the "them" and the consciousness in line 21. The birds are not crying, so what saddens the speaker?

POSSIBLE CONNECTIONS TO OTHER SELECTIONS

Robert Frost, "Design" (text p. 856; question #1, following)

——, "Fire and Ice" (text p. 852)

CONNECTION QUESTION IN TEXT (p. 854) WITH ANSWER

1. Compare what the speaker learns in this poem with the speaker's response to nature in "Design" (text p. 856).

    The speaker in "Design" asks about the influence of a Creator in the natural world, but it focuses on seemingly malevolent creatures and actions. A spider luring a moth into its web raises the question of whether a Superior Being caused that intricate action to happen, although Frost leaves it open to doubt ("If design govern in a thing so small" [line 14]). Nature seems untouched by human emotion in "Country Things" and also opens the question of why a fire would consume a happy home. In both poems, nature seems to follow its own intricate rules, without the moral/ethical sensibility that humans experience.

Neither Out Far nor In Deep (p. 854)

This poem, particularly in its last stanza, comments on humanity's limitations in comprehending the infinite, the unknown, the inhuman and vast. Randall Jarrell's comment in his *Poetry and the Age* (New York: Farrar, 1953, 1972; print.) is useful. He writes, "It would be hard to find anything more unpleasant to say about people than that last stanza; but Frost doesn't say it unpleasantly—he says it with flat ease" (*Poetry and the Age,* 42–43). You might organize a writing assignment around the tone of this poem.

POSSIBLE CONNECTION TO ANOTHER SELECTION

Robert Frost, "Mending Wall" (text p. 843)

Design (p. 856)

The opening octave of this sonnet is highly descriptive and imagistic in its presentation of spider, flower, and moth, all white. The sestet asks the question of design: Who assembled all these elements in just such a way as to ensure that the moth would end up where the spider was—inside a "heal-all" (ironic name for this flower), its "dead wings carried like a paper kite" (line 8)? Frost has in mind the old argument of design to prove the existence of God. There must be a prime mover and creator; otherwise, the world would not be as magnificent as it is. But what of the existence of evil in this design, Frost asks. The final two lines posit choices: either there is a malevolent mover (the "design of darkness to appall") or, on this small scale of moth and spider, evil occurs merely by chance ("If design govern . . ."). The rhyme scheme is *abba, abba, acaa, cc,* and its control provides a tight interlocking of ideas and the strong closure of the couplet.

Randall Jarrell's remarks on the imagery and ideas here are superb; he appreciates this poem with a poet's admiration (see *Poetry and the Age,* 45–49). He notes, for example, the babylike qualities of "dimpled . . . fat and white" (line 1) (not pink) as applied to the spider. Note, too, how appropriate the word *appall* is because it indicates both the terror and the funereal darkness in this malevolently white trinity of images.

A comparison with the original version of this poem, "In White" (text p. 857), should prove that "Design" is much stronger. The title of the revised version, the closing two lines, and several changes in image and diction make for a more effective and thematically focused poem.

As a writing assignment, you might ask students either to compare this poem with its original version or to analyze the use of whiteness in "Design" and show how the associations with the idea of whiteness contrast with its usual suggestions of innocence and purity.

POSSIBLE CONNECTIONS TO OTHER SELECTIONS

Emily Dickinson, "I know that He exists" (text p. 829; question #2, following)

——, "Safe in their Alabaster Chambers —" (1861 version, text p. 805)

Robert Frost, "In White" (text p. 857)

William Hathaway, "Oh, Oh" (text p. 550; question #1, following)

CONNECTIONS QUESTIONS IN TEXT (p. 856) **WITH ANSWERS**

1. Compare the ironic tone of "Design" with the tone of William Hathaway's "Oh, Oh" (p. 550). What would you have to change in Hathaway's poem to make it more like Frost's?

    Hathaway's "Oh, Oh" has a far less serious tone than Frost's poem, as the poet plays a joke on his audience, beginning the poem in a slaphappy, conversational tone, only to change it to a note of impending doom. To be more like Frost's poem, "Oh, Oh" would have to make its audience aware of the entire situation from the beginning.

2. In an essay discuss Frost's view of God in this poem and Dickinson's perspective in "I know that He exists" (p. 829).

    In "Design" the speaker questions the existence of God by suggesting that only a malevolent deity could preside over the relentless mechanisms of nature, whereby one species destroys another to survive. In "I know that He exists" Dickinson's speaker speculates not on the nature of God but just on the hiddenness — the absence against which she must assert her belief. Frost is less comfortable with a God who must be malevolent than with no God at all. God's absence is what troubles Dickinson.

PERSPECTIVES ON ROBERT FROST

ROBERT FROST, *"In White": An Early Version of "Design"* (p. 857)

Many of the alterations Frost made to "In White" to arrive at "Design" have the effect of shifting the poem's focus from an individual occurrence to a more generalized one, from the questioning of a single death to the questioning of the force that caused, or allowed, the death to occur.

Students could begin by noting as many differences as they can find between the two poems. Probably the most obvious is the change in title. Whereas the title of the earlier poem announces a concern with the color white, which seems to represent death, the later title suggests a larger concern: the question of order (or the lack thereof) in the universe.

Frost retained the sonnet form when he revised, but the rhyme scheme for the sestet changes from six lines with the same rhyme to the much more complex *abaabb*. This throws a sharper emphasis on the last two lines of "Design," the lines in which the poet suggests that events are shaped either by forces of evil or not at all.

Ask students to discuss how changes in individual word choices affect the poem. Some of the most striking of these are the change from "dented" to "dimpled" in line 1 and from "lifeless" to "rigid" in line 3 (i.e., even more dead, as though rigor mortis has set in). Another interesting change is that whereas the poem once began with a general observation and ended with the very personal *I*, it now begins with *I* and moves outward to end with a general statement. Also note the use of the word *if* in the last line of the final version of "Design." This is one of Frost's favorite ways of injecting ambivalence and uncertainty into his poems.

POSSIBLE CONNECTION TO ANOTHER SELECTION

Robert Frost, "Design" (text p. 856)

ROBERT FROST, *On the Living Part of a Poem* (p. 857)

Intonation in musicians' parlance refers to pitch and the idea of playing in tune. Does Frost use the word in that sense here? If not, what does he mean later on by the "accent of sense" and how the word *come* can appear in different passages as a third, fourth, fifth, and sixth note?

In introducing this prose passage, you might point out that poets construct poetry out of fairly near-at-hand vocabularies—words we have already tasted on our tongues. One of the appeals of poetry is the physical way we intone its sounds, even when we read silently, so that we become in a sense a resonating chamber for the poem. It might be well to recall, too, that poetry originally was a spoken, not a written, medium, and those things that were regarded as important enough to be remembered were put in verse.

Frost makes several unqualified statements here. Students by and large receive as part of their first-year college training the advice to be chary of the committed word. You might devote some of the class discussion to exploring when and where rhetoric must be unequivocating.

AMY LOWELL, *On Frost's Realistic Technique* (p. 858)

Elsewhere in her review, Lowell describes Frost's vision as "grimly ironic." She goes on: "Mr. Frost's book reveals a disease which is eating into the vitals of our New England life, at least in its rural communities." In discussing the characters in Frost's poems, she calls them "the leftovers of old stock, morbid, pursued by phantoms, slowly sinking to insanity." You might ask students to find evidence for Lowell's observations in the Frost poems in this chapter. Are there opposite tendencies in these characters that save them from what Lowell describes as a "disease eating into the vitals"?

ROBERT FROST, *On the Figure a Poem Makes* (p. 858)

In this introduction to his *Collected Poems,* Frost calls the sounds of a poem "the gold in the ore." Perhaps the best way to discuss Frost's assertion is to put it to the test. How do Frost's own poems stand up? How does he use sound? His more conversational poems, such as "Home Burial," provide insight into individual characters through an imitation of their speech patterns. The contemplative poem, exemplified by "Birches" or "After Apple-Picking," can be analyzed both for the speaker's character as it is revealed in his diction and for the way sounds both reaffirm and undermine the speaker's point.

Poems are, according to Frost, spontaneous in that they are derived from the poet's imagination as it interacts with his surroundings. But the imagination is not groundless because poets take many of their ideas from what they've read, often unconsciously: "They stick to nothing deliberately, but let what will stick to them like burrs where they walk in the fields." Frost's belief in the predestination of poetry involves the idea that the poem is an act of belief, of faith: "It must be a revelation, or a series of revelations, as much for the poet as for the reader." Not entirely the product of either spontaneity or predestination, the poem takes on a life of its own: "Like a piece of ice on a hot stove the poem must ride on its own melting."

In giving up claims to democracy and political freedom, Frost resists the process of naming something that supposedly is without limitation. Once defined as "free," whatever we call free ceases to be just that. Frost uses as an example our "free" school system, which forces students to remain in it until a certain age; it is, therefore, not free. Resisting confining labels, Frost as an artist is more able to reach a world audience; once he states a political bias, his art is one of exclusion.

ROBERT FROST, *On the Way to Read a Poem* (p. 861)

Experience with one or two poems by an author often eases the way for reading other poems by him or her. But will reading "Birches," for example, prepare the way for understanding "Fire and Ice"? Not necessarily. Beyond our literary experience, some of our "life learning" enters into the reading of poems as well.

The image of reader as "revolving dog" also seems a little discomforting, no matter what one's feelings about dogs. Poetry reading requires a certain point of stability. Without it, one might be at a loss to distinguish sentiment from the sentimental, the power of the image from the fascination of the ornament.

You might ask students to try Frost's advice with two or three of his poems. They can read one in the light of another and then write about the experience.

HERBERT R. COURSEN JR., *A Parodic Interpretation of "Stopping by Woods on a Snowy Evening"* (p. 861)

This critical spoof offers a fine opportunity to articulate just what we seek from literary criticism and why we accept one writer's word and reject another's. One important factor in the Frost poem that is not considered here is tone and the speaker's own fascination with the woods, which are "lovely, dark, and deep."

If we were to isolate factors that mark good literary criticism, we might speak of (1) completeness (Are there any significant details omitted?), (2) coherence (Coursen advertises the simplicity of his theory but then talks at length about veiled allusions and obfuscation), and (3) fidelity to experience (No, Virginia, a horse is never a reindeer, not even on Christmas Eve). Good criticism avoids the overly ingenious.

This spoof also lends itself to a review of principles of good writing, which students have probably already acquired in a composition course. You might ask, too, what it was that inspired Coursen to write this essay. What, in other words, is he objecting to in the practice of literary criticism?

ADDITIONAL RESOURCES FOR TEACHING FROST

SELECTED BIBLIOGRAPHY

Bagby, George F. *Frost and the Book of Nature.* Knoxville: U of Tennessee P, 1993. Print.

Bloom, Harold, ed. *Robert Frost.* New York: Chelsea, 1986. Print.

Brodsky, Joseph. *Homage to Robert Frost.* New York: Farrar, Straus & Giroux, 1996. Print.

Cox, James Melville, ed. *Robert Frost: A Collection of Critical Essays.* Englewood Cliffs: Prentice, 1962. Print.

Faggen, Robert, ed. *The Cambridge Companion to Robert Frost.* New York: Cambridge UP, 2001. Print.

Frost, Robert. *Interviews with Robert Frost.* Ed. Edward Connery Lathem. New York: Holt, 1966. Print.

——. *The Poetry of Robert Frost.* Ed. Edward Connery Lathem. New York: Holt, 1979. Print.

——. *Robert Frost: A Time to Talk.* Ed. Robert Francis. Amherst: U of Massachusetts P, 1972. Print.

——. *Robert Frost on Writing.* Ed. Elaine Barry. New Brunswick: Rutgers UP, 1973. Print.

——. *Selected Letters.* Ed. Lawrance Thompson. New York: Holt, 1964. Print.

——. *Selected Prose.* Ed. Hyde Cox and Edward Connery Lathem. New York: Holt, 1966. Print.

Gerber, Philip L. *Critical Essays on Robert Frost.* Boston: Hall, 1982. Print.

Kearns, Katherine. *Robert Frost and a Poetics of Appetite.* Cambridge, Eng.: Cambridge UP, 1994. Print.

Marcus, Mordecai. *The Poems of Robert Frost: An Explication.* Boston: Hall, 1991. Print.

Meyers, Jeffrey, ed. *Early Frost: The First Three Books.* Hopewell: Ecco Press, 1996. Print.

Monteiro, George. *Robert Frost and the New England Renaissance.* Lexington: UP of Kentucky, 1988. Print.

Oster, Judith. *Toward Robert Frost: The Reader and the Poet.* Athens: U of Georgia P, 1992. Print.

Parini, Jay. *Robert Frost: A Life.* New York: Henry Holt, 1999. Print.

Poirier, Richard. *Robert Frost: The Work of Knowing.* New York: Oxford UP, 1977. Print.

Pritchard, William H. *Frost: A Literary Life Reconsidered.* New York: Oxford UP, 1984. Print.

Squires, James Radcliffe. *The Major Themes of Robert Frost.* Ann Arbor: U of Michigan P, 1969. Print.

Thompson, Lawrance. *Fire and Ice: The Art and Thought of Robert Frost.* New York: Russell, 1970. Print.

——. *Robert Frost: The Early Years, 1874–1915.* New York: Holt, 1966. Print.

——. *Robert Frost: The Years of Triumph, 1915–1938.* New York: Holt, 1970. Print.

Thompson, Lawrance, and R. H. Winnick. *Robert Frost: The Later Years, 1938–1963.* New York: Holt, 1982. Print.

32

A Study of Billy Collins:
The Author Reflects on Five Poems

The poems in this chapter, along with Collins's reflections on them, give students insight into one poet's process and how he reflects on what he has made. Just as Collins doesn't want readers to torture poems to get to their meanings (as he makes clear in "Introduction to Poetry," text p. 564), he hopes the writer can create a poem without beating an idea until it breaks. The metaphor of travel he introduces here liberates both readers and writers to relax and see where the poem takes them. The poems gathered in this chapter reveal a number of the poet's techniques. What they have in common is a grounding in the imagery of domestic life and an interrogation of received thinking or speech that leads to surprising revelations.

BILLY COLLINS

Osso Buco (p. 871)

In "Osso Buco" Collins plays the idea of the primitive or instinctual against the idea of "civilization." The opening image of the "bone against the plate" (line 1) brings together the basic act of carnivorous eating with the finer, even aesthetic, work of making dishes. The man leaning back in his chair after dinner is both an animalistic "creature" (12) and a refined "citizen" (11). Collins suggests that our animal instincts get at the essence of life, the "secret marrow" (6) inside the bone. However, the speaker enjoys eating the marrow even more because he has "cold, exhilarating wine" (9), the fruit of culture, to go with it. Collins also comments on the tendency of poetry to be morose, a tendency his speaker gently mocks in the summary in lines 15–16: "You know: the driving rain, the boots by the door, / small birds searching for berries in winter." Yet "Osso Buco" ends with the very poetic strategy by which Collins enlarges the central image of the bone on the plate into a much larger comment on "the broken bones of the earth itself" (48) and "the marrow of the only place we know" (49).

POSSIBLE CONNECTION TO ANOTHER SELECTION

Sally Croft, "Home-Baked Bread" (text p. 636)

Nostalgia (p. 874)

Collins examines the feeling of nostalgia by looking back at periods that no one alive could possibly remember. He notes the kind of things people get nostalgic for—certain trends or styles that seemed to set a period of time apart from others. The real moment of the speaker's nostalgia, "last month" (line 26), comes at the very end of the poem. That moment is dwarfed by the larger movements of history, but it contains the real emotional pull of the poem. As Collins describes in his comment on "Nostalgia," it is after this turn that the speaker changes from a mythical, timeless figure into a real person who longs for "serenity" (26) and who wonders what the future will bring.

POSSIBLE CONNECTION TO OTHER SELECTION

A. E. Housman, "When I was one-and-twenty" (text p. 728)

Questions About Angels (p. 876)

Collins's "Questions About Angels" goes beyond platitudes to ask metaphysical questions about how angels exist in physical space or in time: "Do they fly through God's body" (line 8) or "swing like children from the hinges / of the spirit world" (9–10)? The speaker laments the fact that the conversation about angels has been dominated by "medieval theologians" (23). Their questions are purely philosophical while the ones in Collins's poem are whimsical. The speaker tries to imagine angels both in the "eternal time" (4) of heaven and in the more mundane world in which angels posing as postmen "whistle up the driveway reading the postcards" (22). By ending the poem with the single female angel, Collins turns the abstract idea of a spiritual being into a more personal vision.

Litany (p. 878)

The second-person address of "Litany" raises questions about who the speaker is talking to. Collins's commentary on the poem confirms what the nature of the images also suggests—that the *you* is a beloved, specifically a female beloved. He notes that "Litany" is a send-up of the conventions of love poems, in which fantastic comparisons flatter the object of the speaker's affections. His critique becomes especially clear when the speaker asserts what the beloved is not: for example, "There is no way you are the pine-scented air" (line 11). The act of negation reveals how arbitrary the metaphors are in the first place. Another surprising move is the speaker's turn to characterize himself with equally romantic images such as "the shooting star" (22) and "the moon in the trees" (25). Here he turns from lavishing attention on the beloved to describing his own qualities.

POSSIBLE CONNECTIONS TO OTHER SELECTIONS

Margaret Atwood, "you fit into me" (text p. 645)

George Gordon, Lord Byron, "She Walks in Beauty" (text p. 1003)

Building with Its Face Blown Off (p. 881)

When violence removes the facades that keep up a notion of "the private" (line 1) in urban life, the details of people's intimate domestic lives are suddenly exposed. By comparing the striped wallpaper in one room with "striped pajamas" (7), Collins emphasizes how vulnerable this exposure makes the city's inhabitants. He tries out several figures for the damaged home, first describing it in miniature as if it were a "dollhouse" (19), then comparing it to a theater with "no dialogue or audience" (24). Either way, the scene is empty, with only photographs and "a shoe among the cinder blocks" (27) to represent the people who once lived there. The only human life in the poem exists far away where, at a comfortable distance from the destruction, a couple shares a picnic.

POSSIBLE CONNECTIONS TO OTHER SELECTIONS

William Heyen, "The Trains" (text p. 705)

James Merrill, "Casual Wear" (text p. 682)

33

A Study of Julia Alvarez:
The Author Reflects on Five Poems

This chapter invites a number of approaches—biographical, feminist, and post-colonial readings, analysis of cultural materials and the material products of writing—all in addition to basic close reading. Though academics often treat these as separate endeavors, for the poet they are all part of the one enterprise of making art. This will be especially salient to your students in Chapter 33 because they can hear Alvarez's voice in the text as well as in the poems, interview, and essays. For students who have been taught that a poem is simply a riddle to unlock, this multiplicity of approaches—each illuminating the work in a different way—may seem liberating.

JULIA ALVAREZ

Queens, 1963 (p. 897)

Alvarez's work has such a conversational tone, one that seems to take the reader into its confidence; students may pass over some of her subtle wordplay without noticing it. You might point out to them that the descriptions of how the speaker's family "blended into the block" (line 6) and, later, "melted / into the United States of America" (63–64) call up the idea of America as a melting pot. Have them discuss the extent to which the melting pot is working to incorporate the many different families in the neighborhood. In some cases it seems to work remarkably well. Not only does the speaker's family become acclimated to the new environment, but the Jewish counselor and a German family even coexist peacefully. However, the African American family remains very much unmelted into the common life of the neighborhood.

Another issue that Alvarez points to in this poem is the hypocrisy of America's prejudice given its status as a former colony. The appearance of the "mock Tudor house" (7) at the beginning of the poem is a reminder of America's relationship to Britain. At the end, as the speaker imagines "the houses / sinking into their lawns, / the grass gown wild and tall" (75–77), she has a vision of pre-colonial America before the "first foreigners" (79), the ancestors of those who discriminate against her neighbors, arrived in the country.

POSSIBLE CONNECTIONS TO OTHER SELECTIONS

John Ciardi, "Suburban" (text p. 965; question #1, following)

Tato Laviera, "AmeRícan" (text p. 773; question #3, following)

Gary Soto, "Mexicans Begin Jogging" (text p. 972; question #2, following)

CONNECTIONS QUESTIONS IN TEXT (p. 898) WITH ANSWERS

1. Compare the use of irony in "Queens, 1963" with that in John Ciardi's "Suburban" (p. 965). How does irony contribute to each poem?

    Both Alvarez's and Ciardi's sense of irony comes from the contrast between the idealistic and the realistic. In "Queens, 1963," the traditional images of "Americanness" contrast with the diversity of families in the neighborhood. The sprinkler on the lawn is one of the suburban markers that allow the speaker's family to feel like a part of the neighborhood. However, on the lawn of the new African American family, the sprinkler is confused with a "burning cross" (line 14), a mistake that shows how open such symbols of belonging are to interpretation. For Ciardi, the irony resides in the divorce of domesticated plants like the neighbor's "petunias" (5) from the reality of excrement, that "organic gold" (11). There is also an irony in the speaker's statements to the neighbor. We read these conciliatory moves with the knowledge that he actually thinks her complaint is ridiculous.

2. Discuss the problems immigrants encounter in this poem and in Gary Soto's "Mexicans Begin Jogging" (text p. 972).

The problems of immigrants in "Queens, 1963" have to do with fitting into the community. Through the names of the families in the neighborhood, Alvarez reveals how immigrants from various parts of the world have been stigmatized and then accepted in the course of American history. When most of the inhabitants of America were English (represented by Mrs. Scott in this poem), they discriminated against southern Europeans (like the Castelluccis). As time went on, those families were more accepted as a new group of immigrants (like the speaker's Dominican family) came along. These facts suggest how tensions can arise not just between immigrants and the majority but also among ethnic groups.

In Soto's "Mexicans Begin Jogging," the speaker narrates a border patrol raid that occurs at the factory where he is employed. He describes what happens when the vans arrive: "my boss waved for us to run. / 'Over the fence, Soto,' he shouted" (5–6). Discrimination is so rampant that it doesn't even matter that the speaker is in fact American; when he tells his boss so, he gets the response, "No time for lies" (8). As he runs, the speaker thinks, "What could I do but yell *vivas* / To baseball, milkshakes, and those sociologists / Who would clock me / As I jog into the next century" (17–20). Soto uses stereotypically American iconography—milkshakes and baseball—to draw attention to the irony that it doesn't matter where the speaker is actually from. The perception that he is an illegal immigrant is enough to justify the discrimination perpetrated against him not only by border control, but by his employer as well. The mention of sociologists reminds the reader that though there are privileged, college-educated Americans studying the hardships faced by immigrants, they do little to actually ease this suffering.

3. Write an essay comparing and contrasting the tone and theme in "Queens, 1963" and in Tato Laviera's "AmeRícan" (p. 773).

The tone of "AmeRícan" is exuberant and musical. The poem works as a kind of manifesto for people who identify as AmeRícan, celebrating their heritage and advocating a stronger stand against "marginality" (line 31). Alvarez's tone is more measured and wry. Rather than proclaiming a new way of living, she focuses on memory and on her observations of how people of different ethnicities interact in the world.

PERSPECTIVE

MARNY REQUA, *From an Interview with Julia Alvarez* (p. 900)

One of the most interesting statements Alvarez makes in this interview is that books form a "portable homeland." Have your students talk about how this might fit into Alvarez's feeling that she didn't quite belong either in her adopted country of America or in her country of origin, the Dominican Republic. Does escaping to the homeland of books help a writer to maintain independence from any particular nation? The political implications of this idea are important; taken to an extreme it might exempt a writer from political responsibilities to a country or a region. The "escape" into the imaginary world of books could lead readers away from the problems of the real world. However, Alvarez doesn't seem to be a proponent of art purely for its own sake. The "portable homeland" has allowed her to present a more complicated notion of identity that reflects the values of both of her countries.

Housekeeping Cages (p. 902)

In this essay, Alvarez is ahead of the curve in promoting activities traditionally seen as part of the "women's sphere." In fact, the recent craze for knitting and other needle-crafts has been led by feminists who want to reclaim the domestic arts as a worthwhile form of expression. Alvarez's interest in the forms that art takes is at the heart of this essay. She wants to affirm both the traditionally female forms that became stigmatized at the beginning of the feminist era and to claim her right to enter the traditionally male forms that have often been barred to women. For some artists, adopting forms that have been used by oppressive cultures indicates a conservative point of view, but Alvarez argues that this is a false understanding of art. The artist is free to use whatever form she wants and in fact, by remaking the form, can change its history. For example, the sonnet form began as a way for men to praise their lovers—a function that is flattering but empty, taking away women's voices. Alvarez conveys the problem of the sonnet form beautifully in her phrases "golden cages of beloved" and "perfumed gas chambers" (para. 6), which juxtapose beauty and malice. Once these patterns have been broken though, the form is "totally different . . . from the one [Alvarez] learned in school" (para. 7). The tradition changes not just for the individual poet but for all her followers as well.

"Housekeeping Cages" also calls into question the ownership of language. Since English is not her first language, Alvarez sometimes worries that she is writing in someone else's voice. However, she points out that Spanish, too, was the language of a colonizing power (para. 3). What matters is not the origin of a language, but how the people who speak and write in it are able to inhabit it and make it their own. Alvarez doesn't just preach this idea as gospel; she practices it as well. Though the tone of the essay is casual, she's working hard with the language, and she occasionally has to manipulate it in order to make her point as she does by turning the nouns *muse* and *housekeeping* into the verbs "musing" (para. 5) and "housekeep" (para. 8). These changes reveal Alvarez's emphasis on the active power of the writer and her attempts to wrest the control of the language away from its traditional guardians.

Dusting (p. 904)

The writing that happens in this poem is a kind that can be easily erased. In fact, the writer's mother cleans it away immediately with her "crumpled-up flannel" (line 8). It seems that the speaker is doomed to become, like the mother, "anonymous" (18). However, she refuses this fate. In "Dusting," "fingerprints" (9) are synonymous with "alphabets" (12). In other words, writing is a central aspect of the young woman's identity. At this point, she is only "practicing signatures like scales" (5), but this warming up suggests that she is getting ready to make real art.

The attitude of the mother in this poem is ambiguous. Erasing her daughter's work is a destructive act, but it could also be a protective one, meant to shield her from a world unsympathetic to women's art. In fact, the mother seems like a repressed artist herself. She doesn't just clean, but makes her home "jeweled" (14) and "luminous" (16). Her name has been "swallowed in the towel" (13) along with her daughter's.

POSSIBLE CONNECTION TO ANOTHER SELECTION

Cathy Song, "The Youngest Daughter" (text p. 611; question #1, following)

CONNECTION QUESTION IN TEXT (p. 905) **WITH ANSWER**

1. Discuss the mother-daughter relationships in "Dusting" and in Cathy Song's "The Youngest Daughter" (p. 611).

   Both "Dusting" and "The Youngest Daughter" involve some tension between the mothers' needs and expectations and the daughters' desires for their own lives. In Alvarez's poem, the mother's dusting suggests her need to thwart her child's larger ambition to be a writer. Though this act aligns her with traditional ideas about what women's work should be, it also has a protective quality, as she tries to keep her daughter from taking the risk of entering a profession that hasn't always been open to women. However, the young girl will not be erased and seems determined to keep up with her writing. "The Youngest Daughter" presents a picture of a woman who has been playing along with her mother's expectations and has begun to resent the role. The relationship seems even more strained than that in "Dusting" because the mother knows her daughter is "not to be trusted" (line 44), and that she wants nothing more than to escape from those suffocating expectations.

Ironing Their Clothes (p. 906)

In this poem, as the empty clothes of the speaker's family members become stand-ins for the loved ones themselves, they retain some of the owners' preoccupations and so give us an evocative picture of the family. The father's shirt, "cramped / and worried with work" (lines 2–3), tells the reader that he carries a large burden for the family. The mother, too, has so much work to do that she has *"no time for love!"* (14), but the speaker can "lay [her] dreaming iron on her lap" (20), imagining a time when there would be enough leisure to indulge her affections. Even the sister puts practical considerations first, like keeping her "fresh blouses, starched jumpers, and smocks" (28) neat.

You might have the students discuss which of the characters in the poem they find sympathetic. The love that the speaker lavishes on the clothes certainly makes us feel her sensitivity and affection. Do they feel that the other family members are callous? Or do their many cares make them sympathetic figures, too? You might point out to your class that the speaker has a particular gift in being able to perform these acts of love through the mundane chore of ironing. She is not without duties, but she can find redeeming qualities in them.

POSSIBLE CONNECTION TO ANOTHER SELECTION

Robert Hayden, "Those Winter Sundays" (text p. 547)

Sometimes the Words Are So Close (p. 908)

The fact that several lines in this sonnet end with forms of *be* or *become* indicates how central to this poem are ideas about the existence of the self. The clothing metaphor that Alvarez comes to in lines 5 and 6, saying she is "unbuttoned" and "undressed," suggests that one way she wants to arrive at an understanding of self is to try some different ones on first. However, the most comfortable self is the one "down on paper" (line 2). Here the speaker is more herself than "anywhere else" (3), an interesting choice of words since it indicates that the space of the poem is somehow parallel to the space of a home or city. Though this poem space is comfortable to occupy, it is hard to get to. The finished poem is clear enough that "a child could understand" (8), but she asks, "Why do I get confused living it through?" (9). Through the drafting process, the many versions of the self, which can't be pinned down in regular time, become the poem-self that is "essentially" (13) right, expressing the essence of the writer.

POSSIBLE CONNECTIONS TO OTHER SELECTIONS

Walt Whitman, From "I Sing the Body Electric" (text p. 763; question #1, following)

——, "One's-Self I Sing" (text p. 1027; question #1, following)

CONNECTION QUESTION IN TEXT (p. 911) WITH ANSWER

1. The poem's final line alludes to Walt Whitman's poem "So Long" in which he addresses the reader: "Camerado, / This is no book, / Who touches this touches a man." Alvarez has said that Whitman is one of her favorite poets. Read the selections by Whitman in this anthology (check the index for titles) along with "So Long" (readily available online) and propose an explanation about why you think she admires his poetry.

Whitman's poetry is expansive, and he is interested in encompassing the broad variety of American life in his unique voice. Though Alvarez's poems tend to be formally tighter than Whitman's, with shorter lines and more traditional shapes, the two poets share an interest in how personal experience intersects with communal life.

First Muse (p. 913)

The invocation of the Muse, the goddess of the arts, goes back to Greek poetry. Poets would call on the Muse for help in creating art. In "First Muse," the young poet doesn't know how to appeal to a Muse, but is surprised to discover one, who restores to her the power to write. Her feelings about poetry had been suddenly complicated when she heard a famous poet "pronounce" (line 1) against writing poetry in a second language. Alvarez's choice of verbs here is important, as it not only suggests the famous writer's assertiveness but also brings up questions of what is a "proper" accent for pronouncing English. Suddenly the speaker recognizes boundaries that she didn't know existed before. It is as if a "literary border guard" (19) was keeping her from writing more.

Luckily, the Muse comes with a "lilting accent so full of feeling" (26) to contradict the famous poet's "pronouncement." The Chiquita Banana offers a positive picture of the blending of cultures. You might want to remind your students that when Alvarez was growing up, she would have seen few representations of Latinas in the media. Though there is humor in naming Chiquita as the muse, the discovery is also poignant.

POSSIBLE CONNECTIONS TO OTHER SELECTIONS

Julia Alvarez, "Dusting" (text p. 904; question #1, following)

——, "Sometimes the Words Are So Close" (text p. 908; question #1, following)

Judy Page Heitzman, "The Schoolroom on the Second Floor of the Knitting Mill" (text p. 656; question #3, following)

Julio Marzán, "Ethnic Poetry" (text p. 679; question #2, following)

CONNECTIONS QUESTIONS IN TEXT (p. 914) WITH ANSWERS

1. Discuss the speaker's passion for language as it is revealed in "First Muse," "Sometimes the Words Are So Close" (p. 908), and "Dusting" (p. 904).

   In both "Sometimes the Words Are So Close" and "Dusting," language is intricately connected with the formation of the self. Writing her name over and over, the speaker asserts her individuality through language. Similarly the sonnet allows the writer to move through the "many drafts" (line 12) of her personality to exist "briefly, essentially" (13) in the poem. In "First Muse," language is important not just in asserting the self, but also in understanding its relationship to others. For the young writer in this poem, language is a way of negotiating her allegiances to multiple cultures—her Spanish-speaking homeland and her new life in America. The proclamation of the "famous poet" (line 1) wants to confine the writer to a single identity, but the cheerful image of the Chiquita Banana makes the counter-assertion that she doesn't have to simplify her understanding of herself.

2. Compare the themes concerning writing and ethnicity in "First Muse" and in Julio Marzán's "Ethnic Poetry" (p. 679).

   Each of the poets in Marzán's poem relates a different way of understanding the universe and humans' place in it. Marzán sees this questioning of existence as a crucial function of poetry. His description of the audience's reactions, though, reveals more about his perspective on how poetry is received. Each of the first four responses involves some ethnic marker, which seems to suggest that the work would have an appeal only to the particular "ethnic audience." However, when we get to the famous Robert Frost line in the final stanza, the audience's reaction changes. This ironic last line is a comment on the assumptions about white culture — not only is it perceived as the "norm," but it also often pretends to have a monopoly on "deeply understood humanity" (line 20).

While Marzán is interested in how the ethnicity of the poet affects the audience, Alvarez is more concerned with how the poet herself can be limited by ethnic identifications. The speaker in "First Muse" resists being policed by "a literary border guard" (19). Rather than dividing her native Spanish from the English of people born in America, she wants to speak the new language with her own accent, "the way the heart would speak English / if it could speak" (27–28).

3. Consider the speakers' reactions in "First Muse" and in Judy Page Heitzman's "The Schoolroom on the Second Floor of the Knitting Mill" (p. 656) to the authoritative voice each hears. What effects do these powerful voices have on the speakers' lives?

The voice that cows Heitzman's narrator is one of the first authorities that we encounter after our parents: the teacher. When she humiliates the child for not keeping the line in check, it leaves such a deep impression that the speaker hears her voice again "every time [she fails]" (line 23). The authority of the "famous poet" (line 1) in Alvarez's poem comes not so much from her power over the child's life as from the societal endorsement that calls artists great. Though the famous poet does not speak directly about the young writer, the words are equally devastating. In this case they not only produce a lasting impression but also actually prevent the speaker from writing for months and make her consider burning her "notebooks filled with bogus poems" (6). Luckily, in "First Muse," another voice comes along to contradict the idea troubling the speaker. It is funny that this enabling voice would come from a commercial, but the Chiquita Banana is able to break the spell cast by the older poet. Later the speaker is able to look back on the event not as an instance of failure but as one of triumph.

PERSPECTIVE

KELLI LYON JOHNSON, *Mapping an Identity* (p. 916)

The geographic metaphor Johnson employs in this essay is an illuminating way of looking at Alvarez's poems. The mapping of identity, rather than of rivers or states, suggests that this is an imaginative geography. Indeed, the idea of "'mapping a country that's not on the map'" (para. 1) relates to Alvarez's attraction to the "portable homeland" that books provide (see her interview with Marny Requa, text p. 900). Alvarez's maps avoid the restrictive boundaries of countries but instead provide a view of the creating self through the lenses of multiple cultures. She breaks up the elements of "linguistic, national, and cultural identity" (para. 2) and recombines them in whatever ways are most hospitable to her work as a poet. As Johnson notes, by doing this she also broadens the sense of the word *America*, lessening the hegemonic power of United States culture and applying the term again "across continents and seas" (para. 3) to indicate all of the "New World."

34

A Cultural Case Study: Harlem Renaissance Poets Claude McKay, Georgia Douglas Johnson, Langston Hughes, and Countee Cullen

This chapter focuses on four influential poets: Claude McKay, Georgia Douglas Johnson, Langston Hughes, and Countee Cullen. As contemporaries of the Harlem Renaissance, all four share some common subject matter and influences; however, it would be valuable to discuss with students how each differs from the others. Most notably, Hughes self-consciously puts himself at the juncture of popular culture and the intellectual and political questions of his time, while both Cullen and McKay sometimes resist or reject such associations outright, whether through subject matter or form.

Because of the importance of culture and time period, it may be useful to include audiovisual materials while teaching this section. You may find it useful to provide some background for students or have them do their own research and presentations in class. These presentations might be done singly or as group projects, focusing on such topics as jazz and blues music, the situation of African Americans and the struggle for civil rights during this time, the history of the Harlem Renaissance, labor and radicalism in the 1930s, and so forth. Such presentations have the advantage of making a great deal of information available to the class and of encouraging students to be active contributors of knowledge.

Students' attitudes about race will be inescapable in this section. Nearly every poem could be the focal point of a controversial discussion in class. You might want to foreground these issues early in the discussion, asking students to write about whether or not these poets have any relevance to current racial issues. This will help them articulate their own assumptions about race in a space that is not directly confrontational.

CLAUDE McKAY

The Harlem Dancer (p. 926)

Students might regard the sonnet as a form exercised primarily by Renaissance poets, but in "The Harlem Dancer," McKay provides a twentieth-century example of a Shakespearean or Elizabethan sonnet. (Direct students to the description of the sonnet form in Chapter 27 if they are unfamiliar with its components.) Here, the form seems perfectly suited to organize and emphasize the narrator's observation of the dancer's "perfect, half-clothed body" (line 2).

The Elizabethan sonnet is composed of four parts—three quatrains and a final couplet in which the poet provides an observation about the preceding material. In "The Harlem Dancer," the three quatrains (which display the conventional rhyme scheme of *abab cdcd efef,* complemented by the *gg* of the couplet) provide three different approaches to the description of the dancer. First, the poet provides a sort of general description, incorporating both the dancer's assets—her "perfect" body and her voice, which is "like the sound of blended flutes / Blown by black players upon a picnic day" (3–4)—and a brief indication of the audience as well—"Applauding youths laughed with young prostitutes" (1). The second quatrain dwells on the dancer's movement: "To me she seemed a proudly-swaying palm / Grown lovelier for passing through a storm" (7–8). In the final quatrain, the poet emphasizes her black beauty and her audience's passionate response to her performance: "The wine-flushed, bold-eyed boys, and even the girls, / Devoured her shape with eager, passionate gaze" (11–12). McKay emphasizes the dancer's apparent giving of herself to her audience and their seeming possession of her: in the final quatrain, there seems to be little about her that her audience hasn't grasped. Yet as the "turn" indicates, the dancer has indeed withheld something from those who have watched her performance: "looking at her falsely-smiling face,/I knew her self was not in that strange place" (13–14). In this final couplet, the poet describes one aspect of the dancer that is not mentioned in the preceding lines — her face. The couplet also indicates the speaker's clearer vision of the event, in which he can see what the rest of the audience has missed.

Encourage students to analyze the use of sonnet form in "The Harlem Dancer" as a way of discovering the means by which McKay builds to the climax of the couplet. They might also compare this poem to a Shakespeare sonnet in order to better understand and appreciate the contribution of each component of the form.

POSSIBLE CONNECTIONS TO OTHER SELECTIONS

Langston Hughes, "Harlem" (text p. 941)

——, "Jazzonia" (text p. 939)

Claude McKay, "The Lynching" (text p. 928; question #1, following)

——, "Outcast" (text p. 929)

——, "The Tropics in New York" (text p. 927)

CONNECTION QUESTION IN TEXT (p. 927) WITH ANSWER

1. Discuss the thematic significance of the respective crowds in "The Harlem Dancer" and in "The Lynching" (text p. 928).

   The crowds in "The Harlem Dancer" and "The Lynching" offer a foil to the dancer, the lynched man, and either speaker. In "The Lynching," the crowd is filled with women who show no sorrow at what's taking place, and little boys who "danced round the dreadful thing in fiendish glee" (line 14). In "The Harlem Dancer," the crowd laughs and "devour[s] her shape with eager passionate gaze" (12), with no understanding of her distress.

If We Must Die (p. 927)

The thrust of this poem is in the speaker's injunction to others not to die like animals, but "let us show us brave" (line 10). While this poem was written at a time when violence against blacks was a regular occurrence, McKay does not mention race specifically; discussion might revolve around the treatment of African Americans previous to and into the twentieth century or focus on events of McKay's time specifically. Ask students how they think race might have influenced the writing of McKay's sonnet, and what other peoples or situations it could refer to. Consider the poem's rhetoric, paying particular attention to the metrics of lines like "If we must die, O let us nobly die,/So that our precious blood may not be shed/In vain; then even the monsters we defy/Shall be constrained to honor us though dead!" (5–8). Images such as this add to the urgency and determination in the speaker's tone.

POSSIBLE CONNECTIONS TO OTHER SELECTIONS

John Donne, "Death Be Not Proud" (text p. 781)

Langston Hughes, "Harlem" (text p. 941; question #1, following)

Claude McKay, "The Lynching" (text p. 928)

John Milton, "On the Late Massacre in Piedmont" (text p. 1018)

Wilfred Owen, "Dulce et Decorum Est" (text p. 633)

1. Compare the themes in "If We Must Die" and in Langston Hughes's "Harlem" (text p. 941).

    The call to "meet the common foe" (line 9) in McKay's sonnet has some connection to the ending of Hughes's "Harlem" (in which the "dream deferred" explodes). McKay says "like men we'll face the murderous, cowardly pack, / Pressed to the wall, dying, but fighting back" (13–14). Depending on how students interpret the ending of Hughes's poem, they may find some commonality between the two. If the dream deferred explodes, perhaps it finally moves with positive (though violent) energy, just as McKay's *we* finally decides to go down fighting.

The Tropics in New York (p. 927)

Have students pay attention to the vividness of McKay's images here. The list of fruits is particularly tantalizing. He moves from a current sensory impression into one from memory. The title of the poem tells the reader that despite the vivid images, the speaker is actually in New York, longing for the tropical paradise he recalls. Ask students if they've ever felt longing within their bodies the way McKay describes it in lines 9 and 10. How does such longing translate into the hunger and grief he expresses in the final two lines?

POSSIBLE CONNECTIONS TO OTHER SELECTIONS

Langston Hughes, "125th Street" (text p. 941; question #1, following)

Claude McKay, "The Harlem Dancer" (text p. 926)

——, "Outcast" (text p. 929)

1. Compare how food is used to evoke a sense of place in "The Tropics in New York" and in Langston Hughes's "125th Street" (text p. 941).

    Both men are using food to connect what they see to something they understand. Hughes uses similes to reveal something about the people he watches on 125th Street; McKay lists tropical fruits he comes across in New York City that transport him back to Jamaica in his mind.

The Lynching (p. 928)

McKay's subtle shift in tone in "The Lynching" should be noted. The description of the hanged man doesn't focus on his transgression; instead, McKay describes him using words that invoke Christian ideas, from the spirit in smoke ascending into heaven and returning to the father to the star reminiscent of the star of Bethlehem hanging over the corpse. The tonal shift occurs in line 10 when he speaks graphically of the lynching, referring to the "ghastly body swaying in the sun." Some students might remember Billie Holliday's famous rendition of the song "Strange Fruit," and drawing in other portrayals of lynching might add to general discussion. In McKay's poem, by day the crowds come, full of unsympathetic women and little boys described as "lynchers that were to be" who engage in an evil dance around the body of the lynched man.

POSSIBLE CONNECTIONS TO OTHER SELECTIONS

Countee Cullen, "Yet Do I Marvel" (text p. 944; question #1, following)

Langston Hughes, "The Negro Speaks of Rivers" (text p. 938)

Claude McKay, "If We Must Die" (text p. 927)

CONNECTION QUESTION IN TEXT (p. 929) WITH ANSWER

1. Compare the treatment of religion in this poem and in Countee Cullen's "Yet Do I Marvel" (text p. 944).

   Both Cullen's poem "Yet Do I Marvel" and McKay's piece "The Lynching" have complicated views on religion and God. Both speakers are clearly coming from a Judeo-Christian background, and both question God's cruelty. In "The Lynching," McKay's speaker describes the execution of an African American by whites, saying, "His father, by the cruelest way of pain, / Had bidden him to his bosom once again" (2–3). The speaker in "Yet Do I Marvel" also focuses on God's harsher decisions for life, including, "Why flesh that mirrors Him must some day die" (4). However, Cullen's poem seems more convinced of God's ultimate goodness: "I doubt not God is good, well-meaning, kind" (1). There is more despair in "The Lynching," not only because of the behavior of other humans, but also because of God's seeming neglect of the dead man: though there is a star shining over him all night, the speaker points out, "(Perchance the one that ever guided him, / Yet gave him up at last to Fate's wild whim)" (6–7).

America (p. 929)

Compare this poem in terms of theme with Hughes's "Harlem" (p. 941) and Percy Bysshe Shelley's "Ozymandias" (p. 1022). You might also discuss with the class the inverted word order here and why it strikes our ears now as forced and archaic. Still, some of the language difficulty could be explained by the fact that this is a Shakespearean sonnet that divides, Petrarchan fashion, into octave and sestet. The octave expresses McKay's "love" for "this cultured hell," despite the fact that he receives from it only the "bread of bitterness." In the sestet McKay describes himself as a kind of mute rebel who foresees his country's decline and decay, even though he felt infused by its "vigor" only a few lines earlier. You might explore here the problem of coherence in poetry, and in class discussion try to work toward some resolution of the two parts of the sonnet.

POSSIBLE CONNECTIONS TO OTHER SELECTIONS

E. E. Cummings, "next to of course god america i" (text p. 673)

Tony Hoagland, "America" (text p. 987; question #1, following)

Langston Hughes, "Harlem" (text p. 941)

Claude McKay, "If We Must Die" (text p. 927)

CONNECTION QUESTION IN TEXT (p. 929) WITH ANSWER

1. Compare the themes of this poem with those in Tony Hoagland's "America" (text p. 987).

   Hoagland's poem, which scrutinizes the role of capitalism as oppressor in America, calls attention to those oppressed: "you are floating in your pleasure boat upon this river//Even while others are drowning underneath you/And you see their faces twisting in the surface of the waters" (lines 32–34). McKay, one of the oppressed, insists that he will get the better of America, even with "her tiger's tooth/stealing [his] breath of life" (2–3). McKay will stand up to her, as a David to a Goliath, "with not a shred/Of terror, malice, not a word of jeer" (9–10).

Outcast (p. 929)

Consider "Outcast" as an elegy, and compare it to another McKay poem, "The Tropics in New York," that fits that category. In what way is McKay an elegiac writer? In class discussion, pinpoint words within "Outcast" that connect to ideas of grief or death.

Africa is likened to Eden in this poem, a place of bliss; perhaps it is also akin to descriptions in Genesis before God began to make divisions between dark and light, when all was still and whole: "I would go back to darkness and to peace" (line 5). Ask students to think about the role Christian ideas of life as struggle and death as release play in the subtext of McKay's poem.

POSSIBLE CONNECTIONS TO OTHER SELECTIONS

Langston Hughes, "The Negro Speaks of Rivers" (text p. 938; question #1, following)

Claude McKay, "America" (text p. 929)

——, "The Tropics in New York" (text p. 927)

CONNECTION QUESTION IN TEXT (p. 930) WITH ANSWER

1. Discuss how the speakers' identities are related to time in "Outcast" and in Langston Hughes's "The Negro Speaks of Rivers" (text p. 938).

    In "Outcast," the speaker has lost something of himself in the Western world. He is "out of time," out of his time, in the white man's world. In "The Negro Speaks of Rivers," Hughes's speaker carries his history within himself, complete with the rivers and knowledge of his people.

GEORGIA DOUGLAS JOHNSON

Youth (p. 932)

After first reading this poem, students may be surprised to find that Johnson's style has more in common with Robert Herrick or William Wordsworth than Langston Hughes. This brief poem immediately calls to mind Herrick's "To the Virgins, to Make Much of Time" (p. 599) both because of themes and because of similarities in style. Johnson's verse features classical diction, exemplified in the words "dial-youth" (line 3) and "nevermore" (8). There's no modern slang or racially charged language. Even more so than Claude McKay, Georgia Douglas Johnson's work fits into James Weldon Johnson's vision of African American artists who can work with pre-existing poetic traditions and still make a valuable contribution to literature.

POSSIBLE CONNECTIONS TO OTHER SELECTIONS

Robert Herrick, "To the Virgins, to Make Much of Time" (text p. 599; question #1, following)

Andrew Marvell, "To His Coy Mistress" (text p. 601; question #1, following)

CONNECTION QUESTION IN TEXT (p. 932) WITH ANSWER

1. Compare the theme and tone of this poem with either Robert Herrick's "To the Virgins, to Make Much of Time" (p. 599) or Andrew Marvell's "To His Coy Mistress" (p. 601).

    As mentioned above, "Youth" features formal diction and no slang, giving the poem a similar tone to both of these pieces. The central theme of Johnson's poem is to be aware of the irrevocable passage of time and to seize the day. Both Marvell's and Herrick's poems have the same theme, making a comparison of sentiments between Johnson's verse and either of these straightforward poems. Marvell's poem, however, is directed toward a woman whom the narrator sees as being "coy" or fickle with her affections. Both male poets exhort their readers to use their time wisely and enjoy their youth. Johnson's speaker, on the other hand, simply notes that time passes "swift across our dial-youth" (line 3) and that such youth will quickly "exhale and fade away" (6). Rather than encouraging the reader or the object of affection to *carpe diem*, Johnson's poem simply notes the unstoppable march of time.

Foredoom (p. 933)

Like "Youth," this poem is a brief verse with a simple rhyme scheme and clear diction. These four short lines use metaphors to describe how unhappy the subject's life has been. The speaker conveys this bleak life by comparing it to "shades of night" (line 2) and claiming that "Her soul, a bud — that never bloomed" (4). By starting every line with "Her," Johnson uses repetition to convey a sense that for this mysterious subject, nothing ever changes. The "Her" of the poem seems trapped in a cycle of unhappiness, unable to escape herself and her life. The title of the poem reflects this miserable entrapment as well by describing the woman's state — being "foredoomed" means to be condemned before one even has a chance to escape one's fate. She was doomed from the start of her life.

POSSIBLE CONNECTION TO ANOTHER SELECTION

Countee Cullen, "For a Lady I Know" (text p. 945; question #1, following)

CONNECTION QUESTION IN TEXT (p. 933) WITH ANSWER

1. Compare the portrait of the woman in "Foredoom" with the portrait in Countee Cullen's "For a Lady I Know" (p. 945). How much do you know about each of these women?

   The woman described in "Foredoom" lives a desolate life and feels condemned to suffer through it without reprieve. Without giving any hint of her social status or personal life, Johnson describes the woman's life as "dwarfed, and wed to blight" (line 1), and that "Her every dream was born entombed" (3), or destroyed before she even had a chance to act on it. In Cullen's poem "For a Lady I Know," the subject is the exact opposite of Johnson's woman. Cullen's Lady lives a privileged life as part of a social class that "lies late and snores" (2). She clearly is accustomed to being taken care of and probably has African American servants to do it. Cullen implies this by describing the Lady's idea that even in heaven, "poor black cherubs rise at seven / To do celestial chores" (3–4).

Calling Dreams (p. 933)

"Calling Dreams" is a poem that is almost instantly relatable from any walk of life. Everyone has felt that the odds were against them at one time or another, and that they would have to take a stand to achieve their goals. Because of the universality of this experience, "Calling Dreams" is a very uplifting, inspiring poem. The narrator proclaims, "The right to make my dreams come true, / I ask, nay, I demand of life" (lines 1–2). The rest of the poem is composed of rhyming couplets that lend it a memorable rhythm, almost like a march. Johnson highlights this by making her narrator march as well, as she claims that fate will not "impede my steps" (4).

POSSIBLE CONNECTION TO ANOTHER SELECTION

Claude McKay, "Outcast" (text p. 929; question #1, following)

CONNECTION QUESTION IN TEXT (p. 933) WITH ANSWER

1. Discuss the themes in "Calling Dreams" and Claude McKay's "Outcast" (p. 929).

   As mentioned earlier, Johnson fits well into James Weldon Johnson's aesthetic of black writers using formal diction and poetic tropes to add to the wider literary canon, rather than gimmicks and strictly African American–concerned themes and descriptions. "Calling Dreams" accomplishes the goal of wedding the battle for equal rights that was ongoing during the Harlem Renaissance to this afore-mentioned ideology. The reader can interpret Johnson's poem as a description of a black man or woman who is willing to fight for his or her equality, or alternatively, as anyone, of any race, who has ever faced oppression, whether through social and economic status, gender, race, or simple circumstance. Anyone who has worked against "fate" can relate to "Calling Dreams."

While similar thematically and in tone, "Outcast" describes a more specific situation. McKay is clearly aiming to convey the emotions of displacement and oppression that African Americans experienced. The speaker describes himself as "a thing apart" (line 12) and shows his feeling of entrapment by saying "the great western world holds me in fee" (6) and "I was born, far from my native clime" (13). McKay specifically makes this a racially charged poem by ending with the line "Under the white man's menace, out of time" (14). The final line speaks of the oppression McKay saw himself and others suffering specifically because of their race.

Lost Illusions (p. 933)

In "Lost Illusions," Johnson's speaker longs for her youth explicitly for what many see as its folly: ignorance. She claims that youth had been "Shielding my heart from the blaze of truth" (line 2), and now she has descended "Into the sadness that follows" (4). Still more specifically, she tells the reader precisely what causes this sadness later in life — "to know!" (4). As she ages, the narrator is forced to face the passage of time and her eventual death. Because of this, she wishes she could return to her past and stave off old age longer. She wants to hide behind the "veil" (7) of ignorance that once protected her.

Possible Connection to Another Selection

Georgia Douglas Johnson, "Youth" (text p. 932; question #1, following)

Connection Question in Text (p. 934) with Answer

1. Discuss the perils of youth that Johnson describes in this poem and in "Youth" (p. 932).

   In both "Youth" and "Lost Illusions," the speaker is preoccupied with the passage of time and the descent into old age. In "Youth," the central peril is only that being young doesn't last. Youth is unreliable and fleeting, and time passes as "a shifting shadow" (line 4). The narrator illustrates this further in the lines "Life may renew the Autumn time, / But nevermore the May!" (7–8). She uses the different months and seasons as a clear metaphor for the passage of time in one's life. The central peril of youth described in "Lost Illusions" is not only its temporariness, but also the ignorance that comes with it. However, Johnson does not see youthful ignorance as a fault; her narrator spends the entire poem longing to return to it.

Fusion (p. 934)

In "Fusion," Johnson uses the image of a gardener cross-pollinating roses to create a new species as a metaphor for her own unique background. As discussed on page 931 in the text, Johnson was descended from African, Native American, and English predecessors. Johnson rejoices in her mixed heritage, describing how coming from multiple backgrounds can make one "more gorgeous and more beautiful / Than any parent portion" (lines 4–5). Though she admits she has "warring blood" (7), she views it as a benefit that provides her with "new-born forces" (11). This poem has similar subject matter as Claude McKay's "Outcast" (p. 929), but rather than feeling "a thing apart," Johnson believes she is the privileged one.

Possible Connections to Other Selections

Georgia Douglas Johnson, "Cosmopolite" (text p. 934; question #1, following)
Claude McKay, "Outcast" (text p. 929)

1. Discuss the source of pride that is found in "Fusion" and in Johnson's "Cosmopolite" (p. 934).

   In both "Fusion" and "Cosmopolite," Johnson is proud of her unique family background. In "Fusion," Johnson believes that she is "a new creation" (line 3) and is superior to "any parent portion" (5). She describes her different ancestries as rivers, claiming that within her "The tributary sources / They potently commingle" (8–9). In "Cosmopolite," the theme of Johnson's mixed heritage is still prominent and her pride in it is even more pronounced. Johnson describes herself as "A product of the interplay / Of traveled hearts" (4–5). She also believes that her distinctive background allows her more insight into the race and class struggles of society, which she views as "earth's frail dilemma" (9). Through her experience as a mixed-race woman, Johnson is a "Scion of fused strength" (10).

Cosmopolite (p. 934)

This poem is a powerful self-affirmation, where the speaker recognizes her otherness but embraces it as well. She is "estranged, yet not estranged" (line 6) and sees herself as poised above the more petty aspects of "earth's frail dilemma" (9). She is "All comprehending" (7) and "All understanding" (11), a powerful figure who is self-assured and completely confident. Johnson is speaking here in acceptance of her mixed ancestral background.

POSSIBLE CONNECTION TO ANOTHER SELECTION

Claude McKay, "The Tropics in New York" (text p. 927; question #1, following)

CONNECTION QUESTION IN TEXT (p. 935) WITH ANSWER

1. Compare the speaker's sense of place in "Cosmopolite" and in Claude McKay's "The Tropics in New York" (p. 927).

   In "Cosmopolite," the speaker is not describing a physical place so much as a mental one. There is no literal "estate" (line 8) from which one can "view the earth's frail dilemma" (9); instead, the reader is meant to interpret this as the speaker moving beyond physical place. The narrator is in the unique position of being "Not wholly this or that" (1), and has therefore moved beyond identifying herself with one physical location. The speaker in McKay's poem is torn between two locations, one physical and one mental. Physically, the speaker is located in New York, as the title says, but mentally, he is envisioning the "dewy dawns, and mystical blue skies / In benediction over nun-like hills" (7–8). Though physically in one place, the speaker makes the tropics feel more present than his actual surroundings. The speaker achieves this by vividly describing the paradise he longs for, from the tropical fruit he sees nearby to the "fruit-trees laden by low-singing rills" (6).

I Want to Die While You Love Me (p. 935)

Like "Youth," and "Lost Illusions," this poem is thematically concerned with death. But rather than being ignorant of death, as in "Youth," or trying to escape it, as the speaker in "Lost Illusions" desires to, "I Want to Die While You Love Me" welcomes death. Right away, the speaker tells us she wants to die in the very title. The speaker tells her lover it is better to die "While yet you hold me fair" (line 2) rather than live until "love has nothing more to ask / And nothing more to give" (11–12). Johnson uses words and phrases that could be found in any classic love poem, such as "hold me fair" (2) and "laughter lies upon my lips" (3). Despite the thematic ties to death, the tone of this poem is happiness; the speaker is so in love with her paramour, she can't bear the thought of losing him.

Anne Bradstreet, "To My Dear and Loving Husband" (text p. 956; question #1, following)

CONNECTION QUESTION IN TEXT (p. 935) WITH ANSWER

1. Write an analysis comparing this poem's style and theme with that of "To My Dear and Loving Husband" by Anne Bradstreet (p. 956).

    Stylistically, it is impressive to read Johnson's poem and realize that Bradstreet's was written 250 years before. The diction and rhythms make the two poems feel as though they're from the same era. Both of these pieces have two themes that they tie together: love and death. The speaker in Johnson's poem expresses a desire to preserve the perfection of her love by dying before it has a chance to fade. She would rather die while their love is strong, so she can "bear to that still bed / Your kisses — turbulent, unspent" (lines 6–7). In Johnson's poem, it seems the only hope to preserving such a love is death.

    Anne Bradstreet's "To My Dear and Loving Husband" has a positive twist on the same theme. Bradstreet's speaker is explicitly married to her husband, which means "till death do they part," especially when this piece was written in 1678. Perhaps because of this more concrete commitment, Bradstreet's speaker seems less eager to die than Johnson's. Bradstreet's narrator discusses the love in her marriage, equally crediting herself and her husband, rather than speaking only of what the lover gives her, as in the first poem. The only mention of death is in the last line and has more to do with the way she and her husband live first: "Then while we live, in love let's so persevere / That when we live no more, we may live ever" (11–12). Both speakers see death as a way of preserving the love they possess, but Bradstreet's poem places more emphasis on living fully and accepting death when it comes, rather than seeking it out.

LANGSTON HUGHES

The Negro Speaks of Rivers (p. 938)

Because rivers are clearly the central image in this poem, you might begin discussion of "The Negro Speaks of Rivers" by asking students what ideas they commonly associate with rivers. How do associations such as fertility, life, timelessness, and exploration add to the poem's meaning? Also note that the Euphrates River is one of the rivers that, according to legend, bordered the Garden of Eden. How does this association with the Christian myth of creation add to the poem's meaning? It may be helpful for your students to recognize the geographic locations of these rivers and the fact that they flow in different directions. The Nile and the Congo are African rivers, the Euphrates flows through Turkey and Iraq, and the Mississippi splits the United States. You might ask your students what these diverse locations and directions suggest about the speaker's history.

Another important dimension of this poem is Hughes's use of time. Notice how the speaker stands outside of historical time; the narrative *I* has experienced these times and places over the course of human existence. You might ask students to explore the connection between the timeless narrator and the endurance and timelessness of rivers.

Consider the serious tone of this poem. Ask your students if they think this poem can be interpreted as a celebration. If so, what is the speaker celebrating, and what details contribute to this interpretation? Ask students to consider how the speaker has taken an active role in the history described in the poem ("I bathed..." [line 5], "I built my hut near the Congo..." [6], "I looked upon the Nile and raised the pyramids..." [7], and so on). What do these actions suggest about the history of the "Negro" in the title?

POSSIBLE CONNECTION TO ANOTHER SELECTION

Percy Bysshe Shelley, "Ozymandias," (text p. 1022; question #1, following)

CONNECTION QUESTION IN TEXT (p. 938) **WITH ANSWER**

1.   Compare the meaning of time for this speaker with that for the speaker in Percy Bysshe Shelley's "Ozymandias" (p. 1022).

   For Hughes's narrator, time is not completely linear; the ancient past is not far away and forgotten, but close and important. He speaks of ancient civilizations as though he participated in them directly, as in the line "I bathed in the Euphrates when dawns were young" (line 5). Because of this, the actions of his ancestors take on an immediacy that Shelley's speaker lacks. The speaker in "Ozymandius" is recounting someone else's discovery; he begins his tale by saying, "I met a traveler from an antique land / Who said" (1–2). This traveler describes an ancient, ruined monument he or she stumbled across in the desert. The monument is a ruin, only "Two vast and trunkless legs of stone / Stand in the desert . . . Near them, on the sand, / Half sunk, a shattered visage lies" (2–4). The speaker of "Ozymandius" has no direct connection to any of the events or sights described in the poem, creating an impersonal distance that Hughes' poem lacks.

Jazzonia (p. 939)

   This poem creates both a visual and an aural effect, something like viewing a modernist painting while listening to jazz. On one level the poem serves as a vivid description of a Harlem nightclub in which "Six long-headed jazzers play" (lines 4, 17), but the sense of the poem extends outward with allusions to Eve and Cleopatra and with glimpses of "rivers of the soul" (2, 8, 15).

   The repeated and varied lines about the tree ("silver" in line 1, "singing" in line 7, "shining" in line 14) and the lines about the "rivers of the soul" that follow them are a good way into the poem. What is the relationship between this tree and the rivers of the soul? How do students interpret the tree? What kind of mind might describe a tree as either silver, singing, or shining? The variations within these and other lines in the poem make sense when we consider the title; if you have access to a jazz recording from the 1920s, especially a live recording in which performers allow themselves a good deal of improvisation and variations on a theme, it would be helpful to play it when discussing Hughes's poetry, and especially appropriate when discussing this poem.

   The fourth stanza is likely to provide some difficulties, especially when taken along with the rest of the poem. It stands apart — first because of its odd number of lines but also because its words seem unconnected to the rest of the poem. Point out that these musings about Eve and Cleopatra are initiated in lines 5 and 6 when the speaker describes a "dancing girl." Students may be baffled as to why he would choose such archetypal female figures to describe this dancing girl, but he has, after all, been describing the soul in terms of rivers and trees. Does this poem address universal themes, or is it limited by its setting in a Harlem cabaret?

POSSIBLE CONNECTION TO ANOTHER SELECTION

Claude McKay, "The Harlem Dancer" (text p. 926; question #1, following)

CONNECTION QUESTION IN TEXT (P. 939) WITH ANSWER

1.   Compare in an essay the rhythms of "Jazzonia" and Claude McKay's "The Harlem Dancer" (p. 926).

   Hughes's poem "Jazzonia" features song-like rhythms, emphasized by repetition, punctuation, and end rhymes. The lines, "Oh, silver tree! / Oh, shining rivers of the soul!" (1–2) act as a sort of chorus throughout the poem, breaking up stanzas that act as verses. This is especially appropriate, given the poem's title and subject matter: a jazz club. Hughes's simple rhymes, bold and gold, cabaret and play, add to this musicality. The rhythms in Claude McKay's "The Harlem Dancer" are more traditional to the medium because the poet chose to write in sonnet form.

Lenox Avenue: Midnight (p. 939)

You might begin discussion of this poem by closely examining the first two lines: "The rhythm of life / Is a jazz rhythm." Ask students why jazz and life are so closely connected. Possible responses might include the ideas that jazz, like life, includes solos, improvisations, varied tempos, and melodies that can range from the joyful to the melancholy. Jazz (and life) is unpredictable and often unrehearsed; therein lies much of its beauty and appeal. Ask students to think also about how the word *Honey* (lines 3, 12) functions in several different ways in the poem. For example, *Honey* could be the person the speaker is addressing, or *Honey* could be the sweet heaviness that characterizes both jazz rhythms and life.

You might continue the discussion by asking students why the speaker believes that "The gods are laughing at us" (4, 14). The speaker seems to be describing the vast distance between human and godly experience; gods are so far away, or perhaps are so cruel, that they laugh instead of weep for the pain they see on Lenox Avenue.

Ask students to consider how the setting of this poem — midnight on Lenox Avenue in Harlem — contributes to its meaning. Lenox Avenue is the backdrop for the speaker's (and Hughes's) life — it is the place where his life is "located." Our own Lenox Avenues are the places where we see our own lives, where we see ourselves reflected in our surroundings. You might ask students to explore, in discussion or in a writing assignment, the places that best characterize their own life experiences.

Possible Connections to Other Selections

Stephen Crane, "A Man Said to the Universe" (text p. 673)

Emily Dickinson, "I know that He exists" (text p. 829; question #1, following)

Langston Hughes, "Jazzonia" (text p. 939)

Connections Questions in Text (p. 940) with Answers

1. In an essay compare the theme of this poem with that of Emily Dickinson's "I know that He exists" (p. 829).

   The supreme being in each poem, whether it be God or gods, is distant from humanity and playful at our expense. Hughes's poem implies that the gods are laughing at the way we live our lives. The poem is vital, beginning with "the rhythm of life" (line 1). Dickinson's poem meditates on the relationship between death and life. For her, the game that God plays with us has a deadly serious element that has to do with the relationship between life and the afterlife, a relationship that Hughes does not address specifically.

Ballad of the Landlord (p. 940)

In his poetry Hughes was often concerned with incorporating the rhythms and feeling of blues and jazz. It's not difficult to imagine "Ballad of the Landlord" as a slow blues. Whereas the results of the protagonist's rebellion are anything but unfamiliar, his willingness to fight for what little is his — and the verve with which he speaks of that struggle — affords him a certain nobility even though the landlord undeniably "wins." The poem also shows in derisive terms the idiocy of the landlord's and authorities' overreaction to reasonable and modest concerns about safety (even the landlord's) and comfort.

Ask your students how this poem might be interpreted as political and social commentary. You might point out to them that the tenant is not jailed for his legitimate complaints about the condition of his home but because the landlord unfairly accuses him of being a political radical. As a background for this poem, you might discuss with your students the influence of Senator Joseph McCarthy's anticommunist initiatives in 1950s America and how this poem reflects the rampant political paranoia of that era. Students might also consider manifestations today of a social system that tends to victimize the powerless and defend the privileged.

125th Street (p. 941)

In this celebration of blackness, Hughes sets up three similes to describe the beauty of the people he sees on 125th Street. You might ask your students if the similes at first seem silly: a "chocolate bar" (line 1), a "jack-o'-lantern" (3), and a "slice of melon" (5) may not be entirely flattering comparisons for a human face. In each couplet, however, Hughes turns the quotidian object into a lovely figure, suggesting sweetness, incandescence, and joy. His descriptions of fellow Harlemites don't just capture their physical beauty; they imply a spiritual understanding as well.

POSSIBLE CONNECTION TO ANOTHER SELECTION

Claude McKay, "The Tropics in New York" (text p. 927; question #1, following)

CONNECTION QUESTION IN TEXT (p. 941) WITH ANSWER

1. Discuss the speaker's attitude toward the city in "125th Street" and in Claude McKay's "The Tropics in New York" (p. 927).

   In "125th Street," the speaker describes the street as a face. This may refer to the geography of the street itself or the facades of the individual buildings. He never addresses the city directly as it is, instead only talking about it through metaphors. The speaker calls the city "a chocolate bar" (line 1), "a jack-o'-lantern" (3), and a "melon" (5). These common items have positive associations for most people, especially the festive jack-o'-lantern, so although the speaker never explicitly states his view on the city, it seems positive. Similarly, McKay's speaker never describes New York City; instead, he sees a tropical paradise. Unlike Hughes's speaker, this narrator is not associating the city with the "dewy dawns, and mystical blue skies" (7) he's imagining. Instead, when his fantasy leaves him and he is confronted with the reality of New York, he feels despondent, saying, "I turned aside and bowed my head and wept" (12).

Harlem (p. 941)

Discussion of this poem might be couched in an exploration of how your students define "the American Dream." You might ask your class to compile a list of their associations with the American Dream. Their responses might include education, financial security, hopeful prospects for their children, social status, respect, justice, and so on. You might then ask your students how people might be affected if they found their "dreams" to be unattainable for social, political, economic, or racial reasons. This discussion leads into a consideration of the poetic similes that Hughes uses to describe the results of the dreams themselves when they are "deferred" (line 1).

Ask your students to examine the words that Hughes uses to describe the possible results of "a dream deferred." Words such as *dry up* (2), *fester* (4), *stink* (6), *crust and sugar over* (7), and *sag* (9) offer very diverse images of decay and deterioration. Ask them if they recognize any sort of progression in these images — from the raisin that dries up fairly harmlessly to a sore that causes pain to an individual to rotten meat and sweets gone bad, which can poison several individuals, to a heavy load that can burden many. The final alternative that Hughes offers is that a deferred dream might "explode" (11). Ask students how this final possibility is different from the previous ones and how this violent image of explosion might be related to the social and political realities in the United States at the time Hughes wrote this poem. Although this poem predates the civil rights movement, the 1950s were a time of great social upheaval and tense race relations in America. You might ask your students whether or not this poem could be interpreted as a threat to white Americans who contribute to "deferring" the dreams of minority Americans.

POSSIBLE CONNECTION TO ANOTHER SELECTION

James Merrill, "Casual Wear" (text p. 682; question #1, following)

1. Write an essay on the themes of "Harlem" and of James Merrill's "Casual Wear" (p. 682).

    The theme of "Casual Wear" is that the lives of strangers can intersect randomly and result in tragedy. The theme of "Harlem" also ends in tragedy, but it is not so specific or individualized. It is the direct result of a "dream deferred," whereas the terrorist in Merrill's poem is not necessarily a disillusioned dreamer, although he may be disillusioned in general.

COUNTEE CULLEN

Yet Do I Marvel (p. 944)

This speaker addresses some age-old questions about the mystery of God's works, but concludes the poem by adding his own situation as a black poet to this list of mysteries. The allusions to Tantalus and Sisyphus aren't accidental; Tantalus represents a dream just out of reach and Sisyphus represents eternal struggle. Both of these situations are relevant to the black poet of 1925, and relevant to larger questions of God's goodness. It is interesting to note that, whereas the speaker addresses God, the examples by which he questions God's benevolence stem from the "pagan" classical mythology, mirroring, perhaps, the alienation the speaker feels.

Students have to fill in quite a bit here, though; the situation of the black poet might be difficult, but why is his situation mysterious, or as the title and the penultimate line suggest, marvelous? What is the relationship between God and the speaker? Is this God indifferent, capricious, omniscient, cruel, or all of the above?

POSSIBLE CONNECTIONS TO OTHER SELECTIONS

Countee Cullen, "To Certain Critics" (text p. 947)
——, "From the Dark Tower" (text p. 946)
Emily Dickinson, "Apparently with no surprise" (text p. 830)
Robert Frost, "Design" (text p. 856)
Gerard Manley Hopkins, "God's Grandeur" (text p. 702)

Incident (p. 944)

Ask students to consider how one incident can affect one's perception of a period in one's life. Let this discussion lead to a broader conversation about what spark leads to a poem—if we consider this poem to be autobiographical, which it may or may not be, it reveals to us the kernel from which Cullen's poem grows. Consider the impact of such an event on an eight-year-old child. The speaker says, "I saw the whole of Baltimore/From May until December;/Of all the things that happened there/That's all that I remember" (lines 9–12). Discuss how a memory such as this lasted a lifetime and beyond.

POSSIBLE CONNECTIONS TO OTHER SELECTIONS

Elizabeth Bishop, "Manners" (text p. 582)
Countee Cullen, "Tableau" (text p. 945)
Claude McKay, "Outcast" (text p. 929; question #1, following)
Marilyn Nelson, "How I Discovered Poetry" (text p. 595)

CONNECTION QUESTION IN TEXT (p. 945) WITH ANSWER

1. Compare the themes in "Incident" and in Claude McKay's "Outcast" (text p. 929).

    The themes in these two poems are very much the same; in both, the speaker is the "other" or outcast. The big difference is in presentation. The rhymes of "Incident" give it a lighter, childlike quality (belied by the message within it). "Outcast," a sonnet, also uses rhyme and meter, but they give the poem a weighty feel that matches the more formal diction ("my soul," "alien gods," "among the sons of earth, a thing apart," "white man's menace").

For a Lady I Know (p. 945)

This satirical portrait of whites is brief and to the point. How does the setting of the poem (heaven) infuse the poem with humor? Pay attention to diction. Why is *snores* a funny word here? What does it add to the portrait? Consider the pairing and alliteration of "black cherubs" and "celestial chores," which add to the overall humor of the piece.

POSSIBLE CONNECTION TO ANOTHER SELECTION

Countee Cullen, "Incident" (text p. 944; question #1, following)

CONNECTION QUESTION IN TEXT (p. 945) WITH ANSWER

1. Compare the tone in "For a Lady I Know" with that in "Incident" (text p. 945).

   There is a lightness of tone, largely created by the forms Cullen is working in (the particular meters and rhymes), that belies the overarching message of these poems. That contradiction is important and adds force to the impression left on the reader.

Tableau (p. 945)

This poem was written in 1925. How did it signal the events that were to come with the civil rights movement? In discussion, look closely at the changes that had already occurred for African Americans by 1925. Where does this poem leap ahead of its time (and in fact present "lightning brilliant as a sword" in its subject matter)? Cullen refers to the "dark folk" peering "from lowered blinds," and "fair folks" who "talk, / Indignant." Discuss the issues both whites and blacks have that provoke such reactions when they see these two boys.

POSSIBLE CONNECTIONS TO OTHER SELECTIONS

Countee Cullen, "Incident" (text p. 944)

Claude McKay, "The Lynching" (text p. 928; question #1, following)

CONNECTION QUESTION IN TEXT (p. 946) WITH ANSWER

1. Consider "Tableau" alongside McKay's "The Lynching" (text p. 928). How might the two poems speak to each other socially and politically?

   "Tableau" and "The Lynching" both condemn whites' assumed superiority and treatment of blacks in the United States. Both look forward to a day when such treatment and segregation is not perpetuated and the wrongs perpetrated would be seen for what they were. They may not have foreseen the day of Martin Luther King Jr.'s speech, when the friendship of black children and white children would be announced as a "dream," but they spoke out against the status quo and suggested a new way of living together.

From the Dark Tower (p. 946)

Look at the sestet of this poem while keeping Hughes's "Harlem" in mind. Both men choose metaphors of natural processes of growth and decay to express the state of the black man, aware of his "dream[s] deferred" (Hughes) and white injustice. Consider the "explosion" waiting in Cullen's poem in the lines "So in the dark we hide the heart that bleeds, / And wait, and tend our agonizing seeds" (lines 13–14). The imagery of natural growth offers hope to the reader that something will come forth from these seeds. There is also the suggestion that with the white "light" (12) on them, some seeds will always lie dormant, "crumple, piteous, and fall" (12). Knowing Cullen carefully selected the rhymes "bleeds" and "seeds," ask students if they think he also wanted to suggest the echo of "needs." Consider the end words of the lines and speculate on what other words they suggest.

POSSIBLE CONNECTIONS TO OTHER SELECTIONS

Countee Cullen, "Yet Do I Marvel" (text p. 944)

——, "Tableau" (text p. 945)

Langston Hughes, "Harlem" (text p. 941)

——, "125th Street" (text p. 941)

——, "Ballad of the Landlord" (text p. 940; question #1, following)

Claude McKay, "If We Must Die" (text p. 927)

——, Outcast" (text p. 929)

CONNECTION QUESTION IN TEXT (p. 946) WITH ANSWER

1. Compare how issues of social justice are depicted thematically and tonally in "From the Dark Tower" and in Langston Hughes's "Ballad of the Landlord" (text p. 940).

   Consider first the common expression "ivory tower" and all it connotes. Cullen's "From the Dark Tower" alludes to injustices of the time, beginning with the idea of a *we* who plants while others reap. The ideas in Cullen's poem reach beyond his time, which held injustice enough, and into that of slavery. Both poems draw attention to the unequal state that exists between whites and blacks. Hughes looks at a contemporary situation in which the white landlord refuses to care for the black tenant's property. When the tenant complains (and threatens), the landlord calls the police and the message extends to the whites' fears about the blacks ("He's trying to ruin the government / And overturn the land!" [lines 23–24]). He points to the final insult in the last lines — the black man is incarcerated (no mention of the landlord's slums).

To Certain Critics (p. 947)

Identifying the audience is an important part of understanding this poem. The lines "No racial option narrows grief, / Pain is no patriot, / And sorrow plaits her dismal leaf / For all as lief as not" (lines 9–12), indicate that the speaker should not be bounded in his subject matter, since emotion is not bounded by race. While he doesn't mention his audience or the question of race explicitly, he refers to the "clan" (6), and says he won't "confine [his] singing to its ways / beyond the ways of man" (7–8) which is an allusion to Cullen's earlier "Yet Do I Marvel." Does the speaker argue his position convincingly? How do students respond to his rhetorical question: "How shall the shepherd heart then thrill / To only the darker lamb" (15–16)?

POSSIBLE CONNECTIONS TO OTHER SELECTIONS

Countee Cullen, "From the Dark Tower" (text p. 946)

——, "Yet Do I Marvel" (text p. 944; question #1, following)

Langston Hughes, "Harlem" (text p. 941)

Claude McKay, "If We Must Die" (text p. 927)

Marilyn Nelson, "How I Discovered Poetry" (text p. 595)

CONNECTION QUESTION IN TEXT (p. 947) WITH ANSWER

1. Compare Cullen's attitudes toward writing in "To Certain Critics" and in "Yet Do I Marvel" (text p. 944).

   In "Yet Do I Marvel," Cullen specifically addresses the plight of the African American writer in the lines "Yet do I marvel at this curious thing: / To make a poet black, and bid him sing!" (lines 13–14). Students should consider, given this statement, what Cullen thinks his mission is as a writer, whether he feels he must take on subjects explicitly involving his race or not. In "To Certain Critics," Cullen dismisses the need to become only the spokesperson for his race. Cullen, who also wrote the poem "Tableau," which pictures a white child and a black child walking together, may wish to focus on inclusiveness in his work, instead of excluding a white reader by claiming universal emotions ("grief," "pain," "sorrow") as strictly the provenance of the black man.

PERSPECTIVES

KAREN JACKSON FORD, *Hughes's Aesthetics of Simplicity* (p. 947)

Ford argues for a reevaluation of Langston Hughes's poetry by rejecting the notion that complexity is the most important marker of poetic merit. She proposes that Hughes draws his "aesthetics of simplicity" from the materials of African American folk art. After your students have read this excerpt, you might have them discuss where exactly they see "simplicity" in the preceding poems by Hughes. Is it in the structure of the poems, the diction, or the themes? If a critic says a poem is simple, does that mean that it is missing something? If so, what might be missing in Hughes's work? For a comparison, you could bring in poems like William Blake's "The Lamb" (p. 731) and "The Tyger," (p. 731) which might also be described using the derogatory adjectives Ford lists.

DAVID CHINITZ, *The Romanticization of Africa in the 1920s* (p. 948)

Students may find this passage tough going, but it is worthwhile to spend some time reading it closely. Part of the difficulty may come from the discourse (words like *atavism*), part from their potential lack of understanding of the historical context for such a discussion. It is important that students understand not only the tenets of primitivism but also Chinitz's take on this development (he refers to "clichés" at one point, indicating that he thinks this primitivist strain is a little hokey). Is there any such romanticization of African culture today? If not, do students find post–World War I disillusionment to be a valid explanation of why this romanticization took place in the 1920s?

Many of Hughes's poems from the 1920s can be productively examined through Chinitz's lens. As far as some later poems that show Hughes rejecting this mind-set, "Harlem" and "Ballad of the Landlord" work well.

ALAIN LOCKE, *Review of Georgia Douglas Johnson's* **Bronze: A Book of Verse** (p. 949)

In this short review, Alain Locke, a contemporary of Georgia Douglas Johnson, discusses his opinion of her poetry. Locke mainly praises Johnson's work, saying she "often distills the trite and commonplace into an elixir." While he seems to enjoy her work, Locke emphasizes that Johnson's poetry walks a fine line and that "she succeeds because by sincerity and condensation, her poetry escapes to a large extent its own limitations." Locke specifically points out Johnson's ability to avoid being "preachy and prosaic," though he denies that this is intentional. Instead, he believes that her avoidance of "propaganda" is "more by instinct than by calculation." Students might find this to be an enlightening opinion; it may help them understand some of the virtues of Johnson's poetry as a whole more clearly. Others may take issue with Locke's dismissal of the idea that Johnson could have avoided the "double pitfall" of sentimentality and propaganda by design. You may want to ask students to keep the time period in mind while thinking about this review. Locke and Johnson were both African American, but being a woman and a writer was still a contentious lifestyle at the time. Locke does say, however, that Johnson's poems proclaim, "May the saving grace of the mother-heart save humanity." This is certainly meant as praise, but students may want to further examine this phrase, especially the idea of Johnson's poetic voice being that of "the mother-heart."

COUNTEE CULLEN, *On Racial Poetry* (p. 950)

After reading this excerpt, ask students to respond to Cullen's critique of Hughes's jazz poems. Specifically, have them entertain the idea that they are "interlopers in the company of the truly beautiful poems" and discuss why they are singled out by Cullen. Hughes himself might not exactly quarrel with this idea, since his work grew out of black culture and broke from European poetic tradition, although he might consider himself more of a groundbreaker than an interloper. Until Hughes, American poetry informed itself from overwhelmingly white writers and white themes. While Cullen doesn't deny the great power of Hughes's poems and praises their power, he argues with their reliance on "strictly Negro themes." Are students surprised by his statement, since Cullen, an African American writer of the Harlem Renaissance, was also greatly influenced by Hughes's work? Ask your students to look at examples of Cullen's and Hughes's work and consider where Cullen's poems have absorbed something from Hughes. Which of Cullen's poems are quieter, tamer, or would be regarded as more European?

CONSIDERATIONS FOR CRITICAL THINKING AND WRITING (p. 951)

1. In Cullen's review of *The Weary Blues*, what is his "quarrel" (para. 1) with Hughes?

   His quarrel is with the use of "strictly Negro themes" instead of what Cullen feels poetry should be preoccupied with — subjects that transcend race and are more "traditionally poetic."

2. Given the tenor of Hughes's comments on racial pride in the excerpt from "The Negro Artist and the Racial Mountain," (text p. 921), what do you think his response to Cullen would be?

   In "The Negro Artist and the Racial Mountain," Hughes states that "we younger Negro artists who create now intend to express our individual dark-skinned selves without fear or shame." He also says "if colored people are not" happy about such creations, "their displeasure doesn't matter either." He might not be concerned with Cullen's view of his work. His response would be that the importance his work and role as a trailblazer for other artists of his race far transcends Cullen's opinion of his subject matter.

3. Explain why you agree or disagree with Cullen's view that Hughes's poems are "one-sided" (para. 4).

   Students may agree with the limitations Hughes's subject matter imposes on his work. After all, he has committed to writing about one particular experience. But students may say that Hughes's poetry broke the limitation American poetry had placed on itself by not exploring that side (the black experience) of itself.

4. Do you think Cullen's argument is dated, or is it relevant to today's social climate?

   Cullen's argument is not dated as long as racism exists, and as long as races perceive one another as Other. The issue of race still exists in today's social climate, and all races write not only of their personal experience, but also of their experience of other races — a perspective that can enhance the poetry of black writers, white writers, and writers of all races that make up America.

ONWUCHEKWA JEMIE, *On Universal Poetry* (p. 951)

When discussing Jemie, examine the Hughes quotation included early on. By using it in the essay, Jemie gives him a voice, allowing him his own statement about the "universality" of black experience and black poetry. Hughes asks, "Could you possibly be afraid that the rest of the world will not accept" particulars of black life, use of black themes, in poetry? Ask if your students feel that poems have to follow a particular pattern or shy away from particular subjects in order to be recognized as having value. In that discussion, explore the value, separate from how it calls attention to a particular (black) experience, of Hughes's work. What universal, or human, issues do his poems exemplify? Do students believe that "the long-standing myth of white superiority and black inferiority" that Jemie refers to has clouded our ideas of what makes up "human" experience—and how that experience gets expressed in art?

CONSIDERATIONS FOR CRITICAL THINKING AND WRITING

1. How does Jemie go beyond Hughes's own argument to make a case for the universality of poetry about black experience?

   Jemie goes on to say that the issues Hughes writes about are still relevant today. Jemie points out that a concept of universality is not specific to white and Western experience, and that the fundamental issues of life and death that every human experiences and every poet writes about are felt and faced regardless of particulars of race.

2. How might Jemie's argument be extended to other minority groups or to women?

   Any nondominant writer could use Jemie's argument to claim the universality of his/her experience. Jemie argues against the appropriation of experience by any one group claiming superiority over another. She notes the variety of experience, saying, "The multiplicity of nations and cultures in the world make it inevitable that the details and particulars of human experience will vary according to time, place, and circumstance."

3. Do you think that Jemie's or Cullen's argument is more persuasive? Explain your answer.

   Jemie is much more specific than Cullen, in some respects. Cullen speaks vaguely of poetic tradition and high literary expression as somehow antithetical to poetry dealing with racial themes, but Jemie is clear that all poetry, written by black and white alike, deals with "the circumstances attending birth, growth, decline, and death, the emotions of joy and grief, love and hate, fear and guilt, anger and pain."

ADDITIONAL RESOURCES FOR TEACHING MCKAY

Cooper, Wayne F. *Claude McKay: Rebel Sojourner in the Harlem Renaissance: A Biography.* New York: Schocken Books, 1990. Print.

Egar, Emmanuel E. *The Poetics of Rage: Wole Soyinka, Jean Toomer, and Claude McKay.* Lanham: University Press of America, 2005. Print.

Giles, James R. *Claude McKay.* Boston: Twayne, 1976. Print.

Gosciak, Josh. *The Shadowed Country: Claude McKay and the Romance of the Victorians.* New Brunswick: Rutgers University Press, 2006. Print.

Holcomb, Gary E. *Claude McKay, Code Name Sasha: Queer Black Marxism and the Harlem Renaissance.* University Press of Florida, 2007. Print.

James, Jennifer C. *A Freedom Bought with Blood: African American War Literature from the Civil War to World War II.* Chapel Hill: University of North Carolina Press, 2007. Print.

Maxwell, William J., ed. *Complete Poems: Claude McKay.* Urbana: University of Illinois Press, 2004. Print.

McKay, Claude. *The Selected Poems of Claude McKay.* New York: Harcourt, 1953. Print.

Stephens, Michelle A. *Black Empire: The Masculine Global Imaginary of Caribbean Intellectuals in the United States, 1914–1962.* Durham: Duke University Press, 2005. Print.

Tillery, Tyrone. *Claude McKay: A Black Poet's Struggle for Identity.* Amherst: University of Massachusetts Press, 1992. Print.

ADDITIONAL RESOURCES FOR TEACHING JOHNSON

Bassett, John Earl. *Harlem in Review: Critical Reactions to Black American Writers, 1917–1939.* Cranbury, New Jersey: Associated University Presses, Inc., 1992. Print.

Bower, Martha Gillman. *Color Struck Under the Gaze: Ethnicity and the Pathology of Being in the Plays of Johnson, Hurston, Childress, Hasberry, and Kennedy.* Westport, CT: Praeger, 2003. Print.

Brown-Guillory, Elizabeth, ed. *Wines in the Wilderness: Plays by African American Women from the Harlem Renaissance to the Present.* New York: Praeger, 1990. Print.

Erlene Stetson, ed. *Black Sister: Poetry by Black American Women, 1746–1980.* Bloomington: Indiana University Press, 1981. Print.

Honey, Maureen. *Shadowed Dreams: Women's Poetry of the Harlem Renaissance.* New York: Rutgers, 1989. Print.

Hull, Gloria T. *Color, Sex & Poetry: Three Women Writers of the Harlem Renaissance.* Bloomington: Indiana University Press, 1987. Print.

Johnson, James Weldon. *The Book of American Negro Poetry.* New York: Harcourt, Brace and Company, 1922. Print.

Tate, Claudia. *Selected Works of Georgia Douglas Johnson.* New York: G.K. Hall & Co., 1997. Print.

Tolson, Melvin B. *The Harlem Group of Negro Writers.* Westport, CT: Greenwood Press, 2001. Print.

Wall, Cheryl A. *Women of the Harlem Renaissance.* Bloomington: Indiana University Press, 1995. Print.

ADDITIONAL RESOURCES FOR TEACHING HUGHES

SELECTED BIBLIOGRAPHY

Bloom, Harold. *Langston Hughes.* New York: Chelsea, 1988. Print.

Bonner, Pat E. *Sassy Jazz and Slo' Draggin' Blues: Music in the Poetry of Langston Hughes.* New York: Lang, 1992. Print.

Emanuel, James A. *Langston Hughes.* New York: Twayne, 1967. Print.

Gates, Henry Louis, Jr., ed. *Langston Hughes: Critical Perspectives Past and Present.* New York: Penguin USA, 1993. Print.

Hughes, Langston. *The Collected Poetry of Langston Hughes.* Ed. Arnold Rampersad. New York: Knopf, 1994. Print.

Jemie, Onwuchekwa. *Langston Hughes: An Introduction to the Poetry.* New York: Columbia UP, 1976. Print.

Miller, R. Baxter. *The Art and Imagination of Langston Hughes.* Lexington: University Press of Kentucky, 1989. Print.

Mullen, Edward J., ed. *Critical Essays on Langston Hughes.* Boston: Hall, 1986. Print.

O'Daniel, Therman B., ed. *Langston Hughes, Black Genius: A Critical Evaluation.* New York: Morrow, 1971. Print.

Rampersad, Arnold. *The Life of Langston Hughes.* 2 vols. New York: Oxford UP, 1986–88. Print.

Tracy, Steven C. *Langston Hughes and the Blues.* Urbana: U of Illinois P, 1988. Print.

ADDITIONAL RESOURCES FOR TEACHING CULLEN

Bernard, Patrick S. "Teaching Countee Cullen's Poetry." *Teaching the Harlem Renaissance: Course Design and Classroom Strategies.* Ed. Michael Soto. New York: Peter Lang, 2008. Print.

Cullen, Countee. *On These I Stand: An Anthology of the Best Poems of Countee Cullen.* New York: Harper, 1947. Print.

Early, Gerald., ed. *My Soul's High Song: The Collected Writings of Countee Cullen, Voice of the Harlem Renaissance.* New York: Doubleday, 1991. Print.

James, Winston. *A Fierce Hatred of Injustice: Claude McKay's Jamaica and His Poetry of Rebellion.* London: Verso, 2001. Print.

Shucard, Alan R. *Countee Cullen.* Boston: Twayne, 1984. Print.

Smethurst, James. "Lyric Stars: Countee Cullen and Langston Hughes." *The Cambridge Companion to the Harlem Renaissance.* Ed. George Hutchinson. Cambridge, England: Cambridge University Press, 2007. Print.

35

A Thematic Case Study:
Love and Longing

Students of poetry are usually good at brainstorming. When they get past whatever initial fear of poetry they've had, they often excel at making observations about the poem and connections between those observations. But once they've done this, they need to use their observations and connections to address the poem's central theme. The questions in Chapters 35–38, which follow the poems in the five thematic case studies, encourage students to focus on theme and to back up their statements about theme with specific evidence. These questions should be useful to students who need to make the jump from analyzing specifics to understanding the whole. The questions, however, might also have a reverse application. Sometimes, when discussing themes, students can get a little too abstract. These questions encourage students to ground their abstractions in specifics.

You might decide to use the questions during class time. Try having students spend a few minutes jotting down their responses to the questions about a given poem. Then have them read their responses to the class. In the discussion that follows, try isolating their thematic observations from the more formal observations. Then try integrating the two in a way that would suggest the kind of movement between abstractions and specifics that you'd like to see in a cogent paper. You could even ask students to write their own creative response to the issues of the poem (see question 3 for "The Passionate Shepherd to His Love"). By sparking their interest in the theme, this exercise should get students to relate the poem to the world they inhabit.

Web Ask students to research the poets in this chapter at **bedfordstmartins.com/meyerlit**.

The questions should also help students prepare to write essays on a given poem. You might want to choose specific questions for a paper assignment. Or you might ask students to write a paper that addresses two questions of their choosing. Try making connections between the way you've discussed theme in class and the way you'd like to see your students do it in a paper. Class discussion can be a good primer for essay writing.

CHRISTOPHER MARLOWE, *The Passionate Shepherd to His Love* (p. 954)

Marlowe was the first English dramatist to use blank verse in his plays. He completed a master of arts at Cambridge in 1587 and was stabbed to death six years later, having lived an eventful, though somewhat mysterious, life.

Anyone with an ounce of romance will respond favorably to this pastoral lyric, whose speaker pledges to do the impossible (yet how inviting to entertain the vision in line 10 of "a thousand fragrant posies" on demand!) if only his beloved will be his love. What lovers have not believed, for a time at least, that they could "all the pleasures prove" (2) — that all the pleasure the world offered was there for the taking?

It's significant, of course, that his song is sung in May, the month when spring takes firm hold (in England, at least) and when the end of winter was (and still is) celebrated with great exuberance.

Andrew Marvell, "To His Coy Mistress" (text p. 601; question #1, following)

William Shakespeare, "Not marble, nor the gilded monuments" (text p. 955)

CONNECTION QUESTION IN TEXT (p. 955) WITH ANSWER

1. Compare the speaker's tone in Marlowe's poem and in Andrew Marvell's "To His Coy Mistress" (p. 601).

   Both of these poems are highly romantic, with one lover speaking to another. In Christopher Marlowe's "The Passionate Shepherd to His Love," the speaker is beseeching his beloved to accept him. He uses a combination of pleading and promises, saying, "Come live with me and be my love, / And we will all the pleasure prove" (1–2). His tone is gentle and sweet as he tells the object of his affection of all the things he will do for them. The tone in Andrew Marvell's "To His Coy Mistress" features much more urgency. Marvell focuses on the passage of time, and his images are of opportunities for love lost. For instance, the speaker says, "But at my back I always hear / Time's winged chariot hurrying near;" (21–22). He describes the consequences of being coy and putting off their romance in increasingly grotesque terms, such as, "then worms shall try / That long preserved virginity, / And your quaint honor turn to dust, / And into ashes all my lust" (27–30). The tone of the poem goes from gentle chiding and teasing to more pressuring, whereas Marlowe's shepherd remains romantic and mild.

WILLIAM SHAKESPEARE, *Not marble, nor the gilded monuments* (p. 955)

The central point of this poem — that poetry, more than any monument, possesses the power to immortalize its subject — was a common one in the Petrarchan love sonnets of Shakespeare's day. This same conceit appears in Shakespeare's "Shall I compare thee to a summer's day?" (text p. 743). Have students find conventional images of permanence in the poem. With what destructive forces are these images juxtaposed? Even marble, the most durable of building materials, becomes "unswept stone" when it is "besmeared with sluttish time" (line 4), the most destructive force of all. Yet according to the poet, his lover will live until judgment day in "this powerful rhyme" (2). How do your students respond to this conceit? Can a poem immortalize a person? Do poems last forever? Can students suggest other things that might last longer, other ways of achieving immortality?

Christopher Marlowe, "The Passionate Shepherd to His Love" (text p. 954; question #2, following)

Andrew Marvell, "To His Coy Mistress" (text p. 601; question #1, following)

CONNECTIONS QUESTIONS IN TEXT (p. 955) WITH ANSWERS

1. Compare the theme of this poem with that of Andrew Marvell's "To His Coy Mistress" (p. 601), paying particular attention to the speakers' beliefs about how time affects love.

   While both poets acknowledge the eternal worth of the beloved, Marvell uses "Deserts of vast eternity" (line 24) to convince her to "sport us while we may" (37). Shakespeare's pledges do not have such obvious ulterior motives.

2. Discuss whether you find this love poem more or less appealing than Christopher Marlowe's "The Passionate Shepherd to His Love" (p. 954). As you make this comparison, consider what the criteria for an appealing love poem should be.

   Students will have to choose between the lush detail of Marlowe's shepherd's ephemeral "ivy buds" (line 17) or Shakespeare's speaker's confident pledge that the beloved shall be praised "in the eyes of all posterity" (11). Both have their charms.

ANNE BRADSTREET, *To My Dear and Loving Husband* (p. 956)

Anne Bradstreet, Anglo-America's first female poet, is noted for her Puritan devotion, her belief that all worldly delights are meaningless when placed in the context of the afterlife. Yet there is an ambiguous strain within her poetry that complicates this position; she is human, and thus drawn to worldly things. Note how she describes not only love but heaven in terms of material wealth. With this ambiguity in mind, ask students to assess whether Bradstreet's devotion is directed more toward her husband here on earth or toward the eternal rewards of heaven. The final two lines are themselves ambiguous; she does indicate that she believes in eternal life, but she also declares that at some point she and her husband will "live no more" (line 12). You might also point out that the final two lines compose the only part of the poem not written in heroic couplets (they are eleven syllables each), a fact that adds to their ambiguity. Students might also enjoy discussing the tone of the poem as a dedication to one's husband: Does the speaker seem warm? Rational? Self-absorbed or self-effacing?

POSSIBLE CONNECTIONS TO OTHER SELECTIONS

Anne Bradstreet, "Before the Birth of One of Her Children" (text p. 1002; question #1, following)

Sharon Olds, "Last Night" (text p. 604)

CONNECTION QUESTION IN TEXT (p. 957) WITH ANSWER

1. How does the theme of this poem compare with that of Bradstreet's "Before the Birth of One of Her Children" (p. 1002)? Explain why you find the poems consistent or contradictory.

   "To My Dear and Loving Husband" closes with the hope that "we may live ever" (line 12); "Before the Birth of One of Her Children" concedes, in the first line, "All things within this fading world hath end" (1). Students may find the fear of death contradictory to the faith in eternal life, or they may see both as different facets of a very human and vivid love.

ELIZABETH BARRETT BROWNING, *How Do I Love Thee? Let Me Count the Ways* (p. 957)

The wide scope and specific reach of this poem's depiction of love remains, for many readers, timeless. The extremes of the speaker's devotion, the confident tone established by the simple declarative sentences, and the employment of human nature and the speaker's own "childhood's faith" (line 10) and "lost saints" (12) establish a familiar fulfillment. While the poem acknowledges God's power, it establishes a hierarchy in which love retains the superlative position until the penultimate line, when God is invoked only to permit the love to extend "after death" (14).

POSSIBLE CONNECTIONS TO OTHER SELECTIONS

Christina Georgina Rossetti, "Promises like Pie-Crust" (text p. 1020; question #1, following)

William Shakespeare, "Not marble, nor the gilded monuments" (text p. 955)

CONNECTION QUESTION IN TEXT (p. 958) WITH ANSWER

1. Compare and contrast the images, tone, and theme of this poem with those of Christina Rossetti's "Promises Like Pie-Crust" (p. 1020). Explain why you find one poem more promising than the other.

   Students will have different preferences here: Rossetti's poem provides an open-eyed account of the possibilities of love's disappointment that will strike some readers as honest and accurate, while Browning's presents a heartfelt, earnest declaration of undying love that may be convincing for others. Browning's speaker focuses on the thorough penetration of the "breath, / Smiles, tears" (lines 12–13) attained by the beloved, using an earnest tone and a wide array of comparisons. Rossetti uses a matter-of-fact tone, while she acknowledges previous relationships, scrutinizes her current love and its possibilities, and then chooses "frugal fare" (23). Browning declares her love with the extravagance of "all my life" (13) and proposes to continue "after death" (14).

EDNA ST. VINCENT MILLAY, *Recuerdo* (p. 958)

"Recuerdo" celebrates the joys of youthful romance. The lilting rhythm of its thrice-repeated couplet ("We were very tired, we were very merry — / We had gone back and forth all night on the ferry") establishes and reinforces the couple's childish glee at the silliness and pointlessness of their evening's entertainment. After a night of riding the boat (presumably the Staten Island Ferry) and living in the moment far away from the cares of the city, the exhausted youth consider returning to reality but reject the idea, buying a newspaper but not reading it. Their idyllic escape from the city ends with a potentially sobering encounter with a street woman, but in their exhilaration and exhaustion they either fail or refuse to let the reality of her situation bring them down: they simply give her their food and money and go on their way.

The adventure narrated in "Recuerdo" will almost certainly resonate with your students. Most every high school student has experienced a long night of pointless (even bohemian) entertainment similar in spirit to Millay's, although probably not with the sense of beauty and transcendence that she records. Encourage your students to share stories of their own adventures; as a writing assignment, you might ask them to attempt to describe them in Millay's style.

POSSIBLE CONNECTION TO ANOTHER SELECTION

Emily Dickinson, "Wild Nights — Wild Nights!" (text p. 809)

EDNA ST. VINCENT MILLAY, *I, Being Born a Woman and Distressed* (p. 959)

The humor of this poem is present in the contrast between tone and content; the formal tone belies the harsh sentiments it conveys. The speaker admits that she desires "your person" (line 4) but wants to make clear that this physical desire is "the poor treason / of my stout blood against my staggering brain" (9–10). The "treason" will be overridden once the body has its desires met; the sexual "frenzy" (13) initiated by "needs and notions" (2) and the "propinquity" (3) of "you" does not signify the beginning of a romance. On the contrary, the speaker wants to "make it plain" (12) that she doesn't plan to speak to the object of her desires once those desires have been met.

Students may initially resist the stuffy tone here, especially if they need to turn to the dictionary to look up "propinquity" (3). However, salacious detail can often encourage even reluctant readers to scan a page more thoroughly. Focusing on the cool and cutting remarks hidden in the heightened language of this poem could help students with more challenging work.

POSSIBLE CONNECTIONS TO OTHER SELECTIONS

Elizabeth Barrett Browning, "How Do I Love Thee? Let Me Count the Ways" (text p. 957)

Edna St. Vincent Millay, "Recuerdo" (text p. 958; question #1, following)

CONNECTION QUESTION IN TEXT (p. 959) WITH ANSWER

1. Discuss Millay's treatment of romantic love in this poem and in "Recuerdo" (text p. 958). What do you think a feminist critic would make of these two poems

coming from the same poet (read the section on Feminist Criticism in Chapter 48, "Critical Strategies for Reading," [p. 1477])?

Millay's two poems show, perhaps, different points in the life of a love. "Recuerdo" illustrates the giddiness and pleasure of first love, while "I, Being Born a Woman and Distressed" looks back at the pull of desire and the rejection of love, despite the "frenzy" one feels. "Recuerdo" points to the generosity spawned by love, while "Distressed" ends with a retreat into the self.

JOAN MURRAY, *Play-by-Play* (p. 959)

This series of hypothetical questions makes us consider the effect of older women gazing at and admiring the bodies of young men. One way to begin discussion is to try to answer each of the questions, read exactly as it is written, as a way to determine the speaker's intent in raising the questions. That is, are there implicit answers to the questions? It is a very different thing to ask "I wonder how men would react if they knew that women occasionally scrutinized their bodies" than it is to phrase the questions as the speaker of this poem does, in careful detail with a definite setting. Consider the word "caress" (line 16). If discussion strays too far into general questions of the effect of the female gaze, you might need to bring students back to the specific nature of this poem. It is all about perception, as the final lines make clear. One possible assignment is to have students write a poem from the perspective of these young men — either how they see themselves or how they see the women who are gazing at them. Try to encourage students to recognize the fine line between appreciation of beauty and sexual desire in this poem; how might the poem be different if the poem did not take place at an artists' colony with "marble Naiads" (21) as part of the background?

Possible Connection to Another Selection

Robert Herrick, "To the Virgins, to Make Much of Time" (text p. 599)

BILLIE BOLTON, *Memorandum* (p. 961)

Bolton's poem uses a form very different from the ones described in Chapter 30. You could start by having your students discuss how Bolton's appropriation of the business-world form of the memo contributes to the tone of the poem. They will probably appreciate the contrast between the more formal aspects of business writing and the very personal and detailed gripes Bolton's speaker lists about her boyfriend. The terseness of her statements — this poem doesn't contain any full sentences — also contributes to the humor.

This poem might be a good opportunity to try a creative response with your class, since the form lends itself to imitation. Have students create their own memos to a significant other, parent, roommate, or someone else who inspires their irritation. Emphasize that what makes Bolton's "Memorandum" fun to read is not her speaker's pure ire but rather her clever, indirect characterization of the boyfriend. In their imitations, the students should try to use colorful adjectives and sound patterning like alliteration and repetition to enhance their list of complaints.

Possible Connections to Other Selections

Edna St. Vincent Millay, "Recuerdo" (text p. 958; question #1, following)

William Shakespeare, "My mistress' eyes are nothing like the sun" (text p. 743)

Connection Question in Text (p. 962) with Answer

1. Compare the use of descriptive detail to create tone in "Memorandum" and in Edna St. Vincent Millay's "Recuerdo" (p. 958).

   Bolton uses pop-culture details, including the names of movie stars and discount stores, to create a portrait of the "Boyfriend from Hell." She also incorporates some of his own language into the indictment, which further reveals what kind of character he is. The references to women as "dames" whom he "balled," as well as the comments on the "deep psychological need" of his son and his "long-suffering" mother, portray the boyfriend as someone who depends on stock phrases and has very little original thought.

The detailed descriptions in "Recuerdo" are different from those of Bolton's poem because, rather than invoke the negative qualities of a single character, Millay describes hard-working siblings who remain joyful despite their lack of material wealth. Millay's speaker is one of these siblings, and the details are drawn from their day-to-day toils. The speaker says, "We were very tired, we were very merry— / We had gone back and forth all night on the / ferry" (1–3). This is repeated like a chorus throughout the poem. The siblings leave their home every day, work all night, and when they returned, "We hailed, 'Good morrow, mother!' to a shawl-covered head, / And bought a morning paper, which neither of us read; / And she wept, 'God bless you!' for the apples and pears, / And we gave her all our money but our subway fares" (15–18). These descriptions reveal the family's level of poverty and make the speaker's cheerfulness even more impressive.

LUISA LOPEZ, *Junior Year Abroad* (p. 962)

In this deceptively casual narrative poem, Lopez explores the confused thoughts of a young woman. The narrator, a junior in college, ponders what happened when an old boyfriend visited her for Christmas, not knowing that she had fallen for a new beau. The details of the poem betray her conflicted understanding of her relationships with her "old lover" (line 27), her "new boy" (21), and herself. Most important, she considers herself alone.

This poem offers an excellent opportunity to help students understand the importance of details in narrative poetry. They're likely to empathize with the woman's dilemma: by college, most people have experienced the excitement, guilt, and confusion of casting off an old love for a new one. Have them paraphrase the poem, and ask what is lost when it is reduced to the story line. It may also be useful to explore each of the poem's metaphors and similes in class: What secrets do the phrases and words "shelf life" (4), "muslin" (6), "cocoon" (9), "circus pony" (15), "snake" (18), "two old friends" (31), "traffic" (36), and "currency" (36) reveal about the speaker's perceptions of the visit and of her "betrayal" (18)? Who exactly is she betraying?

"Junior Year Abroad" is also tantalizing in its ambiguity. The final stanzas are unclear: Did the speaker's old boyfriend rape her, or did she guiltily consent to "one last time"? As a writing assignment, pose this question to students and ask them to examine the poem's details to determine what happened.

POSSIBLE CONNECTION TO ANOTHER SELECTION

A. E. Housman, "When I was one-and-twenty" (text p. 728)

CONNECTION QUESTION IN TEXT (p. 963) WITH ANSWER

1. Compare this 2002 poem about young love with A. E. Housman's poem "When I was one-and-twenty" (p. 728) published in 1896. How much has the situation changed in a hundred years?

   Though Lopez's poem is franker about what it means to give your "heart away," both speakers face a similar dilemma. Having found first love with one person, they realize how easily affections can change. For the speaker of "Junior Year Abroad," this results in continuing a sexual relationship with someone she no longer feels strongly about. The young man in "When I was one-and-twenty" meets an older "wise man" (line 2) who gives him advice, but he fails to listen or even understand until he is "two-and-twenty" (15). Lopez's speaker seems to be figuring out relationships on her own, but she comes to a similar conclusion about the problems of committing to love too early.

36

A Thematic Case Study: Humor and Satire

Students often expect poems to express love or to recall childhood experiences, but they may be less used to the idea of poems using humor. If they do have the misconception that all poems are serious all the time, they may miss the poet's humor or even suspect that they're misreading when they do encounter something funny. Grouping these poems together calls students' attention to the fact that amusing the reader is one technique among the poet's many means of communicating. These poems cover a wider range of themes than those in the previous chapter, and they use humor in a number of different ways — from the setup/punch-line structure to an extended series of puns. What brings them all together is a willingness to question orthodoxies and to see the ridiculous in ordinary situations.

JOHN CIARDI, *Suburban* (p. 965)

In "Suburban," Ciardi satirizes the artificial behavior of those who live in the suburbs. Note that Mrs. Friar seems unable to look at or refer to by name the object that incites her to phone the poet — the word *turd* does not occur until the final stanza, when the poet is returning to his own property. Ask students to compare Ciardi's perception of the turd — "organic gold" (line 11) — to Mrs. Friar's — "a large repulsive object" (5). What does the difference indicate about their contrasting worldviews?

How do the poet's tone and behavior alter when he crosses the property line? His attitude when Mrs. Friar first asks him to come over and remove the offending object — a humorous observation that his dog is in another state — is contrasted with his behavior in Mrs. Friar's yard, as he scoops and bows (16). How would Mrs. Friar have responded if Ciardi had shared his vision of what his dog, his son, and his son's girlfriend were doing in Vermont? How would she have responded if he had refused to come over? If Ciardi lacks any respect for the pseudodelicate sensibilities of his suburban neighbors, why does he humor them and conform to their accepted behavior in this instance?

Suburban neighborhoods are noted for being well organized and highly developed; like them, the first four stanzas of the poem conform to a single pattern (note the perfect, standard indentation of the second and fourth lines in each). Yet the final line of the poem stands alone, beyond the conformity of the preceding stanzas. As Ciardi seems to be alone in his ability to accept the "turd" as an aspect of "real life," so this final line presents a different aspect of the suburbs. Ask students to assess the tonal shift and meaning of this final, isolated line, which provides a key to much of the preceding material.

Possible Connections to Other Selections

Louis Simpson, "In the Suburbs" (text p. 616)

John Updike, "Dog's Death" (text p. 548; question #1, following)

Connection Question in Text (p. 966) with Answer

1. Compare the speakers' voices in "Suburban" and in Updike's "Dog's Death" (p. 548).

The speaker of Ciardi's poem is much more satirical than Updike's speaker, which is consistent with the subject matter of each. There is something raw and honest about the way Updike's speaker approaches his topic, but Ciardi's speaker has his tongue in his cheek throughout the poem, emphasizing the "I said" and "she said" of his story to comic effect. The settings of the poems are similar, but the comic presence of Mrs. Friar in this poem and the tragic death of the dog in Updike's poem alter the tones of each considerably.

HARRYETTE MULLEN, *Dim Lady* (p. 966)

Students may find Mullen's "Dim Lady" a refreshing imitation, and her poem may help shed light on Shakespeare's famous "My mistress' eyes are nothing like the sun." Mullen translates Shakespeare's parody into her own diction, replacing his words with slang and images from popular culture. With words like *peepers, noggin, mug,* and *ball and chain,* she creates a comedic effect that distinguishes her version from the original. As a class exercise, ask students to write their own version of Shakespeare/Mullen, after making deliberate choices about how to present their "lady." Or ask them to write a comic version of another Renaissance poem. Decisions about diction, meter, rhyme, and allusion will all have an impact on the final result, and students may see Mullen's choices more clearly as a result of the exercise.

Another avenue for discussion is to interpret Shakespeare's intention in writing "Mistress," with an eye toward why Mullen made the choice to rewrite Shakespeare without his formal constraints. It is important to understand how influential the sonnet and its use as a love poem were for someone of Shakespeare's time. How do Mullen's lines "And yet, by gosh, my scrumptious Twinkie has as much / sex appeal for me as any lanky model or platinum movie idol who's hyped beyond belief" (lines 9–11) encapsulate the essence of Shakespeare but also reveal something about the way the pop culture standard of beauty rules our thinking in the twentieth and twenty-first centuries?

POSSIBLE CONNECTIONS TO OTHER SELECTIONS

Florence Cassen Mayers, "All-American Sestina" (text p. 750)

William Shakespeare, "My mistress' eyes are nothing like the sun" (text p. 743; question #1, following)

———, "Shall I compare thee to a summer's day?" (text p. 743)

CONNECTION QUESTION IN TEXT (p. 967) WITH ANSWER

1. Compare line for line "Dim Lady" to William Shakespeare's "My mistress' eyes are nothing like the sun" (text p. 743). Which tribute do you prefer, the original parody of a love poem or the modern version?

   Students may be drawn to the identifiable music and control of Shakespeare's version. Some may like the classical images of Shakespeare, while others may prefer the modern feel of Mullen's version. Students may like the lack of formality in Mullen's prose poem.

RONALD WALLACE, *In a Rut* (p. 967)

Wallace uses his series of folk expressions to describe an exchange between a man and woman, but in the play of finding new animal metaphors to continue the description, the actual events of the poem become secondary. Wallace reveals the commonness of the scene but also the natural human tendency to describe our experiences in terms of what we see in the natural world. By watching each of these animals, people have observed traits that remind them of human behavior, and the comparisons have been so useful in talking about humans that they have taken on the status of clichés. "In a Rut" shows how people can embody all these traits, even in the space of a few minutes.

The move toward generalization in the last line, where the woman insists that the narrator is "a real animal" (line 45), emphasizes the figurative work of all these common sayings.

POSSIBLE CONNECTIONS TO OTHER SELECTIONS

Billie Bolton, "Memorandum" (text p. 961)

E. E. Cummings, "next to of course god america i" (text p. 673; question #1, following)

CONNECTION QUESTION IN TEXT (p. 968) WITH ANSWER

1. Compare Wallace's organizing strategy in this poem and E. E. Cummings's technique in "next to of course god america i" (p. 673).

    Wallace's poem proceeds through his series of animal metaphors that have become common speech. Nearly every line contains some comparison. Wallace also groups the animals, so that saying "I give her something to crow about" (line 37) leads him to other bird metaphors like "*lovey-dove*" (38), "odd ducks" (39), and "swan- / song" (40–41). Cummings organizes "next to of course god america i" in a similar way, by incorporating language from patriotic songs and sayings. As in Wallace's poem, each phrase seems to remind Cummings of another, but here they occur so quickly that they begin to bleed into one another. In the course of a few lines (2–4), Cummings echoes "Let Freedom Ring," "The Star-Spangled Banner," and "My Country 'Tis of Thee." Rather than reinvigorating these clichés, Cummings emphasizes their emptiness.

HOWARD NEMEROV, *Walking the Dog* (p. 968)

Partly a paean to his dog and partly a rumination on the nature of power, this poem compares "two universes" (line 1): the human and the canine. Some of the details suggest that the human world is the more evolved of the two: man puts the dog on a leash (2), man looks heavenward while the dog inspects the ground (3–4), and of course man "write[s] the poem" (24). But other instances in the poem imply that the dog is actually the master: it determines the pace of the walk, forcing "patience" (10) from the man; it has a "secret knowledge" (5); it is the one who teaches (13); it has a "keener" sense (19). Most significant, the dog causes the man to question whether he really is the "master" (24), whereas the animal presumably has no doubts about the nature of the relationship.

You might want to start class discussion by asking students whether or not dog waste is an appropriate subject for a poem. Some, undoubtedly, will find the subject tasteless and unworthy of any kind of literary attention; others may read deeper meanings into it, perhaps even interpreting the poem itself as the author's own output of shit, as the last line implies. Is shit a metaphor for something else? The first two stanzas of the poem, with their emphasis on "universes" (1) and the relationship between two "symbionts" (11) — or separate entities that are interdependent — privilege a heady interpretation. But the second two stanzas focus on physical, indeed, repugnant — elements of life.

Another possibility for approaching the poem is to explore its comparisons of human civilization and the natural world. Do humans control nature, or does it control them? Which has more to teach, according to the poem, and which has more to learn?

POSSIBLE CONNECTIONS TO OTHER SELECTIONS

John Ciardi, "Suburban" (text p. 965; question #1, following)

Ronald Wallace, "Building an Outhouse" (text p. 660; question #2, following)

CONNECTIONS QUESTIONS IN TEXT (p. 969) WITH ANSWERS

1. Discuss the speakers' attitudes toward the dogs in "Walking the Dog" and in John Ciardi's "Suburban" (p. 965). How does humor inform those attitudes?

The attitude toward the dog in "Suburban" is made apparent in contrast with the stuffy neighbor. While she claims "'I always have loved dogs'" (line 15), she acts repulsed by them. The speaker ironically restates her position when he says "The animal of it" (16). In fact, the speaker values the animal nature of the dog including the "organic gold" (11) it provides his garden. In this poem, Ciardi suggests that there is something unnatural, or even antinatural, in suburban life. The problems of suburbanites can largely be attributed to their humorless rejection of anything that doesn't fit their rigid conceptions of order.

2. Consider the subject matter of this poem and Ronald Wallace's "Building an Outhouse" (text p. 660). Some readers might argue that the subject matter is tasteless and not suitable for poetic treatment. What do you think?

These poems may be blunter than some in the way they deal with excrement, but they both address a broad theme that many poems address: the idea that we can celebrate beauty but can't thereby ignore the rest of life. Wallace's first line, which breaks after the word *pure*, seems to suggest some pious ideas about what is poetic. He reveals, though, that poetry isn't at all as easy as the "mathematics of shape; the music of hammer" (line 2). The artist has to struggle though setbacks in order to produce the final, "Functional" (12) object. In Nemerov's poem, the speaker becomes the one who is impatient, while the dog has the kind of curiosity we expect in poets. His incessant sniffing provides him "a secret knowledge" (line 5), and he has taught his owner to take an "interest in shit" (14). In the last line, Nemerov draws a parallel between the dog's excretion, which is his response to the world, and the poetic act of creation.

PETER SCHMITT, *Friends with Numbers* (p. 969)

Schmitt's imagining of the actions and personalities of numbers seems to begin as an exercise, but toward the end, it becomes a meditation on the difficulty of finding love. He begins by saying the numbers are "not hard to get to know" (line 1), but it becomes clear that two is, in fact, hard, not only to find but to maintain, as it "seems on the verge, / yet, of always coming apart" (24–25). You might call your students' attention to the fact that Schmitt refers to the numbers as "he" until he gets to two, which he characterizes as female. His wry last line suggests that though he has "friends in numbers" (line 29), he lacks the only one that matters.

POSSIBLE CONNECTIONS TO OTHER SELECTIONS

Anne Bradstreet, "The Author to Her Book" (text p. 647)

May Swenson, "A Nosty Fright" (text p. 692; question #1, following)

CONNECTION QUESTION IN TEXT (p. 970) WITH ANSWER

1. Discuss the originality—the fresh and unusual approach to their respective subject matter—in Schmitt's poem and in May Swenson's "A Nosty Fright" (p. 692). What makes these poems so interesting?

Usually, we see numbers only as the visual representation of quantities and measurements. Schmitt's poem is original in that it focuses on the actual appearance of numbers, as they look on a page. Schmitt draws attention to the visual similarity of 6 and 9, and reminds his reader the 8 is similar to an eternity symbol, when turned on its side, by saying, "8 cuts the most graceful figure / but sleeps for an eternity" (lines 3–4). Eight's connection to the concept of eternity is an example of another interesting way in which Schmitt discusses numbers. He draws attention to the non-numerical things that numbers can represent, as when he mentions the number three: "3, for all his literary / accomplishments and pretensions / to immortality" (13–15). This is in reference to such things as three's symbolic importance in literature and religion (for example, the Christian God is "father, son, and holy ghost"). The numbers even develop personalities and desires—three has "pretensions," five "wants to patch his unicycle / tire" (8–9), and two is mysterious and unknowable.

While Schmitt's "Friends with Numbers" finds a fresh approach to what numbers represent, May Swenson's "A Nosty Fright" plays with sound. Swenson's clever swaps between words turn what might have otherwise felt like a childish piece into something more intricate. Often, Swenson trades similar letters and sounds between words, creating new words that sound similar enough to their progenitors, but still carry the possibility of new meaning. The title phrase is an example of this; in line 25, the speaker says, "October was ending on a nosty fright." If readers follow Swenson's pattern of swapping, they know the original words were "a frosty night." But October 31 is Halloween, the holiday dedicated to "frights." Students may enjoy Swenson's playfulness even more if the class rewrites her poem using the "correct" vocabulary and compares it to the original.

MARTÍN ESPADA, *The Community College Revises Its Curriculum in Response to Changing Demographics* (p. 970)

Espada uses administrative language and the conventions of college course listings to make this satirical comment on perceptions of Spanish speakers. The straightforward beginning of his poem takes a turn when the course aligns itself with the needs of the police. We tend to think of higher education as providing pure knowledge, unaffected by ideology, but here Espada reminds us that colleges can't remain completely apart from politics. The "matters of interest" (line 7) to those in power can infiltrate educational institutions as well.

POSSIBLE CONNECTIONS TO OTHER SELECTIONS

Donald Justice, "Order in the Streets" (text p. 777; question #1, following)

Gary Soto, "Mexicans Begin Jogging" (text p. 972)

CONNECTION QUESTION IN TEXT (p. 971) WITH ANSWER

1. Compare the themes in Espada's poem and in Donald Justice's "Order in the Streets" (p. 777).

    The neutral title Espada chooses for this poem belies, but also underscores, its pointed political commentary. The language of both title and poem mimics that of college catalogs and brochures. It sounds purely informational but actually contains significant clues about the values and biases of the curriculum planners. Here, those values include police-enforced order at the expense of fairness to all citizens. The suggestion of the course description is that any "matters" (line 7) conducted in Spanish would be of interest to the police.

    Like Espada, Justice uses a form of public language in his poem. As we see in the epigraph, these statements are from the instructions to a child's toy. Like a course catalog, they reveal much more about the society that produced them than might first be apparent. Also, as in Espada's poem, there is little human agency in "Order in the Streets." All the enforcing work in this poem is attributed to the Jeep, which is controlled not by a driver but by "mystery action" (8). The return to headquarters at the end of the poem suggests a larger power directing military action, but this power is removed from the mechanistic actions of "putting down riot" (14).

GEORGE BILGERE, *Stupid* (p. 971)

The speaker's rendition of a woman's failed attempt to create a simile becomes the engine that runs this poem. A woman is overheard saying, "We were so fucked up, it was… / It was like…" (lines 1–2), and her friend responds with bland agreement. This starts the speaker's reminiscence about the way he and his friends crested through life when they took drugs. The overheard snippet of dialogue leads him into a series of images of himself and his friends "unmoored and adrift, / so hopelessly out of range/Of our calls to the lost/Vessels of each other" (17–20). He describes the "crippled sub of an idea" (25) that emerges when they are unable to speak to each other. In discussion, try to identify how these images of transportation match the impairment he describes. What is funny about his images of flight or floating, and do they accurately describe those who are "permanently" or temporarily "stupid"?

POSSIBLE CONNECTION TO ANOTHER SELECTION

Jim Tilley, "The Big Questions" (text p. 572; question #1, following)

CONNECTION QUESTION IN TEXT (p. 972) WITH ANSWER

1. Discuss the themes of this poem and Jim Tilley's "The Big Questions" (text p. 572).

   Both poems have themes that consider language and how we communicate to one another in a humorous way. Bilgere and Tilley both rely on comic metaphor to articulate what's difficult to put into words.

GARY SOTO, *Mexicans Begin Jogging* (p. 972)

Born in America but mistaken for a Mexican, the speaker of this poem is encouraged by his factory boss to run out the back door and across the Mexican border when the border patrol arrives. Rather than protest, the speaker runs along with a number of Mexicans, yelling *vivas* to the land of "baseball, milkshakes, and those sociologists" (line 18) who are apparently keeping track of demographics.

It is noteworthy that the speaker doesn't protest his boss's orders but joins the throng of jogging Mexicans because he is "on [the boss's] time" (11). Why wouldn't he simply stand his ground and show proof that he is a U.S. citizen? The key may lie in the word "wag" (12), which describes a comic person or wit in addition to its familiar associations with movement: to move from side to side (as in "tail") or even to depart. The speaker's parting gesture, after all, is "a great, silly grin" (21). The joke is on the boss, or the border patrol, or on America in general with its paranoid sociologists. Although the tone is somewhat comic, the subject is serious, whether students take it to be the exploitation of workers from developing nations, or prejudice based on appearance (i.e., the speaker is taken to be Mexican because he looks like he is). What effect does the tone have on a consideration of these subjects? Is there a "point" to the irony?

POSSIBLE CONNECTIONS TO OTHER SELECTIONS

Julio Marzán, "The Translator at the Reception for Latin American Writers" (text p. 770)

Peter Meinke, "The ABC of Aerobics" (text p. 774; question #1, following)

CONNECTION TO ANOTHER SELECTION (p. 973) WITH ANSWER

1. Compare the speakers' ironic attitudes toward exercise in this poem and in Peter Meinke's "The ABC of Aerobics" (p. 774).

   Whereas each poem uses running as a vehicle for meditation, Gary Soto's speaker runs to avoid the border patrol, and the speaker of "The ABC of Aerobics" exercises for exercise's sake. For each speaker, exercise is somewhat futile: Soto's speaker doesn't really need to be running, as he is an American, and Meinke's speaker comes to realize that if he had love, it would replace the exercise. (Meinke's speaker spends lines 1–16 complaining that the city's air is still filthy, and that exercise does him little good anyway because of "tobacco, lard and bourbon" [12].)

THOMAS R. MOORE, *At the Berkeley Free Speech Café* (p. 973)

Our culture is increasingly fragmented by media, data, and stimuli. This fact would have been clear enough in Moore's juxtaposition of "ears wired" (line 4) and "textbooks open/reading for an exam" (12–13), but he punctuates his contemporary scene with a list of gerunds. Gerunds often have the effect of slowing a phrase in context, but they can allow for a strange sort of speed when they are listed one after another. In this list, the speaker inserts references to popular culture, including the ubiquitous iPod and latté, for comic effect. The bodily pulsations that happen when one's attention is divided between all these different technologies is ridiculous, and the speaker captures that ridiculousness in the image (because the fingers are too busy texting) of "toes drumming" (9). The final touch is in the revelation that all this techno-buzz is in preparation for an Issues in Contemporary Culture course exam.

What is the irony in locating this scene at the Berkeley Free Speech Café? What associations do students have with Berkeley or with free speech?

POSSIBLE CONNECTIONS TO OTHER SELECTIONS

Emily Dickinson, "From all the Jails the Boys and Girls" (text. p. 818)

Richard Hague, "Directions for Resisting the SAT" (text p. 767)

CONNECTION QUESTION IN TEXT (p. 973) WITH ANSWER

1. Write an essay comparing the assessment of student life in this poem with X. J. Kennedy's "On a Young Man's Remaining an Undergraduate for Twelve Years" (p. 973).

   In Moore's poem, the speaker is watching students from nearby colleges at a local café. To him, they seem isolated, "one to a table, / at tables for two" (2–3). They don't speak or interact with one another, but are instead completely immersed in technology and media. These robotic students are busy with "ears wired, / laptops humming, / cell phones buzzing, / fingers texting, / iPods thumping," (4–8) among numerous other non-human, non-academic distractions. Even the class the students are studying for is ultra-modern: "Issues in Contemporary Culture 102" (14).

   In X. J. Kennedy's poem, the critique of student life is different. While Moore sees today's students as disconnected from other people, Kennedy's "everlasting kid" (9) is too distracted by others to finish his undergraduate degree. The speaker sums up the subject's philosophy, saying, "Who'd give a damn for earning, / Who'd struggle by degrees to lofty places / When he can loll, adrift in endless learning" (5–8). Despite the mention of learning, the undergraduate is really occupying his time with the "Sweet scent of pot, the mellow smell of beer," (1) and "Pliant coeds who put up no resistance" (4). While Moore's students are absorbed by their digital, information-saturated world, Kennedy's undergraduate is aimless and without motivation, fostered by an academic institution that allows him to remain irresponsible and adrift.

X. J. KENNEDY, *On a Young Man's Remaining an Undergraduate for Twelve Years* (p. 973)

The form Kennedy uses for this poem helps to reinforce his point about the young man in the title. For example, the break between the first and second stanzas separates the description of college's pleasures from the assessment that, for this young man, they "[a]re all life is" (line 5). Kennedy portrays college life as if it were one of those "thrice a year" (3) vacations the young man enjoys. It is a "warm sea" (8) in which the student can "loll" (7). He doesn't want to emerge into cold reality or to engage in the struggle to achieve success in the adult world.

The break between the second and third stanzas abruptly separates what is pleasant about the young man's life from his legend and his effects on the school. Not only does he enjoy staying in college far beyond the usual number of years, he even convinces the deans that in his "ratiocination" (a supremely academic way to describe the process of reasoning) (12) he has figured out a superior way of living.

POSSIBLE CONNECTION TO ANOTHER SELECTION

Richard Wakefield, "In a Poetry Workshop" (text p. 1025)

37

A Thematic Case Study:
The Natural World

Writing poetry about nature is a long-standing tradition, but the poems in this case study focus specifically on the intersection of humans and nature and how each alters the other. Increasing concern about climate change may be one reason contemporary poets are so interested in these meeting points of human progress and the natural world. Poems like Tom Disch's "Birdsong Interpreted" and Robert B. Shaw's "Wild Turkeys" don't explicitly mention it as a subject but are clearly concerned with the changes humans have caused in nature. The range of approaches in this chapter — from the curt and humorous tone of Disch's poem to the elegiac tone of Dave Lucas's "November" — should give students good material for talking about the different emotions our encounters with nature evoke.

TOM DISCH, *Birdsong Interpreted* (p. 976)

The singer in Disch's poem is no romantic nightingale that inspires the poet to verse (though his "Jug jug" does recall the use of the phrase in T. S. Eliot's *The Waste Land*). Instead he is confrontational and something of a smart aleck who uses slang words like "Vamoose! Amscray!" (line 3). Disch makes the bird's speech humorous with elaborate rhymes like "eco-balance" (5) and "Jack Palance" (6), but the core of his message is serious: if humans keep disrupting his habitat, the nest will turn into a "funeral pyre" (11).

POSSIBLE CONNECTIONS TO ANOTHER SELECTIONS

John Keats, "Ode to a Nightingale" (text p. 713)
Mary Oliver, "Wild Geese" (text p. 983; question #1, following)

CONNECTION QUESTION IN TEXT (p. 976) WITH ANSWER

1. Compare the theme and speaker's tone in "Birdsong Interpreted" and that in Mary Oliver's "Wild Geese" (p. 983).

   The speaker of "Birdsong Interpreted" is the titular bird, and, according to Disch, his song is not expressing what most people would think. Usually, birdsong is portrayed as cheerful, beautiful, even sometimes melancholy. But in this instance, the speaker's tone is humorously angry and aggressive. Rather than an affirmation of life or expression of happiness, this bird is trying to protect his territory, the way a dog would bark at a stranger. He is yelling at the intruder, "if songs could sting, / If trills could kill, my dear sweet thing, / You wouldn't linger longer here" (lines 12–14). Mary Oliver's "Wild Geese" expresses a very different relationship with nature. The speaker in her poem articulates a oneness with the natural world, inviting her audience, "let the soft animal of your body / love what it loves" (4–5). Her tone remains peaceful and intimate, asking the reader to "Tell me about despair, yours" (6) and asks for nothing in return. The birds in this poem — geese — are not angry and aggressive as the one in Disch's, but are life-affirming trumpeters. The speaker describes this by saying, "Whoever you are, no matter how lonely, / the world offers itself to your imagination, / calls to you like the wild geese, harsh and exciting—" (13–15).

JANE HIRSCHFIELD, *Optimism* (p. 977)

Hirshfield's poem opens with a statement: "More and more I have come to admire resilience" (line 1). In the speaker's mind, resilience takes shape in "the sinuous tenacity of a tree" (3). Optimism about this resilience is bolstered by the admission that it is "a blind intelligence, true" (6). Students in your class may be familiar with how the concession of a point to an opponent can add to the strength of an argument. How does this logic also follow within Hirshfield's poem? The concession of that weak spot leads to the litany of resilient creatures in the last lines. The "turtles, rivers, mitochondria, figs" have persisted since the beginning of time. Discussion may respond to the optimism about "this resinous, unretractable earth" (8).

POSSIBLE CONNECTIONS TO OTHER SELECTIONS

Emily Dickinson, "Apparently With no Surprise" (text p. 830; question #1, following)

Robert Frost, "Design" (text p. 856; question #1, following)

Gerard Manley Hopkins, "God's Grandeur" (text p. 702)

Mary Oliver, "Wild Geese" (text p. 983)

CONNECTION QUESTION IN TEXT (p. 977) WITH ANSWER

1. Contrast the view of nature presented in "Optimism" with that in Emily Dickinson's "Apparently with no surprise" (p. 830) and Robert Frost's "Design" (p. 856).

   The perspective on nature given in "Optimism" is one of objective appreciation. Hirshfield's narrator does not romanticize nature, admitting that its intelligence is "A blind intelligence, true" (line 6), but she still respects its "sinuous tenacity" (3). In "Apparently with no surprise," Dickinson's speaker is in awe of the strength of nature's unstoppable forces. The flower is killed by frost "In accidental power" (4), but this death does not forestall any other part of the natural world. The "Sun proceeds unmoved" (6) by the changing of the seasons, relentless in its march "To measure off another Day" (7). Frost's view on the power of nature is decidedly more negative. While Hirshfield focuses on its resilience and Dickinson takes even death as a sign of a larger power at work, Frost instead sees the strength of nature as ominous. The speaker in "Design" watches a spider on a flower prepare to devour a moth. To him, this arrangement is "Assorted characters of death and blight" (4) that are "Like the ingredients of a witches' broth—" (6). In this scenario there is no "life will find a way" lesson, as in "Optimism." And where Dickinson's speaker sees the purpose in each natural event, the speaker in "Design" questions if there is a purpose to what he's seeing. He queries, "What but design of darkness to appall?— / If design governed a thing so small" (13–14). To him, nature is either dominated by anarchy or controlled by "darkness."

GAIL WHITE, *Dead Armadillos* (p. 977)

White begins her poem with the simplistic division between "smart" (line 1) and "dumb" (3) armadillos, but it quickly becomes clear that she does not believe lack of intelligence is the problem. Rather, the vulnerable armadillos are failed by humans, who are willing to take up grander causes but don't create a "Save the Armadillo / Society" (11–12). The armadillos are so plentiful that hitting a few doesn't seem to be a problem. White compares the animals to noble "knights / in armor" (9–10), yet they are "blind" (9) and helpless when it comes to the roads they have to cross to "check the pickings" (4) on the other side.

Tom Disch, "Birdsong Interpreted" (text p. 976)

Walt McDonald, "Coming Across It" (text p. 979; question #1, following)

CONNECTION QUESTION IN TEXT (p. 978) WITH ANSWER

1. Discuss the similarities in theme in "Dead Armadillos" and Walt McDonald's "Coming Across It" (p. 979).

   In "Dead Armadillos," the speaker muses on all the armadillos she sees dead in the road on her "daily route" (line 8). She points out that despite the high volume of armadillos that are killed by cars, no one cares; as she says, "There is no Save the Armadillo / Society" (11–12). White is drawing attention to a common human hypocrisy that many people don't even notice: people often do not value something until it's nearly gone. The speaker points out how we will rally around a cause or a species when it's on the verge of destruction by saying of the armadillos, "When we're down to the last half dozen, / we'll see them with the eyes of God" (18–19). McDonald's work "Coming Across It" makes a similar point but from the opposite side of the problem. The people around McDonald's narrator are captivated by an otter because they're in a city, and the animal is an unusual sight. Like an endangered species, the people in "Coming Across It" fear for the otter's well-being; they want to take it to "the river, / the police, the safest zoo" (15–16), and they "wait for someone / with a gun or net to rescue it" (19–20). Still, McDonald carefully introduces the idea of the city-dwellers as "a tribe" (13), and the speaker points out, "But if we had / clubs, we'd kill it" (26–27). In a more primitive time, outside of this urban setting, the very people who claim to want to help the otter would devour it.

DAVE LUCAS, *November* (p. 978)

Lucas mourns the transformation of bright October leaves into piles the color of "copper" and "shale" (line 3). He pays particular attention to the smells of the season as the "cold-tea smell" (2) of wet leaves on the ground is replaced by the "struck-match-sweet" (4) smell of them burning. In the wake of this beautiful but brief "gush" (1) of color, the speaker sees a number of unprotected "orphaned nests" (8) left in the trees. While the poem describes a literal late-fall scene, it also has intimations of a larger elegy. Especially when read in conversation with other contemporary nature poems, it seems to ask what nature is protecting and what will be left bare when the natural world of today passes away.

POSSIBLE CONNECTIONS TO OTHER SELECTIONS

John Keats, "To Autumn" (text p. 637; question #1, following)

William Shakespeare, "That time of year thou mayst in me behold" (text p. 1021)

CONNECTION QUESTION IN TEXT (p. 978) WITH ANSWER

1. Consider the tone and theme of "November" and of John Keats's "To Autumn" (p. 637).

   Though both poems share a common theme, the tone of Keats' "To Autumn" provides a sharp contrast to that of "November." Lucas's version of fall is mired in gloom and decay; the first image is of dead leaves "raked to the curb in copper- and shale- / stained piles, or the struck-match-sweet / of sulfur // becoming smoke." (3–6). On the surface, sulfur and smoke simply connote homeowners burning leaves, but it can also call to mind images of hell. Rather than Keats' cheerful images of "mellow fruitfulness" (1), Lucas's speaker focuses on death, decay, and emptiness, creating a much darker tone. He drives these themes home in the last image of the sky, and "Hung across it, aghast surprise / of so many clotted, orphaned nests" (8–9). Keats' speaker describes autumn in terms of ripeness and plenty, extolling that fall will "load and bless / With fruit the vines that round the thatch-eves run" (3–4) and "fill all fruit with ripeness to the core" (6).

WALT MCDONALD, *Coming Across It* (p. 979)

Like the men stalking an animal in the alley, readers don't realize until they've been observing for a while what the animal actually is. McDonald throws us off by guessing it is "a cat / prowling, or a man down on his luck" (lines 1–2), and then gives up these possibilities and identifies it only as an unknown "something" (8). When we arrive at "*Otter*" (10) in the fourth stanza, we can finally put together the fragmented parts of the animal seen and heard in the dark — the glint of its eyes low to the ground, the way it rattles cans. The name makes the image come "into focus" (11). In the communal activity of trying to track the animal, the people in the poem are bonded "like brothers" (21) or like "a tribe" (13), but what brings them together is partly confusion about what to call the otter (is it cute or ugly?) and what to do with it (the net or the gun?).

POSSIBLE CONNECTION TO ANOTHER SELECTION

Alden Nowlan, "The Bull Moose" (text p. 980; question #1, following)

CONNECTION QUESTION IN TEXT (p. 979) WITH ANSWER

1. Discuss how the unexpected encounter between civilization and nature produces anxiety in "Coming Across It" and in Alden Nowlan's "The Bull Moose" (p. 980).

   The people in "Coming Across It" are startled by the appearance of a wild animal, the otter, in the middle of the city. Though they talk about practical matters like how the garbage in the alley might be a problem, at heart they feel as if they are trapped in a cave and want to club the animal. Unlike the otter, which seems like a vermin to those who want to catch it, the bull moose is more majestic and potentially more dangerous out of its place in the wild. Though he seems tame and "cuddlesome" (line 25) to the gathered crowd, almost like a pet, in the end he asserts his power and strength. When he lets out a roar, the wardens are finally able to shoot.

ALDEN NOWLAN, *The Bull Moose* (p. 980)

This poem describes a conflict between humans and nature, one in which humans, through their actions, futilely attempt to make nature (that is, the moose) look ridiculous but are rewarded only by appearing cowardly and cruel. The speaker, observing the interactions of a lost bull moose and the townspeople, succeeds in making the townspeople and not the moose look ridiculous. The people demonstrate a complete misunderstanding of the moose; they lack respect for creatures of the wild in general and this trapped moose in particular. They condescend to the moose, treating it like a sideshow freak by feeding it beer, opening its mouth, planting "a little purple cap / of thistles on his head" (lines 22–23). Their affection for the animal is utterly skewed; they don't realize the moral problems inherent in so amiably agreeing that "it was a shame / to shoot anything so shaggy and cuddlesome" (24–25). The moose's last act was one of power, strength, and dignity — it refused to die with bottles in its mouth or thistles on its head. As "the bull moose gathered his strength / like a scaffolded king, straightened and lifted his horns" (29–30), it terrified the onlookers, even the wardens. But the final act of the young men, the honking of the car horns as the moose is executed, serves as both a way to mask their guilt by drowning out the sounds of the screaming moose, and as a sort of victory cry upon winning a cruel, unfair, and dishonorable battle.

POSSIBLE CONNECTION TO ANOTHER SELECTION

David Shumate, "Shooting the Horse" (text p. 766; question #1, following)

1. In an essay compare and contrast how the animals portrayed in "The Bull Moose" and in David Shumate's "Shooting the Horse" (p. 766) are used as symbols.

    In both poems there is a violent clash between humanity and the animal world. In Nowlan's poem, the bull moose symbolizes the reluctant power of nature, which humans have abused but which continues to be fearsome. Stafford's speaker thinks deeply and quickly about his ability to influence nature, and though his action is painful, he is ultimately humane in letting the unborn fawn expire.

ROBERT B. SHAW, *Wild Turkeys* (p. 981)

Shaw anthropomorphizes the turkeys, describing them as "dowdy" (line 3) old men, "prim" (9) deacons. Their bodies are inflated with a "fusty basketry of quills and pinions" (18), and the brief flights they can take make them seem pompous. In the end Shaw extends the comparison even further, turning these deacons into "Pilgrims turning out for a hanging" (25). By doing so, he ironically employs the imagery of the first Thanksgiving, but he also suggests a darker side to the self-regard that these promenading turkeys convey.

POSSIBLE CONNECTIONS TO OTHER SELECTIONS

Emily Dickinson, "A Bird came down the Walk —" (text p. 963)

Tom Disch, "Birdsong Interpreted" (text p. 976; question #1, following)

1. Compare the elements of style used to characterize the birds in "Wild Turkeys" and in Tom Disch's "Birdsong Interpreted" (p. 976). How do the poetic styles match the birds' characters?

    The birds in both of these poems are vividly personified, but their characters are almost opposite. Disch's bird is an insult-hurling loudmouth, while Shaw's turkeys are stodgy and self-righteous. Each poet matches the style of his poem to the type of character he is describing. Disch's short lines and virtuoso rhymes convey the smart-aleck song of his bird. Shaw uses long, stately lines and sentences to convey the turkeys' slow pace and their beady-eyed appraisal of the world. His rhymes are subtle and irregular, but the slant rhyme of "Thanksgiving" (line 24) and "hanging" (25) is an incisive way to end the poem.

KAY RYAN, *Turtle* (p. 982)

Ryan's short poem is full of descriptions that portray this luckless creature, the turtle, "a barely mobile hard roll, a four-oared helmet" (line 2), who moves gracelessly, "like dragging / a packing case places" (5–6). There is something humorous yet piteous in the opening line: "Who would be a turtle who could help it?" Students familiar with Franz Kafka may enjoy comparing this turtle to Kafka's Gregor Samsa, who awakens one morning to find himself turned into a cockroach. With this comparison in mind, discuss how Ryan's turtle is analogous to a human being. For whom or what might the turtle be a representation?

Ryan's form is compact, and dense with music. Her sounds add grace while also reflecting the sluggish and toiling turtle. She creates a weighty start-and-stop in the phrase "Her track is graceless, like dragging / a packing case places" (5–6). Discuss assonance and changes in stress. As an exercise, students might seek out her nearly imperceptible slant rhymes: *axle* with *edible* and *patience* with *chastened*, for example. There are alliterative notes in almost every line; for a place to begin discussion, read lines 10 and 11 aloud, examining rhyme and meter: "she skirts the ditch which would convert / her shell into a serving dish. She lives."

POSSIBLE CONNECTIONS TO OTHER SELECTIONS

Anonymous, "The Frog" (text p. 772)

Emily Dickinson, "A narrow Fellow in the Grass" (text p. 2; question #1, following)

Robert B. Shaw, "Wild Turkeys" (text p. 981)

Gail White, "Dead Armadillos" (text p. 977)

CONNECTION QUESTION IN TEXT (p. 982) WITH ANSWER

1. Compare Ryan's "Turtle" with Emily Dickinson's "A narrow Fellow in the Grass" (text p. 2). How do the poems make you feel about the respective animal in each?

   Ryan creates a comical picture of the turtle, while Dickinson's "narrow Fellow" is reflected in the quick, sharp strokes of her lines. Ryan uses words like *graceless*, *dragging*, *stuck*, and *chastened*. Dickinson says the snake "occasionally rides" the grass, as if on water. He is so fast you only see the grass opening and closing as he moves.

PAUL ZIMMER, *What I Know about Owls* (p. 982)

Zimmer describes owls as dual beings. At night they are frighteningly powerful and nearly omniscient. Their senses are so keen that they are almost magical — that is, they seem to go beyond what it is possible to perceive, hearing "a tick turn over in / The fur of a mouse thirty acres away" (lines 2–3) or, even more fantastic, seeing "cells dividing in / The hearts of their terrified victims" (5–6). However, during the day, the owls are feeble, docile, and even subject to the humiliating whims of humans who may want to "gently stroke for luck and life / The delicate feathers on their foreheads" (14–15). Though Zimmer describes the owls as brutal killers, the poem also reveres them. The chill in the blood that accompanies the speaking of their "awesome name" (8) is a proper sign of respect.

POSSIBLE CONNECTIONS TO OTHER SELECTIONS

William Blake, "The Tyger" (text p. 731)

Andrew Hudgins, "The Cow" (text p. 709; question #1, following)

CONNECTION QUESTION IN TEXT (p. 983) WITH ANSWER

1. Write an essay comparing the views of nature offered in Zimmer's poem and in Andrew Hudgins's "The Cow" (p. 709).

   Hudgins's poem ironically describes the domesticated cow as an animal that lives wholly for the benefit of humans. If it suits us to eat her meat slathered in "her own creamy butter" (line 32), then we can do so with impunity. Zimmer is more wary about nature's retribution. Even if we think we can get away with crossing a line like touching the owl's feathers, the owl may remember the "transgression" (18). Unlike the cow, Zimmer's owl is thoroughly wild and cannot be brought within the scope of domestic life. When it enters the sphere of our "lamplight" (19), it does so to exact revenge.

MARY OLIVER, *Wild Geese* (p. 983)

Oliver is one of the major contemporary nature poets, if such a title exists. It might be helpful to compare her with that champion of nature from a previous century, William Wordsworth. Students can discuss the ideas of loneliness and imagination that surface both in this poem and in "I Wandered Lonely as a Cloud" (text p. 1027). They create poems in which transcendence is possible through nature. For Oliver's speaker, humans become one with nature in the description of "the soft animal of your body" which wants to "love what it loves" (line 4) instinctively. Injunctions are offered throughout, and she sets up a Dickinson-like immediacy in her use of second person. A primitive and religious emphasis evolves from repetitive commands and end-stopped lines. The speaker calls the human to shed his or her separateness; ethical and religious trappings fall away as we move as the world moves, open to the sound of the wild geese. In her world, as in Wordsworth's, when people are one with the natural world, nature begins "announcing your place / in the family of things" (16–17).

POSSIBLE CONNECTIONS TO OTHER SELECTIONS

Emily Dickinson, "To make a prairie it takes a clover and one bee" (text p. 803; question #1, following)

Robert Frost, "The Pasture" (text p. 842)

Gerard Manley Hopkins, "Pied Beauty" (text p. 1012)

——, "The Windhover" (text p. 1012)

Mary Oliver, "The Poet with His Face in His Hands" (text p. 572)

William Wordsworth, "I Wandered Lonely as a Cloud" (text p. 1027)

Paul Zimmer, "What I Know about Owls" (text p. 982)

CONNECTION QUESTION IN TEXT (p. 984) WITH ANSWER

1. Discuss the treatment of imagination in "Wild Geese" and in Emily Dickinson's "To make a prairie it takes a clover and one bee" (text p. 803).

   Falling into a reverie is similar to what the speaker suggests in line 15: "the world offers itself to your imagination." Both Oliver and Dickinson look to nature as the source of this imagination. Their creative state does not require one to be "good" or repentant—only to commune with nature, to be open to the sun as it moves "over the prairies and the deep trees, / the mountains and the rivers" (9–10). The world reveals itself to people who are able to open themselves to it.

Poetry and the Visual Arts

Seeing affinities between the aims of verbal and visual expression, readers and scholars have sometimes described poetry and painting as "sister arts." This way of looking at the two different media, as if they were kin to each other, goes as far back as classical Greece and Rome. Horace's *Ars Poetica* gives us the famous formula *ut pictura poesis*—"as in painting, so in poetry." Simonides of Keos is credited with describing poetry as speaking pictures and painting as mute poetry. These claims about the similarity between the two arts also raise questions: What does it mean for a written work to "paint a picture" for the reader? What features make a painting or sculpture "poetic"?

A more recent scholar, John Hollander, in his book *The Gazer's Spirit*, a collection of ekphrastic poems, divides the genre into actual and notional ekphrasis. These two categories divide poems based on real works of art, which readers can observe for themselves, and poems about imagined or invented art that only exists in the poet's mind. As the pairings reveal, each of the poems in this section is an "actual" ekphrasis, and by looking at the art that inspired the poem, students can make their own judgments about how the poets interpret what they see on the canvas.

As the introduction in the student edition indicates, description is one of the key techniques of ekphrasis. However, ekphrastic poems are rarely content to end with description. An important task for students, as they read the poems and view the paintings in this insert, is to consider what other techniques these poems use, beyond describing the work of art. How do they reveal the speaker's attitude toward the scene or the subject of the painting? How do they elaborate on what exists beyond the frame or supply action to a still image? What changes when a poet turns his eye not on a "real" person or object, but a painting of a person or object?

GRANT WOOD, *American Gothic* (p. C)

JOHN STONE, *American Gothic* (p. D)

The two figures in Grant Wood's painting are as inscrutable as they are iconic, so it is no surprise the poets would want to take up the task of imagining the interior thoughts behind these evocative but mysterious faces. (Interested students might want to look up another treatment of the painting, by the poet William Stafford.) The man looks directly out at the viewer while the woman looks off to the side, as if occupied with something out of the frame. Stone seems to assume these two are husband and wife, but some viewers have wondered whether this is a father and daughter pair instead. In either case, their plain clothes and somber expressions mark them as archetypes of the hardworking farm family, and the title of the painting marks them as distinctly American.

Stone fills out the rest of this scene, what lies outside of Wood's painting, by completing the typical image of a small farm, populating it with "chickens, cows and hay" (line 3). He connects the "upright spines" (line 16) of the two figures, which suggest they are proud and perhaps morally upstanding, with the stark lines of the house and the pitchfork in the man's hand. The positioning of the two figures in Wood's painting is static; the man and woman are side by side, facing directly forward at the viewer. However, Stone reads their attitude as restless, eager to go on about their lives. Just as there are many things going on beyond the frame, there are many actions these two long to perform, even as the painter makes them hold the pose. This tension between the stillness of the image and the potential for action in it is a common trope of ekphrastic writing. You might have students discuss why Stone finds it characteristic of these figures in particular.

POSSIBLE CONNECTIONS TO OTHER SELECTIONS

Michael Chitwood, "Men Throwing Bricks" (text p. 989)

Marge Piercy, "To be of use" (text p. 994)

Joyce Sutphen, "Guys Like That" (text p. 993)

CONNECTION QUESTION IN TEXT (p. E) WITH ANSWER

1. Choose a poem from among those collected in Chapter 38, "A Thematic Case Study: The World of Work" (text pp. 985–996) and compare its treatment of work with that of Stone's in "American Gothic."

   Michael Chitwood's "Men Throwing Bricks" (p. 989) sees the grace in physical labor but also acknowledges that for those who perform the labor every day, it is simply a necessity. Outside observers can really appreciate the beauty of the work precisely because they are less accustomed to it. Marge Piercy's "To be of use" (p. 994) also celebrates ordinary labor, elevating work into a calling that gives life purpose. Like both of these poems, Stone's "American Gothic" sees work as an integral element of life; for this pair, it might even be an instinct that is impossible to turn off.

   Joyce Sutphen's poem "Guys Like That" (p. 993) has a more satirical edge than either "Men Throwing Bricks" or "To be of use," as she tries to imagine the inner lives of confidently wealthy men, who seem oblivious about the effects of their work. In fact, the farm that "guys like that" are thinking of selling out for profit at the end of the poem sounds quite like the one where the pair in "American Gothic" resides. Though they take very different tones, both Sutphen and Stone attempt to understand the preoccupations of strangers who live an entirely differ-ent kind of life — and do a very different kind of work.

KITAGAWA UTAMARO, *Girl Powdering Her Neck* (p. E)

CATHY SONG, *Girl Powdering Her Neck* (p. F)

Utamaro's painting captures an intimate moment, and the feeling of private space is enhanced by his close view of the woman, whose head, neck, and back dominate the frame. Against the neutral ground, her dark hair and pale skin draw the viewer's eye. More of her neck is exposed as the patterned robe slips down on her shoulder. The viewer of the painting feels almost like an intruder on the scene, looking at the woman from behind and catching only a glimpse of her face in the conveniently positioned mirror.

Song expands the view Utamaro offers, giving us more of the scene than the tightly framed painting depicts. She details the mood of the room, damp with "mois-ture from a bath" (line 4). She describes the furniture, like the low table at which the woman kneels with "her legs folded beneath her" (10) and the way the woman's articles are laid out as she conducts her beauty rituals. In Song's rewriting of the scene, the woman becomes like a landscape, with her shoulder forming a gentle hill, and her face the "reflection in a winter pond" (35). These figures liken her looks to the beauty of a natural scene, or perhaps a well-executed landscape painting. At the same time, Song emphasizes the act of self-creation the woman engages in by applying makeup. As she looks in the mirror, "she is about to paint herself" (40). While the woman on the canvas is a creation of Utamaro, Song also gives her agency of her own.

POSSIBLE CONNECTION TO ANOTHER SELECTION

Cathy Song, "The White Porch" (text p. 639; question #1, following)

CONNECTION QUESTION IN TEXT (p. G) WITH ANSWER

1. Discuss how the respective points of view in this poem and in Song's "The White Porch" (text p. 639) affect your understanding of the poems.

    Pleasure is central to both of these poems by Cathy Song. In "Girl Powdering Her Neck" the woman prepares herself for the touch of "some other hand" (line 23), expecting to both give and receive pleasure. Similarly in "The White Porch," beauty is a pleasure to the woman as well as to the man whom she waits for. However, in the latter, beauty is also a means of escape. The speaker imagines herself as a modern-day Rapunzel, using her hair as a rope to sneak her lover into a guarded room. Though the woman in "Girl Powdering Her Neck" engages in an act of self-creation, she is also subject to "self-scrutiny" (42) and ultimately finds herself unable to break "the symmetry of silence" (46). She seems to have fewer opportunities, or perhaps less drive, for rebellion than her counterpart in "The White Porch."

MAYA LIN, *The Vietnam Veterans Memorial* (p. I)

YUSEF KOMUNYAKAA, *Facing It* (p. H)

Lin's photograph of the memorial included in this insert conveys the reflective surface of the stone that is so crucial to Komunyakaa's poem. Viewers who come to mourn the loss of lives can literally see themselves in the list of names. Students might also want to search for photos online that indicate the scope of the memorial, which extends over 246 feet, or offer detailed views from the more than 58,000 carved names.

Komunyakaa's "Facing It" is marked by a confusion of the real world and the reflection. The war veteran who speaks the poem seems disoriented by his experience of the memorial, misinterpreting the gestures of fellow visitors, misreading contrail from an airplane as a painter's brushstroke. These images blur the lines between artistic or performative impulses with the "real," what exists in the physical world. The speaker also seems perplexed by the way the polished surface of the stone can both contain and release his own image and the images of other visitors. This visual confusion mirrors his sense of unreality about having witnessed the war but having survived. Looking at the wall, he almost expects to see his own name there in legible but apparently ephemeral "letters like smoke" (line 16). This ghostly feeling is reinforced by the speaker's sense that the white vet with the missing arm looks right through his reflection in the polished stone.

POSSIBLE CONNECTION TO ANOTHER SELECTION

E. E. Cummings, "next to of course god america i" (text p. 673; question #1, following)

CONNECTION QUESTION IN TEXT (p. J) WITH ANSWER

1. Discuss the speaker's tone and attitudes toward war in "Facing It" and in E. E. Cummings's "next to of course god america i" (text p. 673).

    Cummings's poem reflects on the idea of the "heroic happy dead" who gladly sacrifice themselves for American ideals (line 10). Though the poem is full of rhetoric that seems to support this idea, its frantic tone calls the idea of unwavering self-sacrifice into question. In fact, the speaker of the poem seems desperate to convince himself of its truth. In Komunyakaa's poem, questions about loss and sacrifice are vividly embodied in the image of the vet who lost his arm. Rather than a celebrated hero, this man seems as out of place and disoriented as the speaker, who wonders if he has lost the arm not in battle but "inside the stone" of the memorial that also pays tribute to the loss of so many lives (29).

PIETER BRUEGEL THE ELDER, *Two Chained Monkeys* (p. K)

WISLAWA SZYMBORSKA, *Bruegel's Two Monkeys* (p. J)

By posing the monkeys in a window, Bruegel draws a stark contrast between their captivity and the airy, open space outside. They seem to be either oblivious to the freer life that exists outside the circle of their window or else conditioned not to expect it. Both monkeys have their heads down, eyes looking at the ground that is scattered with broken shells. Neither one looks out. The ring that fastens their chain is a central focal point of the painting.

The speaker of the poem imagines herself involved in the scene presented, both as a viewer and as someone on view. Bruegel's monkeys get mixed up in recurring feelings of fear and worry that take the form, in her dreams, of test anxiety. She becomes not only the object of the monkeys' gaze (or, in the case of one, a presence to be deliberately ignored), but the recipient of the message intended by the rattling of chains. This message is ambiguous, but the monkey offers it as a prompt to help her answer a question about human nature, a question that she only seems able to answer with silence.

POSSIBLE CONNECTION TO ANOTHER SELECTION

Kay Ryan, "Turtle" (text p. 982; question #1, following)

CONNECTION QUESTION IN TEXT (p. K) WITH ANSWER

1. Discuss the theme in this poem and in Kay Ryan's "Turtle" (text p. 982).

   Both Szymborska's and Ryan's poems convey something about the human condition by looking closely at animal life, and both force readers to view humans as more humble or, in Ryan's words ,"chastened" (line 14), than is often our tendency. In the case of Ryan's "Turtle," the animal demonstrates a way of life that is so earthbound and plodding that it doesn't allow even "imagining some lottery / Will change her load of pottery to wings" (12–13). The question that begins the poem, "Who would be a turtle who could help it?" (1), might be read as an admission that humans are stuck with our terrestrial nature, even if we might wish for the transports of flight. In Szymborska's poem, one of the monkeys looks ironically on the project of examining "the history of mankind" (5) while the other rattles the chain that holds him. Both attitudes seem to counter human assumptions of superior freedom and intellect.

EDWARD HOPPER, *House by the Railroad (1925)* (p. M)

EDWARD HIRSCH, *Edward Hopper and the House by the Railroad (1925)* (p. L)

In Hopper's painting, the line of the tracks cuts off the house's foundation so that, rather than rooted on the ground, the house seems to be either floating or growing out of the train tracks. A deep shadow on the porch obscures the front door, which makes this look like a place with no entrance or exit, and there are many shaded windows that block the viewer's gaze into the house.

Hirsch's poem anthropomorphizes the house, making it as much of a character as the painter who comes to look at it. He not only gives the house the "gawky" appearance that he connects with "someone / being stared at, someone American" (lines 37–38) but also attributes feelings to the structure. Under the accusing eye of the painter, the house is "ashamed of itself" (5).

Hirsch takes the painting as a window into the painter's mind. He connects the emptiness of the scene—particularly the blank sky and the apparently barren ground—with the emptiness of the house. In fact, he blames the house for this emptiness, as if the only way to explain the desolation is to assume the house has "done something" to offend its former inhabitants, the sky, and the surrounding earth. The house, in turn, begins to suspect that "the man too is desolate, desolate, / and even ashamed" (23–24). Hirsch sees this painting as a starting point for Hopper's career, a font of his typical imagery, a particularly American kind of loneliness that "can no longer stand it" (40).

Possible Connections to Other Selections

Edgar Allan Poe, "The Haunted Palace" (text p. 667; question #1, following)

Jim Stevens, "Schizophrenia" (text p. 657; question #1, following)

Connection Question in Text (p. N) with Answer

1. Discuss the images and themes associated with the house in this poem and in Edgar Allan Poe's "The Haunted Palace" (text p. 667) or Jim Stevens's "Schizophrenia" (text p. 657).

   As in Hirsch's poem, in "The Haunted Palace" the house functions as an emblem of lost time and lost community—in its physical structure, Poe sees the "old time entombed" (line 40). However, while Poe sees the palace as "fair and stately" (3), Hirsch senses that there has always been something awkward or out of place about the house by the tracks, with its "fantastic mansard rooftop / And its pseudo-Gothic porch" (6–7). In Stevens's poem, the house is desolate not because it mourns for an earlier time, but rather because it has been marked by past trauma—the effects of mental illness. Stevens demonstrates how chaos on the inside becomes visible on the house's exterior as "cracking paint, broken windows, / the front door banging in the wind, / the roof tiles flying off, one by one" (16–18), details that help neighbors identify it as a "madhouse" (19).

HENRI MATISSE, *Woman Before an Aquarium* (p. O)

PATRICIA HAMPL, *Woman Before an Aquarium* (p. O)

Compared with Matisse's more eroticized nudes, this woman looks modest and even childlike, sitting at a "plain desk" with her "schoolgirl's haircut" (line 27). However, Hampl imagines that she also contains the memory of "wild nights" and a history of colonial oppression (13). The look on her face might be read as contemplative, or sullen, or angry. In response to this ambiguity, Hampl questions what the goldfish in the aquarium might mean to the woman gazing at them. The fish and the water they swim in seem to have a soothing action, as their image glides over "the hard rock and spiny shells" of the woman's thoughts (5). Eventually, Hampl imagines the woman transformed into a mermaid—not the eroticized "enchantress" that many associate with mermaids, but an emblem of living a "double life" (43–44), both aquatic and terrestrial.

Hampl gives meaning to the pinecones that seem merely decorative in the painting, like elements in a still life. The smell of the crushed pinecone recalls a memory that signifies both ethnic and gender oppression: the "Indian back crushing / the pine needles, the trapper / standing over me, his white-dead skin" (14–16). It also connects the painted scene with the experience of the speaker: "I study my lesson slowly, / crushing a warm pinecone / in my hand" (10–12). The two women are also connected by the fish-bowl as an object. In addition to providing a glimpse into a different, aquatic scene, it also represents the round shape of the globe, even as its glass distorts vision.

Possible Connections to Other Selections

Cathy Song, "Girl Powdering Her Neck" (text p. F; question #1, following)

Kitagawa Utamaro, *Girl Powdering Her Neck* (text p. E; question #1, following)

Connection Question in Text (p. P) with Answer

1. Compare the nature of female identity in this poem and painting with the way it is presented in "Girl Powdering Her Neck" by Cathy Song (text p. F) and the painting by Kitagawa Utamaro (text p. E).

   Both "Woman Before an Aquarium" and "Girl Powdering Her Neck" are deeply concerned with how female identity depends on, or has to negotiate, male desire. In Hampl's poem "the only power of the woman" is "to be untouchable" (lines 24–25). She produces desire but evades its dangerous grasp. By contrast, in Song's poem, the woman deliberately prepares for the touch of another hand through her beauty ritual. In both poems, the woman's ability to create is at issue in this nego-tiation with men: the figure in Song's poem can paint a face for herself but cannot seem to break out of her silence. Hampl's woman can dream of a "double life" but the "paper before her is blank" (31).

38

A Thematic Case Study:
The World of Work

Work, the idea of it and the action, its causes and consequences, is ever-present in American society. Why do we work? Dana Gioia's poem "Money" tells the reader we work for economic gain, but Marge Piercy's narrator speaks of work exuberantly, and claims we desire "work that is real" in her poem "To be of use." Considering the recent economic climate, there are many opportunities for class discussions regarding the poems in this section. Students will find pieces that resonate with their own personal experiences, whether they feel the disillusionment found in Tony Hoagland's "America," or the outright rejection of the nine to five in Baron Wormser's "Labor." Perhaps they will read the experiences of their loved ones and family members in poems like Angela Alaimo O'Donnell's "Touring the Mine," or "My Father Teaches Me to Dream" by Jan Beatty. Since most students already have jobs or are in college for the express purpose of starting a career, this chapter can foster a broad exchange of ideas, experiences, and goals.

DANA GIOIA, *Money* (p. 986)

Poet Dana Gioia was once vice-president of General Foods, and it is no coincidence that the epigraph is by insurance salesman/poet Wallace Stevens. This poem uses a series of clichés to build a picture of "money." And this accumulation literally makes money a kind of poetry. The American phrasing that describes money builds until he comes to the particularly American equation "Money breeds money" (line 13). At this point, the speaker's discussion becomes more clinical and money becomes ubiquitous: "gathering interest, compounding daily" (14). The poem points back to the idea of money as poetry in the final cliché, when "it talks" (18). In what other ways are images grouped effectively? If clichés are likely to reinforce meanings money already holds, how does Gioia's structure make the material new?

POSSIBLE CONNECTIONS TO OTHER SELECTIONS

Florence Cassen Mayers, "All-American Sestina" (text p. 750)

Tony Hoagland, "America" (text p. 987)

Edwin Arlington Robinson, "Richard Cory" (text p. 669)

Joyce Sutphen, "Guys Like That" (text p. 993)

Ronald Wallace, "In a Rut" (text p. 967; question #1, following)

CONNECTION QUESTION IN TEXT (p. 987) WITH ANSWER

1. Compare Gioia's poetic strategy for writing with Ronald Wallace's for "In a Rut" (text p. 967).

   Wallace uses a series of animal-based clichés to describe an exchange between a man and woman. Gioia lists a series of money-based clichés to invigorate our understanding of what money is. By grouping these clichés in a way that allows for movement — in Wallace's case, a dialogue, and in Gioia's case, a new image for each stanza — they avoid the stasis usually associated with cliché.

TONY HOAGLAND, *America* (p. 987)

This poem records a change in attitude on the part of the speaker. The view of America as a country whose culture is one of empty materialism, first expressed by his student, is so extreme that he reacts with cynicism. To perceive America as a "maximum-security prison / Whose walls are made of RadioShacks and Burger Kings, and MTV episodes" (lines 2–3) sounds like a parody of the now-familiar criticisms of popular culture. However, his response to the student is interrupted by the memory of a dream that incorporated a similar kind of capitalist symbolism. In the dream his father's heart is burdened by the weight of "bright green hundred-dollar bills" (15). The speaker remembers Marx's wish that he had spent more time "'listening to the cries of the future'" (28), which suggests a concern not only for the speaker's future but also for that of the student whose attitudes represent a younger generation. You might have your students discuss their own sense of contemporary American culture. Do they feel the emphasis on material goods is a "nightmare" (30), or do they relate more to the speaker's first cynical reaction?

POSSIBLE CONNECTIONS TO OTHER SELECTIONS

Tato Laviera, "AmeRícan" (text p. 773; question #1, following)

Florence Cassen Mayers, "All-American Sestina" (p. 750)

CONNECTION QUESTION IN TEXT (p. 988) WITH ANSWER

1. Compare the perspective offered in "America" with that in Tato Laviera's "AmeRícan" (text p. 773).

   Hoagland's poem expresses a deep disillusionment with the materialistic culture of the United States. The poem purposely mentions things like "RadioShacks and Burger Kings, and MTV episodes" (3), "100 channels of 24-hour cable" (29), and "rivers of bright merchandise" (31) to create images of a culture that is overwhelmed by consumerism. Even in his dreams, Hoagland's narrator cannot escape the presence of capitalism, describing a nightmare in which his father bleeds "bright green hundred-dollar bills" (15). The narrator claims that we are all "captured and suffocated in the folds / Of the thick satin quilt of America" (9–10).

   In contrast to "America," Laviera's poem "AmeRícan" offers a much more positive perspective of the United States. The speaker in this poem expresses appreciation for the way American society "includes everything / imaginable" (6–7) and "salutes all folklores, / european, indian, black, spanish, / and anything else compatible" (10–12). The speaker believes that immigrants and multiculturalism are "defining the new america, humane america, / admired america, loved america, harmonious / america, the world in peace" (50–52). Laviera's focus on the positives of American society (individuality, multiculturalism, and acceptance) is completely opposed to the perspective of America as a materialistic prison in Hoagland's work.

JAN BEATTY, *My Father Teaches Me to Dream* (p. 988)

You might begin discussion of Beatty's poem by asking students about the relationship between the title and the body of the poem. Does the poem render the title wholly ironic? Or is the father's advice actually a way to dream? On one hand, the poem's repetition of words, sentence structures, and concepts suggests that his idea of work is prosaic and limiting. However, within the tautology, "Work is work" (line 3), is a value for the actual effort. One way to read the poem is as austere praise not of the endpoint but of a process.

This poem is one in a series in Beatty's book *Boneshaker* about lessons from a father. If you are interested in hearing the poem in Beatty's voice, a recording of her reading the poem is posted on her Web site: janbeatty.com/boneshaker_fatherdream.php.

POSSIBLE CONNECTIONS TO OTHER SELECTIONS

Robert Hayden, "Those Winter Sundays" (text p. 547)

Baron Wormser, "Labor" (text p. 990; question #1, following)

CONNECTION QUESTION IN TEXT (p. 989) **WITH ANSWER**

1. Compare this father's vision of work with the perspective of the young man in Baron Wormser's "Labor" (p. 990). How might the difference between the two be explained?

   While Wormser's young speaker romanticizes labor, the father in Beatty's poem has an older man's realism about the results of work. The father doesn't invest work with spiritual qualities or describe it with love. He doesn't disappear into the work as Wormser's speaker does by "becoming" the maul or the saw. However, he does seem to have faith in raw effort. Big ideas may go by the wayside, but work will endure.

MICHAEL CHITWOOD, *Men Throwing Bricks* (p. 989)

Some poems vividly capture a moment, like a snapshot. "Men Throwing Bricks" condenses such a moment into a simple description. Notice that there is only one simile—"like a gift" (line 4)—in the entire poem. The power of Chitwood's verse lies in the rightness of his verbs (*chime*, *marvel*) and his attention to detail. When discussing this compact poem, ask students to identify places where stress mimics the action being described. Consider the effect of the rhyme "chimes" from line to line, between *lofts*, *lift*, *gift*, and then *slightly*, *daily*, *marvel*.

POSSIBLE CONNECTIONS TO OTHER SELECTIONS

William Blake, "The Chimney Sweeper" (text p. 687)

Marge Piercy, "To be of use" (text p. 994)

Joyce Sutphen, "Guys Like That" (text p. 993; question #1, following)

Ronald Wallace, "Building an Outhouse" (text p. 660)

Baron Wormser, "Labor" (text p. 990)

CONNECTION QUESTION IN TEXT (p. 989) **WITH ANSWER**

1. Compare Chitwood's treatment of these working men with Joyce Sutphen's perspective on the men and their work in "Guys Like That" (text p. 993).

   Chitwood treats the bricklayers and their work with reverence, while Sutphen exposes the men with white collar jobs, the ones a reader might view with awe, as dishonorable. Chitwood uses words like *rise*, *chime*, and *marvel* in his description, while Sutphen includes the words *slaughter*, *robbed*, and *divide*.

BARON WORMSER, *Labor* (p. 990)

Wormser's ode celebrates both physical labor and the life that led him to it. It begins in his "undestined / Twenties" (lines 1–2), a time when the speaker has not yet figured out the direction his life will take. What could be a romantic retreat into the woods is actually intensive manual labor. However, physical work retains a connection to art throughout the poem. The local workers have "poetically" (3) described the soil as "Stones and rocks" (4), and the act of cutting wood seems to make the speaker more sharply aware of the world around him, as the poem's descriptions illustrate.

Though the speaker gains a heightened attention to nature, he also seems to lose himself in the work necessary for self-preservation. He turns into a tool: "the maul coming down" (9) or the "hellacious / Screeching saw" (10–11). Wormser's simple sentence structures (often just "I" followed by a verb) allow the physical actions he describes to take the most important role in this definition of labor.

Robert Frost, "Mending Wall" (text p. 843)

Michael Chitwood, "Men Throwing Bricks" (text p. 989; question #1, following)

CONNECTION QUESTION IN TEXT (p. 991) WITH ANSWER

1.   Discuss the themes in "Labor" and in Michael Chitwood's "Men Throwing Bricks" (p. 989).

Both Wormser's "Labor" and Chitwood's "Men Throwing Bricks" focus on the theme of physical labor. Chitwood's speaker concisely describes a scene of two men tossing bricks from one to the other, and Chitwood's language mimics their rhythmic, methodical movements. The speaker admires their offhand precision and skill, claiming "You'd have to do this daily,/morning and afternoon, not to marvel." (11–12). Wormser explores the theme of physical labor from the point of view of the worker, rather than the onlooker. Where Chitwood's titular men seem oblivious to the beauty in their work, Wormser's speaker treats his occupation with reverence. This speaker is in love with his job as a lumberjack, describing how he "loved the feel//Of my feet on grass slick with dew or frost" (16–17). He also says, "I loved the moment after I felled a tree/When it was still again and I felt the awe//Of what I had done and awe for the tree that had//Stretched towards the sky for silent decades." (20–22). Chitwood's speaker describes the laborers as unaware of the harmony in their work. On the other hand, Wormser's speaker and his fellow tree-cutters feel passionate about their occupation. He describes himself as "a happy fool" (30) and says of his companions: "Through their proper/Scorn I could feel it. They loved it too" (31–32).

ANGELA ALAIMO O'DONNELL, *Touring the Mine* (p. 991)

"Touring the Mine" begins with a deceptively simple introductory stanza, giving us a first impression of a Pennsylvania coal mine: "Like Disney World, only true. / A tram conveys us / down the earth's dark drop" (lines 1–3). O'Donnell pays particular attention to sound in her clipped three-line stanzas; in a passage such as "only eons of black rock / earth's hull and hammer- / struck walls of oily coal" (13–15), she recreates the claustrophobic mine, the rocky interior of the earth that the miners chipped away.

To start discussion about "Touring the Mine," ask students about the speaker's perspective. The speaker identifies herself as a miner's descendant ("our fathers moved in silence" [17]). How would it be different if O'Donnell removed the speaker, if the poem was written from a miner's point of view, or without an "I"? The speaker acknowledges the great debt owed to miners, who harnessed the power of rocks far below the earth: "Here heavy and inert,/once above the surface/it leapt to light and heat.//They made it so,/shoveled coal to feed the fire/that burnt in every man's cellar" (25–30). Inquire whether or not students think this poem is an ode to the miners.

POSSIBLE CONNECTIONS TO OTHER SELECTIONS

William Blake, "The Chimney Sweeper" (text p. 687)

Michael Chitwood, "Men Throwing Bricks" (text p. 989; question #1, following)

Robert Frost, "Acquainted with the Night" (text p. 665)

CONNECTION QUESTION IN TEXT (p. 992) WITH ANSWER

1.   Discuss the tone in "Touring the Mine" and in Michael Chitwood's "Men Throwing Bricks" (text p. 989).

There is a light beauty to Chitwood's "Men Throwing Bricks" that doesn't match the tone in "Touring the Mine." That's not to say the tone in "Mine" doesn't convey the beauty of the work the miners do; there's a cold, black beauty to the mine itself, and there's nobility in the explanation "They made it so, / shoveled coal to feed the fire / that burnt in every man's cellar." But the tone of "Mine" is heavier, conveyed by the phrase "rush of bone cold" or "rough-muscled alchemy of stone." The ending image encapsulates the overall feeling of the poem: "where we emerge squinting / its black smoke still rising / against the killing cold."

DAVID IGNATOW, *The Jobholder* (p. 992)

The word *wait* is repeated seven times in "The Jobholder." How does this portrayal of waiting reflect the experience of today's jobholder or of modern life? What does this poem reveal about a day in the life of the speaker in the first stanza? How does it express how he sees his life unfolding in the second? Ask students about their experience of monotony in their life routines.

Consider another poetic expression of routine weariness — T. S. Eliot's Prufrock says, "I have measured out my life in coffee spoons." For a writing exercise, let students go line by line through Ignatow's poem, comparing this poem to that famous line. Explain the "measuring out" that's taking place in each one.

POSSIBLE CONNECTIONS TO OTHER SELECTIONS

Jan Beatty, "My Father Teaches Me to Dream" (text p. 988)

Emily Dickinson, "Because I could not stop for Death —" (text p. 814)

T. S. Eliot, "The Love Song of J. Alfred Prufrock" (text p. 1006)

Marge Piercy, "To be of use" (text p. 994)

Louis Simpson, "In the Suburbs" (text p. 616)

Baron Wormser, "Labor" (text p. 990; question #1, following)

CONNECTION QUESTION IN TEXT (p. 992) WITH ANSWER

1. Compare Ignatow's representation of work with Baron Wormser's in "Labor" (text p. 990).

   We're not sure what Ignatow's speaker does for a living, but we imagine it is office work of some sort. In Wormser's poem, the work is manual labor. Ignatow's work isn't worth describing — it's so monotonous that he simply waits "for the day to end." Wormser's speaker, on the other hand, enjoys the work that affects his daily life in the woods. In fact, he loves it so much, he admits, "I lost interest in everything except for the trees."

JOYCE SUTPHEN, *Guys Like That* (p. 993)

Sutphen subtly shifts her tone from start to finish in this poem. In the beginning, "guys like that" are sleek and handsome, the sort of guys who might be thinking about "wine and marble floors" (line 7). They seem ("from / where you sit" [1–2]) to be a desirable choice as a mate. In fact, Sutphen reveals, they are no different than the men who work for a slaughterhouse. By the fourth repetition of the phrase "guys like that," Sutphen announces "guys like that" are in fact "planning worse things than the death / of a cow" (13–14), despite their seeming refinement. Consider the connotations of her pop culture references ("TiVo" and "ESPN") and her diction ("cooking books") when discussing her tonal shift.

Sutphen's accusations against "guys like that" gather force from the use of second person. Ask students to modify the point of view as a class exercise, choosing first-person singular or third person (using "women" or a similar choice for that position, for clarity) to replace her "you." Discuss the effect of second person after trying a different point of view.

Michael Chitwood, "Men Throwing Bricks" (text p. 989)

Tony Hoagland, "America" (text p. 987)

Angela Alaimo O'Donnell, "Touring the Mine" (text p. 991; question #1, following)

Edwin Arlington Robinson, "Richard Cory" (text p. 669)

CONNECTION QUESTION IN TEXT (p. 993) WITH ANSWER

1. Consider the treatment of men's relationship to domestic life in "Guys Like That" and in Angela Alaimo O'Donnell's "Touring the Mine" (text p. 991).

    The men's relationship to domestic life in "Touring the Mine" is deeply pessimistic. In "Touring the Mine," the "tight-lipped men" disappear into the mines, away from a parasitic home life: "women and their worry,/the clamor of children/who ate their wages/before they'd palmed the scrip." Sutphen's speaker warns women away from a domestic life with "guys like that," because they are "planning worse things than the death/of a cow." They are playing with the lives of others for their own selfish ends, and the speaker suggests that they could treat their women the same way—"planning how/to divide up that little farm they just/passed, the one you used to call home."

MARGE PIERCY, *To be of use* (p. 994)

This poem, brimming with metaphor, is a paean to work. In it, the speaker singles out those who approach work with vitality and ease, comparing them with "the black sleek heads of seals" (line 6). Like water buffalo, these workers "strain in the mud and the muck to move things forward" (10). Ask students to describe the poem's work ethic in terms of the animal nature that is singled out. Look also at the image of the Greek amphora or Hopi vase as a symbol for craft, "the thing worth doing well done" (20). List the metaphors and similes made in "To be of use," and look at alliteration and anaphora. Discuss how the poet is one of those who "submerge/in the task, who go into the fields to harvest" (12–13).

Michael Chitwood, "Men Throwing Bricks" (text p. 989)

David Ignatow, "The Jobholder" (text p. 992)

William Blake, "The Chimney Sweeper" (text p. 687; question #1, following)

CONNECTION QUESTION IN TEXT (p. 994) WITH ANSWER

1. Compare the sense of what constitutes meaningful work in this poem with that in William Blake's "The Chimney Sweeper" (p. 687).

    Marge Piercy's poem "To be of use" pays homage to simple, necessary labor. To Piercy's speaker, meaningful work is done by people who "jump into work head first/without dallying in the shallows" (2–3) and who "harness themselves, an ox to a heavy cart" (8). In fact, it seems the only meaningless work is that of "parlor generals and field deserters" (15). She claims, "The work of the world is common as mud" (18) and, like mud, sometimes "crumbles to dust" (19) but often is used to create. Examples of exalted creations composed of such a low substance are "Greek amphoras for wine or oil,/Hopi vases that held corn" (22–23). These once common vessels are now "put in museums/but you know they were made to be used" (23–24).

    William Blake's "The Chimney Sweeper" presents a more complicate view of the same sort of manual labor Piercy's poem seems to praise. The speaker here is a child who loses his mother and is sold into labor by his father. He and other small boys must clean the chimneys of London, a job made dangerous not only by heights, but also through the possibility of illness. Though this work is important and necessary to keep the city safely running, it is tragic that children were forced to perform it. The speaker describes a dream told to him by his friend, where an angel comes to deliver chimney sweeps to heaven once they die. The speaker relates, "And the Angel told Tom, if he'd be a good boy, / He'd have God for his father, and never want joy" (19–20). This vision of holy reward comforts the children, and the speaker ends on the line, "So if all do their duty they need not fear harm" (24). It's unclear whether or not Blake believed this was appropriate work for children, but it does not fit Piercy's definition of meaningful work. These children are not dedicated and adept at a craft or trade; they do not voluntarily "strain in the mud and the muck to move things forward" (Piercy 10). The chimney sweep in Blake's poem is no better off than an indentured servant at best, or a slave at worst.

39

A Collection of Poems

ANONYMOUS, *Bonny Barbara Allan* (p. 999)

Ballads can provide a good introduction to poetry, for they demonstrate many devices of other poetic forms — such as rhyme, meter, and image — within a narrative framework. However, ballads often begin abruptly, and the reader must infer the details that preceded their action. They use simple language, tell their story through narrated events and dialogue, and often use refrains. The folk ballad was at its height in England and Scotland in the sixteenth and seventeenth centuries. These ballads were not written down but were passed along through an oral tradition, with the original author remaining anonymous. Literary ballads are derivatives of the folk ballad tradition. Keats's "La Belle Dame sans Merci" (text p. 1015) is an example.

Notice how often this ballad refers to a broken love relationship. What can you infer about the relationships of the people in this ballad? Is it always one sex or the other who suffers? Is there a relationship between this ballad and modern-day popular songs? "Scarborough Fair" (text p. 690) might provide the basis for a discussion of the romantic situations presented in this ballad and the durability of such old "songs." Despite the list of impossible tasks that the speaker presents to his former lover as the price of reconciliation, the refrain names garden herbs associated with female power. Thyme traditionally is thought to enhance courage, sage wisdom, and rosemary memory, and parsley was used to decorate tombs — but both sage and rosemary had the additional connotations of growing in gardens where women ruled the households. You might wish to have your students speculate on how such "mixed messages" might have been incorporated into this ballad. Also, "Scarborough Fair" was the basis for an antiwar song by the folk-rock duo Simon and Garfunkel in the 1960s. Your students might be interested in hearing how this old folk song was adapted for twentieth-century purposes.

Web Ask students to research the poets in this chapter at **bedfordstmartins.com/ meyerlit**.

Despite their ostensible narrative directness, ballads can be highly suggestive (rather than straightforward) in their presentation. Psychological motivation is often implied rather than spelled out. To explore this point, you might request, for example, that students examine in a two- to three-page essay the reasons for and effects of the vengeful acts of Barbara Allan.

These ballads contain central characters whose awareness (and hence voice) comes into full power near the moment of their death. Again, this observation seems to support the psychological realism and suggestive truth that ballads can convey.

Tip from the Field

When teaching "Bonny Barbara Allan" and other ballads, I begin by reading the selection aloud or playing a recording of it, followed by a recording of early blues music from Mississippi (e.g., songs by Robert Johnson or Howlin' Wolf). In conjunction, I distribute the lyrics from the blues songs to the class. I then ask my students to compare these two oral-based forms.

– TIMOTHY PETERS, *Boston University*

W. H. AUDEN, *The Unknown Citizen* (p. 1000)

In "The Unknown Citizen," Auden criticizes the institutionalization and rampant capitalism of modern Western society. The "citizen" is identified only by a series of letters and numbers, similar to a social security card or driver's license. The poem is written like an obituary or memorial; even the title seems to be a play on "The Tomb of the Unknown Soldier." The only descriptions offered of the citizen are from external organizations. His former employers comment on his satisfactory work record (lines 7–8), and "his Union reports that he paid his dues" (10). Auden never includes the opinions of people who actually knew the deceased, and gives the reader no hints as to what he was like as a person. Auden might be attempting to warn his readers that if we continue to let organizations and external forces rule our lives, this is where the future is heading.

WILLIAM BLAKE, *The Garden of Love* (p. 1001)

This brief lyric poses in customary Blakean fashion the natural, free-flowing, and childlike expression of love against the restrictive and repressive adult structures of organized religion. The dialogue between the two is effectively demonstrated in the closing two lines, with their internal rhyme patterns, in particular the rhyming of "briars" (of the priests) and "desires" (of the young speaker). The process of growing into adulthood is costly, according to Blake; it requires the exchange of simple pleasures for conventional morality.

POSSIBLE CONNECTIONS TO OTHER SELECTIONS

Emily Dickinson, "Some keep the Sabbath going to Church—" (text p. 806)

Robert Frost, "Birches" (text p. 848)

WILLIAM BLAKE, *Infant Sorrow* (p. 1001)

This brief poem uses the voice of an infant to demonstrate distrust of "the dangerous world" (line 2). Arriving "Helpless naked" (3) and "Struggling" (5), the baby is soon "Bound and weary" (7) and has little hope. The parental response is not encouraging: the pain and fear of childbirth preclude a proper greeting. Blake's speaker seems to have been aware of the dangers of the world before his arrival, knowing that the world into which he "leapt" was "dangerous" (2). His first contact does not seem to dissuade him from this bias.

POSSIBLE CONNECTION TO ANOTHER SELECTION

Anne Bradstreet, "Before the Birth of One of Her Children" (text p. 1002)

ANNE BRADSTREET, *Before the Birth of One of Her Children* (p. 1002)

Until Anne Bradstreet's brother-in-law took a collection of her poems to London and had it published in 1650, no resident of the New World had published a book of poetry. Bradstreet's work enjoyed popularity in England and America. She was born and grew up on the estate of the earl of Lincoln, whose affairs her father managed. Bradstreet's father was eager to provide his daughter with the best possible education. When she was seventeen, she and her new husband, Simon Bradstreet, sailed for Massachusetts, where she lived the rest of her life.

As a child Bradstreet contracted rheumatic fever, and its lifelong effects compounded the dangers attending seventeenth-century childbirth. What may seem at first an overdramatized farewell to a loved one can be viewed in this context as a sober reflection on life's capriciousness and an understandable wish to maintain some influence on the living. Perhaps the most striking moment in the poem occurs in line 16, when the only inexact end rhyme ("grave") coincides with a crucial change in tone and purpose. What had been a summary of Puritan attitudes (deeply felt, to be sure) toward life and death and a gently serious offering of "best wishes" to the speaker's husband becomes, with that crack in the voice, a plea to be remembered well.

You might discuss the appropriateness of the poet's choosing heroic couplets for this subject: How does the symmetry of the lines affect our understanding of the subject? You might also consider the way the speaker constructs her audience, like someone writing a diary. Is this truly private verse? Or does the speaker sense that people other than her husband will read the poem?

POSSIBLE CONNECTIONS TO OTHER SELECTIONS

Anne Bradstreet, "The Author to Her Book" (text p. 647)

John Donne, "A Valediction: Forbidding Mourning" (text p. 658)

ROBERT BURNS, *A Red, Red Rose* (p. 1002)

Some of Burns's metaphors have become so familiar that we could hardly imagine poetry without them. Linking love with a red rose has even become a poetry cliché. However, some of his figures are still striking and vivid. The drying up of the seas and the melting of rocks present an apocalyptic scene that belies the poem's gentle beginning. Like many older poems, this one also has a close relation to song. The effects of meter and rhyme are musical, as are the repetitions of phrases like "Till a' the seas gang dry" (lines 8, 9) and "fare thee weel" (13, 14). It might be fun to have your students compare this poem with a contemporary love song. In what ways are the two alike? Besides the obvious dialect differences, how is this poem foreign to the tradition they are used to? Which one seems more original?

POSSIBLE CONNECTIONS TO OTHER SELECTIONS

Anonymous, "Scarborough Fair" (text p. 690)

William Shakespeare, "My mistress' eyes are nothing like the sun" (text p. 743)

GEORGE GORDON, LORD BYRON, *She Walks in Beauty* (p. 1003)

In the nineteenth century, George Gordon, Lord Byron, was commonly considered the greatest of the Romantic poets. He spent his childhood with his mother in Aberdeen, Scotland, in deprived circumstances despite an aristocratic heritage. In *Childe Harold, Don Juan,* and much of his other work, Byron chronicled the adventures of one or another example of what came to be known as the "Byronic hero," a gloomy, lusty, guilt-ridden individualist. The poet died of fever while participating in the Greek fight for independence from Turkey.

The title and first line of "She Walks in Beauty" can be an excellent entrance to the poem's explication. Students might puzzle over what it means to walk *in* beauty: Is the beauty like a wrap or a cloud? The simile "like the night" hinges on that image. You might ask students if the speaker makes nature subservient to the woman, or the reverse. You might point out "gaudy" (line 6), a strange adjective for describing the day, to draw attention to the speaker's attitude toward nature.

Note the mood of timeless adoration in the second stanza. There is really no movement, only an exclamation of wonder. The exclamation is even more direct in the final stanza, where the woman's visage becomes a reflection of her spotless character. Students might explore the images in all three stanzas, looking for shifts from natural to social. How does the speaker move from "like the night" (1) to "a mind" (17) and "a heart" (18)? Why would he want to describe a woman in these terms? What effect does this description have on our idea of her? Do we really know her by the end of the poem?

For discussion of Byron's poetry, consult *Byron: Wrath and Rhyme*, edited by Alan Bold (London: Vision, 1983; print.); Frederick Garber's *Self, Text, and Romantic Irony: The Example of Byron* (Princeton: Princeton UP, 1988; print.); and Peter Mannings's *Byron and His Fictions* (Detroit: Wayne State U, 1978; print.).

SAMUEL TAYLOR COLERIDGE, *Kubla Khan: or, a Vision in a Dream* (p. 1003)

Samuel Taylor Coleridge was born in Ottery St. Mary, Devonshire, but was sent to school in London, where he impressed his teachers and classmates (among whom was Charles Lamb) as an extremely precocious child. He attended Cambridge without taking a degree, enlisted for a short tour of duty in the Light Dragoons (a cavalry unit), planned a utopian community in America with Robert Southey, and married Southey's sister-in-law. He met William Wordsworth in 1795 and published *Lyrical Ballads* with him three years later. Coleridge became an opium addict in 1800–1801 because of the heavy doses of laudanum he'd taken to relieve the pain of several ailments, principally rheumatism. For the last eighteen years of his life, he was under the care (and under the roof) of Dr. James Gillman, writing steadily but never able to sustain the concentration needed to complete the large projects he kept planning.

Reputedly, "Kubla Khan" came to Coleridge "as in a vision" after he took a prescribed anodyne and fell into a deep sleep. What Coleridge was able to write down on waking is only a fragment of what he dreamed. Figures such as the "pleasure-dome" (line 2) and "the sacred river" (3) take on an allegorical cast and suggest the power that inspires the writing of poetry. Although phrases such as "sunless sea" (5) and "lifeless ocean" (28) appear gloomy, they could also suggest mystery and the atmosphere conducive to bringing forth poems.

For a reading of this poem, consult Humphrey House's "Kubla Khan, Christabel, and Dejection," in *Coleridge* (London: Hart-Davis, 1953; print.), reprinted in *Romanticism and Consciousness,* edited by Harold Bloom (New York: Norton, 1970; print.). Another good essay to turn to is "The Daemonic in 'Kubla Khan': Toward Interpretation" by Charles I. Patterson Jr., in *PMLA* 89 (October 1974): 1033–42. Patterson points out, for example, that the river in the poem is "sacred" (3) because it seems to be possessed by a god who infuses in the poet a vision of beauty. Likewise, he identifies the "deep delight" mentioned in line 44 as "a daemonic inspiration." As a writing assignment, you might ask students to explore imagery and sound patterns in order to demonstrate how Coleridge uses words to embody and suggest the idea that poetry is truly a "pleasure-dome" (2), visionary and demonically inspired.

You could initiate discussion by asking students to locate and discuss the way Coleridge uses unusual language to describe the scene and to shape our perceptions of it. What is the effect, for instance, of alliteration in line 25 ("Five miles meandering with a mazy motion")?

POSSIBLE CONNECTION TO ANOTHER SELECTION

John Keats, "Ode to a Nightingale" (text p. 713)

JOHN DONNE, *Batter My Heart* (p. 1005)

Christian and Romantic traditions come together in this sonnet. Employing Christian tradition, Donne here portrays the soul as a maiden with Christ as her bridegroom. Borrowing from Petrarchan materials, Donne images the reluctant woman as a castle and her lover as the invading army. Without alluding to any particular tradition, we can also observe in this poem two modes of male aggression — namely, the waging of war and the pursuit of romantic conquest, again blended into a strong and brilliantly rendered metaphysical conceit. Donne is imploring his "three-personed" God (line 1) to take strong measures against the enemy, Satan. In a typical metaphysical paradox, Donne moreover asks God to save him from Satan by imprisoning him within God's grace.

Rhythm and sound work remarkably in this sonnet to enforce its meaning. Review the heavy-stressed opening line, which sounds like the pounding of a relentless fist and is followed by the strong reiterated plosives of "break, blow, burn" (4).

POSSIBLE CONNECTION TO ANOTHER SELECTION

Mark Jarman, "Unholy Sonnet" (text p. 745)

JOHN DONNE, *The Flea* (p. 1005)

An interesting discussion or writing topic could be organized around the tradition of the *carpe diem* poem and how this poem both accommodates and alters that tradition.

The wit here is ingenious, and after the individual sections of the poem are explained, more time might be needed to review the parts and give the class a sense of the total effect of the poem's operations.

The reason the speaker even bothers to comment on the flea stems from his belief that a commingling of blood during intercourse (here, admittedly, by the agency of the flea) may result in conception. Hence his belief that the lovers must be "yea more than" united (line 11) and that the flea's body has become a kind of "marriage temple" (13). For the woman to crush the flea (which she does) is a multiple crime because in so doing she commits murder, suicide, and sacrilege (of the temple) and figuratively destroys the possible progeny. The flea in its death, though, also stands as a logical emblem for why this courtship should be consummated. The reasoning is that if little (if any) innocence or honor is spent in killing the flea, then, likewise, neither of those commodities would be spent "when thou yield'st to me" (26).

One way to begin discussion is to consider the poem as an exercise in the making of meaning: What does the flea represent to the speaker, and how does its meaning change as the poem progresses? What, in effect, is the relation between the flea and the poem?

POSSIBLE CONNECTIONS TO OTHER SELECTIONS

Sally Croft, "Home-Baked Bread" (text p. 636)

John Donne, "Song" (text p. 706)

GEORGE ELIOT [MARY ANN EVANS], *In a London Drawingroom* (p. 1006)

This poem could more accurately be titled "*From* a London Drawingroom," as the speaker's gaze seems to be directed entirely outward, through a window that makes London (or even the world) seem like a prison. The colors are drab, the people are lifeless, the architecture monotonous. Despite the monotony of the landscape, everyone is in constant motion, which is part of the problem; "No figure lingering / Pauses to feed the hunger of the eye / Or rest a little on the lap of life" (lines 10–12). Ask students to unpack these lines: What do they imply about these people and their surroundings, or about the relationship between this speaker and the rest of the world? What is meant by the phrase "multiplied identity" (16)? And in the last two lines, what do students suppose "men" are being punished for? By whom? The relationship between humankind and nature is also worth pursuing; we have presumably created the "smoke" of the first line and the "solid fog" of the fourth line, yet the punishment seems to come from elsewhere. This poem is a good example of how an outward-looking description really reflects inward psychology.

POSSIBLE CONNECTIONS TO OTHER SELECTIONS

Matthew Arnold, "Dover Beach" (text p. 626)

T. S. Eliot, "The Love Song of J. Alfred Prufrock" (text p. 1006)

T. S. ELIOT, *The Love Song of J. Alfred Prufrock* (p. 1006)

This dramatic monologue is difficult but well worth the time spent analyzing the speaker, imagery, tone, and setting. Begin with the title—Is the poem actually a love song? Is Eliot undercutting the promise of a love song with the name J. Alfred Prufrock? Names carry connotations and images; what does this name project?

The epigraph from Dante seems to ensure both the culpability and the sincerity of the speaker. After reading the poem, are we, too, to be counted among those who will never reveal what we know?

The organization of this monologue is easy enough to describe. Up until line 83, Prufrock tries to ask the "overwhelming question" (line 10). In lines 84–86, we learn that he has been afraid to ask it. From line 87 to the end, Prufrock tries to explain his failure by citing the likelihood that he would be misunderstood or by making the disclaimer that he is a minor character, certainly no Prince Hamlet. Notice how the idea of "dare" charts Prufrock's growing submissiveness in the poem from "Do I dare / Disturb the universe?" (45–46) to "Have [I] the strength to force the moment to its crisis?" (line 80, which rhymes lamely with "tea and cakes and ices"), and finally, "Do I dare to eat a peach?" (122).

You might ask students to select images they enjoy. Consider, for example, Prufrock's assertion that he has measured out his life in the shallowness of the ladies he associates with: "In the room the women come and go / Talking of Michelangelo" (13–14). The poem offers many opportunities to explore the nuances of language and the suggestive power of the image as a means of drawing a character portrait and suggesting something about a particular social milieu at a particular time in modern history.

Grover Smith, in his *T. S. Eliot's Poetry and Plays* (Chicago: U of Chicago P, 1960; print.), provides extensive background and critical comment on this poem.

As a writing assignment, you might ask the class to explore a pattern of images in the poem — those of crustaceans near the end, for example — and how that pattern adds to the theme. You might also ask the class to give a close reading of a particular passage — the final three lines come to mind — for explication.

Possible Connections to Other Selections

John Keats, "La Belle Dame sans Merci" (text p. 1015)
Alberto Ríos, "Seniors" (text p. 573)
Walt Whitman, "One's-Self I Sing" (text p. 1027)

CHARLOTTE PERKINS GILMAN, *Queer People* (p. 1010)

The lilting rhymes in "Queer People" and the repetition of Gilman's strange construction "people people" give the poem a whimsical feeling. However, Gilman also constructs a social commentary on how friendships, marriages, and even families are formed. Once she has pronounced on the strangeness of all the connections people form, both by choice and by birth, she paradoxically suggests that no relationship can be odd. Students may have read Gilman's most famous literary work, "The Yellow Wallpaper." If so, you might prompt them to discuss how this statement on "queerness" might deepen their reading of the story or how the story might help to explain the poem's suggestion that marriage is the strangest relation of them all.

Possible Connection to Another Selection

Lisa Parker, "Snapping Beans" (text p. 546)

THOMAS HARDY, *In Time of "The Breaking of Nations"* (p. 1010)

This poem, published shortly after the beginning of World War I, demonstrates the speaker's belief in the timelessness of domestic life. Nations may break into pieces and kingdoms may be destroyed, as the footnote to this poem suggests, but life and love in the countryside "will go onward the same / Though Dynasties pass" (lines 7–8).

Students may see this as a naive view of international politics, or they may find it comforting. A discussion of this poem could center on what they've learned in history classes: How has the history they've studied been ordered? How do they imagine the speaker of this poem would choose to organize a history of the world?

POSSIBLE CONNECTION TO ANOTHER SELECTION

Dylan Thomas, "The Hand That Signed the Paper" (text p. 650)

FRANCES E. W. HARPER, *Learning to Read* (p. 1011)

This poem, written shortly after the end of the Civil War, eloquently praises the efforts of Yankees from the North who traveled to the South after the war to help teach slaves to read. Harper also recalls her own passion for learning how to read, despite the fact that she "was rising sixty" (line 35). Harper chooses not to characterize any one Yankee or "Reb," but rather focuses on people such as Uncle Caldwell and Chloe to personalize the poem. This technique shows the struggle to be free through the experiences of not only Harper but also those around her.

Students should be reminded of the relationship between the poet and the poem: Harper is writing about adjusting to life as a free woman, and about learning how to read; this poem is a product of that endeavor. It represents a switch from spoken language to written. Expand on this point with students, for the poem takes on more depth as this is fleshed out. Also alert students to what ultimately drove Harper to learn to read: her desire to read the Bible. Although she was "rising sixty," she "got a pair of glasses" (37) and "never stopped till [she] could read / The hymns and Testament" (39–40). The Bible, and the ability to read it, become symbolic of Harper's freedom from slavery.

POSSIBLE CONNECTION TO ANOTHER SELECTION

Philip Larkin, "A Study of Reading Habits" (text p. 557)

GERARD MANLEY HOPKINS, *Pied Beauty* (p. 1012)

It seems appropriate for Hopkins to have used so many innovations in style, structure, and diction in a poem that glorifies God — the only entity "whose beauty is past change" (line 10) — by observing the great variety present in the earth and sky. Ask students to point out examples of poetic innovation in this poem and to suggest their effects on the poem.

In form, "Pied Beauty" is what Hopkins termed a "curtal [that is, shortened] sonnet." Not only is it shortened, but it is shortened to exactly three-fourths of a traditional sonnet: the "octet" is six lines, the "sestet" four and a half. Having compressed the sonnet structure to ten and a half lines, Hopkins must make careful word choices to convey meaning in fewer words. Note the hyphenated words, which are his own creations: Is it possible to understand the meanings of these made-up compounds? Compare Hopkins's practice of creating new words to that of Lewis Carroll in "Jabberwocky" (text p. 704).

Students will need to know what *pied* means (patchy in color; splotched). How do the many synonyms for *pied* in the first few lines emphasize the theme of the poem? How does the repetition of the *le* sound (dappled, couple, stipple, tackle, fickle, freckled, adazzle) add a sense of rhythm and unity to this poem's untraditional metrics?

GERARD MANLEY HOPKINS, *The Windhover* (p. 1012)

At the midpoint of his poetic career, Hopkins considered this poem "the best thing I ever wrote" (*The Letters of Gerard Manley Hopkins to Robert Bridges,* edited by C. C. Abbott, rev. 1955 [New York: Oxford UP], 85). Regardless of the poem's quality, students should be forewarned that this is a difficult work by a difficult poet. It may help them to know that even literary specialists have had a difficult time agreeing on the poem's exact meaning. In fact, Tom Dunne's Hopkins bibliography (1976) lists nearly one hundred different readings of the poem before 1970. With this in mind, you might ask students to discuss the overall feeling conveyed by this lyric, rather than expecting them to be able to explicate it line by line. In general, the poem begins with the speaker's observation of a kestrel hawk in flight. The speaker is drawn from passive observation into passionate feeling for the "ecstasy" (line 5) of the bird's soaring freedom: "My heart in hiding / Stirred for a bird, — the achieve of, the mastery of the thing!" (7–8). It then occurs to the speaker that the bird's creator is "a billion / Times told lovelier, more dangerous" (10–11) than the creature, and his awe expands to consider an even greater power.

Have students note that the poem is addressed "To Christ our Lord." The speaker directly speaks to Christ as "my chevalier" in line 11. Realizing that the poem is addressed to Christ leads to an interpretation of the final lines as references to Christ's suffering and death. Despite Christ's earthly humility (the "blue-bleak embers" of line 13), his true glory — "gold-vermilion" (14) — is revealed when he falls, galls, and gashes himself (14).

One might approach "The Windhover" structurally by comparing it to the less complex poem that precedes it in the text. In "The Windhover," as in "Pied Beauty," Hopkins alters the sonnet form to suit his purposes. Discuss how "The Windhover" conforms to and deviates from traditional sonnet form. In particular, note its division into thirteen lines and the indication of the "turn" not at the beginning of the sestet but with the poet's emphasis on the word *and* in line 10. How do these deviations from the traditional sonnet form affect the poem's meaning?

Also worth discussing are the striking use of alliteration in the first long line and the poet's choices of unusual words, as seen in previous poems. Note that to the poet, a Jesuit priest, the "billion" in line 10 is not hyperbole; if anything, it is an understatement.

Fortunately, a number of glosses and extended critical interpretations of the works of this difficult poet are available. Among these are Graham Storey's *A Preface to Hopkins* (London and New York: Longman, 1981; print.); Paul Mariani's *A Commentary on the Complete Poems of Gerard Manley Hopkins* (Ithaca: Cornell UP, 1969; print.); *Hopkins: A Collection of Critical Essays,* edited by Geoffrey Hartman (Englewood Cliffs: Twentieth-Century Views/ Prentice-Hall, 1966; print.); and J. Hillis Miller's *The Disappearance of God* (Cambridge: Harvard UP, 1963; print.).

POSSIBLE CONNECTION TO ANOTHER SELECTION

Gerard Manley Hopkins, "God's Grandeur" (text p. 702)

A. E. HOUSMAN, *Is my team ploughing* (p. 1013)

This poem is in ballad form, with a typical question-response exchange between the Shropshire lad who has died and a supposedly impersonal voice that answers his queries. The surprise comes, of course, with the introduction of the second "I," who has a decidedly vested interest in the earthly life of the deceased.

You might ask students to trace the development of the worldly objects the speaker is interested in: What is the effect of his beginning with his team of horses and ending with questions about his girl and his friend? Does the development say anything about his sense of priority, or is the effect meant only to heighten the poem's final irony?

POSSIBLE CONNECTIONS TO OTHER SELECTIONS

Stephen Crane, "A Man Said to the Universe" (text p. 673)

Emily Dickinson, "Because I could not stop for Death —" (text p. 814)

BEN JONSON, *To Celia* (p. 1014)

This poem is a laudatory devotion to a lover in which the speaker moves through conceits of drinking in the first stanza and conceits of the tribute of a rose in the second. This poem is in fact a good opportunity to examine a Petrarchan conceit, or rather, two conceits. After students have worked through each stanza, you might ask them if there is a definite relationship between them. Does the poem read like two poems, or do the two stanzas depend on each other in a fundamental way?

You may also want to discuss whether the poem seems to be a bit *too* devotional; students may find the speaker's praise for his lover to be a bit too much, a bit unbelievable. You may want to discuss how poetic conventions change over time. Jonson's Celia is an exaggerated lover (her name connotes heaven), but that type of love or devotion was the subject of poetry in seventeenth-century England. An interesting writing assignment might be to have students trace the way in which such devotion has changed over time by selecting representative love poems from the seventeenth century through the present.

POSSIBLE CONNECTIONS TO OTHER SELECTIONS

Robert Herrick, "Upon Julia's Clothes" (text p. 739)

Christopher Marlowe, "The Passionate Shepherd to His Love" (text p. 954)

William Shakespeare, "Not marble, nor the gilded monuments" (text p. 955)

JOHN KEATS, *To one who has been long in city pent* (p. 1014)

This Petrarchan sonnet is a kind of love poem to the countryside. The speaker moves quickly away from the trap the city represents in the first line to focus instead on the pleasures of escaping it. The "blue firmament" (line 4), "wavy grass" (7), "notes of Philomel" (10), and "sailing cloudlet's bright career" (11) paint a portrait of a pastoral experience that the city dweller longs for, one that slips by as quickly as "an angel's tear" (13). The absence of the city is a presence in the poem, and the vivid description of what the city lacks combines with the first line to depict it as a prison.

Discussion might center on how the speaker's pleasures reflect on the city. Students might enjoy doing a little freewriting from the perspective of one who has been long in classroom pent; what pleasant presences are absent from the classroom?

POSSIBLE CONNECTIONS TO OTHER SELECTIONS

John Ciardi, "Suburban" (text p. 965)

Christopher Marlowe, "The Passionate Shepherd to His Love" (text p. 954)

JOHN KEATS, *When I have fears that I may cease to be* (p. 1014)

The fears described in this sonnet are increasingly human, mortal, and intimate. Keats fears first that death may cut short the writing of his imagined "high-piled books" (line 3); then that he may never trace the "shadows" (8) of "Huge cloudy symbols of a high romance" (6); and, finally, that he might not see his beloved again. In the couplet, love and fame sink to nothingness, but Keats confronts his fear and is deepened by the experience.

There is a subtle order to the presentation of Keats's objects of regret. In a writing assignment, you might ask the class to comment on how one item seems to lead to the next and how their arrangement lends form and substance to this sonnet.

POSSIBLE CONNECTION TO ANOTHER SELECTION

William Shakespeare, "Not marble, nor the gilded monuments" (text p. 955)

JOHN KEATS, *La Belle Dame sans Merci* (p. 1015)

You might read this ballad in connection with other ballads in this book. How is it that ballads have stood the test of time and have continued to appeal to many generations of listeners and readers? Is this ballad any different from medieval ballads? Is it more suggestive, perhaps, of a state of mind?

The opening three stanzas hold a descriptive value for the reader, for they present the knight as pale, ill, possibly aging and dying. The stanzas possess a rhetorical value as well, for they whet our curiosity. Just why is the knight trapped in this withered landscape?

The femme fatale figure goes back at least to Homeric legend and the wiles of Circe. Note how the "belle dame" appeals here to several senses — with her appearance, her voice, the foods she offers, the physical comforts of sleep. Above all else, though, she seems otherworldly, and Keats here seems to insist on her elfin qualities, her wild eyes, and her strange language.

Words change meaning and grow in and out of popularity over generations (even decades). Contrast the way we might use *enthrall* today (with what subjects) and what Keats intends by "La Belle Dame sans Merci / Hath thee in Thrall!" (lines 39–40). Note how the shortened line of each quatrain gives both a sense of closure and the chill of an inescapable doom.

In his well-known essay on the poem, Earl R. Wasserman begins by remarking, "It would be difficult in any reading of Keats's ballad not to be enthralled by the haunting power of its rhythm, by its delicate intermingling of the fragile and the grotesque, the tender and the weird, and by the perfect economy with which these effects are achieved" (from "La Belle Dame sans Merci," in his *The Finer Tone: Keats's Major Poems* [Baltimore: Johns Hopkins UP, 1953, 1967; print.], 65–83, and reprinted in *English Romantic Poets: Modern Essays in Criticism,* edited by M. H. Abrams [New York: Oxford UP, 1960; print.], 365–380). In a writing assignment you might ask students to select any one of these elements and discuss it with several examples to show how it shapes the poem's tone and mood.

Other studies of this poem include Jane Cohen's "Keats's Humor in 'La Belle Dame sans Merci,'" *Keats-Shelley Journal* 17 (1968): 10–13, and Bernice Slote's "The Climate of Keats's 'La Belle Dame sans Merci,'" *Modern Language Quarterly* 21 (1960): 195–207.

POSSIBLE CONNECTIONS TO OTHER SELECTIONS

Anonymous, "Bonny Barbara Allan" (text p. 999)

Emily Dickinson, "Because I could not stop for Death —" (text p. 814)

EMMA LAZARUS, *The New Colossus* (p. 1016)

Students are likely to recognize at least part of the concluding five lines of this poem, which are — of course — inscribed on the Statue of Liberty's pedestal. They're probably so familiar with it, in fact, that you may have trouble getting them to take a close look at the poem as a whole or to move beyond what they think they know about it. You might try a number of different approaches to accomplish this.

For example, consider focusing on the poem's form. "The New Colossus" is a sonnet. Although it mostly conforms to the usual iambic pentameter associated with the form, it also strays from it at signficant moments. You may want to work through a scansion of the poem in class, then ask students to comment on the effects of the poet's departure from tradition. The most notable variation is probably the trochee that opens line 6, where the word *mother* receives the poem's strongest emphasis. Consider also the anapest in "With conquering limbs" (line 2) and the spondee in the first two words of "Keep, ancient lands" (9). What do these diversions from iambic pentameter contribute to your students' understanding of the poem's intent?

Another way to approach the poem is to consider its historical context. "The New Colossus" was written as part of an effort to raise money to pay for the statue's pedestal. What's interesting is that "The New Colossus" had a strong effect on how Americans think about the Statue of Liberty. The sculptor, Frédéric Auguste Bartholdi, conceived of the statue as a bit of propaganda for France, meant to symbolize the friendship between France and the United States. America, at the time, was experiencing unprecedented waves of immigration from poorer European countries, particularly Ireland and Italy; the resulting overcrowding and visible poverty in large cities like New York and Boston strained resources and led many Americans to feel animosity toward its newest residents. But thanks to the cultural influence of Lazarus's poem, we tend to think of the statue as a welcome to beleaguered immigrants. Ask your students if they can think of any other examples of poems (or any works of literature) that had such a profound effect on American cultural perspectives.

A mythological approach to the poem could also lead to an interesting discussion. As the title suggests, Lazarus compares the Statue of Liberty to the famous Colossus of Rhodes, an enormous bronze statue of Apollo, the Roman god of the sun as well as the arts. At the time it was built, the Colossus was one of the seven wonders of the world. As the oracle of Delphi, Apollo was able to cure social ills and prevent plagues. Specifically, he used his ministrations and purification rituals to bring an end to long cycles of vengeance, thereby promoting peace in a war-torn region. Ask your students what political and cultural hopes the poet expresses by making this association between the Statue of Liberty and this tradition.

HENRY WADSWORTH LONGFELLOW, *Snow-Flakes* (p. 1016)

The snow, generally described in terms of emotions and falterings of the human spirit, is taken in this poem to reveal something about "the troubled sky" (line 11) and "our cloudy fancies" (7) at the same time. The air is personified; the speaker insists that the snow is "the poem of the air" (13), which reveals "the secret of despair, / Long in its cloudy bosom hoarded" (15–16).

A good place to begin discussion is with the question of the speaker, who removes himself from the scene as much as possible. The only time he alludes to himself at all is with the plural pronoun "our" in line 7. What type of person must he be? Do we assume that he is feeling troubled, that he is full of grief and despair? What is his relationship to the scene that he is witnessing?

POSSIBLE CONNECTIONS TO OTHER SELECTIONS

Robert Frost, "Stopping by Woods on a Snowy Evening" (text p. 853)
Percy Bysshe Shelley, "Ode to the West Wind" (text p. 756)

AMY LOWELL, *A Decade* (p. 1017)

Amy Lowell was a follower of the Imagist movement led by poets Ezra Pound and H. D. Imagists were known for their spare language — Lowell summarizes "a decade" of a relationship in six lines. To begin discussion, ask students how they feel about the "you" in this poem. Do they mind not having any information about the "you" beyond the extended metaphors of food?

Consider how this poem moves away from Romantic and Victorian poetry. Does it seem, in comparison to contemporary poetry, still to have vestiges of those genres? Lowell's images are spare: wine, honey, bread, nourishment. Over time, the nourishment the "you" provides changes from sweet and new to smooth and expected. Ask students to imagine the celebration of a relationship that exists in which the speaker can "hardly taste you at all" (line 5) but is "completely nourished" (6). Does that seem to match the love of a decade? Is the conceit in a short poem such as this vivid enough to satisfy the reader?

JILL McDONOUGH, *Accident, Mass. Ave.* (p. 1017)

To begin discussion of this prose-like narrative poem by Jill McDonough, ask students what they think of her speaker's use of dialogue and profanity. The other character in the story speaks English, as she does, as a second language. Consider why McDonough used this structure, and what her details and use of internal rhyme reveal about character.

Notice the repetition of *b* in the first six lines — *Boston, blocks, bridge, Buick,* and *being*. This alliteration, coupled with other repeated plosives, adds to the tone of the story and helps build a picture of the angry, swearing speaker; her descriptive details are often about size, gesture, tone of voice, or other types of nonverbal communication. The narrative eventually leads to the denouement, "*Well, there's nothing wrong with my car, nothing wrong / with your car... are you OK*" (lines 34–35). Ask students to think about what might be different if this had been written as a story. Based on her final revelations, how is this both about an individual and an automotive "accident"?

POSSIBLE CONNECTIONS TO OTHER SELECTIONS

Denise Duhamel, "How It Will End" (text p. 677)

Robert Frost, "Mending Wall" (text p. 843)

JOHN MILTON, *On the Late Massacre in Piedmont* (p. 1018)

Born in London, Milton began writing poetry at the age of fifteen. He had a remarkable aptitude for languages, mastering Latin, Greek, Hebrew, and most modern European languages before he completed his education in 1637. After earning his master's degree from Christ's College, Cambridge University, in 1632, he disappointed expectations that he would become a minister and embarked instead on a six-year period of carefully self-designed study in which he read everything he could. (The eyestrain caused by his voracious study eventually led to his blindness in 1651.)

Milton dedicated his literary talent to the causes of religious and civil freedom from 1640 to 1660, writing Puritan propaganda and numerous political and social tracts. He argued vociferously on many issues: "Of Reformation Touching Church Discipline in England" (1641) denounced the episcopacy; his troubled relationship with seventeen-year-old Mary Powell, who left him after one month of marriage, inspired him to support the legalization of divorce in "Doctrine and Discipline of Divorce" (1643); "Areopagitica" (1644), one of his most famous polemics, argued the necessity of a free press; and his defense of the murder of King Charles I in "The Tenure of Kings and Magistrates" (1649), although contributing to his appointment as the secretary for foreign languages in Cromwell's government, nearly got him executed when the monarchy was restored in 1660.

He was arrested, but friends and colleagues intervened on his behalf, and he was eventually released. Blind and unemployed, he returned to his poetry and a quiet life with his third wife, Elizabeth Minshull. It was during these last years of his life that Milton produced (by dictating to relatives, friends, and paid assistants) his most famous and substantial works: the epic poems *Paradise Lost* (1667) and *Paradise Regained* (1671) and the verse drama *Samson Agonistes* (1671).

"On the Late Massacre in Piedmont" is a sonnet of accountability — in an almost bookkeeper sense of the term. The basic premise is contractual. The Waldenses have preserved piety and faith in God over four centuries; now God should avenge their massacre. *Even,* as the first word of line 3, is an imperative verb form, as in "Even the score." Scorekeeping, in fact, matters in this sonnet, and students might find it a good exercise in reading to identify and analyze the numerical images. Nature, moreover, is shown as sympathetic to the Waldenses, for it redoubles the sound of their lamentations. The passage ends with the elliptical phrase "and they / To heaven" (lines 9–10). Syntax again provides the verb *redoubled* (9) and says, in effect, that the hills echoed the moans to heaven. Milton expresses the wish that future generations of Waldenses will augment their number "a hundredfold" (13) to offset the Pope's power.

You might ask students to write an analytical and persuasive essay proving that this is either a plea for vengeance or the expression of a hope that the Waldenses will receive God's protection and strength throughout history.

POSSIBLE CONNECTIONS TO OTHER SELECTIONS

Wilfred Owen, "Dulce et Decorum Est" (text p. 633)

Alfred, Lord Tennyson, "The Charge of the Light Brigade" (text p. 733)

JOHN MILTON, *When I consider how my light is spent* (p. 1019)

This sonnet is sometimes mistakenly titled "On His Blindness." You might begin by asking just what the topic of Milton's meditation is. He seems to be at midlife, neither old nor young. If Milton's blindness comes to mind as the subject, does that idea accommodate itself to the description "And that one talent which is death to hide / Lodged with me useless" (lines 3–4)? It would take some ingenuity to make blindness the equivalent of "talent" here. Far better to let "talent" stand in its old (biblical) and new senses and refer to Milton's poetic capability. At any rate, a discussion of this sonnet should prove useful in developing students' ability to select or discard extraliterary details in connection with a poem.

POSSIBLE CONNECTIONS TO OTHER SELECTIONS

Anne Bradstreet, "To My Dear and Loving Husband" (text p. 956)

Ben Jonson, "On My First Son" (text p. 754)

John Keats, "When I have fears that I may cease to be" (text p. 1014)

CHRISTINA GEORGINA ROSSETTI, *Some Ladies Dress in Muslin Full and White* (p. 1019)

The speaker of this poem transforms herself from a rather benign observer of fashion into a misanthrope who would selectively eliminate men and women based on what they are wearing. You might ask students to locate the precise moments where her attitude seems to shift: Does anything cause it? You might first ask students what they think the poet's tone or intention is. Which words indicate that light humor is the intended tone, and which words make the poem seem a biting satire? The poem may allow you to discuss the aggressive nature of humor, the very fine line between comedy and tragedy. Do students know anyone, or can they think of examples of professional comedians, whose brand of humor reveals antisocial tendencies? What motivates these humorists? Would they put Rossetti's speaker in the same camp?

POSSIBLE CONNECTION TO ANOTHER SELECTION

Emily Dickinson, "The Soul selects her own Society —" (text p. 810)

CHRISTINA GEORGINA ROSSETTI, *Promises Like Pie-Crust* (p. 1020)

This poem's speaker offers a straightforward, no-nonsense response to romantic possibility. Some students may find the crisp tone a pleasure, while others may find her cynicism unwarranted. Do students agree with the speaker's assessment of the risks of relationships? What might the speaker and her addressee be missing if they maintain their relationship as "the friends we were, / Nothing more but nothing less" (lines 21–22)? You may find it productive to focus on that "more" and "less"; what do we have to gain in romantic relationships? What do we stand to lose? Asking students to write a journal entry to consider their own feelings on the matter may help make discussion more productive. An essay assignment could establish correlations between students' own beliefs about love and the pessimistic or optimistic views of romantic relationships found in poems in this collection. Some possibilities for comparison follow.

Helen Farries, "Magic of Love" (text p. 566)

Christopher Marlowe, "The Passionate Shepherd to His Love" (text p. 954)

SIEGFRIED SASSOON, *"They"* (p. 1020)

In " 'They,' " Sassoon, a World War I veteran, creates a satirical dialogue between returning soldiers and those who stayed behind, which reveals the difference between the soldiers' experience of war and the glorified version of it reported at home. One key difference between the two speeches is that the Bishop uses abstractions like "Anti-Christ" (line 4) and "Death" (6) while the soldiers refer to their wounded comrades by name. In this way Sassoon suggests that the Bishop's view of the war from his comfortable distance is simplified and moralistic. His statement about "the ways of God" (12) offers no solution to the real problems of the young men.

WILLIAM SHAKESPEARE

Shakespeare's sonnets have been widely discussed. Useful studies of them include *A Casebook of Shakespeare's Sonnets,* edited by Gerald Willen and Victor B. Reed; Edward Hubler's *The Sense of Shakespeare's Sonnets* (Westport: Greenwood, 1976; print.); and *Shakespeare's Sonnets,* edited with commentary by Stephen Booth (New Haven: Yale UP, 1977; print.).

WILLIAM SHAKESPEARE, *That time of year thou mayst in me behold* (p. 1021)

Images of death and decay predominate in this sonnet. Ask students to identify the different metaphors for death that are presented in the poem's three quatrains. The first quatrain evokes the approach of winter as dying leaves drift to the ground; the image of "bare ruined choirs" in line 4 would probably have reminded Shakespeare's contemporaries of the many monastery churches that had gone to ruin in the wake of Henry VIII's dissolution of the English monasteries in the 1530s. The second quatrain evokes images of falling night and the third of a dying fire whose embers are being extinguished by its own ashes.

The tone of the poem's concluding couplet could be a topic for class debate. Do students find the grimness of the first three quatrains to be mitigated by the poem's last two lines? The speaker seems to be suggesting to his friend or lover that the inevitability of death should sharpen his or her appreciation of the speaker's affections. Ask students to compare the portrayal of love as an anodyne against the inevitability of death in this poem with that idea as expressed in Matthew Arnold's "Dover Beach" (text p. 846).

Matthew Arnold, "Dover Beach" (text p. 626)

Anne Bradstreet, "To My Dear and Loving Husband" (text p. 956)

WILLIAM SHAKESPEARE, *When forty winters shall besiege thy brow* (p. 1021)

"When forty winters shall besiege thy brow" provides another excellent example of the form of an English, or Shakespearean, sonnet. The poem's central concept is expressed through three complementary quatrains, and the rhyme scheme — *abab cdcd efef gg* — adheres to the traditional Shakespearean sonnet form. Students unfamiliar with sonnet form should be referred to Chapter 27, "Poetic Forms," for a fuller explanation of the genre. They should then be encouraged to consider how form and content complement each other in this sonnet.

It may be useful to suggest that the sonnet is a well-organized argument. Generally, Shakespeare marshals his rhetoric to convince his audience — both the person addressed in the sonnet and the poem's readers — of a specific truth. Here the poet warns the poem's youthful subject that age, like winter, offers no true sustenance, and that the best antidote to old age is to have children. The poet's powers of persuasion rest primarily on threats: in the first quatrain he depicts the physical effects of "forty winters" (line 1) and predicts that "Thy youth's proud livery, so gazed on now, / Will be a tattered weed" (3–4). The second quatrain extends this rhetorical approach: the beauty of youth and "the treasure of thy lusty days" (6) are reduced merely to "deep-sunken eyes" (7) and "all-eating shame and thriftless praise" (8). In the final quatrain Shakespeare offers an alternative to what he has depicted as a wasteful life: instead of having nothing to show for youth, the addressee might instead say, " 'This fair child of mine / Shall sum my count and make my old excuse' " (10–11). In addition, the beauty of the parent's youth will live on in the next generation. The couplet emphasizes the advantages of the alternative described by the third quatrain: "This were to be new made when thou art old, / And see thy blood warm when thou feel'st it cold" (13–14). The final line smoothly blends with the opening line, touching on the harsher aspects of "forty winters" and yet contrasting the potential emptiness with the warmth offered by the poet's suggested alternative.

POSSIBLE CONNECTION TO ANOTHER SELECTION

Anne Bradstreet, "Before the Birth of One of Her Children" (text p. 1002)

WILLIAM SHAKESPEARE, *When, in disgrace with Fortune and men's eyes* (p. 1022)

This sonnet posits a future scenario in which the speaker will be outcast because of his fortune. He claims that he will be comforted by remembering his idyllic time with his lover, which presumably occurs in the present. A good starting point for analysis of this poem is its diction, as it contains several words — *bootless, featured, scope* — whose meanings have changed. Another interesting point for discussion is the religious allusion in line 12. Students might be invited to entertain the possibility that the "thee" in line 10 and "thy" in line 13 refer not to the conventional Petrarchan lover but to God.

The sonnet's structure also merits attention. Ask students to compare the arrangement of the quatrains and concluding couplet in this poem with that of the other Shakespearean sonnets in the text. In which of the poems is there a sharp logical break between the quatrains and the couplet, and in which does this break occur after the octave? Is there any obvious relation between structure and content?

POSSIBLE CONNECTIONS TO OTHER SELECTIONS

John Donne, "A Valediction: Forbidding Mourning" (text p. 658)
William Shakespeare, "That time of year thou mayst in me behold" (text p. 1021)

PERCY BYSSHE SHELLEY, *Ozymandias* (p. 1022)

Many students will have read this Petrarchan sonnet in high school. You might begin by asking whether in an unintentionally ironic way Ozymandias may have been right; although he is far from outdistancing the rest of humanity in possessions and power, his statue is a reminder that all things are subject to decay and is thus a source of despair. The sonnet, despite its familiarity, still surprises by the quality of its versification. Observe in line 6 the delayed placement of "well," which underscores the closing cautionary note. The final lines, moreover, with the alliterated "boundless and bare" and "lone and level," do suggest the infinite reaches of both the desert and time.

POSSIBLE CONNECTION TO ANOTHER SELECTION

John Keats, "Ode on a Grecian Urn" (text p. 612)

LYDIA HUNTLEY SIGOURNEY, *Indian Names* (p. 1022)

Sigourney's "Indian Names" points out the hypocrisy in the representation of Native Americans. The "Ye" she addresses herself to talks about them as a "noble race and brave" (line 2). However, it is easy to romanticize a group of people you have removed from the land. As Sigourney points out, Native Americans can only be idealized this way after European Americans have "Crushed [them] like the noteless worm amid / The regions of their power" (43–44). These violent acts of removal are downplayed by the descendants of settlers who "say their cone-like cabins, / . . . Have fled away like withered leaves" (17–19), but they required much more force than an "autumn gale" (20).

In spite of this desire to efface the presence of Native Americans, their language is written into the landscape of the country because so many of the names for geographical places in America — including Massachusetts, Kentucky, and Missouri — come from native words. Though the physical presence of Native Americans has been confined, "their name is on your waters, / Ye may not wash it out" (7–8): they give names to the elemental powers — rivers and mountains — and their mark on Western consciousness endures.

ALFRED, LORD TENNYSON, *Ulysses* (p. 1024)

Tennyson was only twenty-four when he wrote this monologue, magnificently creating the thoughts that must have plagued this hero who had striven with the gods. The poem is written in blank verse and preserves a certain conversational eloquence through its use of parallelism. Consider the infinitives in "How dull it is to pause, to make an end, / To rust unburnished, not to shine in use!" (lines 22–23). Ulysses seems to be passing on his power and authority to his son Telemachus, who will, apparently, have a gentler, less warlike (though no less important) kind of work to do. You might ask the class what they suppose Ulysses has in mind when he says in the final stanza, "Some work of noble note, may yet be done" (52). Could this poem bear some autobiographical reflection on the life of the poet? This question could prompt a brief research paper.

POSSIBLE CONNECTION TO ANOTHER SELECTION

Percy Bysshe Shelley, "Ozymandias" (text p. 1022)

RICHARD WAKEFIELD, *In a Poetry Workshop* (p. 1025)

This poem provides a kind of in-joke for people who are familiar with "the basics of modern verse" (line 1), prosody, the structure of a poetry class, Marx, Plato, and Wordsworth. Students may need a little guidance to understand the humor here; while they are likely to pick up on the tone, they may not see what's going on. You may want to ask what students know about poetry workshops and the concept of bringing poems to read with a group, reading them aloud, and working on them together. The rhyme and meter, in a poem that warns against both, provide tension between the poem's form and content. This tension renders the tone less than serious.

Wakefield's verse provides a good beginning for students' study of poems. One quick lesson learned is the distinction between poet and speaker: Wakefield's speaker may take his or her position as leader of a poetry workshop seriously, but Wakefield himself does not take his speaker's advice. This poem gives students a chance to articulate what they value in a poem. Are meter and rhyme important to them? Do they want to learn about the historical perspective of a piece, how it fits into larger artistic movements? Do they want to understand how Wordsworth and others have affected modern verse? Through humor, this poem provides a productive introduction to these issues.

POSSIBLE CONNECTION TO ANOTHER SELECTION

Mark Halliday, "Graded Paper" (text p. 680)

WALT WHITMAN, *When I Heard the Learn'd Astronomer* (p. 1026)

Whitman's poem sets forth in verse the often-debated argument over the relative values of art and science; true to the traditions of American romanticism, art is the winner in Whitman's view. You might ask your students to recall other instances in which they have seen this issue debated. Which side seemed to have the stronger argument in each case? Is this necessarily an either/or debate? That is, are art and science ever interconnected? What about stanzaic and metrical patterns, in which art depends on numbers? (You might ask students why a poet like Whitman might not be impressed with this particular example.) Can your students think of any poet whose use of imagery or structures depends on scientific principles? Does science owe anything to the power of the artist's imagination?

POSSIBLE CONNECTION TO ANOTHER SELECTION

Emily Dickinson, "Some keep the Sabbath going to Church —" (text p. 806)

WALT WHITMAN, *One's-Self I Sing* (p. 1027)

This poem opens *Leaves of Grass* and is a kind of bugle announcement of several of Whitman's fondly held themes: the individual as both separate and a member of the democratic community; the equality of the sexes; the importance of both body and soul; and the "divinity" of modern humanity, which is not subject to kingly law. Some students will probably hear echoes of the opening lines of a traditional epic poem. Whitman is inverting epic convention somewhat by not singing of arms and men with the requisite bowings to the gods, but hailing the individual self.

As a writing assignment, you might ask the class to describe how and why this brief poem is a good opening for a book of poems. You might also ask students to say what seems particularly American about the poem.

POSSIBLE CONNECTION TO ANOTHER SELECTION

John Keats, "To one who has been long in city pent" (text p. 1014)

WILLIAM WORDSWORTH, *A Slumber Did My Spirit Seal* (p. 1027)

This is one of Wordsworth's "Lucy poems," and the "she" in line 3 alludes to Lucy. Apparently, this poem marks a loss for which the poet was unprepared. He was asleep to the possibilities of aging and death, and Lucy now seems well beyond the province of "earthly years" (line 4) and more the spirit of eternal time. Is there a paradox in this poem? Probably so. The speaker's dream, which he had had in a more pleasant period, when he felt that they were both beyond the effects of time, turns out to be for Lucy ironically accurate, for like the "rocks, and stones, and trees" (8), she is now unaffected by the passage of time.

POSSIBLE CONNECTIONS TO OTHER SELECTIONS

John Keats, "When I have fears that I may cease to be" (text p. 1014)
Percy Bysshe Shelley, "Ozymandias" (text p. 1022)

WILLIAM WORDSWORTH, *I Wandered Lonely as a Cloud* (p. 1027)

The speaker of this poem finds comfort for his loneliness in nature. His connection to daffodils comforts him even in memory. In his preface to *Lyrical Ballads,* Wordsworth describes poetry as "the spontaneous overflow of powerful feelings: it takes its origin from emotion recollected in tranquillity." To some extent, this quotation explains the "wealth" that the speaker alludes to in line 18, for while reclining on his couch he can recall the heightened sense of pleasure the daffodils first brought him. From his mood of loneliness, he moves to a state of gladness. What else characterizes how the daffodils appear to him? Seemingly, they are a token of cosmic splendor in their extensiveness and golden sparkle.

POSSIBLE CONNECTION TO ANOTHER SELECTION

Emily Dickinson, "A Bird came down the Walk —" (text p. 693)

WILLIAM WORDSWORTH, *The Solitary Reaper* (p. 1028)

This poem seems to spill beyond its limits as fit lyric to become a "spontaneous overflow of powerful feelings." Ask the class to note how many boundaries are exceeded here. In stanza 1, for example, the song overflows the vales. In the final stanza the song seems without end, and the listener hears it long after he leaves the singer behind. Implied, too, in the second and third stanzas is the song's ability to transcend place and history. As with other poetic figures of Wordsworth, this solitary reaper and her song provide a way into perceiving an order of existence beneath the surface. You might ask the class if it matters at all that the singer is female.

POSSIBLE CONNECTION TO ANOTHER SELECTION

William Blake, "The Chimney Sweeper" (text p. 687)

WILLIAM WORDSWORTH, *Mutability* (p. 1029)

This poem examines the inevitability of change and the ability to see it clearly. The "unimaginable touch of Time" (line 14) proves everything to be temporary, even the "outward forms" of "Truth" (7). Truth itself "fails not" (7), but the awesome changes in our lives may have some of us fooled; those "who meddle not with crime, / Nor avarice, nor over-anxious care" (5–6) can see change as it is, a nonthreatening part of life.

Among the examples Wordsworth offers are nature and political order; these provide comparisons to the "outward forms" of truth. Frost melts, and "the tower sublime / Of yesterday" (10–11) is no longer so impressive today.

Students are likely to be unfamiliar with the terms of this linguistically dense poem. Reading it aloud and working together on a line-by-line analysis of its meaning may prove helpful. Students may glean much of the meaning through an exercise that includes rewriting or restating the poem in more contemporary terms.

POSSIBLE CONNECTION TO ANOTHER SELECTION

William Shakespeare, "Not marble, nor the gilded monuments" (text p. 955)

STEFANIE WORTMAN, *Mortuary Art* (p. 1029)

In "Mortuary Art," Wortman argues funerary ritual; a mother, who is very much alive, "again" (line 1) makes her daughter promise "never to have her cremated" (2). This leads to the speaker's musings on her own fears, and her consideration of how the dead are laid to rest.

Midway she switches her position against burial, introducing her difficulties with cremation in an allusion to her dead father: "You watch three pounds of ash dissolve / in water and suddenly, he's everywhere" (8–9). In discussion, point out the introduction of second person in those lines and ask how the intimacy of second person changes the poem. She then describes the cremated father "in the rivulet rain makes" (10), leaving him diffuse, like grief, by enjambing the line.

Lines 10–11 recall the ending of Hardy's "During Wind and Rain": "down their carved name the rain drop ploughs." It might be worth bringing the Hardy poem to students' attention, since the rivulet rain makes in his poem is perhaps down a tombstone. The speaker concedes the point that the dead are everywhere for us, whether cremated or buried, in her statement that the dead "are / not folded, are not there, are not" (20). How do students respond to her decision to "instead, allow" (11) the different ways we mark the passing of those we love, and the reasons for her change of mind? What is the tone of this poem?

POSSIBLE CONNECTIONS TO OTHER SELECTIONS

Emily Dickinson, "I heard a Fly buzz—when I died" (text p. 814)

John Keats, "When I have fears that I may cease to be" (text p. 1014)

Dylan Thomas, "Do Not Go Gentle into That Good Night" (text p. 747)

WILLIAM BUTLER YEATS, *Leda and the Swan* (p. 1030)

Some references in this poem might require clarification: the offspring of Leda and Zeus (as swan) was Helen, the most beautiful of women, who married Menelaus but was later awarded to Paris. Paris took her to Troy with him, thus occasioning the Trojan War and the death of Agamemnon, the leader of the Greeks. Agamemnon was married to Clytemnestra, Helen's sister.

According to Yeats's view, this rape marks a turning point in history and the downward spiraling of the gyres. The moment is dark and fraught with the onset of much tragedy that Leda cannot possibly know, yet she does seem to take on a measure of Zeus's power and come closer to assuming a consciousness of the divine than is ordinarily possible. One point to consider in class discussion is Yeats's use of the rhetorical question in this poem. Does the poem suggest any answers to these questions? What do they do to the poem's tone?

D R A M A

The Study of Drama

40

Reading Drama

Before beginning a class unit on drama, you may want to find out if many of your students have seen a play performed. Most of them will probably have had some exposure to drama on stage, but for many that exposure may have been limited to a school or church play during childhood. If possible, arrange for your students to view a live play while they study drama. Many colleges have theater departments that produce a show every semester. If live drama is not available, try showing a video of a play to your class. Seeing a show as a class will give you the opportunity to discuss certain theatrical conventions, staging challenges, casting, and other elements of drama that cannot be represented in a written script.

Web Ask students to explore the literary elements in this chapter at **bedfordstmartins.com/ meyerlit**.

This unit's opening section, "Reading Drama Responsively" (p. 1035), highlights the benefits of reading drama instead of (or in addition to) viewing it. Ask your students about their experiences reading drama. Do they agree that there are some advantages to reading a play over watching one? Discuss the role of imagination. How does their imagination affect the way they read a play they haven't seen?

The sample close reading in the chapter will go a long way in helping students master the demands of reading works that were meant to be performed. The annotations to *Trifles* demonstrate the process of a reader questioning and thinking carefully about a play while reading it. But be sure to remind your students that the annotations are those of an experienced reader, not a student, or they might conclude that the task is beyond their abilities.

Comparing Susan Glaspell's *Trifles* (p. 1038) to her short story version, titled "A Jury of Her Peers" (p. 1050), should generate a good discussion about drama as a *genre*. Have students note the changes from the play to the story, including more detailed descriptions in the story and the story's addition of a third-person narrator who provides background material. Why were these changes made? Is one genre more effective than the other in presenting this plot? By examining ways in which the play differs from the story, you can achieve a good sense of how the elements of drama work and how drama differs from other literary mediums even when it is not being performed.

Web Ask students to research the playwrights in this chapter at **bedfordstmartins.com/ meyerlit**.

Students will probably enjoy reading Larry David's episode of *Seinfeld* (p. 1069). This short reading is a good illustration of the importance of timing in drama. You may even want to have students read scenes from this play out loud to get a sense of how the humor plays to an audience. Starting the unit off with this episode will remind your students that theater has almost always been, and continues to be, entertainment for the masses.

SUSAN GLASPELL, *Trifles* (p. 1038)

A discussion of the elements of drama in *Trifles* appears on pages 1052–1056 in the text; this discussion alludes to most of the questions that follow the play.

The stark, gloomy setting (discussed on p. 1038) evokes the hard life Mr. Wright imposed on his wife. Within this cold environment, the relationship between the Wrights is immediately and subtly recapitulated in the opening scene by Glaspell's having the men dominate the room as they stand by the stove, while the two women remain timidly near the door. The sympathy that we increasingly feel for Mrs. Peters and Mrs. Hale will eventually be extended to Mrs. Wright, despite the fact that she murdered her husband.

Exposition (discussed on p. 1053) is used throughout to characterize Mr. and Mrs. Wright; Glaspell makes us feel as if we know the essential qualities of this couple even though we never actually see them. Just as the dialogue reveals their characters, it displays the insensitivity of the men, whose self-importance blinds them to the clues woven into the domestic setting, which they dismiss as mere "trifles." The women understand what these details reveal, for example, that the bird cage and dead bird offer evidence concerning Mrs. Wright's motive for murdering her husband. The cage (now broken) symbolizes the lifeless, joyless, confining marriage Mrs. Wright had to endure, and the bird (strangled) suggests both the husband and the wife, Minnie Foster, who used to sing in the choir. Although the women recognize the significance of these objects as well as of the identical knots Mrs. Wright used on her husband and on her sewing, they will not give this evidence to the men because, as women, they empathize with Mrs. Wright's circumstances.

Web Ask students to explore contexts for Susan Glaspell and this play—as well as an additional sample close reading—at **bedfordstmartins.com/ meyerlit**.

Trifles is packed with irony. On a second reading, the dialogue takes on a strong ironic flavor, for example when the sheriff says there's "nothing here but kitchen things" (p. 1040) or when the county attorney sarcastically asks, "What would we do without the ladies?" (p. 1041), and expresses mild surprise to Mrs. Hale about her being "loyal to her sex" (p. 1041).

The play's title comments on the kind of evidence that *could* be used to convict Mrs. Wright if the men were not so smugly certain of their powers of observation. What appears to be unimportant in the play — the domestic details and the two women — turns out to be powerfully significant. In the final line, Mrs. Hale answers the county attorney's condescending question about Mrs. Wright's sewing. She is standing center stage while he is by the door so that their positions are the reverse of what they were in the opening scene. She has the dead canary in her pocket and Mrs. Wright's fate on her lips, but she chooses to exonerate her.

Mrs. Wright is tried by a jury of her peers (which became the short story title); Mrs. Hale and Mrs. Peters penetrate the meaning of what appears only trifling to the men and go beyond conventional, shallow perceptions to discover and empathize with Mrs. Wright's reasons for killing her husband. *Trifles*, although written in 1916, has a distinctly contemporary quality because its feminist perspectives make a convincing case for women stepping outside general attitudes and oppressive values to be true to their own experience. This play is well worth comparing with Henrik Ibsen's *A Doll House* (p. 1250), especially in terms of characterization and theme.

TIP FROM THE FIELD

When teaching the play *Trifles*, I divide my class in half and have one half write a final act determining the fate of Mrs. Wright in accordance with the time period of the play. The other half writes a final act in accordance with today's social and legal mores.

— OLGA LYLES, *University of Nevada*

POSSIBLE CONNECTIONS TO OTHER SELECTIONS

Kate Chopin, "The Story of an Hour" (text p. 15; question #2, following)

Andre Dubus, "Killings" (text p. 93; question #3, following)

Henrik Ibsen, *A Doll House* (text p. 1250)

Sophocles, *Oedipus the King* (text p. 1094; question #1, following)

CONNECTIONS QUESTIONS IN TEXT (p. 1048) **WITH ANSWERS**

1. Compare and contrast how Glaspell provides background information in *Trifles* with how Sophocles does so in *Oedipus the King* (p. 1094).

   Glaspell fills the audience in on the background of the crime through the women's conversation. While the men look for evidence, the women talk, and their knowledge of Mrs. Wright's life, even though it is limited, reveals more than the men would imagine. Dialogue also functions to reveal past events in Sophocles's play. As Oedipus struggles to find an answer for the people of Thebes about the curse they are under, he discusses with Creon the murder of the previous king, Laius, and its implications for the future of the city. This past event drives the action of the play as it pushes Oedipus to search for the king's murderer.

2. Write an essay comparing the views of marriage in *Trifles* and in Kate Chopin's short story "The Story of an Hour" (p. 15). What similarities do you find in the themes of these two works? Are there any significant differences between the works?

   In both *Trifles* and "The Story of an Hour" marriage limits women by enforcing a narrow definition of their interests and abilities. In Glaspell's play the male attorney ridicules Mrs. Peters and Mrs. Hale for worrying about "trifles" like preserves and quilting methods. However, their attention to small details allows them to arrive at a theory of the crime while the men remain in the dark about a possible motive. Chopin's Mrs. Mallard is similarly confined by her marriage, so when she is informed that her husband has died, she is overjoyed by the opening of possibilities. Though Chopin does not give the reader many details from Mrs. Mallard's domestic life, the sudden realization that "she would live for herself" (para. 14) indicates that her previous life had been dominated by her husband's expectations of her.

3. In an essay compare Mrs. Wright's motivation for committing murder with that of Matt Fowler, the central character from Dubus's short story "Killings" (p. 93). To what extent do you think Mrs. Wright and Matt Fowler are responsible for and guilty of these crimes?

   In both stories, the murders are triggered by the loss of a loved one. For Matt Fowler, seeing the man who murdered his son walking freely around town is too much to bear. His murder is also an attempt to shield his wife from being reminded of their son's death. The loss of the canary in *Trifles* may be less tragic than having a son murdered. Yet for Mrs. Wright, who has little human companionship, the canary had become a symbol of life and freedom. When her husband cruelly kills it, she reacts violently. The two murders differ in method. The housekeeping tasks left unfinished in the Wright kitchen suggest that Mrs. Wright killed her husband in a highly emotional state, without forethought. Matt Fowler, on the other hand, enlists the help of a friend to make a careful plan for how to murder Strout. Readers also see the extent to which these murders were premeditated in the reactions of the two murderers. Matt Fowler is upset, but manages to concentrate on how his other children will deal with the situation. Mrs. Wright, on the other hand, appears to be in a state of shock.

PERSPECTIVE

SUSAN GLASPELL, *From the Short Story Version of* Trifles (p. 1050)

The play's opening description immediately gives us information about the Wrights' "gloomy" kitchen; the story, however, can take us beyond the kitchen so that we get a larger view of the house from a little hill. We are told that, to Mrs. Hale, the house looked "lonesome." The story, of course, can provide more details through the narrator.

The story begins with characterizations of Mr. and Mrs. Peters ("she didn't seem like a sheriff's wife") as well as Mrs. Hale. The women take more central roles earlier on in the story than in the play. The story also permits us to get inside Mrs. Hale's mind to learn her feelings of guilt for not having visited Mrs. Wright earlier. This intimacy emphasizes Mrs. Hale's perspective and suggests why Glaspell uses the title "A Jury of Her Peers." The story seems to focus more on justice than on the "trifles" overlooked by the men. Perhaps this slight shift in emphasis occurs because the trifles — the sewing, bird cage, and dead canary — make for good stage business.

MICHAEL HOLLINGER, *Naked Lunch* (p. 1057)

Hollinger's short play begins like a romantic comedy. The couple eating lunch together try to get along but are clearly at odds. Vernon's windy opening speech suggests that he is more interested in hearing himself talk than in conversing with Lucy. He does pause long enough, though, to notice that she is not eating her steak. Hollinger plays off traditional associations by aligning the male character with meat-eating, which is linked to hunting as opposed to the more feminine activity of cultivation. As the tension over the issue of vegetarianism mounts, the play takes on a darker mood. The reader begins to see that Vernon's self-centered talk points to a failure to understand Lucy's perspective. His main question is "How do you think this makes me feel?" Hints of his violent nature begin to appear as well. Not only does he verbally challenge her decision to stop eating meat, but he stands over her and pushes the plate into her face. His bullying comes to a climax when he forces her to eat a piece of the steak. The ironic final line, "Nothing to be afraid of," downplays the danger of eating meat but also refers to the danger he poses to a woman like Lucy.

POSSIBLE CONNECTIONS TO OTHER SELECTIONS

Margaret Atwood, "you fit into me" (text p. 645)

Susan Glaspell, *Trifles* (text p. 1038; questions #1 and #2, following)

Fay Weldon, "IND AFF, or Out of Love in Sarajevo" (text p. 173)

CONNECTIONS QUESTIONS IN TEXT (p. 1060) WITH ANSWERS

1. Compare the theme of *Naked Lunch* with those of Susan Glaspell's *Trifles* (p. 1038).

    Both plays concern the way gender roles are played out in individual relationships. To the men in these works, women are baffling creatures. The attorney in *Trifles* turns his surprise at the women's interests into a joke. Mrs. Peters and Mrs. Hale are united in their common understanding of the motive for the murder, but they keep their knowledge a secret from their husbands in an act of loyalty to a fellow woman. In *Naked Lunch*, Vernon's inability to understand Lucy's motives is infuriating. By forcing her to eat the steak, he makes her comprehensible again so that he can feel secure. She acquiesces partly because it is easier than to continue fighting him but also because she has a real fear of what he will do.

2. Discuss the symbolic significance of the steak dinner in *Naked Lunch* and the birdcage and the dead bird in Glaspell's *Trifles*.

The fact that the steak and the bird incite such strong reactions indicates the power of their symbolism. In *Naked Lunch*, the steak represents to Vernon male values, which he fears Lucy has rejected. By inviting Lucy and buying the steak, Vernon takes on the traditional role of provider. The idea that she could find a substitute for him sets off his surprisingly emotional reaction. (And explains why he's so indignant about her eating tofu.) The bird in *Trifles* is a conventional symbol for freedom, but one that is complicated by its being a pet to Mrs. Wright. The caged bird functions on the symbolic level to suggest that Mrs. Wright herself is trapped within her life, but it also has a literal significance because it is her only companion.

ANDREW BISS, *What's the Meta?* (p. 1061)

Biss's play tells the story of two parts — not even yet embodied characters — who "only exist on paper" (p. 1063). They debate over this form of existence, disagreeing about whether their position is enviable or deplorable. The first part sees himself or herself as "just a tool" of the author, with no self-determined needs or goals (p. 1062). The second part thinks that they are both participating in "thoughtfully transcribed literature" (p. 1061). As words on a page, they are the source and origin of whatever the play will become in performance.

Biss jokes around in this play with the kind of praise (often clichéd) that people use when talking about literature: the parts worry about whether they are "fleshed out" enough (p. 1062) and want to appear "multidimensional" (p. 1062). These humorous musings on literary character give way to deeper questioning. What does it mean to be important? Is it enough to advance action, or does one need to feel deep and complicated or have an "arc" that results in transformation? At one point in their discussion, the second part refers to the two as "people" and suggests that humans, like the written parts that approximate them, are often in the dark about their purposes: "We just have to force ourselves. Force ourselves to go on" (p. 1062). At the end, however, these two parts escape philosophical probing and decide to do something very ordinary: they go out for a drink.

POSSIBLE CONNECTIONS TO OTHER SELECTIONS

Rich Orloff, *Playwriting 101: The Rooftop Lesson* (text p. 1346; question #1, following)

Anne Bradstreet, "The Author to Her Book" (text p. 647)

Richard Wakefield, "In a Poetry Workshop" (text p. 1025)

CONNECTION QUESTION IN TEXT (p. 1066) WITH ANSWER

1. Compare *What's the Meta?* to Rich Orloff's *Playwriting 101: The Rooftop Lesson* (text p. 1346) as metafictions exploring the nature and elements of drama.

    Biss's two "parts" are aware of themselves as created by an author. In part, their disagreement stems from how they feel about this: one feels as if he/she is just being used while the other thinks being deliberately created by an author provides a sense of purpose. As they discuss this problem, they keep the audience, who might expect to be absorbed in a play, constantly aware of drama as artifice. In Orloff's play, the characters' knowledge of themselves as created things shifts over time. At first, the teacher has the ability to comment while the two characters are just playing out the drama, but then the characters begin to exert control and challenge the teacher's pronouncements. On some level, both of these works offer negative examples to potential writers. Orloff considers several ways to dissolve dramatic conflict in *Playwriting 101*, and Biss reminds readers of several ways for parts to go wrong in *What's the Meta?*

LARRY DAVID, *"The Pitch,"* a Seinfeld *Episode* (p. 1069)

In this episode, George proposes a show about "nothing," which perfectly describes the much-ado-about-nothing quality of most *Seinfeld* plots. Many of the episodes deal with the fragments that make up our daily lives, such as finding an apartment, standing in bank lines, or coping with needy neighbors. These seemingly mundane incidents become dramatic vignettes of the characters' personal lives. Although these plots about "nothing" are comic, they provide astute observations about human nature and social interactions.

Comedy frequently works by exploiting our knowledge of "types," so you might have your students discuss who in this episode is a "type" and who is an individual. The "suits" at the television network are certainly stock characters. George might be read as the opposite of this confident, successful stereotype. However, through George's actions we learn more about his individual foibles. For example, his childish enthusiasm for spelling Crespi's name correctly suggests the kind of achievement George is able to claim. Later, his misspelling of Dalrymple's name indicates that this particular talent, like George's others, is hit-and-miss. In addition to provoking laughter and making the audience wince, George's spelling sheds some light on his idea that the plot should be about "nothing" because nothing is really going on in his life.

PERSPECTIVE

GEOFFREY O'BRIEN, *On* Seinfeld *as Sitcom Moneymaker* (p. 1077)

The final episode of *Seinfeld* aired on May 14, 1998; your students may be fans of the sitcom, but they may not know the extent to which media pundits and devoted viewers mourned the passing of this "show about nothing." Nick at Nite's *TV Land* paid homage by showing nothing during the hour that the final episode was on, explaining that "nothing is more important than the last episode of *Seinfeld*. . . . *TV Land* is honored to pre-empt an hour of programming for this historic and monumental occasion."

Your students also may not know the enormous sums of money generated around the show, which pulled in 200 million dollars a year in advertising sales. For the final episode, thirty-second advertising spots sold for a record-setting average of 1.7 million dollars.

You may want to start by asking your students whether they like the show and find it funny — and whether they do or not, what qualities they think made it so popular. Is it truly a show about nothing? Does it matter that these are all single, white professionals living in nice apartments in New York City? If, as O'Brien writes, *Seinfeld* is the "defining sitcom of our age," what exactly does that say about our age? You might ask students to think about entertainment other than *Seinfeld.* Why are actors and athletes paid so much? What role does advertising play? What observations can they make about American culture based on the cost of entertainment, whether it be a popular TV show, a blockbuster movie, or a playoff game?

41

Writing about Drama

QUESTIONS FOR RESPONSIVE READING AND WRITING

Considering the "Questions for Responsive Reading and Writing" about drama in this chapter might prove especially useful to your students, many of whom may be relatively new to the study of drama. Remind them, of course, that not every question will speak to the issues raised in every play, but that these questions may be treated as a starting point for a closer investigation into the meaning and significance of a particular play or plays. These questions cannot be answered in a single word; many of them require a paragraph or more of explanation. Thus, you might encourage your students to be as specific as possible when attempting to answer any of these questions; the more details that they can provide, the more interesting and relevant their answers will be.

One way to incorporate these questions into your discussion might be to break up your class into small groups, and ask each group to respond to three or four questions using a play the class has read. By coming up with specific examples from the play to support their answers, students will become more familiar with both the technique of analyzing dramatic literature and the terms commonly used to discuss it. These in-class responses could be turned into short writing assignments and may provide the foundations for more detailed written analyses in the future.

Another way to use these questions effectively might be to assign one question to each of your students and ask them to write a brief, one- or two-page essay answering the given question using a specific play. This is also an important opportunity for students to practice documenting quoted material from the play itself and to become more familiar with the conventions of dramatic literature in general.

A SAMPLE STUDENT PAPER

The sample student paper titled "The Feminist Evidence in *Trifles*" (p. 1083) offers a strong feminist interpretation of the play by Susan Glaspell. Ask your students to examine what makes this interpretation so convincing. You might ask your class to pay particular attention to the way that this student writer incorporates material directly from the play in order to support the main thesis of the paper. And, as no paper is ever perfect, you might ask your class to suggest specific ways that this essay might have been improved in another revision. Using sample essays in this way can not only offer your class a useful model of a well-argued analytical interpretation of a play, but also provide them with some helpful experience critiquing the work of another student writer. This critiquing may prove useful to your students when they revise drafts of their own papers or in any sort of peer-editing situation.

42

A Study of Sophocles

Students (and their teachers) may be surprised at how much they enjoy studying classical Greek drama. Despite the significant barriers of time and place that separate contemporary audiences from Sophocles, these plays continue to hold our fascination. Robert Fagles's accessible translations of *Oedipus the King* should pose no language difficulties for students, and the complex characterizations will draw readers in. Nonetheless, there are important conventions of classical Greek drama that may be puzzling. Have your students read and discuss the section titled "Theatrical Conventions of Greek Drama" (p. 1088) before beginning the plays. Many of them may be familiar with Aristotle's definition of tragedy (p. 1091), but it bears going over in detail. As this section notes, it is important not to reduce tragic characters to a single "fatal flaw," but to see the "hamartia" of Oedipus and Antigone in a larger context.

In order to emphasize the difference between the conventional and the literary use of the term *tragedy*, you might ask students to bring in newspaper articles and discuss them in light of the classic definition. Using concrete and familiar examples, students can then determine, for example, that a car accident is less classically "tragic" than the downfall of a successful politician whose political greatness is overshadowed by a personal flaw or a bad decision.

Many of your students will have read *Oedipus the King* (p. 1094) in the past, and those who have not will certainly be familiar with the story through Freud's "Oedipus complex." No doubt there will be vigorous debate about Freud's interpretation of the play (p. 1138). Do students really see Oedipus's actions as "the fulfillment of our childhood wishes," as Freud claims? In today's talk-show culture, we are all armchair psychologists to some degree, and students should be encouraged to "analyze" the play in light of Freud's assessment. Reading J. T. Sheppard's translation of lines 1433–1550 of the play (p. 1140) will enable them to view the work in another way. How does the elevated language affect their reading? Would students have been as likely to analyze the work in modern terms had this been the translation they read? Comparing the language of the two translations can promote some fruitful discussion about the role of translation in the way we approach a work of literature. Muriel Rukeyser's "myth" (p. 1142) provides a different angle on the same theme, as we read her take on the translation of the word *man*.

SOPHOCLES, *Oedipus the King* (p. 1094)

Student discussions of this play are likely to center on Oedipus's powerful character and the fate that has been prophesied for him. The character and his inevitable end compete for our attention, and the irony raises intriguing questions about human freedom and fate. Oedipus's self-confidence, determination, and disregard for consequences propel him toward his goal and his destruction. His downfall is brought about not solely by the gods or fate but by the nature of his own remarkable character. The gods may know what will inevitably occur, but it is Oedipus's personality — especially his proud temper — that causes it to happen. He is both the victim of the suffering in the play and the one responsible for it. The combination of his virtues and vices contributes to his horror and shame. What happens to Oedipus raises questions of human guilt and innocence and cosmic justice. Students are likely to recognize that, though Oedipus's circumstances are specific to him, the larger issues he encounters are relevant to all people.

The opening scene presents Oedipus as a powerful king who has defeated the Sphinx and ruled successfully for many years. The priest's speech (lines 16–69) offers this exposition and characterizes Oedipus as the "first of men" (41) and the "best of men" (57). As the city faces a plague, the people turn to heroic Oedipus to save it. Oedipus, in his empathy for the suffering of his people, has already sent his brother-in-law Creon to the oracle of Delphi to learn what he can about the curse (81–82). Creon returns with the news that the murder of the previous king, Laius, continues to curse the people of Thebes.

Oedipus appeals to the seer Tiresias for information about the murder, but knowing that the truth will destroy Thebes, Tiresias refuses to tell his "dreadful secrets" (374). Oedipus's fury at this answer establishes his fierce determination to discover the truth. His quick temper and unreasonableness are also revealed when he accuses Tiresias of conspiring with Creon to usurp the throne (431–59). Oedipus's rage renders him figuratively blind to what Tiresias knows: "I say you are the murderer you hunt" (413). When Oedipus also accuses Creon of treason, Creon correctly assesses a significant element — an error or frailty — of Oedipus's personality as a "crude, mindless stubbornness" that has caused Oedipus to lose his "sense of balance" (615–16). Oedipus's absolute insistence on learning who murdered Laius shows him to be a decisive leader while simultaneously exposing him to the consequences of making public the message from Delphi and his cursing the murderer of Laius.

Irony is pervasive in the play, but the greatest irony is that the murderer Oedipus seeks is himself. He sets out to save the city, to appease the gods, and to see that justice is done, but all his altruistic efforts bring ruin on himself. Ignorant of the truth, Oedipus is consistently used as a vehicle for dramatic irony because we know more than he does; this strategy allows Sophocles to charge Oedipus's speeches with additional meanings that the protagonist only gradually comes to perceive. A review of Oedipus's early speeches will yield numerous instances of dramatic irony, as when he declares that if anyone knows about the murder of Laius, that person must report to Oedipus "even if he must denounce himself" (257). His curse on the murderer (280–314) is especially rich in ironic foreshadowings. Tiresias also introduces ironies into the play. His blindness does not prevent him from seeing the truth of Oedipus's past. Oedipus, on the other hand, sees physically but is blind to the pattern of events that defines his life. Once Oedipus does see the truth, he blinds himself, a fitting punishment that will not allow him to escape his suffering.

For a broad range of critical responses to the play, see *Oedipus Tyrannus*, edited by Luci Berkowitz and Theodore F. Brunner (New York: Norton, 1970; print.).

POSSIBLE CONNECTIONS TO OTHER SELECTIONS

Susan Glaspell, *Trifles* (text p. 1038)

Henrik Ibsen, *A Doll House* (text p. 1250; question #2, following)

William Shakespeare, *Othello* (text p. 1156; question #1, following)

CONNECTIONS QUESTIONS IN TEXT (p. 1136) WITH ANSWERS

1. Consider the endings of *Oedipus the King* and Shakespeare's *Othello* (p. 1156). What feelings do you have about these endings? Are they irredeemably unhappy? Is there anything that suggests hope for the future at the end of these plays?

    At the end of *Oedipus the King*, the blinded Oedipus mourns that the curse that afflicted his parents and himself will also be visited on his children. He has little hope that those within his family will be relieved of their suffering, which "wounds [them] all together" (lines 1638). If there is hope at the end of the play, it is for the citizens of Thebes, who had also been cursed by the murder of Laius. Creon's assertion, "here your power ends" (1679), suggests that the city might be released from the evils that have come with Oedipus' reign.

There is even less happiness to be had at the conclusion to *Othello*. With Desdemona, Emilia, and Othello all dead, and Iago in chains, the main characters of the play have reached their tragic ends. There are small mercies in the midst of the tragedy; Iago is discovered to be the mastermind behind the violence and is taken into custody, and though Othello planned Cassio's death, he does not follow through. The only bright spot for the future is Lodovico's knowledge of Iago's plotting, so that when he goes "to the state" (370) to report these events, Oedipus's name will not be entirely tarnished.

2. Write an essay explaining why *Oedipus the King* cannot be considered a realistic play in the way that Henrik Ibsen's *A Doll House* (p. 1250) can be.

The unity of time observed by Greek playwrights is meant to appeal to the audience's sense of reality; the events of the play occur in real time, rather than having a time span of days or weeks compressed into a few hours. However, in some ways the speed with which Sophocles accomplishes this series of revelations is less realistic than a play that allows a greater period of time to elapse. Moreover, Sophocles is not concerned in *Oedipus* with giving the speeches and actions of the play the flavor of "realness" through mundane details. From beginning to end, *Oedipus* is a highly dramatic work. *A Doll House*, on the other hand, is less concerned with dramatizing an archetypal plot than with creating a sense of ordinary life. Even in the detailed stage directions, which lay out the scene down to the smallest household objects, the reader can see that Ibsen wants to represent a mundane world from which drama emerges.

PERSPECTIVES ON SOPHOCLES

ARISTOTLE, *On Tragic Character* (p. 1136)

A tragic figure, according to Aristotle, "does not fall into misfortune through vice or depravity" but through "some mistake" (para. 1). Neither extreme virtue nor vice is appropriate because these characteristics do not produce in the audience the emotional intensity of "pity and fear."

Aristotle argues that characters should be made "handsomer . . . than they are in reality" (6) because a character's qualities on the stage have to be perceived by an audience at a distance.

SIGMUND FREUD, *On the Oedipus Complex* (p. 1138)

Students may agree or disagree with the notion that the Oedipus complex is the "key to the tragedy," but it is certainly an important critical aspect of the play and should not be dismissed too quickly. It is important for students to understand the substantial influence of Freud's ideas about dream interpretation on both psychology and literature; you might ask them to think of other instances in which the Oedipus complex is played out in literature or in some other area.

However, Freud's vision of tragic character differs from Aristotle's in that Freud believes that tragic characters do not necessarily have to make mistakes; they are subject to the mysterious workings of their subconscious minds and act according to their very human reactions to the subconscious.

SOPHOCLES, *Another Translation of a Scene from* Oedipus the King (p. 1140)

Fagles's more modern diction and tone (lines 1433–1549) are less poetically embellished than Sheppard's. Consider, for example, these lines spoken by the Chorus:

Unhappy in thy fortune and the wit
That shows it thee. Would thou hadst never known. (Sheppard)

Pitiful, you suffer so, you understand so much . . .
I wish you'd never known. (Fagles)

Fagles's version is considerably more direct and less mannered than Sheppard's translation, with its many Os and Alases. Although there are no differences significant enough to affect our interpretation of the scene, it is fair to say that in Fagle's translation Oedipus sounds to the modern ear like a man who is truly suffering rather than declaiming.

MURIEL RUKEYSER, *On* Oedipus the King (p. 1142)

The "myth" of the poem's title does not merely indicate a mythical allusion; it also refers to the mistaken notion that "when you say Man . . . you include women." Although Sophocles's play does not address the issue of equality of the sexes, Rukeyser indicates — with good humor — that this unresolved issue is the cause of great unhappiness and even catastrophe. Her colloquial rendering of Oedipus's second encounter with the Sphinx gives the episode just the right updated tone to establish its relevance to the reader.

DAVID WILES, *On* Oedipus the King *as a Political Play* (p. 1143)

In this article, Wiles describes the play's Chorus as a democratic jury, "torn between respect for their divine law and trust for their rules." Wiles discusses how each sequence of dialogue challenges the Chorus's sympathy toward Oedipus, while each dance offers the resulting verdict. You might want to ask students about their personal reactions to each sequence of dialogue. Students could write an essay on how the Chorus's opinions of Oedipus change throughout the play and compare them with their own opinions. What evidence is used to effectively persuade the jury?

43

A Study of William Shakespeare

Most college students have read at least one William Shakespeare play in high school, usually *Romeo and Juliet* or *Julius Caesar*. Recent mainstream movie versions of *Hamlet, Much Ado about Nothing, Richard III*, and *Romeo and Juliet* may have exposed more people to his works, so few students will approach this chapter as true Shakespeare novices. You may want to begin your introduction to this chapter by asking your students to write about or discuss what they already know about Shakespeare and his writings. Many of them will be familiar with his life as a London actor and playwright, his association with the Globe Theatre, and the three basic categories of history plays, comedies, and tragedies into which his works fall. Invite students to contribute their own knowledge to your initial discussion about Shakespeare, then fill in the gaps by reading and discussing the chapter's introduction, which provides important background. Students may be surprised at how much they already know.

Nonetheless, many of them are likely to be intimidated by the prospect of studying one of Shakespeare's major plays in depth. Much of this intimidation stems from Shakespeare's reputation as the "greatest" writer in English as well as the daunting language of his plays. Believing that they need years of schooling and expertise to truly understand Shakespeare's greatness, students may shy away from reading his works. These apprehensions should be discussed openly in tandem with reading "A Note on Reading Shakespeare" (text p. 1154) from this chapter. You may even want to lead a discussion "translating" some passages into "hip," contemporary English to highlight the universal themes that *Othello* encompasses. Once students feel they have permission to "read Shakespeare's work as best [as they] can" (text p. 1156), they will be more open to the pleasure that a study of William Shakespeare has to offer.

You might point students toward the Perspectives at the end of this chapter, which reflect different approaches to Shakespeare's theater from the sixteenth century to the present. And as you conclude this unit, perhaps ask students to account for Shakespeare's continued popularity and even his recent return to popular culture (via movies). Do they see his works and characters, as Samuel Johnson did, as universal (p. 1241)? What about contemporary life in America gives Shakespeare new meaning for your students?

WILLIAM SHAKESPEARE, *Othello the Moor of Venice* (p. 1156)

Alvin Hernan's essay "*Othello*: An Introduction," in *Shakespeare, The Tragedies: A Collection of Critical Essays*, edited by Alfred Harbage (Englewood Cliffs: Prentice-Hall, 1964; print), provides a useful overall assessment of this play, as do the essays following the play in the Signet edition. For an interesting treatment of the black/white theme in *Othello*, see Doris Adler, "The Rhetoric of Black and White in *Othello*," *Shakespeare Quarterly* 25 (Spring 1974): 248–57 (print).

PERSPECTIVES ON SHAKESPEARE

THE MAYOR OF LONDON (1597), *Objections to the Elizabethan Theater* (p. 1239)

Plays, says the mayor, are a bad influence on idle people and the young, who may be inclined to a variety of "lewd & ungodly practizes." They are the cause of diseases of the body, mind, and soul. Examples of similar or related late twentieth-century opinions are readily discoverable. Complaints about violence or sexual immorality in books, movies and, to a lesser extent, plays are heard with regularity from religious organizations, some feminist groups, and the government. Those in favor of restrictions might argue that art affects our perceptions of the world and, therefore, our actions. Those in favor of unrestricted expression might argue that art forms such as Shakespeare's plays do not incite action because they resolve the emotional tensions they create through a cathartic process.

LISA JARDINE, *On Boy Actors in Female Roles* (p. 1240)

Jardine shakes up the conventional view that though Renaissance plays featured female characters played by young boys, the audiences "saw" a woman if the garb were right. She suggests that, in fact, they saw young boys and that many polemics of the period railed against the sexual depravity and perversion stirred up by such transvestites. You might want to start discussion by asking students to imagine how they would see one of Shakespeare's heroines differently if *she* were played by a *he* — if Juliet, Miranda, or Ophelia were played by Leonardo DiCaprio, for example (in a wig and a dress, of course). Many of Shakespeare's heroines cross-dress within the context of the play itself, and mistaken identity is further confused if the girl dressed up as a boy (and winning female attention as a result) is *actually* a boy.

It's difficult for us to imagine Shakespeare — our canonical Bard — being as controversial as heavy metal and horror movies are today, but Jardine offers ample evidence in *Still Harping on Daughters* that such, in fact, was the case. (Students should also read the preceding "Objections to the Elizabethan Theater" by the Mayor of London for another voice of alarm about the evils of the stage.) Have students spend some time brainstorming about potentially threatening or dangerous aspects of *Othello the Moor of Venice* when it was first performed in what we would call today right-wing England. They will probably take Jardine's cue and start by observing that each of the lovers would have been played by men or boys, but encourage them to think carefully about the setting, plot, and characters and try to imagine what warnings the Mayor of London or Dr. John Rainoldes might have offered.

SAMUEL JOHNSON, *On Shakespeare's Characters* (p. 1241)

As an additional writing assignment, you might ask students to consider Iago in light of Johnson's assessment that in the writing of Shakespeare a character is "commonly a species." Ask students to discuss the attributes of the "species" of Iago. What in the world of the play suggests that Iago's treachery is not simply idiosyncratic or confined to one uniquely malevolent figure?

JANE ADAMSON, *On Desdemona's Role in* Othello (p. 1241)

As a follow-up to Adamson's remarks, ask students to write an essay exploring what Desdemona, Emilia, and Bianca represent in the world of *Othello*.

DAVID BEVINGTON, *On Othello's Heroic Struggle* (p. 1242)

In this article, Bevington calls the deaths of Othello and Desdemona "equally devastating: He is the victim of racism, though he nobly refuses to deny his own culpability, and she is the victim of sexism, lapsing sadly into the stereotypical role of passive and silent sufferer." He says that Iago's ultimate intention is to separate Othello from his trust in someone who is good, namely Desdemona. But from this sinister plot, Othello becomes self-aware, conscious of his own destructive jealousy and mistrust. Having experienced jealousy themselves, students often place themselves in Othello's situation. You might have them write an essay on how Othello acquires "self-know-ledge," citing the occurrences that affected him most. Could the deaths of Othello and Desdemona have been avoided if Othello recognized his jealousy sooner?

JAMES KINCAID, *On the Value of Comedy in the Face of Tragedy* (p. 1243)

The irreverent tone of Kincaid's remarks mirrors his thesis, which asserts that comedy is superior to tragedy because of its greater expansiveness. Kincaid calls tragedy "unified and coherent, formally balanced and elegantly tight" (para. 2). He argues that tragedy is constrained by its rigid structure from presenting the human experience in all its complexity and richness.

ADDITIONAL RESOURCES FOR TEACHING SHAKESPEARE

SELECTED BIBLIOGRAPHY

Bradley, A. C. *Shakespearean Tragedy*. New York: Meridian, 1955. Print.

Dusinberre, Juliet. *Shakespeare and the Nature of Women*. London: Macmillan, 1975. Print.

Frye, Northrup. *On Shakespeare*. New Haven: Yale UP, 1986. Print.

Goddard, Harold C. *The Meaning of Shakespeare*. Chicago: U of Chicago P, 1951. Print.

Kermode, Frank, ed. *Four Centuries of Shakespearean Criticism*. New York: Avon, 1974. Print.

Righter, Anne. *Shakespeare and the Idea of the Play*. Harmondsworth, England: Penguin Ltd. in association with Chatto and Windus, 1967. Print.

Schoenbaum, Samuel. *William Shakespeare: A Documentary Life*. New York: Oxford UP, 1975. Print.

Spivak, Bernard. *Shakespeare and the Allegory of Evil: The History of a Metaphor in Relation to His Major Villains*. New York: Columbia UP, 1958. Print.

44

Modern Drama

The characters and situations in Henrik Ibsen's *A Doll House* (p. 1250) will be accessible to most of your students. The everyday concerns of the characters, the natural dialogue, and the familiar domestic settings that characterize dramatic realism should ensure that students have no trouble following the plot of this play.

Modern drama may even seem so accessible that it is easy to forget that the conventions of realism, like those of Greek or Shakespearean drama, are still literary conventions. While we may be more familiar with a picture-frame stage than a Greek amphitheater, we must keep in mind that such settings are used to create the *illusion* of reality and are not actual reflections of reality itself. We are still suspending our disbelief when we pretend we can see through a wall that is really not there, or that the painted background through a window represents an actual outdoor scene. Engage your students in a discussion of the realistic conventions used in *A Doll House*. Is there anything in this play (such as setting, character, or dialogue) that gives the appearance of reality but that, upon further analysis, proves to be a carefully selected artistic technique — and maybe even *un*real?

A Doll House will undoubtedly give rise to some debate among your students as to Nora's morality in committing forgery and her wisdom in choosing to leave her family in order to discover herself. While most students fault Torvald for his hypocrisy in caring more about the way his wife's actions appear to the public than about her reasons for committing them, some students will nonetheless be uncomfortable with any mother who chooses to leave her children. A close examination of Nora's rationale will help students move beyond their initial "gut" response to her decision and analyze it more objectively. Read Ibsen's "Notes for *A Doll House*" (p. 1299) as a class to help you frame the inevitable discussion about the role of gender in this play. He writes that "there are two kinds of spiritual law, two kinds of conscience, one in man and another, altogether different, in woman" (p. 1299). Students may intellectually reject this claim, yet intuitively feel its truth with regard to *A Doll House*. What are the moral and legal implications of Ibsen's ideas? It might be useful to introduce your students to the work of feminist sociologist Carol Gilligan, whose book *In a Different Voice* addresses the difference between male and female morality. For more Perspectives and suggestions on teaching this play, see Chapter 45, "A Critical Case Study: Henrik Ibsen's *A Doll House*" (p. 1305).

Web Ask students to research Henrik Ibsen at **bedfordstmartins.com/meyerlit**.

HENRIK IBSEN, *A Doll House* (p. 1250)

In the final scene of this play, just before Nora walks out on Helmer, he instructs her that she is "before all else . . . a wife and mother." Ever since the play was first performed in 1879, Nora's reply has inspired feminists: "I don't believe in that any more. I believe that, before all else, I'm a human being, no less than you — or anyway, that I ought to try to become one." As a social problem play, *A Doll House* dramatizes Nora's growth from Helmer's little pet and doll to an autonomous adult who refuses to obey rules imposed on her by a male-dominated society. Helmer expects Nora to be a submissive helpmate who leaves all important matters to the man of the house. He treats her more like a child than a wife. His affectionate terms for her are condescending, perhaps even dehumanizing. The title of the play points to the Helmers' unreal domestic arrangement. Nora chooses to stop this game when she realizes that she can no longer play her assigned role.

Ibsen, however, preferred to see Nora's decision in a larger context. In a speech before a Norwegian women's rights group that honored him in 1898, he insisted that

> I have been more of a poet and less of a social philosopher than most people have been inclined to think. I am grateful for your toast, but I can't claim the honor of ever having worked consciously for women's rights. I'm not even sure what women's rights are. To me it has seemed a matter of human rights.

Ibsen is being more than simply coy here. He conceives of Nora's problems in broad human terms, not in polemical reformist ones. The play invites both readings, and students should be encouraged to keep each in focus.

In the first act, Nora insensitively boasts of her family's expectations of security and happiness. However, this sense of well-being will be deflated by the end of the act. When she faces Krogstad's charges of fraud, Nora worries that Helmer will regard her with the same contempt he heaps on Krogstad, and worse, she fears that her husband will judge her to be a destructive influence on their children. The Christmas tree — a symbol of domestic well-being and happiness in Act I — is stripped and ragged at the beginning of Act II when Nora's world is threatened by both Krogstad's possible betrayal and Helmer's possible harsh judgment. Other symbols include Nora's desperately wild dance, her removal of her masquerade costume as she moves closer to the truth of her circumstances, and Dr. Rank's fatal illness.

Although Dr. Rank's character is not directly related to advancing the plot, his interest in talking with Nora and understanding her character provide a contrast with Helmer's behavior. Moreover, like Nora, Dr. Rank has been adversely affected by his father's corruption, which caused his illness.

Just as the Helmers' marriage is breaking apart at the end of the play, Krogstad and Mrs. Linde are reunited in what appears to be an honest, lasting relationship. Krogstad's decision not to expose Nora's secret is motivated by his love for Mrs. Linde. Many readers find this abrupt romantic reconstruction of his character unconvincing, so you might discuss this change with your students.

We don't know what will become of Nora after she leaves her husband. She rejects Helmer's attempts to start over because she realizes that she's never been truly happy as his "doll-wife." Helmer is to some degree sympathetic if only because he is thoroughly bewildered and incapable of understanding the transformation his little "squirrel" has undergone. Although Nora arrives at a mature understanding of herself as an adult woman, that recognition shatters the pattern of her life and forces her to confront her new freedom on her own. Even if we imagine her as fulfilled and happy in the future, her life at the close of the play takes on tragic proportions because she is completely on her own. Ibsen proposes no solutions to the problems he depicts concerning Nora's individualism and the repressive social conventions and responsibilities she rejects. The play does, however, reflect on the kinds of problems we might encounter in our everyday lives. The characters look and sound like real people. Part of Ibsen's realistic method is to leave the ending open, and not to wrap Nora's story up in a neat package.

TIPS FROM THE FIELD

When I teach *A Doll House*, I have students choose a character from the play. You may find it best to assign a group of three or four students to each of the main characters and have the remaining students assume the roles of the children and the nanny. You might also want one or two students to assume the role of Ibsen. At the following class, I group the students together by role and have them discuss their character. I also have them prepare at least one question directed toward another character about any aspect of the play. The class then comes together in a circle with everyone wearing a name tag of their character. Discussion follows with all students "in character" for the rest of the class meeting.

— CATHERINE RUSCO, *Muskegon Community College*

After they read Ibsen's *A Doll House*, I have my students write an entry in Nora's diary. They may choose to date the entry before, during, or after the action of the play takes place. My students especially enjoy tracing Nora's thought process as she decides whether or not she should abandon her children.

— ELIZABETH KLEINFIELD, *Red Rocks Community College*

POSSIBLE CONNECTIONS TO OTHER SELECTIONS

Susan Glaspell, *Trifles* (text p. 1038; question #2, following)

Gail Godwin, "A Sorrowful Woman" (text p. 39; question #1, following)

William Shakespeare, *Othello, the Moor of Venice* (text p. 1156)

——, *A Midsummer Night's Dream* (text p. 1546)

Sophocles, *Oedipus the King* (text p. 1094)

CONNECTIONS QUESTIONS IN TEXT (p. 1299) WITH ANSWERS

1. What does Nora have in common with the protagonist in Gail Godwin's "A Sorrowful Woman" (p. 39)? What significant differences are there between them?

    There is ample material for students to use when writing an essay about Nora and Gail Godwin's protagonists. Both are wives and mothers who do their best to fulfill their roles but become disillusioned with their domestic lives. Both have marriages that are happy on the surface, but deeply troubled by emotional and psychological incompatibilities that have been consistently ignored until the point at which the stories commence. Both women, in their own ways, lie to their families, reveal the truth (whether it be actual misdeeds or thoughts that one might consider "wrong" for a mother to have), and eventually abandon their places in the home.

    However, there are distinct differences between Nora and Godwin's wife. In "A Sorrowful Woman," the main character attempts to overcome her repulsion toward her domestic role in one last flurry of activity. She exhausts herself preparing "five loaves of warm bread, a roast stuffed turkey, a glazed ham, three pies of different fillings, eight molds of the boy's favorite custard, two weeks' supply of fresh-laundered sheets and shirts and towels," as well as several other presents (lines 38–41). But at the end of her desperate attempt to force herself to conform to expectations, she dies. Nora, on the other hand, refuses to sacrifice her life at the altar of self-denial. When her wrongdoings come to light, so does the true nature of her marriage. Nora listens to Torvald's verbal abuse, and realizes that he has never loved her in the way she's loved him, and their marriage is built on falsehoods, surface perceptions, and denial. Rather than kill herself to please him, as Godwin's wife does for her family, Nora makes a decision to strike out on her own and extricate herself from this false existence. She tells her husband that his angry words were correct about her raising children: "I'm not up to the job. There's another job I have to do first. I have to try to educate myself" (p. 1295). She goes on to say, "I have to stand completely alone, if I'm ever going to discover myself and the world out there" (p. 1295).

2. Explain how Torvald's attitude toward Nora is similar to the men's attitude toward women in Susan Glaspell's *Trifles* (p. 1038). Write an essay exploring how the assumptions the men make about the women in both plays contribute to the plays' conflicts.

    In both Ibsen's *A Doll House* and Glaspell's *Trifles*, men treat women as though they're thoughtless children. Torvald calls Nora things like, "my little lark" and "my squirrel" (p. 1251). He scolds her for overspending, constantly belittles her, and calls her "poor thing" (p. 1254). At one point, Torvald admonishes her, "Good—because you give in to your husband's judgment? All right, you little goose, I know you didn't mean it like that" (p. 1273). Torvald thinks of his wife as frivolous, lacking judgment and knowledge, and concerned only with trivialities. Because of this, he never suspects that she is in fact cunning—deceiving him on things as small as her eating macaroons to issues as large as forgery and being deep in debt.

Women are treated in exactly the same manner in Susan Glaspell's *Trifles*. The two women accompanying the sheriff and county attorney barely speak at first, and when they finally do, the men immediately start mocking them. When Mrs. Peters comments that Mrs. Wright was worried her preserve jars would shatter in the cold, the men make light of her concern. The county attorney says, "I guess before we're through she may have something more serious than preserves to worry about" (p. 1040). Hale's response to this comment not only names the play, but also sums up the men's attitude towards women in general: "Well, women are used to worrying over trifles" (p. 1040). Multiple times throughout the play, while the two women are thinking about how Mrs. Wright must have been thinking or behaving, the men assume they're focusing on trivialities and laugh at them. Their disdain and unwillingness to take the women seriously cause them to miss out on the evidence the pair uncovers. Because of their willingness to empathize with Mrs. Wright's trials and thought-process, Mrs. Hale and Mrs. Peters quickly uncover the exact evidence for motive the men are searching for. What's more, they sympathize with Mrs. Wright's actions so much that they swiftly decide to cover for her, without ever needing to confirm it to one another out loud. The two women are quick witted and clever, but the men treat them like silly children.

PERSPECTIVE

HENRIK IBSEN, *Notes for* A Doll House (p. 1299)

Ibsen seems to suggest here that "masculine society" lives by the letter of the law and will not take into account extenuating circumstances, such as Nora's altruistic reasons for forging her father's signature on the loan. This is a correct assessment of Helmer, but whether it is also an accurate observation of today's society is a subject for debate.

When Nora heads for the door, getting past Helmer is perhaps easy compared with facing the disapproval she will encounter on the other side. The social pressures she will have to endure as a wife and mother who has abandoned her family will be formidable.

45

A Critical Case Study: Henrik Ibsen's *A Doll House*

This chapter could ideally be taught in conjunction with Chapter 48, "Critical Strategies for Reading." The critical Perspectives provided on Ibsen's play offer a sampling of several ways to directly apply the various critical approaches discussed in that chapter. As students respond to these readings, they may be surprised at how varied the critical issues are and how open the possibilities for interpretation.

After reading "A Nineteenth-Century Husband's Letter to His Wife" (p. 1306), you might want to go over Kathy Atner's student essay, "On the Other Side of the Slammed Door in *A Doll House*" (p. 1317). If your class has a writing component, you can use this paper to demonstrate certain aspects of writing that you stress in your class. The paper contains examples of a solid thesis statement, well-chosen and well-handled quotations, logical organization, and other characteristics of good writing. This paper can also be a useful tool for modeling peer revision. Have the students critique this paper as they would one of their classmates', with a specific evaluation of the paper's strengths and weaknesses. This activity will give them an idea of what to look for when they help one another revise their work.

This chapter provides a number of options for paper assignments. You could ask students to respond to the ideas in any of the critical articles. Students can write about the importance of economics or the notion of absences discussed in Barry Witham and John Lutterbie's "A Marxist Approach to *A Doll House*" (p. 1308) and Joan Templeton's "Is *A Doll House* a Feminist Text?" (p. 1313), which cites those who dismiss Ibsen's feminism. Your students may wish to develop their own feminist reading of the play in response to these critics. In addition to these possible paper topics, you might invite your students to write a paper on a different play using one of the critical approaches demonstrated in this chapter and discussed in Chapter 48. Or ask students to research *A Doll House* (or another play), and bring in and write about a critical article that uses one or more of the critical approaches they have studied. Regardless of what students write about, the "Questions for Writing" (p. 1315) will help them focus their ideas and get started.

Even if you are not using this chapter as a topic for student papers, the readings provide interesting additional perspectives on the play. In addition to reading them as examples of separate critical approaches, students can also read these essays in conjunction with one another to produce even more interpretations. What happens, for example, when students bring together Carol Strongin Tufts's ideas about Nora's narcissism in "A Psychoanalytical Reading of Nora" (p. 1310) and Joan Templeton's thoughts about Ibsen's feminism? Students will probably find that analyzing these and the chapter's other essays together both complicates and complements their theories.

PERSPECTIVES

A Nineteenth-Century Husband's Letter to His Wife (p. 1306)

Marcus's attitude toward his wife, Ulrike, as expressed in this letter may remind your students of Helmer's attitude toward Nora, especially at the point in the play when he first learns from Krogstad's letter how she has deceived him. Both men place the blame entirely on their wives. Marcus writes, "you, alone, carry the guilt of all the misfortune" (para. 1). He also refers to his wife's "false ambitions" and her "stubbornness." However, Helmer at least displays some affection for Nora in the play. Although Marcus describes himself in his signature as "unhappy," there is little other evidence of affection in his letter. He is possibly being sensitive to her feelings by letting her know that their children are healthy, but in most respects the letter contains only his personal concerns and his list of ultimatums. Do your students see any differences in the ways the two men treat their wives? What does the reader learn about Marcus from his letter? What does his desire to control all the details of the household say about him? Is it possible to infer anything positive about him, such as a talent for organization and efficiency, from his lists of regulations? Encourage your students to try to read Marcus's letter from a nineteenth-century perspective: Why would "many in the world" envy Ulrike if she chose to return to her husband?

BARRY WITHAM and JOHN LUTTERBIE, *A Marxist Approach to A Doll House* (p. 1308)

Witham and Lutterbie's discussion of economics as a subversive force in human relationships could offer important insights into Nora and Torvald's relationship. You might ask your students to consider, possibly in writing, ways in which their marriage has been shaped by financial concerns. Is economics the prevalent shaping force, or are there other powers that must be considered? You might also ask your class to examine closely the idea that "financial enslavement is symptomatic of other forms of enslavement" (p. 1309). Do your students believe that Witham and Lutterbie exaggerate the importance of the play's economics, or are they correct in diagnosing the source of Nora's difficulties?

Consider also the authors' assertion that "the function of women in this society was . . . artificial" (p. 1309). Can your students find evidence of this in the play? Do they see this subservient female role as a characteristic of past societies, or does it still exist today? In what forms? You might discuss with your class whether Nora's desertion of her family might be considered a victory or a defeat, and for whom? In economic terms, what might Nora be facing as an estranged wife?

CAROL STRONGIN TUFTS, *A Psychoanalytic Reading of Nora* (p. 1310)

Tufts uses the American Psychiatric Association's definition of *narcissism* as a framework for presenting her argument about Nora's character. She claims that the application of this definition to Nora will enable readers to see her as multidimensional and complex, rather than as a "totally sympathetic victim turned romantic heroine" (para. 2). One could argue that Tufts's reading of Nora and her discussion of the reactions of modern audiences to the play are reductive rather than complex. Do your students see Nora as "totally sympathetic"? Would the play have remained popular for over one hundred years if audiences considered the characters to be as one-dimensional as Tufts claims? Despite her measured phrases, Tufts clearly wants the reader to "diagnose" Nora in terms of her narcissism and to downplay her heroism. Could any other characters in the play be accused of narcissism?

You might also have students consider Tufts's assessment of Ibsen's words at the beginning of this excerpt. Is he really being "sarcastic" about audience response, as she claims, or is he simply recognizing that authors do not have complete control over how their work is interpreted?

JOAN TEMPLETON, *Is A Doll House a Feminist Text?* (p. 1313)

Templeton's piece incorporates the tirades of several respected critics who do not feel that *A Doll House* should be referred to as a feminist text. However, Templeton's choice of such strident quotations, as well as her presentation of them and her use of the term *backlash* in the title of the essay from which this piece is excerpted, imply that she thinks the various critics are protesting too much. The first line of the Perspective, in which Templeton writes that Ibsen has been "saved from feminism," may well be sarcastic in tone. The quotation from R. M. Adams with which the excerpt closes — "Nora has no sex" — is patently absurd. While the critics Templeton cites may have been responding with extreme criticism to extreme feminist claims, is any purpose served by their vehemence? Does it have the effect of encouraging a reader to take a more balanced look at the play?

R. M. Adams's assertion that Nora has no sex is worth further discussion. Certainly Nora must have universal qualities in order for audiences to empathize with her, but how much difference does it make to the play that she is female? How could Ibsen have written a play with this theme about a man? What kind of man would such a character have had to have been? Who might have been controlling him?

46

A Thematic Case Study: An Album of Contemporary Humor and Satire

This chapter contains six plays that demonstrate twentieth- and twenty-first-century examples of comedic or satiric drama. Like Ives's play, Jane Martin's *Rodeo* is a monologue. It provides opportunities for talking with your students about how writers create interest and tension with only one character. Jane Anderson's *The Reprimand*, on the other hand, gives the audience two characters, but strips their conversation of all context so that the readers or viewers have to fill in all the details that surround it. Rich Orloff's *Playwriting* 101 and Joan Ackermann's *Quiet Torrential Sound* also focus on two characters and their relationship; however, the readers are constantly distracted by an extra character (The Teaches) or the waiter.

Web Ask students to research the playwrights in this chapter at **bedfordstmartins.com/ meyerlit**.

JANE ANDERSON, *The Reprimand* (p. 1324)

This play explores elements of politics and human behavior as two women discuss the hidden meaning behind an off-handed comment. Each character's sincerity is unclear throughout the play, and the dialogue offers the possibility of calculated motives and sinister agendas. Since much of the dialogue is ambiguous, students will have different interpretations of the play, which could facilitate an interesting discussion. You might ask students to write an essay analyzing each character's goals in the conversation. What are these people trying to achieve? How does each person try to manipulate the other? What means do they use to gain control of the situation?

POSSIBLE CONNECTION TO ANOTHER SELECTION

Susan Glaspell, *Trifles* (text p. 1038; question #1, following)

CONNECTIONS QUESTIONS IN TEXT (text p. 1326) WITH ANSWERS

1. Compare the power relationship that exists between Rhona and Mim and that of Mrs. Peters and Mrs. Hale in Susan Glaspell's *Trifles* (p. 1038).

   In Anderson's play, Rhona takes the upper hand by accusing Mim of insensitivity. Her complaint puts Mim on the defensive. Rhona further asserts her superiority in the situation by claiming that she is not concerned for herself but for how Mim's comment could "undermine the project," which casts her as selfless compared to her petty coworker. Finally, Rhona plots to keep her power by creating tension between Mim and another colleague, Jim. Mim lashes out at the end of the scene, which suggests how resentful she is of the control Rhona has over her.

   While the power balance in *The Reprimand* is determined by workplace relationships, the balance between the two women in *Trifles* depends on their respective positions in society. As the sheriff's wife, Mrs. Peters has a position of more importance. Mrs. Hale, a farmer's wife, defends Mrs. Wright's housekeeping and living situation because she can sympathize with the hardships of her life. Throughout their conversation, she attempts to shield Mrs. Wright from Mrs. Peters's judgment.

2. Discuss the ways in which hostility is manifested in characters' dialogue in *The Reprimand* and in Michael Hollinger's *Naked Lunch* (p. 1057).

The Reprimand is a dialogue about dialogue; both Mim and Rhona are expressing anger or hostility, but how it affects their dialogue differs. Rhona expresses aggression toward a specific type of man by saying "Especially when we're working for men like Jim" (p. 1325). She also believes she detects hostility in Mim's offering her "the bigger chair." Throughout the short dialogue, the audience sees Mim as the wronged party and victim of Rhona's misplaced, perhaps even paranoid, hostility. It isn't until the end when, with just two words — "fat pig" — Mim reveals that Rhona was not paranoid. Mim is simply better at hiding her hostility than Rhona is.

In *Naked Lunch*, Vernon's hostility and aggression toward Lucy is more overt. Vernon steamrolls Lucy's attempts at breaking free of him, whether by his opening monologue or later, when he interrupts or talks over her. Eventually, he even ends up shouting at her and physically intimidating her into eating the steak. It's revealed through the dialogue what the source of his anger is: when Vernon asks when Lucy became a vegetarian, she says, "Since we, you know. Broke up." Vernon seems to be antagonizing Lucy for no reason, but the dialogue reveals that his hostility might stem from his fear of her moving on and leaving him.

SHARON E. COOPER, *Mistaken Identity* (p. 1326)

In Cooper's portrayal of an awkward blind date, Steve's first lines reveal him to be naive. His way of speaking, including the way he recites commercial slogans as if they were insights, further reinforces this impression. Steve is well-meaning, but his only knowledge of Indian culture comes from watching a few Westerns. Most of all, he is prepared to jump into a marriage with Kali practically at first sight. However, when Steve talks about loneliness, he turns, as Kali says, "strangely poetic" (p. 1329).

Unlike Steve, Kali is quite canny. She allows her brother to set her up on dates, but she is fed up with them: "you just happened to show up at the end of a very long line of a lot of very bad dates" (p. 1327). She tells Steve that she is a lesbian, with the hope that the news might get back to her brother. Though she is skeptical of Steve from the beginning, when Kali realizes that, like her, he is longing for something, she starts to feel more sympathy. At the end, when he asks whether she thinks he is desperate, she admits, "Not any more than the rest of us" (p. 1330).

POSSIBLE CONNECTION TO ANOTHER SELECTION

Michael Hollinger, *Naked Lunch* (text p. 1057; question #1, following)

CONNECTION QUESTION IN TEXT (p. 1331) WITH ANSWER

1. Compare Steve's character with that of Vernon's in Michael Hollinger's *Naked Lunch* (p. 1057). What is the essential difference between them? Are there any significant similarities?

While Steve is an essentially kind character, if sometimes inconsiderate, Vernon shows that he can be violent and cruel. The final gesture of *Mistaken Identity* is one of sympathy, while the final gesture of *Naked Lunch* establishes Vernon's dominance. The male characters in both plays have a tendency to interrupt and carry on a one-person conversation. However, Hollinger's play is not about a misunderstanding between two characters so much as it is about the power dynamic.

ELAINE JARVIK, *Dead Right* (p. 1331)

The husband and wife in *Dead Right* take two very different positions on what happens after death: Penny is deeply concerned about how she will be remembered, while Bill holds that once you are dead it doesn't matter anymore what people think of you.

Though he humors her by taking notes about what she wants him to say about her, she accuses him of not really caring; the list of obituary items he writes on newsprint will "turn yellow and disintegrate" (p. 1334). As he points out, "So will your obituary," also printed on newspaper and prone to fall apart in time (p. 1334).

As he gets more frustrated with her demands, Bill accuses Penny of vanity. It is true that many of her anxieties focus on what she sees as an unflattering photograph of her friend and her desire to eliminate similarly unflattering pictures of herself from Bill's choices. However, her fears run deeper, too, and many of them are expressed in the writer's complaint she makes about Francine's obituary: "She has no chance to do a rewrite" (p. 1332). The problem is not only that Francine cannot revise what her family wrote about her, but also that her life is finished now, no longer subject to change.

Penny's sympathies as she looks at the obituary are with the complex and interesting woman she knew. She hopes she will be remembered as similarly complex, pointing out to her husband her particular love of Thomas Pynchon, her master's degree from Northwestern, and so on. He, on the other hand, is realistic about what an obituary can really convey about a person: "You can't write about somebody's fantasy life in an obituary" (p. 1333). The best he can hope for is to be remembered as "a decent guy" (p. 1335).

POSSIBLE CONNECTION TO ANOTHER SELECTION

Dylan Thomas, "Do Not Go Gentle into That Good Night" (text p. 747; question #1, following)

CONNECTION QUESTION IN TEXT (p. 1336) WITH ANSWER

1. Compare the tone and theme in *Dead Right* and in Dylan Thomas's poem "Do Not Go Gentle into That Good Night" (text p. 757).

    Both *Dead Right* and Dylan Thomas's "Do Not Go Gentle into That Good Night" are at least in part about resistance to death, but while Jarvik's play takes a humorous view of the obsession with memory, Thomas's poem is grave and fierce. Unlike Penny in *Dead Right*, the speaker of the poem is less concerned with controlling his reputation than with holding on to life with all the strength, physical and emotional, he can muster. Death may prove "gentle," but those who cherish living will not be swayed by its comforts. Penny's concerns about her obituary may seem more superficial — but at their heart are fears about appearing less vital than she feels.

JANE MARTIN, *Rodeo* (p. 1336)

Martin's brief monologue in the voice of Big Eight/Lurlene, a woman whose whole life has been involved in rodeo, hardly seems to be the stuff of engaging drama. However, the author's talent for drawing the audience into the lives of her characters soon makes Big Eight a sympathetic, then an empathetic character. By the time she utters her challenge — "[L]ook out, honey! They want to make them a dollar out of what you love. Dress *you* up like Minnie Mouse. Sell your rodeo" (p. 1338) — the audience is more than ready to accept Big Eight as an individual and her plight as something that is a danger to us all.

Martin presents Big Eight to the audience in such a way as to play into preconceptions about rodeo people. Consider the stage directions, which place her among horse equipment, dressed in jeans and a work shirt, drinking beer and listing to "Tanya Tucker . . . or some other female country-western vocalist" (p. 1336). Big Eight's later comments indicate that she probably chews tobacco, and her dialect stamps her as uneducated and crude. Martin allows, even encourages, the audience to prejudge her character and the rodeo, then works to force us to see the other aspects of both the woman and the rodeo that exist beneath the stereotypical trappings. Big Eight turns out to be funny, touching, and wise, though uneducated. By the time the audience learns that Big Eight has a real name — Lurlene — it is ready to accept her as a human being and to lament the very human problem she exemplifies: that decent and caring people are pushed out of the way in the name of progress and profit.

The aspect of rodeo that Big Eight mentions the most is the importance of family and community. The play opens with the story she tells about how she received her nickname from her father for staying on a bucking horse. The rodeo is "us" to Big Eight: "We'd jest git us to a bar and tell each other lies about how good we were" (p. 1337). The outsiders who come in and change the rodeo are "they." Significantly, one of the things the businessmen have done is to change the character of the people who participate in the rodeo. At the end of the monologue, neither Big Eight nor the Tilson family is involved any longer. The rodeo has been transformed from a closely knit community to a business.

Possible Connections to Other Selections

Stephen Crane, "The Bride Comes to Yellow Sky" (text p. 246; question #1, following)

Dana Gioia, "Money" (text p. 986; question #2, following)

Connections Questions in Text (p. 1339) with Answers

1. In an essay discuss the nostalgic tone of *Rodeo* and Stephen Crane's short story "The Bride Comes to Yellow Sky" (p. 246). In your response consider each work's treatment of the West.

   Both *Rodeo* and "The Bride Comes to Yellow Sky" depict the West as a dying ideal. However, Crane's story is more humorous in its treatment of the mythology. When his brave lone sheriff comes back to town with a wife, it upsets the archetypal situation between him and the villain, Scratchy. Though Martin's Big Eight is certainly a fascinating and slightly eccentric speaker, she is not just the representation of a type. Rather, she is a fully developed character who finds herself in a world that sees her as out of date. Her version of the West is more realistic, so the tone of her remembrance is graver.

2. Discuss the attitudes expressed about money in *Rodeo* and Dana Gioia's "Money" (p. 986).

   Both of these pieces deal with how the need or desire for money can affect people and situations. In *Rodeo*, Big Eight blames the changes to the rodeo on "them"—the corporations, including "Coca-Cola, Pepsi Cola, Marlboro damn cigarettes" (p. 1337). Not only have these commercial interests corrupted the spirit of the rodeo, but in their new vision, people like Big Eight don't belong. They want to replace her with showier women whose appeal has nothing to do with their rodeo talent, because they believe this will bring in more revenue. These corporations are entirely concerned with money rather than talent or skill. Gioia's poem "Money" focuses not on a specific situation, like *Rodeo*, but instead on a general attitude towards financial wealth. The poem is concerned with accumulating and spending cash: "To be made of it! To have it/to burn!" (lines 7–8). Gioia's speaker also emphasizes how important money becomes to those who possess or covet it by saying, "Money. You don't know where it's been,/but you put it where your mouth is./And it talks" (16–18). Like in Martin's play, money is the motivator and influencer of people and events.

JOAN ACKERMANN, *Quiet Torrential Sound* (p. 1339)

Ackermann uses the dialogue that begins her play to characterize two sisters, the main characters of *Quiet Torrential Sound*: Monica is not only more outspoken than her sister Claire, but also more invested in presenting herself as a cultured person, and therefore anxious to manage the way her sister appears as well. Monica is self-denying, avoiding sugar and caffeine, and she tries to impose her austerity on Claire, who resists by ordering a sundae. Monica's tendency to be critical finds its primary outlet in her sister, but she also makes a snide comment about the waiter's dental hygiene. She appears to be forgiving ("I'm sure he has a heart of gold"), but she can't resist pointing out what she sees as his flaws.

Monica's lack of sexual experience, which the audience understands through her response to Claire's revelation, is a further extension of her self-denying principles. The play suggests that maybe her attempt to appreciate high culture is a way of filling in what is missing from her life. Though she phrases her last request for the materials from Claire's workshop as if she is doing her sister a favor, Monica's turn at the end may signal that deep down she does long for a fuller life.

POSSIBLE CONNECTIONS TO OTHER SELECTIONS

Jane Anderson, *The Reprimand* (text p. 1324)

Michael Hollinger, *Naked Lunch* (text p. 1057; question #1, following)

Xu Xi, "Famine" (text p. 123; question #2, following)

CONNECTIONS QUESTIONS IN TEXT (p. 1345) WITH ANSWERS

1. Discuss the ways in which this play and Michael Hollinger's *Naked Lunch* (p. 1057) are stories about power in relationships.

    Naked Lunch considers power dynamics in romantic relationships. In Vernon, Hollinger exposes a male character who relishes his ability to dominate a woman both in conversation and, eventually, physically. *Quiet Torrential Sound* focuses on family relationships — here, the dynamic between two sisters. As in *Naked Lunch*, the way one character dominates the conversation represents a larger need to control the other. Both plays use food as an illustration of how the power struggles play out, possibly because this basic necessity can be a serious means of control. Vernon takes Lucy's vegetarianism as an opportunity to humiliate and eventually to force-feed her, while Monica makes fun of Claire's sundae to suggest that she has no self-control.

2. Compare the themes of *Quiet Torrential Sound* and Xu Xi's short story "Famine" (p. 123).

    In both of these works, food is a significant sign of how family members feel about each other. Xu Xi's narrator longs for decadent Western food and even seeks it out away from home, but as long as her parents are alive she adheres to their austere diet as a form of filial piety. Her gluttonous trip to New York after they die is both an act of rebellion and a way of coming to terms with their deaths. In Ackermann's play, sisters deny themselves food in a way that represents their tentative attitude toward life in general, especially the entanglements of relationships and sex. Monica's refusal to order anything but decaf, and her paranoia about receiving regular coffee instead, make her appear to be pinched and anxious. Though she tries to appreciate classical music, she has a hard time really enjoying more mundane pleasures. In the course of the play, the audience comes to understand that Claire's ordering a sundae, in spite of Monica's protests, is symbolic of a larger change in her attitudes about pleasure.

RICH ORLOFF, *Playwriting 101: The Rooftop Lesson* (p. 1346)

Orloff's play is a clever commentary on what makes a good drama. The teacher-figure begins with a standard lecture on "a typical dramatic scenario" (p. 1346). He or she (notice how Orloff specifies that these characters are not gender-specific) refers to classic dramatic works and seems to have absorbed the language of drama critics, using it to coach students to avoid "[alienating] conservatives" or sounding like "a second-rate David Mamet" (p. 1347). In addition to discoursing on the subject of playwriting, the teacher is able to mediate the action of the scene in an unusual way, using a clicker to pause and resume the action. Yet the teacher is a familiar enough authority figure that we accept this premise. The turn comes when the characters within the scene begin to challenge the teacher's control over the situation. The Good Samaritan gains control of the clicker and thereby gains authority to comment as the teacher had been commenting on him or her: "Notice how organically the teacher's frustration has increased" (p. 1350). When the conflict gets out of hand at the end, it is the teacher who gets shot, a surprising outcome given the authoritative and academic tone of the beginning of the play. You might have your students discuss why Orloff chooses to have the teacher stand and conclude the action of the play with a final click of the remote. Does this highlight the artifice of plays, or does it indicate the teacher's regaining of control over the playwright's creation?

Possible Connections to Other Selections

Joan Ackermann, *Quiet Torrential Sound* (text p. 1339; question #2, following)

Henrik Ibsen, *A Doll House* (text p. 1250; question #1, following)

Connections Questions in Text (p. 1352) with Answers

1. The Teacher claims that "When [Ibsen's] Nora leaves in *A Doll House* [p. 1250], nobody wants her husband to reply — (*upbeat*) 'Call when you get work!'" Why not?

    The teacher suggests that one of the key elements of a good drama is "intense oppositional desires, more commonly known as 'conflict'" (p. 1347). If Torvald accepted Nora's leaving as easily as the line above suggests, then the conflict of the scene would dissolve, and the audience would simply be witnessing the mundane fight of a married couple. The playwright has to keep a conflict going in order to keep the audience's interest. Even to the end, Torvald wants to keep Nora in his possession, which makes her departure necessary.

2. The teacher also claims that "two characters in hostile disagreement isn't conflict, it's just bickering. We don't go to the theatre to hear petty, puerile antagonism; that's why we have families." Consider the value of this assertion in relation to Joan Ackermann's *Quiet Torrential Sound* (p. 1339).

    The teacher's choice of words is interesting because it makes sense, but is ultimately incorrect. Many plays, including Orloff's and Ackermann's, prove that point wrong. After all, what is *Romeo and Juliet* but a play about senseless bickering? In *Quiet Torrential Sound*, the issue is not one of life and death, as it is in *The Rooftop Lesson*. The entire action of the play focuses on a discussion between two very different women. Monica considers herself "cultured" (p. 1344), while Claire, who is slightly younger, is more introverted. Claire quietly puts up with Monica's passive-aggressive criticisms, like when she tells her, "I wish you would make more of an effort to expand your vocabulary" (p. 1340), or critiques her appearance, saying, "that blouse does very little for you... You don't have very strong features so you need more vibrancy of color to perk you up" (p. 1340). Initially it seems ridiculous that Claire would put up with someone like Monica, but then Monica reveals to the audience, "We are sisters, Claire" (p. 1342). Suddenly it changes everything about their interactions. This is a perfect example of how misleading a blanket statement like the teacher's can be. Sometimes characters "bickering" is all it takes to create conflict—especially when they're family.

A Collection of Plays

47

Plays for Further Reading

DAVID HENRY HWANG, *Trying to Find Chinatown* (p. 1357)

Hwang's play gives dramatic life to theoretical questions about race: Is it a matter of genetics or a matter of identification with a culture? Ronnie represents the former view. He is skeptical when he learns that Benjamin, whose biological parents were white, identifies as Asian because he was raised in that culture by his adoptive parents. Benjamin calls Ronnie "Brother" and places himself within the marginalized "we." However, Ronnie doesn't want to be pigeonholed by the ideas of "ethnic fundamentalists" (p. 1360). He gets angry when he thinks Benjamin has assumed he will know where Chinatown is, and he feels more affinity with the African American tradition from which blues and jazz music emerged. Benjamin then labels him as "one of those self-hating, assimilated Chinese-Americans" (p. 1360). The two characters' distance at the end of the play suggests that these two views are difficult to synthesize, and Hwang provides the audience with no answers about which he thinks is more valid. Rather, at the end, Benjamin's monologue and Ronnie's music restate their respective cases, but as the final stage direction says, allow them to "remain oblivious of one another" (p. 1362).

Web Ask students to research the playwrights in this chapter at **bedfordstmartins.com/ meyerlit**.

POSSIBLE CONNECTIONS TO OTHER SELECTIONS

August Wilson, *Fences* (text p. 1420; question #1, following)

Nilaja Sun, *No Child. . .* (text p. 1363; question #2, following)

CONNECTIONS QUESTIONS IN TEXT (p. 1362) WITH ANSWERS

1. How do you think Ronnie in *Trying to Find Chinatown* would assess August Wilson's treatment of race in *Fences* (p. 1420)?

   In Hwang's play, Ronnie thinks that race is a genetic trait, but that it is not closely related to identity. He draws his identity not from the Asian Studies textbooks Benjamin follows, but from the blues and jazz he likes to play. As a musician, he seems to think that interests and talent are more important than race in determining identity. Ronnie would likely be sympathetic to the effect race has had on Troy Maxson's life, preventing him from playing professional baseball and forcing him into harder, more exhausting jobs. Yet there are hints in *Fences* that race was not the only thing holding Troy back. Rose suggests, for example, that he would have been too old to play baseball anyway, even if discrimination had not prevented it. Also, when he confronts stereotypes, Troy gains a promotion to a better job. Finally,

Wilson's portrayal of Troy might escape what Ronnie calls "ethnic fundamentalism." Though Troy has certainly faced racism, his attitudes toward the world are shaped by a complex mixture of family history, social position, and economic hardship.

2. Discuss the perspective offered on white attitudes toward race in Hwang's play and in Nilaja Sun's *No Child . . .* (p. 1363).

   Though Hwang's character Benjamin is the biological child of white parents, his perspective as the adopted son of an Asian family gives him an insider's view of white prejudices toward Asians, and Asian men in particular. He argues that American stereotypes either ignore or exoticize Asians. Sun also complicates attitudes about race in her play. One feature of the classroom that most strikes the new "teaching artist" is the number of ethnic jokes and slurs the students direct at one another and at their teachers. What unites the class, however, is the feeling that whites in other parts of the city expect very little from them beyond having many children, working for the MTA, and so forth. This feeling that they have been underestimated helps them to understand Sun's chosen play, about Australian convicts.

NILAJA SUN, *No Child . . .* (p. 1363)

Like several other plays in this book, Sun's *No Child . . .* gives the audience a backstage view of theater. Though her primary subject is education, we also learn about the power of drama, even for students who start out skeptical about the idea of putting on a play. The audience gets to see the work that goes into the production — both the intellectual work the students put into interpreting the play and relating it to their own lives, and the physical work of staging and voicing it in front of an audience.

The students in the class frustrate their teachers but are also funny and frank. The self-proclaimed worst class in the school contains a range of characters with different interests, but all of them feel disenfranchised. Sun performs the play as a one-woman show, which makes the diverse cast of characters even more remarkable. You can find a video of her performing part of the play on YouTube if you wish to show students how she accomplishes the transformation into different parts.

POSSIBLE CONNECTIONS TO OTHER SELECTIONS

Richard Hague, "Directions for Resisting the SAT" (text p. 767)

Rich Orloff, *"Playwriting 101: The Rooftop Lesson"* (text p. 1346; question #1, following)

CONNECTIONS QUESTIONS IN TEXT (P. 1381) WITH ANSWERS

1. To what extent do Rich Orloff's *Playwriting 101: The Rooftop Lesson* (p. 1346) and *No Child . . .* comment on the nature of playwriting?

   Both *Playwriting 101: The Rooftop Lesson* and *No Child . . .* comment on the ability of drama and playwriting to challenge authority. In Orloff's play, the characters who are seemingly controlled by the Teacher break away and end up exercising control themselves. Similarly, the students in Sun's play use *Our Country's Good* to reclaim their identities, lives, and desires from their prison-like, test-dominated school environment.

AUGUST WILSON, *Fences* (p. 1420)

Troy Maxson's struggles in Wilson's 1985 play make comparisons to Arthur Miller's *Death of a Salesman* inevitable. Nevertheless, *Fences* stands on its own as a work specific to the black struggle in America. Wilson uses a number of details to stress that his play is about the black experience. Among these are the version of American history that precedes Act I, the choices of athletics and music by Troy's sons (Wilson maintained that these are the only fields fully open to blacks), and the story with which Wilson begins the play. Troy's narrative about his coworker's getting away with stealing a watermelon by acting dumb is a "High John the Conqueror" story, a type of story slaves told to one another (but not to whites), that often involved a slave appearing ridiculous while he was stealing from the white master with impunity.

At the same time, the play has a larger, more universal context. Rose tells Troy, "The world's changing around you and you can't even see it" (p. 1439). Troy fails to recognize a number of things. He never accepts that his failure to become a major-leaguer was due to his age as well as to racism; he refuses to recognize his monetary reasons for having Gabe committed; he does not accept his sons' maturity or notice their need for his approval; and he never appreciates his wife's desperation, which matches his own. He wants to control his life, no matter how narrow a definition of life he must accept in order to have that control. His relationship with Alberta, which enables him to see the life of "quiet desperation" he has been leading, is the turning point for Troy; his confession to Rose is the turning point of the play. During the argument with Rose, Cory defies his father for the first time. Afterward Troy becomes isolated from Rose, Cory, Bono, his other friends from work, and Gabe; in a futile gesture to control his life by controlling death, he completes the fence that confines his life.

Troy Maxson attempts to use his large hands to take the world and "cut it down to where I could handle it" (p. 1444). Although the world proves to have forces more powerful than Troy can manage, he finally does what he considers most important in the baseball game that is his life: he "goes down swinging."

POSSIBLE CONNECTION TO ANOTHER SELECTION

Ralph Ellison, "Battle Royal" (text p. 226; question #2, following)

CONNECTIONS QUESTIONS IN TEXT (pp. 1466) WITH ANSWERS

1. Compare the father's sensibilities in *Fences* and in Jan Beatty's poem "My Father Teaches Me to Dream" (p. 988).

    Both Troy Maxson in *Fences* and the father in Beatty's poem "My Father Teaches Me to Dream" highly value work. The first time Troy interacts with his younger son, Cory, he berates him for not doing his chores. When Troy hears Cory is being scouted by college football teams, rather than expressing pride in his son's ability, he says, "I thought you supposed to be working down there at the A&P" (1436). In fact, he objects to Cory becoming a college athlete, insisting, "You go on and get your book-learning so you can work yourself up in that A&P or learn how to fix cars or build houses or something, get you a trade…You go on and learn how to put your hands to some good use" (1436–1437). He calls Cory a "fool" for only working weekends and letting someone else cover the weekday shifts. To Troy, there's no point in anything but work. He's an entirely practical, pragmatic man, who refuses to go into debt or buy luxuries for himself or his family. In fact, he looks at family as another obligation, and tells his son that he provides for him not because he likes him, but because "It's my job" (1438).

    The speaker in Jan Beatty's poem shares the exact same sensibilities as Troy Maxson. He clearly values work above all else, and believes that following one's dreams, like Cory's aspiration to become a pro football player, is pointless. He tells his child to focus his or her life on work and that, "You work all day./You get back on the bus at night. Same thing./You go to sleep. You get up./You do the same thing again" (lines 8–11). It might as well be Troy speaking to Cory when the father says, "There's no handouts in this life./All this other stuff you're looking for—/it ain't there" (lines 13–15). If anything, the father in Beatty's poem is even more stringent about his sensibilities than Troy. The speaker never mentions family or friends, or taking any time to relax or rest. He is entirely fixated on productivity and employment.

2. How might the narrator's experiences in Ellison's short story "Battle Royal" (p. 226) be used to shed light on Troy's conflict in *Fences*?

Ellison's story asserts that, regardless of law, white America has the power and the will to control how far black people will go in realizing their dreams. This is the bitter lesson Troy draws from the experience of blacks in baseball; his belief that there is nothing whatever he can do about the system causes him to narrow his dreams down to a size that will not cause him trouble in white society. Troy's attempt to counter the system, his successful effort to become a garbage truck driver, merely reinforces the lesson when the company allows him to drive but puts him on new and different routes, isolating him from all the people with whom he has worked and become friends over the years.

The young man's experience in Ellison's story can also be applied to Troy's son Cory, who, like Ellison's narrator, is just graduating from high school at the time the play starts. Troy's knowledge of the kind of system that operates in "Battle Royal" causes him to want to protect his son from that kind of humiliation and disillusionment. He sabotages Cory's hopes for a college education rather than allow him to hope and have his hopes destroyed by racist attitudes that are more powerful than his son's talents. He urges Cory to stick to less lofty goals, such as learning a trade: "that way you have something can't nobody take away from you" (p. 1468). His life experiences have taught him not to want anything that white society might *want* to take away from him. Ellison's story shows how well-grounded Troy's fears are.

DAVID IVES, *The Blizzard* (p. 1470)

The storm Ives's title refers to cuts the characters in his play off from the world, with no contact from phones or information from television or radio. Jenny and Neil seem to find their isolation both eerie and promising. Neil asks, "Why don't we all do something different this weekend" (p. 1471), signaling that this break in routine might open up different possibilities. On the other hand, Jenny points out that the atmosphere of the storm is similar to a mystery novel, which raises the specter of murder and mayhem.

The comparison with a mystery story becomes a driving force for the play, as the characters compare their experience both hopefully and fearfully to literary models. Jenny speculates, "I think the reason people like murder mysteries is that, in a murder mystery, everything is *significant*" (p. 1471). At first, this sense of each detail having meaning feels like a refreshing change, but by the time Natasha makes a similar statement about mysteries, Jenny wishes she could escape significance and just go back to her ordinary life. Salim has a different take on the techniques of the mystery writer: "You know what I hate about murder mysteries? It's that everybody in them's got a secret" (p. 1473). Unfortunately, Neil and Jenny are in the dark about what his secret might be. Given these musings on mystery stories, particularly the comments on significance, you might ask students what Neil's profession — as creator of the *Torturama* series — has to do with anything. What is significant about his trade in violence and fear?

POSSIBLE CONNECTION TO ANOTHER SELECTION

Jane Anderson, *The Reprimand* (text p. 1324; question #1, following)

CONNECTION QUESTION IN TEXT (p. 1474) WITH ANSWER

1. Discuss the power struggles in *The Blizzard* and in Jane Anderson's *The Reprimand* (text p. 1324).

   In *The Blizzard,* power comes largely from differential knowledge: Salim and Natasha are apparently intimately acquainted with the details of Neil and Jenny's life, but they offer no information beyond their names that Neil and Jenny can use to form opinions about them. They also wield power in their refusal to acknowledge the strangeness of the situation or the fact that they are out of place in the scene, a strategy that effectively disarms Neil's attempts to get rid of them. In *The Reprimand*, Rhona takes a grievance against Mim and turns it into a source of power. First she puts Mim on the defensive by making her feel guilty; then, she proves to be masterful at manipulating Mim by turning her anger over this guilt-trip against a fellow coworker. She plays on Mim's insecurity while making her own insecurity a weapon.

CRITICAL THINKING AND WRITING

48

Critical Strategies for Reading

Although there is an emphasis on critical strategies for reading throughout the tenth edition of *The Compact Bedford Introduction to Literature*, this chapter brings into focus an increasing tendency in introductory literature classes to make students aware of critical approaches to literature used by contemporary theorists. The treatment of the major approaches discussed in this chapter — formalist, biographical, psychological, historical (including Marxist, new historicist, and cultural criticism), gender (including feminist and gay and lesbian criticism), mythological, reader-response, and deconstructionist — is designed to supplement the more general "Questions for Responsive Reading and Writing" that are provided in each genre section (for fiction, see p. 9; poetry, p. 541; drama, p. 1031). These critical strategies range from long-standing traditional approaches, such as those practiced by biographical and historical critics, to more recent and controversial perspectives represented, for example, by feminist and deconstructionist critics.

By introducing students to competing critical strategies, you can help them to understand that there are varying strategies for talking about literary works. A familiarity with some of the basic assumptions of these strategies and with the types of questions raised by particular ways of reading will aid students in keeping their bearing during class discussions as well as in the deep water of the secondary readings they're likely to encounter for their writing assignments. After studying this chapter, students should have a firmer sense that there can be many valid and interesting readings of the same work. Their recognition should open up some of the interpretive possibilities offered by any given text while simultaneously encouraging students to feel more confident about how their own reading raises particular kinds of questions and leads them into the text. In short, this chapter can empower students to think through their own critical interpretations in relation to a number of critical contexts.

This chapter can be assigned at any point during the course. Some instructors may find it useful to assign the chapter at the start of the course so that students are aware of the range of critical approaches from the beginning. Many students are likely to raise more informed and sophisticated questions about texts as a result of having been exposed to these critical strategies. Instructors who wish to introduce this chapter early in the course may want to take a look at Appendix B in this manual, "List of Perspectives Organized by Critical Strategies" (p. 1441), which organizes the Perspectives throughout the book by the critical strategy they most exemplify. Other instructors may prefer to lead up to the critical perspectives and assign the chapter later in the course as a means of pulling together the elements of literature taken up during the preceding weeks. When you do assign the chapter, however, remind students to first read Kate Chopin's "The Story of an Hour" (p. 15), since each of the critical approaches is applied to that particular work as well as to other texts.

The purpose of this chapter is not to transform students into professional critics; instead, the purpose is to suggest how texts can be variously interpreted by looking through different critical lenses. Despite the intimidating fact that literary criticism is an enormous and complex field, it can be usefully introduced as part of the intellectual landscape to even beginning students.

RESOURCES FOR TEACHING

SELECTED BIBLIOGRAPHY ON THE TEACHING OF LITERATURE

Adler, Mortimer J., and Charles Van Doren. *How to Read a Book*. New York: Simon, 1972. Print.

Bunge, Nancy L. *Finding the Words: Conversations with Writers Who Teach*. Athens: Ohio UP, 1985. Print.

Guerin, Wilfred L., et al. *A Handbook of Critical Approaches to Literature*. New York: Harper, 1979. Print.

Koch, Kenneth. *Rose, Where Did You Get That Red?* New York: Vintage, 1974. Print.

Lipschultz, Geri. "Fishing in the Holy Waters." *College English* 48.1 (1986): 34–39. Print.

Ponsot, Marie, and Rosemary Deen. *Beat Not the Poor Desk*. Upper Montclair: Boynton, 1982. 154–80. Print.

Pound, Ezra. *ABC of Reading*. New York: New Directions, 1960. Print.

Young, Gloria L. "Teaching Poetry: Another Method." *Teaching English in the Two-Year College* (Feb. 1987): 52–56. Print.

Appendix A
Thematic Contents

Love and Longing

KIM ADDONIZIO, *Survivors*, 489

ANONYMOUS, *Bonny Barbara Allan*, 999

ANONYMOUS, *Scarborough Fair*, 690

ANONYMOUS, *Western Wind*, 560

MARGARET ATWOOD, *you fit into me*, 645

BILLIE BOLTON, *Memorandum*, 961

ANNE BRADSTREET, *To My Dear and Loving Husband*, 956

ELIZABETH BARRETT BROWNING, *How Do I Love Thee? Let Me Count the Ways*, 957

ROBERT BURNS, *A Red, Red Rose*, 1002

EDGAR RICE BURROUGHS, *From* Tarzan of the Apes, 70

GEORGE GORDON, LORD BYRON, *She Walks in Beauty*, 1003

BILLY COLLINS, *Litany*, 878

BILLY COLLINS, *Nostalgia*, 874

SALLY CROFT, *Home-Baked Bread*, 636

EMILY DICKINSON, *"Heaven" — is what I cannot reach!*, 807

EMILY DICKINSON, *Wild Nights — Wild Nights!*, 809

JOHN DONNE, *The Flea*, 1005

JOHN DONNE, *Song*, 706

JOHN DONNE, *A Valediction: Forbidding Mourning*, 658

T. S. ELIOT, *The Love Song of J. Alfred Prufrock*, 1006

HELEN FARRIES, *Magic of Love*, 566

DAGOBERTO GILB, *Love in L.A.*, 430

CHARLOTTE PERKINS GILMAN, *Queer People*, 1010

WILLIAM HATHAWAY, *Oh, Oh*, 551

ROBERT HERRICK, *Delight in Disorder*, 728

ROBERT HERRICK, *To the Virgins, to Make Much of Time*, 599

ROBERT HERRICK, *Upon Julia's Clothes*, 739

MICHAEL HOLLINGER, *Naked Lunch*, 1057

Teaching and Learning

Humor and Satire

Culture and Identity

Home and Family

Childhood

Myths and Fairytales

Creativity and the Creative Process

Language and Literature

Ordinary Objects

American Life

Health and Sickness

Grief and Loss

Place

Ethics

Fear

Science and Technology

Religion

Violence, War, and Peace

Race and Stereotypes

Appendix B
List of Perspectives Organized by Critical Strategies

The following list organizes the Perspectives throughout *The Compact Bedford Introduction to Literature* by the Critical Strategies for Reading discussed in Chapter 48. The Perspectives are listed below the critical strategy they best exemplify (though not all Perspectives appear here). The strategies are in the order in which they appear in *The Compact Bedford Introduction to Literature*. By no means comprehensive, this list is meant to serve as a quick reference for instructors interested in teaching the critical strategies by showing them in action, most often applied to specific works that students have read.

BIOGRAPHICAL STRATEGIES (text p. 1484)

Karen Jackson Ford, *Hughes's Aesthetics of Simplicity* (text p. 947, manual p. 262)
Sandra M. Gilbert and Susan Gubar, *On Dickinson's White Dress* (text p. 822, manual p. 223)
Nathaniel Hawthorne, *On Herman Melville's Philosophic Stance* (text p. 158, manual p. 22)
Josephine Hendin, *On O'Connor's Refusal to "Do Pretty"* (text p. 398, manual p. 71)
Edward Kessler, *On O'Connor's Use of History* (text p. 399, manual p. 71)
Amy Lowell, *On Frost's Realistic Technique* (text p. 858, manual p. 236)
Herman Melville, *On Nathaniel Hawthorne's Tragic Vision* (text p. 348, manual p. 64)
Flannery O'Connor, *On Faith* (text p. 396, manual p. 71)
Joan Templeton, *Is* A Doll House *a Feminist Text?* (text p. 1313, manual p. 337)
Richard Wilbur, *On Dickinson's Sense of Privation* (text p. 821, manual p. 223)

PSYCHOLOGICAL STRATEGIES (text p. 1486)

Sigmund Freud, *On the Oedipus Complex* (text p. 1138, manual p. 327)
Carol Strongin Tufts, *A Psychoanalytic Reading of Nora* (text p. 1310, manual p. 337)

HISTORICAL STRATEGIES (text p. 1488)

A. Literary History Criticism (text p. 1488)
A. L. Bader, *Nothing Happens in Modern Short Stories* (text p. 106, manual p. 15)
Edward Kessler, *On O'Connor's Use of History* (text p. 399, manual p. 71)
Kelli Lyon Johnson, *Mapping an Identity* (text p. 916, manual p. 246)
Kay Mussell, *Are Feminism and Romance Novels Mutually Exclusive?* (text p. 44, manual p. 6)

B. Marxist Criticism (text p. 1489)
Barry Witham and John Lutterbie, *A Marxist Approach to* A Doll House (text p. 1308, manual p. 337)

C. Cultural Criticism (text p. 1491)
David Chinitz, *The Romanticization of Africa in the 1920s* (text p. 948, manual p. 262)
James Kincaid, *On the Value of Comedy in the Face of Tragedy* (text p. 1243, manual p. 331)
Kay Mussell, *Are Feminism and Romance Novels Mutually Exclusive?* (text p. 44, manual p. 6)

GENDER STRATEGIES (text p. 1492)

Joan Templeton, *Is* A Doll House *a Feminist Text?* (text p. 1313, manual p. 337)

MYTHOLOGICAL STRATEGIES (text p. 1494)

Sigmund Freud, *On the Oedipus Complex* (text p. 1138, manual p. 327)
Claire Katz, *The Function of Violence in O'Connor's Fiction* (text p. 398, manual p. 71)
Mordecai Marcus, *What Is an Initiation Story?* (text p. 236, manual p. 38)

READER-RESPONSE STRATEGIES (text p. 1496)

Dan McCall, *On the Lawyer's Character in "Bartleby, the Scrivener"* (text p. 158, manual p. 22)

Appendix C
Supplementing the Anthology with
Bedford/St. Martin's Literary Reprints

Instructors who wish to supplement *The Compact Bedford Introduction to Literature* with longer works may be interested in volumes from Bedford/St. Martin's literary reprints, now available with the tenth edition at a special price. Following the list of titles below are descriptions of each series — Bedford Cultural Editions, The Bedford Series in History and Culture, The Bedford Shakespeare Series, Case Studies in Contemporary Criticism, and Case Studies in Critical Controversy.

Jane Addams, *Twenty Years at Hull House* (1910), The Bedford Series in History and Culture, ed. Victoria Bissell Brown

Joseph Addison and Richard Steele, *The Commerce of Everyday Life: Selections from* **The Tatler** *and* **The Spectator** (1709–1714), Bedford Cultural Editions, ed. Erin Mackie

Louisa May Alcott, *Hospital Sketches* (1863), The Bedford Series in History and Culture, ed. Alice Fahs

Jane Austen, *Emma* (1816), Case Studies in Contemporary Criticism, ed. Alistair M. Duckworth

Aphra Behn, *Oroonoko* (1688), Bedford Cultural Editions, ed. Catherine Gallagher

Edward Bellamy, *Looking Backward: 2000–1887* (1888), The Bedford Series in History and Culture, ed. Daniel H. Borus

Charlotte Brontë, *Jane Eyre* (1847), Case Studies in Contemporary Criticism, ed. Beth Newman

Emily Brontë, *Wuthering Heights*, 2e (1847), Case Studies in Contemporary Criticism, ed. Linda H. Peterson

William Wells Brown, *Clotel* (1853), Bedford Cultural Editions, ed. Robert Levine

Frances Burney, *Evelina* (1778), Bedford Cultural Editions, ed. Kristina Straub

Geoffrey Chaucer, *The Wife of Bath* (c. 1387), Case Studies in Contemporary Criticism, ed. Peter G. Beidler

Charles W. Chesnutt, *The Marrow of Tradition* (1910), Bedford Cultural Editions, ed. Nancy Bentley and Sandra Gunning

Kate Chopin, *The Awakening*, 2e (1899), Case Studies in Contemporary Criticism, ed. Nancy A. Walker

Samuel Taylor Coleridge, *The Rime of the Ancient Mariner* (1798–1817), Case Studies in Contemporary Criticism, ed. Paul H. Fry

Joseph Conrad, *Heart of Darkness*, 2e (1902), Case Studies in Contemporary Criticism, ed. Ross Murfin

Joseph Conrad, *The Secret Sharer* (1912), Case Studies in Contemporary Criticism, ed. Daniel R. Schwarz

Stephen Crane, *Maggie* (1893), Bedford Cultural Editions, ed. Kevin J. Hayes

Rebecca Harding Davis, *Life in the Iron Mills* (1861), Bedford Cultural Editions, ed. Cecelia Tichi

Charles Dickens, *Great Expectations* (1860), Case Studies in Contemporary Criticism, ed. Janice Carlisle

Frederick Douglass, ***Narrative of the Life of Frederick Douglass***, 2e (1845), The Bedford Series in History and Culture, ed. David W. Blight

Arthur Conan Doyle, ***Sherlock Holmes: The Major Stories*** (1887–1904), Case Studies in Contemporary Criticism, ed. John A. Hodgson

W. E. B. Du Bois, ***The Souls of Black Folk*** (1903), The Bedford Series in History and Culture, ed. David W. Blight and Robert Gooding-Williams

Olaudah Equiano, ***The Interesting Narrative of the Life of Olaudah Equiano***, 2e (1791), The Bedford Series in History and Culture, ed. Robert J. Allison

E. M. Forster, ***Howards End*** (1910), Case Studies in Contemporary Criticism, ed. Alistair M. Duckworth

Benjamin Franklin, ***The Autobiography of Benjamin Franklin***, 2e (1793), The Bedford Series in History and Culture, ed. Louis P. Masur

Charlotte Perkins Gilman, ***The Yellow Wallpaper*** (1892), Bedford Cultural Editions, ed. Dale M. Bauer

Elliott J. Gorn, ed., ***The McGuffey Readers: Selections from the 1879 Edition***, The Bedford Series in History and Culture

Thomas Hardy, ***Tess of the d'Urbervilles*** (1891), Case Studies in Contemporary Criticism, ed. John Paul Riquelme

Nathaniel Hawthorne, ***The Blithedale Romance*** (1852), Bedford Cultural Editions, ed. William E. Cain

Nathaniel Hawthorne, ***The Scarlet Letter***, 2e (1850), Case Studies in Contemporary Criticism, ed. Ross Murfin

William Dean Howells, ***A Traveler from Altruria*** (1894), The Bedford Series in History and Culture, ed. David W. Levy

Henry James, ***The Turn of the Screw***, 3e (1898), Case Studies in Contemporary Criticism, ed. Peter G. Beidler

James Joyce, ***The Dead*** (1914), Case Studies in Contemporary Criticism, ed. Daniel R. Schwarz

James Joyce, ***A Portrait of the Artist as a Young Man***, 2e (1915), Case Studies in Contemporary Criticism, ed. R. B. Kershner

Eve Kornfeld, ed., ***Margaret Fuller: A Brief Biography with Documents***, The Bedford Series in History and Culture

Gotthold Ephraim Lessing, ***Nathan the Wise*** (1779), The Bedford Series in History and Culture, ed. Ronald Schecter

Thomas Mann, ***Death in Venice*** (1912), Case Studies in Contemporary Criticism, ed. Naomi Ritter

Russ McDonald, ed., ***The Bedford Companion to Shakespeare: An Introduction***, 2e, The Bedford Shakespeare Series

Sir Thomas More, ***Utopia*** (1516), The Bedford Series in History and Culture, ed. David Harris Sacks

Margot Norris, ed., ***A Companion to James Joyce's*** **Ulysses** (1922), Case Studies in Contemporary Criticism

Alexander Pope, ***The Rape of the Lock*** (1714), Bedford Cultural Editions, ed. Cynthia Wall

Jacob Riis, ***How the Other Half Lives*** (1890), The Bedford Series in History and Culture, ed. David Leviatin

Mary Rowlandson, ***The Sovereignty and Goodness of God*** (1675), The Bedford Series in History and Culture, ed. Neal Salisbury

William Shakespeare, ***The First Part of King Henry the Fourth*** (1596), The Bedford Shakespeare Series, ed. Barbara Hodgdon

William Shakespeare, ***Hamlet*** (1599), Case Studies in Contemporary Criticism, ed. Susanne L. Wofford

William Shakespeare, *Macbeth* (1606), The Bedford Shakespeare Series, ed. William C. Carroll

William Shakespeare, *Measure for Measure* (1623), The Bedford Shakespeare Series, ed. Ivo Kamps and Karen Reber

William Shakespeare, *The Merchant of Venice* (1596), The Bedford Shakespeare Series, ed. Lindsay M. Kaplan

William Shakespeare, *A Midsummer Night's Dream* (1594), The Bedford Shakespeare Series, ed. Gail Kern Paster and Skiles Howard

William Shakespeare, *Othello* (1604), The Bedford Shakespeare Series, ed. Kim F. Hall

William Shakespeare, *Romeo and Juliet* (1595), The Bedford Shakespeare Series, ed. Dympna Callaghan

William Shakespeare, *The Taming of the Shrew* (1592), The Bedford Shakespeare Series, ed. Frances E. Dolan

William Shakespeare, *The Tempest: A Case Study*, 2e (1611), Case Studies in Critical Controversy, ed. Gerald Graff and James Phelan

William Shakespeare, *Twelfth Night* (1600), The Bedford Shakespeare Series, ed. Bruce R. Smith

William Shakespeare, *The Winter's Tale* (1610), The Bedford Shakespeare Series, ed. Mario DiGangi

Mary Shelley, *Frankenstein*, 2e (1831), Case Studies in Critical Controversy, ed. Johanna M. Smith

Upton Sinclair, *The Jungle* (1906), The Bedford Series in History and Culture, ed. Christopher Phelps

Bram Stoker, *Dracula* (1897), Case Studies in Contemporary Criticism, ed. John Paul Riquelme

Eric Sundquist, ed., *Cultural Contexts for Ralph Ellison's* Invisible Man (1952), A Bedford Documentary Companion

Jonathan Swift, *Gulliver's Travels* (1726), Case Studies in Contemporary Criticism, ed. Christopher B. Fox

Nat Turner, *The Confessions of Nat Turner* (1831), The Bedford Series in History and Culture, ed. Kenneth S. Greenberg

Mark Twain, *Adventures of Huckleberry Finn*, 2e (1884), Case Studies in Critical Controversy, ed. Gerald Graff and James Phelan

Voltaire, *Candide* (1759), The Bedford Series in History and Culture, ed. Daniel Gordon

Booker T. Washington, *Up from Slavery* (1901), The Bedford Series in History and Culture, ed. W. Fitzhugh Brundage

Ida B. Wells, *Southern Horrors and Other Writings* (1892–1900), The Bedford Series in History and Culture, ed. Jacqueline Jones Royster

Edith Wharton, *The House of Mirth* (1905), Case Studies in Contemporary Criticism, ed. Shari Benstock

BEDFORD CULTURAL EDITIONS

Series Editors: J. Paul Hunter, University of Chicago; William E. Cain, Wellesley College

Particularly appropriate for courses that emphasize a new historicist or cultural studies approach, **Bedford Cultural Editions** reprint authoritative editions of British and American literary works with an abundance of thematically arranged historical and cultural documents. The documents—relevant excerpts from such sources as diaries, letters, periodicals, conduct books, legal documents, and literary works that parallel the themes of the main text—are carefully selected to give students a rich sense of a work's historical and cultural contexts. Each volume also provides a full complement of useful pedagogical aids: a historical and critical introduction to the work, a chronology, an introduction to each thematic unit of documents, headnotes for the documents, appropriate text annotations, illustrations and maps, and an extensive bibliography.

THE BEDFORD SERIES IN HISTORY AND CULTURE

Series Editors: Lynn Hunt, University of California, Los Angeles; David W. Blight, Yale University; Bonnie G. Smith, Rutgers University; Natalie Zemon Davis, Princeton University; Ernest R. May, Harvard University

Introduced in 1993 to meet the need for well-crafted, brief, and inexpensive supplements, **The Bedford Series in History and Culture** has won the high regard of instructors everywhere. Focusing on a specific topic or period, each book uniquely combines first-rate scholarship, historical narrative, and important primary documents. Each volume also offers a full complement of useful pedagogical aids, including text annotations, chronologies, questions for consideration, bibliographies, and indexes.

THE BEDFORD SHAKESPEARE SERIES

Series Editor: Jean E. Howard, Columbia University

Designed to give students firsthand knowledge of the cultural and historical contexts from which Shakespeare's work emerges, **The Bedford Shakespeare Series** facilitates a variety of approaches to Shakespeare. Each volume provides an authoritative edition of a widely taught play accompanied by an intriguing collection of thematically arranged historical and cultural documents such as homilies, polemical literature, emblem books, excerpts from conduct books, court records, medical tracts, chronicle histories, popular ballads, playhouse records, and facsimiles of early modern documents, including play texts, maps, and woodcut prints. Each volume also includes a general introduction, glosses for the play, an introduction to each thematic unit, a headnote and annotations for each document, a bibliography, and a topical index.

CASE STUDIES IN CRITICAL CONTROVERSY

Series Editors: Gerald Graff, University of Illinois at Chicago; James Phelan, Ohio State University

Each volume in the **Case Studies in Critical Controversy** series reprints an authoritative text of a classic literary work, along with documents and critical essays that have been selected and organized to introduce students to the major critical debates and cultural conflicts concerning the work.

CASE STUDIES IN CONTEMPORARY CRITICISM

Series Editor: Ross C. Murfin, Southern Methodist University

Adopted at more than one thousand colleges and universities, Bedford/St. Martin's innovative **Case Studies in Contemporary Criticism** series has introduced more than a quarter of a million students to literary theory and earned enthusiastic praise nationwide. Along with an authoritative text of a major literary work, each volume presents critical essays, selected or prepared especially for students, that approach the work from several contemporary critical perspectives, such as gender criticism and cultural studies. Each essay is accompanied by an introduction (with bibliography) to the history, principles, and practice of its critical perspective. Every volume also surveys the biographical, historical, and critical contexts of the literary work and concludes with a glossary of critical terms. New editions reprint cultural documents that contextualize the literary works and feature essays that show how critical perspectives can be combined.

These volumes provide a useful supplement for instructors who want to cover the different schools of literary theory in more depth than is provided in Chapter 55, "Critical Strategies for Reading," in *The Bedford Introduction to Literature*, Tenth Edition. The critical essays in each **Case Studies** volume can serve as models for helping students understand how to apply a particular approach to works in the anthology.

To obtain complimentary copies of any of these titles, please call the Bedford/St. Martin's College Desk at 1-800-446-8923 or contact your local Bedford/St. Martin's sales representative at bedfordstmartins.com.

Appendix D
Multimedia Resources

The following list of resources is organized by genre (Fiction, Poetry, and Drama), and within each genre section the listings are alphabetically arranged by author. Resources include author blogs, films and videos about an author or a particular literary period, recordings of authors reading their work, interviews, and more. This list is not intended to be exhaustive; rather, it is meant to provide a number of exciting possibilities for supplementing and provoking class discussion. Many of the resources in this list will be most readily available from a local retailer or online. If not, you may contact the distributor by using the addresses, phone numbers, or Web sites provided at the end of the list. For further information, consult your local city or college library, or *The Educational Film & Video Locater of the Consortium of University Film Centers and R. R. Bowker.*

FICTION

Margaret Atwood

Margaret Atwood
VHS, video download (52 min.), 1989.
Atwood discusses her craft with Hermione Lee.
Distributed by the Roland Collection.

Margaret Atwood
Atwood discusses religion in a three-part series.
Part 1: http://www.youtube.com/watch?v=VMrz_ivl8jo
Part 2: http://www.youtube.com/watch?v=QmVD7XcRb6Y
Part 3: http://www.youtube.com/watch?v=TPDt73n7HD0
Distributed by YouTube.

Edgar Rice Burroughs

Tarzan of the Apes [audiobook]
8 Audio CDs (518 min. total).
Read by Shelley Frazier.
Distributed by Tantor Media, Inc.

Ron Carlson

Ron Carlson Interview
Video clip (3 min.), 2009.
An interview with Ron Carlson for Literary Orange 2009.

http://www.youtube.com/watch?v=s9_04uvJijE
Distributed by YouTube.

Raymond Carver

Raymond Carver
DVD (53 min.), 1996.
Fellow writers, Carver's wife, and others discuss his lower-middle-class roots in the Northwest as the source of inspiration for his characters and stories. A BBC Production. From the "Great Writers of the 20th Century" Series.
Distributed by Films for the Humanities and Sciences.

Short Cuts
DVD (189 min.), 1993.
With Jennifer Jason Leigh, Tim Robbins, Madeleine Stowe, Frances McDormand, Peter Gallagher, Lily Tomlin, Andie MacDowell, Jack Lemmon, Lyle Lovett, Huey Lewis, Matthew Modine, Lili Taylor, Christopher Penn, and Robert Downey Jr. Directed by Robert Altman.
Distributed by New Line Home Video (see local retailer).

Kate Chopin

Kate Chopin's "The Story of an Hour"
DVD (24 min.), 1982.
A dramatization of the story, with an examination of Chopin's life.
Distributed by Ishtar.

Stephen Crane

The Bride Comes to Yellow Sky:
A Mystery of Heroism
1 cassette (50 min.), 1984.
Illustrates the contrasting sides of Crane's art — the humorous and the gruesome. Read by Walter Zimmerman and Jim Killavey.
Distributed by Jimcin Recordings.

The Red Badge of Courage and Other Stories
[recording]
8 cassettes (60 min. each), 1978.
Read by Michael Prichard. Includes "The Bride Comes to Yellow Sky," "The Blue Hotel," and "The Open Boat."
Distributed by Books on Tape.

Junot Díaz

Authors@Google: Junot Díaz
Video clip (50 min.), September 29, 2007.
Junot Díaz discusses his novel *The Brief Wondrous Life of Oscar Wao* during a visit to Google's headquarters in Mountain View, CA.
http://www.youtube.com/watch?v
=I-tD45oj1ro
Distributed by YouTube.

Junot Díaz on **The Colbert Report**
Comedian Stephen Colbert interviews Díaz.
http://www.colbertnation.com/the-colbert
-report-videos/174353/june-18
-2008/junot-diaz
Distributed by Colbert Nation.

Writers at Cornell — Junot Díaz
Video clip (6 min.), June 18, 2008.
Interview with Díaz.
http://writersatcornell.blogspot.com/2007/
02/interview-junot-diaz.html
Distributed by Writers at Cornell.

Charles Dickens

Charles Dickens: A Tale of Ambition and
Genius
VHS, b/w (50 min.), 1997.
From the A&E Biography series.
Distributed by A&E Home Video.

The Charles Dickens Show
VHS (52 min.), 1973.
Deals with the writer and his times. Includes dramatization from his life and works.
Distributed by the International Film Bureau.

Hard Times [recording]
9 CDs (12 hrs.), 1993.
Read by Frederick Davison.
Distributed by Blackstone Audiobooks.

Andre Dubus

Andre Dubus Interview [recording]
1 cassette (75 min.), 1984.
The writer reads his work and discusses the writing process.
Distributed by American Audio Prose Library.

Ralph Ellison

Ralph Ellison, The Self-Taught Writer
VHS (17 min.), 1995.
A biography of the author of *The Invisible Man*.
Distributed by Churchill Media.

William Faulkner

Barn Burning
DVD (41 min.), 1980.
With Tommy Lee Jones. Same program available in "The American Short Story Series II" on manual p. 509.
Distributed by Perspective Films.

The Long Hot Summer
DVD (118 min.), 1958.
A film adaptation of "Barn Burning." Directed by Martin Ritt. With Paul Newman, Orson Welles, Joanne Woodward, Lee Remick, Anthony Franciosa, Angela Lansbury, and Richard Anderson.
See local retailer.

The Long Hot Summer
DVD (193 min.), 1988.
A made-for-TV version of "Barn Burning." Directed by Stuart Cooper. With Don Johnson, Cybill Shepherd, Judith Ivey, Jason Robards, and Ava Gardner.
See local retailer.

A Rose for Emily
VHS, DVD (27 min.), 1982.
With Anjelica Huston and John Carradine.
Distributed by Pyramid Media.

Gabriel García Márquez

Gabriel García Márquez: Magic and Reality
DVD (60 min.), 1990.

A look at García Márquez's life and world.
Distributed by Films for the Humanities and Sciences.

Gail Godwin

An Interview with Gail Godwin [recording]
1 cassette (57 min.), 1986.
Godwin discusses the recurring themes and concerns in her fiction.
Distributed by American Audio Prose Library.

Nathaniel Hawthorne

The Birthmark [recording]
1 cassette (63 min.).
Read by Walter Zimmerman.
Distributed by Jimcin Recordings.

The Minister's Black Veil [recording]
1 cassette (82 min.).
Read by Walter Zimmerman and John Chatty.
Includes "Young Goodman Brown."
Distributed by Jimcin Recordings.

The Minister's Black Veil [recording]
1 cassette (40 min.).
Read by Robert Breen.
Distributed by Spoken Arts.

Young Goodman Brown
VHS, DVD (30 min.), 1972.
Distributed by Pyramid Media.

Ernest Hemingway

Ernest Hemingway
DVD (50 min.), 1983.
This program explores Hemingway's life and literary psyche through the eyes of those who knew him. A BBC Production. Part of the "Great Writers of the 20th Century" Series.
Distributed by Films for the Humanities and Sciences.

Hemingway
DVD (18 min.), 2009.
A biography using rare stills and motion-picture footage. Narrated by Chet Huntley.
Distributed by Thomas Klise Company.

Up in Michigan (Hemingway, the Early Years)
VHS (30 min.), 1983.
A literary biography of the writer.
Distributed by WBGU-TV.

James Joyce

Dubliners by James Joyce [recording]
5 cassettes (90 min. each), 1991.
"The Dead" and fourteen other short stories of Irish life, read by Jim Killavey.
Distributed by Jimcin Recordings.

James Joyce
DVD (50 min.), 1996.
Critics and those who knew Joyce trace events in his life through passages in *Ulysses* and other works, including *Dubliners*, the collection of short stories, and the semi-autobiographical novel *A Portrait of the Artist as a Young Man*. A BBC Production. Part of the "Great Writers of the 20th Century" Series.
Distributed by Films for the Humanities and Sciences.

James Joyce's Women
VHS (91 min.), 1983.
Actors portray Joyce's wife plus Molly Bloom and two of his other female characters. Adapted and produced by Fionnula Flanagan. With Flanagan, Timothy E. O'Grady, Chris O'Neill.
Distributed by MCA Home Video.

D. H. Lawrence

D. H. Lawrence, Poet and Novelist, 1885–1930
VHS (30 min.), 1987.
A biographical portrait of the writer. Includes his views on war and censorship. Part of the "Famous Author" Series.
Distributed by Encyclopaedia Britannica Educational Corporation.

D. H. Lawrence as Son and Lover
DVD, VHS (52 min.), 1988.
A biography of the British novelist and poet.
Distributed by Films for the Humanities and Sciences.

The Horse Dealer's Daughter
VHS (30 min.), 1984.
Close-captioned.
Distributed by Monterey Home Video.

Jack London

Jack London's "To Build a Fire"
DVD, VHS (56 min.), 1969.
A screen adaptation of Jack London's famous short story. Starring Ian Hogg and narrated by Orson Welles.
See local retailer.

Katherine Mansfield

The Life and Writings of Katherine Mansfield
Video clip (10 min.)
Short biopic of Mansfield, including a 3-minute film adaptation of "Miss Brill."
http://video.google.com/videoplay?docid
=-4646930032041900975&ei
=U60uSoibA6HWrALO9_TrCA&q
Distributed by Google Video.

Herman Melville

Bartleby
VHS (28 min.), 1969.
With James Westerfield and Patrick Campbell.
Distributed by Encyclopaedia Britannica Educational Corporation.

Herman Melville: Consider the Sea
VHS (28 min.), 1982.
A look at Melville's obsession with the sea, hosted by Richard Wilbur.
Distributed by International Film Bureau.

Herman Melville: Damned in Paradise
DVD (90 min.), 1986.
Documents Melville's personal and intellectual history.
Distributed by Pyramid Media.

Melville: Six Short Novels
[recording]
8 cassettes, digital download (60 min. each).
Includes "Bartleby, the Scrivener," "The Apple Tree Table," and "The Happy Failure." Read by Dan Lazar.
Distributed by Books on Tape.

Rick Moody

Interview: Rick Moody [recording]
Audio clip (41 min.), February 1, 2001.
Bill Goldstein, books editor for the *New York Times* on the Web, interviews Moody.
http://www.nytimes.com/books/01/02/25/specials/moody-audio.html
Distributed by the *New York Times* on the Web.

Joyce Carol Oates

Joyce Carol Oates
DVD (24 min.), 1994.
Oates discusses her work as both a writer and teacher, her craft and methods, and the major themes of her novels, short stories, and poems.
Distributed by Films for the Humanities and Sciences.

Tim O'Brien

Interview with Tim O'Brien
[recording]
Audio clip (43 min.), March 20, 1990.
Don Swaim interviews Tim O'Brien.
http://wiredforbooks.org/timo%27brien/
Distributed by Wired for Books.

Tim O'Brien, Writing Vietnam
[recording]
Audio clip (5 min.), April 21, 1999.

Tim O'Brien's keynote speech at Brown University's Writing Vietnam Conference. Transcript also available.
http://www.stg.brown.edu/projects/WritingVietnam/obrienpreface.html
Distributed by Brown University.

Flannery O'Connor

Good Country People
VHS (32 min.), 1975.
An adaptation of the short story by O'Connor.
Distributed by Valley Video.

Edgar Allan Poe

The Cask of Amontillado
DVD (20 min.), 1991.
An adaptation of Poe's short story.
Distributed by Films for the Humanities and Sciences.

Edgar Allan Poe: Terror of the Soul
DVD (60 min.), 1997.
A biography revealing Poe's creative genius and personal experiences through dramatic re-creations of important scenes from his work and life. Includes dramatizations of Poe classics such as "The Tell-Tale Heart" performed by Treat Williams, John Heard, and René Auberjonois.
Distributed by PBS Video.

Mark Twain

Famous Authors: Mark Twain
DVD (30 min.), 1993.
A look at the life and career of the author.
Distributed by Kultur.

Mark Twain's America
VHS (60 min.), 1990.
A look at Twain's times.
Distributed by Time-Life Video.

John Updike

Remembering John Updike
Audio clips.
Archival interviews with Updike.
http://www.npr.org/templates/story/story.php?storyId=99945565
Distributed by National Public Radio.

Karen van der Zee

A Secret Sorrow [recording]
2 cassettes (180 min.), 1987.
Read by Leslie Saweard.
Distributed by Mills & Boon, Ltd.

General Resources for Fiction

The American Short Story Series I

VHS (45 min. each program), 1976.

Includes five film adaptations of short stories that appeared on PBS: "Soldier's Home," "Bernice Bobs Her Hair," "Paul's Case," "The Music School," and "Almos' a Man."

Distributed by Phoenix Learning Group.

The American Short Story Series II

VHS (50 min. each program), 1980.

Eight programs: "The Golden Honeymoon," "Paul's Case," "The Greatest Man in the World," "Rappaccini's Daughter," "The Jilting of Granny Weatherall," "The Sky Is Grey," "The Man That Corrupted Hadleyburg," and "Barn Burning." With Geraldine Fitzgerald, Brad Davis, and Tommy Lee Jones.

Distributed by MTI and Phoenix Learning Group.

Exploring the Short Story

VHS (37 min.), 1980.

Ancillary materials available. Deals with character, plot, setting, style, theme, and point of view.

See local retailer.

The Famous Authors Series

10 DVDs (30 min. each), 1995.

Ten programs: Jane Austen, the Brontë sisters, Virginia Woolf, John Keats, D. H. Lawrence, William Shakespeare, James Joyce, Charles Dickens, Percy Bysshe Shelley, and George Eliot.

Distributed by Kultur.

The Famous Authors Series
(American Authors).

10 DVDs (30 min. each), 1993.

Ten programs: William Faulkner, Ernest Hemingway, Herman Melville, Mark Twain, F. Scott Fitzgerald, Henry James, John Steinbeck, Walt Whitman, Edgar Allan Poe, and Eugene O'Neill.

Distributed by Kultur.

Great American Short Stories, Vol. I *[recording]*

7 cassettes (90 min. each), 1981.

Includes "Bartleby, the Scrivener," "The Minister's Black Veil," and fourteen others.

Distributed by Blackstone Audiobooks.

Great American Short Stories, Vol. II
[recording]

7 cassettes (90 min. each), 1984.

Includes "The Bride Comes to Yellow Sky," "The Birthmark," and fifteen others.

Distributed by Jimcin Recordings and Books on Tape.

In Black and White: Conversations with African American Writers

DVD (90 min. each program), 1994.

Interviews with African American writers Alice Walker, August Wilson, Charles Johnson, Gloria Naylor, John Edgar Wideman, and Toni Morrison.

Distributed by Films for the Humanities and Sciences.

A Moveable Feast

4 VHS (30 min. each), 1992.

Hosted by Tom Vitale. Profiles eight contemporary writers: Allen Ginsberg, Joyce Carol Oates, Li-Young Lee, Sonia Sanchez, T. Coraghessan Boyle, T. R. Pearson, Trey Ellis, and W. S. Merwin.

Distributed by Acorn Media.

Women in Literature, The Short Story:
A Collection *[recording]*

8 cassettes, audio download (60 min. each), 1984.

Various readers. Includes "The Story of an Hour" by Kate Chopin and other works by Edith Wharton, Willa Cather, Mary E. Wilkins Freeman, Sarah Orne Jewett, George Sand, Frances Gilchrist Wood, and Selma Lagerhoff.

Distributed by Books on Tape.

POETRY

Julia Alvarez

An Interview with Julia Alvarez
Video clip (5 min.).
http://www.youtube.com/
    watch?v=bRbLeRwCnVc
Distributed by YouTube.

Margaret Atwood

Margaret Atwood: Authors Reading
Video clip (17 min.).
Margaret Atwood reading and being interviewed at the International evening at Prague Writers' Festival in 2008.
http://www.youtube.com/
    watch?v=9jyw1fzvn5k
Distributed by YouTube.

Margaret Atwood with Valerie Martin
    [recording]
Audio (1 hr. 22 min.), recorded in Santa Fe, December 1, 2004.
World renowned and much beloved Canadian novelist and poet Margaret Atwood reads "a medley, that is, a mixture of various things" as she puts it, from works published and yet-to-be published, before joining in conversation with her long-term friend and fellow novelist Valerie Martin.
http://podcast.lannan.org/2006/04/09/
    margaret-atwood-with-valerie-martin/
Distributed by The Lannan Foundation.

The Poetry and Voice of Margaret Atwood
    [recording]
1 cassette (59 min.), 1977, reprint 1992.
Available at libraries.

Jan Beatty

Sacramento Poetry Center —
    Jan Beatty
Beatty reads a portion of her poem "Red Sugar."
http://www.youtube.com/
    watch?v=AAusvvw17s
Distributed by YouTube.

William Blake

William Blake: Selected Poems
    [recording]
2 cassettes (180 min.), 1992.
Includes "The Tyger" and "A Poison Tree."
Distributed by Blackstone Audio Books.

Gwendolyn Brooks

Gwendolyn Brooks — We Real Cool
http://www.youtube.com/
    watch?v=jyKF2e2CiMK
Distributed by YouTube.

Elizabeth Barrett Browning

Elizabeth Barrett Browning: Selected Poems
    [recording]
5 cassettes, digital download available.
Read by Nadia May.
http://blackstoneaudio.com/audiobook
    .cfm?id=1661
Distributed by Blackstone Audio Books.

Robert Browning

Robert Browning: Selected Poems
    [recording]
4 cassettes (360 min.).
Read by Frederick Davidson.
Distributed by Blackstone Audio Books.

Robert Burns

Poems and Letters of Robert Burns: On the
    Bicentenary of His Birth *[recording]*
1 cassette, CD, MP3, 1963.
Poems written by Burns, read by Max Dunbar.
Distributed by Smithsonian / Folkways Recordings.

Robert Burns
DVD (35 min.).
Features illustrations, letters, conversations, and music, providing biographical context to Burns's poetry.
Distributed by Insight Media.

George Gordon, Lord Byron

Lord Byron: Selected Poems *[recording]*
2 cassettes (180 min.).
Read by Frederick Davidson.
Distributed by Blackstone Audio Books.

John Ciardi

As If: Poems Selected and Read by John Ciardi
    [recording]
1 cassette or CD, 1956.
Distributed by Smithsonian/Folkways Recordings.

John Ciardi, I, II & III *[recording]*
1 cassette, CD (60 min.), 1983, 1984, 1986.

The author reads poems about war, Italy, and aging.
Distributed by New Letters on the Air.

John Ciardi: Twentieth-Century Poets in English: Recordings of Poets Reading Their Own Poetry, No. 27 *[recording]*
Distributed by the Library of Congress.

Samuel Taylor Coleridge

Samuel Taylor Coleridge: The Fountain and the Cave
VHS (57 min.), 1974.
A biography of the poet, filmed on location. Narrated by Paul Scofield.
Distributed by Pyramid Media.

Billy Collins

Billy Collins: Action Poetry
Watch animated videos of some of Collins's poems.
http://www.bcactionpoet.org/
Distributed by the J. Walter Thompson Ad Agency and the Sundance Channel.

Billy Collins Live *[recording]*
CD, MP3, 2005.
Collins reads twenty-four of his poems at a benefit reading for WNYC, New York Public Radio. Includes "Dharma," "The Lanyard," "Consolation," and others.
Distributed by Random House Audio.

"The Lanyard"
Video clip (2 min.).
Collins reads his poem "The Lanyard." Includes background information about the poem and teaching tips.
http://www.teachersdomain.org/resource/pe08.rla.genre.poetry.collinyard/
Distributed by WGBH Educational Foundation.

E. E. Cummings

E. E. Cummings: Twentieth-Century Poetry in English: Recordings of Poets Reading Their Own Poetry, No. 5 *[recording]*
Distributed by the Library of Congress.

The Voice of the Poet: E. E. Cummings *[recording]*
CD, 2005.
Cummings reads his own work. Includes never-before released recordings, a book containing the text of the poems, and a commentary by J. D. McClatchy.
Distributed by Random House Audio.

Emily Dickinson

Emily Dickinson: Selected Poems *[recording]*
4 cassettes (360 min.), 1993.
Read by Mary Woods.
Distributed by Blackstone Audio Books.

Fifty Poems of Emily Dickinson *[recording]*
1 cassette or CD (45 min.).
Distributed by Dove Audio.

John Donne

Holy Sonnets
An audio download of Donne's Holy Sonnets (23 min.).
http://www.learnoutloud.com/Catalog/Literature/Poetry/Holy-Sonnets/34857#plink
Distributed by LearnOutLoud, Inc.

John Donne: Selected Poems *[recording]*
2 cassettes (180 min.), 1992.
Read by Frederick Davidson.
Distributed by Blackstone Audio Books.

The Love Poems of John Donne *[recording]*
1 cassette, 1994.
Distributed by HarperAudio.

Paul Laurence Dunbar

Paul Laurence Dunbar
Video clip (9 min.).
This segment of the Ohio Reading Road Trip covers Dunbar's life and writing career. Includes readings of his poetry and images of the Dunbar House in Dayton, Ohio.
http://www.teachersdomain.org/resource/odc08.langarts.orrt.dunbar/
Distributed by WGBH Educational Foundation.

Paul Laurence Dunbar: American Poet
VHS (14 min.), 1966.
A biographical sketch of the poet.
Distributed by Phoenix/BFA Films.

T. S. Eliot

The Mysterious Mr. Eliot
VHS (62 min.), 1973.
A biographical film about the poet.
Distributed by Insight Media and CRM Films.

T. S. Eliot Reads "The Love Song of J. Alfred Prufrock" *[recording]*
1 cassette, 2000.
Distributed by HarperAudio.

T. S. Eliot: Twentieth-Century Poetry in English: Recordings of Poets Reading Their Own Poetry, No. 3 [recording]
Distributed by the Library of Congress.

The Voice of the Poet: T. S. Eliot [recording]
CD, 2005.
Eliot reads his own work. Includes never-before released recordings, a book containing the text of the poems, and a commentary by J. D. McClatchy.
Distributed by Random House Audio.

Martín Espada

Fine Print: Martín Espada
VHS (30 min.).
Produced by UMass School of Education. Directed by Liane Brandon, Scott Perry, and John Carey.
Distributed by Cinema Guild.

Martín Espada
DVD (28 min.).
Espada reads a selection of poems from his six poetry collections.
Distributed by Insight Media.

Robert Francis

Robert Francis Reads His Poems [recording]
2 cassettes, CD, MP3, 1975.
Francis reads his poems from *Like Ghosts of Eagles* and *Come out into the Sun*.
Distributed by Smithsonian/Folkways Recordings.

Robert Frost

An Interview with Robert Frost
VHS, b/w (30 min.), 1952.
Bela Kornitzer interviews Frost, who reads from his poetry.
Distributed by Social Studies School Service.

Robert Frost: An American Poet
VHS, DVD, b/w (25 min.), 1961.
Vintage television broadcast of Frost commenting on his art and his country.
Distributed by Films for the Humanities and Sciences.

Robert Frost Reads His Poems [An Evening with Robert Frost] [recording]
1 cassette, CD (55 min.), 1956.
Distributed by Audio-Forum.

Robert Frost: Twentieth-Century Poetry in English: Recordings of Poets Reading Their Own Poetry, No. 6 [recording]
Distributed by the Library of Congress.

The Voice of the Poet: Robert Frost [recording]
CD, 2003.
Frost reads his own work. Includes never-before released recordings, a book containing the text of the poems, and a commentary by J. D. McClatchy.
Distributed by Random House Audio.

Thomas Hardy

Thomas Hardy
See **"Introduction to English Poetry," "Romantics and Realists,"** and **"Victorian Poetry"** (recording) on manual pp. 000–00.

William Hathaway

William Hathaway [recording]
1 cassette, CD (29 min.), 1984.
Distributed by New Letters on the Air.

Edward Hirsch

Edward Hirsch: American Perspectives [podcast]
Podcast (38 min.), September 16, 2008.
Hirsch examines the complex relationships between American poets and painters.
http://www.poetryfoundation.org/journal/audioitem.html?id=571
Distributed by the Poetry Foundation.

A Partial History of Our Stupidity [podcast]
Podcast (8 min.), August 24, 2007.
Two poems (and some commentary) by Edward Hirsch.
http://www.poetryfoundation.org/journal/audioitem.html?id=126
Distributed by the Poetry Foundation.

Poet Edward Hirsch under the Microscope [recording]
Audio clip (11 min.), April 27, 2008.
Hirsch talks about his book *Special Orders*.
http://www.npr.org/templates/story/story.php?storyId=89984960
Distributed by National Public Radio.

Jane Hirshfield

Jane Hirshfield: An Afternoon with the Poet
Video clip (60 min.).
From "Voices" presented by the University of California, Santa Barbara.
http://www.youtube.com/watch?v=acbL-YcBkqY
For additional videos, type "Jane Hirshfield" into YouTube search bar.
Distributed by YouTube.

Gerard Manley Hopkins

Eleven versions of Spring and Fall
CD, podcast.
http://librivox.org/spring-and-fall-by
-gerard-manley-hopkins/
Distributed by LibriVox.

The Windhover
MP3.
A close reading of Gerard Manley Hopkins's classic poem.
http://www.poetryfoundation.org/features/
audioitem/2734
Distributed by The Poetry Foundation.

Gerard Manley Hopkins: Poetry read by Richard Austin
CD, MP3 files.
http://www.richard.austin.sh/free/index.html
Distributed by Here Buckle! Productions.

A. E. Housman

A. E. Housman
See **"Romantics and Realists"** and **"Victorian Poetry"** (recording) on manual p. 000.

Andrew Hudgins

An Interview with Andrew Hudgins [recording]
2 audio clips, July 22, 2003.
Conducted by Troy Teegarden at the Sewanee Writers' Conference at the University of the South. Transcript available.
http://www.blackbird.vcu.edu/v2n2/
nonfiction/teegarden_t/hudgins.htm
Distributed by Blackbird Archive.

Langston Hughes

The Glory of Negro History [recording]
1 cassette, CD, MP3, 1955.
Produced, written, and read by Langston Hughes.
Distributed by Smithsonian/Folkways Recordings.

Langston Hughes: The Dream Keeper and Other Poems [recording]
1 cassette, CD, MP3, 1955.
Distributed by Smithsonian/Folkways Recordings.

The Voice of Langston Hughes: Selected Poetry and Prose [recording]
1 cassette, CD (38 min.), 1994.
Selections from 1925–1932. The author reads poetry from *"The Dream Keeper"* and *Other Poems* and *Simple Speaks His Mind* and narrates his text from *The Story of Jazz, Rhythms of the World,* and *The Glory of Negro History.*
Distributed by Smithsonian/Folkways Recordings.

The Voice of the Poet: Langston Hughes [recording]
CD, 2002.
Hughes reads his own work. Includes never-before released recordings, a book containing the text of the poems, and a commentary by J. D. McClatchy.
Distributed by Random House Audio.

Randall Jarrell

Randall Jarrell
CD (88 min.), 1964.
In this historic and unusual recording, the listener hears how Jarrell gained his reputation as one of this century's most astute poetry critics. Jarrell comments on his own and Elizabeth Bishop's poetry, which he reads on the occasion of her winning the Academy's fellowship.
http://www.poets.org/viewmedia.php/
prmMID/17049
Distributed by The Academy of American Poets.

Randall Jarrell Reads
MP3.
http://www.randomhouse.com/
boldtype/0502/jarrell/audio.html
Distributed by Bold Type, Random House.

Donald Justice

Donald Justice I & II [recording]
1 cassette, CD (60 min.), 1989.
Distributed by New Letters on the Air.

John Keats

John Keats — His Life and Death
VHS (55 min.), 1973.
Extended version of **"John Keats — Poet"** (see below). Explores the poet's affair with Fanny Browne and the events surrounding his death. Written by Archibald MacLeish.
Distributed by Britannica Films.

John Keats — Poet
VHS (31 min.), 1973.
A biography of the poet, with excerpts from his letters and poems. Written by Archibald MacLeish.
Distributed by Britannica Films.

The Poetry of Keats [recording]
1 cassette (90 min.), 1996.
Distributed by HarperAudio.

X. J. Kennedy

X. J. Kennedy: Bookfest 03
   [recording]
MP3 (45 min.), 2003.
http://www.loc.gov/today/cyberlc/feature
   _wdesc.php?rec=3548
Distributed by The Library of Congress.

Jane Kenyon

Donald Hall and Jane Kenyon: A Life
   Together
VHS, DVD (60 min.), 1993.
Bill Moyers interviews these husband-and-
   wife poets at their home in New
   Hampshire.
Distributed by Films for the Humanities and
   Sciences.

Jane Kenyon I & II [recording]
1 cassette, CD, 1987, 1995.
Distributed by New Letters on the Air.

Carolyn Kizer

Carolyn Kizer I, II, III, & IV [recording]
1 cassette, CD (29 min.), 1982, 1985, 1994,
   1997.
Distributed by New Letters on the Air.

Carolyn Kizer: Selected Poems [recording]
1 cassette, CD (63 min.), 1977.
From the Watershed Series of Contemporary
   Poetry.
Distributed by Audio-Forum.

Christopher Marlowe

Christopher Marlowe
See **"Medieval to Elizabethan Poetry"** on
   manual p. 000.

Andrew Marvell

Andrew Marvell
See **"Metaphysical and Devotional Poetry"**
   on manual p. 000.

James Merrill

James Merrill: Voices from Sandover
VHS, DVD (116 min.).
A dramatic adaptation of Merrill's "The
   Changing Light at Sandover." Includes
   an interview of Merrill by Helen Vendler.
Distributed by Films for the Humanities and
   Sciences.

Edna St. Vincent Millay

Edna St. Vincent Millay: Renascence
VHS, DVD (60 min.).
A biography of the poet.
Distributed by Films for the Humanities and
   Sciences.

John Milton

Milton
VHS, DVD (28 min.), 1989.
Looks at Milton's sonnets to his wife
   Katherine and *Paradise Lost.*
Distributed by Films for the Humanities and
   Sciences.

Milton by Himself
VHS (27 min.), 1989.
A biography constructed from Milton's
   autobiographical writings.
Distributed by Films for the Humanities and
   Sciences.

Harryette Mullen

Harryette Mullen: Lunch Poems
Video clip (29 min.), October 7, 2004.
From the Noontime Poetry Reading Series.
http://www.youtube.com/
   watch?v=XYyqqy4BnU0
Distributed by YouTube.

Harryette Mullen Reads "Present Tense"
   [recording]
Audio clip, July 20, 2001.
http://www.poets.org/viewmedia.php/
   prmMID/19326
Distributed by poets.org.

She Swam On from Sea to Shine: Poetry of
   Harryette Mullen
Video clip (28 min.).
From "Artists on the Cutting Edge," presented by the Museum of Contemporary Art, San Diego.
http://www.youtube.com/
   watch?v=n3EUHMO-qgk
Distributed by YouTube.

Marilyn Nelson

Marilyn Nelson: Bookfest 03
Webcast (21 min.), October 4, 2003.
Nelson reads from her poetry at the 2003
   National Book Festival.
http://www.loc.gov/today/cyberlc/feature
   _wdesc.php?rec=3560
Distributed by the Library of Congress.

"A Wreath for Emmett Till": A Poem of Sorrow, and Hope [recording]

Audio clip, August 29, 2005.

Nelson reads and discusses her poem about the 1955 murder of fourteen-year-old Emmett Till.

http://www.npr.org/templates/story/story
.php?storyId=4818586

Distributed by National Public Radio.

John Frederick Nims

John Frederick Nims [recording]

1 cassette, CD (29 min.), 1986.

A reading by the Chicago poet.

Distributed by New Letters on the Air.

Sharon Olds

Michael O'Brien & Sharon Olds [recording]

1 cassette, CD (29 min.), 1985.

Distributed by New Letters on the Air.

Sharon Olds [recording]

1 cassette, CD (29 min.), 1993.

Distributed by New Letters on the Air.

Wilfred Owen

Wilfred Owen: The Pity of War

VHS, DVD (58 min.), 1987.

A documentary drawn from Owen's poems, diaries, and letters.

Distributed by Films for the Humanities and Sciences.

Wilfred Owen: War Requiem [video]

VHS (92 min.), 1988.

Written and directed by Derek Jarman, music by Benjamin Britten.

Distributed by Mystic Fire Video.

Wilfred Owen: War Requiem [recording]

2 CDs, 1993.

Distributed by Deutsche Grammophone.

Kevin Pierce

Kevin Pierce: News and Verse [blog]

Pierce's personal blog, where he transforms everyday news headlines into poetry.

http://www.newsandverse.com/

Distributed by Kevin Pierce.

Marge Piercy

Marge Piercy: At the Core [recording]

1 cassette, CD (58 min.), 1977.

Distributed by Audio-Forum.

Edgar Allan Poe

An Evening with Edgar Allan Poe

DVD, 2003 (3 min.).

Includes "The Tell-Tale Heart," *A Journey in Verse*, and *Stories & Tales I*.

Distributed by PBS.

Rainer Maria Rilke

Rainer Maria Rilke: Selected Poems [recording]

2 cassettes (118 min.), 1988.

From the Spiritual Classics on Cassette Series.

Distributed by Audio Literature.

Alberto Ríos

Alberto A. Ríos reading "A Sustainable Courage"

Video clip (5 min.).

Alberto Ríos delivering an inaugural poem called "A Sustainable Courage" at Governor Janet Napolitano's inauguration at the state capitol on January 4, 2007.

http://vimeo.com/2623947

Distributed by Vimeo.

Kay Ryan

Abusing Animals in the Name of Poetry [podcast]

Podcast (11 min.), May 1, 2008.

Ryan reads and discusses some of her poetry. Includes "Turtle," "Flamingo Watching," and "Blandeur."

http://www.poetryfoundation.org/journal/
audioitem.html?id=399

Distributed by the Poetry Foundation.

Kay Ryan Discusses New Collection of Poems

Audio and video clips.

Ryan on *NewsHour* Poetry Series.

http://www.pbs.org/newshour/bb/
entertainment/july-dec06/
poetry_07-26.html

Distributed by PBS.

Kay Ryan: Essential American Poets [podcast]

Podcast (9 min.), September 11, 2007.

Recordings of poet laureate Kay Ryan, with an introduction to her life and work.

http://www.poetryfoundation.org/journal/
audioitem.html?id=597

Distributed by the Poetry Foundation.

Kay Ryan: Online Resources

Collection of links to print articles, audio, video, and essays by or concerning Kay Ryan.

http://www.loc.gov/rr/program/bib/ryan/
Distributed by the Library of Congress.

Kay Ryan: **On Point** *Interview [recording]*
Audio (46 min.), July 24, 2008.
http://www.onpointradio.org/shows/2008/
07/24/poet-kay-ryan/
Distributed by National Public Radio and
Trustees of Boston University.

Sonia Sanchez

Blackademics January Interview:
Sonia Sanchez
Video clip (8 min.), January 15, 2008.
http://www.youtube.com/watch?v=-NIloz
-2dIQ
Distributed by YouTube.

HBO: Def Poetry
Season 5, Episode 7 includes video of
Sanchez reading "Our Vision Is Our
Voice."
Distributed by HBO.

A Sun Lady for All Seasons Reads Her Poetry
[recording]
2 cassettes, CDs, MP3, 1971 (2 min.).
Poetry written and read by Sonia Sanchez.
Distributed by Smithsonian/Folkways
Recordings.

Carl Sandburg

The World of Carl Sandburg
VHS, DVD (59 min.).
Chronicles the life of Carl Sandburg, based
on Norman Corwin's stage presenta-
tion. Starring Uta Hagen and Fritz
Weaver.
Distributed by The Phoenix Learning Group,
Inc.

William Shakespeare

William Shakespeare: Poetry and Hidden
Poetry
VHS, DVD (53 min.), 1984.
A micro-examination of Shakespeare's
poetry and its hidden meanings.
Produced by the Royal Shakespeare
Company.
Distributed by Films for the Humanities and
Sciences.

William Shakespeare's Sonnets
VHS, DVD (150 min.), 1984.
An in-depth look at fifteen of Shakespeare's
sonnets. With Ben Kingsley, Roger
Reese, Claire Bloom, Jane Lapotaire,
A. L. Rowse, and Stephen Spender.

Distributed by Films for the Humanities and
Sciences.

William Shakespeare: The Sonnets
[recording]
6 cassettes.
Distributed by Recorded Books.

Percy Bysshe Shelley

Percy Bysshe Shelley
See **"English Romantic Poetry"** manual
p. 000.

Charles Simic

Charles Simic [recording]
CD (56 min.), 1974, 1977.
Simic reads from his poetry.
Distributed by poets.org.

Charles Simic [podcast]
Podcast (8 min.), August 10, 2007.
Simic reads and discusses some of his poetry.
Includes "Prodigy," "Fork," and "My
Shoes."
http://www.poetryfoundation.org/journal/
audioitem.html?id=124
Distributed by the Poetry Foundation.

Charles Simic: God Is Annoyed
[podcast]
Podcast (15 min.), May 2, 2007.
Simic reads and discusses Polish poet
Zbigniew Herbert.
http://www.poetryfoundation.org/journal/
audioitem.html?id=109
Distributed by the Poetry Foundation.

Charles Simic: Online Resources
Collection of links to print articles, audio,
video, and essays by or concerning
Charles Simic.
http://www.loc.gov/rr/program/bib/
charlessimic/
Distributed by the Library of Congress.

Charles Simic Reads from Selected Poems
1963–2003
Video clip (6 min.).
Includes Simic reading his poem "Shelley."
http://www.youtube.com/
watch?v=5zKahTbzUwc
Distributed by YouTube.

Louis Simpson

Louis Simpson [recording]
1 cassette, CD (29 min.), 1983.
Distributed by New Letters on the Air.

Gary Snyder

Gary Snyder: After Nature [recording]
MP3 (9 min.).
http://www.poetryfoundation.org/features/
audioitem/461
Distributed by The Poetry Foundation.

Gary Snyder: Essential American Poets
[recording]
MP3 (22 min.).
Recordings of poet Gary Snyder, with an
introduction to his life and work.
Recorded in 1966, Library of Congress,
Washington, D.C.
http://www.poetryfoundation.org/features/
audioitem/3190
Distributed by The Poetry Foundation.

Gary Soto

Gary Soto I & II [recording]
1 cassette (60 min.), 1982, 1992.
The author reads his work and talks about
the rise of Chicano literature.
Distributed by New Letters on the Air.

Bruce Springsteen

Bruce Springsteen: Devils & Dust [recording]
CD, MP3, 2005.
Distributed by Columbia Records.

William Stafford

William Stafford I & II [recording]
1 cassette, CD (60 min.), 1983, 1984.
The author reads his poetry and discusses
politics, poetry, and the writing process.
Distributed by New Letters on the Air.

May Swenson

May Swenson [recording]
CD (35 min.), 1985.
Fourteen poems by May Swenson, most of
which appear in her collection *Nature*.
Distributed by poets.org.

*May Swenson: "That The Soul May Wax
Plump"* [recording]
Audio clip.
Distributed by poets.org.

Alfred, Lord Tennyson

Treasury of Alfred, Lord Tennyson [recording]
1 cassette.
Read by Robert Speaight.
Includes "Ulysses," "The Lotus Eaters," and
"The Charge of the Light Brigade."
Available in libraries.

Dylan Thomas

The Days of Dylan Thomas
VHS, b/w (21 min.), 1965.
A biography of the poet.
Distributed by CRM Films.

Dylan Thomas: A Portrait
VHS (26 min.), 1989.
A biographical film.
Distributed by Films for the Humanities and
Sciences.

A Dylan Thomas Memoir
VHS (28 min.), 1972.
A character study of the poet.
Distributed by Pyramid Media.

The Wales of Dylan Thomas
VHS, DVD (15 min.), 1989.
Images of Wales in Thomas's poetry, prose,
and drama.
Distributed by Films for the Humanities and
Sciences.

Natasha Trethewey

Interview with Natasha Trethewey
[recording]
Audio clip (40 min.), July 16, 2007.
Trethewey discusses writing about her mother's murder and her collection *Native
Guard*.
http://www.npr.org/2007/07/16/12003278/
poet-natasha-trethewey-hymning-the
-native-guard
Distributed by National Public Radio.

*Natasha Trethewey: "Elegy for the Native
Guards"*
Video clip (4 min.), April 9, 2005.
Trethewey reads her poem "Elegy for the Native
Guards," on Ship Island, Mississippi.
http://www.southernspaces.org/
contents/2005/trethewey/1a.htm
Distributed by Southern Spaces.

*Natasha Trethewey: "Theories of Time and
Space"*
Video clip (1 min.), April 9, 2005.
Trethewey reads her poem "Theories of Time
and Space" near Gulfport, Mississippi.
http://www.southernspaces.org/
2005/theories-time-and-space
Distributed by Southern Spaces.

*Trethewey Discusses Poetry Collection, Native
Guard*
Audio or video clip.
http://www.pbs.org/newshour/bb/entertain
ment/jan-june07/trethewey_04-25.html
Distributed by PBS.

John Updike

John Updike, I and II [recording]
2 cassettes, CD (58 min.), 1987.
Distributed by New Letters on the Air.

The Poetry of John Updike
[recording]
1 cassette (47 min.), 1967.
Part of the YM-YWHA Poetry Center Series.
Distributed by Audio-Forum.

Walt Whitman

Walt Whitman
VHS (10 min.), 1972.
Readings of Whitman's poems and a discussion of his life. Hosted by Efrem Zimbalist Jr.
Distributed by AIMS Multimedia.

Walt Whitman: American Poet, 1819–1892
VHS, DVD (30 min.), 1994
Distributed by Kultur.

Walt Whitman: Endlessly Rocking
VHS (31 min.), 1986.
Shows a teacher's unsuccessful attempts to interest her students in Whitman.
Distributed by Centre Communications.

Walt Whitman: Song of Myself
VHS, DVD (31 min.).
Chronicles the life of Walt Whitman (played by Rip Torn).
Distributed by The Phoenix Learning Group, Inc.

Walt Whitman: The Living Tradition
VHS (20 min.), 1983.
Allen Ginsberg reads Whitman's poetry.
Distributed by Centre Communications.

William Carlos Williams

William Carlos Williams [recordings]
MP3.
A large library of Williams reading his own work.
http://writing.upenn.edu/pennsound/x/Williams-WC.php
Distributed by PennSound.

William Carlos Williams Reads [recording]
1 cassette (43 min.), 1993.
Distributed by HarperAudio.

William Wordsworth

William Wordsworth
VHS, DVD (28 min.), 1989.
An examination of the poet's work set against the Lake District, subject for many of the poems.
Distributed by Films for the Humanities and Sciences.

William Wordsworth and the English Lakes
VHS, DVD (15 min.), 1989.
Looks at Wordsworth's use of language.
Distributed by Films for the Humanities and Sciences.

William Wordsworth: Selected Poems
[recording]
2 cassettes (180 min.).
Read by Frederick Davidson.
Distributed by Blackstone Audio Books.

William Wordsworth: William and Dorothy
VHS, DVD (52 min.), 1989.
Explores Wordsworth's poetry and his troubled relationship with his sister. Directed by Ken Russell.
Distributed by Films for the Humanities and Sciences.

Baron Wormser

Baron Wormser: Carthage [recordings]
MP3.
Baron Wormser reads poems from his collection *Carthage*.
http://www.teachpoetry.com/carthage/carthage.html
Distributed by Baron Wormser.

Flash Reading: Poetry [recording]
MP3 (4 min.).
Baron Wormser reads "A Visitation: 1968." Several other poets are recorded on this page as well.
http://mainehumanities.org/podcast/archives/tag/baron-wormser
Distributed by the Maine Humanities Council.

William Butler Yeats

The Love Poems of William Butler Yeats
VHS, b/w (30 min.), 1967.
Selections from the poet's works.
Distributed by New York State Education Department.

Poems by W. B. Yeats and Poems for Several Voices
1 cassette, CD, MP3, 1973.
Includes "Sailing to Byzantium" and features poems by Thomas Hardy, Robert Graves, and Gerard Manley Hopkins.
Read by V. C. Clinton-Baddeley, Jill Balcon, and M. Westbury.
Distributed by Smithsonian/Folkways Recordings.

Yeats Remembered
VHS, b/w (30 min.).
Biographical film using period photographs and
interviews with the poet and his family.
Distributed by Insight Media.

General Resources for Poetry

**An Anthology of African American Poetry for
Young People** [recording]
1 cassette, CD, MP3, 1990.
Arna Bontemps reads poems by Countee
Cullen, Paul Laurence Dunbar, Langston
Hughes, Claude McKay, and others.
Distributed by Smithsonian/Folkways Record-
ings.

Anthology of Contemporary American Poetry
[recording]
1 cassette, CD, 1961.
Includes poems by John Ciardi, Richard
Ebhardt, Theodore Roethke, Howard
Nemerov, Galway Kinnell, Donald
Justice, May Swenson, Richard Wilbur,
Karl Shapiro, and others.
Distributed by Smithsonian/Folkways Record-
ings.

Anthology of Negro Poets
[recording]
1 cassette, CD, 1955.
Includes the poetry of Langston Hughes,
Sterling Brown, Claude McKay, Margaret
Walter, and Gwendolyn Brooks.
Distributed by Smithsonian/Folkways Record-
ings.

**Anthology of Twentieth-Century English Poetry
(Part I)** [recording]
2 cassettes, CDs, MP3, 1960.
Includes poems by Thomas Hardy, A. E.
Housman, W. B. Yeats, D. H. Lawrence,
Siegfried Sassoon, and others.
Distributed by Smithsonian/Folkways Record-
ings.

**Anthology of Twentieth-Century English Poetry
(Part II)** [recording]
2 cassettes, CDs, MP3, 1961.
Includes poems by T. S. Eliot, Wilfred Owen,
Robert Graves, W. H. Auden, Dylan
Thomas, Henry Reed, and others.
Distributed by Smithsonian/Folkways Record-
ings.

Archive of Recorded Poetry and Literature
Distributed by the Library of Congress.

Birthwrite: Growing Up Hispanic
VHS (59 min.), 1989.
Focuses on the achievements of Hispanic

American writers. Includes the work of
Alberto Ríos and Judith Ortiz Cofer.
Distributed by Cinema Guild.

Caedmon Collection of English Poetry
[recording]
2 cassettes, 1998.
Features poetry by William Shakespeare,
John Donne, John Milton, William
Blake, Robert Burns, William
Wordsworth, Samuel Taylor Coleridge,
John Keats; Alfred, Lord Tennyson;
Robert Browning, Elizabeth Barrett
Browning, Gerard Manley Hopkins,
Thomas Hardy, D. H. Lawrence,
Rudyard Kipling, Wilfred Owen,
William Butler Yeats, T. S. Eliot, Dylan
Thomas, and Ted Hughes.
Distributed by HarperAudio.

**Caedmon Poetry Collection: A Century of Poets
Reading Their Work** [recording]
2 cassettes (95 min.), 2000.
Includes T. S. Eliot, W. B. Yeats, Edith Sitwell,
Dylan Thomas, Robert Graves, Gertrude
Stein, E. E. Cummings, Robert Frost,
William Carlos Williams, Wallace
Stevens, Ezra Pound, and others.
Distributed by HarperAudio.

**Conversation Pieces: Short Poems by Thomas,
Hardy, Housman, Auden, Keats, and Others**
[recording]
1 cassette, CD, 1964.
Distributed by Smithsonian/Folkways Recordings.

English Poetry Anthology
3 DVD set (150 min.).
An in-depth look at the life and works of
English poets from the past three centu-
ries. Box-set titles include "The
Augustan Poets," "The Romantic Poets,"
and "The Victorian Poets."
Distributed by PBS.

English Romantic Poetry [recording]
2 cassettes (120 min.), 1996.
Authors include William Blake, Robert Burns,
Lord Byron, Samuel Taylor Coleridge,
John Keats, Percy Bysshe Shelley, and
William Wordsworth.
Distributed by HarperAudio.

The Famous Authors Series
DVD, 42 programs (30 min. each).
Includes D. H. Lawrence, Emily Dickinson,
John Keats, Robert Burns, W. B. Yeats,
William Wordsworth, Walt Whitman,
William Blake, and others.
Distributed by Kultur Films.

Introduction to English Poetry
VHS, DVD (28 min.), 1989.

Introduces students to English verse, with readings from Chaucer, Shakespeare, Herbert, Milton, Swift, Blake, Wordsworth, Shelley, Emily Brontë, Hardy, Yeats, and Ted Hughes.

Distributed by Films for the Humanities and Sciences.

The Knopf National Poetry Month Collection
[recording]

CD, MP3, 2007.

A selection of Knopf Poem-a-Day podcasts from April 2006, featuring poets reading their own work as well as Knopf authors like Joan Didion and Toni Morrison reading work by their favorite poets.

Distributed by Random House Audio.

Lannan Literary Series
83 cassettes, VHS (60 min. each), DVD, 1988–2003.

Includes Carolyn Forché, Allen Ginsberg, Louise Glück, Galway Kinnell, W. S. Merwin, Lucille Clifton, Octavio Paz, Yehuda Amichai, Joy Harjo, Alice Walker, Ishmael Reed, Richard Wilbur, Sonia Sanchez, Sharon Olds, Gary Snyder, Gary Soto, and others.

Distributed by The Lannan Foundation.

Literature: The Synthesis of Poetry
VHS (30 min.).

Hosted by Maya Angelou, who reads some of her work as well as the poetry of Robert Frost, Carl Sandburg, and Matthew Arnold.

Distributed by Coast Learning Systems.

The Master Poets Collection
VHS, 27 programs (30 min. each).

Programs include Millay, Longfellow, Cummings, Lawrence, Keats, Byron, Shelley, Blake, Browning, Frost, Kipling, Plath, Whitman, Shakespeare, and others.

Distributed by Monterey Media Inc.

Medieval to Elizabethan Poetry
VHS, DVD (28 min.), 1989.

Examines trends of the period, focusing on John Skelton, Thomas Wyatt, Chidiok Tichborne, Thomas Nashe, Christopher Marlowe, Michael Drayton, and William Shakespeare.

Distributed by Films for the Humanities and Sciences.

Metaphysical and Devotional Poetry
VHS, DVD (28 min.), 1989.

Looks at the works of John Donne, George Herbert, and Andrew Marvell.

Distributed by Films for the Humanities and Sciences.

North American Poets
[recording]

6 cassettes.

Poems read by Broadway performers George Guidall and John McDonough. Includes "Chicago" by Carl Sandburg, "The Love Song of J. Alfred Prufrock" by T. S. Eliot, "The Road Not Taken" by Robert Frost, and others.

Distributed by Recorded Books.

Poetic Forms
[recording]

5 cassettes (300 min.), 1988.

Includes the list poem, the ode, the prose poem, the sonnet, the haiku, the blues poem, the villanelle, the ballad, the acrostic, and free verse.

Distributed by Teachers & Writers Collaborative.

Poetry: A Beginner's Guide
VHS (26 min.), 1986.

Interviews contemporary poets and examines the tools they use.

Distributed by Coronet/MTI Film & Video.

Poetry by Americans
VHS, 4 programs (10 min. each), 1988.

Robert Frost, Edgar Allan Poe, James Weldon Johnson, and Walt Whitman. Narrated by Leonard Nimoy, Lorne Greene, Raymond St. Jacques, and Efrem Zimbalist Jr.

Distributed by AIMS Multimedia.

Poetry for People Who Hate Poetry
VHS, 3 programs (15 min. each), 1980.

Roger Steffens makes poetry accessible to students. The three programs are About Word, E. E. Cummings, and Shakespeare.

Distributed by Churchill Media.

Poetry in Motion
DVD (90 min.), 1982.

A performance anthology of twenty-four North American poets, including Amiri Baraka, Allen Ginsburg, Charles Bukowski, William Burroughs, Ted Berrigan, John Cage, Tom Waits, and others.

Distributed by Home Vision Entertainment.

Poets Read Their Contemporary Poetry: Before Columbus Foundation *[recording]*

2 cassettes, CDs, MP3, 1980.

Includes poems by Ishmael Reed, Bob Callahan, Jayne Cortez, Joy Harjo, Amiri Baraka, and others.

Distributed by Smithsonian/Folkways Recordings.

The Power of the Word

6 DVD set, 1995 (360 min.).

Bill Moyers's six-volume documentary series explores the power of poetry in language and life. Includes interviews with James Autry, Robert Bly, Lucille Clifton, Joy Harjo, Garrett Kaoru Hongo, Galway Kinnell, and others.

Distributed by PBS.

Romantic Pioneers

VHS, DVD (28 min.), 1989.

Readings of poems by Christopher Smart, William Blake, William Wordsworth, and Samuel Taylor Coleridge.

Distributed by Films for the Humanities and Sciences.

Romantics and Realists

VHS, DVD (28 min.), 1989.

Discusses Thomas Hardy, Gerard Manley Hopkins, A. E. Housman, and Rudyard Kipling.

Distributed by Films for the Humanities and Sciences.

Sounds of Poetry with Bill Moyers

4 DVD set, 2000 (245 min.).

Features readings, performances, and conversations with poets at the Geraldine R. Dodge Poetry Festival. Includes Robert Pinsky, Mark Doty, Lucille Clifton, Jane Hirshfield, Marge Piercy, and others.

Distributed by PBS.

A Survey of English and American Poetry

VHS, DVD, 16 programs (28 min. each), 1987.

A history and anthology of English-language poetry. Programs include Introduction to English Poetry; Old English Poetry; Medieval to Elizabethan Poetry; The Maturing Shakespeare; Metaphysical and Devotional Poetry; Restoration and Augustan Poetry; Romantic Pioneers; The Younger Romantics; Victorian Poetry; American Pioneers; The Earlier Twentieth Century; The Later Twentieth Century; and others.

Distributed by Films for the Humanities and Sciences.

Teaching Poetry

VHS (30 min.), 1990.

A new approach to teaching poetry. Includes discussion questions and homework assignments.

Distributed by Video Aided Instruction.

Twentieth-Century Poets in English: Recordings of Poets Reading Their Own Poetry *[recording]*

33 volumes.

Distributed by the Library of Congress.

Victorian Poetry

VHS, DVD (28 min.), 1989.

An examination of works by Alfred, Lord Tennyson; Christina Rossetti; Elizabeth Barrett Browning; Matthew Arnold; and others.

Distributed by Films for the Humanities and Sciences.

Voices and Visions

VHS, CD-ROM, 13 programs (60 min. each), 1988.

A series exploring the lives of some of America's best poets. Hosted by Joseph Brodsky, Mary McCarthy, James Baldwin, and Adrienne Rich. Programs include Elizabeth Bishop; Emily Dickinson; T. S. Eliot; Robert Frost; Langston Hughes; Robert Lowell; Sylvia Plath; Ezra Pound; Wallace Stevens; Walt Whitman; William Carlos Williams; and others.

Distributed by the Annenberg/CPB Collection.

With a Feminine Touch

VHS (45 min.), 1990.

Readings from Emily Dickinson, Sylvia Plath, Edna St. Vincent Millay, and others. Read by Valerie Harper and Claire Bloom.

Distributed by Monterey Home Video.

The Younger Romantics

VHS, DVD (28 min.), 1989.

Features the work of John Keats, William Wordsworth, and Lord Byron.

Distributed by Films for the Humanities and Sciences.

DRAMA

Susan Glaspell

Trifles
DVD, VHS (21 min.), 1979.
Distributed by Phoenix/BFA Films.

Trifles
VHS (22 min.), 1981.
Distributed by Centre Communications.

Henrik Ibsen

A Doll's House
DVD (73 min.), 1959.
With Julie Harris, Christopher Plummer, Jason Robards, Hume Cronyn, and Eileen Heckart. Hosted by Richard Thomas. An original television production.
See your local retailer.

A Doll's House
VHS (98 min.), 1973.
With Jane Fonda, Edward Fox, Trevor Howard, and David Warner. Screenplay by Christopher Hampton.
Distributed by Prism Entertainment.

A Doll's House
DVD (95 min.), 1989.
With Claire Bloom, Anthony Hopkins, Ralph Richardson, Denholm Elliott, Anna Massey, and Edith Evans. Directed by Patrick Garland.
Distributed by MGM.

A Doll's House
[recording]
CD (180 min.), 1993.
Read by Flo Gibson.
Distributed by Audio Book Contractors.

William Shakespeare

General

Shakespeare's Globe
VHS, DVD (47 min.), 1975.
Provides a montage of Shakespearean background, including scenes from *Hamlet* and the preparation of various actors for the role.
Distributed by Films for the Humanities and Sciences.

Shakespeare and His Theater: The Globe
VHS, DVD, streaming (28 min.).
A history of Shakespeare's life in the theater and an examination of his work.
Distributed by Films for the Humanities and Sciences.

Shakespeare and the Globe
VHS, DVD, streaming (31 min.), 1985.
A survey of Shakespeare's life, work, and cultural milieu.
Distributed by Films for the Humanities and Sciences.

Shakespearean Tragedy
VHS, DVD (40 min.), 1984.
Focuses on *Hamlet* and *Macbeth*.
Distributed by Films for the Humanities and Sciences.

The Two Traditions
VHS, DVD (50 min.), 1983.
Deals with the problem of overcoming barriers of time and culture to make Shakespeare relevant today. Examples from *Hamlet, Coriolanus, The Merchant of Venice,* and *Othello.* Part of the "Playing Shakespeare" series.
Distributed by Films for the Humanities and Sciences.

Sophocles

Oedipus Rex

Oedipus Rex
DVD (90 min.), 1957.
With Douglas Campbell, Douglas Rain, Eric House, and Eleanor Stuart. Based on William Yeats's translation. Directed by Tyrone Guthrie. Contained and highly structured rendering by the Stratford (Ontario) Festival Players.
Distributed by Water Bearer Films.

Oedipus Rex: Age of Sophocles, I
VHS, color and b/w (31 min.), 1959.
Discusses Greek civilization, the classic Greek theater, and the theme of man's fundamental nature.
Distributed by Encyclopaedia Britannica Educational Corporation.

Oedipus Rex: The Character of Oedipus, II
VHS, color and b/w (31 min.), 1959.
Debates whether Oedipus's trouble is a result of character flaws or of fate.
Distributed by Encyclopaedia Britannica Educational Corporation.

Oedipus Rex: Man and God, III
VHS, color and b/w (30 min.), 1959.
Deals with the idea that Oedipus, although a worldly ruler, cannot overcome the gods and his destiny.
Distributed by Encyclopaedia Britannica Educational Corporation.

Oedipus Rex: Recovery of Oedipus, IV

VHS, color and b/w (30 min.), 1959.

Deals with man's existence in between God and beast.

Distributed by Encyclopaedia Britannica Educational Corporation.

Oedipus the King

DVD, VHS (45 min.), 1975.

With Anthony Quayle, James Mason, Claire Bloom, and Ian Richardson. A production by the Athens Classical Theater Company, with an English soundtrack.

Distributed by Films for the Humanities and Sciences.

Oedipus the King

DVD, VHS (120 min.), 1987.

With John Gielgud, Michael Pennington, and Claire Bloom.

Distributed by Films for the Humanities and Sciences.

The Rise of Greek Tragedy, Sophocles: Oedipus the King

DVD, VHS (45 min.), 1986.

With James Mason, Claire Bloom, and Ian Richardson. Narrated by Anthony Quayle. The play is photographed in the ancient Greek theater of Amphiaraion and uses tragic masks.

Distributed by Films for the Humanities and Sciences.

Nilaja Sun

An Excerpt from No Child . . .

An excerpt from *No Child....*, performed by Sun.

http://www.youtube.com/watch?v=RR5v4xUE2Tw

Distributed by YouTube.

Nilaja Sun's No Child . . . at the Kirk Douglas Theatre

Clips from the play with commentary by Sun.

http://www.youtube.com/watch?v=vbx5MNj0a-A

Distributed by YouTube.

Katie Czerwinski Interviews Nilaja Sun

http://www.youtube.com/watch?v=0re3emAyFh4

Distributed by YouTube.

August Wilson

August Wilson

DVD, VHS, color and b/w (51 min.), 1990.

An interview with Wilson and excerpts from his plays.

Distributed by Films for the Humanities and Sciences.

August Wilson

Online streaming (29 min.), 1989.

From Bill Moyers's "World of Ideas" series.

Distributed by PBS Video.

The Piano Lesson

DVD (107 min.), 1996.

With Charles Dutton and Alfre Woodard. A Hallmark Hall of Fame production.

Distributed by Republic Pictures.

General Resources for Drama

Echoes of Jacobean England

DVD, VHS (45 min.).

Re-creates the liberal arts in seventeenth-century England. Features authentically performed music, contemporary literature, scenes of daily life, and period setting to provide a background for the works of Shakespeare, Dryden, John Donne, and John Dowland.

Distributed by Films for the Humanities and Sciences.

The Role of the Theatre in Ancient Greece

DVD, VHS (26 min.), 1989.

Program explores ancient theater design, the origins of tragedy, the audience, the comparative roles of the writer/director and actors, and the use of landscape in many plays. Examines the theaters of Herodus, Atticus, Epidauros, Corinth, and numerous others.

Distributed by Films for the Humanities and Sciences.

DIRECTORY OF DISTRIBUTORS

A&E Home Video see *New Video*

Academy Audio Archive see *Academy of American Poets*

Academy of American Poets
584 Broadway, Suite 1208
New York, NY 10012-3250
(212) 274-0343
www.poets.org

Acorn Media
8515 Georgia Ave., #650
Silver Spring, MD 20910
(800) 999-0212
www.acornmedia.com

AFCI — Association of Film Commissioners International
109 East 17th Street
Cheyenne, WY 82001
(307) 637-4422
www.afci.org

AIMS Multimedia
9710 DeSoto Avenue
Chatsworth, CA 91311-4409
(818) 773-4300, (800) 367-2467
aimsmultimedia.com

AM Productions
1141 South Pasadena Avenue
Pasadena, CA 91105
(626) 403-0258
amproductions.com

Ambrose Video
145 West 45th Street, Suite 1115
New York, NY 10036
(800) 526-4663
www.ambrosevideo.com

American Audio Prose Library see *Western Historical Manuscript Collection–Columbia*

The American Poetry Archive
San Francisco State University
1600 Holloway Avenue
San Francisco, CA 94132
(415) 338-2227
www.sfsu.edu/~poetry/

Annenberg Media
P.O. Box 2345
South Burlington, VT 05407-2345
(800)-LEARNER
www.learner.org

Audio Book Contractors
P.O. Box 40115
Washington, DC 20016
(202) 363-3429
www.audiobookcontractors.com

Audio Bookshelf
44 Ocean View Drive
Middletown, RI 02842
(800) 234-1713
www.audiobookshelf.com

AudioForum
One Orchard Park Road
Madison, CT 06443
(800) 243-1713
audioforum.com

Audio Holdings LLC
197 Wall Street
Princeton, NJ 08540-1520
(609) 683-1774

Audio Literature see *Publishers Group West*

Audio Partners see *Publishers Group West*

Audio Scholar/Learn Out Loud.com
1322 2nd Street, Suite 35
Santa Monica, CA 90401
(800) 550-6070
www.learnoutloud.com

AVCEL (NY), distributed by *CP Media Inc.*
4431 North 60th Avenue
Omaha, NE 68104-0488
(800) 227-5281

Bantam Audio Publishers see *Random House Audio Publishing*

Barnes & Noble.com
www.barnesandnoble.com

Baylor TV
Baylor University
Waco, TX 76798
www.baylortv.com

Benchmark Media
569 North State Road
Briarcliff Manor, NY 10510
(914) 762-3838, (800) 438-5564
www.benchmarkmedia.info

Berkeley Media LLC
2600 Tenth Street, Suite 626
Berkeley, CA 94710
(510) 486-9900
ucmedia.berkeley.edu

BFA Educational Media see *Phoenix Learning Group*

Blackbird Archive
Virginia Commonwealth University
Department of English
P.O. Box 843082
Richmond, VA 23284-3082
(804) 827-4729
www.blackbird.vcu.edu/v5n2/archives.htm

Blackstone Audiobooks
P.O. Box 969
Ashland, OR 97520
(800) 729-2665
www.blackstoneaudio.com

Bloodaxe Books
www.bloodaxebooks.com

Books on Tape
400 Hahn
Westminster, MD 21157
(714) 548-5525, (800) 626-3333
www.booksontape.com

Britannica Films see *Encyclopeadia Britannica Educational Corporation*

Brown University
Providence, RI 02912
(401) 863-1000
www.brown.edu

Caedmon/HarperAudio
P.O. Box 588
Dunmore, PA 18512
(800) 242-7737, (800) 982-4377 (in Pennsylvania)
www.harpercollins.com

California Newsreel
Order Department
P.O. Box 2284
South Burlington, VT 05407
(877) 811-7495
www.newsreel.org

Cassette Works
235 Bellafontaine Street
Pasadena, CA 91105
(800) 423-8273
www.m2com.com/cassetteworks.html

CBS-TV/CBS-Fox Video
51 West 52nd Street, 3rd Floor
New York, NY 10019
(212) 975-4321
www.cbs.com

CD Baby
5925 80 Avenue
Portland, OR 97218-2891
(800) BUY MY CD
cdbaby.com

Centre Communications Inc.
75 Manhattan Drive, Suite 104
Boulder, CO 80303
(303) 444-1166
www.centrecommunicationsinc.com

Chicago Public Radio/WBEZ 91.5 FM
848 East Grand Avenue
Navy Pier
Chicago, IL 60611
(312) 948-4600
www.chicagopublicradio.org

Churchill Media see *Clearvue & SVE Inc.*

Cinema Guild
115 West 30th Street, Suite 800
New York, NY 10001
(212) 685-6242, (800) 723-5522
www.cinemaguild.com

Clearvue & SVE Inc.
6465 North Avondale Avenue
Chicago, IL 60631
(800) 253-2788
www.clearvue.com

Coast Learning Systems
(800) 547-4748
www.coastlearning.org

Colbert Nation
Colbert Report Studio
513 West 54th Street
New York, NY 10019
www.colbertnation.com

Columbia Records/Sony Music
550 Madison Avenue
New York, NY 10022-3211
(212) 833-8000
www.sonymusic.com

Columbia Tristar Home Video/Sony Pictures
Sony Pictures Plaza
10202 West Washington Boulevard
Culver City, CA 90232
(310) 244-4000
www.sonypictures.com

Coronet / MTI Film & Video see *Phoenix Learning Group*

The Cortland Review
527 Third Avenue, #279
New York, NY 10016
www.cortlandreview.com

CRM Films
2218 Farraday Avenue, Suite 110
Carlsbad, CA 92008
(800) 421-0833, (760) 431-9800
www.crmlearning.com

Crossroads Video
65 Church Road
Sherman, CT 06784
www.crossroadsvideo.com

Crown Publishers see **Random House Audio Publishing Group**

Deutsche Grammophon
Baumwall 3
20459 Hamburg
Germany
www2.deutschegrammophon.com

Dove Enterprises
4520 Hudson Drive
Stow, OH 44224
(800) 233-DOVE

Dramatic Publishing
311 Washington Street
Woodstock, IL 60098
(800) 448-7469
www.dramaticpublishing.com

Educational Media Collection
University of Washington
Kane Hall, Room 35
Campus Box 353095
Seattle, WA 98195-3095
(206) 543-9900

Encyclopaedia Britannica Educational Corporation
331 North La Salle Street
Chicago, IL 60610
(800) 323-1229
www.britannica.com

Facets Multimedia Inc.
1517 West Fullerton Avenue
Chicago, IL 60614
(773) 281-9075
www.facets.org

Films for the Humanities and Sciences
P.O. Box 2053
Princeton, NJ 08543-2053
(609) 671-1000, (800) 257-5126
www.films.com

First Run/Icarus Films
32 Court Street, 21st Floor
Brooklyn, NY 11201
(718) 488-8900
icarusfilms.com

ForA.tv
1550 Bryant Street, Suite 700
San Francisco, CA 94103
(415) 868-4310
http://fora.tv

Google Video
Google Inc.
1600 Amphitheatre Parkway
Mountain View, CA 94043
(650) 253-0000
video.google.com

GPN Educational Media
1001 Fleet Street
Baltimore, MD 21202
(800) 228-4630
www.shopgpn.com

Guidance Associates
31 Pine View Road
Mount Kisco, NY 10549
(800) 431-1242
www.guidanceassociates.com

Harlequin Mills & Boon Ltd.
Eton House
18-24 Paradise Road
Richmond, Surrey
United Kingdom TW9 1SR
www.millsandboon.co.uk

HarperAudio see **Caedmon/Harper Audio.**

Harvard University Press
79 Garden Street
Cambridge, MA 02138
(800) 405-1619
www.hup.harvard.edu

HBO Home Video
store.hbo.com

HighBridge Audio
201 6th Street SE, Suite 220
Minneapolis, MN 55414
(800) 755-8532
www.highbridgeaudio.com

Home Vision Entertainment
Image Entertainment
20525 Nordhoff Street, Suite 200
Chatsworth, CA 91311
www.homevision.com

IASTA
IASTA Global Headquarters
12800 North Meridian Street, Suite 425
Carmel, IN 46032
(317) 594-8600
www.iasta.com

ICA Video see **The Roland Collection**

Indiana University Instructional Support Services
Franklin Hall, Room 004
601 East Kirkwood Ave.
Bloomington, IN 47405-5901
(812) 855-2853
www.indiana.edu/~iss/instr_media.shtml/

Insight Media
2162 Broadway
New York, NY 10024
(212) 721-6316, (800) 233-9910
www.insight-media.com

Interlingua VA/Foreign Audio Books.com
P.O. 4175
Arlington, VA 22204
(800) 336-4400, (703) 575-7849
www.foreignaudiobooks.com

International Film Bureau see **AFCI**

Ishtar
15030 Ventura Boulevard, Suite 766
Sherman Oaks, CA 91403
(800) 428-7136
www.ishtarfilms.com

Jimcin Recordings
P.O. Box 536
Portsmouth, RI 02871
(800) 538-3034
www.jimcin.com

KAET-TV
Arizona State University
Box 871405
Tempe, AZ 85287-1405
(480) 965-8888
www.azpbs.org

KCRW
1900 Pico Boulevard
Santa Monica, CA 90405
(310) 450-5183
www.kcrw.com

Kino Corp. International
333 West 39th Street, Suite 503
New York, NY 10018
(800) 562-3330
www.kino.com

Kultur
195 Highway #36
West Long Branch, NJ 07764
(732) 229-2343
www.kultur.com

Landmark Media
3450 Slade Run Drive
Falls Church, VA 22042
(800) 342-4336
www.landmarkmedia.com

Lannan Foundation
313 Reed Street
Santa Fe, NM 87501-2628
(505) 986-8160
www.lannan.org

L.A. Theatre Works
681 Venice Boulevard
Venice, CA 90291
(310) 827-0808
www.latw.org

Library of Congress
Motion Picture, Broadcasting & Recorded Sound Division
101 Independence Avenue SE
Washington, DC 20540-4690
(202) 707-5840
www.loc.gov

Listening Library see **Random House Audio Publishing Group**

MCA Home Video see **Universal Studios**

MGM
1350 Avenue of the Americas
New York, NY 10019
(212) 708-0300
www.mgm.com

Mills & Boon Ltd. see **Harlequin Mills & Boon Ltd.**

Miramax Films see **The Walt Disney Company**

Modern Poetry Association
444 N. Michigan Ave., Suite 1850
Chicago, IL 60611
(312) 787-7070
www.poetrymagazine.org

Monterey Home Video
566 St. Charles Drive
Thousand Oaks, CA 91360
(800) 424-2593
www.montereymedia.com/video

Monterey Media Inc. see **Monterey Home Video**

MySpace
www.myspace.com

Mystic Fire Video
Wholesale Services
687 Marshall Avenue
Williston, VT 05495
(800) 862-8900
www.mysticfire.com

National Public Radio
Listener Services
635 Massachusetts Avenue NW
Washington, DC 20001
(202) 513-3232
www.npr.org

Naxos Entertainment
1810 Columbia Avenue, Suite 28
Franklin, TN 37064
(615) 771-9393
www.naxos.com

Nebraska Educational Television Network and
*Nebraska Educational Television Council
for Higher Education* see **GPN
Educational Media**

New Dimensions Radio
P.O. Box 569
Ukiah, CA 95482
(707) 468-5215, (800) 935-8273
www.newdimensions.org

New Letters on the Air
University of Missouri at Kansas City
5101 Rockhill Road, U-House
Kansas City, MO 64110
(816) 235-1168
www.newletters.org/onTheAir.asp

New Line Home Video
888 7th Avenue, 19th Floor
New York, NY 10106
(212) 649-4900
www.newline.com

New Video
902 Broadway, 9th Floor
New York, NY 10010
www.newvideo.com/aae.html

New York State Education Department
89 Washington Avenue
Albany, NY 12234
(518) 474-3852

The New York Times on the Web
The New York Times
620 Eighth Avenue
New York, NY 10018
www.nytimes.com

Jeffrey Norton see **AudioForum**

Paramount Home Video
5555 Melrose Avenue
Hollywood, CA 90038
(323) 956-5000
www.paramount.com

PBS Video
1320 Braddock Place
Alexandria, VA 22314-1698
(703) 739-5380, (800) 645-4727
www.shop.pbs.org/education/

Penguin Audiobooks
375 Hudson Street, 9th Floor
New York, NY 10014
(800) 526-0275
us.penguingroup.com

PennSound
Center for Programs in Contemporary
Writing
University of Pennsylvania
3808 Walnut Street
Philadelphia, PA 19104
writing.upenn.edu/pennsound/

Pen on Fire
penonfire.blogspot.com

Perspective Films
13381 Danube Circle
Rosemount, MN 55068
(651) 204-2424
www.perspectivefilms.com

Phoenix/BFA Films see *Phoenix Learning Group*

Phoenix Learning Group
2349 Chaffee Drive
St. Louis, MO 63146
(800) 221-1274
www.phoenixlearninggroup.com

Poetry Foundation
44 North Michigan Avenue, Suite 1850
Chicago, IL 60611-4034
(312) 787-7070
www.poetryfoundation.org

Poetry LA
http://poetry.la

poets.org see *Academy of American Poets*

Prism Entertainment
8700 S. Wolf Road, Building F
Burr Ridge, IL 60527-7138
(708) 839-8450
www.prismentertainment.biz

Publishers Group West
1700 4th Street
Berkeley, CA 94710
(510) 528-1444
www.pgw.com

Pyramid Media
P.O. Box 1048/WEB
Santa Monica, CA 90406
(800) 421-2304
www.pyramidmedia.com

Radio Spirits
P.O. Box 3107
Wallingford, CT 06492
www.radiospirits.com

Random House Audio Publishing Group
400 Hahn Road
Westminster, MD 21157
(800) 726-0600
www.randomhouse.com/audio

Recorded Books
270 Skipjack Road
Prince Frederick, MD 20678
(800) 638-1304
www.recordedbooks.com

Rhino Records
10635 Santa Monica Boulevard
Los Angeles, CA 90025-4900
www.rhino.com

Rhode Island Library Association
12 Western Avenue
Providence, RI 02940
www.rilibraryassoc.org

Riverwalk Jazz
12 Western Avenue
Petaluma, CA 94952
(800) 352-7119
www.riverwalkjazz.org

The Roland Collection
22D Hollywood Avenue
Hohokus, NJ 07423
(201) 251-8200, (800) 59-ROLAND
www.roland-collection.com

RTÉ
www.rte.ie

Smithsonian Folkways Recordings
600 Maryland Avenue SW
Suite 2001
Washington, DC 20024
(800) 365-5929
www.folkways.si.edu

Social Studies School Service
10200 Jefferson Boulevard, Box 802
Culver City, CA 90232
(800) 421-4246
www.socialstudies.com

Sony Pictures
10202 W. Washington Boulevard
Culver City, CA 90232
(310) 244-6926
www.sonypictures.com

Sound Photosynthesis
P.O. Box 2111
Mill Valley, CA 94942-2111
(415) 383-6712
photosynthesis.com

Soundelux Audio Publishing
7080 Hollywood Blvd., Suite 1100
Hollywood, CA 90028
(323) 603-3200
www.soundelux.com

Southern Spaces
www.southernspaces.org

Spoken Arts
195 South White Rock Road
Holmes, NY 12531
(800) 326-4090
www.spokenartsmedia.com

Tantor Media Inc.
2 Business Park Road
Old Saybrook, CT 06475
(860) 395-1155
www.tantor.com

Teachers & Writers Collaborative
520 Eighth Ave., Suite 2020
New York, NY 10018
(212) 691-6590
www.twc.org/pubs/

Teachers' Domain
1 Guest Street
Boston, MA 02135
(617) 300-3995
www.teachersdomain.org

Theatre in Chicago
P.O. Box 3713
Chicago, IL 60654
www.theatreinchicago.com

Thomas S. Klise Company
P.O. Box 720
Mystic, CT 06355
(860) 536-4200
www.klise.com

Time Life Video
P.O. Box 6172
Clarion, IA 50526-6172
(800) 950-7887
www.timelife.com

UA Home Video see **MGM**

Universal Studios
30 Rockefeller Plaza
New York, NY 10112
(212) 664-4444
homevideo.universalstudios.com

University of California Extension Media Center see **Berkeley Media LLC**

Valley Video Services
(541) 963-8410
www.valleyvideoservices.com

Video Aided Instruction
485-34 South Broadway
Hicksville, NY 11801-5071
(800) 238-1512
www.videoaidedinstruction.com

Video Learning Library
15838 North 62nd Street, Suite 101
Scottsdale, AZ 85254
(480) 596-9970, (800) 383-8811
www.videolearning.com

Viking Books see **Penguin Audio Books**

The Walt Disney Company
500 S. Buena Vista Street
Burbank, CA 91521-9722
(818) 560-1000
miramax.com

Warner Home Video
4000 Warner Boulevard
Burbank, CA 91522
(818) 954-6000
www.warnerbrothers.com

Water Bearer Films
www.waterbearerfilms.com

WBGU-TV
245 Troup Avenue
Bowling Green, OH 43403
(888) 892-0010
wbgu.org

Western Historical Manuscript Collection— Columbia
23 Ellis Library
University of Missouri
Columbia, MO 65201-5149

WGBH see **Teachers' Domain**

White Star see **Kultur**

Wired for Books
WOUB Center for Public Media
Scripps College of Communication
Ohio University
9 South College Street
Athens, OH 45701
wiredforbooks.org

Women Make Movies
462 Broadway, Suite 500, WS
New York, NY 10013
(212) 925-0606 x360
www.wmm.com

The Writer's Almanac
writersalmanac.publicradio.org

The Writer's Center
4508 Walsh Street
Bethesda, MD 20815
(301) 654-8664
www.writer.org

Writers at Cornell
Cornell University
Ithaca, NY 14853
(607) 255-6800
writersatcornell.blogspot.com

WYEP Pittsburgh
67 Bedford Square
Pittsburgh, PA 15203
(412) 381-9131
www.wyep.org

YouTube
www.youtube.com

Index of Authors and Titles